More praise for
To Say Nothing, V...

"His body ha~
but I have an uneasy susp   gh."

"I have read Mr. Ha.   ...ine."

"Longer than Proust's *In Search of Lost Time*, but not as good."
Norton Critical Editions

"Neil is a true twentieth-century, western yogi: clueless, bumbling, half-hearted,
and cussedly obtuse, but one who never gave up."
Yoga Tribune

"It reads like a lot of sour grapes to me."
Aesop

"It has always been my habit to counsel persistence.
Many is the time I have said, 'Never give up.'
After reading Mr. Hansen's work,
I wonder if it is not time to rethink my policy."
Sir Winston Churchill

"This may be the hippie *Bildungsgeschichte* we've been waiting for,
but for a formation history, a coming-of-age account,
Mr. Hansen shows no sign of growing up and seems to remain quite unformed."
Noam Chomsky

"He appears to be the most incurably lazy devil that ever stood in shoe leather,
and he doesn't seem to care who knows it."
Sir Arthur Conan Doyle

"The Western Canon just got a little bigger."
Thomas Carlyle

"He is a Hideous Man and not ironically. But at least it's not another
f***ing photo memoir clogged with broken Internet links."
David Foster Wallace

Neil Hansen

TO SAY NOTHING

A Diary of Memory

Vol. 2

To Say Nothing: A Diary of Memory, Vol. 2

Copyright © 2014 Robert David Neil Hansen
All Rights Reserved

First edition: June 2014
CreateSpace Independent Publishing Platform

Printed copies of this book can be ordered worldwide from
Amazon.com
Amazon Europe
CreateSpace eStore
Other online retailers

Ask your local bookstore or library to order
a printed copy by providing them with this number:

ISBN 978-1496071866

For more information, or just to chat, contact the author at
rdnhansen@gmail.com or 1-250-885-6093

Cover photo: The author at twenty-nine, Victoria, BC
Photo credit: Brian Atkinson, 1982. Used by permission.

Printed on demand in various locations

For My Girls
Lovena and Naia

Grown-up stories about childish behaviour
and the difficult road to a full heart.

The theme of the work

People have good and bad qualities,
but there are no bad people.
Not even in these stories.

"*Bill*:
[interviewing Hui-yuan, a 71-year-old hermit nun
in the Zhongnan mountains of China]:
What religious practice do you follow?
Tao? Or Buddhist?
Hui-yuan:
Just trying to stay alive keeps me pretty busy."

Bill Porter, *Road to Heaven: Encounters with Chinese Hermits*

Contents

Foreword to Vol. 2 ix

Cranky Preface to Vol. 2 xi

The Proust Questionnaire, Vol. 2 xvii

Ch. 1	Pitching Woo	23
Ch. 2	Forking Potatoes	47
Ch. 3	Science-Drama-Love Dharma	71
Ch. 4	Love-Drama-Science Dharma	95
Ch. 5	Japan, You're Nobody's Sweetheart Now	127
Ch. 6	Return to Normalcy	165
Ch. 7	My Candle Burns At Both Ends	182
Ch. 8	The Thought Sickens	199
Ch. 9	Washing the Pot	213
Ch. 10	Tokyo Owes Me A Good Time	226
Ch. 11	Tokyo Pays Up	244
Ch. 12	Tokyo Confidential, One	256
Ch. 13	Tokyo Confidential, Two	278
Ch. 14	Briefly by the Bay	303
Ch. 15	Holy Toledo	311
Ch. 16	Summer, Sudden and Short	320
Ch. 17	The Last Time I Saw Calgary	335
Ch. 18	Another Hangover	349
Ch. 19	The First Year	366
Ch. 20	Say Cheese	383
Ch. 21	The Pursued, the Pursuing, the Busy, and the Tired	400

Ch. 22	The Bribery of Paris 418
Ch. 23	Meretricious 428
Ch. 24	Trophy Husband 443
	Afterword 458
	Even More About the Author 461
	Of Things to Come 462

Foreword to Vol. 2

by Lovena Morrell
(when she was eight years old)

Me: Daddy, why is Naia at the front of the book and I'm not? I want to be in the book, too.
Daddy: I'll put you at the front of the second book, okay?
Me: Okay.
Daddy: What do you want for supper, honey?
Me: Uhm…can you make something delicious this time?

Victoria, BC

Cranky Preface to Vol. 2

A Brief and Useful Visit to the Past

> If any incident in this little work should appear uninteresting and trifling to most readers, I can only say, as my excuse for mentioning it, that almost every event of my life made an impression upon my mind, and influenced my conduct. For some there is scarcely any incident so trifling that does not afford some profit, while to others even the experience of ages is of no use; and to pour out to them the treasures of wisdom is throwing the jewels of instruction away.
>
> Olaudah Equiano
The Interesting Narrative of the Life of Olaudah Equiano, or Gustavas Vassa, the African, 1792

Not to mention

I've noticed that sometimes second volumes are fronted with a terse, cranky preface by an author who was less than impressed with the reception of his or her first effort. I was unconcerned either way with the public reception of Volume 1. There was practically none, a kind of mass user error. Many authors spend years polishing their work to a high sheen. I left off after a year, part time, satisfied with what I believed to be a competent, if superficial, patina. I should have worked on it longer, I guess.

As for my small private public, my old pals, I sent out a couple of dozen rather amusing book notices, I don't have that many friends, and they were largely met with a wall of silence. I wasn't expecting everyone, or not too many anyway, to actually buy a copy, but I thought I might get a "Congratulations!" or a "Way to go!" Well, from about sixty per cent of them, nothing. Nada. Stone cold. Not a sausage. Nothing but dead air and crickets. I can't think the price of the book was an issue. It's not like I was asking them to lend me money. Again. I hope they got a giggle at least.

If you want to find out who your friends are, or even just who's still friendly, you can either fail at something, or you can accomplish something, even something as mundane as a memoir. Either way, you'll find out. Some people wouldn't give you an "Attaboy!" if you found the cure for cancer.

Nevertheless, I remain in bliss. The year-long creation of a memoir of my early life, in Volume 1, was an interesting, entertaining, and instructive experience for me, if not for anyone else, and at least one category of response from my friends and neighbours was helpful. Several months into the process, about halfway through the first and second drafts, I talked with two of my old friends, separately, about the project, the stories, and the writing of them. One said, more or less, "It's not something I need to do. I still feel like I'm living my life." The other said with a dismissive sniff, "I don't care about memories from the past. I'm still making memories." A couple of other people with advanced university degrees actually asked me why I did it. Why. As if autobiography were not a cultural imperative in an age of increasing uniformity, a lock-step life, educational, governmental, and truly frightening, corporate. As if the timelessness of the humanity of every individual, every life lived, jostling in a time-bound throng, were an airy matter. As if self-fulfillment were not now, for better or worse, a life task.

My friends' half-wit sentiments and knee-jerk reactions might seem like not-unreasonable rationales for feeling no need to attempt such an onerous undertaking as the creation of a written representation of one's overall experience on the earth, to ignore, at some real cost, the desire to throw light on the formation and regulation of one's internal qualities, to catalogue, carefully and intelligently, the effects of external authority and circumstance, how each of us coaxes from existence what we want and what we need, or what we can. But they also smack loudly of, "Writing memoirs is a pitiful activity that people engage in when they can't think of anything else to do that is productive or creative, when they feel their lives are over. I don't have to think about the past or dwell on my memories, or write memoirs, because I'm still living my life. I'm still making memories."

Although it is true that I have lost the desire to produce or create anything except these scribblings, and thus the foregoing criticisms are not unfounded, I was shocked and appalled, yeah, I said it, that I had lived long enough to hear such shallow and fearful views expressed by my peers.

One of these curt critics is a woman of taste and sophisticated judgment, with a tolerable education, a prodigious professional output, a woman who has contributed in no small way to the cultural refinement of her community, and has earned the respect of many. She is nearing retirement, and the grateful citizens of at least one Canadian province, which will remain unnamed, are working on her statue as we speak. I posed the following rather lengthy question to her.

"Haven't you spent the last thirty years, your entire career, trying to convince people that art isn't stupid, that art isn't a waste of time? Haven't you fought tirelessly against the ignorant, the philistines, so many of them, who have said to you, with vehemence, with spittle on their chins, that standing in front of a canvas in a studio for hundreds of hours 'painting some shit my five-year-old could do' is a moral fraud, people who think that art is a criminal waste of valuable capitalist time?"

I went on: "You do accept, don't you, that writing is an art form? I would not even say that memoir and autobiography are the poor cousins of poetry and prose. Creative non-fiction is to writing what photography is to visual art? It doesn't wash in either case. John doesn't have to explain to anyone why he wants to write and record songs. Brian doesn't have to explain to anyone why he has spent a lifetime making breathtaking photographs. You don't have to explain to anyone why you want to paint pictures. Why on earth would I have to explain to anyone why I want to write an autobiography, to bring a life to paper, a reflection of my Self?"

I couldn't resist summing up, then, for her improvement: "I don't think the impetus for these creative pursuits arises from any great defect of character or a lack of imagination in the art of living, from a feeling of giving up. Composing and playing music, drawing and painting, writing, all of these arts are self-constructed means to a thought-free awareness, a bootstrap bump in consciousness. They are human desires, if not human needs, unavoidable. They contract time and expand space as well as giving, not the least, some relief from the pains of life. No stroke you have ever made on canvas has brought you greater joy than what I experience when I am satisfied with a paragraph I have written. When your work takes you away, you must go along with it until it lets you go, a curse and a grace better than any drug. How is art made, anyway? By the hand of the spirit of that which is created. If your work is any good it doesn't come *from* you, it comes *through* you. Is a memoirist not an artist, too? Are songs and paintings not just memories after all? What is memory if not poetry? You, and most of the rest of the world, might not appreciate my artistic efforts, but you, of all people, I would expect to defend to the death my right to make art in any form. This is me dancin'. These are the notes I sing. Giving voice to the eyes and the ears, and the other senses, to hands and feet. You owe me, and Art, an apology. Dummy."

She apologized. We're still friends.

But I had to think about it. Was I really just reliving the past?

Identifying with the past as a pig-headed participant in an *idée fixe* would be torture, and I experienced no such torment during the writing of Volume 1, only joy. I am not a warden of the past. It is not a museum. I did not set out to build walls of self-defence. I am barely presenting my case. I couldn't write these stories if I was reliving them as an apologist, although I see now that something of that nature has not failed to creep in, especially in this second volume. I wanted to make as few statements as possible about what I thought was right or wrong. Apart from the occasional, irresistible cheap shot and the odd anti-materialist rant, I have tried not to trouble anyone overmuch with what I thought should have happened, only with what did happen. Ideally, I wanted to visit these stories anew, for a short time, and let them speak for themselves in a kinder and more judicious context, and a less judgmental one. For me it is not a process of reliving or even recreating the past, but of dissolving it, neutralizing it, putting it to rest, with the benefit of years and perspective, letting it go with a sigh and a blessing, a sigh heaved with a gulp of heavenly breath. Going through a few things in the attic, bundles of memories wrapped up with strings of attachment. Writing them out of my system. Doing the work.

Through the agency of modern technology, I found and contacted people from the very dim past for hints and remembrances and to marvel at the wonder of shared experience, only, in some cases, to be completely ignored. This led me to suspect that some people who reject their past, or who cannot face it, or who dismiss writing memoirs as living in the past, might not really be living in the present as much as they think. They might be living in a state of over-identification with a solidified idea of the past with which they are unable to reconcile themselves. Disappointment or shame or embarrassment prevent them from accepting the reality and the lessons of past moments that were surely present moments when they occurred. Recognizing and accepting each present moment, and its transcendent value, is what allows us to stand at the threshold of love. And at the very least, even the most practical-minded would agree that all of our present moments from the past, lumped together, form the syllabus of our life, its collective educational and evolutionary store. Simone Signoret wrote a wonderful memoir called *Nostalgia Isn't What It Used to Be*. In it she said,

"I'm always sorry for the people who reject the gifts their memories may offer."

God forbid you have lived a life not worth remembering.

Anyone alive and *compos mentis* is still living their life. There is no rebuttal possible, or necessary, to that bit of foolishness. As for memories, I am still making them. Two at a time. One about the past that accepts and heals, and another one, right now.

There are, however, a few good questions that I, or any memoirist, or diarist, should be required to answer before continuing. Have I written enough? Do I need to go on? Is it time to shut up?

And the answer is two-thirds yes. I have written enough, and I do need to go on. It's a story, warts and all, and the story's not over.

Yet for me in particular, there is another problem.

My motivation for writing was not just to get the stories down and retire those memories, but also to entertain a little, as best I could, by writing about the experiences of an obviously deeply flawed human being. The diverse places I lived, the sometimes breathtaking, sometimes clueless travels, the countless episodes of my life, both adept and inept, and the people I met, from the inspiring to the desperate, seemed rich enough, and amusing enough, to record and explore. The icing on the pot brownie was that it was all from the perspective of a bone-lazy stoner.

I have a predicament now, though. At the start of Volume 2, I am twenty-five years old and still behaving like a child. It gets harder to talk comfortably about years of continued bad behaviour lacking the convenient excuse of youth. George W. Bush Syndrome.

By the fall of 1978, I had been a young man, very young, for a long time, avoiding both fortune and responsibility up and down the world, and not surprising, finding neither. I had managed to retain a genial and mildly enthusiastic view of the future, but I was continually confounded by slippery compromise, always off balance. Again and again, how was I to reconcile what I knew to be real, the state of the world, with what I felt to be true, the state of my soul, the matter of memoir versus the stuff of autobiography, and how could I possibly integrate the two into a life of languid self-inquiry and fevered self-indulgence? What seed would grow where there were no labourers? Manure, yes. Labourers, no.

I continued to drift along on the momentum of the old, memories and imagination, heredity and environment, a conditioned life and a conditioned mind, wondering how and where and when I would, or could, find a goal outside myself that I knew was inside, longing for that which I already possessed. I was overwhelmed by my senses and drawn beyond them.

In this befuddled search, on this vague journey, I began to realize, and fear, that I was powered only by a small store of raw, natural gifts, aided by little more than oddly persistent, intermittently sputtering, luck and grace. How long could it be before dark turnings?

But a few funny things happened.

And a few odd things.

Victoria, BC
June 2014

The Proust Questionnaire, Vol. 2
Dating Version

Neil Hansen
by Mia Frank
for *Yellow Jammies Magazine* (Dec 2013)

After a break of more than two years, we were fortunate to find Neil at home again, in Saanich, and I was eager to catch up with him. We joined him in his conservatory.

YJ: Hello, Neil. It's nice to see you again. Thanks for having us. It's been two years since we last talked and a year since the release of your first volume of memoirs. I enjoyed reading it very much, by the way. I understand you are working on a second book. Any thoughts about the process of writing the first volume? Did it have an effect on the way you are approaching the second volume?

NH: Nice to see you, Mia. Welcome. Yes, there was one thing that struck me in particular. One of the concomitants of an exercise in social inquiry, or self-inquiry, is the chance acquisition of unintended self-knowledge. Assembling a long, honest list of the events of one's life in the form of a memoir can be a sobering, if not chilling, experience. It's not the pink cotton candy of a resume.

As I got further into the writing of the second volume, I was a little dispirited, but shouldn't have been, to realize that I have spent fully one-half of my life as a slacker, a drunkard, and a libertine, and the other one-half engaged in continuous and heartfelt, if half-hearted, spiritual exercises, yoga, meditation, and prayer. I always knew there were black-and-white, push-and-pull contours to the topographic map of my life, but seeing it all in one place, shining a flashlight along some of those dark curves, was harder than I thought.

But in addition to reluctantly paying lip service, mostly just lip, to the grim realities of life in twentieth-century North America, in a conservative, WASP society, joyless and colourless, not to say murderous, that has, rather depressingly, and let me quote here from a hundred years ago, "drained away all its spiritual resources in the struggle to survive and that continues to struggle in the midst of plenty because life no longer possesses any meaning," I was able to find joy and colour in other ways.

There were many circumstances of my birth and personality, humble and unambitious, that would prevent my achieving anything resembling greatness, indeed, that might have led me to my grave at an early age by way of the rafters, but thanks to the slow evolution of natural law and liberal democracy in the west, nothing could prevent me from packing up and walking away from that which I found tedious and pointless, or from finding refuge in a school or a library or a bookstore. There is no "friggit" like a book.

A taste for rambling and reading is what has preserved my life. I have scuffed my way through six or seven hundred cities, towns, and villages around the world, and in addition to respectable, if not stellar, academic work, I have, on my own time, happily read a thousand volumes of natural and social science, history, literature, and biography. And I still don't know anything!

In the exercise of writing my own life, I came to disabuse myself of the comfortable fiction that I was an intrepid traveller or a holy mendicant or an intellectual of any kind. I discovered I was just a poly-dilettante hobo, no better, and no worse, than a drifter. I know myself better now. I am not sadder and wiser. I am happier, much happier, and wiser.

YJ: Who have you been reading lately?

NH: Augustine, Browne, Goethe, Equiano, Franklin, Hawthorne, Dickens, Trollope, Twain, Kipling, the Goncourt brothers, Galsworthy, Scott Fitzgerald, Joyce, Hart, Mowat, Newby, Dinesen, Berton, and as always, a steady diet of history and religious commentary.

YJ: Do you read modern authors?

NH: Not until they're dead.

YJ: Do you still work one day a week at the seniors' home?

NH: No. I quit after two years, hoping to leave them wanting more of me, but I stayed a little too long for that. I turned sixty this year, and as Haldane remarked when he retired, "Sixty years in socks is quite enough."

YJ: This will leave you more time for reflection. (*Both laughing.*) Any recent travels?

NH: Only six-week, low-budget, winter getaways to Mexico, Costa Rica, and Hawaii. Quiet retreats for yoga and meditation. Thermal therapy. Nothing very adventurous. My schedule in Victoria with my girls, now nine and ten years old, is pretty steady.

YJ: We covered a lot of serious points in our last meeting. May I ask you a few rapid-fire questions in a lighter vein with perhaps a few repeats from last time, just for fun?

NH: Shoot.

YJ: Now that you are fully retired, let me ask again, what would you be if you weren't retired?

NH: Cattle baron.

YJ: Your current obsession?

NH: Aviation.

YJ: What are you working on next?

NH: In vitro organ replacement.

YJ: Do you have an iPad yet? Can we follow you on Facebook or Twitter?

NH: Next question, please. (*Both laughing*.)

YJ: What talent would you like to have?

NH: Mesmerism.

YJ: What place on earth inspires you?

NH: Fukushima.

YJ: What place in BC inspires you?

NH: The Legislature.

YJ: Secret indulgence?

NH: Girl-on-girl.

YJ: What is your greatest fear?

NH: Tumours.

YJ: You are, or have been, a self-described libertine, although I'm sure you were just being immodest when you said that.

NH: Filthy as charged.

YJ: Any new romantic relationships?

NH: No. I was hoping there might be something of that nature after my divorce, but fate has decreed otherwise. I have made myself unf***able by choosing to live a hermitic and abstemious, if not ascetic, life. I can't think of any other reason why the girls would be staying away in droves, can you? Oh well, there's time now to give my battered parts a rest.

YJ: No regrets?

NH: Some in the past. None now. The herpes, I guess. Maybe one other.

YJ: Your new life as a hermit virgin aside, how would you respond to a potential sweetheart if she were to ask you questions about your favourite foods, books, music, and movies?

NH: Stop! I would rather have an open mind and a sense of humour than a favourite anything. But for some reason, try as I might, I just don't like eggplant. It's my least favourite.

YJ: Name a few things you are good at.

NH: Accepting reality. Not judging or commenting on other people's lives or behaviour. Not having strong opinions about things that don't matter. Not telling other adults how to perform trivial tasks. Resisting the temptation to turn every want into a need and every need into an emergency. Minding my own business. Being quiet, at last. I've always been flip. I'd rather be that than dull, but now I shut the f*** up and put it on paper.

YJ: If she asked you the most private thing you were willing to admit in public?

NH: My memoirs would indicate there is very little I will not admit in public! How about this? I owned a lemon-yellow Renault Le Car for ten years.

YJ: Do you laugh when somebody trips and falls?

NH: Of course, but I feel bad after.

YJ: Does intelligence turn you on?

NH: I prefer wisdom to intelligence, but try finding it!

YJ: Assuming no unusual risk of injury, are some sex acts between consenting adults inherently wrong or immoral?

NH: No. The important word is consenting.

YJ: Is there such a thing as having had too many sex partners?

NH: Yes, but I don't know what that number would be. A hundred is too many, right?

YJ: Are some human lives worth more than others?

NH: No, it just seems that way.

YJ: What is your opinion of sarcastic humour?

NH: Sarcasm is not humour. Sarcasm is for young people who aren't very good at conversation yet.

YJ: Beards. Cool or ugly?

NH: Depends. Into most men's lives, and some women's, a little facial hair must grow.

YJ: As an adult, have you ever worn a leash and collar in public?

NH: No, but I'm not ruling it out just yet. Where did you get these questions?

YJ: OKCupid.com. (*Both laughing.*) Just one more?

NH: All right.

YJ: Do you brush your teeth twice or more daily?

NH: Of course! How many teeth can you afford to lose?

YJ: Oh, and finally, in case you've changed your mind since last time, what actor would you like to portray you in a movie of your life?

NH: Harris Milstead.

YJ: How would you like to die?

NH: Laughing.

YJ: Well, thank you so much for your time, Neil, and for your very entertaining responses. Thanks for playing along.

NH: You're very welcome, Mia.

YJ: Again, talking to you has meant a lot to me personally, and I know our readers always enjoy catching up with you. One last question, on a more serious note. You mentioned mini-strokes in our last interview.

NH: I am happy to say that after four years of symptoms, it has been determined that I was not having mini-strokes, but acephalgic migraines, two or three times a year, a migraine headache without the headache. With them I get the classic migraine visual aura, for me a late-life migraine accompaniment. It's a very spacey, shimmering, just-in-time reality, the physical world coming into focus in a dazzling, dancing, as-needed way. I was just as glad it wasn't mini-strokes, but I was a little disappointed. I was hoping it was *samadhi*. I am more concerned now about this rash on my bum.

YJ: Where?

1   Pitching Woo

Laverne lived just up the road in the next town, only seven miles away, but I had forgotten how to woo, how to flirt, how to be relaxed with women. After several years of fairly successful, but mostly drunken, forwardness with women, I had forgotten how to be clever and funny around girls. Maybe I never was. Normally, I was so greedy for the fruit of womankind I couldn't hear a cluck without putting my hand under the nearest layer.

I had met Laverne in Sedgewick when we were both just fourteen. She was all eyes and lips, flawless skin, cute and skinny, utterly bosomless. Unlike the other girls in town, she didn't have dyed blond hair backcombed a foot in the air, but we had a couple of heated necking sessions anyway. She had grown up, gone to university, and now she had a grown-up job as a social worker. She had shortish brown hair, a bit wavy, casually maintained, and was still slim, but she had finally grown from a skinny teenager, at last, we were all waiting, into pleasantly noticeable contours. I had always liked Laverne. She was intense and easygoing at the same time, a laid-back firecracker, persistent sensuality in very casual clothing. Her relationship with my moody friend Dan, the naked hippie, had been a mystery to me, but I let that slide. Laverne and I were about the same age, so I was far too young for her.

I was nervous, unusually so, when I wandered into her small, plain, non-governmental office in the town of Killam, but I knew why. In your twenties everyone you meet who is about your own age is a potential lover. By simply telephoning her and going to see her, I presented myself to her as such, by evolutionary default. But I was suffering from a debilitating case of mental over-seriousness. I was a reformed drunk and a meditator, a sure-fire formula for pious solemnity. It was just as well I had been so thoroughly chastised and expelled by India. If my journey there had been at all successful, I might have been, surely would have been, insufferably unctuous. In spite of my recent lessons in humility, I still held forth frequently, to anyone who would listen, on diet, yoga, meditation, religious practice, and Eastern philosophy. There is no arrogance like the beginner's. I lectured and extolled. I abjured. I came close to exhorting. The passing years have shown that I was dead right and ineffably wise on all those topics, but that was not generally recognized when I was twenty-five and was therefore irrelevant. My grandfather, the golfer, now in his eighth decade, and enjoying God's gift to the elderly, comfort in his own skin, said, "Well, that stuff doesn't make any difference to me now. I've lived my three score and ten. But hell, you should have been a preacher." My grandmother's only comment was, "You have achieved a level of verbosity I could never hope to match."

Laverne had that very enticing, but maddening, combination of womanly features, attractiveness and brief periods of availability. Very brief. She was not the kind of girl to be single long. There was a small sign in her office that read *Sex is Spoken Here*. She liked the company of men, and there were always suitors in the wings. Amazingly, right now, in the fall of 1978, the timing was good. She and Dan had broken up in the spring of '76 when he moved from Edmonton to the Okanagan Valley to live in an orchard in my tipi, become a roofer, and build a gypsy wagon. She had had other relationships since then of course, but she had recently found a job in Killam, a hundred miles from Edmonton, and the city boyfriends of the intervening seasons were now faded with the fall. My window of opportunity, like the coming days, would be short.

Laverne made it clear to me that she was available. I was twenty-five years old and hadn't had sex in a year. There was definitely lead in my pencil, but I was no longer romantically cursive. I hesitated, and that was that. I thought I would have more than a week to consider the matter, but I was wrong. She was snapped up by someone I never met. At a dozen other times in my life, a week would have been more than enough. One date was often sufficient. Sex was the natural and predictable direction to take, but I knew it was pointless, and for the first time in my life I didn't have the inclination to start something I knew I couldn't finish. And I liked Laverne. Part of me just wanted to be friends. As a couple, we were never to be. It might have been the first time I had ever knowingly left an attractive, available woman undisturbed by my advances.

I was living once again on the frozen rolling parkland of East Central Alberta, but my mind tended ever southward. My experience over the last eighteen months with the meditators of California had been delicious and satisfying, life-changing, but somewhat contradictory, a little confounding. What was I to do with the warm, loving, skinny, shirtless, unperfumed hippies of Northern California, or with the churchy, ultra-clean, alternately surly and somnambulant meditators of Los Angeles? The life of an illegal alien at Ananda under the direction of the oily Kriyananda, Smarmy-ji, was as difficult to imagine as one in the very tempting, year-round warm climes of Southern California with the creepy, robotic clones of Self-Realization Fellowship. In spite of these general and specific aversions, I knew I had to try. There was nothing for me on a street of bungalows and white picket fences. When it comes to the material world, all I've ever wanted was a pocketful of money and a bus ticket out of town. That has never changed.

I had given Ananda a try. It was now time to make my feeble assault on SRF. I found myself filling in the many pages of application forms required to enter the ashrams of a bona fide, New Age, California religious cult. I wrote to US Immigration and requested the thick package of forms necessary to apply to live in the United States. I had to use my full name when dealing with the US government, and my first name is Robert, my father's name. When the forms arrived at my parents' post office box in Sedgewick, my father opened the package thinking it was for him, and he wondered what the hell was going on. A thousand people committed suicide, or were murdered, at Jonestown that fall. Religious cults were in some disrepute.

I was honest in my application. Too honest. I bared my soul to the gatekeepers of SRF. For me, if life wasn't about honesty, it was about nothing at all. This is a common superstition. I valued blunt openness and knew diplomacy only by its poor reputation. I never cared that honesty makes you seem indiscreet and defiant to those who do not see it as a virtue. At the very least, I was as yet unfamiliar with the advisability of revealing my passions and inclinations slowly and with caution. I was fairly certain Brahmachari Gary, my exasperated guide at the Mother Center earlier in the year, wouldn't be reading my application. I had yet to learn the story of Thomas Merton, rejected by the Franciscans, the Order of Friars Minor, for being too honest about his past, which included drunkenness, profligacy, and bastardy. He was less forthcoming when he then applied to the much stricter Order of Cistercians, the Trappists, where he spent twenty-seven notable years before he died young and accidentally in Bangkok. In rejecting him the Franciscans had done him and the Cistercians, and the world, a favour.

The application process took most of the fall to play out, but I finally received a long letter from SRF telling me they were concerned about my history with drugs, and they could not accept me at the ashram at the present time. They felt it would be better if I reapplied in a few years providing evidence of continued drug-free and healthful living, possibly a course of psychotherapy, and a deep and sincere study and practice of the SRF lessons. I couldn't argue about the wisdom of any of this, even the drugs, and I didn't need to, that was behind me, but I thought they were rather marvellously ignorant of their own heritage, the ritual consumption of entheogenic substances, the *soma* of the *Rigveda*. Psychotropic drugs had been as good a friend and teacher to me as anyone, or anything, in my past.

I thought it would be inconsequential to reveal to SRF, in frank detail, the full range of my experiences. Weren't honesty and willingness, grace and potential, the key features of this process? Wasn't my past what I was leaving behind? What did my very brief past have to do with the present or the future, or with anything? What were a few years of slightly wacky, experimental, youthful behaviour compared to the arising and nurturing of awareness? Arnold Schwarzenegger's use of bodybuilding steroids, performance enhancing drugs, hadn't disqualified him from becoming a four-time Mr. Universe, they weren't illegal then, and they wouldn't keep him out of the California Governor's Mansion. Why should my use of meditation enhancing drugs, consciousness steroids, keep me out of SRF? I also thought that being a counterculture outsider would be an excellent background and preparation for living in a yoga ashram. Who else was applying? This wasn't the Junior Chamber of Commerce or the Rotary Club, or even the Knights of Columbus. SRF was an outsider organization. They knew that, didn't they? Since when does God reveal Himself to the prudent and the wise?

Eventually, I realized that Yogananda had been preaching to the people of his time, the dissenting, xenophobic, and fearfully conforming Americans of the 1920s and '30s, and later, to the galvanized, hyper-patriotic, and fearfully conforming Americans of the 1940s and '50s. His church was still run by the disciples who had come to him fifty years ago as upright and virtuous women in dresses, girdles, and hats. Serious and sober men in suits, ties, and hats. They were over-conditioned saluters of flags, idolaters of rectitude. And always in hats. His pre- and post-WWII listeners were subject to all the misinformation and propaganda, the social pressures and prejudices, of a narrow, conservative, and not generally well educated society. Yogananda poured into them what he could, and it was a lot, but he could give them no more than what they could handle. Each generation, each cup, only holds so much. And now that old guard was in charge of SRF. In 1979, Sri Daya Mata had already been president for twenty-four years. She would serve in that office for another thirty-one, until she died in 2010 at the age of ninety-six.

When the stoned, wild-eyed hippies of the 1960s and '70s came along, they were drawn to Yogananda's neo-Vedantic teachings. Alarmed by these longhaired devotees, SRF closed further in upon its fretful self to present a secretive, monolithic face to the world with a soporific, unconvincing smile. They cultivated a stifling, over-rehearsed blandness so as not to attract attention to themselves, and to dissociate their organization, and its activities, from the drugs of 1967 and the violence of 1968. They were terrified of dilution, and their goal was to avoid infiltration by hiding in plain, tame sight. They wanted no endorsements from a generation of spaced-out flower power and radical protest. Also, they insisted that all applicants to the ashrams be able to type at a professional secretarial level. This was not a good sign.

It was very disappointing, and I was very sorry there would be no further opportunities in that direction. Their letter was polite, but clear and final. I was a wide-eyed applicant. My desire to live a life centred around daily spiritual practice was genuine. Exercise, yoga, meditation, meaningful labour, and good company was what I wanted. Heart to God, hand to work. I thought then that it was still possible. And I was willing to forgive them their stupidities. All they had to do was forgive mine, but they had evolved a different view of their guardianship role in this give and take.

Poor Yogananda. Such followers. They say the Devil never has to worry about the awakening of new buddhas. He simply sends them disciples who build churches around them, disciples who create errors and then strengthen them. God makes the rapture. Satan makes the churches. The guru points toward enlightenment, but unfortunately the ashram's existence depends on no one's ever finding it. The shell of the teaching, inevitably, becomes more important than the kernel. Temples and churches degenerate into egoic madness, dogma, secrecy, division, paranoia, and violence, and nothing ever comes of it. And when the guru is gone, like a passing ship, the water of ignorance and absurdity flows in again behind, often enough during his or her lifetime. Business as usual. Yogananda's breathtaking teachings were in the hands of a tense, conservative, hyper-vigilant curia, spiritual drones and bureaucrats. They would have none of me.

Although, in fairness, how sincere was I? And how suitable? They had had many years to figure out who would fit in and who wouldn't. I don't question their decision now. They did me, and themselves, a service. It was no service to the world, though, which would now bear the burden of my formation.

It was a blessing in heavy disguise. In an atmosphere of subjective unaccountability, in a church, in an ashram, you live in a culture that, however spiritual, is paramilitary. In an organization whose goals are a state of mind beyond judgment, there are nothing but judgments. There are no checks and balances, and no courts of appeal. I know now that if I had been accepted to the ashrams of SRF my involvement would have been short and painful. I was too ornery, too lazy, and too horny, for girls anyway, to be a monk.

And really, was I just as interested in moving to a warmer climate as I was in joining an ashram? Probably. It was likely I was just as tired of living in the cold of Canada as I was drawn to either of these yoga communities. I already had reason enough to be chary of them, Ananda and SRF, and there were more reasons to come. They sniped and squabbled and sued each other for years, a disgraceful squandering of money on litigation. SRF was accused, on good grounds, of unfaithfulness to Yogananda's teachings. Ananda was accused, on good grounds, of condoning a culture of sexual abuse. A plague on both their houses. I wanted to seize what they had to offer, and I couldn't, and there was my mistake, the grasping. But neither could I live without it. In spite of everything, to this day, I still have warm feelings for them both.

And it did get cold in Alberta. Winter wasn't here yet but when it came, I thought my nylon parka would crack walking the few hundred feet from my little apartment to the bar at the Pioneer Hotel on the southeast end of Main Street, the same bar where my uncle drank beer while I, eleven years old, waited for him in the parking lot in the sweltering cab of his grain truck. My aunt and now sober uncle, living in Sedgewick again after a few years in Kelowna, owned a busy insurance and real estate business in a new building on Sedgewick's one-block-long downtown, and there was a tiny apartment behind it that they rented to me. Living on Main Street in quiet little Sedgewick was not noisy. I went to the bar to socialize, but I wasn't drinking.

In a few days at my new job at the Co-op, I learned the intricacies of taking goods from the small warehouse and placing them on the shelves of the small grocery store, and how to bag them at the checkouts. In the canned goods aisle, being careful to rotate the stock, I turned all the cans and jars to make sure the English side of the labels faced out and the

French side faced in. After about a week of this, I thought I had a pretty good grasp of the mechanics of retail food transfer principles, and now would be a good time to begin my managerial training. Shadowing the grocery manager, Janet, seemed like the place to start. Standing next to her one day, I was politely waiting to be introduced to a visiting sales representative. She said, "What do you want?" I told her. She said that wouldn't be necessary. I realized then there was no plan in place to train me to do anything other than stock shelves and bag groceries.

I went immediately to see the tall, thin, good-natured general manager, the man who had held out the shiny bauble of a career in retail management. He said it would be best if we talked again in the spring. We were not on the same page. I nearly quit that day, but I thought I could use a few more paycheques, so I let it go. The end of my commitment to the Co-op did, however, coincide with the end of my first week on the job. I had decided not to be choosy in finding employment, and there I was, in spite of my rather high opinion of myself, a 25-year-old bag boy in a grocery store.

There are usually one or two simpatico souls in any workplace. God help you if there aren't. Julie was, among other things, the produce attendant. She was in her mid-thirties and had moved from the rainy, grey climate of Northern England to the sunny, cold climate of Alberta with her husband and children, and was unlikely ever to return. She was slim, cheerful, had a good sense of fun and humour, and was energetic and diligent in her duties. She had worked in a glove factory in England, and when she had her babies, she took her machine home and worked there, one baby dandling on her ankle, the other burbling in a playpen, while she sewed hundreds of pairs of gloves a day. She told me she never had to look at the clock. She always knew what time it was, to within five minutes, by the number of gloves she had sewn. It seemed to me a mildly Dickensian sketch of the Industrial Revolution. I think she preferred working at the Co-op in Alberta, in spite of the cold.

Before the oil and gas started to flow on the prairies, workers in small towns, workers for wages, lived a very humble life. If you wanted to break out of the lifelong, dismal routine of earning just enough money for food, rent, an adequate or just-reliable car, and no savings, you had to be a farmer or be in business, or move to the city and try your luck there. No one earned a decent wage in a small town. Well into the 1950s, people built their tiny shack-houses with their own hands using salvaged wood and bent nails. Sedgewick was full of small, decrepit, and strangely built dwellings. The early days were not glamorous. Some of the old coots in the area had spent as much of their lives in a wagon pulled by a horse as they had in a car. Although now you could see old farmers on Main Street, who, if you saw them in the city, you would swear were down-and-outers, driving around in big new cars, their serendipitous reward for finding in recent years that fields of oil and gas lay beneath their fields of wheat and oats. The general manager of the Co-op was right when he said they didn't pay the moon. For a 40-hour week, I was making about twenty per cent of what I made as a taxi driver in Calgary. I wasn't overly concerned about the comparison, but after a couple of paycheques I realized I wouldn't be saving much money at this rate, or any. I wasn't interested in a job that didn't pay enough to bank savings, and I started looking for other work.

Oil and gas were now making a lot of people in Alberta rich, or very comfortable, even on wages, and I thought I may as well be one of them. The local gas plant had nothing open, but one day Bozo came into the store. He was six feet, five inches tall and weighed three hundred and twenty five pounds. His name was Danny, and when he entered adulthood most people stopped calling him Bozo. I liked Danny, and I hesitate to seem unkind, but I have to say he was not, to put it mildly, a handsome man. To be honest, his appearance was a little frightening. He had just finished high school when I moved to Sedgewick at fourteen. He was so big no one ever messed with him, and he never had to prove anything to anyone or straighten anyone out. No one was crazy enough to challenge him. Consequently, he lived without conflict in an easy manner. Not that he didn't have his own problems, but he had no competition in the community, and therefore he had no beef with it, an enviable position for a young person of irregular size and features living through the hell of high school. As a teenager I played two hundred games of snooker and eight ball with his father, Bob, at the pool hall on Main Street, part of the intergenerational socializing that goes on in small towns. I liked their sense of humour. And Danny must have liked mine a little. We hung out a few times. He was head and shoulders, literally, above the other small-town louts who tormented my teen years in Sedgewick.

Danny was only two years older than I, and he was now a driller of oil and gas wells. If he had an opening, and if he felt like it, he was in a position to give me a high-paying job as a roughneck. I had already asked him about employment at least once on the telephone, but I hadn't been able to corner him closely in person. When he walked into the Co-op, I realized I had a chance now to make an impression, and I wasn't going to let it slip by. I said, "Hey, Danny, how are you? Any jobs going on the rigs these days?" I couldn't have been friendlier.

He feigned interest in his rare shopping duties, avoiding eye contact to sidestep the discomfort of having to say no to me again. "No, nothin' going. Got a pretty good crew right now."

I said, "Well, Danny, if you ever do need anyone, give me a call. If you hire me I'll give you such a blowjob your eyeballs will fall right out of your head."

The foulest profanity and the crudest sexual references were commonplace in male conversation in rural Alberta, but this comment was on its own distinct level of outrageousness. I had his attention now. Danny wasn't gay and neither was I, but he probably wasn't sure about that, so to make this kind of remark, in a public place, although that was of course the safest place to do it, was truly shocking, which was my intention. I needed to establish an unforgettable point of reference between us, say something to him that no one had ever said before. I think I was perhaps a little over the top on this occasion, but it was definitely a *bon mot* beyond the banalities of your average job-seeker. I had only a few talents, most of them unmarketable, but if you ever needed someone to blurt out something that would stop everyone in their tracks, I could usually be counted on. It stands out as the shortest and weirdest employment pitch I ever made. Will woo for work.

I think he laughed, I don't remember, but less than a week later I was awoken by a telephone call at five o'clock in the morning. It was Danny. His motorman had just quit, and he asked me if I could start on the rig that day. I was scheduled to work at the grocery store, but there was someone I could call to cover my shift. The Co-op and their four dollars an hour would have to muddle along without me. I said, "Hell, yeah."

Danny said, "I'll pick you up in fifteen minutes."

It wasn't my first thought as I scrambled half-asleep to get ready to start my new job on an oil rig, but from the back of my mind I was suddenly reminded that I had told Bozo I would give him a blowjob if he hired me. I thought, "Holy shit, I hope he doesn't want to collect." More about that later.

I had something resembling a pleasant family experience over the fall while waiting patiently for news from the yogis of California and putting in my mildly annoying, but not terribly disagreeable, shifts at the Co-op. I went to Edmonton a few times with my mother and aunt and grandmother, at least once to the Citadel Theatre. Their production of *Richard III* was riveting. Literally. The set featured a giant wall of riveted metal. On one of those trips, I explained to my grandmother what muff-diving was.

And speaking of carpet, I took her into Edmonton once to shop for new carpeting for her apartment. We went all over the city to half a dozen stores, had a very late lunch, and then returned to one of them to pick up the roll of Autumn Rust broadloom she had decided on. It was the seventies. It went well with her Harvest Gold kitchen appliances and her traditional maple wood dining room set. She had one wall of her living room papered in a fall forest scene. My grandfather said it reminded him of the path to the old outhouse, a remark that made my grandmother steam a little. The roll of carpet fit beautifully into the tipi pole holders I had built two years earlier. They were still mounted on the top of my camper. Later in the week, my father and uncle both took me aside and thanked me for driving my grandmother to Edmonton for a twelve-hour day of shopping. That was not something they had wanted to do with their mother-in-law.

On one trip to the theatre, after the Sunday matinee, I dropped my grandmother and her good friend Betty at a house in the city to visit old friends. They all had dinner together, but I didn't join them. I left them there and picked up Maura, now in her fourth year of studying clothing and textiles at U of A. The two of us went to a restaurant where we had a long chat and found we had absolutely nothing in common anymore. Afterwards, since they were on the way, we picked up Helen and Betty first, before swinging by Maura's apartment. On the highway back to Sedgewick, my grandmother and Betty couldn't stop talking about what a lovely girl Maura was. They went on so long I finally had to ask them why they were so surprised. Did they think I was incapable of getting a nice girlfriend? They clearly thought she was out of my league. Lucky me, I guess. Myself, I didn't feel Maura was too good for all of me, but she was definitely too good for parts of me.

On one of those trips to Edmonton, I visited briefly with a fellow apprentice from Ananda, my one compatriot from the program. There we both were only a year later, post-Ananda, both still a little lost after such a wonderful experience. We were both working, but in a grander sense neither of us had any idea what to do next.

My grandmother was not overly maternal, but she did bring me cookies once at my little apartment and a casserole dish of scalloped potatoes, which I enjoyed very much. My mother didn't dote at all, but I went to my parents' place, only a few blocks away, a couple of times a week to visit. My father didn't have to worry about my stealing all his beer anymore. I bought some housewares at the Co-op using my employee discount and cooked brown rice, and baked bread and pumpkin pie. I lived right across the street from the store, so I went home for lunch and usually fell asleep on the couch for half an hour. Janet, the grocery manager, said, "Gee, nothing much bothering you, is there?" I routinely fell asleep in the bathtub after work, before doing yoga. Schlepping boxes all day was good exercise.

Before the snow flew my grandfather golfed Sedgewick's nine-hole prairie course almost daily, often twice a day. He would pick up our good-natured, now very old dog, Sparky, a golden Cocker Spaniel, the one I had covered in soot when I nearly burned down the garage apartment, and take him along for the walk. My father and a couple of other businessmen in town had got together and built several houses on the golf course, small, three-bedroom bungalows. This was mostly a low-profit, civic-minded exercise to provide housing for potential new residents. My parents had bought one of them at the end of the fourth hole. Sparky used to walk the whole course with Hector, but now, when Hector putted out at the fourth green, the old spaniel went home to sleep in the shade of his house and left my grandfather to finish the round on his own.

Two of the businesses on Main Street in Sedgewick were owned by two German brothers, Fritz and Werner, who had come to Canada after the war. They both spoke fair English with heavy accents, had families with their German wives, and were friendly enough during the workday, but I rarely saw them anywhere else in the community. They kept to themselves socially. One brother was a baker who owned the cafe and bakery next to the men's wear store, Hansen's Men's Wear, which my father had just sold after ten good years. The other was the town barber. He had a small shop another two doors down.

I kept my hair short while working at the Co-op and one day, sitting pumped high up in Werner's barber chair, it occurred to me, suddenly and for the first time, that he must have been in the war. I asked him about it, a little tentatively. He said, "*Ja, ja,* of course, I vass in za army." I asked him where. He said, "Stalingrad."

I stopped still in amazement while he continued to clip. After a pause I said, "You were at Stalingrad?"

"*Ja, ja.*"

Still amazed, "You were in the German Sixth Army?"

"*Ja.* You know about ziss?"

Again, not trusting my own ears, "At Stalingrad?"

"*Ja, ja.*"

I had learned a little about the Second World War over the years especially in my twentieth-century history course at UVic four years earlier. I had always wondered at what point 3.8 million men thought it would be a good idea to get up one morning and march into Russia. The Battle of Stalingrad, ruin and slaughter for control of Asian oil, is considered to be the third bloodiest urban siege-battle in the history of warfare, with casualty estimates nearing two million soldiers and civilians over the course of five months, a butcher's bill exceeded only by the Siege of Leningrad and the Battle of Berlin, both in the same war.

Over a period of six years, 65,000 Canadian soldiers were killed in World War II. At Stalingrad, in the winter of 1942–43, in one season's battle, 13,000 people were killed or died of sickness and starvation *every day*, the equivalent of Canada being at war for five days. The loss of life was so overwhelming the Germans never managed to achieve another strategic victory in Russia. I learned that the Sixth Army, 110,000 men, was cut off and surrounded by the Soviets in November. It was the first German army of the war to be completely destroyed in the field. A hundred thousand men were captured by the Russians, and two-thirds of them died within a month, frozen, starved, and diseased. Only 5,000 ever returned to Germany, most of them not until years after the war had ended, as late as 1955, prisoners of the Russians for thirteen years. Germany's allies in the Italian Eighth Army lost another 115,000 killed and wounded. The barber on Main Street in Sedgewick, Alberta, the man cutting my hair, was one of the very few survivors of an unimaginable horror. Of the overall battle, on the German side, eighty per cent were killed or wounded. Of the German Sixth Army, ninety-five per cent. Werner was one in twenty to live.

I said, "My God, Werner, I read that the German prisoners were marched out of Stalingrad and died by the thousands."

"*Ja.*"

My respect for the privacy of his memories was now completely overcome by fascinated and morbid curiosity, and I asked him, "Where did you end up? How on earth did you survive?"

Still clipping away Werner said, "Vell, I lived for two years in an old bunker somewhere in the country. We had nothing, no food, no clothing even, just rags. The Russian peasants used to bring us something now and then. They had nothing themselves, but they felt sorry for us, we were in such bad condition. I did not die because every day I dragged myself out of the bunker, *auf meinem arsch*, on mine ass, to lie in the sun, no matter how hard it was, or how long it took, no matter how sick I was. Once outside I would expose as much of my skin to the sun as I could, almost naked. The others laughed at me, but they died, *ja*, and I lived."

I was speechless. Werner, a skeleton aided only by the kindness of his enemies and the rays of the sun, had crawled away from a mountain of two million corpses somewhere in the middle of Russia. It had never occurred to me that these two brothers in Sedgewick had fought in the war, on the side that killed my uncle before I was born.

Werner didn't seem upset talking about the war, but he didn't dwell on it. He was an old-fashioned man, and he had raised a pretty and old-fashioned daughter. She went out with my friend Ken for nearly three years in high school. Ken was straight as an arrow, hardworking, sincere, and he loved Brigitte. He would have married her, worked all his life to support her, and given Werner six grandchildren. But when Brigitte was nineteen, Werner reverted to the romantic nationalism of his fathers. The *Blut und Boden*, the Blood and Soil, of the Fatherland called to him, and no Canadian would be good enough for his only daughter. He sent Brigitte back to Germany to live with relatives and marry a good German boy.

Canada, geographically, is the second largest country of the modern world, but in the 1930s and '40s the openly anti-Semitic officials of the Immigration Branch, ignoring the pleas of much of Canadian society, the Anglican Church, the United Church, the YMCA, local service clubs, and the Co-operative Commonwealth Federation, argued fiercely and intractably that there was no room in Canada for any of the half-million pre-war Jewish refugees of the Nazis, not even children. Children were of no use in the concentration camps, and the Germans sent them immediately to the gas chambers upon arrival at the killing centres, particularly Auschwitz. One and a half million Jewish children, and thousands of Roma and Sinti children, were factory murdered in these German slaughterhouses. Others were killed slowly and horribly, tortured to death, in medical experimentation.

Canada accepted fewer than one per cent of the total number of refugees, a third of the number accepted by Bolivia and Chile, countries with one-fifth of Canada's population and one-tenth the arable land. The number accepted into Canada was twenty-five per cent of that of the US *per capita*. Mackenzie King, the long-serving, wooden-headed, vacuous, foot-in-mouth, racist, superstitious, bachelor prime minister died without writing an autobiography, but he kept a very candid diary. He was an open admirer of Hitler, likening him to Joan of Arc, and in 1938 he wrote, "This is no time for Canada to act on humanitarian grounds." In 1939 he said to a Jewish delegation, "*Kristallnacht* might turn out to be a blessing." I picture King and Hitler singing in the same choir. The Nazis murdered six million Jews in twenty-two countries. By the end of the war, Germany had roused the hatred and determination of fifty-six nations around the world to grind it into dust. The Allies levelled the country and killed eight million German soldiers and civilians, a tenth of its population, a precise mathematical decimation for which all were eligible. There was no room in Canada for Jewish children, but in spite of all-out war with Germany there was room for Fritz and Werner, later, to immigrate. There was room for their children to play and learn and grow, to thrive. There was room for old German soldiers to practise their trade in Sedgewick, Alberta, and look down on their daughters' Canadian suitors.

The snow fell. The temperatures plummeted. I had driven a snowmobile before, but not often. My aunt and uncle had three or four of them, and I and my eighteen-year-old cousin, Clint, went for a 25-mile ride one very cold night. Our destination, gained partly across country and partly along tiny rural roads largely unused in winter, was my aunt's brother-in-law's farm a dozen miles south of town. We would visit there for a while and warm up before heading back home. Snowmobiles have headlights, of course, and you can see much more at night on the prairies by the light reflected off the snow than you can on the rainy, pitch-black coast, but it was a very dark night. Coming back to town we were travelling fast along a small, narrow country road. Clinton knew the way, so he was a hundred yards ahead of me, snow billowing in his wake. I saw him zoom through a deserted intersection and then noticed the very unexpected headlights of a vehicle approaching rapidly through the dark from the right. I realized I had to stop immediately, or I would collide with it as it crossed my path. In spite of the snow, the truck was probably going forty miles an hour. I was going thirty. One way or another, at best, one of us was going in the ditch.

In a panic I hit the brakes and shifted my weight to turn and wound up doing an uncontrolled 360-degree flat spin at full speed, creating a tornado of snow. The pickup truck sped by only a few yards in front of me and vanished again into the dark on my left. With the way suddenly clear, I hit the gas again and raced through the intersection in a flourish of speed to join my cousin on the other side who had stopped, wide-eyed and anxious, looking back. All he had seen from his vantage point was a storm of snow and crazy, whirling lights, and the blur of a passing truck. He was expecting to hear the sound of a collision at any moment. He was certain I would hit the truck. So was I. I missed it by no more than three seconds, maybe two, the amount of time it took to pirouette on my Ski-Doo at thirty miles an hour. As the flurry of snow settled around us, we howled together into the night sky, hearts racing, both of us exhilarated by this rapid and startling event and its astonishing outcome. Each of us had missed the truck by mere seconds. Mostly, you never know how close you are to a random, potentially life-ending event. But sometimes you do. Less than four years later my cousin, Clinton, was killed in a motorcycle accident. Not his fault.

I socialized a bit with people I had known when I lived in Sedgewick as a teenager. I didn't drink, so there wasn't a lot of partying. This was before home VCRs, so you went to the movies in the drafty, old theatre in Killam. There was a television in the little suite I rented, but the reception was almost non-existent.

When I was a high school student in Sedgewick, I scoffed at my country contemporaries and the dismal prospects that lay before them, a miserable life of work, ignorance, and conformity. Marriage, children, in-laws, small-town life. Not more than half a dozen of them went to university. I knew for a certainty that I would escape Sedgewick as soon as I possibly could and would, somehow, immediately begin living a life of sophisticated freedom and adventure while they rotted within a hundred-mile radius of where they were born. I don't think I have ever been so spectacularly wrong about anything.

I would have been right in the 1950s and '60s, but by the mid-seventies oil and gas had changed everything. Young men from small towns all over Alberta, men who might never have ventured farther from their homes than Calgary or Edmonton, the provincial capital, were now travelling the world drilling for oil. They often started locally then moved on to the Arctic, where oil had been discovered at the mouth of the Mackenzie River in 1970. There the money was legendary. Then, if they wanted, they could go on to Africa, Central Asia, East Asia, and Southeast Asia, international postings where the money was spectacular.

One of my few hippie friends from my early days in Sedgewick moved his wife and kids to a suburb of Athens and regularly flew in and out of Iran to work. He was twenty-four. He travelled so much he had a special-issue, accordion-paged passport with a hundred leaves. He said he knew Heathrow Airport like the back of his hand. I had been there twice, six years earlier, once going to Europe with a backpack, once coming home without a dime in my pocket. He said Iran in 1978 was a madhouse. If a truck broke down, the driver would simply dump his load in the middle of the highway heedless of the hazard to other drivers, even at night. He told me he saw fenced-off compounds of hundreds of vehicles out of commission, in need of only minor repairs, but there weren't enough qualified mechanics to service them. They simply bought new ones with the billions of dollars in oil profits they were now making. He said the population was seething and angry. There were strikes, demonstrations, and civil resistance. He flew directly to the drill sites where he was working. It wasn't safe otherwise. It was the last year of the Shah.

My shirt-tail cousin Dale drilled for oil in the Congo. Every time he came home, he turned his suitcase upside down and emptied another two dozen carvings and crafts onto the floor. He said it was nearly impossible to run a night shift on a derrick in the tropics because the locals they hired fell asleep the minute the sun went down. He said he saw one man fall asleep while climbing a ladder, and he couldn't get any of them to wear shoes, never mind steel-toed boots. He was making so much money he bought three houses in Edmonton. He had the same hundred-page passport.

This was epically and criminally ironic. All I ever wanted to do was travel, to lay eyes on every square foot of the planet, and I could barely manage a trip every few years. And now all these uneducated, small-town ruffians were surfing their way around the world on a wave of oil, making a fortune.

We had a family Christmas at home after which my parents fled to the Caribbean for a two-week frolic. After four months at the Co-op, I had less than two hundred dollars in the bank. Something had to change. Working on the rigs was a horrific prospect, but tales of bags of money and seemingly limitless travel were bound to pique my interest.

My father was very pleased that I was working, but he made no attempt to hide his disgust that I was working for the Co-op. He hated the cooperative movement, its principles and goals. He was a free enterprise chauvinist. To him it was as clear as the nose on your face that large, vertically integrated, multinational corporations were the biceps of capitalism, the strength of all human good, but large, member-based, collectivist corporations were the tumours, the cancer. He was a small, conservative businessman. If he was going to be crushed by big business, he wanted it to be right-wing, not left-wing. If it simply came down to different methods of supply-chain management, low-cost mutual insurance, coordinated marketing, and government lobbying and manipulation, his perceived differences seemed to me to be overwrought and picayune, but he was endlessly vociferous in his objections to the cooperatives' political influence and any taxpayer support they received. At the same time, quite inexplicably, he generously pardoned the very same tactics and benefits on the part of free enterprise.

It has always amazed me that the most strident supporters of free enterprise have not the slightest notion of, or blithely ignore, its origins. "Free" enterprise would never have existed in the first place without early and continued government support, and corruption of course. It is inextricably intertwined with every level of government and couldn't reasonably exist for a minute without it. It is a blissful myth that glows preternaturally in the minds of the devotees of capitalism that the pure, God-given principles of free enterprise are spiritually self-contained and above the moral life of the community, like gun rights, and that the unrestrained functioning of the free market, its mere presence, magically optimizes all other natural and social systems. Even Adam Smith said, somewhere, as well as Marx, that the incentives and mechanisms of free markets favour the owners of capital, and consumers would always have to be protected from producers. My father believed in the durability of civilization and the future of human enterprise, but he also believed in social fascism and enterprise anarchy, industrial Darwinism. I have had to remind him a couple of times over the years that when he bows down and worships before the Golden Calf of Capitalism, it makes Baby Jesus cry.

For my father poverty was everything, and all, that was wrong with life, and money was the thing that could make it right. For me, for all that I had thought about it, poverty was admittedly wretched, but to be rich was simply to be less wretched on the same relative scale. My father never accepted the possibility that to be rich, to have a rich life, a life less wretched than being poor, was still just life. Fathers talk a lotta shit.

And now he was astonished, as astonished as I was, that I had started working as a roughneck on an oil rig. In his trucking days he used to haul drilling mud and diesel to the rigs, and he was always shocked at the unbelievably filthy state of them, the workers covered in dirt and mud from head to toe. He was himself so neat and tidy that, getting out of a car or a truck or leaving a room, he would dust himself out the keyhole.

I was seated in Danny's pickup truck at five thirty in the morning along with the young man who, with the recent loss of the motorman, or chainhand, had just been promoted to that position. He was asleep. He was young and kept a young person's hours. He was always asleep if he wasn't actually working. His old job was floorhand, and that was now my new position. It was February, but it was fairly balmy, no more than twenty degrees below zero. We drove through the dark to a town only forty miles away where we met up with the derrick man and had a big breakfast at a busy gas station restaurant surrounded by fifty other men on their way to work, eating and drinking coffee, and smoking. I ordered a cheese and mushroom omelette and was immediately quizzed about my eating habits. No point in lying. I told them I was a vegetarian. The derrick man, about thirty years old, was generally good-natured but never in a good mood, and he said, "I hate vegetarians. They won't buy my cows." He was a farmer from Saskatchewan working on the rigs for the winter. A big breakfast at a gas station, at six o'clock in the morning, with lots of coffee, in February, in a small town in Alberta, is a manly way to start your day, and I was fuelled, if not ready, to start my new job.

The four of us drove a few more miles out of town to the rig. It was still dark, and the derrick stood alone in a field, five storeys high, lit up like a Christmas tree on land leased from another farmer made rich. A short access road had been bulldozed through the skinny trees and scrubby bushes, the site had been cleared, the mud pits dug, and the ancillary buildings, trailers, tanks, and sheds were in place. It had all just been moved here from the last drill site, and the derrick had been erected the night before by the other shift crew. I had been a labourer for the railroad and in a couple of sawmills, so I had been around huge, noisy machinery before, but this was new.

There were giant diesel generators to provide electricity to the huge motors that turned the drilling pipe, and to power the enormous block and tackle system that hauled the hundreds of pipes into place and held the weight of them all in the hole, 100,000 pounds or more for a depth of one mile into the earth's crust. The derrick was a single, meaning it was tall enough for one 30-foot pipe at a time to be changed, added to, or removed from, the drill string, the pipe in the hole. Danny told me that in the Arctic, where he had been a derrick man, the rigs are taller, doubles or triples, where two or three lengths of pipe at a time are changed. He said they go slowly and more carefully in the high North, and that every rig in Canada was safer and better run than any in Texas or Oklahoma.

It so happened that my start on the rig coincided with the start of a new hole, and we drilled for a week. Before you can add another length of pipe to the drill string, you have remove the very top pipe, the rectangular drive pipe, with its large stabilizing mass of steel at the bottom of it, the Kelly. You first secure the drill string already in the hole with a heavy, three-piece, articulating, conical plug that you throw around the top of the second pipe, the one directly below the drive pipe, jamming it all into the floor. This prevents the drill string from falling into the hole. The plug is called a slip. It's the lightest thing you lift on a rig, and it weighed as much as I did. Giant tongs on cable supports hold the drive pipe fast while the driller reverses the motorized rotary table in the floor to unscrew the drill string from the drive pipe, which is then placed safely out of the way. Another set of tongs are then used to prevent the drill string from turning. The floorhand removes the enormous hauling block from the top of the side-lined drive pipe and swings it onto the top of another section of free pipe positioned horizontally nearby, if the derrick man doesn't already have one in place pulled from the vertical pipe rack. Either way, the new pipe hangs high and free in the derrick, and the floorman manoeuvres its bottom end into the exposed end of the drill string secured near floor level. The power of the drive motor is needed to unscrew the pipes, but for the gentle task of screwing them back together again, a length of chain is wrapped around the new section of pipe, and the driller uses a small motor to draw it quickly back, spinning the single pipe into place. The floorhand removes the slip, and the drill string is lowered into the hole, now one length of pipe longer. When the top of the drill string is at floor level again, the floorhand re-inserts the slip, removes the hauling block and places it back onto the top of the drive pipe sitting off to the side. The drive pipe is raised up the derrick again, its bottom end is seated into the newly added length of pipe, and spun in with another pull of the chain. The Kelly, the big lump of steel at the bottom of the drive pipe, is then seated into the motorized rotary table in the floor of the rig and the drilling starts again. Adding a new section of pipe to the drill string takes less than five minutes. About the time it takes to read a description of it. Or it should.

Not exactly angry, but definitely emphatic, Danny barked at us with advice and commentary, and called us many choice names, a sailor would blush I suppose, while the new motorman and I, the new floorhand, slipped and slid and lost our balance wrestling with slips and tongs and chains. I, of course, never knew what was coming next. The motorman had been on the job for a while. He was miles ahead of me. But he was still learning too, and my incompetence ate away at some of his own expertise and momentum as he tried to make up for my lack of them. It was an amazing dance of steel, motors, cables, chains, and pipe. You couldn't lift the slip out of the rotary table unless it was first loosened by the driller raising the hauling block, and he couldn't safely raise the block any farther until the slip was pulled out of the way by the floorman. The pipe, the tongs, the chain, and the block, all forward progress, were under the control of not one man, but four. The driller's actions and the floorhand's movements, along with the chainhand's and the derrick man's, were carefully timed, and when they were in sync, it was fluid and beautiful and productive. And when they weren't, the air was blue with Danny's many jests and merry sayings.

When another thirty feet of depth had been drilled, another pipe was added. Drilling thirty feet sometimes took only a few minutes, and other times it took an hour, and then we got to sit in the shack and warm up a bit until Danny thought of something else for us to do. When the bit had to be changed, you pulled the entire drill string out of the hole, no matter how long it was, making a hundred pipe changes as fast as you could go. You replaced the bit and reinserted it all again, another hundred changes. Every minute the drill bit wasn't turning at the bottom of the hole was time and money the company didn't want to spend.

Drilling mud is pumped down the hollow centre of the pipes and pumped back out again from the cavity around the pipe. It performs a dozen crucial functions in the drilling process, and the science and engineering of mud are impressive. It is also the source of the typical appearance of roughnecks, muddy from head to toe.

Oil or gas, when struck, could be pumped out through the drill pipe, but drill pipe is expensive, and it is removed from the hole and replaced with a cheaper, thin-walled casing pipe. The casing has to be cemented into place, and this was a job I was dreading. Like all concrete work, it is a time sensitive operation, and on a rig it is severely labour intensive as well. A hundred bags of cement have to be carried manually by two men, at a dead run, from where they are stacked on the ground near the rig, up a flight of stairs, along the staging deck by the horizontal pipe rack, up another flight of stairs to the drilling floor, ripped open, and quickly dumped into the space around the top of the casing pipe. Each bag weighs a hundred pounds. I estimated I could manage five bags before I collapsed. Not fifty. Not even at a walk, never mind a run.

We struck gas in just a few days, and to my immense relief it fell to the other shift crew to run in the casing pipe and cement it in. I knew I would not be that lucky again. The odds of having to perform the job were a straight fifty-fifty. Danny told me and the motorman to go cut the casing, and armed with the biggest pipe cutter I had ever seen, we scrambled below the floor of the rig and slid down the wide, muddy crater to the top of the drill hole beneath the BOP, the blowout preventer. The Bee-Oh-Pee is a giant, bulbous pressure valve, as big as a car, mounted directly below the drilling floor. It is designed to regulate the extreme and erratic pressures encountered during drilling. A blowout is a full-on catastrophe where anything in the hole, pipe, casing, mud, water, oil, and gas can be blown out and upwards, and ignited, destroying the rig and killing the crew. Danny told me not to depend on the BOP too much. Some of the time at least it wasn't even hooked up. It took us forty-five minutes to turn the giant pipe cutter twenty-five times, constantly slipping in the mud, pulling it a quarter of the way around with your arms and then pushing it with your feet and legs another quarter of the way to get it halfway around the pipe and into position to be grabbed by your partner. Danny felt we had taken our sweet time performing this task, and he had some colourful phrases for us when we were finally done. He told us he could cut a pipe by himself in fifteen minutes. I believed him. He was three hundred and twenty-five pounds.

Small contractors come and go on a derrick site to perform a variety of specialized operations not undertaken by the drilling crew. Mostly, I never knew what they were doing. One day I was hanging onto some damn piece of steel or other, standing next to one of these contractors during the warmest five minutes of the winter day. He took off his coat to adjust the many layers of insulated clothing you wear on a rig in the winter. He wasn't much taller than I was, but his arms were three times the size of mine. I was pretty sure he didn't go to the gym or work out. He was just big and strong, born that way. I was five feet, six inches tall, and of moderate build. I would never be as strong as this man, no matter what I did or how hard I worked, not at the peak of physical fitness. I didn't really care about my own size and strength, except as they affected my ability to attract women and make this kind of living. Better to be smart than big, most of the time. I had made half-hearted efforts at physical jobs in sawmills, in railroad locomotive shops, in construction, and now in the oil patch, and I found that I couldn't compete. I never could fight worth a damn, never did get those boxing or Taekwondo lessons. Plus, I was way too pretty to risk injury to the face. Some small men are able to compensate for their size and participate successfully in a physical arena, but I wasn't one of them. On an oil rig I was a Lost Boy amongst the pirates, maybe even Tinker Bell, but not as resourceful.

Roughnecks make a lot of money, but mostly because they work so hard. I don't remember the details of the shift schedule, but Danny had called me on a Saturday morning and we worked four twelve-hour shifts in a row, and then three more eight-hour shifts through to the next Friday. I enjoyed making good money, but I never wanted to work too hard for it. There was short change and there was long change. On short change you had only eight hours off before starting your next exhausting shift. At eight dollars an hour, the wage was only double what the grocery store paid, but with regular overtime and a substantial per diem, it worked out to eight times as much. In one week I made twice as much money on the rig as I made in a month at the Co-op. You can see the attraction.

When the Friday shift ended, we had the weekend off. But by Friday I had come to the obvious-to-everyone conclusion that I was not cut out to be a roughneck, or built to work on a rig. This was a dangerous, difficult job involving mostly lifting. I could feel the vertebrae in my spinal column crunching together every time I picked anything up. I imagined every one of my vertebral discs prolapsed and herniated, flattened into bone-dry mini pita pockets after no more than a couple of months. I had torn cartilage in my knee two years earlier, while golfing. I weighed a hundred and twenty-five pounds. To a newcomer the drilling floor was a maze of cables that would cut you in half, chains that would take your head off in a second. Each length of pipe was six hundred pounds. If one fell on your foot, you would never walk straight again. Injuries on oil rigs were frequent and usually serious. I could barely lift the slip. I could barely move the block. You had to grab swinging pipe and settle it to connect one joint to the next, and when the pipe swung across the drilling floor, I swung with it hanging on to the bottom. It was madness.

I had been born a hundred miles north of the forty-ninth parallel in a time of relative peace and had therefore escaped becoming military cannon fodder. There was no World War II, no Korean War, no Vietnam War for me, but I was just another young man of no particular ambition or social privilege in a resource-based economy. I would be hard pressed to escape becoming industrial cannon fodder, well-paid but expendable labour in the armies of rich men getting richer.

And I was pretty sure the toolpusher didn't like me. He was the general manager of the rig. I only saw him a couple of times on the drill site, but I had spent an evening with him at the same big table in the bar one night, with several other people, where he was awkwardly and unsuccessfully attempting to attract the attentions of a young woman who was more interested in talking to me than to him, and he glared at me then. I knew he was a toolpush but I didn't realize he was Danny's push. A couple of days after starting, I was surprised to see him walk through the door of the drill shack, and he glared at me again. He remembered me well, and he took the opportunity to make me feel as unwelcome on the rig as he had in the bar. Bad luck.

I thought I may as well make a clean break of it and give Danny as much notice as I could, although very little, so I telephoned him right after I got home from our Friday shift and told him I would rather walk to South America than spend another day on the rig. I wasn't going to tell him that in person. I think Danny liked my company, but I wasn't going to test it. He wasn't happy, of course. He would need to find someone else by Monday, but he didn't seem too upset. He was probably relieved. He knew I wasn't likely to become a good floorhand, and dealing with turnover was part of his job. I thought about leaving a bottle of whisky at his door by way of apology, but I was broke. I could expect a nice fat cheque from SEDCO, the Seaman Engineering and Drilling Company, but I had just bought a very expensive stereo at a good discount through the Co-op, and I owed them almost exactly what my one-week cheque would be for working on an oil rig. I was a bum but I paid my bills.

Thankfully, Danny never mentioned the blowjob I had promised him for hiring me, but I discovered, in 2013, that one of the founders of SEDCO was a man named, oddly, B. J. Seaman.

I only ever saw Danny once more, seven years later. He had kids by then and had quit the rigs. I asked him why he had given it up, all that good money, and he said, in his laconic way, "I seen guys work all their lives and never get rich." One friend remarked that in order to succeed on the rigs all you needed was a good supply of "stupid-stamina." Danny died in 2002 at the age of fifty-one, too big to live.

On one Saturday I had quit one job, started another, and by the next Saturday, I had quit that one as well. Hell of a week.

What now?

As always, my default strategy was simply to start walking. Working for a living in Sedgewick was bad enough. I wasn't going to be unemployed there. There were better places to do that.

It was time to go.

2 Forking Potatoes

When I got back to Calgary from California in 1977, and showed up on my sister's doorstep for the winter, I had seventeen dollars in my pocket. I wasn't concerned. I would start driving a taxi the next day. When I got back from India in 1978, and showed up on my parents' doorstep for a visit and to pick up my truck, there was actually a fair amount of money left in my pocket. I had been nursing along a student loan from the University of Victoria for a few years, and when I got the job at the Co-op, I decided, bravely, to pay it all off at once with my remaining funds. This left me debt-free but without a penny. I had spent five months treading water financially in Sedgewick, and when my grandmother expressed concern that I was leaving town with no prospects on the horizon, I told her not to worry. I had ten times more money than I had when I got back from California, a hundred and seventy dollars. She tried to joke about it. She said I was a member in good standing of the IWW, "I Won't Work," but there were tears in her eyes when I walked out the door. She worried about my future. She said, "You're having a heck of a time finding your niche, aren't you?"

I replied, "Niches are for statues, Grandma."

I was packed up and driving south in a couple of days. When I got to Calgary, I went to Gay's place. She said I could surf her couch at her duplex apartment for a while. The weather had turned nasty. It was bitterly cold. I had always been warmly attracted to Gay, everyone was, and to my pleasant surprise she was happy to see me. She gave me a more avid reception than I had anticipated. She was a gorgeous young woman, and particularly appealing to me, she was petite. I knew her from grade school. She was my best friend Gordon's younger sister. Gay and I were the same age, but I was a year ahead of her in school, so she was just the generally annoying and invisible kid sister of one of my pals. But even then I knew she was pretty. She had a pixie face, a high forehead, and fine hair. Her childhood features remained remarkably unchanged over the years, a felicitous neoteny, and she grew into a pretty woman. She was a dancer all through her teen years and was lean and strong. By the time she was seventeen I, and everyone else, really started to notice her. She was an occasional member of our little drug-addled circle entering adulthood, or at least leaving adolescence kicking and screaming, and we had all lived together for a few tumultuous months in the early seventies. She wasn't particularly fond of me during that time, but I had grown a little, or at least had stopped drinking, and she was a forgiving soul. She had been married briefly and now had a three-year-old girl, Sarah. The husband was history. There was a lineup of men at Gay's door begging her to let them take care of her, but she was sick of suitors.

A few years earlier, I had met Gay for lunch one day. I picked her up in my truck at the graphics shop where she worked, and we drove to a hotel pub nearby, in southeast Calgary's light industrial area. She was pregnant. We ordered lunch and ate it, and for forty-five minutes I never said a word while Gay nearly drowned me in a non-stop torrent of complaints about the discomforts and unfairness of pregnancy. I then uttered, very gingerly, but very foolishly, the only sentence I was able to get in over the hour, "So Gay, I'm curious, given the obvious strength of the feelings you have just expressed, did you ever consider having an abortion?" I was genuinely interested in knowing. She then unleashed a fifteen-minute firestorm of vituperation chastising me for being a heartless, hateful, miserable excuse of a human being for even thinking of such a thing, and that was the end of our lunch date. I drove her back to work and went about the rest of my day in a state of shock. I ran into her ex-husband some time later, and I told him about my very one-sided lunch with Gay. He said, "Yeah, they tell you women get a little moody during pregnancy. They don't tell you they turn into monsters from outer space."

I hadn't seen Gay since our blistering lunch date, but she had survived pregnancy and childbirth and now had a beautiful little girl and seemed quite level-headed. She gave me better accommodation than I deserved and went about her workweek as usual. I filled her refrigerator with groceries, made suppers, and bought her a new teapot. I did yoga and meditated for hours and drank gallons of tea while she was away during the day. I stood staring out the window of her living room at the bleak and frozen Calgary winter. "Good taxi weather," I muttered to myself, and for a couple of days I seriously considered renewing my taxi licence, but in the end I couldn't do it. I couldn't jump back into it. It did not call to me.

I took my time at Gay's. There was no need to rush out the door. She didn't seem to mind much that I was there although Sarah vigorously resented my presence. She waged a pitched battle against my incursion into her home and her little family. She scowled at me continuously and dumped out an entire bottle of my shampoo. She washed her feet and scrubbed her toenails with my toothbrush, but Gay tried to comfort her, telling her that I was only there for a short visit. Staying in Calgary was too awful to contemplate, and after three weeks I moved on.

Anne, Gordon's former girlfriend of many years, was in town and wanted to go to Brisco for a visit. Gordon wasn't living there anymore. He was still going to school in Castlegar, but we could visit John and Renee at the XN Ranch. I packed up, said good-bye and thanks to Gay and Sarah, and together Anne and I made the familiar drive through Banff and Kootenay National Parks, on icy roads, to the Columbia River Valley.

John had returned to Brisco from his carpentry course in Nelson, and he and Renee were living in an old, yellow school bus they had bought and converted into a recreational-cum-residential vehicle. John had designed and built a wooden addition, a hippie penthouse, for the bus. He peeled away the back quarter of the roof of the bus, like opening a can of tuna, and fitted the prebuilt loft into place without having to adjust his construction by a hairsbreadth. It turned out he was a pretty good carpenter. Unfortunately, he hadn't been able to find work in carpentry, and he was piling lumber at the local sawmill. The money was good, but it wasn't what he wanted. He petitioned his employers regularly for a chance to work as the carpenter's helper, and eventually he was successful.

The cabin at the XN Ranch had new hippie tenants, a family of four, but arrangements were always loose at the XN, and John and Renee had parked their bus just slightly out of sight from the highway on a level spot behind the small barn on the side of the hill.

And the XN Ranch was where I ran out of gas and money.

Anne and I knocked on the door of the bus, and it was a wonderful reunion. John asked Anne how long she could stay before she had to get back to university, and she said a couple of days. He then asked me the same question, except for the university, and I announced, and confessed, that I was broke. I asked them if I could hang around and look for work at the local sawmill or at least wait until some Unemployment Insurance money caught up with me. They were a little alarmed at this request, but if I had the nerve to put the question, the answer was a foregone conclusion. I was a friend in need.

No one ever paid rent at the XN, or none to speak of. John and Renee were living there without the landlord's knowledge or consent, in much the same way people had been living there for the last six years, ever since the day Sandy and I drove out from Calgary with the mayor and his aide to look the place over. I hardly had a right to be there, but no one really did, other than through the right of covert occupation, or long occupation, or general amnesty. It had been a place of fluid residency for a long time for a lot of people. Even though I only lived there for a few weeks over the years, I had known it from the beginning of its recent history, and it always had a special place in my heart.

They say fish and houseguests start to stink after three days. This was an aphorism to which I did not subscribe. I had read Austen, Dickens, Eliot, and Hardy, where I discovered that visits of a few weeks to a few months were commonplace in civilized society in former days. We were civilized, weren't we? When we were younger, John had made himself comfortable at two of my apartments in Calgary, at all hours, for many months, often enough overnight. We were hippies. Overnight parties and crashing were part of the culture. Our friend Ray had dined at my table, and Gordon's, many times when he didn't have a penny in his pocket for groceries. Alex and I once paid Gordon's rent for three months, and we never saw a nickel of that again. I've bummed a lot of couches in my life, but I always paid rent of some kind. There was always somebody in the young community who was broke. Looking after a broke friend was a meritorious undertaking. This was changing as people got older and more insulated, with serious jobs and families, but John and Renee had no children yet.

Mind you they did live in a bus. I spent a few nights on their little couch and then moved into my camper to sleep when I realized I could make it fairly comfortable before retiring for the night by turning on both burners of my portable propane camp stove for half an hour. The temperatures in the mountains, on the west side of the Rockies, were still cold but not as horrifically frigid as those on the prairies, and in just a few more weeks the snow began to melt and spring was in the air. I actually liked the idea and the reality of living in my truck in the winter. It was like winter camping. It was liberating to be responsible for so little. I think John and Renee felt lucky to have a good place to park their bus, near the old cabin, and I felt lucky to have a good place to park my truck, near them and their bus. It was a bizarre hippie pecking order. And I was at the bottom of it, "the least among you."

I was an inveterate, unapologetic couch surfer. I would not play by the economic rules, and I was experiencing the consequences. Unfortunately, so were my friends and acquaintances. I wasn't a bum. I always paid rent. But my behaviour cost my friends time and patience. And then it cost me my friends. A "leaner," my sister called me, without anger.

So I slept in my tiny, low, insulated camper. You couldn't stand up in it, and it had no fittings of any kind, so I was much dependent on John and Renee. I ate their groceries at their little table in the bus for many weeks before I was able to make any contribution of money, after the dole started to arrive. Tom, living in the cabin, and John, got up early to go to work, laboured the entire day outside at the sawmill while I visited and lounged about with their wives, Renee and Cathy, chatting and drinking tea, mostly in the warm bus, baking bread together, cooking, reading, doing the shopping. Having another vehicle there, mine, proved handy. This was not a situation likely to give John and Tom any consolation, but I knew they weren't worried a jot about their wives' affections or about any competition from me. John knew I was a horny little bastard, but I was no threat. And we had been friends for eight years through a lot of experiences. If I hadn't wound up staying with them for thirteen weeks, we probably would have remained friends.

Thirteen weeks was a bit unexpected, by all of us, and is to this day my personal best, and worst, for sponging. Housing in the Columbia Valley was terrible. There was nothing. People lived in ramshackle houses, log cabins, tiny hovels, run-down trailer homes, miserable little motel rooms, shacks, tipis, buses, and campers. There were expensive new housing developments going up at a slow but steady rate farther south around Radium and Invermere to accommodate the oil-rich Calgarians who had made the Columbia Valley their backyard playground, but they were not for the locals. And I couldn't get my own place until I found work and had some income.

I filled out an application immediately at the local sawmill, in Brisco. I introduced myself to the office staff and managers and made friendly chat. I asked them if it would be all right if I checked in every morning to see if there were any openings. Shows determination, right? They told me they were probably going to put on another shift in about a month. I had sawmill experience, so I was likely to be hired. It always amazed me that you would need previous experience to get a job piling lumber. What difference could it possibly make? I asked John if I should tell the managers I had worked on the oil rigs in Alberta, since I had only managed to last a week. He said, "Yeah, definitely. They love that shit."

A month. It was a long time to be flat broke and without income, sponging off friends at close quarters. I went every day to the mill office first thing in the morning wearing my hardhat and presented myself in a straightforward manner for the ritual of asking if there were any openings that day, although I rolled in a little later each day as the weeks went by. They got to know my face, but it was still a bit of a gamble. The managers might have enough nephews between them to fill an entire shift. Or what if they didn't give me a job in April even if they had one?

I drove up and down the valley investigating every possibility of housing that I heard of, finding nothing. And I wasn't fussy. I was living in a truck. Anything with a roof would be acceptable. Wood stove, creek water, unfurnished, outhouse, no electricity, it didn't matter, but there was nothing.

I found one day of work with a local farmer and spent nine hours in a small, dark shack in the middle of a field shovelling potatoes onto a conveyor belt with a pitchfork, where they were sorted and bagged by two or three women also working for the day. I was exhausted halfway through the day, and by the end of it I was in agony. I didn't know how I would make it through the afternoon. I thought I might weep in the last hour. It was a scene out of Thomas Hardy, the human labourer spent and broken trying to keep up with electrically powered agricultural machinery, steam-powered in Hardy's day. It was brutish labour. I had never felt more like a peasant. I could never understand how a labourer continues to work when all the energy is sapped and gone, the well dry, the muscles fatigued beyond flexion. It was worse than labouring on the rigs because the motions were immediately and endlessly repetitive. I haven't had a pitchfork in my hand since that day. Satan can keep them.

There was no hot water at the bus or the cabin unless you heated a pot on the stove. When you wanted a good soak and a shower, you drove twenty miles down the narrow valley over the roughly undulating, frost-damaged highway to Radium, then into the national park where for a few dollars you could rest and heat yourself into mush in the hot springs and shower in the change room. You were supposed to pay a fee to get into the park, as well as the pool, but the locals always just told the toll booth attendants that they were driving through the park to Calgary. There was no fee for through traffic, and the attendants never checked when you left the park again after your swim, a couple of hours later. I went an experimental two weeks once without a visit to the hot springs, a true mountain man.

Joe and Doris ran the store in Brisco, one of those little places in the mountains where everything costs twice as much as in town. The Post Office was there and they had gas pumps, but they didn't sell much gas. They had to charge so much for it in their remote location that the locals couldn't afford to buy it, and you timed your gas purchases with shopping trips to Radium or Invermere. Joe was over seventy years old. There was another Joe, Joe's dad, living forty-five miles north in the town of Golden in a home for seniors. He was a hundred and five. I don't know where he was born, but he first saw the light of day in 1874. That was a year after the founding of the North-West Mounted Police and the same year they marched from Manitoba to Fort Whoop-Up, Alberta, to bring order to the Canadian West.

No one wanted to buy Joe's expensive gas, but everyone wanted to use Joe's washroom, especially the well-heeled tourists being ferried in small buses up to the breathtaking granite spires of the Bugaboo Range in the Purcell Mountains only an hour west of Brisco. Lawyers, oil men, and engineers brought their families from Calgary, Houston, and Stuttgart, and spent more money on a few days of heli-skiing than I would in a year on rent, groceries, and gas. One day Joe had had enough, and when the bus stopped, and the passengers made the usual indications of purchasing nothing but making mass use of his facilities, he stepped behind one man and put his hand on his shoulder, thinking he might ask him what he thought he was doing. The man turned around and it was Pierre Trudeau, the Prime Minister of Canada, obviously under light security. Joe decided he would let him use the washroom.

Michael and Rebecca lived on the other side of the valley on a sunny acreage where they raised Rebecca's kids and garden-farmed. Michael came by the cabin one day looking for paying passengers to take a flight with him. He had just got his pilot's licence and was trying to rack up hours. I couldn't afford it, but I decided to go anyway, and we all drove thirty miles south to the little airport at Invermere, where Michael rented a four-seater plane, and we flew for an exhilarating hour up and down the valley. Thirteen years later, Rebecca introduced me to Amanda, the only woman I ever married.

And then it happened. After six weeks of daily checking in at the sawmill, I heard the words I needed to hear, "Start on Monday." Hallelujah. It had been a long six weeks, only a little fretful, not unpleasant, but I was seriously in need of income. The non-union mill paid union rates, nine dollars an hour, a good wage, far in excess of everyday expenses. Unfortunately, I still couldn't find a place to live. I was still hanging out at John and Renee's, but now I was making money which actually made the situation worse. They weren't looking after a broke friend anymore. They were putting up with an unwanted roommate who could easily afford to live somewhere else. They were tiring of my presence. It was getting tense. There were words.

Finally, in a stroke of luck, I was able to rent a disgusting little house with two tiny bedrooms only half a mile from the sawmill. I could walk to work, something generally unheard of in rural employment. The great thing about the valley was that even though there were practically no places to rent, when you finally found one, the rent was negligible. That's how awful most of them were. I paid fifty dollars a month, three and a half per cent of my gross salary. It was a cockeyed economy. A month earlier I had no place to live and no income. Now I had a ratty, but liveable, house to myself and a salary that was triple the minimum wage. In 2014 dollars I was making $60,000 a year piling lumber, and my rent was a hundred and sixty dollars a month.

And what luck, my house had electricity. It blazed into service a few days after I moved in. I retired my oil lamps and set up my expensive new stereo. It was heaven. There was no stove or heat in the house, but I put my camp stove on the counter for cooking, and the spring was now so far along I was able to get by with no other source of heat than the few BTUs it produced. There was a kitchen sink, but no water came out of the tap. With a sudden spike in temperatures as May arrived, one day I came home from work to find gravity-fed, ice-cold spring water pouring out of the faucet. Unfortunately, I had inadvertently left the open faucet swung over the counter, not over the sink, and the whole damn house was flooded. I was so happy I didn't even care.

There was no refrigerator, and I couldn't find a used one anywhere in the valley, so one weekend I made the three-and-a-half-hour drive to Calgary to buy one at one of the many used appliance stores there. And was lucky to find one. Buying a used fridge didn't seem like it should be a problem, but they were very scarce. At the sixth and last store on my list, where I was fortunate to find one, the owner told me it was artificial insemination season in the cattle industry, and the artificial inseminators had shot into town and scooped up every used refrigerator they could find to keep their collections cool.

I had a toilet in my tiny bathroom, flushed with a bucket of water, but there was no hot water tank and no bath or shower, so I kept a routine of ad hoc home ablutions, bathing in a saucepan of water in the middle of the living room, which was also the dining room and the kitchen. I drove at least twice a week to Radium for a luxurious, long soak at the hot springs. Now that I had money I could, after my soak, dine in leisure and luxury at the Radium Lodge on the hill just across the way. I brought a book with me and ordered the all-you-can-eat salad bar and a baked potato and French onion soup, the vegetarian's three-course feast. My first paycheque from the sawmill covered my small financial debt to John and Renee. My second paycheque was completely unattached, and my purchasing power soared. It wasn't rags to riches. I still wore rags, that was just my style, but my wallet was full now.

The first month was not easy. I went from the brutal labour of the oil rigs and the potatoes to piling railroad ties on the green chain at the sawmill. The ties were only eight feet long, but they were either 8" x 10" or 10" x 12" at the butt end. The wood was still wet. The eight by tens were very heavy. The ten by twelves were nearly unmanageable. If you dropped one it was a serious problem to get it off the floor again. My arms, especially forearms, were frequently numb during the day and constantly so at night. It made sleep difficult. I went to a doctor, but he had no idea what it could be. My back was killing me. I didn't know how long I could last piling railroad ties, but I had no choice now. I couldn't quit this time.

There were, mercifully, occasional breaks from the railroad ties, and I piled long pieces of light lumber at the end of the chain with an old man who had lived in the area for decades. He had been a guide for hunters of bears, and he told me hair-raising stories of ursine encounters. They're big, bulky creatures, but they can run, climb, and swim fast, and he had more than a few close calls with them. There are only eight living species in the Family Ursidae, but they are widely dispersed, especially in the Northern Hemisphere, and they are a familiar and fearful motif in art and myth, not least, I imagine, because both humans and bears lived for such a long time in caves, in competition for shelter. The taxonomists call bears dog-like carnivores and say their closest living relatives are the Pinnipeds, the seals and walruses. This is hard to imagine in the Rocky Mountains, but it did used to be a vast sea, or so I understand. They come and go.

I think the managers saw I was fading fast on the green chain, and to my great delight they moved me to the edger saw where I became the edger tailer.

Raw logs are lifted from the yard onto a huge outdoor platform where they are spun through the debarker on giant rollers. Our pal Benjie ran the debarker from a little hut where he sat and listened to music on his boombox. It was a rare non-physical job in the sawmill, and we thought it had to be a sweet gig, but it must have been dull, and hard on the back as well, but in a different way.

Milling big logs, up to six feet in diameter in the old days, requires a primary head saw, usually a band saw, to make the first cuts and turn the logs into giant planks. The planks then go to the edger, an adjustable bank of up to eight circular rip saws. The edger man quickly estimates the optimal way to cut the plank into four-sided, dimensional lumber. He moves each saw into place, electrically or hydraulically, and feeds the plank through on powered rollers. Tailing the edger, my job, involved removing the irregular pieces of edging that came off the sides of the freshly cut lumber after it came through the rollers, landing on a large steel table in front of me. The edgings weren't heavy, but they were either long, awkward, and floppy, or short and inaccessible. I had to remove all of them, quickly, pushing and tossing them down onto a conveyor belt below the table where they were moved off to the chipper. There they were ferociously masticated, and the chips stockpiled for sale. The cut lumber, now unimpeded by slash, went off at a right angle to me along the transport chains to be piled by the green chain gang.

Once again I found myself doing a non-stop, eight-hour dance, two or three steps in any direction, in primary industry, babysitting large, loud, dangerous steel machinery. Once in a while a piece of lumber coming through the edger would be mis-sawn, or for some other reason require a re-saw. Then I had to lug, as best I could, an enormous piece of irregularly-sized wet wood back to the edger saw. The edger man, himself as big as a bear, didn't like me much, and more than a few times he expressed his disgust at my face and performance by raising both hands high over his head and spitting dramatically onto the floor. He wore an enormous T-shirt that read *You don't work, You don't eat.* I thought to myself it should probably say *You don't have money, You don't eat*, and there had to be a better way to make a living.

After a few weeks of tailing the edger, I was transferred to the dry chain. I didn't like the edger much, but it seemed better than the dry chain. It didn't really matter. 'Twas all shite. I spent the rest of the summer piling dry wood, none of it very heavy, thank God, but the pace was relentless, and the work was so crushingly boring I could barely stand it, hour after hour after hour.

Early on, the management decided to cancel the evening shift and start a new schedule consisting of a single ten-hour shift, every day of the week, manned by two separate crews, each one working four days out of eight. A list went up on the bulletin board outside the office, labelled *Red Shift* and *Blue Shift*, concepts I would encounter again when studying physics, but their only significance now was to let us know when to show up for work. Working four ten-hour days in a row was very trying, but four days off in eight was refreshing, if you kept yourself busy. John said it never stopped being a source of amazement to him, seeing my name on the list outside the office. He told me it just didn't belong there. He knew as well as I did that I didn't belong, or fit in, in a sawmill. It wasn't a great job for him either, but at least he was a carpenter's helper, not a labourer. I laughed when he told me that. He was right, but good God, where did I belong?

There continued to be plenty of time for reading. I wasn't always busy on my four-day stretches of time off. In the winter I had read Germaine Greer, June Singer, Marilyn French, and Erica Jong. I was curious about women. In the summer, I discovered Robert Graves and read *I, Claudius* in two sittings, as well as *Claudius the God*, and Graves's autobiography, *Good-Bye to All That*, much of it about his young years in World War I. There was a tasty little bookstore in Invermere, and I had the money now to buy new books. Raymond Chandler's novels had just been reprinted. I bought all of them, and we shared them amongst ourselves.

We also read, with gusto, James Clavell's exotic and bloody novel about Japan, *Shōgun*. It was twelve hundred pages long. It sold six million copies in its first three years, and another nine million over the next decade. There were fourteen hardback and thirty-eight paperback printings. I read it while living at the bus. We only had one copy, John's, and we all vied energetically for chunks of time to be alone with the heroic John Blackthorne as he encountered and endured the trials of shipwreck on the shores of Japan, and sudden exposure to the bizarre and violent society he found there in the early Edo Period, the start of the Tokugawa Shogunate. The fictional Blackthorne was based on the historical William Adams, probably the first Englishman ever to reach Japan, in the year 1600. In the novel Blackthorne and his crew endured what they rightly considered to be the horrific savageries of the Japanese, boiled alive, multiple beheadings, ritual suicides, incomprehensible social and political structures and allegiances, plots, ruses, earthquakes, ninjas, and all those unhealthy hot baths. The Japanese in the novel see the English, Dutch, and Portuguese sailors, quite rightly, as filthy, flea-bitten, pox-ridden barbarians. Critics and analysts called the book "a half-million-word encyclopedia of Japanese history and culture." Also, "In terms of sheer quantity it brought more information to the non-Japanese public than anything, or everything, that came before it."

I took the book with me into town one day on the chance I might have a few minutes to read some of it between errands. John was at work. Renee was busy. I was in the clear to claim it for my own for the day. Unfortunately, there was a rare occurrence of trouble-at-mill that day, and most of the workers were sent home before lunch. John was beside himself in anticipation of a day off and free time to go home, lie on the couch, and read his book, *Shōgun*, uninterrupted, for several delicious hours. When he got home, found the book was gone, and realized I must have taken it to town with me, he was very disappointed, and not a little annoyed. I returned home by sawmill quitting time, as I had intended, to make sure John got his daily ration of titillating, mouth-watering historical melodrama, but the damage was done. This did not increase my popularity with John.

It occurred to me to stay in the valley and work at the mill until I was inevitably laid off for the winter. With some time, effort, and money, I could winterize the house and live peacefully through another season of snow and occasional deep-freeze temperatures. I might take up skiing, downhill or cross-country, or both, get in a winter's supply of good pot, read fifty good books, and live comfortably on UI for the winter. That's what you did in the valley. If I lived there long enough, I might even be able to weave a nest for female inspection and find a girlfriend. But single women were very scarce. When a new woman arrived in the valley, usually in long skirts, rubber boots, wool socks, and shapeless woollen sweaters, men you hadn't seen for months would come down from out of the hills, dressed in their finest, come a courtin'. John had been very lucky. Renee was good-natured and attractive, sweet and sexy. Is there a better combination?

But there I was, out of place, like John said. We hung out a lot of course while I lived at the bus, warmly renewing our old friendship. And I found, no surprise, that I really liked Renee as I got to know her better. John made genuine attempts to introduce me to his friends and to the social life of the valley. Wherever John and Renee went, I went. I enjoyed Benjie's bright and generous company especially, and on most days I found myself at least briefly in one group or other of generally easygoing valley residents. We played tennis at a new, local, so-far-underused court built for tourists. We went to the two local pubs, twenty and thirty miles away. There were many evenings of music and drinking and mushrooms and pot, although I was still on the wagon.

John and I went a few times to the auto wreckers to strip cars for parts to rehabilitate the many vehicles he liked to buy and sell. We hung out at the garage in Spillimacheen where the crusty old owner, Don, gave me tips on how to tune my engine and install a stereo. I bought six new radial tires from him, with my income tax refund, in a show of support for local business, and I was amazed at how much better my truck handled with them. I wished I had had them when I was racing Ben to the hospital in Grass Valley two years earlier on winding roads and tall, skinny tires. Don lived in a trailer home behind the garage and had a wife I never saw, not once. I drove by the garage in 2012 for the first time in twenty-eight years, and the owner at the Spillimacheen store, next door, told me that Don, now very old, still lived out back, but I saw the service station had been long abandoned, the yard full of junked cars. Don had worked in Canada's far north, like so many young men, putting together a grub stake to be able to marry and settle farther south. His garage business couldn't have made any more money than being on welfare, but he ran it for many years. It didn't seem to make him happy. One day, commenting on all the music these new hippie residents in the valley liked to play, he said, "There must be a lot of music in me…," pause for effect, "because none ever came out."

I didn't see John and Renee much after I left the bus and settled into my new house, although I saw John every day at the sawmill. They had had enough of me for a while. Their friends were my friends while I was living with them, but when I moved on, only three miles down the road, I found I hadn't met anyone I felt particularly close to, and vice versa. In the last half of the summer I saw only a few people, and most of my four-day periods of time off were spent alone. I had thrown myself on friends for aid when I was broke, and I found there was a price to pay for that. John has always been the first to admit that his memory is pretty poor, but he has never forgotten my unasked-for, thirteen-week visit in the spring of 1979. I and my actions had had an isolating effect.

Apart from a mild general regard for the angelic nature, endless variety, and ingenuity of humankind, my particular interest and enthusiasm for people were genuinely, if annoyingly, reserved for those I thought of as seekers of truth, and I was becoming spiky in my social expectations. Often enough I put my most challenging foot forward, not my best. I sought the bow that shoots the farthest, there's a saw for you, and I had little interest in the mass of humanity. Daring people to awaken to their infinite inner selves is always a conversation killer, sincere people are such a bore, but it seemed better than the usual fare. I wasn't that obnoxious. I merely cast out my topics for heartfelt dialogue and reeled them back in disappointed, my wormy bait still on the hook. No one, certainly not John, was interested in anything I had to say about yoga or meditation or vegetarianism. John was a lifelong, hilariously dedicated meat eater. He once ended a discussion about the merits of vegetarianism, years earlier when he was still young, with an inarguable, "Shut up! Shut up! Shut up! Shut up! Shut up!"

One day John said to me, in a gentle way, that he was sometimes embarrassed when he introduced me to his friends. He said he never knew what I was going to say. This was true. The mountain hippie lifestyle had always attracted me, but it was starting to look like just another set of cherished ideas, another meandering channel through which attachment and judgment flowed. The mountain longhairs were non-mainstream and counterculture, for me a sort of minimum qualification, but I found no one looking for anything beyond that, beyond their own level of identification and comfort. I wasn't interested in the banalities of polite, or hip, conversation. Saying whatever came into my mind seemed the only proper way to address and dispose of the uninspired claptrap and twaddle of daily banter and boilerplate conversation, and I indulged my pointed preferences as a matter of principle. As Fitzgerald rather delightfully put it, "If I didn't tell at least one person a day to go to the devil, I wouldn't have had anything to do at all." Not everyone appreciated my sense of humour. I still had a primordial, biotic need to be liked, and without that I might have given up speaking altogether, but I didn't have the courage to shut up and go my own way. Mostly, people in the valley drank and smoked dope and partied and played music, "without a cry, without a prayer." A common saying was that the only thing that changed in the valley was lovers. And all I wanted was change.

Forgive me if I sound condescending. I did not parade myself about in a sandwich board sign proclaiming to be a man of consecrated goals, but for me there were no other sirens within hearing distance. Self-knowledge and its vague pursuit were unnerving and often hard to explain, but I saw nothing noble in the endless, tiresome grasping and soporific specificity of consumerism and conformity. I was a *sadhu*, a religious wanderer, of some kind. I believed the core of the hippie lifestyle was valid and had been since pre-history. In the two million years between the time humans first started to walk upright and when they started painting on the walls of caves, someone must have thought cooperation and non-violence were ideas worth considering, in spite of the violence of nature all around them. Among the old and familiar: "They shall beat their swords into ploughshares, and their spears into pruning hooks: nation shall not lift up sword against nation, neither shall they learn war anymore." Meeting the new and strange: "Barrels of flour instead of barrels of gunpowder, biscuits and bread instead of gruel, implements of husbandry instead of guns for destruction, rapine, and murder, and articles of usefulness to substitute for the torturing thumbscrew and the galling chain." Peace and love, man, was a calling to which I had responded religiously, deeper, I hoped, than the trappings of fashion and manifesto. But I found the mass of hippies to be just as timid and superficial, just as subject to group-think, as the supporters of any other ideological molehill turned into mannered facade. In the lunchroom at the sawmill, the rednecks sat in one group and the hippies in another. Hooray for our side. Of all the hippies and progressives I met in the valley, I'm not sure there was a meditator among them. Not that being a meditator is any guarantee of skilful living. Meditators are some of the most cloying cretins in the world. Case in point.

So I found myself no more at home with the mountain hippies than I had anywhere else. From my early teen years, trusting no exterior source, trusting no one, not even myself, I had developed and managed a mindset and a *modus operandi* of rejection which I focussed in specific directions on specific topics, an over-exercised strain of the general contempt of youth. But I started to see that that approach, which I had by now cast very wide, had other consequences. For a long time, I had thought that one way of being was better than another way of being, that one set of ideas was better than another, and that because I belonged and adhered to the one I thought was better, I was better, a common judgment and a common error. I now began to think that this might not be true. At the rate I was going, even that which I believed would, in the end, have to be rejected. Another twenty-five years would pass before I was able to reconcile these overlapping, ontological Venn spheres, discovering that by both not accepting and not judging, you can position yourself at the dimensionless point that creates the particular and the universal, embodying and dissolving them both, the centre everywhere, the circumference nowhere, that sets of ideas are not what make you free. It also looked like my very unpleasant Grade 6 teacher would turn out to be right. I would always be on the outside looking in. Like would be met with like. That which I rejected, rejected me.

So I decided not to stay in the valley for a winter of improving books, good dope, yoga, meditation, bracing outdoor exercise, and unchallenging company. Or none. There would be no fabulous life in the theatre for me, no down-to-earth trade as a carpenter, no organic gardening in an Arcadian country ashram, or even secretarial work in an urban one, I couldn't type that well, and no buckets of money and delicious travel in oil exploration, the endless search for fossil fuels. I didn't like being around straight people and I hated rednecks. I didn't feel like a failure because I didn't think in those terms. I wasn't throwing my life away, as some people thought, my family especially. To me, working nine-to-five was throwing your life away. But I was at yet another crossroads. I needed a prod. I needed to be challenged and to learn something.

Brian, my UVic theatre buddy and Mexico travelling companion, had said, "You have to love university. It's like Mom. It'll always have you back." I wrote a short letter to Camosun College, Victoria's two-year vocational and university-transfer institution, established only eight years earlier, containing a mildly worded query about a possible course of study in science, my only remaining area of occupational interest. Camosun was much cheaper than UVic and had smaller classes. In a matter of days, I received a package of forms in the mail and the following precipitate, concise, and very helpful letter.

"Dear Mr. Hansen: Thank you for your interest in attending Camosun College. I have enrolled you in the following courses. Please fill in the forms and return them with a cheque for $25.00 for the registration fee. In-person registration for your classes will begin at 9:00 a.m. on September 4th. I wish you the best of luck in your studies. Sincerely, (Mrs.) Kay Kelly."

I had asked for no such thing. When I wrote to them I thought I would receive a calendar of courses in the mail, which might then have been discouraging to examine. Somehow, the clerk or counsellor at Camosun had decided that I, and they, would benefit from a nudge, and taking the matter into her own maternal hands she had made it all very simple for me. Math, chemistry, physics, biology, and French. I was slightly stunned, a little confused about the French, and very amused. Well, why not? I wasn't looking for a sign. I am not one of those New Agers always on the lookout for omens, but this was as close to one as I was going to get. I sent her a cheque and stopped thinking about winterizing the house.

The rest of the summer took on an easier tone. I could count readily the number of long days of physical labour that remained before I could walk away from the sawmill forever. I needn't spend money on the house now or take time to repair it. There was no point in trying to find a girlfriend if I was moving away with no intention of returning. This takes some weight off the male mind. I went to the hot springs in Radium, to restaurants and movies in Invermere. I went swimming with the summer tourists at Windermere Lake. I read endlessly. I socialized hardly at all. There was a baseball picnic of hippies and an evening at the bar, where everyone drank. I left early to go home to meditate. The silence was essential and satisfying, except for the mice and the packrats poking around in the spare bedroom.

I got sunburned jumping off a short, wooden bridge and floating around on an old inner tube for a hot afternoon in the Columbia Wetlands, the interconnected pools of clear water set amongst many square miles of grassy and bushy marshes. I went to a couple of small mountain lakes with Renee's brother, Michael, and some of his many kids. He was a genial hellraiser, a serial producer of children, and a well-known valley resident. Renee and Michael's father had been the town doctor in Invermere for many years. The water in these little lakes was so sharply frigid they were only swimmable during the two or three hottest weeks of the year, and I was glad Michael had invited me along to experience these mountain jewels.

I bought camping equipment with the idea of making a solo, multiday hike of a north-south, highline trail in Kootenay National Park, but I was scared off by reports of the continued presence of aggressive bears in the area. This suited my general state of laziness and exhaustion anyway. I wasn't sure I wanted to use my days off to go alpine hiking after working four ten-hour days in a row at the sawmill.

I decided to do at least one full-day hike in the park, the Sinclair Creek-Kindersley Pass Circuit. I bought bear bells, which I realized were useless as I walked the winding and bushy path next to noisy Sinclair Creek. I could barely hear their tiny, tinny clanking myself. I was sure a bear on the trail, just around the next tight corner, would never hear them. Or worse, a bear cub, the last thing you want to see at close quarters in the woods. As usual, I lost the trail, after it left the forested creek, and I was only vaguely sure of where I was. I was a very good taxi driver. There was no urban destination I couldn't find as easily as a homing pigeon, but I was a bit hopeless in vistas off the grid.

I wound up scrambling straight up the south side of a very steep slope for nearly an hour, along and around avalanche paths, to the top of Kindersley Summit, at 7,800 feet. The view to the northeast was a sea of white peaks, the long, magnificent procession of the Brisco Range. I am terrified of heights. I can stand on a chair to change a light bulb, but don't expect much useful work out of me on a rooftop. It was a moving and antsy experience to sit alone for half an hour at the tippy-top of this windy, cold peak in thin, sharp air in a state of breathless awe.

I could see the Kindersley Pass Trail far below me but no indication of how to join it. I knew I was supposed to go a little north first, along the ridge, and then, at the bottom, swing back south again with the path, assuming I could find it. I decided I may as well short-circuit this occult, northerly loop of the trail and just head straight down the west side of the peak. I had scrambled up for an hour, and now I scrambled down again for another hour. Once at the bottom of the very steep, pathless side of Kindersley Summit, I had to traverse a dipping half mile of dense forest and underbrush. Once in it, I couldn't see anything other than the trees and the undergrowth in front of me, but I knew if I kept a generally westward direction I would find the trail.

It was in that dense, scrubby patch of alpine forest that I first understood why you don't see more animals in the mountains. In the thick of the woods, there were dozens of faint trails over and under the deadfall, obviously used by the creatures of the forest. These were their primary routes. When I got to the human trail, I realized that from the perspective of a furry quadruped, a human trail is as big as a freeway, obviously dangerous and to be avoided. Rambling the four or five miles back along the trail through the forest and down to the highway would have been easy, but I had to walk knee deep through snow for much of it. It was July. The entire hike was no more than ten miles, but it was a strenuous day, a gain of over 3,000 feet in elevation. I was very sore and quite satisfied with myself at the hot springs that night. I hadn't seen another soul all day. Hiking alone is not a good idea.

One evening after the movies in Invermere, I was very surprised to see two prostitutes standing on the street. There was no mistaking their profession. They favoured the full-on LA hooker look. This was unusual. Invermere is a small town. My windows were rolled down to let in the warm night air, and I could hear a couple of blades chatting with them. There was no one else on the street. The girls said they were from Calgary. They had come out for a few days of R & R, and they needed to earn a little money to cover expenses. They ran down the items on their very tempting menu. I hung my head over the steering wheel in agony and wondered if I could afford to bring one of them back to my very shabby mountain house for the night. She would need a ride to town in the morning, but I wasn't working the next day. I drove very slowly, and alone, out of town. I was twenty-five then. I am sixty-one this year, and I have never yet felt a need of sufficient urgency to actually employ a sex worker, but I'm not ruling it out just yet. I had renounced Satan's pitchforks, but I will wait until my deathbed, like Constantine, before renouncing the rest of his works.

After three months of employment, I was eligible for the company dental plan, and I went immediately to the young, very professional-looking dentist in Invermere. We made a plan to remove my last two wisdom teeth and replace the dozen poor fillings I had got eight years earlier. My experience over the years with incompetent, greedy, and alcoholic tooth-pullers had been sketchy, but I felt safe with this young, hang-gliding dentist, and I didn't even mind sitting in his chair for four or five appointments for a complete dental makeover, rid of all my wisdom teeth at last. He also assured me that amalgam had come a long way in recent years, and I could expect a much longer life from this new set of fillings. When it comes to your teeth, any good news is very good news.

Earlier in the spring, when I was still living in my truck by the bus, my old friend Dan came by and stayed a couple of nights at the XN Ranch, sleeping in his own little camper. I had spent some recuperative weeks the previous summer at his place in the Okanagan, on my way back from India, sleeping in his gypsy wagon in the yard at his little house. He had quit the Coca-Cola warehouse while I was there and had been collecting Unemployment Insurance for many months. The counsellor at the federal government office said, with disgust, when he finally cut him off, that it was, in his experience, a claim of disgraceful and near record-breaking length. Dan was a competent worker and never seemed to have any trouble finding a job, but he wouldn't work if he didn't have to. I was myself on a bum and couldn't even offer my friend indoor accommodation. I was glad to see him, but I quickly realized that his demons were getting the better of him. He was bitter, rigid, contrary, humourless, and mean. And he was twenty-six years old. He was probably the unhappiest man I knew, and I was broke and living in a truck.

One evening John and Dan and I went to the movies in Invermere in John's Volkswagen Beetle. When the movie was over, and we piled into the tiny car to head home, I got in the back. John and Dan were both over six feet tall. I was small. I always sat in the back. Dan was a hopeless, unapologetic tobacco addict, and before the engine was even started he had lit a cigarette. I had quit years earlier, and John had kicked the habit as well. The car was so small we weren't going to tolerate Dan's smoking in it, and we both piled on. We howled at him, in a friendly barrage, to put his cigarette out, but he absolutely refused. Laughing, I grabbed Dan from behind and put him in a choke hold, and John relieved him of his cigarette, throwing it out the window. This was fairly typical grab-ass behaviour for young men. We assumed Dan would accept that he was outnumbered, morally and physically, and take it in good part, but he was enraged. He wasn't up for a pile-on, friendly or not. He got out of the car and started walking. John drove slowly along beside him, and we urged him again and again, in an exasperated and pleading way, to quit being a dick and get back in the car. It was eleven o'clock at night and thirty miles to the cabin. What was he going to do, walk? It was still spring. It wasn't that warm. After five or six blocks, John had had enough. He stepped on the gas and drove away. I thought he might stop up the way a bit, but Dan was my guest, not John's, although they had met before, and John left him to his own childish devices. He had to work in the morning. He had no more time for this silly game. We were not much sorry to leave the crazy bastard behind to hitchhike home on his own after such a ridiculous display. I thought Dan might have to stay at one of the many motels and inns nearby that were starting to open up again for the tourist season. He would be very annoyed to have to pay for a room, he was so cheap, but there was nothing I could do about it.

John had made the call, and I felt bad about it, but I didn't disagree with him.

We were perplexed, the entire drive home, by this sudden turn of events, and when we got back to the XN we were astonished to find that Dan was already there, packing up his truck and camper. We were dumbfounded. He had beat us back to the cabin, hitchhiking, and we had not delayed a moment or stopped anywhere along the way. I could hardly remember a car passing us the entire thirty miles. We thought it unlikely Dan would even make it back to the cabin that night, never mind beat us there. That possibility never crossed our minds. It was eerie and a little creepy, like he had teleported home. I looked about me in the dark for angels and demons, weird minions. We apologized endlessly, not because we felt we were wrong in our abrupt and corrective behaviour regarding his rudeness about smoking in the car, but because we had no desire to see him, or anyone, drive away at midnight with nowhere to go. It was crazy. But Dan's dignity had been offended beyond repair. He said not a word to us. We watched in amazement as he rolled slowly down the dirt road in front of the XN Ranch, turned north onto the dark, empty highway and drove away. It was the damndest display of infantile behaviour I had ever seen, and given my own histrionics over the years, that was saying something. It was also accompanied by a downright spooky exhibition of validation of his rage, a supernatural leapfrog through the night by the aggrieved party. It was so strange overall that I have never forgotten it, and it was also the last time I ever saw Dan. I understood a little of the pain of living, but the depth of Dan's pain was, to me, deep-rooted and unfathomable. His pain was acute and had a medical name. Everyone else's pain is the same in kind but is chronic and low-grade and is called normal. He definitely couldn't take a joke. He died less than ten years later of a heart attack, a kind of suicide. I believe he drank himself to death. It takes about thirteen years, and it's a shitty way to live and die.

I had been to Castlegar twice in the spring to see Gordon, the second time to attend his graduation. Through previous part-time employment, and now a junior college diploma, he was well positioned to find a lifetime of steady government work, reasonably well-paid, outdoorsy, and pensionable, in parks management, provincial or federal. This was his practical solution to the common problem of the wedding of personal inclination to impersonal survival. Gordon had always been a quiet man, but after two successful years at college he was transformed. He was energized and confident. At the graduation ceremony, when he ran up to get his diploma, he grabbed the microphone from the speaker's hand, and to everyone's surprise and delight, made a cheeseball speech. I think he actually said, "But seriously folks, I know there's a lot of love in this room."

Later in the summer, Gordon was getting married. I had met his fiancée in the spring when she was still just a pretty blonde girlfriend. Gordon asked John to be his best man, and I was so hurt and pissy about it I didn't go the wedding. I had been out to Castlegar twice already, in a visit of friendship and nobly attending his graduation milestone, and I thought I was as good a friend as John, who hadn't gone out with me either time. Gordon and John had spent a lot of time together in recent years, but I had known and loved Gordon since childhood. I told myself that I couldn't afford another trip to Castlegar, and I had to get ready to move to Victoria in only another week. This was all true, the timing was bad, but it was a miserable excuse. I drove all the way to Cranbrook to buy a wedding present for them and after an hour, in a tortured frame of mind, walked out of the store and drove all the way home without one. Talk about childish displays. I don't think Gordon and his new wife were together for more than a few months, maybe a few years. You don't have to be too embarrassed about missing the nuptials of your friends' starter marriages, do you? Still, not my finest hour.

Our only significant source of news in the valley was magazines like *Time* and *Newsweek*, and we usually read them cover to cover and swapped them in the lunchroom at the sawmill. Subscribing to magazines was not a practical option for me because I moved so frequently, but the previous fall I had signed up for a year of the Canadian magazine *Maclean's* to try to get a better perspective than that offered by most American publications. Journalism south of the border routinely ignored much of the world's news if it didn't involve the US directly. I received one *Maclean's* magazine after another with cover banners shouting "The New Lawyers," "The New Scientists," "The New Students," "The New Accountants." Everything was New! like laundry detergent, and I let my subscription lapse.

Nineteen seventy-nine was a hell of a year. Pol Pot was overthrown in Cambodia by the Vietnamese after dictating an autogenocide of two million people. Egypt became the first Arab country to recognize Israel, ending thirty-one years of a state of war. Idi Amin fled Uganda when Tanzanian troops took the capital, Kampala. Margaret Thatcher became the first female Prime Minister of the United Kingdom, Saddam Hussein became

President of Iraq, and the Nicaraguan dictator, Somoza, was overthrown by Daniel Ortega and the Sandinistas. Pope John Paul II became the first pope to visit a communist country, his own, Poland, an event which catalyzed the nascent Solidarity Movement that led to the overthrow of communism in Europe. His visit was called "nine days that changed the world."

Smallpox was declared officially eradicated, and the One Child Policy was introduced in China which has since prevented 400 million births. There was a partial nuclear meltdown at Three Mile Island in Pennsylvania, the first space shuttle was delivered to the JFK Space Center, and the *Gossamer Albatross* was the first human-powered aircraft to cross the English Channel. The Compact Disc was introduced by Philips Electronics, and the Sony Walkman went on sale in Japan. Guessing where the US space station *Skylab* would land when it fell out of its six-year orbit was an international news story. Parts of it landed in Western Australia, and the local government fined NASA four hundred dollars for littering. They never paid.

Patty Hearst was released from prison after two years' incarceration, John Wayne died, and McDonald's introduced the Happy Meal, which has since killed 400 million people.

But until the Soviet Union invaded Afghanistan on Christmas Eve, Iran dominated the news of 1979. After "2,500 years of continuous monarchy," the Shah, the King of Kings, the Light of the Aryans, the American Puppet, fled Iran in January, and two weeks later Ayatollah Khomeini returned after an exile of fourteen years, most of it spent in Iraq. Five million people lined the streets of the capital, Tehran, to greet him. He was *Time* magazine's Man of the Year, and nearly everyone on the planet knew the unsmiling face of the man with the long, white beard. Only two months later, Iran declared itself an Islamic Republic in a referendum carried by ninety-eight per cent of the votes. By the time Iran started writing its new theocratic constitution in August, I was only a few delirious days away from moving to Victoria and ending five months of dismal labour at the sawmill, piling lumber all day on the dry chain and all night in my sleep. I never worked in a sawmill again, never had another physical job. By the time Khomeini was made the Supreme Leader of Iran, its Guardian Jurist, I was settling blissfully into the fall semester at Camosun College and the diligent and busy lifestyle of a sober student, renting a room in the basement of the Victoria Buddhist Dharma Society Centre in Fairfield, a short stroll of only two deliciously cool, moist blocks under the chestnuts from both Beacon Hill Park and the Strait of Juan de Fuca.

On October 22, President Jimmy Carter reluctantly allowed the ailing Shah into the United States, the Great Satan, for gallstone surgery. Three weeks later, the Iran Hostage Crisis began. It lasted fourteen months until January 1981.

In the fall, in Victoria, I met a beautiful young woman from Japan at the Dharma Centre named Shizuka, it means "peaceful," and plummeted precipitously and hopelessly into love. Her last name was Isayama, "admonish mountain," and I thought of her full name, optimistically, as "peaceful advice from the mountain." Our relationship was coeval with the Iran Hostage Crisis and was not unlike it, "an entanglement of vengeance and mutual incomprehension."

Shizuka and I were lying in bed together on the morning of May 18, 1980, the next spring, when Mount St. Helens, nicknamed the Mt. Fuji of America, erupted a hundred and thirty miles away in the state of Washington. It was the second of only two eruptions in the twentieth century in the lower forty-eight states of the USA. The other had been sixty-four years earlier at Lassen Peak in California, a giant stone magma-plug in the earth's surface. Lassen Peak is at the southern end of the same Volcanic Arc as Mount St. Helens, both in the Cascade Range. On that Sunday morning in 1980 in Washington, one-quarter of a cubic mile of ash was blown into the stratosphere, fifteen miles straight up, in under fifteen minutes. It spread across the United States in three days, circled the globe in two weeks, and killed fifty-seven people, 7,000 big game animals, and twelve million fish. Volcanic ash was found over an area of 22,000 square miles.

For many people the Iranian Revolution, the Hostage Crisis, the Soviet Invasion of Afghanistan, and the Mount St. Helens eruption, were kind of a big deal.

They hadn't met Shizuka.

3   Science-Drama-Love Dharma

Victoria has a long history of scenic and climatic seduction. If, as a visitor, you experience one of the few sunny days of the year in Victoria, you may return home to whatever frozen part of Canada you were visiting from and work single-mindedly for the rest of your life to be able to move to the coast. All you need to accept in exchange for the mildest, warmest winters in Canada, as well as year-round greenery and stunning floral extravagance, is limited and viciously competitive employment prospects and a breathtakingly expensive cost of living, including scarce, over-priced housing, which for students is usually improvised, quirky, and sometimes downright shabby.

But nothing could dampen my spirits as I fondly renewed my acquaintance with the short drive from the ferry terminal to the small city. I had been away for three and a half years, and I wasn't sure I would ever return. It was a much longed for reunion. I knew this climate and this lifestyle, and it could only be better now that I had stopped drinking and was free of a life of physical labour. I had spent most of the last year working at physical jobs, and I never wanted to do that again. And I had never lived in Victoria sober. I was looking forward to seeing it through temperate eyes.

Susan had a couch I could sleep on for a while. She was one of my brother-in-law's six cute sisters. We had met eight years earlier, when we were teenagers, at our siblings' wedding. We had a brief, torrid, and confusing affair then, and we had been friendly, again, as recently as this spring, in Calgary. She moved to Victoria over the summer. I wondered idly if I might not be able to strike up a longer term relationship with her in Victoria. She was pretty cute, and I was willing to make the offer. But she was already being wooed by a much older man, a naval officer. Susan thought it would be a good idea to have a baby when she was eighteen, and she was still only twenty-three years old now, a single mother. The naval officer looked like a better prospect than a broke student. He was nearly twice her age and as aggressively conservative as my father. I was a little puzzled by their relationship, but I didn't have time to think about it. Each to their own, or better, *chacun ses goûts*. I was studying French now.

Susan's apartment was at the far end of a long bus route from Camosun College, and I was able to get a seat first thing in the morning every day and study my new textbooks for forty-five minutes, largely uninterrupted, on the way to school, valuable time. I had been to college and to university but never to study sciences. Seated a little nervously in my first chemistry class, someone asked a good question. "What do we need to know already in order to be able to pass this class?" The instructor wrote a long equation on the board. He said, "If you can't balance this equation, you probably shouldn't be in this class." I couldn't remember what the letters stood for, the names of the elements, never mind balance it. I went immediately to the library and checked out the same textbook I had used in my Grade 10/11 combined night class in chemistry two years earlier. I read it cover to cover, twice, in the first week of classes. With a sigh of relief, I found most of it still made sense. I left Susan's apartment at seven o'clock in the morning and worked on her couch until ten o'clock at night. Math was trying. I found I was quite inept with numbers, and it seemed the solutions to these puzzling queries would be found only in complete immersion and dogged repetition.

Fortunately, Susan was in no hurry to be rid of me. Her romance with Captain Jones was in its early stages, and from her point of view there was no down side to making him a little jealous by having a much younger male houseguest, a suspected former lover, hanging about. It did serve to sharpen his interest, and I was glad to be able to help. Once again, finding accommodation in Victoria at the beginning of the school year was a quiet, tense misery, but after about ten days I finally found a room at the Victoria Buddhist Dharma Society Centre, also called Sakya Thubten Kunga Chöling, at 1149 Leonard, a flat street in Fairfield only one block long.

The door was answered by Margaret, also called Sister Margaret, also called, rarely, Dechen Drolma. She had taken vows as a Buddhist nun in the Tibetan Sakya lineage only two years earlier and was the major-domo of the house. One of the benefits of expensive housing in Victoria is that many homeowners have to rent rooms to be able to pay the mortgage. These rooms, often in houses in the nicer parts of town, allow students to live in beautiful neighbourhoods, at high but manageable rates, close to the college and the university. Not one in a hundred students, in later life, could afford to buy a house in these same neighbourhoods. For many students, their years in college in Victoria were halcyon days spent in the lovely, expensive, tree-lined streets of Fairfield, Rockland, Oak Bay, and Cadboro Bay, occasionally even the very pricey Uplands. There are hundreds of small rooms for rent in the fine old houses in these areas, some pleasant, some ridiculously makeshift, some positively grisly.

The Dharma Centre house, built in 1912, newly acquired and mortgaged by its current owners, was badly in need of rental income, and there were two bedrooms on the main floor available to students and one in the basement. Margaret and the resident lama, Tashi Namgyal, occupied the two bedrooms on the second floor. The three renters shared the main-floor bathroom. There was a simple, good-sized, eat-in kitchen with a plain table that would accommodate six diners, the scene of many ad hoc meals and friendly, spur-of-the-moment discussions over the next nine months. The in-line living room and dining room, separated by heavy sliding wooden doors, a common feature in Victoria houses built before World War I, had been converted together into the Dharma Centre's temple area with a full-on Tibetan Buddhist shrine and altar.

If you have never seen a Tibetan Buddhist shrine, I recommend having a look at one. The constituent parts together form a profuse, but subtle, delight to the senses, primarily in both strong and muted burgundy and gold colours, with splashes of blue and green and sharper reds and yellows, all representing the body, speech, mind, and enlightenment of the Buddha. Usually covering an entire wall, top to bottom and side to side, in ascending tiers of covered tables, they are made up of a regularized medley of fabric images, *thangkas* in cotton or silk brocades with copper, silver, and gold threads, embroidered and painted with scenes from the Buddha's life, or the images of other buddhas and bodhisattvas. There are also statuary, incense burners, candles, and numerous bowls and plates, often in brass, for offerings of rice, fruit, and flowers. There are baldachins, cloth canopies. And always scriptures. Typically, the devotees sit on the floor.

I turned the corner in the kitchen and was shown the temple area. I was amazed, and after a moment to adjust to this visual feast, delighted to see it. I had my own little altar that I set up wherever I lived consisting of a smallish, black travel trunk and half a dozen photos of the SRF gurus, but this profusion of Buddhist imagery was new to me and pleasantly overwhelming. Sister Margaret told me that most of the people who came to look at the rooms for rent took one look at the shrine and ran for the street as fast as they could go. I told her I was a yogi and meditator in the Vedantic tradition and a devotee of Paramahansa Yogananda, and that while I would not be participating in any of the Buddhist services held four or five nights a week at the Centre, I would be happily practising my own *sadhana* in my room. She had friends who were followers of Yogananda and was happy to rent a room to a sympathetic soul. She told me to call her Margaret.

The lama was usually called Geshe-la, a title given to accomplished scholars, *geshe* meaning "virtuous friend," and *la* an honorific. We also called him Tashi or Lama-la. He was not more than five feet, four inches tall, and a hundred and twenty pounds. He was fifty-six years old, but I couldn't have guessed his age. He had brown, weathered skin like many Tibetans, very short hair, small hands and feet, and big ears. He wore strong glasses and had a full set of false teeth. He had a degree in Buddhist academics, was ordained at twenty-four, and was appointed abbot of a monastery in Tibet at thirty-four. Later, when he was forced to flee his own country, he earned another degree at the Sanskrit University in Varanasi, India.

The lama's knowledge of English, however, was very rudimentary. He had been in Canada for maybe eight years, and I couldn't imagine his English was any better now than when he first stepped off the plane. I estimated that he had a vocabulary of about eighty words and very little understanding of grammar. His pronunciation was often indecipherable. It seemed he had decided it was pointless to try to learn another language in his fifties.

It was easy to dismiss Geshe-la as a foreign oddity. Tibet. I knew nothing about Tibet. Who did? It was tempting and easier just to see him as a curiosity, a gnomish little man of mysterious and sorrowful background, an object of pity, imprisoned by the Chinese, tortured certainly, a man damaged mentally and physically by history and war. He had escaped to India over the Himalayas in 1960 under conditions I could not imagine. And I had seen those mountains. There was a copy of Harrer's *Seven Years in Tibet* lying about the house, but I was so busy at school I was unable to read it all. I did manage to read most of it at the kitchen table in a couple of sittings, mesmerized by the account.

There was no translator handy while I was living at the Dharma Centre, but occasionally visitors from the larger Sakya community in Seattle would come over, and Geshe-la's talks were then translated, live, to much larger groups than usually showed up for the Centre's evening meditations. Margaret told me that his discourses, when translated, were erudite, powerful, and inspiring, so unlike what we knew of the odd, sing-songy little man with the small hands who smiled easily, burbling about the house talking baby English. For lack of a common language, I and many others were foolish enough to grossly underestimate him. Although there were quirks.

The drama started almost immediately. There was a slim, handsome, voluble Venezuelan man, not very tall, with very long, straight, jet-black hair, who had just moved in. He was renting the good-sized bedroom at the front of the house on the main floor. When Margaret introduced us, she made a point of telling me he was waiting for money from home and had yet to pay his rent. She mentioned this within public hearing a few times over the next couple of weeks to keep the matter in the air, not wanting to let the facts slip from anyone's awareness. The Dharma Centre suffered from a problem not normally experienced by Victoria landlords. They actually had difficulty filling their rental rooms. I had nothing for or against the Venezuelan, although to me he had a shifty look about him. His English was good, he was in fourth-year biochemistry, and he told me he planned to go to graduate school to do research in cosmetic oils. I suspected he would do well in business. He seemed like the kind of man who, going into a revolving door behind you, might very well come out in front of you.

One day near the end of September, I came home from classes to find Geshe-la and Margaret in heated confrontation with the Venezuelan. He was packing up his few belongings and loading them into a friend's car. His money had failed to arrive, or more likely it had arrived, and he decided he would rather spend it elsewhere. He was now in the middle of a bold, daylight bunk. On his last trip out the front door, as he was running for the car, amongst anguished and agitated imprecations from both Margaret and Geshe-la, and threats of calling the police, Geshe-la ran after him into the street and took him by the arm attempting to hold him there while the Venezuelan struggled to free himself. Margaret was beside herself, calling to the lama, "No, Geshe-la, no! No, no! Geshe-la, stop!" I was stunned to come home and see the lama in this undignified brawl in the street. He let go of the Venezuelan who promptly jumped into the car and fled the scene. The look on Geshe-la's face was one of utter bewilderment. He and Margaret returned to the house huddled together in a state of distress and disbelief. At that moment I wondered if ours was a culture Tashi Namgyal would ever understand.

The Venezuelan had forgotten something in his hasty departure, and a week later he appeared at my window, tapping quietly, and asked me if I would retrieve it for him, on the down-low. It was an inexpensive piece of homemade exercise equipment, of no value. He thought I would be a natural ally against these strange people in burgundy robes, but I wanted no truck with an oily thief and liar, and when I referred him to Margaret, and could not be persuaded otherwise, he skulked away.

I had taken the small bedroom on the main floor, but I decided I needed more room, and I was willing to pay higher rent for the much bigger room in the basement. There was a queen-sized bed, an ample closet, a desk, one good-sized window, and enough room to do yoga on acceptable carpeting. It was still occupied by a pleasant, but unsmiling, man, a little older. I would be able to take the room when he moved out in a couple of weeks. He had been there for a year, and I asked him how he had enjoyed his stay at the Dharma Centre. Standing with him and his girlfriend in the kitchen, just the three of us, they said in agreement with a long, unsmiling sigh, "Well, I won't go into details but I will say, to keep it simple, Margaret has been a handful. She can be difficult. It's been an experience." They wished me luck, and I got the unmistakable feeling they were very glad to go. I could make no mountain of this. I had things to do, and I would get along with the residents as best I could, keeping to myself, doubly glad now to be moving out of the traffic of the upstairs area to the privacy and quiet of the large bedroom in the basement.

In North America, Buddhism is to religion what jazz is to music. Incomprehensible to the general public, it initially attracts contrary, overwrought, technically-minded practitioners, and every congregation contains noisy beginners who are simply elitist wannabes and pious, chatty hepcats. Like jazz, it seems at first both disjointed and repetitive, mannered and stupid, but then, if you're ever going to get it, you just get it. It is a practice of compassion, and eventually the posers and the hipsters fall away. But it does attract weirdoes. All that chanting and incense, the lure of the exotic and the foreign, the multitude of buddhas and teachers, the different sects, the robes, the prostrations, the visual hypnosis of the shrines. If you were a troubled individual living in a world of your own making, some distance from yourself, over-exercised and flustered about spiritual matters, new in town, looking for something weird to do, you would be immediately attracted to a listing in the telephone book under "Victoria Buddhist Dharma Society Centre." I began to dread hearing the doorbell ring. Margaret had told us that when the wild and woolly appeared on the doorstep, and they would, we were to tell them clearly and firmly that there was no accommodation at the Centre for visitors, however pious or however much in need they were. Every time the bell rang, and I opened the door, I had no idea who or what might be standing there.

The Venezuelan was quickly replaced by Ginnie, a stout and sturdy, round-faced, busty, happy young woman from Mexico, of wealthy family. She was in Victoria studying English. Her father sold agricultural fertilizers in Sinaloa, a land of tomatoes and marijuana. The baseball team in the capital city, Culiacan, is called *Los Tomateros*, the "Tomato Growers," although they could just as easily be called The Buds. Her English was very poor, but she tried very hard. If she found she couldn't climb over a problem in communication, she would go around it. She was sweet and loved to talk.

I moved downstairs, and the little bedroom I had vacated upstairs was rented to one of the strangest people I have ever met, a man attempting to get into the Faculty of Graduate Studies at UVic to continue work on a Master's thesis in Greek philosophy that he had already begun somewhere else. He was having a hell of a time convincing any of the professors at UVic to take him on as a graduate student because he was so extremely odd. He was about five feet, ten inches tall and much too thin. He had a small head, floppy wrists and ankles, and thin arms and legs. He was all sharp angles, like a crane. Like Ichabod. I'm sure I could have picked him up myself and carried him like a child. He was effeminate, without perhaps knowing it, and he talked in a high-pitched squeal, occasionally overcome with delight, occasionally with complaint and regret. At the kitchen table, where everyone gathered spontaneously over meals and for company, he told us a few stories of his life, bizarre and sad. Everyone stared at him wide-eyed, our mouths hanging open, responding as best we could, but who had ever seen such a stick-creature before? He could think and read and write well enough to get a first degree in philosophy, maybe a second, or a third, but what then? I couldn't imagine him ever employed. Where would he work? Who would give him a job? Who would ever marry this man? Of what sex? It seemed if he wasn't giggling, he was in tears. I had met Shizuka by now, and one day we were all sitting at the table chatting, the Philosopher included. Shizuka's English was still quite horrible, and she turned to me and said, in her horrible English, "Is he a man?" She was genuinely perplexed.

Shizuka was a friend of Ginnie's from English class, and she came to the Dharma Centre to visit Ginnie or to pick her up, and together they would go out to eat, to movies and plays, to gatherings and parties with friends. Shizuka was also from a rich family, Japanese, very wealthy, and she and Ginnie had the money to toddle about Victoria entertaining themselves freely. I estimated Shizuka spent $2,000 that fall on shopping, when she was bored and lonely, the equivalent of about $6,300 in 2014. By Christmas, her parents had told her she had to stop spending so much money. Money's nice to have. It will attract people, but it doesn't really keep you company. The friendship of fellow students can save your life when you are far from home in a strange, new place, but it isn't the same as having a lover. People from other cultures, speaking other languages, are fascinating to an open-minded host, and they often find friends in their new surroundings, but there always remains a cultural core that is rarely if ever penetrated, and national loneliness sharpens to a fine edge the yearning to share from the deepest recesses of the heart.

The Philosopher didn't last long. And now I saw Margaret at work. She despised him, probably because he was gay, or who knows what, and obviously unstable. He was a wounded member of the human herd, and Margaret harried him to death like a one-woman pack of wild dogs. She sniped and sneered, insulted and disparaged, openly and under her breath. It was astonishing. It was appalling to see. She was a Buddhist nun? But the Philosopher would have to defend himself. I was busy. One day, he told us in a tearful and excited flutter that he had found a room with a professor at UVic. I helped him move. I had a truck.

Margaret was, so she said, a Buddhist nun, but she was also a deeply damaged human being. She was about my mother's age. She was twelve years old at the end of World War II, but she was born in Holland, not Alberta, and she damn near starved to death with 18,000 others in the Dutch famine of 1944, the *Hongerwinter*. She told me that when the war was ending and she was finally able to bicycle to the country in a desperate search for food for her family, she was unable to refrain from eating some of the little she found, before returning home to share the rest. She said she had never been so hungry and never felt so guilty. Margaret suffered from Stockholm Syndrome. She expressed an open admiration for the Germans, their efficiency and order. Dutch is a close linguistic cousin of German, closer than English, all of them West Germanic languages. The Dutch people would probably have been welcomed by Hitler, eventually, into the Master Race, but Holland was in a crucial military position, only a hundred nautical miles from England, and it was fully subjugated by the Nazis and brutally occupied from the first days of the war to the last. The Netherlands capitulated after only five days of military action in May 1940, and the police and the civil service then collaborated with the Nazis, too willingly, in killing seventy-five per cent of Holland's Jewish population, a much higher percentage than in France or Belgium. Twenty-five thousand Dutchmen volunteered to serve in the German military, and every other able-bodied man was forced to labour in German factories or build coastal defences. Two hundred thousand Netherlanders died in those five years, the highest per capita death rate of all Nazi-occupied countries in Western Europe. It is a shocking number considering Holland's armies only fought for five days, with fewer than 6,000 battle deaths of soldiers and civilians. The entire country suffered badly, and its citizens experienced multigenerational, war-related emotional problems for years afterwards.

That was all Margaret told me about her life, except that she had lived in the Yukon for many years before her husband died and she moved to Victoria.

When the Philosopher was gone, Werner moved in. He was a friend of Margaret's and the lama's, and other members of the Dharma Society. He was in his late twenties and was a deep-sea navigator. When he was between ships, he would take short courses at Camosun College to upgrade his officer skills, staying at the Dharma Centre if they had a room available. He planned to take a little time off on this visit and stick around for the fall before signing on to another ship. He had been born in Austria and moved to Montreal as a child. His English was easy and natural, and Margaret made fun of his German, which he had forgotten over the years. He took flying lessons in Montreal as a teenager and became interested in navigation. As a young man he was bumming around Central America, sitting in a saloon in Panama City one day, when a man came into the bar and shouted, "Any man here want to work on a tuna boat?" He spent the next two years gutting tuna and smoking dope at sea. When he ran out of pot, he figured he may as well take a few more courses in navigation, and he was now a well-paid second officer on merchant ships.

Werner had anglicized his name to Warren, but mostly we all called him Navigator. I couldn't resist asking him about Margaret and the lama. They were mysterious creatures, and he seemed to know something of them. When Warren had known me for a while and decided I was a low risk for gossip, he told me more about Margaret.

She had moved to Canada after the war and married a Canadian in the Maritimes somewhere, maybe Nova Scotia, and had four children. This was news. The marriage was a nightmare, and one day she slipped away by herself and travelled as far, as fast, and as quietly as her money would take her, stopping only when she ran out of funds somewhere in the Yukon. There she found a German man, Wolf, a man she could understand, and together they made a life for themselves somewhere in the woods southeast of Whitehorse, running a souvenir shop and store on the highway, doing whatever else might come along to make a little money. After many years together Wolf developed diabetes, and Margaret nursed him for many more years until he finally died one day, and she found herself free to move again.

I was astonished, and all I could say was, "She has four kids?" And it turns out, thirty years later, I *am* a bit of a gossip.

Warren had his own problems. He had been involved, off and on, with a married woman, a member of the Dharma Society. She had two children with her loving and dull husband. Warren had money, was free and handsome and single, and travelled the world, riches she could not resist, a treasure she could not put away. What I wasn't expecting was that, when I met her, I found she was so beautiful I was actually unable to speak. My eyes were insufficient to the sight of her. I believe I grunted. She wore no makeup, and was so soft-spoken you could hardly hear what she said, but I nearly fainted when I first saw her. She was physical perfection united to a tired and unhappy soul. The difference between the inner and outer person was so obvious it was jarring to see. She was a beautiful woman who had married a dull man to escape the aggressive attentions of every other man on earth. Everyone knew that she and Warren had been linked before and were now involved yet again. It was a sad, silent scandal that no one would condemn, and no one could bear to talk about. One day Warren showed up on a motorcycle that he kept in storage in Victoria, and I saw him and his paramour riding together up the street, holding close, nowhere to go.

Warren told me he also took Geshe-la for a ride on his motorcycle one day, but he wouldn't do it again. He said the lama had made obscene gestures to young girls. More disturbing news about my landlords. I think Geshe-la was so appalled by the behaviour of westerners, especially the young, that he thought his own outbursts were merely an imitation of his host culture, in keeping with his surroundings. In an immoral society what did it matter if a teacher was inappropriate, if he made a feint of immorality, an ironically immoral display? This was just crazy wisdom. He was simply communicating and teaching at their own rough level, a level they could understand, mirroring their own faults. He was playing the intoxicated mystic. There is value in crazy wisdom. Unfortunately, its excessive use almost always leads to compromise, and the forfeiture and burial of the source and intention of the lesson. It is the contemptible technique of a dozen, or dozens, of discredited teachers and gurus. How long can you pretend to be a jackass and a scoundrel before you become one in fact? Not to mention, in our culture, in spite of its other shortcomings, crazy wisdom in the form of obscene gestures to minors in public is, quite rightly, a criminal offence.

The first house that Margaret and the lama occupied in creating the Dharma Society, only a few years earlier, was on Elford Street, and the lama would stand at the windows of the empty house, staring into the rain, waiting in vain for people to show up for devotional services. Margaret said he would shake his head looking out at the lights of the city and say wonderingly, "So many people no come."

They were coming now, if only a few every evening. There were not only Vajrayana Buddhists, but Zen practitioners as well. There was hardly a Tibetan among them. They were all westerners. There probably weren't more than a dozen Tibetans in all Victoria in 1979.

TC was one of them. He dropped around the Dharma Centre now and then. He was a humble man, short and stocky, with a bright eye and a tired face. He was a little older, and he had just become a new dad. One day he stopped by in the afternoon. He was sitting at the kitchen table, and I asked him what he had been doing. TC was a modest man, and he showed only a hint of twinkle when he said, "Well, I just had tea with Prince Charles at the Empress Hotel, but I must go home now to look after the baby." The Prince of Wales was indeed in town for a visit, but I didn't know he and TC were friends. TC explained that he had been a translator for the Dalai Lama in Dharamsala, India, the seat of the Tibetan Government in Exile, and he had made the acquaintance of the Prince during that time. When HRH learned that TC had moved to Victoria, he arranged to see him again during his visit. You never knew who you were going to meet in the kitchen at the Dharma Centre.

Some of the meditators were pleasant enough, but some were a sour-faced lot. Others were arrogant and angry, others just quite obviously self-deluded and nuts. This was common. The variety of demanding and needy egos you found in an ashram or a temple was exhausting. After a five-minute harangue from a wild-eyed acolyte, it was all I could do sometimes not to roll my eyes, slap my forehead, and walk away muttering, "What an asshole." Margaret always served tea and cookies after the services. I think it was her favourite part of the evening. By that time, around 10:00 p.m., I was finished with my books and came upstairs for a snack of peanut butter and honey on toast before bed. I was putting in a fourteen-hour day, and I stopped doing yoga and then stopped meditating. I fell into bed at eleven at night.

Geshe-la rarely answered the telephone because he couldn't usually understand the barrage of English coming out of the handset, but one day, while I was standing at the sink doing dishes, the telephone rang and Geshe-la decided to give it a try. He then talked for a full ten minutes in Tibetan. Obviously the caller was a compatriot. I didn't often hear Geshe-la speak for extended periods in his native language, and I noticed there was a definite tone of confidence and aloofness coming through in his voice, qualities I didn't normally associate with him from hearing him struggle along, day-to-day, in his few words of English. By the time he hung up the telephone, I was under the impression that he had very elegantly told his interlocutor that he might get back to him someday, and in the meantime he could hold his breath if he felt like it. It was such a curious and notable incident that I mentioned it to Margaret a few days later. When a small smile of satisfaction appeared immediately on her face, I knew Geshe-la had talked to her about it.

Margaret told me the call was from a Tibetan man living in Calgary. Geshe-la had come to Canada, in the early 1970s, as a minister of divine words, a Buddhist shepherd for a flock of refugees that settled in Calgary, part of the very first wave of immigration. The understanding, or profound misunderstanding, with the Canadian government, which had to invent an ignorant and condescending new category for their paperwork, "Nomads," was that the Tibetan refugees would support their own priest since the lama could not be expected to find other employment. No such thing happened. The Tibetan community of refugees was not a community at all. It was small and scattered across Canada, some were sick and malnourished when they arrived, some had tuberculosis and were hospitalized for months. They were in no condition to support anyone. They struggled with language, culture shock, and isolation. Geshe-la was soon forgotten and left to fend for himself while the rest of the refugees dealt with trying to understand their strange new home, find jobs, and stabilize their families and their lives. And over the years they succeeded. The seventies was a good decade to work in Alberta, and eventually they found themselves, just as I had, making more money than they had ever seen in their lives. They worked with Canadians, made Canadian friends, bought houses and cars and clothes, earned and talked about money. They sent their children to public schools, and in less than ten years they found their offspring could no longer speak Tibetan, and had no idea of the Three Jewels, the Buddha, the Dharma, and the Sangha. They had been invaded to death by the Chinese, and now they were being assimilated to death by the Canadians. The flag went up and the call was made, "Geshe-la, come home!" I got the feeling from the sound of Geshe-la's voice that after all he had been through, he felt quite comfortable telling them to piss up a rope.

Margaret had become interested in Buddhism while living in the Yukon and had travelled occasionally to Seattle to participate in the activities and devotions of the Sakya Buddhist community there. When her husband died, she sold the little house and the little business they had built together, and with her life savings in her pocket, she put on a backpack at the age of forty-two, and told her friends she was going to India, moving to Dharamsala to study and pray with the Tibetan community there. Her friends in the Yukon feared for her life.

She would stop in Seattle first, and on her way through Vancouver, she crossed paths, at long last, finally, with Tashi Namgyal. Tashi was a Tibetan man, from a land so high, pointy, and gabled it was called the Roof of the World. Margaret was a Dutch woman, from a land so flat and low it was called the Low Countries, much of it below sea level. They were two refugees far from home, displaced by war and unimaginable suffering. They had each been swept along for a lifetime by a river of pain. It is not too strong an image. They found each other, in confluence, on the wet, west coast of Canada. Margaret told me that Geshe-la was living in terrible conditions in Vancouver, in a shabby room with a cardboard box for a shrine. He needed new glasses, new teeth, and new shoes. And worst of all, he was washing dishes in a Chinese restaurant, listening daily to the language of the invaders of his country, the murderers of his people, his jailers and torturers, the destroyers of his religion and culture. Margaret realized now she did not need to go to India.

She and Geshe-la moved to Victoria. Margaret used her savings to meet the lama's most urgent physical needs, and then, trying not to look too overtly Buddhist, she got a job in an office downtown. Together they established the Victoria Buddhist Dharma Society and moved to a rented house, and eventually, recently, they bought the old house on Leonard Street.

Sweet Jesus Howard Christ on a rubber crutch.

I had not a complaint in the world to compare with the problems these people had encountered in their lives. It was no great wonder they occasionally exhibited wildly inappropriate behaviours and frequently seemed to be as mad as hatters.

I had always had a vague notion that Buddhists were vegetarians, but I was very wrong about that. Several times a week there was something horrible boiling on the stove, something that used to walk the earth, and I only made the mistake once of lifting the lid to peek. Geshe-la lived mostly on white rice and boiled meat. I thought if he liked meat he would enjoy the fresh fish you could buy in Victoria, which he pronounced "pish," but Margaret told me that in Tibet fish is considered unclean, and Tashi wouldn't look at it. At night, Margaret would appear in the kitchen in her housecoat, skinny and bent, squinting and sour, and butter two pieces of white bread, open a can of apricot halves, and place four of them on each slice, humpy side up. She would then pour a full quarter-inch of white sugar on top of it all and scurry back upstairs with it to her bedroom. I lived mostly on brown rice, soybeans, *miso* soup, broccoli and cheese sauce, eggs, and toast with peanut butter and honey. We kept a peculiar galley.

The Navigator lost interest in staying the entire fall in Victoria, and after receiving a telephone call one day, he was gone the next. He had an offer on a ship, and he decided to go. In the time it takes to fly to San Francisco, steam across the Pacific Ocean on a freighter, and then fly back to Victoria, he was back in his old room at the Dharma Centre. He didn't like the ship, and he left it in Yokohama.

When the Philosopher was gone, Margaret needed another outlet for her anger, and eventually she turned on Ginnie. Margaret liked me, though. I was steady, Nordic, paid my rent, and caused no problems. The lama smiled and said, "He is careful man." Later, when he saw me falling head-over-heels in love with Shizuka, my feast and my folly, he smiled again and said, "Now 'beery, beery' happy. Soon 'beery, beery' sad." I laughed and said, "I know, Geshe-la, I know," but nothing could prevent me from throwing myself in front of that train.

If I called Shizuka tempting, bewitching, seductive, false, and manipulative, a devil in a skirt, there would be at least three dozen women in Victoria who would agree with me, but the context was not overtly sexual. Shizuka was not Mata Hari. The boyfriends and husbands of her three dozen potential accusers did, nevertheless, swarm around her in bunches, buzzing in open and rapt admiration, animated and attentive, while their wives and girlfriends scowled together across the room. There are now hundreds of students from Japan studying English in Victoria at any one time, but in the late 1970s, they were a novelty. And Shizuka was not a typical Japanese student. For one thing, she was not a girl, she was older, twenty-seven, a few months older than I. This made her a spinster in Japan, a Christmas Cake, "unsold after the twenty-fifth," but not in Canada. She was also embarrassingly tall, five feet, six inches, my height. Her eyes were not narrow. Her cheek bones were set high and wide, her nose was not flat, her face not particularly round. She didn't favour the mincing walk or speak in the annoying, high-pitched tone of most Japanese women in their twenties. She didn't exhibit giggling and childish behaviours. There was nothing *kawaii* about her, the sick-making Japanese culture of cuteness. She wasn't routinely shy or sycophantic or cloying around men, but she did know the drill, and she could turn it off and on at will. And that was the key.

In Canada, in 1979, there were a lot of men, especially of broadly defined liberal characteristics, who hadn't seen a piece of lingerie in a long time, if ever. On the BC coast in particular, arguably the worst-dressed part of Canada, the art of seduction was nearly dead. I rarely met a woman who wore a dress or shaved her legs, rarely met one who would agree with anything I said without first seriously considering cutting my throat, if only to silence another man, even a stranger, even at random. Most of a generation of men had grown up without a trace of teasing admiration from women, without a thimble of flirty compliment. Most of us had spent years just trying to figure out how not to offend women with our chauvinistic attitudes. We had been called MCPs for a decade, Male Chauvinist Pigs. You could be raked over the coals at any time for your sins, or those of your fathers. Every time I turned around, I was offending a woman without knowing it, even sober. For us, every interaction with a woman had the potential to end badly. We were a cowed and jumpy lot.

Shizuka was a different kind of dangerous. She was the youngest, the fifth of five children, the third girl. She had been raised by a traditional Japanese mother, a woman who never worked outside the home, and whose husband was tremendously wealthy. Her mother didn't have a job, but she had many duties. Her role was to be refined and beautiful, to produce children and train them, to run a beautiful house, to be at her husband's beck and call, day and night, to serve him without question, putting his socks on his feet in the morning, literally on her knees, and never complain. She taught Shizuka that "the highest woman is only as high as the lowest man." Her very words. Most of the female employees in Shizuka's father's companies would be clerks and secretaries, office ladies. He might have had a rare woman on staff in a position of authority, an engineer or a project manager, but once outside the office, on the street, she would defer to any man. In a society where women have no power, their power lies in their ability to manipulate men, to make men think that whatever the wife wants is the husband's idea, a common enough practice worldwide. In Japan, it was a social mechanism raised to a high art.

In Canada, many women of my generation, and older, hadn't thrown their man a bone in ten years. They may or may not have been right in thinking they had nothing further of value to learn from men. But Shizuka was skilled in the old ways and could bring a man to his knees in ten minutes, then make him sit up and beg. She was astonished at these loud, opinionated, mannish, hairy-legged women in Victoria who were so sharp and critical with their men, and she thought them outright fools for resorting to such brute techniques to get what they needed and wanted. The feminists in their turn despised Shizuka's blatant use of seductive femininity. And having no experience of it, their husbands and boyfriends were particularly vulnerable. They had no idea how to resist it, no idea they were being manipulated. What Canadian women saw as progress had simply turned their men into boys. They had not been inoculated against feminine wiles, and they were now susceptible to childish diseases. Over the twelve months Shizuka was in Victoria, she began to see the other side of the argument, but her overall opinion of the situation changed very little. She had no respect for a woman who didn't know how to use the gifts God had given her. She may have singlehandedly set feminism in Victoria back ten years.

Her attitude towards sex was also a revelation to me. Sex was a lot of fun in North America, God knows everyone was doing it in the seventies, but somehow it was still considered bad. It had the baggage of untold generations of Christian condemnation, and that was part of the reason it was so much fun. It was naughty. When asked if sex is dirty, Woody Allen said, "It is if you're doing it right." He would know. I was getting the impression sex was not considered dirty at all in Japan. It was impractical, yes, owing to the housing shortage, but they had love hotels for that. To the Japanese, sex seemed to be a more natural part of life, less entwined with guilt and retribution, not a part of religious prohibition. But it was just an impression. I didn't have time to make an anthropological study of it. Japanese girls were definitely not as sexually active, as early in life, as North American girls, but when they did start having sex, it seemed they had not been deliberately taught any reason not to "lay aside their modesty with their petticoat."

I remember the first time I saw Shizuka. It was early October. Ginnie had moved in, and she started having visitors right away, pretty Spanish-speaking girls from Mexico and Chile, also studying English. And one day I came home and Ginnie's friend Shizuka was sitting at the kitchen table. Her English was very poor, and she had a dictionary in her hand for months. The three of us made simple table talk, while I made myself something simple to eat, and as always the conversation was accompanied by a lot of repetition and laughing and arm-waving. I could see that Shizuka was a very attractive woman, but I also noticed right away that while her clothes were obviously very expensive, each item outstanding in quality, they were mismatched and too old for her, the sort of overpriced, cheeseball items you find in the shops of expensive hotel lobbies, aimed at rich, conservative, older women. Her fashion sense was very haphazard, as if someone had just thrown money at her without a thought for overall effect. Her hair was appalling. It was thick, rich, healthy, and jet-black of course, but it was shellacked into fantastic waves and curves, and not ironically, not a homage to classical Japanese hairstyles, neo-geisha, but simply the result of bad hairdressing choices. It was as crunchy as cardboard. Her makeup was excessive and inexpertly applied. There was no hint on that first day of the spells she could cast on the unsuspecting manhood of Western Canada. I said a pleasant good afternoon and descended to my room in the basement to study for the next six hours with barely a thought of wanting to see this mishmash of a woman again.

Shizuka became a regular visitor, warmly welcomed, at the Dharma Centre. Margaret and the lama both liked her, probably because she was well-mannered and respectful. Warren liked her too, of course, but for different reasons. I got used to seeing her at the kitchen table, and we talked as best we could, slowly, interrupted by constant referral to the dictionary. When we did manage to get an idea across, it was a happy little victory of cross-cultural understanding.

Both Shizuka and Ginnie were amazed at my devotion to work. I studied every day, every night, and at least one full day on the weekend. They wanted me to come out and play with them, but I would only agree to give them rides to their many social events and then make these little rich girls take a taxi home.

And then late one Saturday morning, everything changed. I came home to find Shizuka sitting at the kitchen table, reading, the rest of the house quiet as death. She had come to meet Ginnie, they had made a date, but Ginnie had forgotten all about it and wasn't at home. Margaret and the lama had gone out and left Shizuka on her own to wait, in case Ginnie came back, but Ginnie was still nowhere to be found. I told Shizuka I was sorry I couldn't keep her company. I had to go downstairs and study. She asked me if she could sit in my room with me, so she wouldn't be lonely, and write a letter to her mother. She promised she would not disturb me, the little liar.

I opened my books at my desk, and just to my right, at the foot of the bed, Shizuka sat on the carpet, in her expensive clothes and her goofy hair, her legs tucked under her skirt to one side. She was writing on a sheet of airmail onionskin, top to bottom and right to left, in exquisite *kanji*. On this day, for the first time in weeks, the mysteries of biology and physics and chemistry did not call to me. I looked at this quiet, beautiful, strange woman in my room, sitting demurely at my feet, and wondered what kinds of sounds and images were going through her head, what assumptions, what memories, as she wrote to her wise and sainted mother in her mansion in Hofu, a small city in southern Japan.

I loved school, I was happy, I wanted to study. I didn't have time for fooling around with girls although the nineteen-year-olds at the college were driving me crazy. I was twenty-six, and I didn't feel I was too old for them, but they seemed to think so. Here was Shizuka, my age, as mysterious a being as I had ever met. Even speaking very little English, probably because of it, her manners and bearing were intoxicating to the men around her, and she was beginning to create something of a sensation in her widening circle of acquaintance as she realized that Canadian men were just boys in her classically trained hands. And here she was in my room.

This was an opportunity that could not be ignored. I knew very well that one move on my part would change my life and hers. Even though Shizuka had never made any sign that she was particularly attracted to me, I knew if I could manage some kind of physical contact with her she would open to me without reservation. I had not courted her in any way, but it never crossed my mind that an advance would be rejected. If I waited another day, she would be gone. Men were lined up at her door. She went out every night of the week. I suspected, and later confirmed, that her many beaux had been cautious so far, uncertain of how to proceed with this exotic beauty in the odd clothes, but eventually they would figure it out. I knew what she wanted, and not because that's what I thought all women wanted or needed, although there may be some truth to that. She was twenty-seven years old, and in spite of all her friends, and dates with men, I knew she was lonely. So was I. In the last two years I had been the tearful recipient of pity-sex exactly three times, from three different women. She was not a child. She wanted kisses and touches, and she wanted them until there were none left in the expanding universe. We fell into each other's arms like two wild streams of water into one rocky pool, inseparable by any means known to science, like any two stupid young lovers who ever lived.

I have never made a more conscious decision in my life to begin an affair. After no more than a few minutes at my desk gazing at her on the floor, I put my pencil down, turned off my calculator, and sighed, "And so we begin."

Shizuka looked up at me with an open expression, possibly unaware, if only for a moment, of how beautiful she was. "Paw-dawn me?" On the other hand she may have played me like a fiddle.

I said, "Would you like to see some pictures of my trip to India last year?"

She said, "Oh yes, please, very much," and she quickly put her letter away.

We sat close together on the floor, touching, arm to arm, laughing and marvelling together over the rich, fuzzy photos of my abortive trip to India, the elephants and the monkeys. In five minutes we were necking like teenagers. We spent the next twelve hours in bed. This wasn't a desire to have sex with someone, this was the desire to consume another person whole, and then feast again, and then again.

Our wild coupling was not a secret that could be kept for a minute at the Dharma Centre. Over the next few weeks, Margaret said they were having trouble concentrating on their meditations in the evenings, and perhaps we could try to keep it down just a little in the basement. But she smiled. Two people who are obviously crazy in love are easily forgiven many indiscretions.

I hadn't had a steady girlfriend in two years and I was "beery, beery" happy.

My grandfather died on October 16, almost seventy-six. He had lived his three score and ten. He golfed nine holes in the morning and went home for lunch, measured out on a scale by my grandmother, a diabetic regimen of carefully weighed portions. After lunch, he was sitting in the plush chair in the living room, another nine holes of golf on his mind, when my grandmother asked him a question from the kitchen. He didn't respond, and my grandmother told me later that she was annoyed with him, thinking he was deliberately ignoring her. She dried her hands in the kitchen and went into the living room to see if there was a reason he could not pay her the courtesy of an answer, and there she found him in the chair taking off and putting on his sunglasses repeatedly, otherwise unresponsive. She called the doctor, only half a block away. Dr. Meer said, "Helen, he's had a stroke. Call an ambulance right away. I'll be right over." He died in hospital a week later. My father offered to buy me a plane ticket to travel the nine hundred miles home for the funeral, but I was up to my neck in schoolwork. It was early days for me for a return to academic life. I was working non-stop, training myself to be able to handle the constant flood of new information. Midterms were only days away. I couldn't miss a single class, never mind most of a week. So I didn't go to either of my grandfathers' funerals. And now I was glad I had been able to spend most of the previous winter in Sedgewick.

I had thought the Dharma Society members were an odd bunch, but then we had a very odd visitor from Japan. He was a Buddhist monk, probably still in his twenties, and he looked so bored I thought his eyes might roll completely back in their sockets one day, signalling his departure to the Pure Land of Amitabha Buddha, the Paradise in the West. I asked Shizuka how someone so obviously uninterested in his chosen path could stand to wake up and meet it every day. She talked with him at some length in Japanese and then said to me, "His father owns the temple where he works." It was a family business.

The Japanese monk gave a few talks at the Dharma Centre, and a translator was required. A Japanese man, an instructor at the university and a teacher of *kendo*, the Way of the Sword, volunteered. When he showed up for the first time at the Dharma Centre, he took one look at Shizuka and immediately fell in love with her. He was lonely, too. A modern Japanese woman, traditional to the core, was the nutty and savoury fermented soy he was missing.

So I had yet another rival. Shizuka gave every indication of being in raptures about our new relationship, but it didn't stop her from going out on dates. I wasn't concerned about fidelity. I knew I was her only lover, but I did mention to her that it made me uncomfortable that she was so frequently, and so happily, in the company of other men. Her rebuttal was watertight and delivered with her usual beguiling charm. She said, "I must do my suitors the honour of going out with them for dinner one last time so I can explain to them that I cannot go out with them anymore." It took a couple of months to run through the list of hopefuls, and I'm sure the *kendo* instructor proposed marriage at least twice during that time. That's the problem with beautiful girlfriends. Other men will walk up to them and ask them out on a date right in front of you. What was I going to say to a man who taught sword-fighting?

Eventually, the crowd of Shizuka's admirers thinned out, and we spent every moment we could together. Between school and Shizuka, I was exhausted. One day in the kitchen, I said to Margaret, only half joking, that what I really needed was a girlfriend who would leave me alone during the week so I could study, show up on Friday night, and go home on Sunday afternoon. Margaret laughed. "Oh, I think Shizuka is the kind of girl who is going to need a lot more attention than that."

Geshe-la said, "Now 'beery, beery' happy. Soon 'beery, beery' sad."

In the summer, in the valley, I had bridled at the uniformity of my cultural surroundings and the bland, widespread notion that thinking the same, being in constant conflict-free agreement, was a virtue. Now I lived in a house of thoroughgoing cultural diversity and personal eccentricity, and I loved it. You never knew what anyone was thinking. You never knew what to expect, how anyone would respond to a given situation. I was surrounded by non-native speakers of English. Tibetan, Dutch, Spanish, German, and Japanese were the first languages of my daily companions. The conversation could go in any direction.

When I was fleeing India the year before, I had thought about stopping in Japan to try teaching English, but I was too sick and exhausted to consider it seriously. It was at the Dharma Centre in Victoria that the idea was resurrected. I spent a year informally tutoring basic English at the kitchen table, and in bed, and I found it very enjoyable, especially the latter. I liked the socializing, the exposure to different ideas and customs, and the openness that you usually find in second-language learners. Teaching English is fun. I found later that it's not something you would want to do for the rest of your life, but a couple of years of teaching English when you're young can be a very pleasant and rewarding experience.

My first term at Camosun College was winding down. The fall semester had been exhilarating. When I was in high school, I fractiously assumed that the teachers and administrators were conspiring together in a nefarious and relentless program of brainwashing, their goal to mould the students into pliable mediocrity. It seemed to me that Compliant Attitude and Learning to Conform were the most important courses you took, even if they didn't appear on your transcript. At SAIT and UVic I studied theatre, also a strongly flavoured work culture that trains its postulants in an obvious program of corrective behavioural assimilation. At Northern Lights College, in carpentry, we had been lectured daily by our over-opinionated instructor on every moral topic under the sun. But at Camosun College, studying science, I found that the instructors seemed utterly indifferent to the social consciousness of their students and didn't much care if we lived or died. It was a thoroughly refreshing breath of disinterested air. They were there to teach us the miracles of arithmetic, the periodic table, DNA, and kinetics. What we did with that information was of no concern to them. There seemed to be no hypocritical mission among them to improve us other than through straightforward instruction. They were scientists, not moralists, and for them the mystery was not that things are not the way they should be. The mystery was that things are the way they are.

And in science, I discovered knowledge that cried out to be known, tantalizing and delicious. I swam in it to satiety. The act of study itself, day after day in a classroom or a laboratory, or at a desk, was soon as routine as piling lumber, but it was infinitely more stirring to the mind, if not as physically healthful. Eventually I discovered, of course, that science is not the cure-all it imagines itself to be, that it has its own very narrow set of prejudices, mental blinders, ridiculous assumptions, philosophical stupidities, vanities and pretensions, a lack of elementary logic in a field that should know better, scientistic rather than scientific, as well as moral and societal stupidities, extraordinary intelligence in the service of absolute wrong. The phrase "tobacco scientist" comes to mind. That used to be a job. The results of seeking only profitable truths are the invention of lethal ingenuities and intricate, self-serving humbug. In the academic world I would find heated and violent controversies, hatreds, persecutions, and much else that is unpleasant. But that would come later. For the time being I was enthralled by what I was learning. I never hesitated to open my books and dive heart and soul into the strange new things I encountered there. I also had good teachers, and for a change, I don't think any of them were fucking the students.

Shizuka was booked to meet her parents in Hawaii for three weeks over Christmas. I was crushed to see her go. I would spend the near month-long break between semesters at the Dharma Centre reading and listening to books on tape, vinyl albums actually, that I borrowed from the public library downtown. It was housed in a 1905 building at the corner of Yates and Blanshard Streets, a small, two-storey, neo-Classical stone edifice, Richardsonian Romanesque, with creaking floors. It was the gift of Andrew Carnegie, one of the 2,500 libraries he built around the world. Carnegie was born in Scotland in a one-room cottage, and by the time he ended his life in the United States, having the good sense to acquire an astonishing fortune in the steel industry, and having the further good sense to live to the age of eighty-three and then die quickly of pneumonia, he had given away the 2014 equivalent of six billion dollars.

I became obsessed with Vietnam over the holidays. It was 1979. The war had ended in 1975, and North Americans were just beginning to deal with it mentally and emotionally. In 1968, John Wayne directed and starred in *The Green Berets*, a movie that was a box-office success, but one that was so fanatically anti-communist, and so excessively glorified the war, that it was called "cowboys and Indians," "clichéd," "heavy-handed," "old-fashioned," "vile and insane." Roger Ebert gave it zero stars and put it on his Most Hated List of movies. John Wayne visited Victoria in 1975, in his yacht, *Wild Goose*, a converted wooden US Navy minesweeper, and he was booed on the street when he went for a walk downtown. The photographs of the Fall of Saigon were still fresh in everyone's mind. The movie *Coming Home* was released in 1978, and audiences in the US left the theatres weeping, struggling to come to terms with the aftermath of the war. I saw *The Deer Hunter* in the spring of 1979. Susan and I walked out of the theatre nearly sick to our stomachs from the scenes, fictional we hoped, of Russian roulette, which so vividly and garishly represented the randomness of death in war. We had all been reading for years about the filming of *Apocalypse Now*, and it was finally released in Victoria that fall. It was a dark, surreal meditation on the horror of war, like being caught in a Dali painting in a novel by Kafka. Or Conrad. Michael Herr wrote the narration for the film. Over Christmas, I also read his book *Dispatches*. It contained a hundred stories of his time in Vietnam as a correspondent for *Esquire* magazine. It has been called the best book written about the war. In one story, he describes two soldiers, best friends, walking down the beach side by side. A mortar landed nearby and killed one of them, the other completely untouched. What does the survivor think after that? Who does he become? In another, he talks about an American soldier who, after a firefight, wandered the field of battle emptying a full clip of bullets into the head of each fallen enemy. "Would you let your daughter marry that man?" said one reviewer. I also read Tim O'Brien's *Going After Cacciato*. For that novel he won the National Book Award for Fiction, beating out John Cheever and John Irving. It was an ambiguous, dreamlike tale of a soldier who had had enough of the war and decided to go AWOL, walking from Vietnam to Paris, pursued by the rest of his platoon in an effort to bring him safely back.

In dark movie theatres, and in my dark bedroom in the basement of the Dharma Centre, during the darkest time of the year, I was alone and lost for days in wartime dramas, morality plays, and bizarre, horrifying imagery. I had to stop. I was starting to think that war was normal.

To recover, I got out LPs of Mark Twain's funny stories from the library and chuckled over them for hours, especially, since I was studying French, *The Jumping Frog: in English, then in French, and then Clawed Back into a Civilized Language Once More by Patient, Unremunerated Toil*.

And there I waited, in Victoria, as patiently as I could manage, for Shizuka to return from Hawaii.

4   Love-Drama-Science Dharma

Camosun College is a place where you can get certificates and diplomas in accounting, communications, a dozen areas of office administration, jazz, a dozen healthcare fields, cooking, photography, calligraphy, flower arranging, welding, mechanics, public relations, golf management, and a hundred other subjects of technical and vocational study. Clown college. It is also a place where you can go back to school to study academic arts and sciences as an older student without the horror of jumping straight into university. The math, physics, and chemistry I was studying were high school equivalents. The French and biology were university level. By the time I started the second semester in January 1980, I had adjusted to the all-consuming lifestyle of the student, and I realized I could now relax a bit. I also realized I wasn't interested in French, so I didn't re-enrol in that subject, and now I had a lighter load of only four courses. I still worked day and night, the work and the anguish expand to fit the time, but the pace was easier, and I was much more confident now that I was capable of keeping up with the enormous volume of new information that comes with an all-science curriculum, if I just showed up and did the work. Stephen Hawking estimates that he worked three hundred and fifty hours a year to finish his first-class BA Honours degree in physics at Oxford University. I worked 1,400. I was no Stephen Hawking.

I tightened up my game in math and stopped making mistakes. I was usually two weeks ahead in the textbook. I had always wondered what trigonometry was. Our instructor was a visiting teacher from England with a lovely, bone-dry sense of humour. Addressing the class he said things like, "Machines are usually used to solve these kinds of problems," referring to cubic equations, "since they are too complex for human beings," and then, witheringly, "or *you*."

My second physics course was taught by Eugene Tong, a Chinese man with a PhD in high energy physics. He always came quietly to class at 8:30 in the morning with a large cup of tea with a lid on it. He started slowly but by the middle of the class, after covering the board with proofs and formulae, it was not unusual for him to whirl about and exclaim excitedly, to his still sleepy students, "Is this not amazing? Is this not incredible?" And *this* was just Grade 12 physics. I loved his sense of wonder.

Biology continued to astonish me, but being a vegetarian and a bit squeamish anyway, I was nervous about the upcoming dissections we would be required to perform in one or two of our three-hour labs. The day arrived, and by the time I was finished with my own specimen and had examined half a dozen others in detail, I wanted to grab the next person who walked down the hall and dissect *him*, or her. It was utterly fascinating. I could easily have committed, that day, to a career as a vivisectionist. I may have been woozy from the formalin.

The biology instructor gave me a prize in the fall for being so bloody brilliant, I did get straight A's, in the form of a day out with the second-year students. An old Norwegian fisherman donated a day to the college, and we bobbed up and down on his boat in the Strait of Georgia, dragging things up from the bottom of the ocean to look at. I spent hours talking with him. He had been raised on the west coast of Vancouver Island. As a child, he spoke Norwegian at home, English at school, and Japanese on the playground with his friends. There were many Japanese fishing families living there before the war.

I loved my day on the water, and I asked Warren, the Navigator, how I could get a job on deep-sea ships. I listened eagerly to his stories about life at sea. I told him to telephone me from anywhere in the world, if he was on a ship with a job opening, and I would fly to his location on a day's notice, but he told me entry-level positions were shit jobs, and I would hate it. Warren had a new, very expensive, handheld Hewlett-Packard calculator, the first I had heard of the brand. He bought navigational modules to go with it and was using it in his classes, and recently on board ship. It was seven hundred dollars in 1979, well over $2,000 in 2014. He said his fellow navigators and officers, old-school, disapproved of these new methods, sometimes strongly, and mocked him without humour for using a calculator. They thought he might forget how to navigate by the stars.

I was now in university-level chemistry, taught by John Ward. He was a pleasant-enough fellow with a recent PhD in inorganic chemistry. He developed a new arsenic compound during his doctoral research, and as he shopped his results around at scientific conferences, his new compound was inevitably referred to as Ward's Arse.

I didn't miss French class.

Make no mistake. I had no particular goal in mind, not a thought for how a few years of studying science might roll out in the real world. I went back to school for the breathtakingly impractical, but to me quite valid, and rather lofty, purpose of investigating how western scientific knowledge compared with eastern spiritual learning. I shit you not. Yogananda talked about, and constantly stressed, the *science* of *Kriya* yoga. The word "science" appears seventy-five times in his autobiography. With no sophisticated understanding of physics or metaphysics, it was unlikely I would be able to make a noteworthy judgment about the relationship between the two. So what? What did I care? I wasn't selling anything. I wasn't getting paid to do it. I didn't care what anyone thought. You can do whatever you want in life, until your hair turns grey, as long as you don't ask anyone to agree with you. I didn't talk about it much, but I made no secret of it. I wasn't trying to fool anyone or take advantage of anyone. It was just brain candy, something to ruminate on, sugar-free gum. I had read and read and done yoga and meditated for nine years. And all that dope, of course. I was genuinely interested in seeing what the western paradigm had to say about all this yoga business. I knew science pooh-poohed religion in general, but I was also becoming aware that subatomic physics was a seriously mystical topic. I started out with laughably airy motives, but I kept getting straight A's, and I became addicted to that little achievement. Two years later it crossed my mind that I quite enjoyed crushing my competition, and I really wouldn't mind receiving a Nobel Prize.

There was an older guy in physics, about my age, and we got together on Saturday afternoons to study. Mostly I tutored him. He got straight C's. He had left Victoria after high school and gone to Australia where he found a slack job in pipeline construction and made so much money he bought a brand new BMW motorcycle and circled Australia on it, and then skied for a winter in New Zealand. He got a job on a private yacht and sailed around the South Pacific, stopping at little atolls, scuba-diving, working for three or four men who had made a fortune in Vietnam during the war, something they never talked about, not once. They were engineers and worked for Caterpillar Inc. He wound up in Thailand and got a job as an extra during the filming of *The Deer Hunter*. He was a stand-in and body double. Among other things, he portrayed one of the movie's heroes hanging onto a log floating down the river after escaping from the Vietcong. He was now back home, living in his parents' basement in Victoria, hoping to do a degree in engineering so he could travel again and work anywhere in the world. Straight C's in Grade 11 physics. Not a good start.

There was still plenty of drama at the Dharma Centre. Margaret drove Ginnie, the sweetest of girls, out of the house with her sneering and insults.

When Ginnie was gone Tom moved in, a tall, polite, unemployed young man with no idea what to do with his life. He soon ran out of money, which caused Margaret to scowl again, and he had to move out of the Centre. He lived in his truck-camper, as I had a year earlier, parked on a different street in Fairfield every night. He couldn't find a job, but he knew that art was prayer, and he was beginning to live more and more in an anguished mezzanine of his mind, obsessed with the lure of beauty, or with the potential of it, always just out of reach.

One of the gravelly Zen meditators who frequented the Centre was aggressive in his understanding of the so-called non-religious interpretation of Buddhism, and when he found out I was a tepid Vedantist he enlightened me with a glower that there was no God or soul in Buddhist philosophy, no Brahman, no atman, and therefore no kinship between these traditions. Or, by extension, us. He was often accompanied by his pudgy younger brother who was welcome in the Zen group but was considered mentally slow. The second time the muscular Buddhist volunteered to chauffeur out-of-town dignitaries around Victoria in his vintage Mercedes-Benz, he remarked that his car had now been blessed by the presence of a few important Buddhist personages. The pudgy brother immediately commented, "Gee, maybe it will come back as a person in its next life." Not so slow after all.

Brian had moved back to Victoria after a few summers in California and winters in Mexico, and Ron, the drummer from our Grade 7 garage band, had moved here from Calgary, so I had at least a couple of companions who were native speakers of English.

Other than my brief obsession with Vietnam and listening to Mark Twain's stories, I don't remember much about that long Christmas break, except that Brian and I went to the lounge of an expensive hotel and had a couple of drinks on New Year's Eve, soda for me. We talked about women, of course, our favourite topic. I bemoaned the mental and spiritual state of the young girls I went to school with and their inexplicable indifference to my many obvious charms. Thank God for Shizuka. Brian agreed that girls didn't seem to be quite as interested in sex, or him, as they used to. He was twenty-eight now. The ages eighteen to twenty-five, spread across the early 1970s, had been, for some, a boiling orgy of sex, drugs, and rock 'n' roll, which now seemed to be simmering down. We raised our glasses to January the First, and the new decade, and Brian gave a toast and a lamentation. "Happy New Year! And the zipper goes up on the '80s!"

He didn't know how right he was. Several thousand men in San Francisco and New York had already been infected with HIV in the last two years. The first clinical cases would be identified in 1981. In 1978, passing through San Francisco on my way to India, I had seen a small, handwritten poster in a bar window in the Castro district that read *Gay Cancer: If you have a sore like this on your leg, see your doctor immediately*. There was a 3" x 5" photograph glued to the little handmade poster showing the typical lesions of Kaposi's sarcoma. It wouldn't be called AIDS for another four years.

Shizuka and I had our ups and downs, the beginnings of the "beery, beery" sad part of our overheated relationship. Dropping her off at her new shared house on Taylor Street one night, I mooned into her eyes and told her I was hopelessly in love with her. She interpreted this to mean our relationship was hopeless, which was true, but that wasn't something that needed to be addressed just yet. She was speechless and shattered, fled into the house, and avoided me for two miserable weeks, until I managed to corner her and explain the difference. The language barrier was definitely a problem. Every word created misunderstanding.

One of Shizuka's friends, from one of her English classes, invited us for lunch at her apartment one day. She was seventy-seven years old and lived in a seniors' residence in Oak Bay. Her name, as near as I could make out from Shizuka's pronunciation, was Fenya. She was my grandfather's age and was born in Albania or Romania. She married a man who built hydroelectric dams and moved with him to Iran, where he worked for many years, and she was widowed there. Her successful sons wound up in Canada. They wanted her to be closer to them in her old age, and away from the unrest in Iran, so they moved her to Victoria, but she said she missed Tehran. She knew all the streets and the markets. She missed her friends. She bent in front of her refrigerator and pulled out a dozen tiny plates of scant leftovers, covered in foil and clear plastic, and placed them on the table for our lunch. She talked of her husband and her sons and Iran. In simple English she told us she was too old to learn another language. She had learned half a dozen in her life and had forgotten three or four of them. She was polite, but she had little energy for guests. Only a few years later I was cutting through Ross Bay Cemetery, and I saw a tombstone there. *Fatemeh Atlasi-Roshan (Tso Tso Fenia), 1903 — 1983. In God's Keeping*. There was a photograph of Shizuka's friend embedded in the stone under half an egg of clear acrylic, already scratched and marred by vandals. I found her gravestone again today with the help of the groundskeepers. I was surprised it was so weathered after only thirty years. The lettering was almost impossible to make out, and the picture was gone.

My days at the college were delicious. I never tired of them. When I wasn't in a classroom, or at a study desk somewhere, there were films, readings, displays, events, discussions, other lectures, always something to do if you got tired of homework and wanted to have a completely different topic wash over you. Plus, there was no television at the Dharma Centre. If I wanted to see video, I had to go to the movies downtown or at UVic, or to the various showings at Camosun, which were usually educational in one way or another. There were no sitcoms.

One day, I was outside a small attic meeting room waiting for a documentary film to start on the subject of the use of analgesic acupuncture in China. It was showing in one of Camosun College's handful of funky old buildings, this one just an old house on a high outcropping of rock. I was standing on the little interior landing at the very top of the stairs, at the very top of the building, looking down through the window onto the roof of the three-storey Fisher Building below. The Fisher Building was under construction that winter and was nearing completion. When it opened later in the year, it would be Camosun's largest building, housing mostly sciences. There were half a dozen workmen scattered about the wide, flat roof preparing to begin roofing. They were warming up the large, rectangular tar kettles, and before my eyes I saw the burner mechanism under one of the kettles break loose, and the propane, pouring from hoses attached to pressurized tanks, ignited in snaky, random fury. In seconds, the situation was out of control, and the workmen fled the rooftop. Several of the propane tanks were now engulfed in flames, and I knew there would be an explosion very soon. I ran to every room in the small wooden building, stuck my head into each doorway, and announced, "There's a fire on the roof of the Fisher Building next door! Everyone should leave this building now and move towards Richmond Road!" I might not have been that articulate.

Quickly down the stairs I went with the pottery students and moved westward and then south to take cover in front of the Young Building, the oldest building at Lansdowne Campus. It was three solid storeys of brick and concrete, with a tall clock tower in the middle, and I wanted it between me and the Fisher Building, if the Fisher Building was going up in flames that day. What I hadn't anticipated was that when the propane tanks blew, the burning fuel and debris flew high up into the air, and it was now all coming over the top of the Young Building and landing on the spacious lawns in front of it. I had run directly into a field of falling debris. As I scurried east just south of the Young Building, enormously loud explosions were followed by flaming metal and tar landing intermittently both in front of and behind me. I was doing a very poor job of avoiding the threat of injury and death, but there were only so many propane tanks on the roof, and eventually the explosions stopped, and the fire department arrived. The damage was mostly contained, and soon all that was left of the fire was the remains of a tall, thin, black mushroom cloud drifting over the city to the north. Needless to say, it was a topic of excited conversation for the rest of the day. Everyone had heard the explosions, but not everyone had run through a rain of flaming wreckage, like the few of us unlucky enough to be caught out on the lawns. I got a pretty good idea that day of just how useless I would be on a field of battle.

Eventually, Victoria's landscape changed from grey and green to blue and green, as it does in the spring. I had spent the winter at the Dharma Centre in a very entertaining, occasionally alarming, potpourri of languages and cultures, with eccentric companions of disparate histories and wildly varying world views. In the kitchen one day, Shizuka casually told us that her father and brothers used to get up very early in the morning in the winter and pour ice-cold water over themselves in the back yard, nude, some sort of *samurai* thing. Ginnie's eyes nearly fell out of her head as she exclaimed for about a minute and a half, *"Al noooood-oh!??!!!* She was from warm and very Catholic Mexico, very modest, and could not imagine such a sinful thing taking place in a family not certifiably insane or facing excommunication. She had probably never seen a penis, never mind the horror of her father's or brothers'. To her the Japanese may as well have been from Mars.

Mars was where I wanted to go. I couldn't imagine any scenario where I would give Shizuka up without first enduring, willingly, every possible manner of personal humiliation. I loved her insanely. I was addicted to her physically like a prisoner chained to a wall. I was a drunkard in love with love, and there was liquor at her breast. I had never met a woman who, hang on, that's not quite true. I had been almost as crazy about Terri, my beautiful, maddening, twenty-year-old girlfriend in Calgary. I had adored Shelagh and Carol and Gay. It is quite possible that when it came to women, I was simply as shallow as paint, paralyzed again and again by a pretty face. I had indeed known this intensity before but not to this degree. With Shizuka, once I fell into her arms, I was barely aware there were other women on the planet.

There was only one way I could stay with Shizuka, to be with her for any further length of time. And that was to go to Japan with her when she had to leave in August, when her visa expired. It was possible we could see each other that way for many more months. I would have followed her anywhere in the world just to spend one more day with her. Shizuka and I both knew at heart that ours was not a marrying kind of situation. I was just a broke, too-old student with no goals, but who knew what might transpire once I had been in Japan for a while? Her father had made a fortune in construction and trucking. There was more money in Shizuka's family than they knew what to do with. Hell, maybe he would give me a job and welcome me into the family as a son-in-law. I obviously didn't know that much about Japan, or money. Her family was stinking rich and mine wasn't. I was lacking in every kind of capital.

Shizuka had gone to university in Japan and done a degree in something or other and then a Master's degree in law. I was a little surprised on learning this, until she told me her brother wrote her thesis for her. There was never any plan that she would actually become a lawyer. She was just being indulged. She was the youngest child, and her older siblings had already made her parents proud. The boys were an architect and a physician. She said her father built her brother, the doctor, a "hospital," but I'm sure she meant a clinic. Maybe not. Her sisters had married well, one into the Morita family, the Sony family, and there were already many grandchildren. Shizuka did not have to be successful to be loved. She was spoiled and was allowed to do whatever she wanted. Her siblings had satisfied the family honour, and her parents could afford to let their last child experiment. A throwaway graduate degree? A slacker ESL year slumming in Victoria? Dodging marriage into her late twenties? No children yet? No problem.

She told me that a driver picked her father up every morning at their house and always brought a sizable stack of cash for him, her father's healthy per diem. The driver would leave the envelope of cash on the table in the entryway and then return to the car to wait for his very big boss. Every day for ten years, Shizuka stole a hundred dollars out of her father's per diem. Being a loving father and a wise man, he never said a word about it. She only ever had one job. When she graduated, she worked for a year at Japan Airlines, in the legal department. I asked her what she did there and she said, "Make tea for the men." When she received her first pay packet, an envelope of cash, she went home, bowed deeply to her father, and offered it to him on her knees, a symbolic token of appreciation for a very comfortable upbringing. He declined, of course.

All of this was neither here nor there, just fruit for tasty and idle speculation. What mattered to me was Shizuka. I knew two things. It was unlikely I would ever be able to stay with her, and I would never willingly part from her.

The only thing I could do in Japan was teach English. I wrote a letter to the Japanese Consulate in Vancouver innocently asking them for advice. They sent me a photocopy of a few pages from the Tokyo English-language Yellow Pages, the entries under *Schools, Foreign Language*. There were a hundred and ten of them. I chose fifty-four schools, for no particular reason, and typed out fifty-four short letters on Margaret's electric typewriter upstairs, saying that I was twenty-six years old, a university student, and I wanted to teach English in Japan. While waiting for responses, I put together a lengthy, largely insubstantial, but showy, curriculum vitae, heavy on recommendations, light on qualifications, and employing a lot of white space. I got a letter of reference from Margaret, on Dharma Centre letterhead, more in Spanish from Ginnie and her friends, and of course one from Shizuka, in Japanese, attesting to my natural abilities as an English tutor. And many more, from former teachers in speech and drama and science. My CV was twenty-six pages long.

Over the next six weeks, out of fifty-four schools, I received a dozen responses to my simple letter of enquiry. A couple of them said they required a Master's degree in something to do with English, and they would be happy to hear more from me. A couple of others said they required a Bachelor's degree and would be happy to hear more from me. And two included long, thick contracts in Japanese. These responses said they would be happy to give me a job, sight-unseen, and all I had to do was erase the words in the contract written in pencil that said "Erase this and sign here," sign my name, and mail it back. When Shizuka had finished giving me a rough translation of the first contract, I realized it said, more or less, "We can do whatever we want and you have no say in any of it." The second contract was more straightforward and was accompanied by a letter from the school, which said, more or less, "Don't worry about the contract. It's just a formality. When you get here I may have a job for you, but if I don't, you can get one anywhere." It was signed "Kiyosumi Owada, Director, Yotsuya Foreign Language Institute." This was the one I was looking for. I erased the many instances of words written in pencil, signed my name several times, and mailed the contract back to Mr. Owada, telling him I would arrive at the end of August.

I wrote my last exam, in biology, in the middle of April. I had worked diligently at school from the first day of classes in September to the last, and I had my reward. I had taken eight courses in science, and one French class, and I had a flawless transcript. And more importantly, I had finally proved to myself that I could concentrate on something constructive for more than a few weeks. A couple of semesters of school at twenty-six is no great accomplishment, but it was something, and it was a beginning. "The heart thus asking favor from its God, / Darkened but ardent, hath the end it craves, / The lesser blessing...." In other words, those who pray to lesser gods, receive the blessings of lesser gods. If you pray for a Volkswagen, one day you might get one, but you'll never get a Mercedes. It was unthinkable that I would not spend the night before a final exam studying, but on the last night before the last exam, I finally let go of the drive to succeed in this first year of school, and instead, Shizuka and I went to see all four hours of *Gone With the Wind*.

I was eighteen and of blithe spirit when I went to Europe and Turkey and Israel, but these were not hard places to be. In Mexico and especially in India, I was unprepared and had suffered for it. This time I was determined, with Shizuka's help, to be as ready as possible. I bought large sheets of construction paper, and together we made posters of the fifty basic characters of the Japanese syllabary, in which I drilled myself repeatedly, with and without Shizuka, and practised writing them frequently until, after a few weeks, I had all of them, and their combinations, thoroughly memorized and could, miraculously, read Japanese, or at least sound it out. There were two scripts that I could deal with immediately, *katakana*, the blocky script used for sounding out foreign words, and *hiragana*, the slightly more flowing script that is taught to Japanese children as a stepping stone to the beautiful, but utterly incomprehensible, pictograms used by adults called *kanji*. If I saw something written in the one hundred characters of *katakana* or *hiragana*, I was master of the sounds, but that didn't mean I knew what the words meant.

I read Ruth Benedict's book *The Chrysanthemum and the Sword*. It was commissioned by the US government during World War II in an effort to understand the Asian enemy. Without benefit of ever having set foot in Japan, Benedict wrote a massively influential book about Japanese culture, with an eye to what America could expect in the final days of the war, as well as the occupation, a period nearly twice as long as the hostilities. Under the circumstances in which it was written, and considering the period of time in history, it is not surprising it has been called "politely arrogant and condescending," but what is perhaps more surprising, is that it was not worse, given the open racism of the day. It was a best seller in English and Japanese, and was selling well in China as recently as 2005, when Japan and China started bickering again. I read Ooka, Kawabata, and Mishima. We went to a Japanese film festival at UVic. Between *Shōgun*, *Chrysanthemum*, post-war authors and cinema, and my increasingly surreal life with Shizuka, my view of Japan that summer was fascinating, and slightly Cubist.

I knew someone who was living in Japan. I had heard that a man I had known vaguely in high school, David, was living there with his English girlfriend. I hadn't seen him in years, and we were hardly pals, but we knew a lot of the same people from the old drug days in Calgary. I wrote to him and let him know I was coming. Of course, I said we might get together for a visit in Tokyo and then asked for any advice he might have. I received a short response of little enthusiasm, but people living in Japan were always getting letters from strays at home looking, anxiously, for advice about jobs and housing in the land of rising employment opportunities. After I moved there, I received a few myself, and it was tedious to respond at any level of reassuring detail to their nervous authors. Japan is a rather long story. I didn't think it likely I would be seeing much of Dave and his English girlfriend.

I knew virtually nothing about the structured aspects of teaching English, and I enrolled in two three-week summer courses in Second Language Acquisition in the Department of Linguistics at UVic. They were third-year courses, and having no prerequisites, I was only able to attend as an auditing student, which was fine with me. I had no desire to write essays or exams, and I didn't need course credits. I could simply list the courses in my curriculum vitae, and that would be sufficient for my purposes. I assumed the public servants in Tokyo reviewing my thick application for a work visa would simply put it on a scale and weigh it. This would be much easier than reading it.

These short summer courses met every day for three hours and proved valuable in the end. We discussed such earnest matters as the nature of learner language, individual differences in language acquisition, the role of input and interaction, similarities and differences in first and second language acquisition, instructed acquisition and the relationship between acquisition research and second language teaching, curriculum development, lesson planning, instructional strategies for teaching different language skills, including listening, speaking, reading, writing, grammar, and vocabulary, and the use of classroom materials for language teaching, language assessment, interactive and socio-cultural approaches to language teaching and learning, form-focused instruction and computer-assisted language learning, as well as classroom discourse and pragmatics. I had very little idea what all of this meant, but I made sure to list it at great length in my CV, much as I have done here. I didn't do a lot of extra reading, or any, but I went to all the classes, and by the time I was done I had a paper-thin knowledge of Teaching English as a Second or Foreign Language. I had now heard the terms and the jargon once or twice. I had done theatre for eleven years as a young person, and in that business the barest familiarity with a subject and a knack for mimicry are the tools of your trade.

I wanted to get into a classroom for some observation, and I could have just shown up at a couple of Shizuka's ESL classes, but I thought it would be good form to ask permission first. Not always a good idea. The director of language programs at Camosun was a middle-aged English woman named Beryl.

"Pronounced like 'Pearl'?" I asked her secretary.

"Pronounced like 'Barrel,'" she said.

I requested an appointment. My own classes at Camosun were over now, and in a state of sunny bliss, on a morning in early May, I was shown into Beryl's office.

I thought I would do her the favour of getting right to the point, so after a very brief introduction, I told her I had a job lined up in Tokyo to teach English, starting in September, which gave me the rest of the summer to prepare. Was she aware of a short course in TESL that I could take over the next four months?

This unleashed the bear in Beryl.

She was cold and sharp. She said, "What subject do you study here?"

I picked one. "Physics."

With a snarl and a naked tooth she said, "Do you think someone could teach physics after a taking a four-month course?"

"Of course not," I replied. "Well, not advanced physics."

"Then what makes you think you can teach English after taking a four-month course?"

I was confused. "Well," I started slowly, "I would only be teaching basic English, and I already speak it, quite well. I learned it as a child at my mother's knee, and other low joints, and I have been practising it for twenty-five years. To teach physics you have to learn it first, and that takes at least four years at a university as an adult." The difference seemed pretty obvious to me.

I don't remember what she said next, but I do remember it was all very unpleasant and bitterly expressed. She told me she had a Master's degree and twenty years of experience and several other things I didn't really care about.

When she was finally done blowing hot, and the hair on my head had settled again, I said, as charmingly as I could, "Yes, well, I see, but the fact remains that I *am* going to Tokyo on August 25, and I *have* a job, and I *will* be teaching English starting in September. Would it be possible to sit in on a few of your ESL classes?" I smiled sweetly.

She gave me a look of mixed disgust and bemusement, mostly disgust, at my presumption. She told me I could visit two classes on one day, and no more. She was obviously not in the mood to help me, someone she saw as polluting the profession, or the unfortunate students I would eventually be teaching. She finished by saying, thoroughly sickened, "Fine. Go to Japan and teach English, but for God's sake, don't try to pass yourself off as an English teacher!" And that was the end of my meeting with Beryl.

I was pretty sure if I had been an English major asking the head of the Physics Department if I could sit in on some physics classes, because I was going abroad to teach basic science to the benighted, he or she wouldn't have given a toss. Richard Allen, the co-founder of the African American Episcopal Church, born a slave, said, "We think it a great mercy to have all anger and bitterness removed from our minds." He forgave the slave-owners of Delaware Bay. But here was a very white woman, living in a very free society, affected to the core, negatively, by a job to which she was not chained, consisting of undemanding tasks, for which she was rarely beaten, a job that kept her in a life of substance, paid her mortgage, fed her children, and sent them to college, a career and a profession that provided her with social standing in the community. Yet she was so distressed by the course her life had taken, and so threatened by the likes of me, she couldn't summon a moment's courtesy to answer a simple question in a professional setting. Some days, it just seems that every person you meet in a position of authority is a cunt.

Before I went to Camosun's ESL classes, I went with Shizuka to her English class at the YWCA. It was taught by a short, middle-aged, busty, over-dressed, operatic woman from Eastern Europe who gave me a reception just as frosty as Beryl's had been hot. She let me stay for one class, and no more, and addressed me in a snarky and condescending tone. I started to wonder how many angry, bitter, middle-aged women there were in the ESL profession. I seemed to be stepping on painted, old toenails everywhere I went.

When I did get up to the old Carey Road school, the site of Camosun's ESL program, I sat in on a couple of classes. Geshe-la was in one of them. The one taught by an older man was old-fashioned and dull, chairs all in a row. The one taught by a young woman was fun and loose, more like a language festival. Neither of them cared one bit about my presence in the classroom. The woman was the only teacher I had seen yet under the age of fifty, and she offered me a ride back to town, which I happily accepted. I felt comfortable with her simply because she was younger, and I told her about my experiences so far in researching the ESL business, especially the downright unfriendly reception I had received, and my scolding interviews with Beryl and the opera singer. I asked her why everyone I had met so far seemed so angry. She said, "Oh, God, ESL is awful! Nothing works! We study, we read, we go to conferences and workshops, we try new techniques, and year after year the success rates are just as dismal as the year before. It's a heartbreaking profession. People get very touchy after years of so much effort and so little success. I'm looking for something else to get into. I can't do this much longer."

"Ah," said I, and returned to my linguistics classes at UVic. I also got a book of English grammar out of the library and read it cover to cover, relieved to find, after fourteen years, the last time I looked at anything to do with grammar, that nothing in it was unfamiliar to me.

The spring and summer of 1980 were sunny and pleasant. I saw no need to spend the four months from May through August working. I was eligible for many healthy cheques from the federal government because I had worked at the sawmill the summer before at a very good wage. I also sold my truck. This would finance my move to Japan with a comfortable cushion. Shizuka was practically living at the Dharma Centre now, and the other students and tenants had moved on. I saw no reason why we couldn't live there, quietly, through the warm, idle months, going out to the movies and for dinner, socializing, studying a little Japanese, reading and relaxing, until it was time to take up our exciting and uncertain new life in Japan.

I had managed to live in an easy, but cautious, peace with Margaret for eight months, while she turned savagely on every other tenant and drove them from the house. I was now the only one left. Inevitably, her withered heart and tortured mind turned in my direction. Since school had ended in mid-April, Shizuka had been at the house five nights out of seven for a month, but she had no intention of moving in. She kept her own place. I was just about to bring the matter up with Margaret, suggesting an increase in my rent for the summer to cover the extra consumption of utilities due to Shizuka's now very frequent visits. So many showers.

Then, one day, shortly after Mount St. Helens erupted, Margaret exploded at the kitchen table. We were all, coincidentally, seated for a friendly lunch that day, and she suddenly let loose a stream of vitriol at me and Shizuka, mostly Shizuka, on the subject of our abuse of the lodger's terms. Geshe-la was swept along by Margaret's vicious harangue, and he threw in a few admonishments of his own, but he might have been more disturbed about having two tireless fornicators in the basement than he was about the money. As always, with Geshe-la, it was hard to tell. We were both unprepared for this, utterly taken aback. Margaret had never been shy before about asking for slight increases in household money, to which I always acquiesced, and money was not a problem for Shizuka. She could have paid my rent from her change purse. Margaret's bitter attack, the accusations and name-calling, were motivated by pure malice. Money was not the issue. She hadn't been in a fight for a while, and she was missing the adrenaline. Shizuka was a well-mannered woman, beautiful, graceful, charming, and privileged. Margaret had initially been attracted to her well-heeled and cheerful poise, but the spell was broken now and was replaced by an inrush of bile. She was no longer happy for us as a couple. She couldn't stand our youth and joy, carefree and self-indulgent.

After the tirade at the table, Shizuka and I retired, staggering, to the basement to recover, and there I received a further earful from Shizuka, because I had not adequately defended her dignity. I had tried to be reasonable during Margaret's onslaught, telling her I was just about to bring up the matter of compensation for Shizuka's frequent visits, but the only thing Margaret wanted to hear was the satisfying sound of her own vituperation. I've been called a few names in my life, but Shizuka had probably never been on the receiving end of such a deliberately hurtful outburst. I was appalled and speechless, but Shizuka was shaken and pale.

There was nothing to do but move out. Margaret had behaved abominably. Her lack of control in her relations with people was shocking, pathological. She was ill and unrestrained, of this there was no doubt. A continued residence was impossible. I went to the provincial government department that handled landlord-tenant disputes and told my story in someone's office. The advice I received was simply to move out, and if I chose not to pay the rent on my way out the door, Margaret could sue me for it. I could then countersue her for harassment in small claims court. Worth a try. I always paid my rent, but I was damned if I was going to pay to see the object of my affection, and myself, so roundly and unfairly abused.

Shizuka fled to her own house, never to be seen at the Dharma Centre again, a terrible shame after the affection and good feelings that had prevailed over the previous winter. I packed up and moved out in a matter of a few days. As I was leaving the house for the last time, Margaret was smiling, all sweetness and light, still expecting me to put my next month's rent into her hand, less the return of my deposit, on my way out the door. She knew I was honest, generally, and she trusted me to pay. Instead, I said exactly what I had been advised to say, adding that I knew where Ginnie lived, and the young man who wanted only beauty in his life, and the Philosopher, and the previous unsmiling tenant of my basement room. I told Margaret I was sure they would all be happy to give me a letter stating the unpleasant circumstances of their time at the Dharma Centre, and their departure, driven out by her scowls and insults. If she wanted to pursue me for the measly ninety dollars I owed her, I would be happy to spend the summer suing her for a thousand. I may have gone a little overboard when I then gave her some further choice words concerning her conduct. She ran wailing to her room, in her nun's robes, in a fit of absurd dramatics, weeping and shouting baby talk, looking for the lama who, unknown to her, was standing right behind her as she fled up the stairs yelling, "Geshe-la! Geshe-la! He say I Big Evil!" It was indescribably bizarre and grotesque. I cannot recall the like of it. I have been appalled by, and gladly set sail from, many of my landlords over the years, but there has been nothing to match that particular day. I also can't believe she thought I would actually pay her after her deliberately hateful and revolting behaviour. What did she see when she looked in the mirror? What did she honestly expect? What did she learn that day? I don't think I learned anything at all. Geshe-la stood in the hall with his eyes wide and his mouth open, aghast, I imagine, at yet another intense and ridiculous conclusion to the tenancy of someone under his roof. I think he was also beginning to realize that he was now alone in the house with Margaret for the summer.

I stayed a few nights at Shizuka's, but one of her roommates was moving out to rent a two-bedroom apartment with her five-year-old son, and she wanted to rent us her second bedroom for the rest of the time we would be in Victoria, three months. I moved from Leonard to Taylor to Bank in a matter of a few days.

Not long after arriving in Victoria, Shizuka had become an exotic social butterfly, and she was still constantly asked to lunches, dinners, garden parties, soirees, theatrical and musical events, casual get-togethers, schools, and intercultural activities, and I accompanied her to all of them. We went to an astonishing performance of *Ankoku-Butoh* at the Open Space artists' centre downtown, the grotesque and mind-numbingly slow Japanese dance performed nearly nude in full-body white makeup. We dined frequently in what can only be called your finer restaurants, employing the magic of the single person's thrift. When you have no mortgage, no car payments, no children with expensive futures, no college fund to feed, no garage to fill with recreational and sporting goods, no credit cards, no debt, no money for foreign vacations, you can spend your entire small income on personal entertainment. Restaurants, even good ones, are always full of young people who have the price of an expensive meal in their pockets, and it doesn't matter if it's gone at the end of the evening. Of course, Shizuka always had a big wad of twenty-dollar bills jammed into her purse, but I tried not to let her pay all the time.

The little apartment on Bank Street was on the second level of a small house. Our bedroom, at the front, had a balcony looking out at the quiet street, and the kitchen overlooked the back yard. The entry was at the side of the house, up a straight flight of fifteen steps.

There was an English couple, recent to the country, renting the suite on the main floor. They were a little older and were an established concern with an apartment full of heavy furniture. He was a glazier, and she was an esthetician. I don't know much about English accents, there are so many of them, but between them they definitely had one or two. He was blond and sour-faced, and she was pretty and olive-toned, with the slippery skin and big hair estheticians seem to have. She told me her husband was an accountant, but he had taken work as a glazier until he could get sorted out professionally in Canada. In a matter of a few weeks, he was fired from his job as a glass cutter, and she told me it was because he had pilfered a few dollars from a customer's cash payment, money he had intended to replace, but the misdeed was noticed before he could do so. She was quite candid with me. I wondered what kind of accountancy he practised back in England. Freed from a life of nine-to-five labour, he took up curbsiding, selling cars from his home pretending to be the legal owner, probably under the assumed name of the previous owner. Every few days a different used car showed up in the driveway, and he sold it privately. The practice is illegal for many reasons.

These downstairs neighbours had an enormous dog named Caesar, part Saint Bernard and part Great Dane, the biggest dog I think I have ever seen, with a head the size of a basketball. He didn't bark much, thank goodness, but he was an incorrigible and serial producer of stools, which were about the same size as his head. They littered the back yard in the dozens. Late one morning, I looked out the kitchen window and saw the attractive esthetician sunning herself in the middle of the back yard, on a chaise longue, wearing tiny shorts and a skimpy top. Her hair was in a towel-turban, and her entire face was hidden under a green mask of moisturizing goop. She was smoking a cigarette surrounded by a hundred giant dog turds in various stages of desiccation. She seemed utterly at peace. Paradise on the west coast.

The accountant-turned-glazier-turned-curbsider was responsible for paying the water bill, since the meter was in their apartment downstairs. We would split the bill with them when it arrived. One morning, seated happily on my balcony, I saw an unmarked pickup truck pull up in front of the house. A man in unmarked working clothes got out, flipped up the lid of a small wooden box buried in the front yard, did something with a tool, closed the lid, returned quickly to his truck, and drove away. It took him all of fifteen seconds to accomplish this task. I had no idea what he had done, but I was sure it had nothing to do with me. In about two minutes, there was a howl from the bathroom, where Shizuka was having a shower. I went in and saw her standing, deliciously naked, in the tub, with a giant white ball of sudsy shampoo about her head and face. There was no water coming out of the showerhead. I realized immediately that the contemptible English git downstairs had not paid the water bill. I ran down to his side of the house, where he was selling yet another curbside car. I proceeded to encourage him to get his fuckin' ass down to City Hall and pay the goddamn water bill right fuckin' now. I don't know if this had a cooling effect on his sale or not.

It also turned out that our roommate, Linda, had an alcoholic boyfriend, perhaps the father of her child, I'm not sure, who showed up once or twice in the middle of the night screaming drunkenly to be let in so they could "just talk things over!" I stood at the top of the stairs, inside the house, with a baseball bat, Shizuka cowering behind me, and we called the police. I'm sure Shizuka wondered if she would survive the night. Neighbours from half a block down the street yelled, "Shuuuuut uuup!" Bank Street is in a pleasant enough part of town, but we all got a lesson in trailer-park living that summer, an eye-opener for Shizuka.

There were preparations necessary to going to Japan other than wondering how I was actually going to teach English. I didn't know what Thoreau was thinking when he said, "Beware of all enterprises that require new clothes." I hadn't read *Walden*. What he meant was that new clothes won't do you any good unless there is a new man underneath them. I was definitely a new man, through the "internal industry and expansion" of a year's work. I had one very nice navy blue suit, purchased when I was a wealthy cab driver, and it was time for a couple of new additions. There was a sale at a clothing store downtown, where I could buy two for the price of one, so I bought two three-piece suits, one in French blue, another in soft grey. I was a peacock in subtle, but not wholly false, colours. Standing in the busy store on a Saturday afternoon, at this very good sale, I was looking at the back of the suit jacket collar, and I wondered idly what that piece of material was called that lines the collar and joins it to the body of the coat. I knew it wasn't "yoke." I asked the salesman if he knew. He struggled a bit and said he couldn't remember. I didn't much care what it was called, but he was determined to satisfy my curiosity, and he shouted loudly across the crowded store to a fellow salesman, "Bob! What's this piece of fabric behind the collar called?"

Bob yelled back over the heads of two dozen customers, "The hymen!"

It got very quiet in the store, but it made sense. A piece of material that covers and holds together other pieces of like material. My salesman said, "Right. The hymen. How am I supposed to remember that?"

I said, "How could you forget?"

I also bought a shiny, light, hard-sided, very swish, Samsonite attaché case in elegant burgundy. No more leather aprons and yellow hardhats for me.

The dream of every Japanese person, if they think about Canada at all, apart from a bizarre obsession with Anne of Green Gables, is to take a train across the Rocky Mountains to Jasper, travel by bus down the scenic highway to Banff, stopping at the Columbia Icefields, and then return to Vancouver on the train again. I could not deny this sacred pilgrimage to Shizuka, with a few minor variations. We took the train the many hundreds of miles to Jasper and then another three hundred miles east to the tiny village of Viking, just north of the tiny village of Sedgewick. There, my father picked us up, and Shizuka became one of the few Japanese people in history to visit Sedgewick, Alberta. Mile after slow mile, referring to the breathtaking expanse of the Canadian prairies, Shizuka could not stop from remarking, again and again, in wonder, "Nee-du, it is so wide, so wide!"

A word about "Nee-du." Japanese is a syllabic language. With the exception of "n," occasionally pronounced "m," most common perhaps in the honorific *san*, as in Shizuka-san, no syllable or word or sentence in Japanese ends with a consonant. It's all open vowel sounds such as ka, ki, ku, ke, ko, ma, mi, mu, me, mo, etc, all pronounced, more or less, with equal emphasis. The pronunciation of final consonants in foreign words, then, usually has an involuntary vowel added to it. The final "l" in Neil would become "lu," "Nee-lu," but unfortunately, on top of that, although the Japanese can say an "l" sound, there is no "l" in the written language. The final "lu," then, is written and pronounced "ru." And since the "r" in Japanese is tapped lightly on the hard palate behind the top front teeth, it comes out as, I hate to say it, a soft "doo" sound. These compound problems make "Neil" almost impossible to pronounce in Japanese. What starts out as "el," in English, is transformed into "du," in Japanese, an unpredictable result to those unfamiliar with the language. Shizuka called me Nee-du throughout our relationship, and some people who met me during that period wickedly called me Nee-du for the next ten years.

Native speakers of English find almost no sounds in Japanese that are unfamiliar to them, although speed and accuracy are, of course, always stumbling blocks to native-like delivery. Native speakers of Japanese, on the other hand, encounter all kinds of problems pronouncing English. Stress, pitch, intonation, diphthongs, and certain letters are all challenging. They can say "r" and "l." They just never seem to know when to use them.

Instead of London and Rome, you get "Rondon" and "Lome." In World War II, in the Pacific, the English front-line military challenge, the shibboleth, was "lollapalooza." If you mispronounced it, with even a hint of an "r," the sentries opened fire. Three consonants in a row can prove insurmountable. The temptation to insert and add vowels is irresistible. What do you do in Japanese with an eight-letter word in English that has seven consonants and one unstressed vowel? "Strength" becomes *tsu-ren-su*, almost unrecognizable. "Gal" is *gya-ru*. English spelling, of course, drives everyone mad, native and non-native speakers alike. In Japanese, as in other syllabic languages, and especially languages made up mostly of pictographs, spelling can hardly be said to be an issue.

A few months later, when I was in Japan, my landlord made me a present of a *hanko*, a small bamboo stamp or chop, with my last name carved in the end. They came into use hundreds of years ago to replace fingerprinting and handprinting as a means of signing documents and are still widely used in Asia in place of handwritten signatures. My last name consisted of two characters, 板 and 泉, accompanied by an explanation from my landlord that I did not understand. The first character means "board" or "plank," and is pronounced "han" in *onyomi kanji*, the Chinese reading, but in *kunyomi kanji*, the Japanese reading, it is pronounced "ita." The second character means "spring" or "fountain," and is pronounced "sen" in *onyomi*, but in *kunyomi* it is pronounced "izumi." The difference between *onyomi* and *kunyomi kanji* has melted finer brains than mine. Suffice it to say that people's names in Japanese, naturally enough, take *kunyomi* pronunciations, so my name in Japanese *kanji*, 板泉, is indeed "Han-sen," meaning "board-spring," but a Japanese person reading these characters and saying my name would address me as Mr. Ita-izumi. It is, at the same time, both confusing, and I think you'll agree, not very interesting, except to a linguist or a serious student of the language. Moreover, the literal translation of my last name evokes nothing more interesting than the utterly prosaic image of a plank floating in water. But I digress, and painfully.

I was as proud of Shizuka as new shoes, and I loved showing her off to my family and to the few other people in Sedgewick we ran into while we were there. My aunt and uncle gave us a barbeque of freshly caught Arctic char, and we celebrated outdoors in the evening of a long June day, swatting mosquitoes all the while. I had left town broke and disgraced eighteen months earlier although I was largely unconcerned on that account. Since then, I had completed a year of college, even if it was only junior college, and I was always the only one in the room moving to Tokyo that fall with a beautiful Japanese woman. It was safe to say I had redeemed myself somewhat. Mostly people asked me what I had been up to, not the other way around, and I am only mildly embarrassed to say I loved it. I sprinkled my conversation with Shizuka with the few tidbits of Japanese I had learned, and everyone thought I was genius. I have always been content to let people think so if it makes them feel better.

My father had sold his clothing store and was so sick of working indoors for the last ten years that he had bought land to grow trees, and equipment for a tree-moving business. He was never shy about employing family members when they showed up at his door. "Welcome home, make yourself useful."

Shizuka and I found ourselves down in the dirt one day, in the fresh air, weeding many rows of trees at my father's little tree farm. I don't suppose she had ever had a hoe in her hand before. I wonder if she remembers that day, getting filthy in the good clean dirt of the prairies, under the hot Alberta sun. She looked at my father's very large workshop, as big as a barn, the sheds, the tractor, and the other strange, tree-related machinery. "Your father is a farmer," she said, in a tone of increased respect and admiration. The Japanese have a positively mystical regard for agriculture. So many people to feed, so little land. This was an adventure for her. I had always spoken of my father as a retailer of clothing, so she wasn't expecting a trip to a working farm, or a facsimile of one. This was not a normal part of the well-beaten triangle of Japanese tourism, Vancouver, Jasper, and Banff. I lived in Japan twice as long as Shizuka lived in Canada, and I never visited a farm while I was there.

My father had left us on our own for a few hours under the wide prairie sky to play in the dirt. We weren't much good as farm labourers. When he returned to check on our progress, Shizuka found she was suddenly very hot under the many layers of clothing she had put on in the cool, early morning. Standing only a few feet in front of me and my father, she quickly turned around, panting, and tore off her sweater and shirt and T-shirt, to rearrange them. Her naked back, beigey, olive-brown, and smooth, was uninterrupted, from neck to waist, by any sign of a bra strap. Hints of her uncovered breasts were unavoidable, to the east and to the west. My father's trees were still too young and too small for her to hide behind, but I was surprised she had stripped to the waist right in front of us. My father was even more surprised. He has always had a good head of hair, which I didn't inherit, and when he saw Shizuka in a state of dishabille, his eyebrows went up so far his browline met his hairline at the top of his forehead. With a great sigh of relief at being instantly cooler, Shizuka turned back around and bowed. "Paw-dawn me," she said. Her coy smile was practiced but no less exquisite for being so. Not many Japanese boobs have seen the Alberta sun, unless you count the salarymen tourists.

Shizuka had definitely had a change of heart about clothing and fashion. I had made a few very careful comments over the last eight months about her odd fashion sense. She could see that the prevailing styles of Canada's west coast were very casual compared with the overblown ones she was used to. They were also a lot easier in terms of preparation, maintenance, and expense. She slowly and steadily began to favour a more youthful, less fussy look. She showed up at the Dharma Centre one day, fresh from a downtown hair palace, with a new perm in long, loose, Mediterranean curls, a style that was perfect for her magnificent head of thick, black hair. The makeup all but disappeared. Fashion-wise, she went from a slightly disturbing theatrical mix-up to an off-the-cuff girl next door. When I put her on the plane back to Japan on August 15, at the Victoria Airport, I watched her moving along in line with the other passengers, until she passed through the door out onto the tarmac. She was wearing blue jeans, a T-shirt, a pair of old Adidas sneakers I had given her, no socks, no bra, and no makeup. Her hair was still long and loose, past her shoulders. She looked as relaxed and at home as anyone I knew, and Shizuka relaxed was a beautiful thing, although I wondered what her mother would say when she picked her up at the airport in Tokyo.

We did my parents the courtesy of sleeping in separate bedrooms in their little house on the golf course, at least until they went to bed, and then I slipped down the hallway and joined Shizuka. My parents were always gone by the time we crawled out of the sheets in the morning. One morning, though, we realized they were at home and in the kitchen when we woke up, and we quietly got dressed and went in separately to join them. It was the weekend, and we knew they had been out late the night before. We were expecting them to have a lie in. Yet here they were, both fully dressed at eight o'clock in the morning. It took only a moment to piece the situation together. Shizuka said, very surprised, "Did you just get home?" They were having breakfast in their evening clothes. My father said, "It must have been a hell of a party. We stayed for the whole damn thing." I was a little surprised, but Shizuka was amazed at these Canadian prairie folk who could work all day and party all night. My father was forty-nine, my mother two years younger.

We caught a ride to Red Deer with my father, where the two of us said good-bye without a hint of ceremony, even though I was going to Japan and didn't know when I was coming back. He had seen it all before. From there we took the bus to Calgary for a couple of days to visit my sister. We saw *Star Wars: The Empire Strikes Back*, the second, the best, and the last good *Star Wars* movie. I wanted to visit John and Renee in Brisco, and we took another bus to BC. Shizuka's national wish was fulfilled when we saw the Rocky Mountains on a spectacular summer day, as we rode the bus through Banff National Park. At Radium, we hiked the short, spectacular trail through Sinclair Canyon to the hot springs. Along the way, we stopped to yield to a standing temptation but were interrupted by other hikers. In the pools we melted together, an experience Shizuka knew very well. There are thousands of *onsen*, hot springs, in the 2,500 islands of the volcanic archipelago of Japan. They are the source of much of Japan's obsession with cleanliness, and mixed bathing, traditional into the twentieth century, is partly the source of its very casual attitude towards nudity. In general, Japanese people are blessed with a thick head of straight black hair and very little hair on the rest of the body, also straight. Shizuka was typical in this regard. A little shaving cream and half a dozen swipes of a safety razor would have removed every hair on her body below the neck. I regret now that this did not occur to me at the time.

John and Renee had finally found a decent house to rent, decent for the Columbia valley, and John's mother was visiting from Ontario. We all behaved ourselves and had a pleasant time. John's mother had always looked askance at me, obviously thinking I was leading her son astray, which was true, but only in the beginning. Of recent years, little did she know, and better were it so.

John gave us a ride to Golden, and we caught the train there back to Vancouver. We talked for a long time with a group of Japanese tourists and their insolent tour guide, the first of many repulsive Japanese men I would meet over the next couple of years. Japanese men live a life of humourless servitude to rigid custom and expectation, and in some it breeds an anger that smoulders just beneath the surface and manifests as sneering and aggressive rudeness, which they often take great pride in, the Japanese version of *machismo*. It is particularly hard on Japanese women.

Our trip to Alberta and the mountains had been restorative, but back in Victoria we returned to the long, slow arc of the aching decline of our relationship. We had sparred many times over the last eight months, often not even in the same ring, the square circle of boxing and relationships. Shizuka expected me to respond appropriately to a panoply of cultural cues that I didn't even know existed. Every day, I said or did something that offended her Japanese-ness. She knew how to manipulate a chauvinistic man into thinking he was in charge, but she didn't know how to deal with a passive man who wasn't in charge of anything and didn't want to be. I had found, in my short life so far, that cultural leanings and party lines could, and did, easily fall into strongly held, useless, and misguided opinions, and worse, into the most hateful bigotry. I made an active point of watching carefully, and discounting, if not rooting out, my own cultural prejudices. I was content to let the world look after itself, in its own way. I wasn't a Japanese man. I was barely a Canadian man. I was an outsider in my own society. Even western women don't like that. From a Japanese viewpoint, not only was I not in the game, I didn't even have a glove on. Shizuka couldn't figure out who the hell I was. For her, Canada's easygoing, lukewarm culture had lost its charms, and the closer she got to returning home the more devoted she became to her own country's customs. To me, those strange customs seemed like a weight around her neck, and mine. Each of us was an isolated other, and she mistook her every cultural viewpoint for the only truth. I had learned not to be over-impressed with my own culture, so I didn't care who was right or wrong. People think that's a sign of weakness. It isn't. It's a sign of wisdom. For the two of us, our souls had met and then turned away. I was only waiting now for the end I knew was coming.

I had slightly long hair and a beard when I met Shizuka. I had let it grow while working at the sawmill the previous summer, but in the fall, after a while at school, I cut it all off, hair and beard. In the early seventies, if you had long hair it meant you were going to college. By the late seventies, if you had long hair it meant you had never set foot on a campus. My longhaired days were over. Shizuka had fallen for a broke, scruffy student, and when I presented myself to her clean-cut, her eyes nearly fell out of her head. "Oh, Nee-du, too handsome!" she exclaimed. And I'm sure she meant it.

Our relationship was primal and impossible. Shizuka knew how to reward a man and how to punish one, and she had decided by now that I had to be punished for something. I wasn't bride-stealing. Why should I be punished? Since when has stealing a woman's heart been a crime? But there was some truth to the charges. I had made her fall in love with me, I was addicted to sex, I wasn't rich, and I had come upon her unawares in a strange land and dragged her into a hopeless relationship. I would need a good lawyer.

She was alternately ecstatic and angry, and Shizuka angry was a terrifying thing. One day euphoric, the next day bitter. She would gush, "Oh, Nee-du, when I walk down the street with you in Japan, it will be the proudest day of my life." Then, resentful, "When I get back to Japan, I will marry the first man my father introduces me to." I gave her a brooch for her birthday. She threw it out the window. This was not a relationship of manners, it was not a social or economic arrangement, it was purely carnal, and the result was carnage and the profound disruption of two rudderless lives. Neither of us had the faintest notion of how to navigate a relationship in healthy ways. There were no boundaries between us, sensible or otherwise. My heart was on her hook, and the more I squirmed, the more I bled. My spirit and mood were roughly reeled, this way and that, by her constantly shifting charms and favours, indifference and contempt. The depth of our erotic art was no deeper than the canvas on which it was splashed, no matter how often. At Bank Street our relationship took a painful turn into the netherworld. It became a threat to decency and social order. There is an insufficiency of metaphors to mix together to match the mix of emotions I felt. I was profoundly confused. I guess we all fall in love from time to time.

Shortly after we moved out of the Dharma Centre, it was Swiftsure Weekend, the Swiftsure International Yacht Race, its fiftieth anniversary, but not its fiftieth running. There were over four hundred entrants that year, still the third highest number for the event. You could walk all the way across Victoria's picturesque Inner Harbour, stepping from one beautiful sailboat to the next. It was a spectacular sight. We bought tickets for a day trip on a 50-foot ketch, ferrocement and gaff-rigged, to watch the boats race home, but finding wind in Victoria can be a problem, and the race is just as often referred to as Driftsure. Over four or five hours, the skipper and crew of our sightseeing vessel, and its dozen or so passengers, motored out into the Strait of Juan de Fuca, put the sails up for a disappointing hour, had lunch, and motored back to the harbour. We saw a few racing ships in the distance floating slowly homeward toward the finish line. Paint dries faster.

One of the passengers was a man I would very much like to have met under different circumstances. I was becoming quite interested in the vasty ocean, wondering if I might not one day have the opportunity to sail upon its challenging and rewarding waters. This man was a friend of the skipper's and had just sailed, alone, across the Pacific Ocean, from Japan to Victoria, in his 35-foot sailboat, a gutsy undertaking. What was perhaps more interesting was that, coming from Hong Kong, he and his boat had been run over by a freighter in the East China Sea, which then steamed away leaving him crippled and without assistance. He managed to limp into a harbour somewhere in southern Japan, where he was immediately taken in by the local yacht club and given every aid in repairing his boat. It took a few months to get shipshape again. He told stories of his time in Japan with great fondness and gratitude for the kindness and generosity of his hosts. Shizuka listened with attention and appreciation to his praise of her countrymen. He, in his turn, was dazzled by Shizuka, everyone was. He was a handsome enough fellow, and he had a boat and spent his days travelling the world. This looked like a lifestyle that Shizuka could be interested in, perhaps her next adventure. He flirted with her openly, and flirting with men was something Shizuka knew a thing or two about. The burden of beautiful girlfriends. When we got back to the harbour, I almost had to drag her away from the boat, while the lonesome sailor threw out every invitation he could think of to get her back within his compass, even if it meant inviting me as well. As I yanked Shizuka down the dock with me, he shouted a final, quick, "That's my boat over there! Come down any time!"

Here was a way to punish me.

The next day after a leisurely morning, I realized Shizuka had been in the bathroom for quite a while, and when I finally looked in, I saw she was applying more makeup than I had seen in a long time. I asked her what she was doing. "I am going out," she said. Without me. This was unusual.

"Where?" I asked.

"For lunch."

"Oh. With who?"

"With a friend."

"Oh, who? Which friend?"

"You don't know her. A friend from school."

"Shall I come with you?"

"No, no. It's okay."
"I'd like to meet her."
"No, no. I will go alone."
"Are you sure?"
"Yes, yes. I will go alone."
"Where will you go?"
"I don't know. Downtown."
"You're sure you don't want me to come?"
"No, no. That's fine."

She was going to find the sailor. This I knew beyond a doubt. If she showed up at the dock around noon, lunch would be on the table. After that, who could say? The idea of such calculating and deliberate betrayal left me stunned. What could I say to this? I grasped at something, "Really, Shizuka? For a sailor?"

Still standing in front of the mirror, she turned her head slowly in my direction and gave me a look that no man ever wants to see. It says, without an ounce of pity, merciless and cold, "You see what I can do to you?"

I didn't know what to do, but I knew I had to do something, and it had to happen soon. I couldn't let her leave the house. I knew as clearly now as I had known when she first sat in my basement room at the Dharma Centre, writing a letter to her mother, that if I let another day pass I would lose her.

But how the hell could I stop her? I made stalling conversation in a slightly wounded but still reasonable tone. Our roommate Linda was a cleaning lady. She worked for Howard Petch, the president of UVic, and she had cleaning supplies in the closet. While Shizuka was still getting ready, I opened the closet door and saw there was a bucket handy. I made my plan.

She was nearly ready to go. If this was going to happen, it had to happen right now, and it would require split-second timing. When Shizuka turned away from my last words of conciliation and compromise, turned her back to me, and started down the interior stairs, I ran for the closet, grabbed the small bucket and raced to the kitchen sink to fill it. I had to fight back the very strong urge to fill it to the top, knowing I would have to propel it through the air a goodly distance to accomplish my goal, and it was taking too long. With no more than half a gallon of water in it, lukewarm, I wasn't that cruel, I ran down the interior stairs to the landing at the top of the outside stairs. Shizuka hadn't dawdled and was already down the stairs and a few feet up the walk to the street. Stopping at the top of the stairs, I called to her, and to my horror she ignored me and kept walking. It didn't occur to me to run after her. My sense of the dramatic dictated that a dousing from the top of the stairs was the only fitting form of retaliation, and I wanted her facing me. I modulated my tone. "Shizuka, please, I would like to ask you something before you go." I was relieved to see her stop and turn around. She started to say something, but the second she began to turn, I swung the bucket out from behind me, where I had been hiding it, and flung the water out of it, and through the air, in a beautiful sparkling arc towards her. It took all my strength. If she had been a foot farther away, I would have been unable to reach her.

I would like to say my accuracy was flawless, but it wasn't. It was, however, effective. The bulk of sixty or so ounces of water landed squarely on her left shoulder, drenching her expensive blouse, and enough water splashed onto her head and face to spoil both hair and makeup. I don't think I ever saw Shizuka's eyes and mouth open so wide. After a huge in-breath of air, and a pause of three or four seconds to realize what had happened, she looked up at me with murder in her eyes. She flew up the outside stairs in a fury, and I flew for my life back into the apartment. There was no place to go except the bedroom, and she ran in after me. I fell down on the bed. She leapt on top of me with both fists flying, in a frenzy. I grabbed her wrists, of course, to stop the pummelling, and you can imagine what happened next. We spent the afternoon in bed, and by evening we were more in love than ever. It was a wild ride with Shizuka.

I give myself full perverse marks for the moral appropriateness of my solution that day, also high marks for the practical application of quick and critical thinking. I had disarmed Shizuka in the most effective and efficient way possible. It was quick, clear, pointed, painless, and economical. She wouldn't show her face in public in such a drizzled state, and it would take another hour to put all that warpaint back on. Crisis averted, problem solved. We never saw the sailor again.

I'm not exactly sure when I started drinking again, sometime in July. After three and a half years.

Nineteen-eighty was the year of Abscam, short for Abdul Scam, when the FBI ran a sting operation that convicted more than a dozen US politicians of bribery and conspiracy, including senators, congressmen, and city councillors. More than 100,000 Cubans departed from the harbour at Mariel, just west of Havana, on anything that would float, bound for Florida. One of Hemingway's granddaughters was named after the town.

Archbishop Óscar Romero was assassinated while saying mass in San Salvador. He was killed by a military, or paramilitary, death squad for denouncing human rights violations and the murder of thousands of civilians by the US-backed Salvadoran government. Two hundred and fifty thousand people attended his funeral. The Salvadoran civil war lasted another twelve years. San Romero was declared a Servant of God by Pope John Paul II. He is the unofficial patron saint of Latin America, and his canonization process continues. Terry Fox ran 3,300 miles, halfway across Canada, on one leg, before his cancer came back and forced him to stop. He became a Canadian hero, and his foundation has since raised half a billion dollars for cancer research. The US boycotted the Summer Olympics in Moscow over the invasion of Afghanistan, the pot calling the kettle black. In 1980, Zimbabwe was the last country in Africa to gain independence from Britain. Over a period of a thousand years, the tiny nation of the United Kingdom ruled more than two hundred countries, colonies, dominions, protectorates, mandates, bailiwicks, and seigneuries. Robert Mugabe, a guerilla leader, was elected Prime Minister of Zimbabwe, and thirty-three years later he is still in power, as President, reviled the world over, an insane and murderous dictator. The Communist Party of Peru, The Shining Path, began operations in 1980, a brutal and barbarous guerilla war that lasted twenty years. CNN commenced 24-hour news broadcasting that year, and Richard Pryor set himself on fire freebasing cocaine, or "having milk and cookies," as he later said. The Unabomber was buying one-dollar stamps in Montana, and a heat wave in the southern plains of the US killed seventeen hundred people. The Solidarity Trade Union Federation was founded and soon recognized by the Polish government. Somoza was assassinated in Paraguay. The eight-year Iran-Iraq war began. I didn't have access to a television in 1980, and I never saw a minute of TV news coverage the entire year. Everyone in the televised world was wondering who shot J.R., but I hadn't seen a single episode of *Dallas*.

My friends from San Francisco, Dan and Mickey, had visited Seattle in 1978, but I was living in Sedgewick then. They headed east from Vancouver, thinking they might make a side jaunt to Alberta for a visit. They drove a hundred and thirty miles, then telephoned me from Manning Provincial Park. After we chatted awhile, and they realized it was another eight hundred miles to Sedgewick, they decided a visit would have to wait for another time. In the summer of 1980, they made another trip to Seattle, and Victoria, and I was delighted to see them. Brian, who had also met them in Mexico, was out of town, and he gave them the use of his apartment. We lounged at the beach, lunched on the deck at the Oak Bay Beach Hotel, went for dinner, and amused ourselves in the lazy summer weather. One evening at Brian's apartment, we found a board game of some kind, and we played and drank on the floor, lolling about on cushions, until we were useless of body and mind. When Dan stopped rolling the dice, and started sucking on Mickey's toes, Shizuka and I thought it was time to go, but we were too drunk to get home, so at their insistence we took the bedroom, and Dan and Mickey slept in the living room.

I was called, once again, to the Unemployment Insurance office to explain to a federal bureaucrat why I felt the taxpayers of Canada should continue to pay my rent. I hadn't been looking for work in Victoria, but I had an impressive collection of correspondence from Japan. I put on one of my new suits, stuffed my lovely new attaché case full of letters, and presented myself bright and early one August morning at the UI office. I stood out amongst the other scruffy unemployables in the waiting room, and as I explained my situation to the officer, I dumped out half of my attaché case onto his desk. He was delighted to see I would soon be off his roll, and he said he would schedule my claim to end in a few weeks, when I had left the country. In the meantime, we would say no more about my previous three months of tax-funded indolence, travelling and going to school, drunkenness and watersports. It was as smooth a meeting as I could have asked for.

A few days later, a cheque arrived in the mail, General Delivery, Victoria, from my mother. She sent me five hundred dollars for my birthday, an unprecedented sum. I suppose, after India, she was worried about her nitwit son travelling overseas again.

About ten days before Shizuka left for Japan, we went out for dinner with Brian and his girlfriend. We started early and went long, and we drank the entire time. Brian fought with Sue, and I fought with Shizuka. It turned into a summer night's inferno of argument and madness. We were a raging foursome, the kind of table of drunken asses I despised when I became a waiter the next year. To their obvious disgust, our shouts and arguments interfered with the jazz combo playing on the little stage. A couple of times, the management nervously encouraged us to leave, but we ignored them all and raged on. In a white heat, Brian finally bolted the restaurant, leaving us with a huge cheque and his small girlfriend. He was given to dramatic exits, but I knew he was good for his share of the bill the next day.

When Shizuka and I got back to Bank Street, she was drunk and unrestrained. She tortured me with threats and taunts of desertion and betrayal. I was close to blackout drunk, and I snapped in a way that I never had before and never did again. The sex that night was nearly an auto-*crime passionnel*. The bucket-of-water incident paled by comparison. I will never say out loud or in writing what happened that night, but I know there are counties in the state of Nevada where I would have been sent to prison for ninety-nine years. The next day I awoke and found Shizuka in the kitchen having breakfast. I was half expecting to see a police cruiser on the street, but all she said was, shaking her head, "Nee-du, you were crazy last night."

Maybe I wasn't a new man in my new suits after all. Maybe I was just the old man all over again, thrown back five atavistic years, the worst man, a binge drinker and a pervert. Or was I simply going to be a different person every two years, whirled from one extreme to the other? New or not, I met an unwelcome stranger that night. This couldn't have been what Shizuka meant by taking charge. Maybe it was.

Our angry, frenzied, panicked, drunken sex and brawling was forgotten as fast as it had arisen. I took Shizuka to the airport on August 15 in her casual clothing and waved good-bye. She had been away from her family and her country for a year. She was proud of her adventure abroad but happy to be going home.

I had a garage sale and sold most of my carpentry tools for what Shizuka and I would have spent on one dinner in a restaurant. I stored a few boxes of books and things in Susan's empty storage locker at her apartment building. Ten days later I boarded a plane for Los Angeles and left my current acquaintances, Dr. Petch's cleaning lady, the accountant-glazier-curbsider, the esthetician, and Caesar, to do what they did best.

I was excited and nervous, and I wondered what the hell I was doing, chasing a woman halfway around the world in a turbulent and dying relationship. My heart was a sick child, and I was a foolish parent. I granted its every wish. Goethe said that when a woman draws back from a difficult relationship her reasons always appear valid. In this, at least, I think Goethe was something of an idiot. In another month, Shizuka would leave me for reasons that were impossible for me to comprehend, because they were impossible to accept, dirt in my soul.

I heard a gurgling sound in the distance. I felt a swirling motion about me. I knew what it was. It was my life circling the bowl.

5   Japan, You're Nobody's Sweetheart Now

At a hotel by the airport in Los Angeles, I treated myself to one very cold beer by the sunny pool and shook my head in exhausted wonder at the events of the previous year. If I hadn't met Shizuka I would now most likely be getting ready to go back to Camosun College, or UVic, for another year of studying science. I might even still be living at the Dharma Centre. I knew nothing good could come of my blind, driven, lustful pursuit of Shizuka, but that wheel was in motion and there was no brake upon it.

In the morning I took the hotel shuttle van to the airport. It was driven by a talkative young man culturally compelled by his life in Southern California to tell us as much about himself as he could in the time he had available. Still in the parking lot, we drove slowly by a shiny, black muscle car, a Camaro. A family of tourists, a Black family, was lounging about the hood consulting a map. The blond California surfer driving our van pulled up and asked them politely not to lean on the car because it would leave marks on the finish. The car was his. As we drove away he said, "It's worse because it's black." Then he laughed. "The car, not the people."

And in no time I was on another Korean Air 747 flying high over the Pacific Ocean, heading west on my way to the East. Sitting next to me was a Japanese student who had spent the last year at UBC. He ordered the western lunch, a chicken sandwich, and I ordered the Japanese option, *soba*, buckwheat noodles. I saw a blob of green paste on the side of the plate, and it was so intriguing I scooped it up with my chopsticks and threw it into my mouth. I boiled and wept and leaked liquid from every pore of my body for the next fifteen minutes. It seems incredible that after ten months with Shizuka I still had no experience of wasabi.

At Narita Airport, in one of the long hallways in the arrivals area, I was delighted to see a message with my name on it, pinned to a board. The message read *Please come directly to the office. We will wait for you here until you arrive. Mr. Owada*. I felt like a small VIP.

Unfortunately, I wasn't wearing one of my lovely new suits, and the man at the transportation information kiosk didn't think I looked like a VIP at all. When I asked him how to get to Yotsuya, he gave me a scan, head to toe. In good English he said, "You better take the train." It was the cheapest option. It was also the longest and slowest option, but I took him at his word. I was on three trains over the next three hours, and it was nearly ten o'clock at night by the time I reached Yotsuya station in the centre of Tokyo. I then staggered three blocks up Sotobori-dori and through the front doors of the PL Yotsuya Building, along with all of my luggage, none of it on wheels.

On the long goose-chase journey into the city, I had stood exhausted and sweltering on train platforms, my God it was hot, in the countryside east of Tokyo, trying to decipher Japanese script. I stared out the windows of the trains, not yet plunged underground, and saw the enormity of Tokyo in the distance at night, a megacity massive and unknown to me, sprawling to the horizon. I thought of Bangkok and New Delhi and murmured to myself, "Oh God, I'm back in Asia. What have I done?"

Mr. Owada, the owner of the school, had gone home and left Mr. Hayashi, the manager, to meet me and take me to a cheap hotel, a hostel. Mr. Hayashi was a six-foot Japanese man with a gentle air and a face like an unmade futon. He told me I could have arrived much sooner if I had taken the direct bus from the airport, which they assumed I would do. I blamed the man at the kiosk.

Mr. Hayashi was anxious to get home, and he kept up a furious pace as we dragged my luggage the three blocks back to Yotsuya station and reboarded the subway for three more stops, a transfer, and another two stops on a surface train, the Yamanote Line, to Okubo, where he had to ask directions a couple of times to find the hostel, many blocks away. Mr. Hayashi then had to retrace this entire route, back to his car, and drive nearly two hours home. At the hostel, I would like to have collapsed in slumber, but I couldn't sleep because of the time difference, and it was August in Tokyo, hot and humid as a steam bath, and I lay on the uncomfortable futon, awake and nervy, most of the night.

Mr. Hayashi had told me to come to the school at my leisure the next day, and by mid-morning I was able to find my way back to Yotsuya and the Yotsuya Foreign Language Institute.

I was looking for this sign: 四谷外語学院. It's no wonder I was lost.

When I was young, I used to hate coming across snippets of foreign languages, French, German, Latin, or Greek, in the books I read, academic or classic or just pretentious, although I didn't often run into Chinese or

Japanese. If no translation was provided, you would be hard-pressed to come up with one on your own. You really had to want it. To me, it seemed a ridiculous waste of everyone's time. Now, with the Internet and Google, if you are so uneducated you don't know what *inter alia* means, among other things, you can find out in about ten seconds. *Moi* will continue to be just as pretentious as I feel like, and you can look it up, even in Japanese.

At the school, I met Mr. Owada. He was short, with a slightly squashed face and thick lips, wearing glasses, maybe sixty years old, and had a fine head of thick hair. He had had an interesting life. After the war, he went to work for the Americans, where his English improved greatly. His job was to travel Japan and survey business activity for the purposes of economic planning during the occupation. He told me every business in the country was keen to be reported in a positive light, and he was shamelessly housed, entertained, and bribed by company owners. He had a government per diem, but he never spent a night in a hotel or paid for a meal. He was waited on hand and foot by the families of the companies he visited. As time went by, and the Americans finally left Japan, in 1952, he realized there was money to be made teaching English. He started his language school, Yotsuya Gaigo Gakuin, and in the sixties and early seventies he had ten floors of classrooms and 2,000 students, practically a private university. Then language schools started popping up everywhere. By 1980, Mr. Owada had an office staff of three, all stuffed into a tiny space in the lobby of the PL Building, two floors of classrooms, a handful of teachers, and a hundred students. I met the pretty young women who worked at the front counter, Ginger and Mariko, and saw Mr. Hayashi dutifully back at his post after no more than four hours' sleep. After a brief welcome, Mr. Owada said, "Can you teach tonight?" He spoke quickly and seemed slightly anxious.

"Of course," I said. There was nothing else to say. Today was the day I would start teaching English.

But not until 7:00 p.m. Most private English classes are scheduled around the students' work day or school day. I looked over the small, slightly shoddy, now empty, classrooms upstairs, on the fifth, sixth, and eighth floors. I poked my head into the very plain teachers' lounge, also empty, and then had the rest of the day to myself. I went back to the hostel to try to rest, stopping briefly at Shinjuku, utterly overwhelmed by the size and number of the buildings, the crowds of people, and the maze of streets both above ground and below. You can walk for blocks underground around the main subway stations, sometimes as many as eight floors below street level.

Tokyo in 2014 is famously weird on a planetary scale. In 1980, it was still relatively quiet. It had the feel of the world's largest village. There remained many similarities between city dwellers and country folk. The habits of centuries prevailed. Men still worked six days a week, fifty-one weeks of the year. Women, unless in small business, worked for a couple of years after high school or university and then married, after which they worked at home seven days a week for the rest of their lives. The country had prospered over the last thirty years beyond anyone's expectations, but the reality of day-to-day life was that every able-bodied man and woman in the country got up very early in the morning and went to work for no more than a living wage, half of the women working in the home looking after the house and every generation of extended family.

Unceasing work was still Japan's only hope of survival, and the work was paying off. By 1980, the partnership of government and corporate old boys in industry that had built Japan Inc. was responsible for creating some of the biggest and richest exporting companies in the world, first in manufacturing and then in finance. Their international trade surplus was the envy of the world. They made the world's most reliable cars and the finest home electronics. "Japan Number One!" was becoming a phrase in common use. Commentary appeared in Japan about the decline of the US due to the "lazy American worker." Lewis Lapham called it "wind from the east," but if you owned an American-made automobile or television in 1980, you probably agreed with the Japanese.

Wages in Japan were still very low. As a pampered foreign English teacher I made twice as much money as the average salaryman for half the hours, money for old rope. Typical houses in Tokyo were running up to $800,000 in 1980, eighty times the average annual wage, and 50-year, multigenerational mortgages were being issued so families could afford to buy them. Idolizing and mimicking the west was still a major force in Japanese society, but they were starting to flex nationally, and they had reason to crow. If the bubble hadn't burst in the late 1980s, followed by Japan's economic ten lost years in the nineties, it's hard to say just how much more obnoxious they might have become. I left Japan in 1984 and have never been back. It seemed then like there were a billion lights on the streets of Tokyo. The city was so successful and so crowded, and the infrastructure so stressed, that the government's message to Tokyo business was, verbatim, "Move or die." In 1980, a young person in Japan could look forward to a lifetime of low-paid, but successful and uninterrupted work, and take pride in inheriting the world's most impressive economy. All those old dreams are faded now, but when I see pictures of Tokyo today, economic slowdown notwithstanding, it looks like yet another billion light bulbs have been added to the skyline, each one at ten times the wattage.

In a daze of jet lag, I reappeared at the school on that first evening, an hour or so before classes started, and introduced myself to the teachers as they drifted in, one by one. Tom was the head teacher. He was a bit gruff and quite a bit older, meaning perhaps thirty-nine. He had bright silver-white hair, amazingly thick, but only in a ring around his head a couple of inches high above the ears. It was all combed over into a large, smooth, solid, glistening helmet that never moved. I asked him how he had come to Japan. He told me that after high school, in the mid-1960s, rather than wait to be drafted and sent to Vietnam, he had volunteered for the US Navy. The navy had the least involvement in the war and was the safest branch of the military to be in. As it turned out, he wasn't sent to Vietnam but was posted to the US Navy Base at Yokosuka at the mouth of Tokyo Bay. He had been in Japan for many years and was dead fluent in the language. He said he never took a language class, but after about six years, one day, he just woke up speaking Japanese. It was a long tenure for the typical English-teaching riff-raff that usually floated in and out of the country. Teaching English abroad didn't seem like something you would spend a lifetime doing, and I asked him why he had stayed so long. He was quite direct. He said, "I fell in love with Japanese pussy and never left." It was time for evening classes to begin. As an afterthought he said, "I guess I could have given you a few tips on teaching since it's your first day. Oh well. You'll be fine. Good luck."

Modelling for advertising billboards and posters in Japan has long since been taken over by professionals, but in 1980, it was still possible for amateur westerners to get casual modelling jobs, especially if you were a lookalike. Princess Diana's hairstyle and complexion were very much in demand. One of the teachers was a tall, striking woman, with wavy, long, blond hair. I used to walk by enormous posters of her in the subway, where she was posed lying on her stomach in nothing but a little underwear and loose, white, cotton socks. Another teacher was a Stanford University student doing a study semester in Japan, another was a refugee from the Soviet Invasion of Czechoslovakia in 1968. Another was a recent graduate of art school in the US. He told me he had come to Japan naively thinking that his fine US education would immediately get him a job in graphic design, but he found very quickly that the Japanese were "miles ahead of us in all areas of design," and he was now teaching English wondering what to do next. There was a gorgeous young American woman with long, black hair and olive skin teaching at the school, and she was constantly harassed by love-sick Japanese men who followed her home and mooned outside her window. There was Rosie, a busty, confident, short-bobbed blond who had been in Tokyo for quite a while and was a little weary, and there was Jean who was new and very tall. She had played centre for the University of Chicago women's basketball team. Go Maroons! She was a towering sight on the sidewalks of Tokyo.

I taught two or three classes on my first night. The rooms were tiny, like everything in Japan, just big enough for ten little desks in two facing rows, and I sat with six or eight high school and university students, businessmen, and office women. I taught a little grammar from the textbook, and then we practised it in structured exercises and then in conversation. The next thing I knew the time was up, and you might not have guessed I had never done it before in my life. The classes I taught that first night, in terms of friendly informative exchange, were as good as any I taught over the next two years. There are long periods in the process of acquiring a second language where it doesn't matter a hoot if your teacher knows what he or she is doing. Show up, be nice, teach 'em a little English, and send 'em home. Big deal.

Housing was my primary concern, and Mr. Owada was on the job. In less than a week, he informed me that a former student of his knew a young family who would be willing to take me in for a little rent, likely hoping I would teach their children some English as well. I had no reason to say no. It was better than the hostel in Okubo. The arrangement was completely informal and free of the many expensive deposits and strict contracts you normally had to enter into. Until I knew what Shizuka was doing, an interim arrangement suited me fine. The former student was an attractive woman named Kazuko, probably thirty, single, with a perfectly round face, very long, straight hair, and exquisite hands and feet. She had a refreshingly straightforward and independent attitude, not typically Japanese, competently communicated in clear, simple English. Needless to say, I liked her right away.

She took me to meet Mr. and Mrs. Kaneko, it means "golden child," and their two little girls, about four and five years old. They lived in Higashikomagata, near Honjoazumabashi, a working class neighbourhood in Old Tokyo, in the Sumida Ward, by the river of the same name, just across from the famous old shrine at Asakusa. Their house was new, in concrete and brick, very narrow, and four storeys high, each floor encompassing a very small space, a bizarre, abrupt, and vertically laborious separation of function. There was a bath on one floor, a kitchen on another, the parents' bedroom on the third floor, and the children's on the top floor. And somewhere, there was a bedroom for an old woman who was, I believe, Mr. Kaneko's mother. There was no yard, just more of the same kind of house-cum-office building on either side. I was to share the third floor next to Mr. and Mrs. Kaneko's bedroom. They had blocked off a space in the little living room area, with curtains and luggage, and this and that, and if I wanted, I was welcome to come and live with them and their family. It was clean and humble, but substantial, and about as typically modern-urban, working-Japanese as you could imagine. Kazuko didn't know the Kanekos very well, but she shook her head and said they were the probably the sweetest people she had ever met. I had no trouble deciding, and in only another day I was underfoot at the Kanekos'.

Unfortunately, I now lived quite a distance from where I worked, and there was, as yet, bugger all of interest to me in Sumida-ku. It took the better part of an hour on three subways to get to Yotsuya, or anywhere else I wanted to go. Riding the trains was a steam-baked hell in a sardine can in the mornings but no trouble returning home in the evenings, unless I missed the last train. They stopped running early in 1980, before midnight.

For the first many weeks, my new landlords knew exactly which train I would be on after work, since I rarely went anywhere after classes were finished at nine o'clock. On a couple of occasions, I forgot my umbrella at home in the morning, only to find it pouring rain later in the day. When I emerged from the subway at 9:45 p.m., imagining I would have to sprint through the rain the last couple of blocks home, there was Mrs. Kaneko standing in the rain, waiting for me with my umbrella, which she had noticed sitting at the bottom of the long, steep concrete stairs in her house. One day, I mentioned that I loved fruit, and the next day, when I arrived home from work at night, and every night thereafter, Mrs. Kaneko had a plate of peeled and sliced fruit, neatly arranged, waiting for me. She did my laundry. She ironed my shirts and underwear. I had a little wastebasket in my living area, and I asked Mr. Kaneko to show me where I could empty it outside. He was the gentlest Japanese man I met and was probably as kind a husband a Japanese woman could ask for, but he knew the value of tradition and the division of labour. He tried and failed to give me a stern look. "That is Mrs. Kaneko's job." He absolutely refused to show me how to deal with the garbage. Shizuka had said many times in Victoria, "Oh, Nee-du, when you go to Japan, you will see. It is a paradise of man." I tried to tell her that the correct phrasing was "a paradise *for* men," but she never caught on to that particular point of grammar. I suppose she might have if I had been a better teacher.

Shizuka was very much on my mind. She had gone to the south of Japan to see her parents and had then moved to her sister and brother-in-law's house in Ichinomiya, just outside Nagoya, Japan's third largest city. It's south of Tokyo, west actually, most of the way to Osaka. If you look quickly at a globe, or a small-scale map, it is reasonable to assume that Japan is mostly a north-south country, but much of it, the big part in the middle, actually runs east and west. It's confusing. Like Panama. It was two or three weeks before I was sufficiently settled to be able to plan a trip out of town, and it took a while for Shizuka to meet her family obligations, after a year away, and get settled in Ichinomiya. Each weekend that passed without a reunion was an agony to me.

It is only two hundred and twenty miles to Nagoya, and one Saturday morning in late September, I finally boarded the Shinkansen, the Bullet train, in Tokyo, and sped west at a hundred and twenty-five miles an hour, non-stop, to see Shizuka. It took less than two hours. At the station in Nagoya, there was a glitch with the doors, and they wouldn't open for a few minutes. I could see Shizuka waiting on the platform a few cars down, but she didn't know which car I was in, and she looked up and down the train for me, wondering why the doors weren't opening. My patience was tried to the limit before they finally slid apart. Japanese people tend to be moderate in their displays of public affection, but we hugged and kissed and held hands, wringing them together in relief. She had been Canadianized. We took another train to Ichinomiya and a short taxi ride to the house.

It was the biggest house I was ever to see in my two years in Japan. I suppose it was about twenty-five hundred square feet, spacious enough by Canadian standards, but not spectacular. In Japan it was enormous. Shizuka's brother-in-law, I don't remember his name, let's call him Takeo, was some relation of the Morita family, the largest shareholders of the

Sony Corporation. He was about thirty-five and was a senior manager, or director, at Sony's Ichinomiya Plant, the factory that produced the Trinitron TV, a colour television so good it won an Emmy Award for technology in 1973. Takeo knew where his bread was buttered. He had a small, framed painting of *kanji* on his bedroom wall, done and given to him by Akio Morita, Sony's co-founder and chairman. He performed a mock prayer in front of it and laughed stupidly at his own good fortune. By that time, we were all drunk and lying around in the master bedroom in our pyjamas.

The house might have been only modestly spectacular in Canada, but there was no mistaking the wealth in it. In the afternoon on my first day there, Shizuka's sister opened the front door and received a team of three furriers who had brought a large selection of their goods to the house for a private viewing. Shizuka and her sister tried on one mink coat after another, and Takeo rolled his eyes, wondering no doubt how much this was going to cost him. A little later, there was a delivery of new futons and linens for the entire house. I guessed it had to cost in the thousands of dollars. The bar fridge was full of liquor, and I asked Shizuka to teach me how to tell her fat little nephews, in Japanese, all four of them, to bring me another beer. They couldn't take their eyes off the yellow-haired *gaijin*, the foreigner, and they were my faithful servants while I was there.

The house may have been large and expensive, but it was situated next door, at the back, to a textiles factory. The noise of the machinery was constant. Such a thing would never have occurred in Canada, but in Japan, of necessity, there is little regard for zoning and separation of industrial and residential areas. You could be rich at home but still have noisy and smelly factory neighbours.

In the evening, we all went into Nagoya to an expensive restaurant and dined in family luxury. I couldn't help but notice the bill was well over two hundred dollars, about seven hundred dollars in 2014. Obviously, I was not picking *this* cheque up. We had all had drinks at the restaurant, and by now Shizuka and I could hardly maintain an acceptable level of decorum. Shizuka's sister laughed and slapped our hands and told us to behave ourselves, but she was tipsy, too. Dinner was finally over and a taxi was hailed in the street. I was champing to go home and be alone with Shizuka, but my ever-expanding bubble was burst when she leaned in close to me. "No, no, my sister and I will go home now with my nephews. From here you and Takeo-san will go out drinking together."

I whispered back, "Oh, no. Oh, fuck! No, no, no, no, no. I don't want to go out drinking with Takeo. I appreciate his generosity, but he's kind of a dick, you know. And he doesn't speak English. I don't speak Japanese. What are we going to say to each other? This is nuts. I *want* to go home with you."

Shizuka said, "This is Japan. You are a man. This is what you must do."

A paradise of man, indeed.

I said, "What are you going to do while I'm out getting drunk against my will with your brother-in-law?"

She knew how to mollify me. She gave me a demure smile, the one I loved, the one that made me crazy. "I will go home and warm the bed." This she said as if it were the most obvious thing in the world.

The women and children got into the taxi, and I steeled myself to carry on clinking glasses with Takeo-san, consoled now by the thought of an enthusiastic response waiting for me at home.

In Japan, it is common to buy an entire bottle of liquor in a bar. It is labelled with your name and left on the shelf for your exclusive use when you come in. The bar feels more like a club that way. The practice is called, sound it out, *botorukiipu*, "bottle keep." Takeo probably had a dozen bottles with his name on them, in a dozen bars. We walked by a few little places. He stopped a couple of times but after some thought continued on. Many of them were nothing more than an unmarked door. The less known, the more fashionable? Or, possibly, he was avoiding his usual haunts because of his disreputable guest. He finally decided on one, but when he opened the door, he didn't let go of the handle. Before entering, he shouted out to the occupants of the tiny, smoky room, something like, "*Gaijin, daijoubu desu ka?*" He was asking the tightly packed room of drinkers if it was okay to bring in a foreigner. We waited long enough to hear a few shouts of indifference before going in. He ordered a new bottle of Johnny Walker scotch. The proprietor asked if he wanted Black Label or Red Label. He hesitated. Red would be fine. Even I knew this was a slight insult to me. It was an indication that while I was welcome to roger the daylights out of his sister-in-law, and drink all his beer at home, that didn't mean I was going to get the good stuff at the bar. I was a visiting curiosity, not a visiting dignitary. I didn't care. I just wanted to get this macho bullshit over with and get back to Shizuka. And the prices were insane. Even Red Label was over a hundred dollars a bottle. In 1980! There wasn't much to talk about and inevitably the karaoke microphone came our way.

Everyone insisted I sing a song, and I found the words to "You Are My Sunshine," in English, in the grubby book that was passed around. There was no video karaoke yet. When I was done butchering the 1930s Louisiana State Song, I received a small round of applause, but they took the microphone away.

I thought we might be out for hours, but fortunately Takeo lost interest in our men's night out fairly quickly. We taxied back to Ichinomiya after visiting no more than one or two more bars, and I thanked him profusely for his hospitality. I was very grateful that I wasn't completely drunk when I saw that Shizuka had made up a luxurious new futon for us on the main floor, away from the rest of the family. It had been a long day, but we hadn't seen each other in six weeks.

I learned that the house was actually owned by Shizuka's father, but I don't remember asking Shizuka if it was the house she grew up in. When her mother finally grew weary of her husband's mistress, she left and returned to southern Japan. He gave up the house to his daughter and son-in-law and their many children. His housekeeper of two decades quit when the family of boys moved in, and Takeo's tribe was now frequently, and currently, without household staff.

It was even hotter and more humid in Nagoya than in Tokyo, and we were all limp with the heat when out of the range of air conditioning. Nevertheless, somewhat hung-over, the next afternoon, Auntie Shizuka and I walked a few blocks to a very urban baseball diamond, not a hint of grass, to watch her nephews play. One of the teams had been thoroughly coached in the art of chatter, and kept up a constant barrage of noise and ten-year-old verbal harassment, trying to fret the other team. "Hey, batter, batter!" I noticed nothing amiss. This was standard practice in my Little League days. I was a third baseman. "Pitcher's got a rubber arm!" I did notice murmurs of disapproval from the crowd of parents scattered about the diamond and in the stands, and around the third inning, the umpire stopped the game. He gave a full two-minute speech to a completely silent audience, after which the chatter stopped. Shizuka translated. The umpire had told the noisy team that if they did not conduct themselves in a more sportsmanlike manner, he would call off the game. The Japanese loved baseball, but they would not tolerate impolite behaviour on the field.

It was a short, amazing, wonderful weekend, and I was aglow from our reunion and even a little heartened by it, but we had discussed nothing of the future or Shizuka's plans or where she might live. It could wait, I suppose, but for how long? As it turned out, there was nothing to discuss.

It would be too much to visit again the very next weekend. I would have made the journey, happily, but I couldn't throw myself on their hospitality again so soon. I waited two weeks.

My second visit went much like the first but with quite a bit less attention to impressing the foreign visitor. Takeo, my generous host, was mostly just showing off the first weekend. He was, sorry to say, truth be told, a vulgar, self-centred ass, a style of deportment too common among Japanese men, wealthy or not. He smoked and hawked and snorted and was gruff and arrogant. He made very crude jokes, strutted and bragged shamelessly, and ignored his children, all of which caused no reaction at all in the members of his family.

The adults were all sitting in the living room one afternoon when Shizuka and her sister left to attend to something in the kitchen. Takeo also thought of something he needed to do and got up to leave. He realized I would then be left alone in the room. This meant he was now responsible for maintaining good form. He paused a moment, handed me a photo album of a recent trip to Europe, and excused himself. The album contained forty pictures of Takeo, alone and in a group, the distinguishing feature of all of them being that it was obvious, to Takeo, that he was the only one in the picture, no matter how many others surrounded him. In his own mind, if not physically, he stood head and shoulders above the others, and his posture of pre-eminence and superiority jumped off every page. His wife was nowhere to be seen in these photos, and I learned later that she had not accompanied him. Why would you take your wife with you on a vacation? It would be very inconvenient in sampling the shores and whores of other nations. Although Takeo, blowing smoke in my face, did tell me that his wife still had "a very good pussy." He was a distasteful man.

I didn't envy him his money. He had a worrisome job and responsibilities. While I was there, he showed me proposals from three manufacturers, from three countries, one of them Canada, competing to supply Sony with very expensive assembly equipment for the high-volume production of printed circuit boards. He had to make a decision by Monday. I looked them over and patriotically recommended the one from Canada, although I couldn't have told you the difference between a circuit board and sea biscuit.

I wanted to see the Sony Ichinomiya Plant, and I asked if it would be possible to have a tour. I would not be averse to VIP status. Takeo-san mumbled and chuckled and mumbled some more. There are fifty ways to say no in Japanese without actually saying no, and he was running through the list. Shizuka explained that he was concerned about just how I would be introduced at the plant. How would he explain who I was and why I was there? His sister-in-law's Canadian Boy Toy? There would be no tour.

Shizuka and I spent every moment of the weekend together, but when I left for the train station in Ichinomiya on early Monday afternoon, to be back in Tokyo for evening classes, she did not accompany me. I knew the way now, and I got into the taxi and turned immediately to wave good-bye through the back window. Shizuka and her sister stood in the middle of the sunny little street, in front of their big house, dressed in long aprons. There was still no housekeeper, no one who would work for this unruly brood, no matter how rich they were, and the co-chatelaines were, themselves, preparing to launch into an afternoon of cleaning. My eyes never left Shizuka as her form became smaller and smaller, and we never stopped waving, not until we were out of each other's sight.

It was the last time I saw her. As I waved good-bye without stopping, not wanting to, unable to, I suspected it might be the last time. When I finally turned face-forward in the back seat of the taxi, my heart sank, and I trembled in dread at the thought. We hadn't fought over the weekend, but we were tense and edgy. We talked in fits and starts, wringing each other's hands, draped together, staring off into the distance one moment, trading desperate kisses the next. We had sex in the bathroom and in the bedroom. We couldn't get enough of each other, but I had no place in her life, and we both knew it. We also knew we would never leave each other as long as we were in each other's company. Neither of us could do it. We were both stressed and exhausted. We had lived for months in a highly charged, overwrought situation, void of sense or solution, focussed on nothing but each other, over-sexed, over-sensitive, apprehensive, and panicky. We dove into a rocky pool together and crawled out a year later breathless and bruised.

In Japan, Shizuka had a world of possibilities at her fingertips, not all of them enviable, but she could go where she wanted and do what she pleased, as long as it involved marriage and family in the very near future. She had turned twenty-eight. She was rich and beautiful and would have no trouble attracting a husband, even at her age, but time was running out.

And now was the time to leave me, when she had the courage to do it, and the ease of movement, things I would never have. We were entwined together for exactly twelve months. When she was gone, I thought about her every day for seven years.

    I spent the next three months drunk to disguise my condition. If I had been sober, I would have crumpled to my knees and wept every day. I couldn't have grieved more if she had died in my arms. It was the first time in my life I had felt such a shattering sense of lack. She got under your skin like that, just one of those things. It was a sentimental attachment.

    Of course, I didn't know right away that I would never see her again. I telephoned and wrote two dozen times and received no response. Neither of us could utter the word that would part us, and for my sins of the previous year, I received only silence. I knew Shizuka. Some of this was cruelty. I put my feelings away as best I could and drowned them in Yebisu beer, but by the end of November, I asked my landlord, Mr. Kaneko, in a maudlin state of defeat, if he would do me the great favour of making an embarrassingly personal call on my behalf. I had a telephone number for Shizuka in Hofu city, in southern Japan, and I suspected she had fled there for refuge. I told him I was very sorry to ask this of him, but I had to try one more time to find her. He said he understood, and even if he didn't, he saw me depressed and suffering before him, and he agreed to the task with kindness and the utmost gravity. I sat across from him in the living room in Sumida-ku and listened, while he spoke in polite and serious tones with someone on the other end of the line. He had to introduce himself first, and explain the intrusion of a stranger into their lives, and the mission he had undertaken for his depressed and lovesick tenant. He spoke and listened attentively for a full fifteen minutes, and when he put the receiver down and looked at me, I could see no hope in his face. I asked him what they had said. He hesitated and replied gently, "They said she is not there." I knew enough not to torture Mr. Kaneko with more questions about what they had actually said in fifteen minutes of conversation, what Shizuka's unidentified relative had chosen to share with him, and what to hide, under the easy lies of linguistic convention. He didn't deserve that. The message was clear. She was not there. In the two months that had passed, she could have become engaged to be married, been admitted to a mental hospital, gone to Hong Kong to study Chinese, or to the US to study more English, something she had talked about before, or simply decided that the only way to end this madness was never to speak to me, or see me, again. I wondered, idly and perversely amused, if I had actually, for the first time, managed to drive a woman right out of an entire country. She could have been anywhere in the world.

In the meantime, however, there was another life I led, almost normal, my ravelled and ragged emotions in a shambles just beneath the surface. I had a job and a place to live, the two legs you stand on whether you want to or not, and I was learning, sometimes the easy way, sometimes the hard, about a new place and the people of the place, at work and at home. It wasn't obvious at the beginning of October that Shizuka had disappeared forever. I could not imagine or accept that I would never see her again. I clung to hope, even as hope put on its sneakers and fled from me as fast as it could go. I made new friends at work, and now that I was drinking again, I had plenty of opportunities to get to know them better.

Jean, the basketball player from Chicago, expressed an obvious physical interest in my company, and we made an interesting pair, Mutt and Jeff, noodling about Tokyo before and after work, going to cafes and restaurants and bars. She was a sombre young woman, pleasant in her way, and we were an odd couple. She told me her feet always stuck out the bottom of any futon you would normally find in Japan, and she had to wear wool socks to bed. I, on the other hand, was able to buy shoes in Tokyo that fit my small feet perfectly, for the first time in my life. In a group of Japanese people I was sometimes the tallest person in the room. I told Jean about Shizuka and all that sadness.

My having a girlfriend, or possibly not, in another city in Japan wasn't a matter of any great importance to Jean, and unlike a lot of tall women, she wasn't prejudiced against short men. She had no more choice in the matter of height than I did. She invited me, on a couple of nights, to her apartment, well out in the suburbs, and I accepted her invitations. It seemed impolite not to, but my heart wasn't in it. She was so tall I hardly knew where to begin. I felt it was a bit unfair of me not to love her, but I didn't, and she didn't mind. Even though she had a spacious, self-contained, and separate apartment, her landlady came over one day and told her that it was not acceptable for her, an adult American woman, to have male visitors overnight in the biggest village in Japan. After a couple of more nights in a by-the-hour Yotsuya love hotel, we lost interest in each other as easily as we had found it, and we just stopped conjugating our verbs together. Sex is more like callisthenics, a healthy, sporty workout, when you're young, and

Jean was an intercollegiate athlete. The zipper hadn't quite gone up on the '80s.

Jean had spent her college years playing basketball, and one day she said, "You know all that stuff you hear about women athletes in college?"

I was confused.

She said, "You know. That they're all lesbians?"

I astutely caught her meaning.

She said that, herself excepted, "It's true, tons of lesbians."

Jean had a plan, a good one. She had just graduated from the University of Chicago and was now going to live and work in Japan for four years, studying Japanese. Once fluent, she thought her degree, combined with her Asian work experience and bilingualism, would put her in a good position to find well-paid, career-oriented work in international business of some kind.

In my first week at the hostel in Okubo, I met a fine young fellow from New Zealand by the name of Kim. He had been travelling around Asia, and like so many others, he had drifted into Tokyo on his way home to see if he could extend his travels by teaching English. At nineteen, he was fearless handling a sailboat by himself in the high winds of Wellington Harbour, but he lacked the years and poise to stand up in front of a classroom of language students. I tried to give him a few tips, and we went to an interview together, but both he and the interviewers felt he was just too young. Before he flew home to the antipodes, we went out and drank until three in the morning with a couple of shifty, but funny, Australians. I had just moved in with the Kanekos, but I missed the last train, and we were hopelessly intoxicated. I thought I would pay for a night at the Okubo hostel, where Kim was still living, and go to work in the morning from there. We staggered bent double down the street, arms around each other's shoulders, shouting at nothing, and for some reason the hostel, and every other accommodation on the block, refused to open their doors to us. It cost a fortune to take the long taxi ride back to Sumida-ku, but it was a quick trip at that hour along the strangely empty streets. Kim assured me he was capable of wandering about Okubo until the hostel opened in a few hours.

His decision might have been unwise in a different city of eleven million people, but in Tokyo, the odds of coming to harm alone on the streets in the middle of the night were small. There is a creepy and disturbing underworld in Japan, a shadow society buried under layers of cultural convention, a corrupt and violent substratum of organized criminality. Although rarely seen by average Japanese citizens, and I never saw it, it is structurally pervasive and deeply entrenched, shored up by the widespread public acceptance of outward appearances and shameless, unmitigated hypocrisy. Everyone knows about it. No one talks about it. This lack of honest discourse, in favour of the maintenance of a facade that everyone knows is just that, arises from the tension between *honne*, "true feelings," and *tatemai*, "facade," and *giri*, "duty," all key parts of Japanese culture, seen as arising from, and essential to, a country with so many people living in such a small space. In a country where there are fifty ways to say no without saying no, the truth is always buried in darkness, no matter how honest you are on the surface.

The Yakuza, pronounced Yah″-ku-zah′, not Ya-koo′-za, is Japan's thriving version of the mob, twenty times the combined size of America's crime families at their height. They operate mostly in gambling, sports fixing, the sex trade, extortion, loan sharking, and political and corporate manipulation, especially in real estate and banking. Some sell drugs, some don't. To maintain favour with the community, they participate frequently, and lavishly, in local festivals, and their members are forbidden from engaging in petty theft. Assaults and muggings in Japan are, therefore, very rare, in spite of Japan being a cash society. I found that chequing transactions, personal or business, were relatively uncommon. I saw a man standing on the street casually counting thousands of dollars in yen without a care. I saw another man in a bank empty a large paper bag full of cash onto the counter for deposit.

Japan still has a reputation for public safety and its citizens for honesty, even gullibility. At the end of the day, the street sweepers left their brooms on the street wherever they happened to finish up, and picked them up at the same place when they started again the next morning, never imagining anyone would disturb them. Corporate and even military espionage were always potential problems because Japanese businessmen and professionals would naively attempt to give an honest and thorough answer to any question, even those posed by new foreign friends with whom they were not yet well acquainted. I saw a news report on national television of an overnight break-in and robbery of a couple of hundred dollars from a ferry toll booth, an event unusual enough to be worthy of national notice. Everyone in Japan was working. There was no need to steal.

I spent two years in Tokyo and was never uncomfortable on the street, day or night. There were other issues, such as women always in danger of being groped by greasy strangers on crowded subways, and the overwhelming presence of armoured vehicles and riot police at every large gathering in the street, but in general, every westerner I talked to, including women, said they felt quite safe in Tokyo. As a man, I never blinked once.

The food supply was abundant and safe to eat, the elevators and the air conditioners worked, the trains were on time, and no one ever asked for money in the street. This was not the Asia I knew from my last trip. True, Tokyo had a homeless problem, but it was minuscule compared with North America, and not for lack of employment. Alcoholics and the mentally ill suffered from a lack of government support, or refused it, and wound up sleeping in the subways. Were it not for illness and addiction, they could just as easily have been working there.

Not everything in Tokyo was safe. I knew there were earthquakes, and I knew I would experience one sooner or later. It was sooner. The first week I was at the Kanekos', asleep on my futon in the middle of the night, I was awoken by the building shaking. I smiled and thought to myself, "Ah, here we are. A Tokyo earthquake already." I actually closed my eyes and prepared to go back to sleep, thinking that nothing ever came of a little earthquake, when I heard Mr. Kaneko get out of bed, run into the living room, and shout "Hey!" I reasoned that Mr. Kaneko had been living here all his life, and if he thought the appropriate response to the continued shaking was to get up, run into the living room, and shout "Hey!" then perhaps that's what I should do, too. Just then, the hard-sided suitcase I had brought with me, which I had placed on a shelf above my bed, fell and landed heavily, inches from my braincase. I bolted out of my futon and joined Mr. and Mrs. Kaneko in the living room, catching things as they fell off the walls and shelves, pictures and knickknacks. After a heart-pounding minute, the shaking stopped, we all let out a huge breath, laughed nervously, and went back to bed. The next day, eleven million tired people could talk of nothing else but the earthquake of the night before. The next night I was very tired and sleeping soundly when it happened again! We all leapt from our beds and ran into the living room, shouting "Hey!" and caught and juggled tchotchkes as they fell. The day after that, everyone in Tokyo was exhausted, but I was assured that two nights in a row of earthquake-interrupted sleep was unusual.

One other thing that was a little dangerous for me was that they drive on the left in Japan, and for some reason, on that first trip, I never got used to it. The main streets were wide and well-maintained, mostly clean and clearly marked, but for Tokyo drivers, as in most of Asia, traffic lanes were merely suggestions. I never knew where the cars were coming from, or where they were going, and there were a lot of them.

The public launch of new developments in engineering, and especially electronics, were a couple of years ahead of North America, and it was in Tokyo, not Canada, where I first encountered ATM machines, direct deposit salary, motion-activated water faucets, on-demand, gas-heated hot water, automated window washing machines, and the most impressive army of vending machines I had ever seen, most of them outdoors, selling every imaginable item that could fit into a vending machine, including beer with a snack of sea urchin in a little plastic cap on top of the can. And there were other mechanical oddities. Taxi doors, on the cleanest taxis I had ever seen, were opened for you by the driver, using a small hand lever, like a school bus. You learned to stand back, or you got a sharp smack on the knees.

I went to Akihabara, Tokyo's major and dazzling shopping area for electronics, and got a very good discount on the most expensive watch I was ever to own, a Seiko. It was the exact model worn by Roger Moore in a couple of *James Bond* movies, although you'll just have to believe me when I tell you I didn't know that until many years later. I was developing my new plan for ultra-urban living. If, in the mountains of BC, all you needed to be self-contained was a roof that didn't leak too much, a wood stove that didn't smoke too much, and a truck that would start in the winter, in Tokyo, all you needed was a good watch, a good overcoat, and a good umbrella. If you had these three things under control, the rest of your life would be taken care of by Tokyo's half-million small businesses, including more than 100,000 restaurants.

For all Japan's breathtaking array of engineering and electronic gadgetry, the housing for most of the population was still very primitive. Household heating was expensive and archaic, and I froze indoors when winter came. On the Canadian prairies, in winter, at forty below outside, everyone's house is seventy-two degrees Fahrenheit inside, burning inexpensive natural gas that comes out of the ground locally. In Japan, a country without fossil fuel reserves, there is an endless convoy of expensive shipping that arrives hourly, from around the world, carrying precious oil, gas, and coal to burn in houses and factories. After World War II, Japan's energy consumption doubled every five years. At any given time, there are half a billion barrels of oil stockpiled in Japan, in tank farms, enough for five months, but a persistent typhoon can disrupt delivery by sea to the point where airports start to run short of specialized aviation fuel after only a few days.

In most Japanese houses, it's as cold inside as it is out, except for the one room of the house which is heated, usually not well. Mr. and Mrs. Kaneko didn't have one, but many people still sat on the floor under a *kotatsu*, a low table covered by a blanket with a heat source underneath, charcoal in the old days, electrical now. Your legs were deliciously warm, sometimes too warm, and on top you wore a quilted jacket with three-quarter-length sleeves, a *hanten*. Often enough, if you turned your head away from the table, you could see your breath. Portable kerosene heaters were common, as well as natural gas heaters, if you had a gas line into your apartment, but of course you could never leave them turned on overnight, or when you left the house, because of the danger of earthquakes. In Tokyo, getting up in the morning and coming home from work in the evening, were chilly times, colder than living in the log cabin at the XN Ranch in the mountains of BC. At least in the cabin, the wood stove would provide heat for a couple of hours before the fire went out. Mr. Kaneko told me that keeping a deliberately cold house in winter is "training" for the children.

I was quite enjoying teaching, although my voice was hoarse by the end of the week. Even in small classrooms, you make an effort to speak clearly, enunciating carefully, and at a slightly elevated volume, so everyone can hear you. More than a quarter of my weekly classes fell on Friday, six hours, three in the morning and three in the evening, not allowing enough time to go home to rest during the day, and I was spent by the time they were over at 9:00 p.m.

There was at least one larger classroom at the Yotsuya Foreign Language Institute for groups of a dozen or more. The open tables were placed in a squared-off U shape in front of me, and I looked out at twelve young Japanese women and twelve pairs of panty-hosed legs under the tables, all closed at the knees. There were always a few men, too, some older, some younger. I felt for these people. I was tired on Friday nights, but they had been up for fourteen hours before classes started, riding the trains to work early in the morning, and working all day, all week. They were sitting in an English class in the evening, and I found that admirable. If they were feeling dozy, I didn't work them hard. I reserved the last fifteen minutes of most classes for games, and they always looked forward to them. On hearing me say, "Alright, we need two teams," I would hear the sound of a dozen textbooks slamming shut, and they would confer and jockey amongst themselves over team membership, maximizing strategic advantage. We played our language games, the students energized and engaged, and I gave the winners little prizes of toys and balloons and candies. The first night I gave out a balloon for a prize, it went to a 55-year-old Japanese man who had ridden a train for three hours a day, and worked six days a week, fifty-one weeks of the year, for thirty-five years. His classmates applauded, and his face fell as he took the balloon from my hand. A lifetime of stifling social obligation and unceasing commitment to his business and his company fell away at the sight of a single red balloon, as though he suddenly remembered the boy he had once been, so long ago. Fellini couldn't have filmed a sadder face, fractured by memory and emotion into old and young.

I taught schoolgirls in the late afternoons, all in their modest sailor-suit uniforms, long, wide-pleated skirts, black loafers, white socks, no makeup, no jewelry, and lifeless hair. One day, a school holiday, they came, even so, to their private English class, but out of uniform. I did not recognize any of them. Each was attired in the latest fashions and accessories for seventeen-year-olds and wore full makeup, with completely different, shiny hairstyles. The transformation was utterly bewildering. These were girls I had taught for several weeks. I knew them all by sight and by name, but I had to ask them their names during class that day, and they laughed at me for my ignorance. It was as though a group of Amish girls had gone for a makeover and then on a shopping spree at Suzy Shier. I hadn't looked twice at these girls in their dowdy, shapeless uniforms, and here they were, painted pop-star beauties out of a teen magazine, in wildly colourful Cyndi Lauper tops and skirts and tights. Somehow I recognized them when they were all dressed the same but not when dressed as individuals. Too much distraction. They couldn't have been in heavier disguise in their makeup and sexy outfits. I saw the value that day of school uniforms in keeping young natures calm.

There was a university-aged woman in one of my larger classes named Ayako. To me she stood out. I thought she was a dazzling beauty. She was reserved, her manners and dress modest, quite in keeping with the tone of the rest of the group. She showed none of the signs of female vanity you might expect in a beautiful woman. No one in the group seemed envious or paid her any special attention, and I wondered whether the other Japanese people in the class, and not just the men, thought she was attractive. I wanted to know if they felt the same emotion and sensation I experienced, if they had the same esthetic regarding a pretty face. One night, during the break, I casually asked one of the younger men if it was just me, or was Ayako considered to be an attractive woman to Japanese eyes? He said, in simple English, more or less, "Are you kidding? She is stunning. Everyone in the class calls her Princess Ayako, even the women, and they all mean it sincerely." That answered my question. Later, I asked Ayako if she knew that her classmates called her Princess. She blushed and everyone laughed.

One evening, I was riding home on the train after class and one of my male students was on the same train. We sat together on a long, upholstered bench, side by side, in an almost empty car. I knew he was about to graduate from university, and I asked him what his plans were. He was twenty-two years old and after a sixteen-hour day, he was exhausted at 9:30 at night. He stared straight ahead speaking slowly and dully. "I am going to get a job for a company." He paused here, turning his head equally slowly to look me fully in the eyes. "And work for the same company for sixty years." Ouch. Education and career were serious matters in Japan. I saw television coverage of families gathered around large bulletin boards at high schools. There were long lists of names of students followed by the names of the colleges to which they had been accepted. Whether the news was good or bad, the reactions were not unlike families reading lists of soldiers killed in battle, relief and sorrow, weeping and hysterics. I saw a news story of a father who was discovered writing his son's university placement exams for him, dressed in his son's clothing.

To lighten the mood, I said, "Ayako is quite pretty, isn't she? Do you know her?"

He said without interest, "Yes, she is my sister." I changed the subject.

And then I ran into David and Jude. I had called David, my old acquaintance from Calgary, when I first got to Tokyo, and we had a lacklustre conversation, ending with a very non-committal, "Yeah, let's get together sometime." At Yotsuya station one evening, I was walking up the stairs going to work, and I saw, in the sea of black hair, a tall blond man and a much shorter blond woman, walking down. I hadn't seen Dave in years, and I couldn't be sure it was him until I had had a good look. Later, Jude said she thought I must be gay, since I couldn't take my eyes off Dave and didn't have a glance for her. We had written to one another and spoken on the telephone, but it was still a tremendous coincidence to see each other by chance in a city of eleven million people. I could easily have lived there for two years and never laid eyes on him. For all the reticence David had exhibited in our previous communications, meeting in person turned out to be a catalyst of good humour and spirit. I hate to think that we were drawn to each other simply because the three of us couldn't have been blonder or whiter, because we simply looked alike, but whatever it was, we were delighted to meet from the moment we met. We finally agreed in earnest to see each other, later that same evening. I brought Jean with me after classes were over, and we all chatted joyfully in a small bar, drinking beer, while it rained in the little street outside. Once again, I had forgotten my umbrella, and the proprietors gave me one when I had to make my way to the station for the long ride back to Sumida-ku. David and Jude had just moved to the area, Yotsuya-san-chome. They were only a few blocks up Shinjuku-dori, a major thoroughfare, from where I worked. I saw them many times over the next many weeks, before I packed up and headed home to Victoria, wasted by my experience in Japan, shattered by the loss of Shizuka, and by my own roaring stupidity.

How many lost weekends could I take?

Kazuko, the lovely woman who had introduced me to my landlords, called one day and invited me on a trip to Nara and Kyoto with her and two of her friends. They all worked in the travel industry and wanted to do a refresher tour of the area. I was thrilled at the chance to see these amazing monuments of old Japan, in the company of tourism professionals no less, and also to spend time with Kazuko. Jean and I knew by now that we were not chemically compatible, and Shizuka was gone. I had a propensity to fall madly in love when the circumstances were right and here was Kazuko, a Shizuka replacement before my very eyes, a beautiful, independent, English-speaking Japanese woman, with experience of living in the US. My troubled mind was filled with imagined ecstasies.

I met her late on a Friday evening, in the pouring rain after classes, with a bag packed for the weekend. I got into her car, and she immediately produced a towel and proceeded to dry off my overcoat for me. The personal attention Japanese women pay to men is astonishing. In Japan, superficial courtesies are extended to men by women, not the other way around. Women help men on with their coats, pour their beer for them, light their cigarettes, and insist they pass through doors, and get into elevators, ahead of them. By western standards, Japanese men are rude to women, and this is normal. Competitive over-politeness is the woman's domain, and it was not unusual to see two women in the street engaged in a bowing contest. The winner bowed lower and more often.

We drove a long way to pick up Kazuko's friends in Tokyo, at different apartments, and they were both late. We waited an hour in the car for one of them to appear, a petite young woman. It was midnight, or later, before we were on the freeway for the 300-mile drive to central Japan, Kazuko's male friend at the wheel. I was surprised they wanted to drive all night, but they said it was the best way to avoid traffic. I didn't see the advantage. The freeway was full of trucks anyway. It poured rain the entire way, and we hydroplaned between semi trucks at seventy miles an hour, in zero visibility. This forced race through the black of night would save money since we wouldn't need accommodation, but it didn't seem worth the risk. Riding all night in the back seat of a small car, after working all day, in a violent and frightening monsoon, was not my idea of how to travel. I had walked through the foothills of the Himalayas with explosive diarrhea and a bleeding penis, but I never missed a night's sleep. Kazuko and I were in the back seat, and she was so tired she slept with her head in my lap. This did not help me relax.

We arrived in Kyoto very early in the morning. The rain had stopped and the sun was shining. I had been up for twenty-four hours. I assumed we would go to a hotel right away to nap and refresh ourselves, but this was out of the question. We had to start sightseeing immediately, and in a thoroughly shattered state we made haphazard visits to one magnificent temple and estate after another, where we were treated to exquisite views of parks and lakes, statuary and Zen gravel gardens. We went to a museum and saw the art, armour, and shards of earlier ages, and part of a tea ceremony. After the ceremony, I signed the guest book in *katakana* with my right hand, ハンセン ニール, Han-sen Nee-ru, my left hand resting lifelessly in my trouser pocket. Kazuko gave me a little slap on the offending left hand because she felt my slouching attitude was louche and disrespectful. I was full of respect. I just couldn't stand up straight from exhaustion. I was concussed by culture and the frequent indecision displayed by my companions in their endless discussions about what to do next. I thought this must be the famous Japanese group consensus I had heard so much about, but they didn't bother asking me what my preferences were.

Late in the day, thoroughly exhausted, we drove the short distance from Kyoto to Osaka. From a road mounted high along the edge of one side of a long, broad, open valley, the dusk turned to night, and I could see the sleek

Bullet train speeding along its track in the opposite direction on the other side of the valley, a couple of miles away. There were huge flashes of electricity in constant eruption from the rooftop pantographs, where they made contact with the overhead line, white lava against the black background of the night. It was a breathtaking sight.

We found a hotel in Osaka without difficulty, new, central, and efficient, the Do Sports Hotel, a better establishment than I was used to, in spite of the silly name. I was able to bathe and rest a bit, and change, looking forward only to supper followed by an early night and a long sleep. No one had set a time to meet again, but I happened to walk past the small bar on the second floor and there was my travelling companion, the driver. I remember thinking, "Oh, God. No drinks. Let's just go out for dinner and come back and go to bed." I walked into the bar and started drinking scotch. It went down like apple juice. The driver and I were barely able to communicate, but I sat next to him in the empty bar and we became very merry.

Nothing is better than scotch for calming frayed nerves when you are tired, and on an empty stomach, nothing will get you drunker. After two or three quick ones, I was magically revived and very hungry. The four of us grabbed the subway for a ride of only a few stops to the incredibly busy pedestrian streets of Osaka's main entertainment and shopping district, Dotonbori, on a Saturday night. There, we stopped in front of twenty restaurants, where my friends engaged in long discussions on the merits of every menu. I was starving unto death and would have gone into the first restaurant we saw, but to my extreme frustration, they spent an hour picking just the right one. There were hundreds of them, and they all seemed exactly the same to me. I couldn't believe these people were travel professionals. They were so indecisive and made such laboured and foolish planning decisions, I thought they would be hard-pressed to organize a piss-up in a brewery. I guess they were doing research.

By the time we sat down, I hadn't slept or eaten a decent meal in thirty-six hours, and by then it was too late. I ordered a gallon of sake, ate very little, became leglessly drunk, and eventually waltzed passionately around the entire establishment with one of the waiters, who told me he was a "homosexualist." I'm not sure why I was so interested in dancing, but I remember continuing to caper on the subway and all the way back to the hotel. I think I was close to insane. I knew I wouldn't be much good in a torture chamber. Deprive me of slumber for only a day, and I would betray my comrades, man, woman, and child, for an hour of sleep or a glass of whisky.

The next day, with a hammering hangover, we made the short drive to Nara to visit its famous park. It covers fifteen hundred acres and is home to the Nara National Museum, noted for its collection of Buddhist art, home as well to Buddhist temples and shrines, including Todai-ji, the world's largest wooden structure, begun in the eighth century, making it and other temples in the area, the oldest wooden buildings in the world. We were all too hung-over to go to the museum, and Todai-ji, very big indeed, was closed for renovations. We wandered in a dull and painful state around the park and to other sites. As the day wore away, we found ourselves standing on a 1,000-year-old balcony of heavy wood at a temple on the side of a hill. The eves of the roof curled up at the corners like the nose of an Irish child. From there, we saw a sunset I will never forget. Its reds and golds, purples and blacks, were as deep and rich as any you ever saw painted onto framed velvet leaning against a van parked at a service station in the American southwest. Everyone on that balcony might have died that night and gone straight to heaven without a single regret, were it not for the ceaseless, blaring commentary of a loud-mouthed, middle-aged, dyed-blond American woman who had obviously taken an art course at a junior college. "Ow, look at the crimson and ruby! Now here comes a barn red. Oh my, burnt orange. Tangerine!" If I had been standing closer to her, I would gladly have pushed her over the edge for the benefit of all.

It is a bad idea to get alcohol-poisoning drunk. It is a really bad idea to do it two nights in a row. Somehow, it seemed normal to drink more that day and then go to a restaurant and drink even more. The weekend had turned into a horrific binge. I was at the point, where in order to recover from a hangover, I had to drink more just to feel normal again. Hair of the dog until I was coated. My companions were also toxically inebriated. We returned to the lovely, wooden Japanese inn, the *ryokan*, that we had arranged earlier in the day and then all fell out in terrible misunderstandings of a very personal nature. We were all black-out drunk, with the exception of Kazuko's girlfriend. I can't imagine what she must have thought. Early the next morning, while everyone was picking themselves up after battle, I think we all slept in our clothes, I decided I couldn't spend another day with these insufferable idiots, and I grabbed my bag and bolted into the street. A taxi appeared from nowhere, and in twenty minutes I was at the station and on the Bullet train for Tokyo, wretchedly ill. It was one of the strangest weekends I had ever passed. The booze didn't help. I wouldn't be surprised if there are three or four businesses in the Kansai area that have never allowed another westerner through their front doors. My apologies. The Ugly Canadian.

And then there was another. In my first week at the Kanekos', they had asked me if I would like to join them, in eight weeks' time, for a weekend at Shirakaba-ko, "White Birch Lake." It's a family-friendly, ski-resort area in Nagano, surrounded by 8,000-foot-high volcanic mountains, the Japan Alps, only forty miles from the site of the 1998 Winter Olympics. I knew nothing of the area and had some suspicions about the wisdom of such a journey in November, but I agreed to go anyway, just to be sociable.

The night before we were to leave, Tom, the Japanese-pussy-loving head teacher at Yotsuya Gaigo Gakuin, had a party at his house, and I couldn't resist going. It turned into another debauch. There were several westerners in attendance at Tom's small apartment and several Japanese people, many of them students from the school. Misbehaving with students is never wise, but it was at least as common in the English language schools of Japan as in North American universities.

You can't help but be impressed by the cultural depth you encounter in Japan. The country is blanketed in temples and shrines, the calendar is red with festival days. My students burst into song when an important life event was announced or celebrated. I could hardly think of a song I knew for such occasions besides "Happy Birthday," and "For He's a Jolly Good Fellow," or was it "The Bear Went Over the Mountain"?

I was third generation Norwegian-Scottish, the grandson of people who had deliberately left their countries behind, often enough in disgust. They, and their children in Canada, wanted nothing to do with the Old Country and its unending wars, its harsh social divisions, a homeland that couldn't give them a decent life, all that goddamn history. As young men, my Norwegian grandfather and three of his brothers knew that if they stayed at home they would never have a pot to piss in or a window to throw it out of. As they travelled from Oslo to Liverpool to New York to Kansas, they were probably in more than one punch-up because they couldn't speak English. Once in North America, no one wanted to stand out. My grandfather only spoke Norwegian, his mother's language, the first sounds he ever heard, until he learned English, and he didn't teach his mother tongue to his children. He never went back to Norway, not once, never saw his parents again. My father, only second generation Canadian, knew almost nothing of Norway. In the third generation, for me, watching *Howdy Doody* on television was a cultural event, and the Friendly Giant was a mythical character. Cartoons were my heroes of legend. Superman, Batman, Spiderman, Iron Man, the Fantastic Four, and coincidentally, one from the Norse myths, Thor. Patriotic ceremony was mumbling through "Oh, Canada," and "God Save the Queen" at school assemblies, and until the late 1960s, before the start of movies in theatres.

At Tom's party, I found an album by the Eagles, *Their Greatest Hits*, and put it on the turntable. Every westerner in the room immediately began to sing along to every song, in loud, drunken harmony. We knew all the words. The Eagles sold 150 million records, and this was my culture, California pop music. We enjoyed the experience so much, we flipped the record twice more and sang all the songs again. I missed the last train, the evening dribbled to a close, and I slept on Tom's floor in my good overcoat, wearing my good watch, but I knew I had to get up very early to get home and join the Kanekos for the train to Nagano.

Tom lived in Shibuya. Two million people a day go through Shibuya station, but on that day, at 5:00 a.m. on a Saturday, I was the first. It is the western terminus of the eight-mile-long Ginza subway, the oldest line, and therefore the shallowest, on the Tokyo Metro. At peak hours, the trains run every two minutes, during off hours, every three minutes. You didn't have to wait long for a train on the Ginza line, and it would take me all the way to Asakusa, just a few blocks from home, without having to transfer. Approaching the above-ground terminus in Shibuya, on the third floor of an enormous department store building, overpasses flying in every direction, I walked the wide, empty streets in a scene from a science fiction movie. I was the last man left alive after the mysterious depopulation of the planet. Seeing the streets of Tokyo without cars and people on them was always disturbing. A city without people is a strange, useless thing. The weather was cold but clear, the garbage drifted about in the streets, and I couldn't have felt worse.

The Kanekos were busy preparing for departure when I arrived, and they were surprised to see me. They thought I was a no-show. I had little desire to accompany them, and God knows I was painfully hung-over, but I was sure Mr. Kaneko had already bought my train ticket and made reservations for me at the lakeside hotel. I would never have left them in the lurch, in spite of my deteriorated state of body and mind.

It's a mere one hundred thirty miles to Shirakaba-ko, but with all the stops and transfers, it took three and a half hours to get there, and we were lucky, I found out later, to have seats the entire way. We were met at the station by one of the managers of the hotel, possibly the owner, a friendly, chatty, middle-aged woman. She picked us up in a four-wheel drive vehicle and took us the rest of the way up to the lake, twelve miles of rising, bare switchbacks, with breathtaking views. I had little ambition but to go to bed for a while, but I was denied this necessity. No one seemed to have any respect for my hangovers.

The manager had told us that there was a Canadian working at the lodge, but I was not expecting the sight that greeted us when we walked into the lobby of the rustic, mostly deserted hotel. Giselle was French-Canadian, and she was a fashion model working in Japan. She had long, blond, healthy, straight hair, and of course was ridiculously gorgeous. She had fallen in love with a Japanese man who worked at the lodge, and when she wasn't doing photo shoots in Tokyo, she stayed at the hotel and worked there doing odds and ends. Her English was good and her Japanese even better. She greeted me courteously, but I was, for various reasons, bereft of conversation.

I found my initial suspicions about the wisdom of travel to Nagano in late November justified. It was a ski area, but there was no snow yet, and it was very cold. All the vegetation was dead and brown, the skies leaden. Outdoor activity was unappealing. I don't know what we did that day, but I do know I was in bed only minutes after supper. It was 7:00 p.m., and I wanted to sleep until the next morning, maybe the morning after that, and surely would have, but for a knock at my *shoji* door. There was no lock on it, and when it slid open, there stood Giselle. I was already in bed. Why on earth was there a fashion model standing in the dark at the door of my bedroom, and what on earth did she want? I would be lying if I said my little heart didn't leap when I saw her, but I was pretty sure it wasn't me she wanted. She said, "Hi. Mrs. Kaneko asked me to check on you. Why are you in bed? It's too early. Come and join us in the bar. You should come down. Come and have a drink with us." I made a few attempts to refuse, but in the end, it was unlikely I would say no to an offer of drinking with a beautiful, blond model with a French accent. Mrs. Kaneko knew that, too.

The bar was in a small, separate building and was designed to resemble a trapper's cabin in the Yukon. The owners were very proud of it. They had done a good job of decorating it with traps and furs, rough wood, and rustic bits and pieces. There were three or four staff and only seven or eight guests, but everyone was there for a good time. It was going to be a party. The Kaneko children were safe in their beds in the hotel, under the eye of the front desk clerk, and Mrs. Kaneko, a typically exhausted Japanese housewife, was looking forward to having a drink. One or two days and nights away from home was a big weekend for my landlords. I think Mrs. Kaneko sent Giselle to get me because she wanted to show off her handsome *gaijin* tenant to the other guests, and she also knew that when it came to padding out a party, I would probably provide good entertainment. I was familiar with the medium. Who knew what the strange foreigner might do next? We drank liberally and mingled freely, sitting at tables or at the bar, chatting with everyone.

I got into a long, drunken conversation with the bartenders, translated by Giselle, about the reality of mountain life, or life in the North of Canada. I had no intention of insulting what they had so carefully recreated in the mountains of Japan, but I wondered how much they really knew about Canadian pioneer life, the ignorance and brutality of it. It was not so much a historical discussion as a history lesson, from me, on the domestic manners and social consciousness of early settlers, and their current descendents. The owners spoke with unreserved admiration of, and had built their little Disney shrine to, the independent spirit of the immigrants of Canada, so different from their own life experience, never once not part of a group. I knew the asshole rednecks of Western Canada, especially Alberta, and I hated them. At their best, they were hardworking. At their worst, they were racist and sexist, white supremacists, Holocaust deniers, secessionists, bigoted and violent, intolerant and prejudiced, knee-jerk, hate-filled, obtuse, ignorant, and proud of it, sneering at, and willing to destroy, anything they didn't understand. I was pretty sure none of these Japanese men would want to spend a winter in a trapper's cabin with some of the Neanderthals I had had the misfortune of meeting in the small towns and rural areas of Alberta and BC, Sedgewick, Medicine Hat, Prince George, Giscome, and Brisco. I told them stories of several incidents of violence against people, some of them friends of mine, in the late 1960s, simply because they had long hair. I told them that the independent spirit they admired so much was only part of the story. I didn't even get to examples of illegal taxation and other forms of legalized white racism against the Chinese who worked on the railway, the East Indians who worked in the forests, or the internment of Japanese civilians during World War II, many of them already Canadian citizens, many born in Canada, and the confiscation of their property. By this time, Giselle was becoming concerned about the direction the conversation was taking, and she stopped translating. I told her that if we were going to have a discussion, both sides of the story needed to be told. But she and Basil Fawlty were probably right. Whatever you do, don't mention the war. I mentioned it once, but I think I got away with it all right.

We spent the next day in a listless tour of the small artificial lake in frigid weather. The Kanekos booked to come back again at New Year's, when there would surely be snow. Mr. Kaneko had been unable to get train reservations for the trip back to Tokyo, even two months in advance, and it was a long and very difficult journey, standing the entire way on slow, local trains, no seats to be had. And somehow, I was still viciously hungover.

I wasn't drunk all the time. I never drank before teaching a class. I often didn't feel much like going to work, but I always felt better afterwards, cheered and energized by contact with my students. I asked Mr. Owada if there had been any complaints or suggestions from the students regarding my performance in the classroom over the course of the term. He hesitated a moment, and if he had anything in mind, he declined to pursue it, telling me that all was well. It's possible none of his teachers had ever asked him that question before. Ex-patriot English teachers are a pretty self-satisfied lot. He did inform me that student enrollment was typically lower in the January semester, and I could expect to have fewer hours after the holidays. Mr. Owada's school was in the mid-range of reputation and expense and consequently provided an income to its academic staff in the lower mid-range of Tokyo English-teaching salaries. I wasn't concerned about money. I was having no difficulty meeting my monetary obligations. My lifestyle was self-indulgent, perilously close to disaster, but not extravagant, and I easily maintained a revenue-neutral position in the trying world of personal finance.

I worked about twenty-two hours a week and had plenty of time to go to the YMCA at Kanda, halfway between work and home, where I played solo racquetball, and pick-up handball and badminton, and ran around the indoor track, counting my laps in Japanese. The cold war was still everywhere, and the old war, if not mentioned, was not forgotten. When I slipped into the men's hot baths in the basement of the YMCA, everyone over the age of fifty got out.

I was invited for a driving tour of Mt. Fuji by some of my students, and we drove to the Fifth Station, around 5,000 feet, the usual starting location for the gruelling climb to the top. The climbing season is July and August, and in November, it was cold and uncrowded. No one felt much like walking. I think we got out of the car, nothing more.

I went to movies and museums, to department stores and markets, to parks and shrines, and to an enormously crowded festival in Asakusa, with some of my other students. I took the train north to Nikko National Park. It's five hundred square miles of mountains, lakes and waterfalls, breathtaking switchback roads, and fabulous fall colours, as well as home to Buddhist temples and Shinto shrines.

I was utterly miserable. I tried to keep busy, but the nights became difficult. There was a Shizuka-sized hole in my heart, left there by a shotgun. That form was gone, those hands, those eyes, those lips. I was love-longing for the love-worthy, for the perfectly lovable, in a world of fear and desire, contradictions and opposites. The longing I felt from three years of meditation had shifted with a vengeance, from the inside to the out, and fell ruinously, confused and selfish, on both Shizuka and me. For the first time in my life, I lay awake in bed at night and encountered mountainous waves of self-pity, titanic glooms, chasms of regret. For a month, as I came to realize, if not accept, that Shizuka was gone forever, I saw and tasted the deadening bitterness of mind, the black dogs of depression, that would return again in later years. Not since the biological misery of my teenage years had I been so humourlessly unconscious, so mired in human drama, unable to detach myself philosophically, pitifully bound to what I knew was illusory, desperate for what I could not have. There was a helplessness and intensity to it that took me by surprise. I was seized and borne away in the sleepless nights by dark fantasies and murderous plots, searching for something or someone to blame, brooding over old harms and resentments, things I hadn't thought about in years, drawn to recalling past evils rather than endure the present. I was on a black train that never stopped, one that went nowhere, and never arrived.

I sought solace and refuge at David and Jude's apartment. Two or three times a week, for many weeks, I showed up at their door with a shopping bag full of beer and a gallon of ice cream. It was freezing in the mountains of Nagano, but in Tokyo, the days can be very mild even into late November. David said he always knew when I was dropping by. He could hear the clanking of Yebisu beer bottles through the open window of their second-floor apartment, as I turned the corner and walked up their little street.

We felt immediately at home in each other's company and talked easily and endlessly. We went to bars and clubs and parties, had dinners at home, and in restaurants. I passed out on their floor half a dozen times and spent the night in their little *tatami* living room. They introduced me to the friends they had made in the year they had been in Tokyo. We spent a Sunday afternoon walking through the enormous park in Shinjuku, a short distance from their apartment, kicking our way through two feet of fallen autumn leaves. David took a photograph there of Jude and me that could not have been more emblematic of the season, two blonds with big, bright smiles on sun-lit faces in the crisp, sun-warmed air.

We got along famously. I told them everything, rattling on unrestrained, things I would never have told anyone else. Jude was from northern England and had a personality the likes of which I had never seen, emotion, love, and spirit so close to the surface, so freely and easily expressed, so quick. She had studied social work and counselling and had a way of helping people work through things without their being aware of it, and I adored her. This was transference behaviour, of course. But it was also obvious that she liked me, too. To see the light of pleasure in her eye when we were together opened in me a floodgate of friendship, devotion, and intimacy. She was a silver-tongued angel with a Teesside accent. She doted and flattered at a time when I couldn't have been more susceptible, and I was buoyed up and swept away. When we think someone loves us, one of the side benefits is that we tend to find ourselves quite adorable as well.

But it was even stranger than that. I fell in love with David and Jude as though they were one person. Together, they became the single object of my affection. I rarely thought of either of them as an individual entity. I didn't sexualize my feelings, although inevitably, we did make a couple of jokes about threesomes. We were frequently in company, and later we lived together for a while. They became, for me, an unattainable love. It was not unreciprocated, they were open and affectionate, but it was unrealized and unrealizable. How could they be one person? It was absurd. Three years later, when I was back in Japan for a second tour of duty, my new girlfriend, from Oklahoma, suddenly turned to me and said, "Oh, my God! I finally get it! You're in love with *Jude*. You always have been!" I denied it, of course, and scoffed at the suggestion. She was, after all, only half right. My feelings for David and Jude became something unfinished and unresolved. It was slightly mad, and it took me thirty years to be able to verbalize this view. Visiting them occasionally over the next three decades was always bittersweet, like seeing an old girlfriend from an old relationship that you felt should have turned out better, like a short summer.

A year earlier, in Victoria, busily studying chemistry in my basement room at the Dharma Centre, I was as happy and self-contained as I had ever been. Now I was fragile and needy, an emotional black hole. When I ran into David and Jude at the train station in Yotsuya, they inherited, whether they wanted it or not, the Wreck of the Hesperus. I was as shipwrecked on the shores of Japan as John Blackthorne in *Shōgun*, but far less heroic.

Jean called one evening, out of the blue. I hadn't seen her for several weeks. It was a Sunday night, and she wanted to meet for coffee. I preferred beer, and we settled on a bar I knew in Ginza. I was standing on a corner waiting for her on the, again, strangely deserted streets of a massive shopping and entertainment area. The Japanese were all safe at home getting ready for bed in anticipation of another Monday morning. I looked up at a department store window, and there was Giselle, the beautiful, blond French-Canadian model, on a glossy and expensive poster, eight feet high. She was lit and made-up and air-brushed into natural perfection, striking a quirky pose, dressed in casual, but expensive, clothing. She had a brilliant smile on her face and was holding a book awkwardly on her head, with one hand, indicating by this posture that she was so genuinely delighted with the new fall and winter fashions, they had made her positively kooky.

When Jean arrived, we sat for a couple of drinks in the empty bar on the cold, wet Tokyo night and she broke up with me. I hadn't actually realized we were together, but she said she felt bad that she had been ignoring me, and she wanted to let me know in person that she had started a relationship with one of her students. I knew who he was. Jean and I shared some of the same classes. He was a very forward, and occasionally amusing, young man of nineteen. One day, he brought a book to class that he was eager to show me. It was an absolutely foul and hilarious 100-page glossary of English swear words and phrases. I had never seen such a creative and idiosyncratic use of the vilest profanity in such convoluted variations, and I was from Alberta. I told him not to show it to anyone else. I was surprised that Jean, who was probably twenty-four, was attracted to Kuniyuki. She said she liked his youthful, outgoing, heterodox attitude, and I imagined her Japanese would improve rapidly in his company.

I told Jean some of my recent adventures, and that I had just about come to the conclusion that there was no point in my being in Japan anymore. I had spent one evening at home alone in my little living room drinking beer, thinking it over, stacking the empty cans on the coffee table in front of me until they nearly fell over. When Mr. Kaneko came home he did a double-take at my tall shrine of dead soldiers. Jean said, with her mouth open, obviously and spontaneously titillated, "My God, what must he have thought?" I was surprised at her concern, or even the notion, that I would care what he thought. I had not a smidgen of disquiet about what my reckless, drunken behaviour looked like to anyone. To me, the opinions of others were no more than the fluff of so many navels. Let the dead bury the dead. I was in a battle for my senses. I couldn't waste time or energy explaining my actions or reasons to others, appeasing the sensitivities of the unknowing. I was more troubled, for good reason, about what I was than what I might be taken for.

One day at work, Richard showed up with a giant cast on his leg, hip to toe. He had come to Japan from Czechoslovakia with his parents as a young teenager, refugees of the Prague Spring. He was fluent in Japanese and went to a local university. His English was also good enough, his accent light enough, that he could get ESL teaching jobs. He liked to drink as much as I did, and because he spoke Japanese he went frequently to bars with his students after class, something I rarely did. The previous night, they had been particularly hammered, and he stumbled off the curb walking to the subway and broke his leg. His drunken companions thought he was faking it, and they dragged him down the sidewalk by his broken leg a considerable distance before his screams managed to convince them he was genuinely, and seriously, in pain. At the hospital, he said the doctor told him he had better pay him in cash, or he was going to give him a shitty cast, and he kept taking his pants off in front of him. It was a bad night for Richard.

I had a brief dalliance, in the late fall, with a Japanese woman, a little older, named Toshiko, and she fell for me the way I had fallen for Shizuka. I had to stop sweet-talking girls. The trouble it caused.

John Lennon was murdered in New York on December 8. He was forty years old. I read every word of coverage I could find, mostly the reportage in *Time* and *Newsweek*. In one of the articles, the writer ended by saying that John "wanted only what so many others have, and take for granted. A home and family. Some still center of love. A life. One minute more." I wondered about that last phrase, "one minute more." I wondered if all of us were that desperate for life.

David and Jude went home to Calgary for a few weeks over Christmas. They threw themselves a going away bash in the party room of a lovely, old restaurant in Iidabashi. I wasn't sure I would survive long in Tokyo without them. I was shipwrecked, and together they were my personal flotation device, my Mae West, a substantial and comforting poitrine, which might be the nicest possible way you can inadvertently refer to your saviours as a pair of boobs. I was also beginning to suspect I had a drinking problem. I couldn't get drunk enough. I used to drink knowing it would make me happier, and now I drank hoping it would make me less sad. It was a bad kind of growing up.

David and Jude were gone, and the Kanekos were about to depart for a few more days at Shirakaba-ko. I reasoned that if I bolted now, I could be back in Victoria in time to start another semester at Camosun College in the first week of January. I made Mr. Kaneko a present of my sleek, and mostly useless, Samsonite attaché case. He was wide-eyed that I would give him such a treasure, but he was nearly overcome when I thanked him for his patience and generosity and told him that he and his wife had been too kind to me. In his cultural mindset the literalness of the phrase "too kind" was impossible to process. I left them extra money for natural gas and other utilities, and a couple of large, pre-addressed envelopes, with money for postage, to forward any mail that might arrive after my sudden departure. I never saw the Kanekos again, and I can only wonder, as Jean did, what on earth they must have thought about the drunken, lovesick mooncalf who blundered into their lives for four months, from out of nowhere, and disappeared again just as suddenly. What a strange little encounter in the briefly crossing trajectories of two life paths.

I told Mr. Owada and Mr. Hayashi I was going home and wouldn't be available for the next semester. Mr. Owada didn't seem concerned, but Mr. Hayashi and the office girls, Ginger and Mariko, pretended to be disappointed and asked me why I was leaving. I teased the girls by saying, "Well, Mariko won't marry me so there's no point in staying."

I gave notice to my one private class, a couple of middle-aged rich ladies. Every Tuesday night, I was received by the maid at the door of an impressive private house. Halfway through the class, the maid would reappear, on her knees, with tea and snacks. It was a new experience for me to be seated in a pleasant drawing room and waited on by an older woman on her knees, although my mother might not have thought it was entirely new for me.

I went to a cheap travel agent in the crowded streets of Harajuku and bought an Air China ticket for Seattle and Victoria. I sat in a funk at the Kanekos', alone, for three days, drinking, until it was time to go to the airport at Narita. I got drunk on the flight home, but fortunately the 747 was only half full, and there were plenty of empty seats to stretch out on. When we approached Seattle, we circled SeaTac for over an hour, trying to find a break in the fog to land. Eventually, we were allowed to land at Boeing Field. I suppose we were out of gas. From there, security staff had to be rounded up to convey us, on buses, under lock and key and guard, to SeaTac, to go through customs and immigration. When we finally entered the arrivals hall, through a maze of back stairs and hallways, we did so at the same time as one thousand other passengers from three other 747s that had just landed. It was Sunday, January 4, 1981, and there was one immigration officer on duty, one booth open out of twenty-five. It was eight hours, most of it standing, without food, from the time we landed, to the time my passport was stamped. My air connection to Victoria was long gone, and I ran for the airport bus to take me into Seattle, knowing that I could just make the last Greyhound to Vancouver.

At midnight I wandered from the Greyhound station in downtown Vancouver to the Niagara Hotel, the same dangerous dive Maura and I had stayed at on our way back from Mexico. There was no chance I could sleep, and I was famished. The only 24-hour restaurant the front desk clerk could think of was Denny's on Burrard Street. I wasn't sure I wanted to walk ten blocks through downtown Vancouver at one o'clock in the morning, but I kept to the bigger streets and found myself going by the new Four Seasons Hotel on West Georgia, in sight of the Hyatt Regency Hotel, where I had attended the World Symposium on Humanity four years earlier. The streets were practically empty, but in front of the Georgia Hotel, across from the lovely, neoclassical columns and dome of the Vancouver Art Gallery, once the old provincial courthouse, and the blocky, less attractive, but still impressive, French chateau immensity of the Hotel Vancouver, the third hotel of that name, I passed a cluster of twenty-five of the most beautiful women I had ever seen, all prostitutes, all wearing expensive clothing, many in fur coats.

I had heard about this recent renaissance in Vancouver prostitution. These were all very attractive women in their twenties, no obvious drug addicts among them, none of them looking abused by pimps or police. I had read that many Vancouver prostitutes were now making tremendous sums of money and driving Mercedes-Benzes. I had decided not to repeat the mistake of dressing down while travelling, and it was easier to wear a suit than to pack one, so I looked quite presentable in my good overcoat and good watch, nice suit and shoes, as I walked by. One of them asked me, cheerfully and politely, if I was looking for a date, but I knew I didn't have the price of admission, and I was sure not one of them would want to accompany me back to the Niagara Hotel. My generally dapper appearance was a little misleading regarding my financial situation. Being of a perpetually puerile nature, I am fascinated by prostitution, but I have never been interested in it as a personal pastime, or as a sociological study, so for me it was simply an odd and mildly titillating encounter, something to muse over while eating soup and salad at Denny's on Burrard, jet-lagged at two o'clock on a black winter's morning.

The next day, in Victoria, I showed up at Susan's door and begged a few nights on her couch. It had been four and a half months since I left Victoria in August. I had met seventy-five westerners from Canada, the US, England, and Australia, and had taught English to a hundred Japanese adults of all ages. I had seen a hundred new sights and things in a place I had never been before. It was an amazing and difficult fall, full of adventures and odd events and sorrows, and destructive, exhausting behaviours, mostly mine. I was still shattered and sick at the loss of Shizuka. Everyone falls in love and some are destroyed by it. I had fallen into an Iñárritu film, a dark, slow-moving tableau of deep disappointments, melodramatic love and lust, loss, sorrow, and despair, grim, intense, unrelenting, and vulgar, a sad, continuous, silent scream, *Love's a bitch*! I felt matters were not quite what they should be.

I was still a long way from better, but I had had enough. I knew I didn't want to drink myself to death, and it was time to stop, but I was still well in it, with no clear idea of how to get out of it, other than a handful of dull and dim notions about plain, unemotional matters, some small, some large, an attempted return to "normalcy." Sometimes it is better to avoid thinking about the unthinkable and concentrate on equally vague notions of practical improvements. If survival cannot be attained by salvation, it might be attained by increments.

If you had told me then that I would be spared for some future purpose, I would have been very skeptical.

6   Return to Normalcy

Susan wasn't as happy to see me as she had been the last time I rolled into town, a year and a half earlier. She and the aggressive old Canadian Forces captain still weren't living together, but their relationship was now long established, and he exercised his right to be annoyed at the intrusion of an old boyfriend. Susan had other things to do besides putting up with annoyed, and annoying, boyfriends, old or new, and she encouraged me plainly, and daily, to be out looking for a place to live. Fair enough. I was exhausted in general and particularly from the gruelling journey home, more than twice as long as it needed to be, thanks to fog in Seattle, but I quickly found a place to live in Oak Bay and got myself smartly out of Susan's hair, to her obvious relief.

I lived in the basement of a house at the corner of Pentland and Falkland Roads for the next four months. The young, immature family of landlords upstairs and my disturbing roommate downstairs were people in whose company I would not willingly have spent another second.

Two other things required my immediate attention. I hadn't saved any money in Japan, but I did come back with eighty more dollars in my pocket than I had when I left, thanks to the exchange rate, so my second Journey to the East hadn't been a financial disaster, but I didn't have quite enough money to get me through a semester of school. I applied for a student loan right away, but they were notoriously slow. I could easily starve to death before I heard anything from them, and I was very hesitant about asking my parents for money. I had been to that well a little too often. I needed a job, and I needed it this week.

With determination and desperation I put on my best suit and my subdued and elegant disco boots, my overcoat and watch, steeled myself, and headed downtown in the rain. I had somehow avoided becoming a waiter over the last ten years, a job that many young people did, especially when going to school, but it seemed like it might now be the wise thing, or the only thing, to do in Victoria, a tourist town. It was January, the worst time of the year to be looking for a job in tourism, or anywhere, but I had no choice. I shopped my resume, with no restaurant experience on it, other than working in the retreat kitchen at Ananda, to the restaurateurs of Victoria. After two or three bold and falsely self-confident, and unsuccessful, chats with managers in various restaurants, I walked into Bartholomew's in the Executive House Hotel. It was an English-themed bar and restaurant, one I had never patronized.

The maitre d' invited me to sit at a table in the empty dining room and brought me a cup of coffee. I explained my situation to him, and he seemed impressed by, and interested in, my travels. He was also a fan of nice suits. He could tell I was sincere in my desire to work and learn the business in order to be able to support myself during semesters at school and over the summers, at least that's what I told him. I guess he thought I might turn out to be a good long-term investment, or maybe it was just the suit. Either way he told me he could take me on as a bus boy and give me a shift or two for training and then maybe one shift a week until the tourism season picked up in the spring. I might have been the only person ever hired, in Victoria, in the first week of January in the restaurant business.

I also needed to convince the bureaucrats and educators of Camosun College to admit me to classes. Obviously, I had not registered in advance. I knew many of the classes would be full, but I also knew that there were always people who dropped out in the first couple of weeks when they realized they were in over their heads and there were still no financial penalties for withdrawing. I asked the instructors if I could sit in on classes until someone inevitably dropped out, and they all agreed, pleased to see an enthusiastic student. The college administrators were easily bought off with an extra fee for late registration.

Over a period of two weeks, I had cold-called and approached two dozen professors, administrators, landlords, and employers. In just a few days, I had managed to sort myself out in terms of housing, school, and employment. Energetic activity often finds its feet. I was very relieved. I considered having business cards made up. *Have Ego, Will Travel.*

Rick, the maitre d' at Bartholomew's, surprised me, and I found myself working three and four nights a week as a bus boy right away. This was good for my bank account, but it was more time at work than I was expecting. Fortunately, I guess, I had only been able to get into three courses at Camosun, math, chemistry, and physics, so I was able to manage without a great deal of strain. I may have been too busy to notice.

I was only a little embarrassed about being a 27-year-old, first-year student and a bus boy in a restaurant, mostly the bus boy thing. But Bartholomew's wasn't a hash house. It was an upmarket establishment with an expensive menu. I worked only evenings and was required to wear a tie under my long, burgundy apron. I worked in a darkened setting of candles, fresh flowers, and table cloths. Everything was served on a plate with a doily under it, no squeeze bottles of ketchup to be found, and bus pans were not used, or permitted, on the dining room floor. Somehow, I had managed to start my career as a waiter in an up-market restaurant, and my dignity was appeased. Never underestimate the power of a nice suit.

I had experienced considerable culture shock when I went to Japan the previous August, and I found now, even after so short a time away, I was experiencing it again, in reverse, on my return to Victoria. The streets and sidewalks were too wide and empty. Where were the people? Where were the eleven million bicycles? Everything was too big, the houses, the cars, and classrooms. The buses were empty, enormous, and lumbering, the stores understaffed, the women positively not deferential. Why did women walk through doors in front of me, and why weren't they helping me on with my coat? How come no one brought me tea when I sat down? Why wasn't my underwear ironed? In some respects Shizuka was not wrong when she said Japan was "a paradise of man." Why did no one shout "*Irrashaimase!*" "Welcome, honoured customer!" and hand me a hot towel in bars and restaurants? Where were the elevator girls in white gloves to push the buttons for you and announce the floors, the pretty young women in uniform at the bottom of the escalators, bowing and welcoming you to the store? Where were the countless tiny shops with half their inventory placed on the sidewalk in front of them every morning and tucked away again at night? Where were the uncountable pairs of slippers outside every door?

One day in Tokyo walking into the school, I saw a young man in a suit presenting Mr. Owada with a tray of expensive-looking pens. I asked Mr. Owada about it later, and he told me he had recently bought a pen, and it had leaked in his pocket. The store sent someone over immediately to apologize and reimburse him for his ruined shirt and present him with a tray of replacement pens to choose from. In Japan the customer is God. In Canada? Not really. More like a sheep for the fleecing.

I was glad to be back in Victoria, if only because it was so quiet and the air was so much cleaner than in Tokyo. I was unimpressed with myself for giving up and coming home so soon, but I felt the circumstances had warranted it. It was a tough breakup. I was re-acclimated to west coast living in Canada in only a few weeks, but it was amusing to me that I had grown so used to my pampered lifestyle in Japan in so short a time.

I bought a lovely new, white Peugeot Mixte bicycle with a step-through frame, a unisex arrangement, easier on the testes for a man with short legs. I relied on it extensively, the hills of Victoria notwithstanding. I bicycled downtown and worked until midnight, spent my minuscule tips on beer, and then bicycled home, weaving.

To get to physics class at 8:30 in the morning, I bicycled up a long steep hill to school in the rain at eight o'clock, too early for breakfast. I then had to climb three flights of stairs in the new Fisher Building, wishing now it had burned down the previous spring. I slept on the floor of my bare basement bedroom and wrote differential equations on pieces of paper and tacked them onto the walls to try to memorize them. I developed a taste for Harvey's Bristol Cream Sherry added to yogurt and fruit smoothies. I wasn't proud of being a bus boy, but without that income there wouldn't have been any sherry smoothies.

Toshiko, the Japanese woman I had a brief affair with in the fall in Tokyo, came to Victoria for a few days, and I took time off to show her the city. We walked through Christ Church, the gothic cathedral on Quadra Street, where we saw the carved robin's nest. During construction of the Anglican cathedral in the late 1920s, building operations were suspended when a robin and her eggs were discovered in one of the partially completed pillars and the work didn't resume until the babies had hatched and were able to fly. This little bird family was then memorialized in stone by the masons. From there we strolled over to a popular new restaurant, Pagliacci's. "*Solidarność*" was painted boldly across the front window. The Polish trade union, the first non-communist union in the Eastern Bloc, was still only six months old and on its way to a membership, in its first year, of nine million workers. I tried to be cheerful, and we chatted as best we could, but on recollecting the story of the robin, Toshiko started to cry in our little booth.

She stayed with me in my basement room in Oak Bay, but insisted we spend one night at the Empress Hotel, so she would have a receipt to show her mother. I flew to Seattle and back on the same day to put her on the 747 to Japan. I watched it take off at SeaTac and was tired and ashamed of myself for such foolishness. She telephoned and wrote to me constantly, until I was able to convince her that I would never return to Japan. She wrote back, "It's okay. I had adventure."

I barely remember those four months at Camosun studying science. I was taking all university courses now. I had finished my high school catch-up. I was depressed and lonely and made no friends, although I drank and behaved badly on occasion with others who liked to drink. I had a couple of dozen classmates who must have been familiar to me, but when I returned in the fall semester and saw many of them again, I couldn't remember their names. It was as though the whole semester had never happened. Following the acute agony of the previous autumn, the four months of late winter and early spring were a long, dull ache. My roommate, also a Camosun student, was a complete slob and rarely spoke, a skinny, sour-looking, rat-faced girl from Kamloops. The landlords were sickeningly middle-class and offensively uninteresting. I kept as busy as I could. Going home at the end of the day was nothing to look forward to.

I do remember walking into a midterm exam in chemistry one day. I was already late, but not in a hurry, and when I entered the lab where the test was being held, I saw a new *Time* magazine on one of the benches near the door. I hadn't seen this issue yet, and I stopped to look at it. I then spent fifteen minutes bent at the waist, leaning on my elbows on the lab bench, reading the magazine while the minutes ticked away and my classmates struggled, heads down, with the mysteries of inorganic chemistry. Eventually the instructor, Graham, an Englishman, sidled my way. "Anytime you think you might like to start." He was dry. I wrote the test and got my A.

My kind of intelligence is impressive in a school setting, but it doesn't transfer well into the real world. I got A's on all my tests, all the time, and for the most part, I had no idea what the courses were about. I was just good at reading and memorizing large chunks of new information and answering written, time-limited questions. Beyond that, the subjects were often a mystery to me. Over the years I studied calculus, general chemistry, inorganic chemistry, organic chemistry, biochemistry, general physics, electricity and magnetism, thermodynamics, basic engineering, statistics, biology, microbiology, economics, administration, law, and many other subjects, and I couldn't have told you a thing about them the day after the last class. It's no wonder I spent so many years in school. It was easy for me. "Except for a few bits of knowledge here and there, I am almost a halfwit, scarcely fit to vote." I was to prove again and again, over the years, that I couldn't pull my prick out of a bucket of lard.

From my second week as a bus boy, I bugged Rick to make me a waiter. Bus boys didn't make money, waiters did. He stalled, telling me I needed more experience on the floor, but I wasn't worried about the complexities of the job. I could stand at the front of, and manage, a classroom of students in a foreign country, teaching them a second language. I was pretty sure I could take a food order, even in a fancy restaurant. He finally relented, and I was a good waiter from my very first shift, with a few ups and downs over the summer.

The semester wound down, and as I predicted, my student loan arrived on the last day of exams. I could have given it back. I didn't need it. I had survived the semester under my own steam, but instead I used it to buy a brand new motorcycle, a gorgeous 1981 Honda CB 400 Hawk in red and black. Somehow I thought I deserved a treat, and I was thoroughly sick of unmotorized transportation. I love bicycles, but I never got used to them as a daily-commute vehicle.

I started working full time at the restaurant, and I stopped drinking.

The little rat-faced girl from Kamloops moved out of the basement suite and left a horrific mess, which the obtuse young landlady blamed on me. I had had enough of these white-bread fools, and I found myself a tiny room, really tiny, in a lovely, at least from the street, 1908, Queen Anne-style, heritage house in Rockland. It was chopped up inside into eight suites. I had to share, with two other suites, a tiny toilet on the main floor. Up one flight of stairs was a spacious bathroom, shared by the entire house, with an old clawfoot bathtub and no shower. The building manager lived in the unattractive 1960s in-fill house next door. He was tall and heavy, and he was a fat-headed creep. May his wife live forever. May he be food for the crows. I seemed to be meeting a lot of very unpleasant people. This was the world I was creating now, with my consent, self-selected and self-imposed. Maybe I was the ass. My new place was clean and had some storage space in an outdoor closet on an unlikely little balcony, but the suite was so small, just one tiny room, I didn't see how I could possibly survive there for an entire school year. It was furnished, and full, with a single bed and a small kitchen table. There wasn't enough room to swing a cat. No room to study.

I let it slide for the summer and spent as much time as I could outside, going to work, motorbiking, going to the gym, nearly always eating in restaurants. I occasionally had the free staff meal at work, "bones and ketchup," but more often I devoured a double Greek salad at two o'clock in the morning in late-night pizza places, after swimming and lifting weights at the Oak Bay Rec Centre, which was open until 1:00 a.m. For my one other meal of the day, I breakfasted on filling omelettes at Goody's Restaurant on Broad Street, at two in the afternoon, just before starting work again.

I spent the summer waiting tables five evenings a week and made a comfortable living doing it. My old friend from Calgary, Ron, had bought himself a 21-foot sailboat the previous summer, and I had been out with him a couple of times. Shizuka and I went with him once, and we were pounded by sudden wind and waves as we left the harbour. Shizuka fled to the tiny cabin below in fear of certain death by frigid drowning, but Ron told me what to do and he got us safely out into the strait.

I was exhilarated by the water. I could afford to take sailing lessons now, and I enthusiastically completed Canadian Yachting Association courses in basic coastal cruising and navigation. I bought and read Bowditch's *American Practical Navigator*. It is nine hundred pages long, and much of it is charts and tables, but it is also an encyclopedia of maritime knowledge in piloting, oceanography, meteorology, celestial and electronic navigation, mathematics, and safety. It's okay to be a little obsessive when you're researching a new topic. I had time. Once I finished the courses, I was allowed to rent the school's 24-foot C&C sloop, *Tiercel*. Many times over the summer, I endeavoured as best I could to stock the little boat with cocktail waitresses from work for an afternoon flap around the Strait of Juan de Fuca. I loved sailing and handled the boat with confidence from the beginning, except for one early incident where I lost the wind and way while approaching the dock and hit the wharf embarrassingly hard. I might have got away with it, but the entire staff of the Victoria Sailing School were seated on the floating pier in a circle, having a meeting, and I nearly knocked them all off their folding chairs. The beginner's confidence I felt that summer was shredded forever one stormy night seventeen years later, in a 50-foot yacht a hundred miles off Cape Mendocino.

I spent the summer smoking pot and reading Heisenberg and Planck, their autobiographies, which included a smattering of their physics. Heisenberg was thirty-one years old when he got the Nobel. Planck was sixty. For balance I read *The Adventures of Tintin*. I went to the gym and rode my motorcycle. And I went sailing and read about sailing and thought about sailing. I was dying to be on a boat. My very amiable instructor, Daiquiri Jim, had spent a lot of time on the eastern seaboard, and he told me you could practically stand on the dock in Morehead City, North Carolina, and thumb a ride to the Caribbean for the winter. It was the point where snowbird recreational boaters stopped on their way south in the fall to gear up, and crew up, before leaving the safety of the Intracoastal Waterway. With Cape Hatteras, the Graveyard of the Atlantic, behind them, they could strike out into open water and make way for Florida and the Keys, the Bahamas, Puerto Rico, the Virgin Islands, and Bermuda. These sounded like places I would very much like to see and spend the winter. Good dope, loose shoes, and a warm place to squat. I was crazy enough to take my few savings and try my luck as a winter deckhand in the Caribbean, but I also knew it would be just one more self-indulgent adventure, leading where? For some reason I thought my life was in need of a solution or at least some kind of commitment. So a dreamy life as deck candy, which sounds better than rail meat, became just that, another pipedream, happy thoughts to think while chasing the dragon, smoking a joint every night after work at 2:00 a.m. by the dumpster behind the restaurant, or in Michaeljon and Louise's living room. "2 a.m." was our "420," and it was always 2 a.m. There was very good pot in Victoria that summer. As August came to a close, I let out a sigh of profound disappointment and came back down to earth. I gave up on my dreams of island hopping in a tropical paradise and registered for school. I wasn't happy about postponing the present for the sake of the future, but I liked school. Didn't I? It hadn't made me happy lately and waiting for the future can take a long time.

Mark came to work at Bartholomew's in July. He was nineteen, slim, well-muscled, in very good shape, a tall, handsome sprout with short, shiny, curly black hair. He was so energetic he used to run ten miles at one o'clock in the morning after working eight hours at a run in the restaurant as a bus boy. Sometimes, instead, he ran up and down all eighteen floors of the hotel half a dozen times. At first I was astonished by his energy, until I discovered he drank ten-ounce glasses of Coca-Cola non-stop during every shift. It was free to the staff. We started to hang out together a bit, sitting on the roof of his sister's giant mansion after work, another grand house in Rockland chopped up into little suites, smoking pot and staring at the stars. His conversational choreography was bouncy and highly caffeinated, and broadly and eccentrically selective when it came to subject matter. I found his company very refreshing in small doses, but it was a lot like being around a child. He constantly skipped from one topic to another. One harebrained scheme was suddenly proposed and just as quickly abandoned in favour of another. He was a young buck in a china shop, full of awkward energies, always tangential, sometimes obtuse and disturbing. He exuded a vitality of incoherence and chaos.

Mark had spent half of his short life in the US. He was born in Canada, but when his father died at a young age and his mother remarried, he and his four brothers and sisters moved to Springfield, Oregon, the actual "Springfield" of *The Simpsons* television series. I have found that if a Canadian spends even a few years in the US as a child, they are forever different from all other Canadians, like a Catholic is always different from a Protestant. To me he seemed more American than Canadian, a result of growing up with all that liquor in the corner stores, all those freeways, all those handguns and assassinations, all those wars. And he had indeed been born and raised Catholic, all that smoke and Latin in both church and school.

I didn't realize it then, but I see now that he had all the signs about him of a true American crank. He was still very young then, just finished his first year at the University of Oregon. He took a year off to work in the restaurant and then went back to school, changing majors from business to international studies, switching ideals in midstream. He graduated and later did a year of law school at UBC, but he didn't care for it. Over the years he continued to work in restaurants and as a bicycle and motorcycle courier, a salesman, a variety of jobs. He was no more interested in the treadmill of conformity and the constraints of a career than I was. Like Dorothy Parker was suspiciously and "prematurely" anti-fascist before the Second World War broke out, like Benjamin Button living his life in reverse, Mark and I were both prematurely mystical, inappropriate to our stage of life, and we stayed that way. We were in the unsatisfactory position of having adopted mature judgments with immature minds. We had no mundane goals. We had the vigor of youth, especially Mark, but we were already old, without the consolations of age.

Mark is one of the funniest people I have ever met. I have been bent double in tears of laughter more often in his company than in anyone else's. He doesn't tell jokes. He talks infectiously and non-stop about life and the goofiest adventures I have ever heard, describing them in absurd and brilliant detail. Later, he became another North American to go to Japan to teach English. I drove him to the airport in 1992. He spent many years there over the next decade successfully employed and even managed to find a woman forgiving enough to marry him.

His eccentricities became more pronounced as the years passed and were accompanied by an inevitable lessening of youthful charm and a rise in contrariness, the normal progress of the crank. He became an obsessed writer of self-published books, the refuge of the oddball! His written work is highly personal and occasionally moving, but every page is filled with italics and underlining, quotation marks and exclamation marks, grammatical errors, typos, awkward constructions, and jarring transitions, a tendency to rant. I believe that with the help of an editor, or a co-author, his books, especially the first one, would be a good read. He's a unique and interesting man, but when he writes he falls into common and uninteresting traps. Don't we all. To write pleasingly, you must exhibit clarity, perspicuity, and insight, or at least be comprehensible. Writers always hope for a creative, nimble-minded readership, one that can keep up with them as they jump around, but they are in trouble if they count on it.

Starting in the late nineties, Mark and I fell out a bit. His eccentricities began to compound other stresses I was experiencing, not the least of which was that my wife didn't find him very amusing. We didn't see each other for several years. I've always been glad I met Mark, and I thoroughly enjoyed most of the time we spent together. There were difficult times as well, and he hasn't always been easy to be around, but neither have I.

He was sharp. At the end of one very busy evening at work in the summer of 1981, I was counting my checks and cash at the hostess's desk. She had fled somewhere, so I was covering for her briefly. Even in a higher-end establishment, a busy bar and restaurant at midnight can be a disturbing sight. The customers are drunk and sometimes disorderly, the staff are exhausted and giddy, and the premises have been abused for hours on end, often with only patchy janitorial service. We had been swamped that night, and the restaurant was greatly dishevelled. A well-dressed, middle-aged woman who wasn't drunk, one of the few, came out of the women's washroom and leaned toward me to inform me that the facilities were "shocking" and badly in need of attention. I knew there was no one left at this hour, anywhere in the building, who would attend to this chore, and even if there had been the chances were they would tell me to go to hell anyway. I wasn't the boss. By midnight, young minimum-wage summer workers are often less than enthusiastic about their duties, when they know that a few minutes' absence or procrastination can get them out of an unpleasant task and on their way to an after-work party. Even the maitre d' was gone. I knew it was pointless, but I thought I would have to make some response, so I assured her that I would see to the matter. I was exhausted and giddy myself. Something in my tone led her to doubt my sincerity. She said, "Tsk. Well, it's just a shame that a cute place like this is brought down by poor maintenance." Just at that moment Mark came hurrying by the desk, busy with some task. I shouted, "Mark!" which brought him to an abrupt halt. I said, "I am informed by this customer that the women's washroom is a disgusting state. Please see to it immediately!"

He tilted his head back, furrowed his brow, then lowered it again. He looked at us both and said, "*New Jersey* is a disgusting state." He sped off. I erupted in laughter, fell off my stool, and our customer was left unsatisfied.

There were many unsatisfied customers that summer, as there are in general in the restaurant business. It seems that because everyone eats, everyone thinks he knows how to run a restaurant, and the paying public holds strong opinions on the matter. In some instances, though, the case for dissatisfaction is more open and shut.

I had avoided becoming a waiter over the years because, although it paid fairly well and there were always jobs to be had, I have never enjoyed being pleasant to people, subjectively, for money. Driving a taxi was as close as I had come to a customer service job, and each encounter in that business had the advantage of being brief and well-defined. For a short period of time, I could be as charming as a psychopath and the tips, while valuable, were not essential, a mere ten per cent of my income. As a waiter I earned minimum wage and tips formed a full two-thirds of my income. I also spent up to two hours, or more, with the same customers, often enough while they became drunker and ruder. This was trying.

The prices at Bart's were high, and some people were angry from the moment they sat down. Americans in particular were often surprised by the prices. Ah, Americans. Every tourist town has a love-hate relationship with its tourists, and I truly hated them by the end of June. A couple of examples will suffice.

For some reason I expected people to behave themselves in my restaurant, as though they were eating at my house. In this I was to be disappointed again and again. One day, the hostess absent somewhere, I showed a party of four well-dressed, leathery old Southwesterners to a spacious booth, one of only two in our establishment. As we rounded the corner and I indicated the proposed table, a loud, obnoxious drawl made its appearance. One of the women said, "Ow! It's a *bewth*!"

"A *bewth*!?" said another.

The tallest man, very tall indeed, said, "We don't wanna sit in a gaaaddaaam *bewth*!"

It is amazing to me how loudly and how slowly some Americans can speak without expiring before the end of the sentence.

I couldn't help myself when I said, "Very good, sir. Let me see if I can't find you a different *gaad-daam* table." There seemed to me to be no reason at all for such language and behaviour in a public place.

One very large gentleman from Texas wasn't rude, just appalling. He and his family were seated in the lovely Garden section of the restaurant, and when I approached the table I couldn't help but notice the eight-inch cigar sticking out of his mouth. It wasn't lit, thank goodness, but it was a kind of pacifier for him, and the four inches of it that were generally resident inside his mouth were truly disgusting to behold when he occasionally extracted the whole from his very large head on the top of his very large body. He asked me for a ten-ounce steak. He said he wanted it "RAHR." I didn't understand him at first, but he made himself clearer by differentiating "RAHR" from "MAY-JUM." He asked me how we cooked our steaks up here in Canada. We discussed colour and depth, and when he made his decision I confirmed his order by saying, "Very good, sir. One ten-ounce steak, rahr."

On Sunday mornings, you could hear the bells of the downtown churches ringing, calling the faithful to brunch. Half of them were coming directly from church, the other half were hung-over from the night before. Don't get me wrong. With forty-nine out of fifty customers, I was polite, cheerful, efficient, and helpful. When I was rested, and up for it, I was a fine waiter. I was nominated for, and received, a pin from the Ministry of Tourism to prove it. "Superstar!"

But there were days when I was not up to it. It was very popular practice to introduce yourself by name. "Good evening. I'm Neil and I'll be your waiter tonight." I didn't feel this was necessary, and it wasn't restaurant policy. It seemed fairly obvious who I was in my white shirt, black vest, and black tie, and I never bothered with it. Customers occasionally asked for my name, and I would say, "Elmer," at which point they would laugh. Not a common name. I would remain straight-faced, and in a moment they would stop laughing, a little embarrassed, and apologize. When I had finished taking their order, I would mutter, while walking away from the table, "Fudd."

One evening, before I was quite up to speed, I found myself having to repeat the daily specials, for the fifth time, to a group of very elderly ladies, mostly deaf, and out of exasperation I said, surprising even myself, "Curried *rat*, madam!"

"What? What did he say? What?"

I thought this ad-lib was up there with Woollcott who, when asked to repeat his order to a waiter, said, "Muffins filled with pus!"

Some days I was tired. Some days I was angry.

I felt quite unfairly judged one evening in the quality of my service, not only by the insulting amount of the tip that was left on the table, but also by the snooty attitude of the diners as they took their leave. I had worked hard to make sure they had a pleasant experience, and they had had one. In short, what was their fucking problem? As they left the restaurant walking by the noisy bar, I took the opportunity to shout enthusiastically, "Thank you! Thank you very much! Good-night! Thank you!" Although it did come out sounding a lot like "Fuck you! Fuck you very much! Good-night! Fuck you!" The alpha male of the group, well over six feet tall, was the only one who heard me. He flinched, but he didn't stop.

My foulest customer over the year I worked there, even more so than I, was a tall, evil-browed brute. He was openly bullying and rude, both to me, and more distressingly, to his girlfriend. It was embarrassing, repulsive, and maddening to see him abusing her at the table. I took great pleasure in spitting on his entree before serving it to him. Seriously, don't piss your waiter off.

One day just before starting work, I was feeling raw, and I saw a customer berating one of the day-shift bus girls. He had that satisfied look that men get when they know they are in a position to chastise their inferiors uninterrupted and with impunity. He was also a small man and that's what made me mad. Being small myself, I have always hated the physical bully, or any kind of bully, and I have always felt that small men should eschew aggression in the few instances when it may play to their advantage. Somehow a small bully is even worse than a big one. The bus girl was five feet tall and fifteen years old. The man was older than I and about my size. I walked over to where they were standing, and I made it clear to him that if he had a problem, he could take it up with me instead of abusing a child. The bus girl fled. He was flustered by my challenge and demanded to see the maitre d'. When we enquired at the hostess's desk where Rick was, we were told he was in the bar. I turned and walked away to get him, and unknown to me, the customer followed close at heel. I thought he would wait at the desk. In the bar, I said to Rick, "There's a guy at the front. He was being rude to Sadie. Get him out of here before I smash his face." Too much adrenaline. I wheeled about and nearly walked into the customer. He had followed me into the bar, right up to Rick. I glared at him and left. Rick then had to listen to some fairly legitimate complaints and apologize for his staff's rudeness, and I got a week off to collect myself. I thanked Rick profusely for the suspension. I really needed a break. He called me back after a couple of days anyway, because the restaurant was busy.

I was not an ideal employee, but I was honest. Food and booze were always walking out the door. The dishwasher stole fifteen-pound prime-rib roasts at the end of his shift, one under each arm, and the bus boys made off with dozens of cases of beer in their cars. Inventory is always a concern in the restaurant business.

Hiring practices were less than admirable. The restaurant employed only women during the day, and in the evenings only men. The servers in the bar were always female, day or night. If a woman was hired by the management, and later, when seen by the owner, didn't meet his standards for physical appeal, she would be fired for no other reason. The women working in the restaurant wore uniforms of long skirts with low-cut frilly tops, and goofy English hats. In the bar the servers wore black, scoop-necked body stockings and short wrap-around tulip skirts. There was gold in those legs and bosoms. Tips in the bar ran up to a hundred and fifty dollars a night, close to five hundred in 2014 dollars. I suppose the bar and restaurant business will always attract young women working for tips.

And speaking of women, I was having terrible luck again. Month after month I couldn't get a live, breathing female to look in my direction. In the bar and restaurant business, it's not hard to meet women, there are so many of them. I met a lot of available women with a good sense of humour and a pretty ankle. They just weren't interested in me. I thought being a student would present a promising face to potential sweethearts, neutral at least, hell, I even went sailing once a week, surely that was a plus, but the attractive young women who work in the hospitality industry are looking for men with real jobs. They see the disposable income flashed around by young executives on their evenings out, and poor student suitors, rather short-sightedly, are sent to the back of the line. I decided to try a bulk, scattershot approach. They say if you ask enough women to come back to your place to look at your etchings, one of them is bound to say yes. I managed to debunk this theory entirely. The summer was very frustrating. Finding someone to love me was becoming a full-time job.

Then, out of nowhere I got a cold sore on my lip the size of a golf ball. By now, cold sores were called herpes. This was embarrassing for me, and it couldn't have been pleasant for my customers. I asked Rick for time off to let it pass but it was high summer, the restaurant was busy, and he needed all of his waiters on the floor. Where it came from I had no idea. There were no sexual partners in my life although I have a vague recollection of getting one or two little cold sores as a teenager in the sixties. We thought nothing of it then. Herpes. A friend for life.

And then, of all the gin joints in all the towns in all the world, who should walk into mine but Carol. I hadn't seen her in six years. She worked just a block away at the museum so I guess it wasn't that startling to run into her.

I was standing at the busy bar sorting out drink orders for thirty-eight Japanese tourists in the banquet room, my mind racing, when I heard someone say hello. I glanced briefly behind me, saw a pretty girl standing there, didn't recognize her, assumed she wasn't talking to me, and turned back to my business. She said hello again. I looked at her again, said hello this time, and still didn't recognize her. I went back to my high-pressure arithmetic. Then she said with a big smile, sweetly amused, "You don't know who I am, do you?"

If you could hear a jaw drop, you'd have heard mine hit the boozy hardwood. "Carol! Oh, my God!"

Two weeks earlier, one of the managers from the BC Provincial Museum had come in to the restaurant and was seated in my section. We chatted and caught up a bit on the six years that had passed since I had worked at the museum in the summer of 1975, patching the cobblewood street in the Old Town exhibit and trying to look busy. He had obviously told Carol that I was working at Bart's, and she had dropped by to say hello. It was an agony to me, but I had to tell her that I couldn't talk now. I had thirty-eight Japanese people in the banquet room, and they all wanted a piece of me. She gave me her number and left. I was ecstatic.

Needless to say, I called Carol as soon as it was decent to do, meaning the next day, and when we got together over the next few weeks, canoeing, talking endlessly, making love, I thought I had come back to life and might live again. Unfortunately, I was wrong about that.

It was a while before I figured it out, but Carol had a steady boyfriend, and she was cheating on him with me. It was "beery, beery" sad. For a couple of weeks, I had positively glowed at the thought of having Carol as a steady girlfriend. I had loved her warmly and closely when we had our affair back in 1975, the snow falling softly in the night in huge fluffy flakes outside the black window of my little room on Pandora Avenue, but to her I was still just a confection. She lived only a few blocks away, and she visited me at my apartment over the fall, when she felt like it, but we never went to dinner or to the movies, never went out. She couldn't be seen with me in public. I was only at her apartment once or twice, and she was nervous the whole time I was there, afraid her boyfriend might drop by unannounced.

I went back to school in September and continued working at the restaurant. I saw Carol once every three weeks or so over the fall, and by the end of November I was mad with desire and frustration. I ached and longed for her. I wanted to see her every day, to smother her in kisses and touches. I couldn't stand it. I came to the painful and reluctant conclusion that it would be easier to live without her than to have my longing for her so cruelly governed. To see her only once every three weeks was torture, worse I felt, by just a little, than not seeing her at all. Half is always worse than nothing, and I wasn't even getting half. I had to try to put her out of my mind, try to stop being crazed by anticipation and disappointment. I stopped calling her. There is no one more desirable than someone who doesn't want you, and no one less desirable than someone who does.

Before Carol walked back into my life, there were at least four women at work I was trying very hard to get to know romantically, with no luck. Shea was a sweet, down-home girl from Saskatchewan who loved to party. I liked her in a friendly way, and we flirted off and on, lackadaisically. After a comic siege of a few too many weeks, our little dance had become a joke between us, and I was content just to be friends. I was very surprised then when she indicated to me one day that she had decided to submit to my blandishments. I guess she couldn't find anyone else either. By then I felt our casual courtship had been going on too long to be a matter of dizzying passion. It was such a long time that I was a little annoyed. Ladies, take note. The shelf life of seduction has a best-by date. In addition, by this time, Carol had also reappeared, and my head snapped so hard in her direction it was nearly spun off my shoulders. But I didn't see Carol very often. There was plenty of time in-between to see Shea. This was a just-workable arrangement for the fall until I decided, for my own good, not for Shea's, that I had somehow to tear myself away, with a wrench, from Carol. Shea and I settled for each other and spent the rest of the winter together in a loveless, usually friendly, occasionally dismal, relationship where she was forced to watch me start drinking again and become thoroughly overworked and miserable at school, obnoxious to myself and others. I haven't always been easy on my girlfriends. But she *was* a smoker, the last one I ever went out with.

I was looking forward to the start of the school year in September, but dreading it as well because I had such a tiny unworkable closet of an apartment and then, on the last day or two of August, I saw the woman in the front suite on the main floor moving out. I ran immediately next door to see Mr. Jones, the miserable building manager, and asked him if he had rented it yet. Amazingly, he hadn't. He wouldn't, on principle, willingly do another human being a favour, but he now had an opportunity to hurt and insult his departing tenant, something he couldn't resist. She had asked him if a girlfriend of hers could have the apartment, and he had agreed, at least with a shrug of his shoulders. He now decided he would give the apartment to me on the fiction that I had precedence as an existing tenant. He didn't give a toss about my rights or precedence. He just didn't like women. The girlfriend in question could have my tiny suite if she wanted it, which she didn't, of course. It was unliveable. I felt terrible about scooping the apartment out from under these girls in such an abrupt manner, more bad karma, and I apologized sincerely, which was no consolation to them. I had no choice. The apartment at the front of the house was three times the size of mine. It had high ceilings, a couch, a chair, a dresser and closet, a bay window, a double bed, a good-sized kitchen table for eating, and more importantly, for studying, and room to swing a cat. In the dog-eat-dog world of Victoria student accommodation, I had to take it.

It's hard to imagine a shabby bedsit without a bathroom was a Godsend, but it was. It was almost a pied-à-terre. I was so ecstatic about my new digs I went to the store and bought half a dozen plants to adorn the place and make it look more loved-in.

In six weeks they were all dead.

7   My Candle Burns At Both Ends

It was time to settle in to a new semester, but I wasn't quite ready yet. I still had a few hundred dollars worth of the best marijuana I had smoked in a very long time. After years of putting up with the cheap, skunky grass that flooded the market in the 1970s, twigs and seeds, there was finally some righteous shit on the street. It was smooth and easy, very clean and very high, no jitters, no paranoia, no headache, a very pleasant change, but a lot more expensive. We called it Mexican Red Hair, but really, we had no idea what it was. There were no cultivators in my circle of acquaintance.

I kept busy. I was only taking three classes, but they were all chemistry, so there were three labs as well. A single lab course takes about twelve hours a week, every week, to keep under control. It was still busy at the restaurant in September, so I was also working there three or four nights a week. Add gym and racquetball time to that, plus "420," and I was putting in an 80-hour week, this for a guy who in any season of the year didn't have twenty hours a week in him to give.

By the time midterms rolled around, I realized I was seriously unprepared for my organic chemistry exam. For a week before the test, I swore every day that I would study that night, and never did. I had been to all the classes, but I hadn't looked at my notes since I first wrote them down, hadn't cracked my 1,400-page textbook, *Organic Chemistry*, by the two Roberts, Morrison and Boyd. On the night before the midterm, I had no choice but to accept with a fearful sigh that time had run out. I had six hours to learn the basic structures and properties, the isomers and nomenclature, of the compounds of carbon. I was just ill. I did what I had to do. I rolled the biggest joint I could, using the finest marijuana I had smoked in years, and spent six hours becoming one with organic chemistry. The next day I wrote my test. A couple of days later, our Dutch professor, Rintje, pronounced "Rin," returned the exams expressing disappointment in the overall results. Our instructors knew how to mark on the curve and inflate grades. They were scientists. They could do the math. But the classes were too small for that. Frequency distribution, percentiles, and relative performance mean nothing in a class of eleven students. I got ninety-eight per cent on my organic chemistry midterm. Everyone else got C's. I thank the Red Hair.

Rintje finished a PhD in organic chemistry at the University of Alberta at the age of twenty-five and worked in pharmaceutical research for ten years before taking up teaching. He was a long distance runner, and he had the skeletal build and the slow, blissful, over-oxygenated demeanour of a runner. He had shoulder-length hair, wore Birkenstock sandals and wool socks, and walked so slowly it occasionally made him late for class. He ran ten kilometers six days out of seven, and I asked him how he managed to fit it in. "You simply decide that no matter what else happens on any given day, you run." He also talked slowly. He said he would never pay more than twenty dollars for a pair of runners. When I asked him about the difference between doing original research, being a chemical explorer, and teaching at a junior college, a little less prestigious, he said, "It doesn't matter what you do, you still have to get up every morning of your life and go to work." It was a philosophy of the equality not of all men, but of all human conditions, the mere fact of existence being the main point, the rest indifferent and accidental. Molecules, atoms, subatomic particles, peas, beans, rice. It's all just counting. He told me I was capable of doing a PhD in chemistry.

I wasn't as smart as I pretended to be, but I knew now I could graduate from any university in just about any program. I could get a job. I could work. So what? What did that prove? What did it mean? It meant nothing to me at all. Why exert yourself in the pursuit of something extraordinary when the result of nearly every human effort was mediocrity? My empty capacities, undeveloped and destined to remain so, bridled at the overwhelming likelihood of achieving nothing more than survival. How would that achievement make me better? There seemed a very good chance it would have the opposite effect. In the throng of human experience, ambition was a stranger to me, a cold I never caught.

Over the winter I wrote one fairly brilliant exam after another, and one of my classmates asked me how I managed to do it. I said, "Don't fight the material. You don't always have to understand it. Don't expect to. Just *be* with it." I'm not sure that helped. I went to every class, and I took careful notes, but often I wasn't actually paying much attention. I would teach it to myself later when I looked at it again. I noticed that the other students in the class asked surprisingly pertinent questions, clearly following along, while I was daydreaming and had no idea what the instructor was talking about. Yet come exam time, I knew I would be whipping their asses when it came to grades. Graham, once again my instructor in inorganic chemistry, gave up asking me questions in class when I once responded, "I'm sorry, Graham, I really wasn't listening." To the other students he said, "Neil gets good marks because he can write three clear sentences in a row." This was not a skill shared by most of my classmates.

Biochemistry was taught by Howard, a gentle, friendly man with a PhD from McGill University in Montreal. He was always able to put me at ease, and biochemistry, frankly, is fascinating, all pathways and reactions, like life. I loved the class. Howard was so pleasant to be around I could have sat in his office every day just to chat about anything and everything. I asked him why he hadn't studied medicine, he would have made a lot more money. If you can do a PhD in chemistry, you can handle the academics of a degree in clinical medicine. Or as Graham put it, "PhD chemists don't take any shit from MDs." Howard told me he was tempted to try medical school, but he didn't want the worries that come with being responsible for other people's health. He said he realized later that sixty per cent of a general practitioner's patients are women and their children, and sixty per cent of them have an infection of some kind, treatable with drugs. If you get a more complex case, you send them to a specialist. You make an income in the top five per cent of the country writing non-stop scrip and referrals. He also told me not to worry about the difficulties of doing graduate work, it's mostly an assembly line. You look up what someone has already done and repeat their experiments changing a single parameter, perhaps just running them all at a different pH. Most of the time your supervisor will tell you exactly what to do anyway, since your work is part of his or her research and integral, if not crucial, to their funding. Howard made these mildly jaded comments in such a cheerful, off-hand way that I might have been, probably should have been, undismayed, but I was still a bit nervy and uncertain about the unknown terrain of future academics.

The instructors taught their own labs, and their office hours were any hours they weren't teaching. I could walk into Graham's office at any time during the day and ask him to help me get to the heart of, and articulate the essence of, say, the Jahn-Teller Effect, or other mysteries of transition metal chemistry. Three or four of us worked at our studies every day in the prep room of the main lab, where there were four chairs and a table available. There we prepared for labs, wrote lab reports, and did other homework.

I rode my motorbike to school every day, and in the winter of 1981–82 it rained every goddamn day. To keep dry I used the cheap, stiff, two-piece yellow rain gear I had bought for sailing, and I looked like a commercial fisherman on a scooter, riding to and from the college in the pouring rain, freezing.

When it was still warm and dry in September, I made the acquaintance of Tom. He lived upstairs in a shameful little room, smaller than the one I had just managed to escape, smaller than a dorm room. It was criminal that such miserable accommodation could command rent of any kind. The landlord should have paid his tenants to live there. I would see Tom sitting on the front steps of the house when I came home from classes, and we took to chatting and smoking pot together. He was about my age, taller, well muscled, blond, and his experience of life had included trouble with the law and time in jail, as well as time in the army, where he had fired howitzers at the snowpack in the mountains to induce controlled avalanches. He lacked education and maybe compassion growing up. I'm not sure. He was unemployed now and concerned about how he would pay his rent. He had no transportation and was forced to buy his groceries at the corner store. They charged outrageous prices. More than once he came home with a small bag of groceries, and an empty wallet, and barked, "Those fucking Wong Brothers did it to me again!" For lack of kitchen appliances and space in his ridiculous room, he bought convenience foods, a further unnecessary and crippling expense for the poor. On Sundays, I did my shopping at a cheap supermarket in Esquimalt, since the stores were still closed on the Sabbath in Victoria, and I hauled my groceries home in a cardboard box bungeed to the back of my motorcycle, the same way I hauled my laundry home from the laundromat in Cook Street village. I invited Tom to my place for supper one night and gave him soy burgers, which I made inexpensively by the dozen and kept in my freezer. I'm not sure Tom had a fridge. We were very stoned by the time dinner was ready. He wasn't sure what a soy burger was, but when he tasted it he exclaimed, "Holy shit, it's bean cake! I'm back in the joint!" He laughed. "You're feeding me prison food!" He made me a little nervous. He was under stress, and he had anger issues and a criminal past.

One day, he ecstatically informed me he had found a job at Zellers department store stocking and selling women's clothing. He came home from work a few days later to find an eviction notice on his door. He hadn't worked long enough yet to be able to pay his rent. He knocked on my door in an agitated state with the notice in his hand. I went to Mr. Jones and asked him to give him a break. I told him Tom was working now and would pay his rent with the first cheque from his new job. In a rare moment of kindness, Mr. Jones relented. For a couple of weeks, I saw Tom going to work in sandy-coloured trousers, a golf shirt, and a tweedy sport jacket he had bought at a thrift store, perfectly presentable. The clothes became more and more dirty as the days passed, and one day he told me he had been fired. He had lied about his retail experience in order to get the job, and he was unable to learn the ins and outs of women's clothing fast enough to perform to Zellers standards. I asked Rick to give him a job as a bus boy at Bartholomew's, and was pleased when he did, but on Tom's first shift, which I was also working, I saw him in the dining room in his tie and his long burgundy apron looking like a man who has just realized he has made a huge mistake. We all had to agree that this was not going to work. The rigours and details, the public exposure, of being a bus boy were too much for him.

He came to my door late one evening stoned on acid and told me the story of his trippy adventures that day. It ended when he walked up to a policeman sitting in a cruiser and wildly asked him if he knew where his parents were. The policeman wisely and calmly said, "Have a seat in the back. Let's see if we can find them." Tom got into the car, and then panicked when he realized he was locked in. He punched the window out with his substantial fist. He had been released from jail, but he now had a court date. Happily for Tom, when the appointment came up a week or two later, the policeman was on holidays and failed to show. No witness, no charge. Tom showed up at my place bounding with joy. If the matter had come before a judge, he would surely have gone back to jail.

But he was now unemployed and broke again and Mr. Jones kicked him out once more. I told Tom he could appeal the eviction, but he couldn't face filling out forms and dealing with bureaucrats. There was nothing more I could do for him. I was working non-stop. I had befriended him and fed him and got him a job. He said I was the only "mad scientist" he knew. He had smoked a lot of my good pot, and I had given him the best advice I could about landlords, employers, governments, and the law, but I had only enough money for a year of school, with a student loan, and no more. I couldn't pay his rent for him. I knew the date of his eviction, and when I came home from school that day he was gone.

A couple of months later, I ran into him. He told me that the day he left the house for the last time he wandered around downtown until midnight. At the main bus stop on Yates Street, the last bus was leaving, and he had nowhere to go. He was pacing back and forth, and he decided that when the last bus was gone, and the streets were empty, he would rob the 7-Eleven store near the bus stop. A young woman saw him pacing. She said, "You seem kind of upset. What's wrong?" He told her his situation, and she said, "Well, I guess you could sleep at my house." Together, they got on the last bus to the quiet neighbourhood of Willows, where she rented a small basement suite not far from the beach. When I saw him again, he was with his saviour, Carolyn, who worked as a janitor, and they were a happy couple. They were living together, and she had found him a job as a janitor at a shopping mall, but he still lacked the common, non-criminal, sense to be able to function in a system he just couldn't understand. One night, he was late for work and the premises were locked, so he broke a window to get in. He was fired, of course. He and Carolyn were now moving to Calgary with happy expectations of better days. I wished them the best of luck. I couldn't remember hearing such an odd story of just-in-time romance and anti-recidivist kismet, a doubly happy deliverance from a return to a life of crime.

    By the end of November, I had been sober for many months and yet was depressed again, as much as I had ever been in my life. I ached for Carol, I was dismayed witnessing Tom's struggles with basic survival, Shea and I brought each other little joy, and although I loved science, I hated working, or at least, being overworked. I had hoped time and sobriety would be enough to replenish the natural store of diffused delight that surely everyone is born with but not everyone can command. I practised yoga as often as I could manage, but my meditations brought me no peace of mind. I went to a house party somewhere with Brian on a Saturday night and decided there was no point in not drinking if not drinking offered so few rewards. It was easier to smoke a joint and be above it all or take a drink and be beneath it all. Thereafter, until the next April, I drank to spectacular excess as often as was compatible with my schedule, and sometimes more. In early December, in order to prepare for final examinations, I stopped taking shifts at the restaurant and then resigned altogether. Starting in the January semester, 1982, I would be taking five science classes, four with labs, and I wasn't in the mood to handle more than a 70-hour week.

Call me idle. My time as a waiter was over. I never worked in another restaurant. Once was enough.

I went home to Sedgewick for Christmas, flying first to Calgary and then taking the bus from there, still another nine or ten hours' journey. I treated myself to a salmon sandwich for lunch at a health food restaurant in downtown Calgary before getting on the bus. I soon felt unwell. Eight long, uncomfortable hours later, closing on Sedgewick while chatting with the bus driver, an old high school friend, I had for hours been ready to explode, nearly overcome with waves of nausea and hot flashes, and I knew I had eaten the wrong salmon sandwich. My father picked me up at the bus stop in Sedgewick, and I tried to remain casual as we drove the few blocks home. I entered the house and sat on the couch after greeting my mother. After only a moment or two, I excused myself and went into the bathroom where I spent the next forty-five minutes in the most violent expulsions imaginable in what is referred to as "two-bucket disease." My mother called gently from outside the door, "Are you all right, dear?"

I replied, upbeat, "Just glad to be home, Mom!" It was a memorable entrance.

Over the next ten days, I lay in my father's La-Z-Boy recliner reading fiction until my back hurt. My father now had a new business and a new house right across the road from it. He had given up on the tree-growing and tree-moving business and bought a bulk fuel and fertilizer dealership. He was now an agent for Esso Oil. "S.O." Standard Oil. The money was very good but the hours were horrific, and my father would always rather work two shifts himself than hire someone to work one of them for him. He had a few employees to deliver fuel in big trucks to farms and businesses, and in the spring, summer, and fall, especially the spring, he sold dry fertilizer and liquefied anhydrous ammonia, a very dangerous gas fertilizer, by the tonne. He rented out the equipment the farmers needed to apply it to their fields, spreaders for the dry product, and for the ammonia, pressurized tanks and tillers mounted with injecting knives. It was a new business for him, and I never set foot in his office while I visited over the holidays. I was far too self-obsessed to be interested. And I had seen it all before. He was exhausted and so was I, and we snapped at each other over dinner. He had the nerve to say to me that there was nothing more important than family. In my experience this was a man for whom nothing was less important. I wanted to reach down his gullet and pull out his liver with my bare hands.

To my grandmother I bemoaned the unhappy state of my love life. She remarked that I was at a good age now, the end of my twenties. I could have my choice of marriageable women from the age of twenty on up. I sighed a little and told her you couldn't fill a thimble with what I had in common with a twenty-year-old woman. This she acknowledged.

Coming back to Victoria in early January, I breathed in the heavy, wet air, a delicious relief after the smoky, dry indoors of Alberta, but there was snow on the flowers newly planted outside the Empress Hotel and on the seat and speedometer of my motorbike parked in the driveway at my house. My mental image of the next four months was baleful. Five science classes, sixty hours a week of non-stop reading and writing and studying new material. My chemistry instructors said, "Oh God, Neil, don't do it. Just take four. Drop one of them. Five is too much," but I wanted to get it done. If I had to be in school, I would make the most of my time. I wanted to make progress and be in good shape to transfer to the University of Victoria in the fall, which seemed to be the next logical step. My motorbike was temporarily immobilized by the snow. After registering for January classes, I walked down the long, straight pathway in front of the Young Building on my way to catch the bus home. I turned around, looked at the campus buildings, and muttered to myself, "It's only four months. You can do anything for four months. And there will be a sunny day in April when you will walk away from this place for the last time."

In the dead of winter, I saw my grandmother again, along with her friend Betty. She telephoned me out of the blue. They were staying in a hotel downtown for a couple of days waiting for a flight to Hawaii. On the previous Sunday, they were walking home from church in Sedgewick, and it was so cold that by the time they got home, they were determined to fly to Hawaii for respite as soon as possible. Shea and I joined them at the hotel for Bloody Caesars. My grandmother always carried a small bottle of homemade Caesar mix when she travelled, just in case.

Day in and day out, without a break, I went to classes and did homework at the table in the chemistry prep room. I had integral calculus at eight o'clock in the morning, from a young teacher who had taken up body building. His over-muscled neck was wider than his head. He was a pompous ass, a fool, and a jerk. One day he lied to my face and the experience stirred me to coin the following pithy maxim, "Never trust a man whose neck is wider than his head."

Happily, I took physics from an old favourite, Dr. Tong. I loved the way his eyes bulged when he marked my exams, every question answered to perfection. He thought I was brilliant. He said I would have "a brilliant career," but I knew it was impossible. What did I want with a brilliant career in a world of bleak, shallow, and destructive materialism, a civilization that had lost its mind, a "thought-tormented age"? I cared not a jot for living well in a sick society, a never-ending routine of intense, narrow responsibilities, channelled through life's most obvious patterns, the craving and grasping that drive us to stuff ourselves with the delicacies of survival, our thoughts no longer than our greedy fingers, reaching like infants for everything we see, endless evaluation and acquisition, dreaming our lives away in a distracted state of being busy, the annoying bastard fortitude of the happy materialist, the exasperating genius of the uneducated, filling every unoccupied moment with activity, wearing ourselves out because others want us to, sick with stress, exhausted and trembling in the line-up at the cafeteria, living only for our own safety's sake, dead already. The very idea of an average life in a deeply demonic age, violent and covetous, the shortcut and the broad road together, going through the motions without question, seeking a chain of pleasures rather than a seat of joy, made me sick to my stomach. How durable could our civilization be? How much apparatus do we need on the road to bliss?

As far as I knew, I had only one life or only one kick at the can in this life, and I was damned if I was going to spend it in the company of the fucking bourgeois. Only those who have much and those who have little can afford to be bold. The fat balloon around the middle of society is filled, intellectually and culturally, with so much cheap custard. In a previous decade, I might have been an abstracted anarchist or a slapdash socialist, a unionist, a nervous commie, a bootlegger, an opium eater, or a second-rate actor in any age. If I had been a teenager in the 1950s, I would have been a beatnik, but I was a teenager in the 1960s, so I was a hippie instead, and admirably suited to the smoky lethargy that entailed. In any lost generation, as long as the personal danger was slight, the pleasures more frequent than the pains, and the girls generally available, I would have tended to indifferent membership, of lackadaisical standing, posing mildly disingenuous, in one bohemian group or another, whatever constituted the counterculture or subculture of the day. I would never swim in the mainstream, but I was always suspicious of the alternative. When you accept and support the alternative, it means you accept the reality of the mainstream and thereby reinforce its existence and the illusion of duality, the continued orgy of self-definition, self-defence, and exclusion.

I was tired and not a little cranky. I craved independence from irksome constraints. "This is the trouble you catch, that where you itch you must not scratch." It's possible I was smoking too much dope and listening to too much Bob Marley.

The days were long and unvarying, eight in the morning until eleven at night. I gained weight, some of it beer, some of it soy burgers, some of it owing to physical inactivity. I found an old, tan cardigan sweater and wore it every day. Its buttons, one of them missing, barely met at the vertical centre of my expanding belly. I listened to my new Sony Walkman, the size of a small breadbox clipped to my belt, while doing homework in the prep room, and lusted after Rosemary, a woman my height, my age, a handsome, carrot-topped girl with a slightly raspy voice, and a twinkling eye. Don't ask me what colour her eyes were. I've never noticed irises. Small amounts of colour seem to mean nothing to me. They were the colour it pleased God and her genes to make them. Unfortunately, she was espoused. Although I don't suppose I presented much temptation in my shabby clothes and beer gut, my unhappy visage.

In September, I had decided to rent a television and entered into a year-long agreement with the Granada company. When I told the young man how much money I made, as part of the lease application, he said, "God, is that all?" and I came home with a thirteen-inch colour TV.

I hadn't had access to a television for most of the 1970s, and I now watched every episode of *M*A*S*H* in reruns, two back-to-back, Monday through Friday, while cooking supper. Then I would turn the TV off and work until 10:00 p.m. drinking weak tea all the while, listening to Bob Marley and the Wailers, Toots and the Maytals, Peter Tosh, Talking Heads, the Blues Brothers, and *The Rocky Horror Picture Show*. At ten, I would grab my child's beach pail of bathroom necessities and head up the wide, beautifully panelled, turnaround flight of stairs in the house's entryway, past tall stained glass windows in the landing, and take a bath in the shared tub on the second floor. It was used by a lot of people, and I washed it before using it, not after. I drank so much tea in the evenings I always had to pee at least twice during the night. Fortunately, the toilet I shared was on the main floor just outside my door, but I couldn't bear to get up and leave my apartment in the middle of the night, so I kept large pickle jars by my bed. I would roll off the mattress, eyes closed, still asleep, and fill the jars to the brim using my penis as a sensory gauge to know when the jars were full, a flesh-and-blood plumber's ballcock.

When it got cold for a couple of weeks, I used my gas oven to supplement the feeble heat coming from the radiator. Gas was included in the rent. Mr. Jones walked by my suite one day when the door was open and saw my oven door down. He realized I was using it for heat, and the next day I came home to find that the burner had been removed. Without my permission, or even telling me, he had entered my apartment while I was gone and removed the burner to stop me from using it during the cold weather. He was a bald-faced prick, but I didn't have the time or energy to squabble with him. I never used the oven for cooking, so I didn't care that it was now out of commission, and for heat I just used the range burners instead. He must have known I would do that.

In October 1981, the eleven-episode British television production of Evelyn Waugh's novel *Brideshead Revisited* was shown on PBS. Public television was new to me, but there it was on my screen. I had read the book and loved it, and Jeremy Irons and Anthony Andrews played the hell out of Charles Ryder and Sebastian Flyte. The mini-series has been widely praised and ranks high on many lists of the best television programs of all time. For some reason it never occurred to me that the characters were gay although Waugh never really tells us one way or the other. I enjoyed PBS that fall and winter. I watched a rebroadcast of the excellent, but depressing, 26-episode series on World War Two, *The World at War*, narrated by Laurence Olivier.

I don't recall watching much in the way of news in 1981, but Northern Ireland was a hot spot that year, again. In and around Belfast, Bernadette Devlin was shot and wounded, Bobby Sands died on a hunger strike, and the first DeLorean car rolled off the assembly line in a plant built with one door opening onto a Protestant neighbourhood and one onto a Catholic, a coincidence they said. There were race riots in Brixton, and 700 million people watched the wedding of Prince Charles and Lady Diana Spencer on television. Belize gained independence from Britain, and South Africa invaded Angola. Sandra Day O'Connor became the first woman to sit on the Supreme Court of the United States. Madame Mao, the leader of the Gang of Four and a major influence in the Great Proletarian Cultural Revolution, which paralyzed the country for ten years, was sentenced to death in China. She committed suicide in 1991. Israel bombed and destroyed a nuclear reactor in Iraq. Anwar Sadat was assassinated, and Hosni Mubarak became president of Egypt for the next thirty years until he was deposed in the 2011 Egyptian Revolution, part of the Arab Spring. He was sentenced to life in prison for corruption and abuse of power. Poland declared martial law in a long, failed effort to stop the Solidarity Trade Union. The first space shuttle, *Columbia*, was launched in April, and the first IBM Personal Computer, running PC DOS 1.0, was introduced in August. Six children in Yugoslavia claimed to see a vision of the Virgin Mary at Medjugorje, the video game Donkey Kong was released, and MTV began broadcasting from New York City. Muhammad Ali fought his last fight, in the Bahamas. But all I remember about 1981 is that assassination attempts were made on Ronald Reagan and John Paul II in the spring, only six weeks apart, resulting in serious injuries for both of them. I had no love for either of these old white men, but I was saddened nonetheless. I read now that it is impossible to overestimate their contribution to the fall of communism. The pope openly roused the Polish people, and the president secretly funded the Solidarity Movement. The irony could not have been lost on Reagan. He saw his greatest wish achieved, the defeat of communism, by using US tax dollars to fund a union.

My thoughts grew darker every week, and I didn't know how much more I could take. Most days I would rather have ridden my motorbike into a retaining wall than go to another class. By Reading Week in February, I was in a low state of mind. On the last day of school before the holiday, a Friday, I recruited three or four students to come sailing with me on Monday. It was slightly mad. No one sails in February. I said, first as a joke, "Rain or snow, people! See you at the dock at one o'clock sharp. Bring ten dollars. You *cannot* dress too warmly." To my surprise they all showed up. Rod was a married student, with children, and he had the downbeaten demeanour to prove it. He was trying to maintain a family and improve his life by going back to school. I was miserable, but he was perpetually exhausted. I couldn't imagine the stress he was under. And there he was, ready to try sailing for the first time in his life. At my hands. Foolish man.

The strait was in gale or near-gale conditions, 30 to 40-mile-an-hour winds, heaping seas, whitecaps, moderately high waves with breaking crests. And it was snowing! No joke. I'm surprised the sailing school allowed us to take the *Tiercel* out, but out we went, and the strong wind was exhilarating after a summer of very gentle air. These conditions demanded everyone's constant attention and fully-engaged participation in managing the boat, and we shot back and forth across the water for two hours in the

24-foot C&C, with no jib and the mainsail double-reefed, no more than a handkerchief to the wind, all of us wearing every piece of winter clothing we owned. It was delicious madness.

Under my able instruction Rod took the tiller for the first time while the rest of us crouched in the cockpit out of the gale. He faced into the wind and snow with a smile plastered on his face until his hair and beard were completely iced over. I had never seen him happier. We tacked for the safety of sheltered water off Albert Head and hove to for half an hour to recover and then went out again. After four astonishing hours in the storm, we surfed an eight-foot-high standing wave all the way back to the harbour until we were past the breakwater. It was the best day I had ever had on the water, and it was mid-winter! It was the purely elemental, thought-free, faux-survival experience we were all badly in need of, something to take us away from the drudgery of non-stop deskwork and the endless linear thinking involved in memorizing the details of introductory science. That day alone may have saved my life that semester.

Graham had started discussions with the chemistry department at UVic, and there was now a plan in place to allow students leaving Camosun College in April, with the intention of transferring to the university in the fall, to start directly in May in the UVic chemistry co-op program. This would give the students a summer semester of credited chemistry employment before starting classes. I fell into this category, and I was allowed to submit a resume and go to co-op interviews at UVic with an eye to finding employment for the summer. My resume was eclectic, and not in an impressive way, but the coordinator plugged me into some of the lower-level job interviews.

I dragged myself up to the university campus in the rain, in a suit and tie, five or six times and interviewed for summer jobs that I didn't want, all of them involving exposure to horrible chemicals on a daily basis. One interviewer asked me if I thought I could handle spending every day in a very noisy room testing gasolines on unmuffled, constantly running V-8 engines. "It's a horrible job," he said. One petroleum engineer from Calgary wanted to know if I would be opposed to spending a hundred days setting up an experiment at a research centre affiliated with the University of Calgary, something to do with oil and rock, and one day blowing it up. When I asked him what the salary was, he said he was not allowed to discuss it. How was I supposed to plan a summer not knowing how much money I would have? Another wanted to know if I would be comfortable eight hours a day head-to-toe in a mask and cleanroom apparel in a pathogen lab at the BC Cancer Agency or at the Institute of Ocean Sciences. One exhausted looking woman only wanted to talk about my travels to Asia, obviously envious. Behind a face that was prematurely old and worn with care, she gushed, "Tell me about Bangkok!" For at least one of these interviews I was drunk at eight o'clock in the morning, still up from the night before.

I liked the names of some of these employers. They would look good on my resume, but they all paid just over half of what I had made as a waiter the previous summer. If I took a chemistry co-op job outside Victoria, I would incur moving and storage expenses and return in four months' time with nowhere to live and not a penny of savings. It was absurd and perversely counterproductive. I literally could not afford to take a career-oriented job. I would be better off financially staying in Victoria and working in a restaurant again, although I couldn't imagine another summer of American tourists.

Eventually, I received an offer to work at an oil refinery fifty miles outside Prince George, the Northern Capital of BC. The city is actually in the centre of the province, but that still meant the refinery was fifty miles from nowhere. I had worked in a sawmill outside Prince George ten years earlier. I had no desire to see the area again. A few days later, in the Victoria *Times-Colonist* newspaper, there was a photograph of a street scene taken in Prince George. The snow almost buried the Stop signs. In Victoria, apple and cherry blossoms were dusting the street.

One day near the end of the semester, Howard wandered over to where I was working, with a blank application form in his hand. He said, "Neil, I was going to nominate you for the Governor General's Academic Medal, but when I got to the part about your history of community service, I didn't know what to write." I laughed. "Yeah, it's hard to volunteer for the Suicide Hot Line when you're the one who's always on the other end of the phone."

Classes finally ended. In twelve weeks I had been to a hundred and eighty lectures and performed more than forty lab experiments and written the same number of lab reports. I was utterly sick of it. The weather had finally broken, and it was warm and sunny just in time to be sequestered for preparations for my five final exams. I went to the bar one afternoon and met several of my old friends and acquaintances from Bartholomew's restaurant. While sitting on the arm of a comfortable leather couch in a downtown oyster bar, I realized I would have to spend the next three weeks studying, six to eight hours a day, or the work of the last twelve weeks would be in vain. There was no point in going to school and not getting A's. I wanted to drink with my friends but I couldn't. I had to go home and study. I envied them their carefree lifestyles, concerned only about which shift they were working next and counting their tips. They were content to work in the hospitality industry and were untroubled by delusions of improvement. I went to school for many more years, off and on, and wrote five or six hundred quizzes, tests, midterms, and final exams. It was astonishing to me that there were people in the world who never wrote another exam in their lives after leaving high school. It seemed that writing exams was all I did, and all I knew how to do.

I thought I had better quit drinking. So I did. For another three years.

I gave myself over to a steady review of the work of the previous four months, and when I was finished writing my finals I had a GPA of 4.0, a transcript of twenty courses and twenty A's, all but one of them sciences. I was one course short of earning Camosun College's newly instituted Diploma in Arts and Sciences (Chemistry), and I went to the administration office to provide a little feedback, to complain, that my failure to qualify had been through no fault of my own. There had been scheduling problems. The right classes had not been offered at the right time. How could they offer a diploma and not provide the classes necessary to earn it in a timely fashion? The sweet, middle-aged woman I was talking to indicated with a little smile that I should wait just a moment. When she returned, she had a blank diploma in her hand. She wrote my name on it, signed it, smiled again, and handed it to me. I misplaced it long ago, so I can't check the signature, but it might have been (Mrs.) Kay Kelly. And thus I graduated from Camosun College. It wasn't Harvard.

I walked down the long, straight pathway in front of the Young Building on a beautiful, sunny day in April. I turned around to look at the campus buildings. Then, I walked away for the last time.

I was sick to death of school. The thought of working in a remote oil refinery doing bucket chemistry for the summer, for pauper's wages, and going back in the fall to another gruelling year of non-stop study and poverty was utterly repugnant to me. It made me ill. At Shea's apartment I found a book on her coffee table called *The Thorn Birds*. I read it in two sittings and after eight months of reading nothing but math, chemistry, and physics, thought it was best book ever written in the English language.

My mind was thrown back to halcyon days in California, the peace and joy, the contentment, of my blissful summer at Ananda Cooperative Village five years earlier. Prince George is five hundred miles north of Victoria. Sacramento is a thousand miles south. I made a new plan. I told Graham and the Co-op Coordinator at UVic I was resigning from the program and unlikely to return in the fall. They both expressed concern that I was going to California "to live with the Moonies." For good reason I suppose. A few weeks later, Reverend Sun Myung Moon, known for performing mass weddings, and for matching the couples himself, was sentenced to eighteen months in prison for tax fraud and conspiracy to obstruct justice. Another in a long line of egregious gurus.

With short notice I told Mr. Jones that I would be vacating the apartment. I knew a man who wanted it, and I asked Mr. Jones if he would consider returning my security deposit since I had saved him the trouble and expense of advertising for, and finding, a new tenant. Nor would there be any expense incurred by the owners for cleaning or repairs since my tenancy had been peaceful and without incident. Although I don't know how anyone could have failed to notice the constant cloud of marijuana smoke billowing out into the hallway, and I did throw my calculator at the wall one day, as hard as I could, when it stopped working during a marathon study session in physics. He summarily denied my request. I knew the house had been sold recently, and I telephoned the new owners and repeated my request. The young, sweet-natured wife of the couple who had bought the house came over to meet me and my proposed replacement. She looked at the apartment and agreed that, as a kindness to me for being a good tenant, there would be no problem returning my security deposit and allowing my friend to move in, in spite of the short notice. She and Mr. Jones were only newly acquainted. Sitting in my little suite, she whispered to me, "He's kind of a redneck, isn't he?" She confided in me that they couldn't afford to keep him on as manager, and in future they would be handling rentals and maintenance themselves. The next time I saw the small-minded, high-handed Mr. Jones, happily also the last, he gave me such a scowl.

I placed an ad in the newspaper to sell my motorbike, and the head driver at Greyhound agreed to my price. The night before I was to deliver it to him, I met Brian and his friend Bob for a drink at the Six Mile Pub in Colwood. I consumed no alcohol myself. Riding home in the rain, wouldn't you know it, it rained for my last ride, I was sitting at a red light at a black, deserted intersection in downtown Victoria at ten o'clock at night, when I noticed the headlights of a car behind me, to one side. The car then changed lanes and was now a few yards directly behind me. I remember thinking, "I hope this guy doesn't crash into me. Wouldn't that be stupid," and a few seconds later the car crashed into me. We were the only vehicles at the intersection. It was the only motorcycle accident I was ever in, and it was one hundred per cent not my fault. The driver of the car was a drunk Asian woman. She hit me just hard enough to knock me off the bike, which then fell on my leg, which was quite painful. She was young and pretty, and when the cop showed up, in short order, she told him, all of us sitting in his cruiser out of the rain, that her shoe was wet and her foot had slipped off the brake. She told him she had been drinking, and I felt quite strongly he should give her a breathalyser test, but as I mentioned she was young and pretty, and was a government employee, and the policeman didn't think it was necessary to cause her any embarrassment or legal upset just because she had knocked a student off a motorcycle. The pain in my knee disagreed.

The motorbike was towed to the shop where I had bought it, only a block away, and the cop gave me a ride home. The cute Asian paid for the repair of my broken turn signal and a bent shifter. When I went to her office to pick up the cheque, I told her she was very lucky she hadn't been found impaired. Fortunately, the Greyhound driver was satisfied with the repairs, and he bought the bike in spite of the mishap.

I limped for the next two months. I had no desire to pursue the tipsy bureaucrat, or the provincial insurance corporation, for compensation for a painful knee, the same one I was always bashing and tearing, although it hurt like hell for far too long this time.

I was leaving in only another two days, and I had no idea when I was coming back, or what I would do when I did.

8 The Thought Sickens

Shea had moved to Calgary to find work, and she had a storage locker in Victoria where I threw a few boxes and then limped onto a plane for Sacramento. There, in the waiting room at the bus depot, looking for the Greyhound that would take me to Grass Valley, in the foothills of the Sierra Nevadas, I saw a young man studying a copy of Morrison-Boyd, the thick, standard text for introductory organic chemistry. I said, "Hey, how's it going?" I nodded solemnly at his book and added, "I just spent a year with Morrison-Boyd." Without further speech we exchanged a knowing look, like veterans of foreign wars, whole on the outside maybe, but with a shared inner derangement few others would understand.

I planned to stay at the retreat at Ananda as a working volunteer for two months, all I could afford. I was desperate to meditate and practise yoga, sober and uninterrupted, hoping to recover from my thoroughly dismal winter, looking for some clarity and peace of mind, a level ground of relief from which to contemplate the future.

My injured knee was a problem. I was physically handicapped and of little use for a couple of weeks. The staff at the retreat were somewhat understanding. They gave me a couple of days' grace, in addition to the week of free classes I was entitled to, before starting my volunteer duties. I spent five full days and evenings with the current cohort of nine or ten new students who had just arrived to begin a six-week course in yoga teacher training. This gave me time to stretch and heal and get to know the people who would be resident at the retreat during my time there.

I was soon dazzling my new friends with specious little lectures on the mysterious aspects of quantum physics, the contradictions of nature beneath the animate and the inanimate. I had studied some of the terminology, and by using it in support of my own notions and experiences, I believed, lightly, if not rightly, that I was actually saying something, if not actually understanding it. I had been told all my life that I was marvellously bright, and as soon as I learned anything I became immediately didactic. Besides, even though I knew little about the subject, I knew more than they did, and I wanted to let them know that science, although it understands little of awareness, was on their side. I knew some people at Ananda struggled with belief. I never did, and I wanted to show them that there is a belief that arises from, and is the partner of, knowledge.

It wasn't long before I realized Ananda had changed in the last five years, a lot. The swami had exhibited some disturbing behaviours of late, and several people had left the community. Many of the early followers had also left to start a new sister community on the coast of California, preferring the deeply-felt, shared experiences of the conceptually simpler and more intense process of founding, as opposed to maintaining, an intentional spiritual community. I noticed right away that some of those who had remained, and some who had joined Ananda since I was last here, had a smug and self-satisfied air, a pride of achievement and belonging they may or may not have deserved. The people I had known in 1977 were uniformly warm and loving, even-keeled, and obviously sincere. Now that the early difficult days were over, many of them were gone and Ananda seemed to be attracting kooks, the wild and woolly that Sister Margaret had warned me about at the Dharma Centre. The very smug leader of the teacher training program said, "Ananda attracts all kinds of people, and the good ones stay."

There were other opinions. I was assigned a counsellor, and we met informally two or three times while I was there. I think his job was simply to make sure none of the volunteers was completely mad. He was a genial, sincere young man with a degree in religious studies from a Midwestern university. I told him of my concerns about the changes in the community since I had last been here, and he said, in a humorous and refreshing parallel to the patronizing opinion of the smarmy head teacher, "Yes, it seems Ananda does attract a lot of weirdoes. And they're the ones who stay!"

In short order some of the senior members of the retreat staff were giving me sour looks. I believe my error was not showing sufficient admiration for the hierarchy. Although comments and reviews occasionally came down in my favour. One man I scarcely knew from my previous time at Ananda was delighted to see me again, and without knowing anything about my life of the last five years, he told me I was an example of the teachings successfully at work. I said, "Obviously looks can be deceiving!"

I was brooding, carefree, depressed, and relaxed all at the same time.

I saw Shivani again, the intense madwoman of Ananda's gardens, circa 1977, and now found her, from mere observation, she didn't recognize me and we didn't talk, in an inspiring state of calm, teaching and lecturing, although there was also a withdrawn, robotic air about her words and movements. It seemed as if Ananda now felt itself to be the elder statesman of the yoga community movement, a rare survivor, and its dicta and maxims were not to be questioned. But over the next twenty years, there would be many questions, accusations, and judgments by its own residents, by the yoga-practising public, as well as by local governments, and the courts. Behaviour at Ananda was starting to go badly awry, and it was poised for a tremendous comedown.

The Swami was in residence. This was new. I had been here twice before and had never laid eyes on hisse'f. There would be an opportunity to hear him speak at Sunday services and at one-off afternoon teas open to the public.

Swami Kriyananda was now fifty-six years old and had enjoyed the adulation of his followers since the late 1960s, particularly the unconditional support and protection of a small core of people dedicated to his, and the community's, success. His ejection from SRF in the early 1960s had never been discussed by either party. The reasons eventually given by SRF were straightforward and severe, "desire for personal power, ulterior motives in his service, and setting himself up as the new guru," attempting to establish a cult of personality. Swami now issued a short tract discussing the reasons for his expulsion and copies were available, free of charge, at the retreat office. I dutifully read the case he put forward and was unable to decide who was right and who was wrong. I was not a witness to the events that led up to his expulsion, there was no evidence before me other than testimony, and I was no judge of character. Most days I would rather just go for a walk than try to figure out why people do what they do. Everyone has their reasons.

There was another tract available in the retreat office in the form of a letter from Swami to the community informing the members of his marriage to Woman #7, or an explanation as to why the marriage had failed so quickly and so suddenly. I never knew her name. She is identified as Woman #7, or maybe it was Woman #3, it's hard to keep track, in the hundreds of pages of depositions and declarations filed in the 1994 sexual misconduct lawsuit brought against the swami.

Kriyananda married? This was a bombshell. Kriyananda had thrown himself at Yogananda's feet in 1948 and taken the final vows of *sannyas* in 1955. He was an avowed monk. His marriage was impossible to explain or justify. He wrote, "What then of my monastic vows? I feel that in a very real sense, I have completed them." He said he and his new "spiritual wife" were soul mates and had known each other in many past lives. She was less than half his age. I had a sinking feeling that Kriyananda and the community were slipping off the rails.

His wife fled the community only a few weeks after she arrived, only weeks before I arrived for my visit in 1982. I asked a member why she had left so suddenly. His response was that Swami had placed her too high, too fast, in a position as Mother of the Community, and that it was too much for her to handle. She was twenty-five. Years later she testified, "He claimed that we recited holy vows of marriage [after reading poems to each other on the beach at Half Moon Bay, California]. He said this to the community at a community meeting. I was shocked! I never agreed to marry him! I wasn't legally divorced from my husband, there was no wedding, no witnesses, no legal papers signed, no blood test, no invitation, no reception, nothing! This was said without my consent. This man was thirty years older than me. He was old enough to be my grandfather, and I did not want him to be a stepfather to my child! [She was pregnant. The father was her first husband.] He thought children were a nuisance anyway."

Something was definitely rotten in both the state of Denmark and the World Brotherhood Colony of Ananda Cooperative Village.

In later legal proceedings in the nineties, Swami Kriyananda was described by an expert witness as falling "clearly within the profile of a clergy sex offender on the most destructive, predatory end of that spectrum, a multiple repeat offender who deliberately seeks vulnerable women." Several women made legal declarations claiming to have been manipulated, under the guise of spiritual counselling, into dozens or hundreds of situations involving indecent exposure, erotic massage, sexual intercourse, even "sexual slavery." These events took place repeatedly over a period of many years. Eventually, Kriyananda admitted to having sexual relations with more than a dozen women at Ananda, but he claimed to be the victim, not the perpetrator, an innocent prey to their aggressive and misguided desires to be at one with the guru, saying the sex was initiated by the women hoping to gain spiritual or organizational advancement. The expert witness disagreed, as did the jury, pointing out that there was strong evidence that Kriyananda requested the sexual activity himself, and that he framed it in terms of being a privilege and a sacred service, justifying it in spiritual language using his ministerial authority. He responded to objections and confrontations from the women by blaming them for seduction and consent. He threatened them with ostracism and ejection from the community, and therefore loss of employment, along with public shaming and the stigma of failure as spiritual disciples.

He was found liable, in 1998, of "constructive fraud," "intentional infliction of emotional distress," "malice and fraudulent conduct," and "despicable conduct." In short, sexual exploitation over a period of thirty years by the father figure of a church-family-community, a father engaged in persistent, predatory, incestuous abuse. The court awarded the plaintiff over $600,000 in compensatory damages and one million dollars in punitive damages. Punitive, or exemplary, damages are awarded "to serve as a warning to others that certain conduct will not be condoned." They are typically awarded in lawsuits where a defendant has acted in a willful, intentionally malicious way. From the verdict: "During the three and a half years of this lawsuit and continuing to date, Ananda vilifies anyone who dares to speak out, condemning them as 'negative', 'liars', 'embodiments of evil' or in league with dark secret conspiracies. Kriyananda and Ananda leaders have consistently refused to accept any responsibility or accountability for their actions."

Ananda also agreed to pay an additional $200,000 to settle two other lawsuits. In one of these lawsuits, Ananda admitted hiring someone, and paying them with church tax-exempt money, for the theft of trash from the plaintiff's lawyers' office, searching, obviously, for privileged client-attorney information. Ananda sought to avoid payment of the awards by declaring bankruptcy, and Swami moved to Italy and then to India.

Unknown to me some of the worst sexual misconduct was taking place while I was at Ananda in 1982. Thirty years later, the swami still has dozens or hundreds of apologists and staunch defenders including deniers, rationalisers, and the intractably angry. Some of them believe that all of his accusers lied. Some accept that there were unfortunate incidents, but the swami was the victim, not the perpetrator. Others say it wouldn't matter if he had sex with a hundred women, or a thousand. The teachings are not invalidated or weakened by the human failings of the teacher.

The separation of church and sex is arbitrary and conditioned by culture. Monks marry in other religions. Some priests marry. What's the problem? Why begrudge your guru the little bit of sex he or she gets? A lot of people, myself included, like both sex and yoga. Why can't you have both? Even at the same time? Why couldn't you have all the sex in the world and still meditate? Meditation is just meditation. Sex is just sex. There's no compelling reason why sex should be forbidden to religious teachers and gurus. If, however, Swami Kriyananda had a "problem" with sex, as many people in the community knew, and as was stated many times, he could have renounced his vows and married. I suspect he did not want to become a householder because it would diminish his own sense of specialness and his place in the community as a high and revered practitioner of yoga. And he didn't like children.

But it's not the sex, it's the predation, the conspiracy, the abuse of power, the lies, the cover-up, the denial, the remorselessness, and the hypocrisy. Jesus forgave every kind of sinner and ate with tax collectors and prostitutes, but even the Model of Forgiveness had no use for a hypocrite. By just about any standard, Kriyananda turned out to be a narcissistic Fully Enlightened Bastard. Many wear the Robe but few keep the Way.

Some members of the community who remained adopted the swami's inventive approach to monasticism, and there had been other unexpected marriages. Prakash, the leader of the volunteer program in the seventies, a man I truly admired, had ceased to be a monk and had recently taken a wife, but was already divorced. This was almost more astonishing to me than the swami's change of heart. When I ran into a woman I had worked with in the retreat kitchen five years earlier, a young, pretty Englishwoman, she told me she had been working "very closely with Swami." She followed this with "very, very closely." And then she said it again very, very slowly. Her meaning was so theatrically obvious I laughed out loud. "You make it sound sinful," I said. I had no idea how right I was.

It wasn't until 2002, surfing the Internet at work one day, that I became aware of the charges against the swami and the verdicts of sexual misconduct, and at the same time, the shameful squandering of millions of dollars in the nineties, on both sides, in Ananda's multi-year legal battles with SRF over copyright issues. The devil take them both. I was once again in a rather poor frame of mind after many years of marriage to a difficult woman and many years in a largely meaningless, occasionally unethical, government job. I was saddened to hear of these egregious behaviours although I suppose I shouldn't have been surprised. Recently, in a moment of lurid and voyeuristic weakness, I attempted to read the six hundred and thirty-three pages of Swami's depositions concerning the charges of sexual exploitation. Unfortunately, half of it consists of lawyers sniping at each other, every third line an objection by Kriyananda's lawyer, and I was unable to stomach it.

In 1982, besides Swami's marriage and the obvious change in atmosphere at Ananda, there were two other things I became aware of. One was that Swami had recently gone through an intensification of his survivalist writings and preaching in preparation for Armageddon. One day, for some reason, as part of my duties, I had cause to venture under the bunkhouse I was staying in, and I discovered, in the crawl space, a small cache of food and supplies. I asked someone about it. They responded casually, "Oh, yeah, for a while Swami was talking about the need to prepare for a coming disaster of social breakdown and chaos, and we should be ready to survive on our own for many years. We started stockpiling food and equipment, but eventually everyone just lost interest. It was kind of weird."

Narcissism usually involves a behavioural style of specialness, and the consequences of feeling special can evolve into a battle against the evils of the world. What we see and love in others is ourselves, and when we begin to hate others what we are looking at is a mirror. The projection of what we hate about ourselves, the darker aspects of the personality, onto another person or onto the community, or the community onto the world, creates enemies. We don't see things as they are, we see them as we are. Ananda, promoting yoga, meditation, self-realization, virtue, restraint, and selfless service to the world, saw its own shadow-self, its own faults and failings, in the outside world, threatening and dangerous. Where there is a bright spirit there is the risk of a dark spectre. Ananda could easily have retreated and regressed into a very dangerous self-obsessed paranoia, the dark side of any organization, spiritual or not, that purports to enjoy a superior lifestyle, where money and power are concentrated in a small hierarchy, where the people at the top are more equal than the people to whom they should be accountable. Fortunately, not even Kriyananda could convince his followers the bogeyman was coming to get them. His program of Apocalyptic preparedness was shrugged off and forgotten. This is no small testament to the remaining good sense of the residents. The community leadership was already secretive and manipulative, engaged in lewd and harassing behaviours, mischief and villainy. It was just as well they didn't slip into a culture of violent survivalism on top of that. The mass suicides and murders at Jonestown in the same era had had a cooling effect on these hyper-defensive enthusiasms.

I learned also that there had recently been a long and expensive attempt to incorporate Ananda as a town in Nevada County. There are only three towns in Nevada County, and if successful in its bid Ananda would have become the fourth largest, with all the legal, financial, and political ramifications that would entail. They attempted to convince the County Board of Supervisors that Ananda was a democratic institution, a laughable misrepresentation. Ananda was obviously a theocracy where Kriyananda or his representatives made all the decisions. Kriyananda persisted in this charade, encouraging his followers to come out in force to ongoing meetings chanting, "Where there is righteousness, there is victory!" The supervisors saw through this ridiculous pretence and ruled against Ananda's request as a clear violation of the separation of church and state. The affair caused tension and bitterness in the county, and there had been physical attacks on the community, vandalism and threats. Ananda had challenged its redneck neighbours and lost. They were losing friends fast.

One other very troublesome concern for me was the pointy end of the overall weirdness that had overcome Ananda. There were a few recent, and slightly older, members who had quickly found high positions, or status, in the community, and they enjoyed the open admiration of many of the newer and younger members. Five years earlier, it seemed to me the focus at Ananda had been on Paramahansa Yogananda, the community, and the practice of yoga and meditation. There were no outlandish or nefarious goals. Now too many eyes and minds were turned to the question of who had power and prestige in the community and who was close to Swami, who was in his inner circle.

One evening, the retreat guests were invited to observe, or participate in, a ceremony in the Temple Dome, its blue carpet now much the worse for wear. It was something I had never heard of. I had an academic, devotional, and experiential interest in religious ritual, and I arrived on time expecting to see a yoga, or Hindu-based, service of some kind. I was the only guest who showed up.

There were just a few people in the temple, two of the older male members, community rock stars, and three or four adoring younger people. The ceremony turned out to be a show of ridiculous charlatanism, nothing to do with traditional yoga teaching. I was appalled and speechless, but I stayed until the end. In a small circle, while the younger people gazed on in rapt attention, the two older men, one a physician, one resembling a soap opera star, engaged in an exchange worthy of, no better than, a circus sideshow fortune teller or a murder mystery séance. There was a lot of pointing of crystals and throwing of energy and deep twitching and convulsing. I may as well have been at a Pentecostal or Charismatic orgy of glossolalia, speaking in tongues, or in this case, grunts. I couldn't believe such foolishness was sanctioned by the swami or his senior teachers, and I had never seen anything like it before at Ananda. I could only conclude that I knew as much about God, and the world, as these bilkers. When the other guests asked me about it the next day, I couldn't stand to talk about it. "All I can say is that at no point during the evening did I have any understanding or appreciation for what was taking place." This was as charitable as I could be. Ananda had taken a serious turn to the bogus, the pompous and theatrical.

I spent my two months at Ananda in 1982 in a state of dismay and gently expressed skepticism following, occasionally, in the newspaper, the depressing events of the Falklands War. I had little fellow feeling for any of the retreat guests, little kinship. Some of them were repugnantly immature, and apart from my personal counsellor there were no obvious reasons to look up to any of the retreat staff. My knee stopped hurting so much, and I was walking better, but carefully. I spent my time sweeping and cleaning, digging, swinging an axe, chopping wood, working a few days in the kitchen. I was generally productive in my duties but not always enthusiastic.

I skipped out on work one day to go to town, for a semi-legitimate reason, and was busted on the street in Nevada City by a retreat manager who was also in town that day. We had had a civil relationship so far, and when I apologized for neglecting my retreat duties, I fully expected to be forgiven for playing hooky. After all, he was too. It wasn't that important. I was much taken aback, then, when he said, "I wouldn't mind at all if I didn't dislike you so much personally." I was not cut to the quick by his low scowl, but I was a little hurt and confused by his animosity. I had done nothing to him. And what a thing to say! A manager of a spiritual retreat! I couldn't help mentioning it to one of the other guests, an older simpatico woman from Vermont named Priscilla. She said, "Well, it's not hard to see where that is coming from." I wasn't sure what she meant. She continued. "You have many blessings. You're young and good-looking. You have a good sense of humour and a good sense of a balanced life. You know how to work and how to rest. I think we can safely chalk his anger up to jealousy." I was surprised to hear her say these things and was glad to know that someone thought I was alive and well inside.

The unfriendly manager was quite funny, though. He told us the story of how he had come to Ananda. He had been devoutly resident at Swami

Muktananda's ashram, somewhere in California, but had started to think he might be more in tune with Yogananda's teachings at Ananda Cooperative Village. He made the decision to change gurus and homes, but he agonized long and hard before making the move and joining the retreat staff at Ananda. His last hurdle and his last argument to himself against severing ties with his old community was that he couldn't leave because he had many important ashram duties left to perform. He couldn't abandon his friends, his spiritual brothers and sisters, not when there was still so much work to be done, so much unfinished. He closed his story by saying, "And then I remembered I was the ashram's garbage man."

Swami spoke at a Sunday service at the new temple at the farm, built over the exact spot at the top of the hill where I had erected my tipi five years earlier. I don't remember the subject. It was diffuse. He sidetracked further into a short lecture on English grammar and then commented in a smarmy way that you never knew what you were going to hear at one of his talks. This made his devotees nod and laugh warmly, but I knew for a certainty that his knowledge of grammar was misinformed, completely wrong, unimportant but off-putting to me, a lifelong lover of language. This old guru-fraud, the writer, "all I know how to do is write," couldn't even get a minor point of grammar correct. His trifling mistake, however, was suggestive of a larger problem. I have nothing against using reflection and intuition as a means of establishing perspective. Knowledge without reflection is not knowledge, it's just information, but when you get most of your store of knowledge from intuition, as opposed to actual learning, without any specific concentration of mental effort, it is tempting to picture yourself as more knowing than others. If you see beyond the facts, it is unnecessary to be familiar with them. We all live in some fear that someone knows something we don't, and most of us will sit up and listen if we are told that we, too, can possess knowledge without toil. This is handy for gurus. If you save people the trouble of thinking, you can do anything with them. If you decide to give preference to intuition, rather than learning, you need to prepare yourself to be wrong, occasionally, in matters of fact.

One Sunday, the retreat guests were invited to Swami's dome-house, far back in the hills, a place I been before as an apprentice in 1977. It was deserted on my last visit, but it was now full with fifty or more people crowded together on the floor. Ananda was attempting to mend fences and regain friends outside the community by offering free, informal dialogues with the swami. I found a spot just to the left of Swami's chair and a little behind. From that vantage I was able to observe him closely, but he never saw me. The crowd was undemanding. He was challenged once or twice by non-members voicing small objections and criticisms, thrusts easily parried. Tea was served afterwards. And it was then that I uttered the only words I ever spoke to Swami Kriyananda. Standing with him in a small circle after his talk, I said that this was the third time I had been at Ananda and the first time I had found him at home. He chuckled. "Yes, I am often away." Driving away from Swami's dome, one of the retreat guests, an older woman from Australia, a woman of constant complaint, said teasingly, "Ooh, I liked Swamiji, quite dishy. I could see taking that on." My head drooped in profound disappointment as we jostled in the crowded car along the hot, dry, bumpy road back to the retreat.

My experience at Ananda in the summer of 1977 had been the most blissful of my life. Working at the kibbutz in Israel was a close second. Besides the clear skies and hot weather, the wonderful people and California New Age culture, the appeal for me had been that I was in a peaceful place where spiritual techniques were practised in the community. And practice is perfection. It was a home, a job, a church, and a community all in one, and the residents showed many signs of benefit from their efforts. It seemed clear to me that the likelihood of living a meaningful life was greater where a sensible and wholesome psycho-physical religious practice was routine, focussed, and integrated into daily life.

Now, in 1982, I saw the semblance of sense at Ananda slipping away. Everyone was so obviously *not* enlightened that the notion of anyone finding it there disappeared from my field of view forever. I had become a little frightened of the place. Before my two months were up, I realized there was no point in staying any longer. I informed the retreat staff that I would be leaving a week early. As an easy excuse I told them I had to get back to Canada to see a doctor about my knee. Free health insurance.

Given my generally rebellious feelings about obedience, and my distasteful experiences with corrupt hierarchies in schools, jobs, and governments, it is not surprising that I had no more respect for these features in a religious organization, indeed less. Because of an ingrained and intractable abhorrence of authority, I was never in danger of irretrievable indoctrination into a cult, destructive or otherwise. I knew there was liberation in surrender, but I also knew that you never give up your right to make your own decisions, and that surrender is not helplessness. And I was too lazy anyway, so lazy I couldn't even get into a cult. I loved the meditation and the easygoing lifestyle, but too much of being a back-to-the-land hippie was just manual labour, bad weather, dirty feet, and body odour.

I was at little risk of success or failure in my half-assed searches over the years, in churches and ashrams, with gurus and cults. My searches outside myself were always destined to be of an unconvinced nature because I knew from the beginning that the goal, the treasure, was not outside, but inside. Although I would not have articulated it in quite the same way, I knew even then, from both science and religion, that all objects exist in a transitional state of infinite causation and infinite interconnection. Therefore, no single object has an identifiable self-cause or a separable self-substance. We always fancy ourselves, and every field of human endeavour, to be finished and complete in this moment, but a single object is an illusion. No atom is ever knowable in a static state. A group of objects is a constantly changing, temporary system, congealed briefly into a myth. At what fixed point in time is a tree a tree? At what point am I me? "The magisterial and the masterpieces of the Creator, the flowers of Creation, are the best part of nothing actually existing."

In 1982, I knew all this to be true, but it wasn't woven into the fabric of my being. It wasn't marrow in my bones. I had been an outsider for many years. I always pointed and shrieked when I saw bullshit. Still, I wanted and needed to belong to something. Being perpetually unconvinced, I was safe from all cults, but that only meant I still had a desire for convincing. There was, at my core, a craving for reassurance. There was a vacuum, and there was yearning.

I began to realize with sadness that I was leaving Ananda for the last time, saying good-bye to the gentle pace, to the people, the quiet and the peace of the bright blue sky, the Ponderosa pines, the red dust, the fresh, dry air of the Sierra Nevada chaparral, the big grey squirrels, the big raccoons, the deer, the manzanita, the coffeeberry honey, and the tumbling waters of the South Fork of the Yuba River.

The day I left the retreat, I was at the farm waiting for a ride into town. One of the retreat staff, an attractive woman, slightly older than I, slightly taller, a woman of style and peaceful demeanor, just a little mannered, asked me if I had enjoyed my stay. She was expecting to hear only compliments, but I said, "To be honest, not really. I find the community much changed since my last visit." To my great surprise she roared, leapt on me, and threw me into a headlock for a moment, a violent response, decidedly unyogic. When the dust settled and she pulled herself together, she said,

"Well, take care of that knee." She was embarrassed by her outburst, and rightly so.

I was stunned by this awkward incident, and I brushed myself clean searching for a response. "Right. Thank you. Well, you know, I'm actually more concerned that I have recently started bleeding from the anus." In my final week or two at Ananda, I had become aware that there was definitely something wrong south of the Mason-Dixon.

Finally, speaking of assholes, and to put the matter to rest, James Donald Walters, a.k.a. Swami Kriyananda, died in April 2013 at the age of eighty-six, still seeking justification, still childish and whining, a tawdry, despairing offender, petulant to the end, still publishing hundreds of pages of arguments on the Internet, refuting every utterance ever made against him, deny, deny, deny. If he had accepted any responsibility and made any apology, it would have gone a long way towards redemption, but when you are infallible, you never have to apologize. I don't mind people who never explain as long as they don't complain. He was a man despicable to every reasonable and moral being, to all the world, to all but a handful of crackpot devotees blind to the heinousness of his crimes, a disgrace to himself and his family, to the guru and the religious organization he claimed to love, and to the movement and the communities he founded. If Yogananda was waiting for him on the other side when he died, the swami had some explaining to do. And for the first time, I am concerned about reincarnation. Let the swami squirm awhile on the Devil's lap before he comes back to trouble the world again.

He wrote fifty books, none of them very good, the ones I read, but some of them were translated into twenty-eight languages, and they have sold three million copies in ninety countries. He also composed four hundred pieces of music, produced six films, and took 15,000 art photographs. He lectured around the world. He founded schools, temples, and communities. To this day he has thousands of followers.

Kriyananda's decades-long, controlling, condescending, and abusive attitude towards women has at least one obvious source. In 1962, he was fired from SRF as vice-president by an all-female board. He was surely in line for the president's chair. This would have been hard for a man to swallow at that time, or any time, especially in religion, not the most tolerant of businesses, and typically male-dominated.

Did he do more harm than good or more good than harm? Why did he make it necessary for anyone to have to ask the question? Why did he do harm at all?

In 1994, Swami's spiritual wife, his soul mate, stated in her legal declaration that she only had sex with him once. When he raped her.

What do you do with a kind and gentle man who devotes his life to the realization of idealistic practice, to writing and teaching, helping thousands of people, most of them strangers, one who then also cruelly and heartlessly hurts, in the most intimate way, a dozen other people, maliciously and fraudulently, women who have placed themselves wholly and trustingly in his service?

You put him in jail.

9   Washing the Pot

I was light of heart riding the bus for the three-hour journey from Nevada City to San Francisco. I started telling my beads almost immediately, *japa* yoga, *Aum Namah Shivaya*, the Indian version of the western rosary, and when I next opened my eyes I could see the magnificent view of the bay and the city skyline as we drove south past Berkeley. I spent a few nights on Michael's couch again in the Castro district. He still lived in the same big house on upper Market Street but had moved down the long flight of stairs from the third floor to the apartment on the second floor, which he was now sharing with his new girlfriend, Mia, and I believe, a Marxist lesbian. Maybe the Marxist lesbian had already moved out when Mia took up with the enemy.

It is always a small shock for a man to see his male friends newly adorned with female company. Although Michael was a good-looking man, men often see their bachelor friends as rather unattractive overall. We see them so often at their least appealing, and we are surprised to find that a woman might actually be interested in them. Who would kiss this man? And why?

But I was soon delighted with this new arrangement. Mia. What a woman. Taller than I, a feat not hard to accomplish, with very long dark hair, a narrow face and quick eyes, willowy and busty, a dancer with elegant arms and legs, always deliciously barefoot and braless. She worked at home transcribing taped court proceedings at lightning speed on an electric typewriter, a better option than having to put on pantyhose and take the streetcar downtown to work in a law office. Michael was a musician and worked odd hours. For them their three-bedroom apartment was a home and an office, a studio, a place where they spent nearly all their time. The noise from the traffic on Market Street, very steep just below Twin Peaks, was horrific in their living room at the front, but not bad towards the back of the in-line apartment, in the bedrooms and kitchen, and they lived in this tall, old, narrow, crumbling, rent-controlled character building for twenty-three years. The plumbing was so bad it took an hour to run a bath.

Mia was from New York and had only been in San Francisco for a year or two. She was thus still a New Yorker, articulate and whip smart, and she made fun of the laid-back California culture. You had to be on your toes around her. Like me, she loved language and I liked her, not from the first day, she was a New Yorker after all and took some getting used to, but from the second.

Larry and Cathy, Michael's former roommates upstairs, were avid sailors. I leapt at the chance for an afternoon sail when they asked me to join them on San Francisco Bay. It was a long drive to Richmond, the closest place they could afford to keep their 23-foot boat, and they didn't have a motor for it, so it took a little finessing to get it out into the air, but once we caught the wind we shot back and forth across the bay for hours. It was a Sunday and there were hundreds of pleasure craft on the water. Larry and Cathy handled the boat beautifully in all this traffic, and I sat back and enjoyed the ride. We passed a long yacht with fifty practically naked gay men sprawled about the deck, not a woman in sight. Hello, sailor! It's what you might expect in San Francisco. Two years later, Larry and Cathy were skippering yachts in the Caribbean for pay.

To our mutual surprise, I ran into Sarah on the street in San Francisco, along with her mother and young brother. She was one of the beautiful nineteen-year-olds from Camosun College who used to drive me crazy, especially in chemistry class in a light T-shirt and no bra. Besides that obvious attraction, I liked Sarah because she had a rough and tumble personality, and when she rejected me she chose from among her many suitors a quiet, gentle man I liked as well. We were both three years older now, and I had forgiven her for not being interested in me. We made a date to spend an afternoon together, which included standing in line for an hour to see *E.T. the Extra-Terrestrial*. "Ouch." It had opened only the day before in the old theatre on Van Ness Avenue, across from Tommy's Joynt. Afterwards, I walked Sarah back to the Jack Tar Hotel where she was staying. It was "the world's most modern hotel" when it opened in 1960.

My time at Ananda, so eye-opening and disappointing in so many ways, had nonetheless been a slow-growing success in the accumulation of ideas, my main reason for going there. I now had three or four ideas, which was three or four more than I had when I left Victoria.

By the time I bolted from Ananda at the end of June, I had come to at least four conclusions. First, it was unlikely I would ever set foot there again. They had given me the best summer of my life, in 1977, the "high and far off times…the days beyond compare," taught me some yoga, how to meditate, and some Indian philosophy, but I now felt that the best of Ananda was behind them and therefore behind me. I knew somehow there was nothing but strife in their future, well-deserved, as it turned out. They were on their own to twist themselves inside-out in their delusions until they were exhausted. As was I. I was done with the yogis of California. There had to be a connection closer to home.

Second, when it came to employment, I had several options, and they were all terrible, the same as having none. I began to think, slowly and carefully, with disbelief at first, and then with guarded enthusiasm, that Tokyo owed me a good time. I had no money to speak of. I wasn't sure how I would get back there, but I knew I could make money if I did. I wasn't committed to the project yet, but the idea persisted in the back of my mind and grew less foolish, less downright crazy, as the summer wore on. Third, there was no way in hell I was going back to school in September. I was sick of that foolishness.

My fourth conclusion was that if a channel was needed perhaps the form wasn't that important. In Victoria, I wondered again about the Catholics. They had *japa* yoga, the rosary, mantra meditation, mystical experiences, rites and rituals, miracles, and incense. They had saints and gurus, ascetics, hermits, and mendicants. They even had Jesus. How were they, including 2,000 years of the most horrifying political behaviour, different from any other religion? They had the juice, this much I knew, in their otherworldly traditions, in their spiritual theology, in the Desert Fathers, and the medieval mystics. They had *bhakti* yoga, devotion. Yogananda exalted the Divine Mother, the Catholics the Virgin Mary, the Mother of God. I understood these Catholic concepts and experiences from the point of view of a yogi. There seemed to be parallels between east and west at every significant point of inquiry. In western civilization the only wisdom ever produced was the contemplative tradition of early and medieval Christianity, and it meshed nicely with its counterparts from the east. Western art and culture, the scientific method, and representative democracy are all fine things, but they are not wisdom. Where were these east-west parallels to be best encountered and how best utilized? Where were they hiding this spiritual treasure? Where were the entry points to the modern church for an experienced adult? I wanted somewhere to meditate and someone to meditate with. Someone who knew what I was talking about when I talked about religious experience rather than, or in addition to, religious observance. And I didn't want to have to travel to California to get it. How would I find out if the Catholics had something usable for me if I never walked through the door?

I was looking for organizational universality and simplicity. If I was going to become a mystical Christian, then "one holy, Catholic and apostolic church" was what I wanted. The original would be fine. It couldn't be any worse than its progeny. The Protestant sects were too numerous to keep track of, too many crazy charisms, too many internal schisms. They were a jumpy bunch, quick to hive off at a moment's notice. The evangelicals and the bible thumpers were always yelling about Satan, more often than about God, and were actually, in that sense, Satan worshippers, the angry devotees of bigotry. The Catholics, at least, were "at ease with the Awful." And they were everywhere, which suited my wandering lifestyle. I wanted to be able to go anywhere, walk into a church, and feel at home.

Growing up in the suburbs of Calgary, Alberta, I had felt no history, no culture, nothing to belong to but a fractured family and the Cub Scouts, nothing to believe in but consumerism, living in a community of fearful uniformity, jostling through a pedestrian education with the rest of the Baby Boom generation, the Pig in the Python, in preparation for a treadmill career, bracing myself for the corporate autogenocide of the twenty-first century. I was trained by western suburban society to be eager for amusement, to strive after the irrelevant, to be jealous and grasping, trained to be anxious, sad, desperate, and greedy, trained to react angrily to whatever provoked me. These were the fruits of rugged individualism and the advance of industrialism. Was it any wonder I wanted to escape from this barren prison of desire? To be in love with your destiny, you must have some idea of what Life was thinking when She made you. I was a walking wounded outsider by history, by disposition, and by choice, but not content to be so.

I had read a few Catholic things. *Seven Storey Mountain* by Thomas Merton, *Saint Francis* by Nikos Kazantzakis, *The Imitation of Christ* by Thomas à Kempis, the New Testament, much of the Old Testament, most of it incomprehensible. I knew of the famous British conversions, especially in the twentieth century. If it was good enough for Greene, Muggeridge, Sitwell, Waugh, Sassoon, Tolkien, and Beardsley, in addition to Hopkins, Mahler, Hemingway, Toklas, Alec Guinness, and Gary Cooper, maybe it was good enough for me. This was company in which I need feel no shame.

In early July 1982, I found myself standing at the door of the rectory on View Street behind St. Andrew's Cathedral. I rang the bell, was shown to a little waiting room, and in just a few more minutes, I met Fr. John Mott.

There I was, one of Sister Margaret's wild and woolly, washed up on the doorstep, drawn to incense and altars and rituals in a church that was unlikely to do me any good, and vice versa. I have wondered occasionally at the happenstance of my meeting Fr. John that day rather than any of the other priests at St. Andrew's. If I had met any of the others first, I would have had a brief, formal chat with them and never darkened their door again. But John Mott was a charmer.

He was forty-seven years old when I met him and had been a priest since before he was twenty-five. He told me he was so young when he was ordained it required a dispensation from the Pope. His hair was fair and fine, weightless, always clean, the colour of sand and salt. He was pale-skinned, not tall, and a little thick around the waist. He had bright eyes, an active, animated face, and a tendency to smile. We talked for an hour. He said he would be happy to meet me once or twice a week for what I thought of as general discussions about religion, and what he naturally thought of as preparation for conversion. From years of reading and meditating, I had a rare appreciation of mystery, without actually having accrued many of its benefits. But what are the benefits of mystery? I was comfortable with contradiction and paradox, with leaps of a quantum nature. Fr. John saw this right away. He suggested I also come to a weekly class he was giving, already in progress. I had walked through the door.

I started going to mass every day, often twice a day, the first time not without trepidation. I was half-expecting to trigger searchlights and the release of hounds when I traversed for the first time the small narthex at St. Andrew's. There were no lights and there were no dogs, but I found, in the mass, the same quiet and peace I had found when meditating at Ananda.

This was crazy enough to work.

I found a room to rent in the house that Shizuka had lived in two years earlier, near Camosun College, a bizarre coincidence of no particular significance to me. I had met the landlord when Shizuka lived there, an unenergetic wet blanket who had inherited the house as a young man and lived there unemployed for years on the paltry income of renting bedrooms to the usual variety of odd people, single, often depressed, usually students, who find themselves in need of cheap, temporary accommodation. He was in Calgary now, gone there to work for a time as a bus driver, obviously in need of an infusion of cash. There were no students now, in July, but the house was full. There was an aggressive young man with an unknown job, and an alcoholic cook occasionally employed. There was a brilliant recent graduate of computing science, a man so socially backward and contrary I couldn't imagine anyone ever giving him a job. There was a young mother, also sketchily employed, with her five-year-old son, and a young woman who got up very early every day and made a thousand sandwiches at 7-Eleven, not forgetting the unemployed wild-eyed Satan worshipper in the basement, and me, also in the basement. It was a diverse group.

I looked for work in Victoria, but it was hopeless. In April, I had asked Rick, the maitre d' at Bartholomew's, to hire me back for the summer, but he told me he was staffed up. In July, in spite of my year of local experience as a waiter, part-time and full-time, there was nothing to be had. I survived on the small amount of Unemployment Insurance money I was eligible for, from working in the restaurant for minimum wage the previous summer. By now I was just killing time until I went back to Japan.

I went to mass every day at the cathedral, or at St. Joseph's Friary on Joan Crescent next to Craigdarroch Castle, or at St. Patrick's Church in Oak Bay. At St. Patrick's I met Kay Davies. She lived by herself in a house on King's Road, not far from Taylor Street, and was closing on eighty years old. She picked me up one day on the walk home from noon mass and invited me in for tea. Over the summer I drank about ten gallons of Kay's tea, served in lovely old teacups, with cat hair, and we talked for hours about every topic under the sun, especially the Church. She told me she nearly lost her job teaching in Britain in the 1930s when she converted to Catholicism, and she was expected to resign, and did, when she got married. No respectable married woman with a working husband would dare take a job from a man with a family to support, there were so many unemployed. She told me of her conversion and her experience as a Catholic, of her life as an information officer in the Canadian federal government, and of her marriage to a difficult alcoholic. She was charming and practical, a worldly and saintly woman, not far now from finding out if all that rigmarole about purgatory and heaven and hell was true. She agreed to be my sponsor and gave me a rosary of olive wood from the Holy Land that I have used now, off and on, mostly on, for thirty-one years. It has been repaired many times.

The RCIA, the lengthy Rite of Christian Initiation of Adults, was still fairly new in 1982 although it was designed to reintroduce principles and practices dating back to the earliest church times when joining the church was a risky business for everyone. Fr. John took a more immediate approach to saving souls, and he eschewed the process. He admired St. John

Vianney, the Curé of Ars, a French parish priest of the nineteenth century, the patron saint of all priests. He took a much more practical approach to conversions. Fr. John told me the Curé's technique was to invite people to the parish hall, teach 'em a little religion, give 'em a cookie, and send 'em home. Big deal. This was a style I understood. The RCIA program, on the other hand, is a protracted, year-long process of parish posturing. Fr. John felt that if you were *compos mentis* and stood up before the congregation and renounced Satan, all was well. Another soul was saved. The contract was primarily between you and God, secondarily between you and the Church. What the other parishioners thought about it was a distant third. God was the goal, not the Church, a goal that pastoral councils sometimes lose sight of in their concern for the forms and preservation of the Church Militant.

I went to Fr. John's classes, which were very casual, we talked for hours once or twice a week at the rectory, we went for dinner. He knew a lost soul when he saw one, and he knew I was ripe for the picking. Half a dozen people from his class agreed to join the Catholic Church on the evening of September 8, 1982, the birthday of the Virgin Mary. The bishop could come if he wanted, but if he didn't approve of Fr. John's precipitate approach to conversion he could stay at home, and he did. Fr. John wasn't going to wait until Easter and jump through all the hoops of the RCIA when he had a chance, right now, to increase the flock. He knew I was going to Japan, and he had a strong suspicion he would lose me if he didn't act before I left. He was a wily priest, and it wasn't his first time at baptism.

Fr. John was gay of course, so very many priests are, but he had at least as much trouble with alcohol as he did with celibate homosexuality. He told me that of all his burdens doubt was never one of them, and for that he was thankful. He had never in his life had a crisis of faith. Nor have I. As for sex, well, he would rather be a fully formed, functioning human being than a eunuch, unexcited and never tempted. What victory is there in that?

I had been baptized in the United Church as an infant, and my mother, slightly horrified by this recent turn of events, found my baptismal certificate and mailed it to me. This made the conversion paperwork easier. I expect a copy of it is still in the files somewhere at St. Andrew's Cathedral. Only seven or eight weeks after crossing the threshold of the rectory and meeting Fr. John, on the night of the great event, Kay stood behind me in the sanctuary as my sponsor with her left hand on my shoulder. She was supposed to use her right hand so obviously the ceremony was invalid. I and a few others renounced Satan and pledged ourselves to Jesus and to the Church before a small turnout of the congregation. The Monsignor gave a sermon about how new converts can be more Catholic than the Pope and were often a pain in the ass to those born to the faith, but beneficially it was hoped. My old friend Ron, from Calgary, and a friend of his were in the pews that night, and they both came up for communion although they weren't Catholics or anything vaguely Christian. Ron's New Agey female friend wore a blue and white *dupatta*, an Indian scarf or veil. Fr. John joked afterwards that he thought she was one of Mother Teresa's Missionaries of Charity.

At the reception after the ceremony, there was a fabulous feast in the basement of the rectory. I asked Fr. John where it all came from. He said he had but to mention the upcoming ceremony to the office staff and volunteers, food, and money appeared from every direction. There was a special guest that night, a deacon from Botswana. He wore a white clerical collar and was a man of ebony black skin. He sang a song for us, unaccompanied, in heavily accented English, a soulful tune common amongst his Christian countrymen. He was so sincere and obviously filled with love and devotion that I thought anyone in that room would willingly trade places with him. We thought we had faith, but we were just too damn white. No one really believed Jesus had blond hair and blue eyes, did they?

Later, I walked into the kitchen where three or four women were cleaning up and washing dishes. I hadn't come to help them. I had a question. They were in their early twenties, stout, young, happy virgins, overexcited, all laughing and talking at the same time in very loud voices. When I appeared at the door, one of them noticed me and shouted vigorously to her friends, "It's a man! Quiet, girls! Quiet! It's a man! He wants to speak!"

So that was that. I was now a newly minted Catholic, and I was more or less at home with the idea. I knew there was still much more to learn, and I was looking forward to it. Catholicism is a subject so big that I would never stop learning about it. It was something I hoped would never grow old. I could now go anywhere in the world, walk into a Catholic church, and claim my right to teaching, belonging, participation, discussion, friendship, and space to meditate. Much of their hocus pocus was absurd, and no sensible person would believe a word of it at face value, but I knew the value of myth, metaphor, symbolism, and poetry, and at that level it made perfect sense. And I was quite certain that I had a much better understanding of the mystical experience than ninety-nine per cent of the world's Catholics. This was a practical hubris on my part combined with awareness and resignation. I breathed a sigh of relief, thinking, at least tentatively, that I had solved a fundamental problem in my life. The thought of a state which lasts for a lifetime always brings a little peace in the beginning, usually short-lived.

Years earlier, when I went so often to "the Church" in Victoria, the Churchill bar, or any other bar, I always went on the weekdays and weeknights. That's when a bar is a bar. Going on the weekends and fighting the crowds, surrounded by strangers and tourists, was an unholy experience, a betrayal of the purity of drunkenness, the devotion to alcohol. I went to some pious effort to get to the bar every night of the week, and the affected, over-dressed dilettantes, the yuppies and hipsters who showed up on Saturday nights simply took up valuable space and made it hard to find a seat. I couldn't consider them true devotees.

I felt the same way about real church. I went happily to mass every day, but I did not enjoy Sunday services. The pews were then full of people I never saw, obviously, during the week, clean and well-dressed, Hallmark Card Christians. Who were all these people? Where were they all week? I didn't know them, and I wasn't keen to meet them. Why were they all dressed up? They seemed like dilettantes, weekend warriors, dabblers. Was the church built for them? Probably not, although it was likely paid for by them. I understood that most of them were upstanding members of society with jobs to go to, the "paying laity," but to me they were just tourists, once-a-weekers, toddler Catholics. Fr. John said of them, "We teach the catechism to children and for most of them, that's where it ends. They never become adult Catholics." I had grown up in a world of lukewarm Protestant Churchianity where the Lord's people went to church every week of their lives without internalizing a single Christian idea or feeling. Sunday in a Catholic church seemed no different.

I felt the same way about Sunday Catholics as I had about Saturday drinkers. They weren't my people. I wasn't born into the Catholic Church. I wasn't stuck with it. I was a willing convert, and I would be a full-time, renovative practitioner, not a Sunday stick figure. I wanted to become a social Catholic no more than I had wanted to become an actor, a carpenter, a Co-op manager, a roughneck, or a scientist. There wasn't a chance in hell. Serial abandonment, the act of vacating, was my hallmark.

Many people said, "A Catholic?! Jesus, Neil, why the hell would you want to join that degenerate organization?" I usually responded that I had joined the good church, not the bad one, and I would work with its good members, not its bad ones, for as long as I could. So far, so good. I would take from the Catholics the best they had to offer, the mystical traditions, the contemplative prayer, and would happily ignore their sillier doctrines, virgin birth, all-male priesthood, and a hundred others, the stuffies they needed, and I didn't, to sleep at night. I fervently hoped their best, and mine, would be enough to balance out the foolishness.

I remained quiet about the dogmas of the church. They were, as the dogmas of all churches are, at best, of only mild academic historical interest, comforting to some. They were otherwise childish, mostly irrelevant, and too often misleading and harmful, endless babble and squawk attempting to describe the indescribable. Monotheism, tri-theism, polytheism, pantheism, panentheism, and atheists who never shut up about God! "Isms" on pinheads. Formed or unformed. Created or uncreated. Predestination versus free will. Nature versus grace. Incarnation, reincarnation, inlibration. Orthodoxy versus orthopraxy. East or West. And worst of them all, wherever it is found, the enfeebled and violent egotistical belief in a God so personal, "He may as well be Me." For Christ's sake, what did it matter? What fool would waste a lifetime attempting to define that which, by definition, is indefinable?

To the individual the only useful aspect of religion is personal transformation through practice. The theology wasn't important, the discussion was but brain candy, only occasionally noteworthy, and the bickering ludicrous, if not sinful. I was willing to listen to anyone talk about religion, but I kept a supply of salt in my back pocket. "Love, and do what you will. We are talking about God. What wonder is it that you do not understand? If you do understand, then it is not God." I was just looking for a home, and from recent experience I thought the Catholic Church couldn't be any worse than Ananda Cooperative Village. Unfortunately, in the end, it was no better. Although it is the church of the poor, it is no place for the weak or the vulnerable, for women or children, or indigenous cultures. For them a different saviour is required. Persecution is no way to propagate the faith. The issue of child abuse in residential schools, and child sexual abuse by clergy and religious of the orders and parishes, was still low on the horizon in the early eighties. Those horrifying scandals, symptoms of a deadly sickness in the Church, would arise later. There were thousands of victims, eighty per cent of them boys under the age of fourteen. Many wear the Robe but few keep the Way.

I had written to Mr. Owada, my old boss in Tokyo, asking him if he would sponsor me again in my application for a work visa. He could have said no and given me any excuse, but he didn't. I had been a reliable employee during my first visit, and he knew if he didn't have any classes for me himself, I would be capable of finding other work on my own when I arrived, without risk to his official endorsement of me. He had his office ladies fill in the volumes of paperwork required, and in just a few weeks I took the bus, in a state of profound serenity, to the Japanese Consulate in Vancouver to have my passport stamped. I wrote my parents a long letter, not too cloying I hope, and told them that as far as employment was concerned, I was screwed, and that if they could lend me fifteen hundred dollars I would go to Japan, get a job teaching English, and pay them back over the next year, which they did, and I did. My mother sent me a cheque, quite smartly, for $2,000, and I spent the rest of the summer going to mass and to the movies.

I wrote to David and Jude and asked them if I could occupy their *tatami* living room in Yotsuya for the time it would take me to find accommodation in Tokyo. They were generous to a fault, and coincidentally were heading home at Christmas for nine weeks. I could babysit their apartment for them and take several of their classes while they were gone. This would be a benefit to both of us. Often, for western teachers in Japan, in order to take a holiday, you have to find your own replacement to cover your absence.

I spent the summer blissfully relaxed, drinking tea with Kay, going daily to mass for meditation, and frequently to the movies in the evenings at the Oak Bay Cinema, always a double bill, changed every couple of days. One night, I ran into Carol. I hadn't seen her in nine months. We walked around the corner to a side street to chat in private, and I involuntarily covered her face in kisses. God, I had missed her. She said, "You never called."

One day at the cathedral, an old woman pressed a small parcel into my hand, overstuffed with tissue paper and bound with an elastic. She hurried away with no more than a "God bless you." When I opened it I found a crucifix of frightening design. There was a graphic skull in silver metal mounted on it. It was a ghastly thing. I hung it on the outside of my bedroom door in the basement where, on the warm summer afternoons, when I wasn't drinking tea at Kay's, I lay on my thin piece of foam on the floor, surrounded by cardboard boxes filled with my worldly goods, and was so horny I could ejaculate, impressively, without ever touching my penis, all the while aware of the young woman next door, the Satan worshipper, puttering around, quite possibly in a schizophrenic haze.

Good times.

My winter weight began to shed as early as May and with the summer sun I was, by the end of August, as slim as ever and able to get into all my little suits again. At that age gaining and losing fifteen pounds, twelve per cent of my body weight, was but the work of a moment.

Sometime late that summer, on a street downtown, I ran into Geshe-la, the Tibetan monk, my old landlord. He was often downtown during the day, a chance to get out of the house. I approached him with only a little hesitation. I didn't think he held a grudge for my hasty departure and partial non-payment of rent two years earlier. I was sure he understood. I told him what he had predicted from the beginning, that Shizuka had left me, and I had been "beery, beery" sad, but I was now going back to Japan just to work. We chatted briefly, and as our short conversation wound down I ventured to ask how Margaret was. He gave a little wince. He said, "You know. Old woman."

I would have left for Japan immediately after my conversion ceremony, but it was my paternal grandmother's ninetieth birthday in late September. I had been firmly instructed to be in attendance. As far as my parents were concerned, my buggering off to Japan could wait a month. The party was in Sedgewick at the community hall. It was a beautiful fall day, and every one of the children, grandchildren, and great-grandchildren walked to the head table and presented my grandmother with a carnation. When it was over you could hardly see her behind the pile of flowers. John Arthur Hansen's and Sophia Amelia Abrahamson's descendants now run into the hundreds.

And not least, there was the matter of my bleeding anus. It took several visits to a general practitioner and to a couple of specialists over the summer, but it was eventually diagnosed. A small surgical procedure was required, one serious enough to warrant general anesthesia. Back in Victoria, on October 4, the Feast Day of St. Francis, at the old Victoria General Hospital on Fairfield Road, the proctologist and I got that sorted out.

I went to say a fond farewell to Fr. John. He blessed my new rosary and wished me good luck in Japan. "You can do a lot of things in the Catholic

Church. There is a lot of future ahead of you. But whatever you do, do *not* become a Jesuit!"

A few days later I flew across the Pacific Ocean, from Seattle to Tokyo, for my fourth trip to Asia and my second visit to Japan.

10 Tokyo Owes Me A Good Time

David and Jude met me at the airport in Narita. It was sweet of them to make the long trip out on that late Sunday afternoon in mid-October 1982. From the bus back into town, we all gazed in amazement at the darkening, and then twinkling, Tokyo skyline, the lights, the urban sprawl created by eighteen million people living and working in a megacity of low-rise buildings.

Tokyo was a city of thousands of five-storey buildings, a hundred main traffic arteries, and thousands of very narrow streets, all scrabbled together after sixty per cent of it was burned and levelled by bombing during the Second World War. Until the 1970s, the threat of earthquakes and the state of architectural engineering prevented the mass construction of super-tall skyscrapers. When I lived there, there were only seven of them, all in the 50-storey range, all in Shinjuku. Thirty-four have been built since then as well as dozens or hundreds of others in the high-rise category. The metro population is now 35 million, the population of Canada in a single urban area.

I barely slept, of course, on David and Jude's futon and *tatami* floor, because of jet lag, and they were off early to work the next morning. I decided to walk to Yotsuya instead of taking the subway, only one stop, to stretch my legs and get a look at the familiar, if not very rewarding, sights of Shinjuku-dori, the wide main road. I wanted to clear my head before presenting myself at Yotsuya Gaigo Gakuin, my old school. I was suddenly very nervous as I saw once again the buildings, the crowds of people, the uncountable bicycles and cars of Tokyo, and I muttered to myself for the second time, "My God, I'm back in Asia. What have I done?"

I received a civil welcome at the Yotsuya Foreign Language Institute from Mr. Owada, Mr. Hayashi, Ginger, and Mariko, but there were no classes to be had. Mr. Owada was staffed up. There would be nothing until at least January. It was a short visit and I promised to keep in touch. I was told of the school Christmas party that was scheduled for early December, only seven weeks away, and I planned to go.

I made general enquiries here and there about teaching jobs, but I was committed to taking many of David and Jude's classes while they were away in Canada which would make it difficult or impossible to commit to any others in the meantime. I thus found myself at considerable leisure for the month of November since David and Jude weren't leaving until December. This allowed me time to settle a bit, get used to Tokyo again, enquire locally about accommodation, and thoroughly enjoy myself. I went to a couple of modelling auditions, with no luck. I wasn't that photogenic.

I wanted to live in Yotsuya. After nearly three years in Tokyo, David and Jude were seasoned veterans of expat survival. They knew Yotsuya and Shinjuku very well indeed, where to eat cheaply, the cheap movie houses, fun and interesting places to go. They had a dozen Japanese business contacts at their fingertips who were often, if not always, looking for teachers. They knew a hundred westerners as well, pleasant and interesting people from the UK, Australia, New Zealand, Canada, and the US. Some of them were ambitious go-getters, but most westerners teaching English in Tokyo worked no more than twenty-five hours a week, often less. My schedule was occasionally as light as fifteen hours a week, by choice. This left plenty of time for social encounters over coffee, lunch, and dinner, visiting and chatting, going to bars and cafes. In addition to giving me good contacts for finding work and good tips for cultural survival, David and Jude introduced me to a ready-made, relaxed, and satisfying social life. I owed them a lot.

I was a different creature from the one my friends had met two years earlier. For one thing I wasn't drinking. There was no clattering of bottles of Yebisu beer as I rounded the corner into their little street. Instead I clattered my rosary in the living room at night before going to bed, and I explained to them as best I could my recent odd conversion to the Catholic faith. I went to mass at St. Ignatius church on the campus of Sophia University, one of Japan's leading universities, a Jesuit institution across from Yotsuya station. Jude had little taste for religion of any kind, old or new, but she managed to hold her tongue. For a while. Some people wouldn't believe in God if you showed up on their front lawn with the Virgin Mary in a wheelbarrow. Jude was one of them. David, on the other hand, said, "Hey, whatever you're doing, keep doing it. I've never seen you more clear-eyed and relaxed."

I had a delightful few weeks in Tokyo before David and Jude went home to Canada for their long holiday of nine weeks. Without much stress I lined up work and accommodation for January. I searched out and found the Franciscan Chapel Center in Roppongi, a place where more English was spoken than at St. Ignatius.

I noodled confidently about Tokyo by bus after David suggested I buy the thick but compact map of Tokyo bus routes that was only available at a little booth under an overpass in Shibuya. It was six hundred yen, about three dollars. It was the cheapest and most detailed map of Tokyo you could find. I started taking buses, when practical, instead of the subway. One of the truly disorienting problems with taking the subway, the easiest way to get around, was that you never knew where anything was in relation to anything else. You are constantly in a tunnel underground while travelling. You find yourself with a good knowledge of the few blocks around any given subway station but you never see anything in-between. Tokyo, overall, is therefore reduced in your mind to a schematic of subway routes. Taking the bus is much more informative and engaging except at rush hour when you're stuck in traffic. Most of Tokyo's old people take the bus. You rarely see them on the subway. It's too challenging physically. And since there wasn't a word of English in the book of bus maps, you were forced to learn all the station names in *kanji* and *hiragana*. It was an immersion class in geography and language.

The fall weather was a delight, warmer than Victoria in the summer. In late November, we sat in the apartment with the windows wide open at eleven o'clock at night enjoying the warm, moist breeze, listening to that damn dog barking next door above the drycleaners and to cool new eighties music, Dave Edmunds, Soft Cell, Blue Rondo à la Turk, the Thompson Twins, Squeeze, Prince, David Bowie reinvented for the umpteenth time, with umpteen more to come, Joe Jackson, China Crisis, Culture Club, Thomas Dolby, Stray Cats.

David and Jude and I got along effortlessly. At least on my part. Who knows what exertions were required from them to endure my company? One afternoon, not long after I arrived, I got a hint when there was an incident of supreme disharmony. Jude came home rocket-fuel hormonal and was mean as fuck to me for no reason at all. She lived life close to the surface in all its intensity, and it was not surprising that things other than loving-kindness should have an occasional airing. I, addicted to the bovine, had drunk the last of the milk when Jude arrived home after classes, gasping for a cup of tea. The store was a hundred yards away, and I made to go replenish the supply of milk when she pounced on me unleashing a stream of abuse. I cowered before her until the heat of her roar pivoted away with a swivel of her head. She then clopped on cloven hoof down the short hall to shriek and swear at various articles in the bathroom. I turned to David in horror. "Holy *shit*, Dave! Should I start looking for an apartment right away?" He said, "Forget it," in a voice of utter unconcern. He had been married less than two years and was already a seasoned husband. Later in the evening, as I sulked and waited, quite reasonably I thought, for an apology, she took the opportunity to lash out at me again, through the horizontal pupils of her flaming eyes, not for an omission, on my part, of cooperative deportment or obliging disposition. It was a personal attack, twisting the knife. I had never known anything but flattery and kindness from Jude, and the appearance of this vicious darkness left me reeling. I understood that I was treading on the shadow of her bloody pain, but when you accept someone as a roommate you expect some mitigation of territoriality. I realized that Jude was a woman to be loved but not to be trusted to keep the peace emotionally. It was not the first time, I imagine, that a man has made a similar observation about the frightening goddesses in our midst. I never did get that apology.

And speaking of women, David and Jude knew some of the single variety. They introduced me to Gillian and Sue.

I met Sue first. We went for dinner one evening. I gussied up a bit for my blind date and met her at a train station, a common practice in Tokyo. She was blond and not hard to spot. When I saw her, I approached and said, "Hello. Are you Sue?" She said, "No, sorry," and when I muttered my apology and turned to walk away, she grabbed me by the arm. "I'm kidding! Of course it's me. I'm the only other westerner here!" She thought that was funny. We spent the evening talking easily. We didn't hate each other, but there was no great mutual spark in evidence. She was very New Agey, so we communicated well on that level, and she could respect my history with yoga and the ashrams of California and travelling in India, even my new interest in the old Catholic ways. She had a Master's degree in speech pathology and had worked for six years in the public schools of California, so she was highly qualified to teach English in Japan, unlike me. She had a pleasant, pear-shaped face with a wonderful profile, and bouffy, curly hair falling lightly past her shoulders. It was the eighties. She was a little substantial in the bottom and had thick ankles, but none of this bothered me. I was no prize, short and squeaky. She was smart and had bright eyes and an easy impish smile, and I love her to this day. She did, however, have a boyfriend. Or at least she thought she might, and after meeting me she couldn't think of any reason not to continue to pursue her first option. He was a handsome, athletic Japanese man, a skier, and I could tell she was very attracted to him. I would have to wait my turn.

Then I met Gillian. She was from New Zealand, from Britain before that, but she had moved to New Zealand with her family as a young teenager. Our affair lasted three weeks, and it seemed like a lifetime. She told me she had lost her virginity on the ship from England to New Zealand when she was date-raped in the cabin of an older teenager. She ran into him a few years later, and when she confronted him his response was, "So what?"

Gillian started studying Japanese in high school, developed an unstoppable devotion to the culture, and moved to Japan right after college. She had now been resident for four years and had no intention of ever leaving. Not many people can thoroughly adopt and adapt to another culture, but Gillian was one of them. After two years in Japan she was dead fluent in the language and was now working for the Japan Professional Golf Association, the JPGA. She was one of the few westerners I met in Tokyo who wasn't an English teacher. She had perfected her Japanese in male company, and when she talked with the old woman who lived across the hall from her, the old lady, appalled by Gillian's rough, masculine usage, would correct her speech to make it more feminine. She had brown wavy hair, shoulder length, a brilliant smile, and an upper-incisor diastema, a gap between her top front teeth, which in English folklore indicates a "lustful character." She was not tall but wonderfully proportioned, "balanced" she called it. She told me that Japanese women in the *sento*, the public bath, often complimented her on her breasts. She was modest and soft and gentle, never brash. She had an elfin smile and shameless dimples and a way of casting her eyes downward that might have been a deliberate imitation of her adopted culture but which was, of whatever origin, very appealing to me. I wish I had a picture of her, but even without one I can see her now, thirty-one years later.

After an evening or two, or a lunch or two, in short order, she invited me to join her on a trip to Kamakura, a popular tourist destination just south of Tokyo. It is a former *de facto* capital of Japan, a 1,000-year-old beach town on Sagami Bay. There is an enormous, and famous, iconic statue of Amitabha Buddha there, *Kamakura Daibutsu*, often referred to as "the face of Japan." There are many Buddhist temples and Shinto shrines in the area. Gillian had family friends visiting from Australia, and the four of us would go to Kamakura together and stay in private rooms at the hostel. Her friends were actually her parents' friends. They were older, near retirement. They had letters of introduction to various Japanese people, from Buddhist monks to military personnel. Gillian was of great assistance to them as a translator.

We took the train down, and on the way Gillian taught me sign language, at least the signs for the letters of the alphabet, and we spent the weekend signing flirty, secret messages to each other. The four of us toured the sights of Kamakura. I had been there before, but it is well worth more than one visit.

As we checked in at the hostel, Gillian's friends teased her when she modestly insisted on getting two rooms for her and me. We weren't lovers, not yet, and she wasn't going to be rushed into anything. Her Aussie friends, although older, were shameless, and they laughed and dared her to share a room with me. I only pointed out that it would be less expensive. She accepted the dare.

We went for dinner nearby and everyone drank except me. When we got back to our room, it was time for a bath. To my great surprise, when we found the hostel bathing area in the basement, Gillian simply walked into the men's rooms with me, removed her *yukata*, the thin housecoat provided by the hostel, and naked, joined me in the very hot tub. There was no one there at that late hour, but in a few minutes a Japanese man walked in, and he was very surprised indeed to find a young, balanced western woman in the tub. Gillian's fluent, slightly drunk, Japanese assured him that all was well, and he joined us, but he didn't stay long. He had a story now to tell his friends on Monday morning at the office, one they would never believe. I would be surprised if he has ever forgotten it.

Liquor and a hot familiar bath form as good an introduction to physical intimacy as any, and the sun was rising before we slept a wink. We were very tired the next day. We had a full schedule of touring and visiting and a train ride back to Tokyo. Our flirty sign language was now a matter of many blushes.

It is a tendency of mine to fall in love, and I was certain beyond a doubt that if I didn't already love Gillian with all my heart and mind and soul, give it a day or two and I would. We saw each other every day for the next three weeks, and in only three weeks we went from head-over-heels to knocked-out-cold. We spent every moment we could together, wasting none of it in sleep. When we weren't making love, we were talking. We probably learned everything there was to know about each other in that brief span. We were up all night, every night. I raced from Gillian's bed for a taxi or to the subway to arrive at work with only seconds to spare, barely prepared. I was then a walking, or sitting, zombie in my classes. My supervisor for one of my classes picked the worst day of them all to show up and evaluate my teaching, a day when I could hardly hold my head off the table. He told me I should stand more while teaching. I told him I normally did but I had not slept well.

One night I left Gillian's place at a sensible hour, for a change, by taxi, and as the cab rolled into my own neighbourhood, I was pulled back to her by an unquenchable thirst, involuntarily, inescapably drawn to her. I got out of the taxi, bought a bouquet of freesias, and took another taxi straight back to her apartment.

We went to the last-round, sold-out, semi-final matches of the *Hatsu basho*, the New Year's sumo tournament, at Kuramae Kokugikan, the sumo hall built after the war, in 1954. Gillian volunteered to line up at five o'clock in the morning to buy four of the last, worst seats available. There we saw Chiyonofuji fight. He was one of the best wrestlers of his day and one of the lightest and strongest ever at only two hundred and sixty pounds. He won two of his six tournaments that year but not the one we saw at New Year's. We did, however, see him pick up a man twice his weight and throw him out of the *dohyo*, the ring of clay, straw, and sand, where these behemoths slap each other with a force that would send any normal person to the hospital.

We went to my favourite curry restaurant in Ginza, Mr. Nair's. We went to the very expensive Imperial Hotel where a bowl of soup cost a hundred dollars, to the swanky lounge on the seventeenth floor. We were nearly always well dressed because of our office occupations, and "westerners can get into anything," remember? We ordered drinks and strawberries, and ate them out of each other's mouths. We were insufferable. She introduced me to the Whisper Bar in the back streets of Harajuku, a cafe where you were not allowed to speak above a whisper. The proprietor stood in front of rows of unique cups, and you selected the one you wanted. He made every cup of coffee freshly ground and very strong, playing only classical music softly on the stereo. He never left his post behind the counter ready to instruct quiet to anyone who let the caffeine animate them into a conversation above a whisper.

We went to a notorious porn movie, much talked about, and Gillian translated the odd bits of dialogue for me although I got the gist of it anyway. She offered in the most obvious way to oblige me in the theatre, with people sitting all around us, this sweet, quiet woman, but I had to decline. I am a Virgo after all. We took the bus back to my apartment ready to burst. It has been my experience that women like men who can't get enough of them, for a while anyway, although ultimately no one in their right mind wants to be worshipped.

Eventually, in the long night hours, spent and naked in every sense, I began to piece the situation, and my fate, together. I found myself once more in the role of the other man. I was not Gillian's only lover and not her principal one. She had been having an affair with a married man for at least three years. He had been out of town for the last three weeks. Her mad, sweaty, uncharacteristic affair with me had been a desperate effort to tear herself away from him, and now that he was back in town she found she couldn't do it. Slowly, in bits and pieces, she gave me the history.

Her lover was her boss at the JPGA. He had children. Gillian knew he would never leave his wife. And she knew now that she could never leave him. His wife didn't know about this long-running affair. I asked Gillian what her lover's wife would do if she found out. She said, "She would probably kill herself." My heart dropped a full two inches in my chest. And then, just as gruesome, Gillian told me she had been pregnant three times in the last three years and had just had her third abortion, a common occurrence in Japan. Easy access to abortion was that nation's ridiculous policy alternative to legalizing oral contraceptives. The Pill wasn't approved for use in Japan until 1999, and it is still only used by one per cent of Japanese women compared with rates of up to eighty-five per cent in western countries. I was speechless. I was shocked. I was shattered. Only a year earlier, I had suffered the same fate at Carol's hands. Like the walking wounded I staggered out of Gillian's apartment in Jingumae, but not before, I am ashamed to say, unleashing a few much deserved, and then much regretted, oaths and profanities, observations and advice. "He say I Big Evil." When I am hurt and angry, those I accuse, for a while, are not fit for heaven.

I thought I would never see Gillian again, but she surprised me about a week later and telephoned. I wasn't expecting a change of heart from her, but I would have taken one. She told me she had promised to go with me to Yokohama to see the *Queen Elizabeth 2*, and she wanted to keep that promise. I had forgotten all about it. It was now in port. One of her English cousins was a waiter on the *QE2*, and he had told Gillian a few weeks earlier, by letter, that if she wanted to come down to Yokohama when they arrived, he would give her a tour of the ship.

I wanted to see the *QE2*, and I couldn't resist being once more in the melting warmth of Gillian's company, but it wasn't a comfortable ride down to Yokohama on the train. We took a taxi to where the impressive liner was docked. We then had to jostle our way through a few thousand curious, admiring, and milling spectators to a small gangway where Gillian's cousin waiting for us, and we were ushered aboard, little VIPs. There were very few people on the ship. Most of the round-the-world passengers were ashore on excursions.

The outside of the ship was painted white which didn't seem familiar to me. I remembered it as blue. Gillian's cousin, a mildly distasteful young man, no fault of his own really, explained that it had just been painted in Hong Kong. The light colour proved unpopular, and the ship was repainted navy blue the next year. It had been grey for the last several months until a few weeks ago. It had been used for troop transport in the Falklands War in the spring. Before sailing off to the conflict, the ship's company was asked if they wanted to volunteer for the upcoming tour of duty, and Gillian's cousin had gone to war, a wine waiter to the officers. He had a medal to prove it. The passageways of the ship were lined with photographs of its livery and protective measures during the conflict. A helicopter landing pad had been installed, the floors were covered inside to protect the carpets, and guns were mounted on the decks. The wine waiter told us he had been allowed to fire off a few rounds himself. Pouring wine for officers seemed like a silly way to wage war, but the danger was real. Sixteen ships, including two destroyers, went to the bottom of the South Atlantic in the Falklands War. The *QE2* could have been one of them.

After an easy tour of the ship, we were seated in one of the dining rooms while Gillian's cousin hovered nearby. He wasn't allowed to sit down, but he could treat us to a complimentary meal. There was so much cutlery I was at a loss where to begin. I had used only a pair of chopsticks and a wooden bowl for years. The young waiters sorted us out. We chatted. The cousin told funny stories about the idiosyncrasies of the wealthy passengers. I said it must be difficult for the crew to be away from home for such long periods of time. He said, "Oh, hell, most of the women are single and most of the men are gay. You don't work on a ship if you have a family."

The conversation wound down to a desultory prediction of the wine waiter's life after cruising, and Gillian and I made the long trip back to Tokyo, again just in time for me to make my evening class. I wish I could say I was more even-minded, less spiky, on the way home, but I can't.

After that day I never saw her again. Not once.

Fortunately, a three-week affair is not that hard to get over. I spent every afternoon for another three weeks buck-naked at the gym baths, twenty minutes in the sauna and ten minutes in the cold pool, repeated half a dozen times. The small, one-man cold pool was kept at four degrees Celsius, colder than the ocean in Victoria in January, but I routinely cranked it down to one or two degrees above freezing, amazing the naked, locker-room *samurai*-salarymen of Tokyo. I did yoga. I went to mass. I took the train to the western suburb of Nakano and tracked down the Hare Krishnas. I spent an hour chatting with one of them and bought a cassette tape of chants. At home I threw out everything in my house that Gillian had touched, and in a few more days the beauty and the shock of my affair with her were gone.

But I am a little ahead of myself.

When David and Jude left for Canada and I took over their classes, I was suddenly very busy. My days went from empty to full overnight. For a few weeks I worked very hard, made a good income, and then caught a bad cold. I slept twelve hours on Christmas Eve. David and Jude had left me a present which I kept by the side of my futon until I woke up on Christmas morning, alone, and rolled over and opened it without getting out of bed. It was a *hanten*, a quilted jacket for indoor winter wear. I put it over my head and went back to sleep for another twenty-four hours.

I found a four-month house-sit not far away in Akebonobashi, "Daybreak Bridge." It wasn't ideal. In four months I would be looking for accommodation again, but in the meantime I had a comfortable, fully equipped apartment on the second floor of a small house while the regular renters, English teachers from New Zealand, were taking a break back home. It was comfortable and fully equipped, but it didn't have a bath and the tiny shower room had no heat. It was easier to go to the *sento*.

And thus began what would become a sixteen-month regimen of evening baths at the local *sento*, the public bath. For nearly five hundred nights in a row, I left my apartment to wash and soak in tubs of both warm and very hot water with up to two dozen Japanese men, rarely any other westerners. The women were on the other side of the wall.

The wall was tall enough to block the view, but it didn't go all the way to the ceiling. If you were so inclined, you could get the tiniest peek at the women's side when you were standing at the desk near the door buying your ticket. The desk was positioned in the middle, between the men's and women's entrances, and faced inwards. The vendor, either male or female, sold tickets to both men and women, from either side of the desk which was always in an elevated position, like a pulpit, affording the attendant a view of the proceedings on both sides of the wall, including both change areas and both bathing areas. Most western women wouldn't tolerate using the public baths and found apartments with working showers. I heard them say that the guy who sold the tickets was always ogling them. When Sue complained about it, I said, "Hon, male or female, the attendant sees everyone naked at the bath. Just turn around, bend over, and show it to him. He'll stop looking."

"No!" she exclaimed, mortified. We had different attitudes about nudity.

I never did find an apartment with a decent shower and came to enjoy my visits to the *sento* immensely. In winter, they warmed you after a chilly walk home, and in summer, when I thought a hot bath would be unbearable, they opened your pores and washed away the sweat of the hot, sticky day. It turns out there's nothing better than a hot bath on a hot day when the weather is humid. The *sento* were open six days a week and closed one day for deep cleaning. You thus went to your closest *sento* most of the time, and on the night it was closed to your second-closest one. They were usually family-owned, and sometimes the husband sold tickets, sometimes the wife. Walking up the street one day coming home from work, I saw an attractive woman in her thirties doing her family shopping. We recognized each other, smiled, and said hello, but I couldn't for the life of me think where I knew her from. Then I realized she was the *sento* lady. "Good God," I thought, "that woman has seen me naked."

I was completely moved out of David and Jude's apartment when they arrived home from their long holiday. I didn't go to the airport to meet them, it didn't seem necessary, but I did blow up a hundred balloons with no mechanical aid and stuff them into their tiny bedroom, three feet deep. I was waiting for them at the apartment when they staggered in exhausted. I presented them with many little gifts, and best of all I told them I had found my own place. When they opened the door to their bedroom, the balloons spilled out into the apartment. After a short visit of chatting and playing with balloons, I left my exhausted hosts in peace. I had hidden a stash of money in the apartment as a small payment of rent, and David found it in only a day or two. I was grateful as a puppy dog for their timely and generous assistance and forbearance, in spite of the milk incident. They had helped, in no small part, to make my next year and a half in Tokyo tolerable and profitable, pleasant and successful.

So January began and I was fully employed, which is to say I worked four hours a day. There were a couple of different styles of working in the English teaching business in Tokyo. You could put in twenty or more hours a week based at a single school, the one sponsoring your visa, for good but not spectacular pay, and try to get one or two private classes on the side at much higher rates, which is what I did on my first visit to Japan. The alternative was to be unfettered and itinerant, getting as many classes as you could, at the highest pay you could find, at half a dozen different schools and companies, and with individuals, which is what I was doing now. Each style had its advantages and disadvantages.

I had five or six often changing sources of income, a situation that was more difficult to keep track of, but they always paid on time and mistakes were rare. I had to travel more now as my classes were all over town. The goal was therefore to have as many classes as possible close to where you lived. The more unpaid time you spent on the subway, the more time you wasted and the more tired you got. In general the less time you spent commuting, the happier you were. Fortunately, nearly every company in Japan pays transportation expenses for its employees, usually in the form of a monthly subway or bus pass. Living in Yotsuya, so close to several major business districts, was perfect. After a few months I weeded out all of my classes in the farther reaches of Tokyo until I was no more than a couple of subway stops, or bus stops, to work on any day of the week.

I bought myself a brand new mama-san bicycle, a girl's bike with a bell, a simple spoke-lock, and two large baskets, front and back, to solve the problem of getting groceries home. It also served as transportation to my classes nearby. For more than a year I rode up and down central Tokyo's major thoroughfares, in and out of bumper-to-bumper traffic, onto the sidewalk and off again, without a care. Once at your destination you flipped the flimsy spoke-lock, removed the key, and walked away from your bicycle without a thought for its security. I once accidentally left my bike unlocked in the middle of the sidewalk for three days, outside a restaurant in Yotsuya, when I went out of town. When I came back, I didn't see it in its usual spot outside the subway station, and I thought it had been stolen. When I rounded the corner to walk home, I saw it sitting exactly where I had left it in my rush to get out of town, untouched and unlocked for three days in a city of twelve million people.

I bicycled the main streets fearlessly, and foolishly, I suppose, but what was most enjoyable was riding through Tokyo's back streets, either going to work or just exploring. Tokyo has a few hills and valleys, little dips in the road, and the odd dead end, but it's mostly flat, and if you know where you are and where you want to go, you need only find the first side street away from the main roads and start pedalling. You will veer a little this way and that, and occasionally you are stymied by an unexpected cul-de-sac. But in the end you will come out where you want to go, you will have avoided the heavy traffic, and you will have seen a lot of little neighbourhoods that would otherwise have remained unknown to you.

I loved riding my bicycle in Tokyo. One day in the summer, I was wheeling easily down a secondary route on my way to Sterling-Winthrop, a pharmaceutical company, right across from the National Diet Building, the home of Japan's government, in the hectic and wealthy Akasaka business district. I was steering with one hand, and holding a popsicle in the other, enjoying the sun and the season and my pampered, carefree lifestyle. When I got to the Sterling offices, one of my students, a single woman of forty, told me she had seen me riding from her window on the fifth floor, and the image had created, for her, the very picture of freedom. It was so un-Japanese. A grown man, thin, with blond hair in need of a trim, dressed all in white with burgundy shoes and suspenders and a dark tie, riding a bicycle and eating a popsicle, overpaid and going to work at noon. No two-hour commute on the train, no six-day work week, no company song to sing, no stifling social obligations, no crushing business and company concerns. Japanese salarymen work themselves to death, literally. Sterling owned and manufactured Astringosol mouthwash, my favourite kind, and my students presented me with a case of it. It's sold as a concentrate, and I used it daily for at least two years, long after I left Japan.

My schedule was unusual, though. Over Christmas, I substituted for David and Jude at Sony Language Lab, at their Shimbashi location, and then worked there for the next sixteen months. Among their other offerings they held short classes before the business day commenced, for early birds and the truly ambitious. I had to be at the school, three stops away, at 7:50 a.m. I didn't bicycle that early in the morning, and I knew to the minute when I had to get up and which train to catch to be on time. I did two classes and was finished at quarter after nine. David and Jude worked there, as well as Sue, and we would chat together in the very short five-minute break between classes. At 9:15 exactly I would make for the subway and be home frying French toast in my tiny kitchen by quarter to ten. Once a week, with or without company, instead of heading home, I would go to the Imperial Hotel for breakfast in their western-styled cafe, only a few blocks away from Sony LL. Here you could order familiar versions of hot oatmeal, and eggs, as well as unlimited amounts of rye toast, for 2,000 yen, ten dollars. That was expensive, but it was worth it to me. I went many times and once ordered, and ate, so many slices of toast with jam they actually cut me off, in violation of their own policy.

Four days a week I had a private one-hour class at noon which I could bicycle to. I then had the afternoon off when I went to the gym or exploring or shopping or doing errands and then home again for a nap. And then, every evening, I had a full two or three hours of classes. I was home by 9:40 p.m. for a quick trip to the *sento*. At 10:00 p.m. I turned on my stereo and started doing yoga postures. Five nights a week The Far East Network, the US Armed Forces Network in Japan, broadcast *CBS Radio Mystery Theater*. I listened to two hundred episodes of the fourteen hundred in total, most of them introduced by E. G. Marshall and the ominous sound of a creaking door. "Come in…! Welcome. I am E. G. Marshall." And then his other standard phrases, "The sound of suspense," or "The fear you can hear." At the conclusion the door would creak again and Marshall would intone, "Until next time, pleasant…dreams?" They were sometimes cheesy but almost always entertaining.

I then did readings and meditation for at least another two hours. In bed at one or one-thirty, I was up again at seven for early morning classes. When I described my schedule to some of my students, one or two of them said, "That is a *horrible* schedule." It didn't bother me a bit. I was quite content to be bouncing around Tokyo as long as I didn't have to go too far for any given class. I loved having the late mornings and the long afternoons to myself.

I had a kerosene heater in my little apartment, and I woke up half an hour early in the freezing winter mornings so I could light it and try to warm the room a little before getting out of my futon. My shirts, clean and folded from the laundry, were nearly frozen and had to be pried apart before I could get them on. I ran the few blocks to the subway in a frozen shirt racing for the warmth of the tunnels. Every two or three weeks I carried, with considerable difficulty, a five-gallon container of kerosene the few blocks from the vendor's to my apartment, until I figured out they had free delivery. There was a blazing neon sign on a giant building across a shallow valley and up a big hill to the north of my apartment. It was many blocks away, but the sign was so big it fully lit my room at night. When Gillian was over one time, I asked her about the sign. She said, "Women's Hospital." A week before I moved out of my house-sit, I realized there were light, sliding, aluminum typhoon shutters on the outside of the windows which, when closed, completely blacked out the apartment. I had slept in blazing neon light for four months. After I discovered the shutters, going to sleep at night was like falling down a well.

By the time the New Zealanders returned to claim their apartment, I had been assisted by an English-speaking Japanese man, Mr. Kohno, a language-school associate, in finding another place to live. There are rental agencies galore in Tokyo, and they are the primary source of rental accommodation. Language is a problem. Without assistance in Japanese you are unlikely to get far. Also, many landlords won't rent to foreigners. It can be touchy. Up-front payments to the landlord, outrageous sums under such make-believe names as "key money" and "gift money," can be as much as half a year's rent. Moving in Tokyo is thus prohibitively expensive. I was told there is a phrase in Japanese which translates roughly as "poor through moving." Consequently, families in Tokyo often move into an apartment and never move out, renting it for thirty years or more. Most Japanese singles, especially women, lived at home until they got married, or for the men, in large company dormitories, a loveless, dismal existence. Overworked, underpaid, and not getting laid.

My local Yotsuya agent found a landlord nearby who was willing to accommodate me with no more than a couple of months' bribe money up front. It was a single room with a nine-square-foot kitchen and a shared squat toilet that was also used by Mr. Sasaki, the occupant of the room next door, the only other one. This little two-room house was an oddity in Samon-cho only three short blocks from Yotsuya-san-chome subway station. It was on a small double lot, surrounded by bigger apartment buildings on three sides. On the side separating me from very busy Gaien Higashi-dori, "East Park Street," the main road to Roppongi, one of Tokyo's centres of young night life, there was a very tall, very wide apartment building which provided a very effective sound curtain. I spent the next year in an ultra-urban area living in a quiet cottage. The rent was two hundred dollars a month, a little less than what I had paid for my student bed-sit in Victoria. I made the same amount of money teaching English as I had as a waiter at Bartholomew's restaurant, for half the hours and no American tourists. My expenses were generally low, in this very expensive city, and for the next ten months I sent four hundred dollars a month home to pay back the money my mother had lent me and the small student loans I had incurred while going to Camosun College. The first time I re-negotiated a payment schedule for a student loan, at a bank in Victoria a few years earlier, the clerk and I stood on opposite sides of the counter, and without using calculators we both worked out the weighted average of my interest rate using pen and paper, like the NASA scientists in the movie *Apollo 13*. We then checked our figures with each other to make sure they agreed. The word "calculator" used to be a job title describing someone who did calculations for a living. The height of Mt. Everest was first estimated by human calculators.

I moved from my house-sit in Akebonobashi by taxi at the end of March 1983 and spent the next twelve months living next to my landlord's house and office on a quiet street in Samon-cho. He was a veterinarian, but from what I could make out his practice was very slow. I rarely saw clients or pets about the place.

My young neighbour, Mr. Sasaki, spoke almost no English, and my Japanese didn't get much better while I was there, so we only said good morning and afternoon and evening when we occasionally ran into each other. We had no relationship at all although I would gladly have throttled him. He absolutely refused to help keep the squat toilet clean. If you gave it a swish every couple of days, it was fine, otherwise it would become very third-world in no time. In Japan, the men work outside the home sixteen hours a day, and the women and girls do all the housework. All of it. The boys inevitably grow up helpless, useless, and arrogant.

But I was settled now and could anticipate a year or more, as much as I wanted, of well-paid, undemanding work, my favourite kind, stable housing, and easy living. My new little room had a sink in the minuscule kitchen but no hot water. There was, however, a gas line into the apartment. In the confusing final days of my affair with Gillian, I called her and asked her to call the gas company for me and request a small boiler for installation over the sink. It was expensive, but it was worth it to me, plus I owned it. When I left Japan I was able to take it off the wall and sell it.

Having gas in the apartment was a tremendous benefit. I bought a portable gas heater, far stronger and more efficient than a kerosene heater, and I was able to survive much more comfortably the next winter. And when it was really cold, I even risked leaving it on overnight.

The room was completely empty when I rented it, and I found a going-away sale where a foreign couple living nearby were leaving Japan and selling everything. I stumbled across a lumberyard and bought wood and four small wheels and built myself a little moving wagon. When the day arrived, I loaded up my wagon with the refrigerator and carpeting and tables and the other household items I had bought, and with David's help pulled it fully laden to my new apartment through the back lanes of Yotsuya. It broke down, of course.

In 1982, there was a war in the Falklands and in Lebanon, where Lebanese Christians, under the eye of the Israeli military, massacred Palestinians by the thousands at the Sabra and Shatila refugee camps. Ariel Sharon was one of the greatest soldiers of the twentieth century, the saviour of Israel in both the 1967 and 1973 wars, but in 1982, as Israeli Defense Minister, he was deemed to be personally responsible for the Phalange militia massacres. He knew they were likely to happen, and he did nothing to stop them. He was known as the Bulldozer and the Butcher. He might have been the toughest son of a bitch with two girl-names ever to live. On the verge of becoming prime minister in 2006, he suffered a stroke and was in a permanent vegetative state until his death in 2014.

Brezhnev died in November of 1982. Only Stalin had ruled longer in the Soviet Union. He was succeeded for just over a year by Andropov and then for another year by Chernenko. Hard-line cold war rhetoric escalated in the Reagan White House. American media fed the world a steady diet of "evil empire," "totalitarianism," "the ash heap of history" (stolen, oddly, from Trotsky), "rollback," "the struggle between good and evil," "the failure and collapse of global communism," "writing the final pages of the history of the Soviet Union," and the Star Wars program, a bellicose and unrealistic plan which threatened to put anti-ballistic missiles in constant orbit over the godless enemies of freedom in the Soviet Union. The next year, only seventy-five miles off the coast of Japan, the Russians shot down Flight 007. They must have thought James Bond was on board. It was a Korean Air Lines 747 passenger plane en route from New York to Seoul via Anchorage. All on board were killed including a US congressman. All of this was making everyone nervous. Reagan had no use for the *détente* of the seventies. He was committed to the destruction of communism, not only in his lifetime, but during his administration. In Tokyo, now living only six hundred miles from Vladivostok, I had for the first time, vivid nightmares about nuclear attack. There were three long, unsettled years to go before the era of Gorbachev and the start of *perestroika* and *glasnost*.

In the spring, the British Parliament passed the *Canada Act 1982*. And thus the Canadian Constitution was finally brought home, "patriated," a new word few people had heard before. I was unaware of all of this.

What I do remember from the muddle of 1982 was that Claus von Bülow was found guilty of attempting to murder his wife. Lawn Chair Larry flew 16,000 feet into the air in California in a lawn chair with weather balloons attached. And someone named Michael Fagan walked past every guard at Buckingham Palace to have a chat with the Queen in her bedroom. The Vietnam Veterans Memorial was dedicated in Washington, D.C., and Michael Jackson released *Thriller*, the biggest selling album of all time. I stood on a little street in Shinjuku in the winter outside an electronics shop, and with a shifting audience of several others, watched, through the window, the one-hour documentary, *Making Michael Jackson's Thriller*. For the longest time I couldn't figure out who the girl was who was doing the voiceover.

Barney Clark became the first person to receive a permanent artificial heart which allowed him to live for another three months, the Toyota Camry was introduced, and *Time* magazine's Man of the Year was the personal computer.

Roberto Calvi, God's Banker, was found suicided in London hanging from Blackfriars Bridge. He was involved in a sickening financial and political scandal, the collapse of Italy's second-largest private bank, the Banco Ambrosiano. With the participation of the mafia, which was the bank's largest shareholder, and an illegal black, or covert, Masonic Lodge, which was implicated in numerous other crimes including murder, a billion dollars disappeared, much of it through the Vatican Bank, much of it the small deposits of the faithful.

Henry Fonda and Ingrid Bergman died that year, but I was only really aware that John Belushi was gone. Overdosed. The wrong drugs. Again.

11 Tokyo Pays Up

The variety of people I met in Tokyo was probably the most interesting feature of the time I spent there. It wasn't the quality of the air. Or the steam-bath summers. Tokyo is not a northerly clime, but it's far enough north to have four seasons, something Tokyoites are happy to tell you over and over. Spring and fall are the best, cherry blossoms in the spring, falling leaves in autumn. Winter can be bitter, but the stiff winds blow the clouds and pollution away, and the skies are clear. I never had to walk more than a few, brisk blocks from a warm subway or bus, and I now had a gas heater at home to take the chill away. It snows a little in Tokyo, but it doesn't usually stay long.

Soon after arriving, I went to one of David's employers looking for work, but the International Language Centre, headquartered in London, was an earnest operation, and my scanty qualifications were not up to their standards. David had decided to take English teaching seriously and had been accepted at ILC as an employee while doing a course offered there under the aegis of the Royal Society of Arts, an "enlightenment organisation" dedicated to, among other things, civilizing the world through the teaching of English. The RSA certificate evolved into the Cambridge CELTA. It is now the world standard and minimum qualification for people wanting to travel the world teaching English. When I arrived in Tokyo, David was writing an essay on the fascinating subject of the present perfect tense and the use of "have" as an auxiliary verb. I read one page of it and decided it was unlikely I would ever take the RSA course.

The standards at ILC may have been high, but the hiring process had its flaws. David told me one day that a new teacher had arrived on Monday and was gone by Friday under a cloud of suspicion. Apparently he had been teaching his students, a group of beginners, a few stock phrases about names, jobs, introductions, etc, a typical way to start a new class. It became clear, however, after a couple of days, that his commitment to excellence was overshadowed by his cultural discontent. His new students were overheard practising in the lounge. "My name is———. I am an office worker, and I will never be anything else." "Nice to meet you. My name is———. I am an office worker, and I will never be anything else."

One of my early assignments was also one of my most interesting and lucrative. Sony Language Lab hooked me up with the Senior Managing Director of AGF, a joint venture of the Japanese food giant Ajinomoto and the US giant General Foods. Ajinomoto made MSG and spice mixes that could be found on every table in Japan, and the company name was another genericized trademark, as in "Pass the Ajinomoto, please." AGF made mostly instant coffee, Maxwell and Maxim, in freeze-drying factories outside Tokyo. Their head office was next door to Yotsuya Gaigo Gakuin, handy to my apartment.

At 5:00 p.m. on Tuesdays, I took the elevator nine floors up to AGF's executive offices where I was unfailingly met by two bowing secretaries as the doors opened. They escorted me to a large, beautiful waiting room with a view of the lights of Chiyoda-ku, the heart of Tokyo and home to the Imperial Palace. They brought me tea and cookies. When Mr. Kusumi was ready, I was shown into his office. On a couple of occasions, he was busy for our appointed hour together, and I read a book or fell asleep and then went home without seeing him. For this I was paid about thirty-five dollars, eight times BC's minimum wage in 1982. If you can make eight times minimum wage, you're doing all right.

Mr. Kusumi's English wasn't very good, and for our first few sessions I prepared lessons and exercises which he reluctantly practised with me. Eventually, he told me he would rather just engage in casual conversation, so we spent our time together discussing every topic under the sun in simple English. I always asked my students to tell me about life in Japan or to give me the Japanese perspective on a given topic. This was an easy, and for me, informative way to get them talking. Occasionally, if they were tired, I would utter an outrageous statement of some kind which would rile them into a rebuttal. On more than a few occasions, I felt I was being fed a personal, idiosyncratic viewpoint under the guise of a fictitious national trait. It is convenient for anyone to give weight to their own actions and thoughts by passing them off, to unknowing foreign visitors, as widespread cultural practice.

In just a few months, Mr. Kusumi was promoted to CEO. He was in his fifties and was able to give me the perspective of a seasoned and successful businessman, and I was not shy about asking questions that I would never get to ask in North America. When would I find myself chatting comfortably for hours with the CEO of a major corporation in Canada? Teaching English gave foreigners, many of them of dubious origin and scant accomplishment, access to privileged domains in Japan, crossing many social barriers, although Mr. Kusumi was unlikely to invite me home for dinner. He told me that in Japan it was not always the most knowledgeable candidate or the most qualified who was promoted, but the one who was the most trusted. I was impertinent enough to ask him what his salary was, and he didn't hesitate to reveal it, about $110,000 a year, only ten times that of the lowest-paid employee in his company. In North America the CEO often makes up to 5,000 times the income of entry-level employees. Hiring senior officers from outside the company was unheard of, and the idea of employing an outside consultant was offensive. One evening after class he wandered away for a few minutes looking for someone to go for drinks with. He came back saying he was astonished to find that everyone had gone home, the first time he had ever seen it happen. In Japan it was very unusual for middle managers to pack it in before the highest-ranking managers left the office. Informal discussions over drinks in the evening amongst different levels of management are the source of much of a company's internal, vertical communication, and a place where the young men can try to impress the old. The gym, the golf course, and the bar. Most of the women in the office were single, and if they went to the bar at all, it was to pour drinks for the men.

Mr. Kusumi and I talked for many weeks about business, family, styles of life, education, and culture. One evening he told me he was taking his wife to Hawaii for two weeks. This was unusual. It was their first vacation of any length in thirty years of marriage. He said, "I have to…," and then he spent a moment looking in his dictionary before saying, "make amends." Eventually, Mr. Kusumi's duties as CEO became too numerous, at least that's what they told me, and he cancelled our class. I was sad to lose him as a student. He was the highest ranking businessman I got to talk to in Tokyo and was a fabulous source of information about Japanese life and business. He took me to the New Otani Hotel for lunch one day, very expensive. We were chauffeured over in a company car, black of course, with white antimacassars on the seat-tops, a necessity in Japan since most Japanese businessmen still favoured the liberal use of pomade. The chauffeur, along with a hundred others, waited in a large parking lot in front of the hotel until we were done. The driver was then called back to the front door using a public address system. Being financially successful in Japan is a bizarre combination of privilege and snobbery, of homogeny and uniformity, but it is usually more money-rational than in the west.

On one of my many visits to Mr. Kusumi's executive office, I noticed a box of Jell-O on one of his shelves, encased forever in a rectangle of acrylic. It was engraved *From the 500 millionth case of Jell-O produced by General Foods.* Jell-O is made from sugar and flavourings, and powdered gelatin extracted from the boiled bones and connective tissues of animals. It is a generic name for any gelatin product. It was a baby-boom standard, and I knew it well from my childhood. To this day gelatin salads and aspics make me gag.

I taught a group of engineers who worked at a dredging company. They were currently involved in extensive liquefied natural gas harbour works in Indonesia and were required to know, and be able to discuss in English, the volumes of plans and contracts involved. Their supervisor was a particularly obnoxious man, and I quit after a month or so. In general I tried not to be too capricious in my demands when it came to my pampered profession, and I tried to overlook this particular man's utterly insensitive rudeness, but the job just wasn't worth it to me. Quitting a job in Tokyo was pretty easy. You just told them that you had emergency family business at home and you had to leave the country. Everyone's face was saved. It was the only time in my life, when, if I didn't like the way my boss said "Good morning," I could respond with a dignified "I don't have to take that from the likes of you," walk out the door, and have another job by noon.

I taught a group of actuaries for a while, a class I inherited from Jude. She said they were "the most boring bastards on the face of the earth," and she was glad to be rid of them. They seemed like perfectly normal, average Japanese people to me, but I could see her point. We met in a room completely lined with books. One evening I started to look through them and discovered that every page of every volume contained only numbers and formulas, the mathematics and mechanisms of assessing risk and uncertainty, actuarial ambrosia.

I taught a wealthy man who owned a small chain of cookie stores who wanted to talk about his mistresses. He made me rather uncomfortable one day when he told me that he was having trouble getting erections lately. This was another class I covered for Jude. She laughed. "Yeah, he's always nattering on about that." She called him Biscuit Man.

I spent a few crushingly boring days assessing the English levels of engineers at Toyota. Several of them had spent three or more years in offices in South America, and they spoke Spanish. They had also studied English while working in these Spanish-speaking countries and spoke it with a

Spanish accent. This was a perplexing thing to hear coming from Japanese faces.

For a while I had a gruelling all-day schedule of seven classes in a row at a school that trained unexceptional high school graduates to be travel agents. They had to know some English to be in this business, and they had daily classes. Absenteeism was not tolerated, and I was required by the school to take attendance without fail. The classes were large, and I found myself reading out a list of twenty or more Japanese surnames at the beginning of every class. One day I was so tired and giddy I started to get the giggles while reading out the students' names. The syllables, meaningless to me anyway, became more and more ridiculous sounding as I went on. I nearly cried trying to keep from laughing out loud.

One of my students was a young man obviously in great physical shape. He was in his early twenties, taller than I, and very trim. He was not big, but he looked Bruce Lee strong. He usually wore a black, form-fitting leather jacket and beneath the jacket were muscles of cabled steel. He was gentle and soft-spoken like many Japanese men, very well groomed, polite and cooperative in class. He was a likeable fellow, but I had the feeling that if he wanted he could cross the length of the room as fast as a panther and break my neck or cut my throat before I knew he had left his chair. One evening at the end of class, I asked him about his job. In simple English he said, "Oh, I told you already, didn't I? I thought I did." I apologized for not remembering, and he said, "I am Imperial Guard Man." Ah. That explained it. His job was to guard the Emperor with his body and his life and to train daily for that duty. He was as close to a real-life ninja as you could get, and not a man you would want to disagree with in matters of the Imperial Household.

Costumes could be misleading in Japan. Like the dowdy high school girls dressed in Cyndi Lauper fashions on their day off, like the Disney trapper's cabin in the mountains of Nagano, like the band who sang flawless Country and Western songs at Yotsuya Gaigo Gakuin's Christmas party but didn't otherwise speak a word of English, you often never knew who was hiding under that brilliant mimicry. I saw a Japanese woman give a concert on an Andean harp at the Franciscan Chapel Center, and I would have sworn she was Peruvian. The Japanese are generally reluctant to leave the comfort of their own culture, but the few who do often seem to create a seamless simulacrum in their area of study. Also, cosplay is huge in Japan.

I started a new class one evening and was a little alarmed to see four Japanese men walk in suited entirely in American outlaw, biker-gang clothing. They were genuinely intimidating. I couldn't imagine what would happen in a classroom situation, or why they were taking the class at all. I used humour and joking and lighthearted conversation in my classes to get my students relaxed and unafraid to speak. I wondered how these soft techniques would play to an audience of hard-ass bikers. After fifteen minutes I realized they were only bad-ass outlaws in appearance. They cooperated in class, participated conscientiously, and were polite and friendly. Like the "trappers" of Nagano they really had no idea what they were mimicking.

I went to Yoyogi Park, near Harajuku station, on one or two Sundays to watch young people dance in costume, mostly Rock 'n' Roller and *Grease* style in those days. Up to 10,000 people in small groups danced in front of hundreds of boombox stereos, the boys in black leather jackets and slicked-back hair, the girls in poodle skirts and flip wigs. The girls snuck out of their homes in the morning when their parents weren't looking, their costumes in a bag, and changed in the bushes in the park. Harajuku is the centre of Tokyo's, and probably all of Japan's, youth fashion culture, from retro to extreme. The styles and names change every few years, but there are always one or two dozen street fashions trending in Harajuku, an area chock-full of cafes and clothing stores. As you walk east to Omotesando and Aoyama, the shopping becomes much more expensive in upscale, high-fashion flagship stores in architectural showcase buildings. There are boutiques and beauty salons, corporate headquarters and embassies. An hour or two in these areas can be exhausting although I slipped in and out almost daily to go to the gym or food shopping or to my favourite health food restaurant.

I had a private student, briefly, who was a registered patent attorney in solo practice. He spoke excellent English. He told me that when he finished his engineering degree, after working for a couple of years, he decided he wanted to go to law school. He said he had to get permission from his former engineering professors to change careers. I thought he must be confused about English terminology, and I questioned him about his use of the word "permission." He then explained to me in some detail the process and the meetings involved, the formal nature of it all, and in the end I was forced to conclude that permission was the right word. I told him that in Canada no such permission would be required. He said in Japan even in the absence of written requirements one was obliged in the handling of important life decisions to take a formal and respectful approach, and reach a consensus involving people from one's family, schools, companies, and professional associations. Once again I was just as glad I had not been born into such a rigid society. Mr. Sugahara told me there was a saying in Japanese, "Even sitting on a rock for three years will bring some benefit." I told Mr. Sugahara that if you sit on a rock for three years you will surely get hemorrhoids. He nearly leapt out of his chair. "Who told you?!" I wasn't sure what he meant, but he then said that he had hemorrhoids and he wanted to know who had told me. "Was it my wife?" I also gave her English lessons. I laughed and said it was just a joke. He went on to explain that in Japanese "hemorrhoids" is *jishitsu*, no kidding, and if you have a very good friend he is your "*ji* friend." This means he knows you so well he even knows if you have hemorrhoids. He told me another Japanese saying, "Three days, three months, three years," meaning that for every enterprise you embark upon, there will be a personal crisis of doubt, some loss of heart, at three days, three months, and three years, and you should be prepared to persevere during these critical times. True enough. You never quite knew where the conversation was going to go in a private language lesson. There were always unexpected misunderstandings as well as little found treasures.

I often taught groups of people who all worked for the same company, as well as groups composed of people from several different companies and different walks of life. There were highway engineers, oil engineers, a man who flew frequently to Vancouver to buy fish, a nuclear engineer, administrators and bureaucrats of every ilk, and many, many secretaries, office workers, and students.

I taught at JASRAC for quite a while, the Japanese Society for Rights of Authors, Composers and Publishers, Japan's music copyright organization. One day I showed up to find them all on strike. I thought I would get to go home, but they informed me the strike was only thirty minutes long and was nearly over.

The Japanese are devoted to the formal and ritualistic exchange of business cards, *meishi*. They are usually printed on both sides, *kanji* on one side and English on the other. There are complicated ass-sniffing behaviours associated with these rituals that only a born Japanese could understand. When I asked my students about their jobs, they would dive for their *meishi* and begin a set speech about their company and their position, formal and impressive. When I was finally able to convince them that what I really wanted to know, beyond their job titles and descriptions, was what they actually did when they got to the office, many of them said, "Oh, I usually have a cup of tea and read the paper."

I taught a class of rich housewives, the Real Housewives of Tamagawa, for a year. They came to the expensive department store next to the train station on Tuesday mornings for a class in English followed by lunch and shopping. One of them had lived in Manhattan for five years and never learned a word of English. She socialized with other Japanese women, the wives of wealthy businessmen and diplomats, and spent her days playing bridge and mahjong. I had thought mahjong was a Chinese game, and it is, but it is also the most popular table game in Japan. Mahjong means "sparrow." No one knows why. It was banned in China by the Communists in 1949, and in 1983 it was still illegal there. It wasn't officially reconstructed until 1985. At least one of these rich women had been to Banff, a stunningly beautiful natural landscape, but she said she didn't like it because the shopping wasn't very good. One day after class I tried a different subway route on the way home to see if the attractive older student I was accompanying would invite me home for the afternoon. She didn't.

It was at Tamagawa, the Tama River, where I saw a Japanese shantytown, clusters of wooden shacks along the shoreline obviously occupied full time. I hadn't imagined such a thing could exist in Tokyo, otherwise so rich and new. In the 1980s it was easy to forget that until the twentieth century Japan was a poor, non-industrialized country.

Mr. Owada, my visa sponsor and the holder of my official employment contract, eventually gave me one class at Yotsuya Gaigo Gakuin, probably to be able to prove to the authorities, if necessary, that I was actually working for him. I didn't really want the class. Mr. Owada didn't pay very much. But I took it as an obligation and with gratitude and kept it for the next sixteen months. I got a couple of classes at Shibuya Gaigo Gakuin for a semester, but the head teacher, a humourless Englishwoman, was a pest, so I declined to accept another contract. I think they declined to offer. Another school, IMI, one that David and Jude worked for, also stopped offering me classes. It's possible I wasn't as good a teacher as I thought. It might have had something to do with my performance on the morning I couldn't keep my head off the desk when the supervisor showed up unannounced.

Change was constant, anyway. When it comes to language learning, no student wants the same teacher year in and year out. Tokyo schools were well aware of the value of switching teachers frequently in order to maintain the interest of continuing students. It was also a bit of a beauty pageant. Nice-looking young teachers are the ones in demand. After a year or so, some of my students were surprised their English had not improved very much, and it was easier for them to accept their lack of progress if they thought it was the teacher's fault. I was usually a little less tired of them than they were of me since the money that was exchanged in our relationship came out of their pockets and went into mine.

If you think about Japan at all, you can't help thinking about nuclear energy, at least for a moment, and I had a small, strange connection to the subject. My last student in Japan, the very last, the one I saw on the morning of my last day ever in Tokyo, was Mr. Mukai, an assistant senior engineer at the Power Reactor and Nuclear Fuel Development Corporation. His office was in Tokyo, but their small, new, fast-breeder reactor development project, the Joyo MK-II, a research reactor with a core about the size of a barrel of oil, was at Oarai, in Ibaraki, halfway up the Pacific Coast from Tokyo to Fukushima.

The reactors at Fukushima, what's left of them, and those in most of the rest of the world, are thermal reactors, moderated and cooled by water. The energy from the fission in the core heats the water, the water forms steam, and the steam drives the turbines that turn the generators that make electricity. Fast-breeder reactors are much less common, about one in twenty. They're harder to build and manage, and they require more highly enriched uranium to get them going, but they offer the advantage of breeding, that is creating, their own fuel once the reaction has started. They can't be cooled by water because water slows down the fast neutrons in the reaction. Liquid sodium is often used as a coolant instead of water, and the heat has to be transferred in an additional step from the hot sodium to the water that drives the turbines. Sodium is a nasty metal. It burns on contact with air and explodes on contact with water. Its boiling point is eight hundred and eighty degrees Celsius. Safety is an issue. It has always amazed me, and should amaze anyone, that two very obnoxious elements, sodium and chlorine, together make table salt.

When I was hired at Sony Language Lab, the interviewer, Mr. Namikawa, asked me if I had a four-year degree. Taking my cue from Japanese practice, not wishing to say no outright, I told him I had studied science and had an Associate Diploma in Chemistry. I referred him to my 26-page curriculum vitae. He looked at me with earnest concern and then began nodding his head slowly up and down, never taking his gaze from my eyes. "Yes, but you have a four-year degree, correct." This he said very slowly and it wasn't a question. I joined him in his slow nod, and after a moment said only, "Ye-es." He then continued the paperwork. When Mr. Mukai came to Sony looking for a few sessions of English tutoring, he was looking for someone with a background in science, not just English. It turned out I was the only person in Sony's stable of ESL teachers who had ever taken a science course.

At our first session Mr. Mukai presented me with a list of ninety-five questions that he wanted to pose to nuclear scientists and engineers in the great state of New Jersey during an upcoming fact-finding mission. I knew more or less what a radioactive isotope was, and I had a vague understanding of nuclei and neutrons and what they were doing in a nuclear chain reaction. I had seen the diagrams in my first-year textbooks. But looking over Mr. Mukai's list of questions, I realized my handwritten, two-year Associate Diploma in Chemistry wouldn't be holding much water, light or heavy, in our discussions of nuclear engineering. I told Mr. Mukai he would have to tell me a great deal about the workings of fast breeder reactors before I could begin to assess whether or not his questions were actually asking what it was he wanted to know. I was unconcerned about passing myself off as an English teacher in spite of the blistering lecture I had received nearly four years earlier from Beryl, the head of Camosun College's ESL program. What harm could it do? In the end, perhaps, I should have been more concerned about passing myself off as a physicist.

Mr. Mukai and I spent our next six sessions standing over large blueprints and diagrams, rolled out and hanging over the edges of a table in one of Sony's small classrooms, and together we went over his questions one by one. Prepositions, and there are about a hundred and fifty of them in English, are very important in asking questions about step-by-step processes. Whether something happens across, or along, or before, or after, or behind, or between, or except, or following, or opposite, or through, or within the various components of a nuclear reactor constitute very important distinctions in those very dangerous environments. Mr. Mukai was particularly concerned about keeping very hot liquid sodium away from air and water and concrete although, happily, sodium is not corrosive to steel. A sodium spill is a full-on catastrophe, but he informed me that the word "accident" is never used in the industry. An accident involving renegade sodium would be called a "spill event."

The next year, 1985, construction started on the full-sized Monju reactor, ten times the size of the Joyo MK-II. It took nine years to build and it achieved initial criticality in 1994. In 1995 it was connected to Japan's electric grid, and four months later there was a spill event of thousands of pounds of sodium which caused a large, intense fire. Many Japanese citizens were understandably outraged and then further incensed when it was discovered there had been a subsequent cover-up, a scandal that included falsified reports, edited footage of security videos, and employee gag orders. The plant was shut down. After fifteen years of court battles, it was restarted in 2010 by which time Mr. Mukai was its director general. Four months later, there was another accident. A 7,000-pound transfer-machine fell into the core during a fuel replacement procedure, and the plant was shut down once again. It took a year to retrieve the transfer-machine from the core. Monju was a demonstration plant. The stated goal was to demonstrate the "safety and reliability of fast reactor power generation and sodium handling technology." So far, more than eleven billion dollars have been spent on the plant, and it has generated no more than a few weeks of electricity.

The Tokyo Electric Power Company has decided to scrap all six reactors at the Fukushima Daiichi nuclear plant although only four of them were damaged in the earthquake and tsunami of March 11, 2011. The decommissioning costs could run to four billion dollars with other compensation costs in the tens of billions. In 2013, groundwater containing radioactive particles was still leaking into the sea. In spite of the accidents at Fukushima and Monju, the Japan Atomic Energy Agency has plans to develop another fast-breeder reactor, a successor to Monju, to be built by Mitsubishi and currently scheduled to open in 2025. Other fast reactors are under development in several other countries.

Japan is the only country, so far, to have experienced, twice, the horror of nuclear attack. Little Boy, the bomb dropped on Hiroshima, contained a hundred and forty pounds of enriched uranium, but when detonated, less than a gram of it actually underwent fission releasing the equivalent heat and radiation of 30 million pounds of TNT in an airburst over the city. The nuclear weapons industry uses the kiloton as a measure of yield. It's easy to forget that a kiloton is 2.2 million pounds, as if that were easier to imagine. The Fat Man bomb, named for the character played by Sydney Greenstreet in the 1941 film of Dashiell Hammett's novel *The Maltese Falcon*, and dropped on Nagasaki three days after Hiroshima, contained only fourteen pounds of plutonium but was two-thirds more powerful than Little Boy. One hundred thousand people were killed by the acute effects of these blasts. By September of 1945, the US military was able to build an atomic bomb every ten days, and more attacks were planned before Hirohito, the Emperor *Showa*, the Heavenly Sovereign, decided that now was a good time to end eight years of total war with China and the Allies. Between the atomic blasts of World War II, the ongoing financial fiasco and dangerous disappointment of Monju, and the disaster of Fukushima, the worst nuclear accident since Chernobyl, Japan has had a sad and bizarre history with nuclear energy. Fukushima was a Level 7 accident. There is no Level 8. I never visited Hiroshima or Nagasaki in the two years I was there.

There is a very nice writing implement with several others less impressive in a mug on my kitchen table, next to my laptop. It's a Pilot brand, manufactured in both brushed and polished metal. There is a pen at one end and a pencil at the other. Mr. Mukai gave it to me thirty years ago, in 1984. The side is imprinted with the classic image of an atom, a nucleus with three electrons in orbit around it, followed by *PNC JOYO MK-II*. PNC. Power Nuclear Corporation.

Without nuclear power Japan would have to import eighty-five per cent of its energy fuels. For them, nuclear power generation may be an absolute necessity. But what a dangerous, unhappy, intolerable industry of ruinous cost and slim, desperate hopes of sustainability, a heap of waste, failure, stupidity, and misery. Fifty years of shame and sorrow and a complex, toxic legacy of uncertain duration. I liked Mr. Mukai, but if I had had his disturbing, depressing, and unsatisfying career, I would have switched to selling hotdogs on the beach long ago.

12   Tokyo Confidential, One

I hesitate to go on about my penis, it seems a bit juvenile, but I simply have to mention ten very uncomfortable minutes I spent on the subway one morning. For several Thursdays, I took two short subway rides to Tokyo's main business district of Chiyoda-ku, to a company I knew nothing about in a building I don't remember. I sat on a small couch in a small waiting area on the second floor of the strangely empty building, and a very serious man whose job I didn't understand, a manager of something, would appear at 8:00 a.m. We would then go to one little meeting room or other and practise sepulchral English for forty-five minutes. Throughout this arrangement I was never able to establish any rapport or fellow feeling with this man, and when he cancelled after eight or ten lessons, I was relieved. Not least because of the horrendous subway journey required to get to his office.

Most of us have seen the video images of Tokyo subways packed to bursting, with uniformed men on the platform wearing white gloves forcefully pushing commuters into the cars so the doors can close. I was usually able to avoid such extremes, but on this particular route it happened every morning. There was no different place on the platform where I could stand to wait, no alternate selection of cars, that would make any difference. The subway line I was on for a couple of short stops was always packed tight at 7:30 in the morning from the front of the train to the back. If you were only going a couple of stops, you had to resist the temptation to struggle to the centre of the car, where it was usually a little less suffocating, because you would not be able to make it back to the doors to get out before they closed again at your stop. You had to stay near the doors and be crushed together with fifty other people in a space the size of a galley kitchen. There was no danger of falling even if you were nowhere near a bar or a strap to hang on to. You were packed so tightly you simply couldn't fall over. A smaller person could be lifted up by the crush and ride the whole way without touching the floor. It can be a gruelling experience.

Getting touched up on the subway has always been, and still is, a problem for women in Tokyo. Women were always in danger of being groped and manhandled in these crowded conditions. One morning, we all packed ourselves into the subway car, and after the crushing ebb and flow had settled, I found myself immobilized and face to face, or crotch to belly, with a short young woman. We were ground together more forcefully by the pressure of the crowd than if we had been lying on top of each other. It was still warm weather, no need yet for coats, and my private parts were more than intimately in touch with her midriff for ten very long minutes. I didn't look at her and she didn't look at me. There was no need for introductions. Imagine a man in North America in random, suffocatingly close contact with a complete stranger, a younger woman in summer clothing, in public, and pressed against her as hard as possible in the most intimate way for ten full minutes. Criminal charges would be inevitable. It was something I had never experienced before, or since. It was unacceptably personal and unbelievably embarrassing for both of us. Not even I was a big enough pervert to enjoy this.

There was then a campaign afoot in Tokyo, one renewed every few years, an ongoing fruitless attempt to put an end to, or at least curb, subway groping. There were posters in the subways and newspaper articles highlighting the issue. A few women had had the courage to make a complaint, and a few men had been charged and convicted but probably not jailed. As the rocking motion of the subway ground my genitals into her abdomen, and her breasts into my stomach, neither of us able to move a centimetre in any direction, I was hoping and praying, first of all, that I would not have a further unbecoming response to the situation. I had good reason to be concerned. My penis has always done pretty much whatever it wants with very little regard for instructions from my brain. Happily, I remained master of my domain. Secondly, that this young woman was not in a mood to press the issue on this occasion. I was terrified that if she were hyperaware of the current anti-groping campaign, or if she had had other bad experiences recently, her nerves might snap and she could react in a way that would get me into a world of trouble. The critical moment was when the doors opened and everyone tumbled out of the subway car. It would be at that moment, when she could call for a platform attendant and make her accusations, that things could go very badly. It would have been an unreasonable charge, of course, but I had heard, and lived, stories of profound misunderstanding between Japanese women and foreign men. I also lacked the necessary language skills to make a convincing, on-the-spot defence. When we reached the next station, I sighed in huge relief as she turned away and bolted down the platform. John Lindsay, the mayor of New York, visited Japan in the early 1970s. Commenting on the Tokyo subway system, he said that if they had the same conditions in New York there would be riots and shootings every day. Try pushing someone into a subway car in New York. It is a tremendous testimony to the patience of the Japanese that they endure these conditions on a daily basis. What a way to have to go to work every morning!

However difficult, taking the subways and trains was better than driving. Mr. Hayashi, the manager at Yotsuya Gaigo Gakuin, told me that once during a subway strike, he had had to drive his car to work. He sat in traffic for eight hours, reported for work for one hour, and spent another eight hours driving home. He lived no more than thirty miles from the school. In 1983, I went to his apartment to celebrate New Year's Eve with him and his family. I took the train.

Sue, the woman I had met at the same time as Gillian, the one who had decided she would rather pursue a relationship with a handsome Japanese skier than with me, had a Thursday morning class at the same office. Once in a while, I saw her sitting on the same small couch on the second floor waiting for her older, unsmiling student. Whatever it was they did in this office, no one was happy about it. It occurred to me one day to ask her how her love life was going. Tears sprang suddenly to her eyes. She said, "I don't have one." The skier had declined to continue their connection. This was a great and pleasant surprise. Just at that moment, my humourless manager-student appeared, and I was obliged to follow him quickly and humorlessly down the hall in servitude. While walking reluctantly away from Sue, I turned my bright eyes back to her. "I'll call you!"

I was not averse to trying again with a woman who had previously shown no interest in me. I liked her. She was smart and funny. When I asked David to describe her to me before we went on our blind date a few months earlier, he said, "Well. Average. Really. It's the most appropriate word I can think of. She has average looks. She looks completely average. Nice. Average." This from a man who was often referred to as Pencil Neck. But he was right. Her facial features were unexceptional in the older sense of the word, nothing to which you could take exception, nothing out of place. What's to dislike? I see now from looking at old photographs that we had very similar smiles, and we were almost exactly the same height. We could put our arms around each other and kiss nose-to-nose, eye-to-eye, rarely the case between men and women.

We went out for lunch and coffee a few times, decided we liked each other after all, timing and availability now being more cooperative, and I was looking forward, very soon, to a meeting of profound physical intimacy. But there was a complication. Sue was a New Age kind of gal, and she had recently begun exploring the mysterious world of tantric celibacy. Aargh. I understood. This was how she was getting over her short, failed relationship. I had used hot saunas, ice-cold plunges, Catholic mass, the Hare Krishnas, *CBS Radio Mystery Theater*, yoga, and meditation. Whatever it takes.

I was familiar with the concept of celibacy for the sublimation of physical urges. I just wasn't up to it personally. And what was tantric celibacy, anyway? Was it just the technical, esoteric Eastern version of the West's dismal obsession with virginity? I really didn't know what she was doing, I couldn't bear to think about it, but she had met some people and joined a group, a very small group, that included a Mexican man who said that being celibate and doing tantric exercises gave him so much energy he was "jumping around like a Mexican jumping bean." His words. Sue probably, genuinely, wanted a greater supply of blissful spiritual energy, who wouldn't? But she might also have just been tired of men and sex, like other single, twentieth-century, North American women over the age of thirty, and needed a break. We continued to go out together. Eventually, the notion of not being intimate in private, a 29-year-old man and a 32-year-old woman, both healthy and attracted to each other, became absurd. We spent a year in each other's company with hardly a moment's unease, until I flew away from Japan for the last time, to San Francisco. We parted but we never broke up.

My relationship with Sue was not as passionately insane as with Gillian. She was less tortured and more forthcoming. She was calmer than Jude. Our relationship was warm and even and loving. She was just right, my third bowl of porridge, which made me Goldilocks. One day the bears would nudge me awake, but we were at peace for now.

Sue was from Oklahoma. She told me she never wore shoes until she was ten years old, but she may have been pulling my leg. In her childhood Sue and her mother and her two brothers had spent some time moving quickly and quietly from one apartment and motel to another in the American southwest, on the run from her stepfather. They finally lost him and found refuge in Helena, Montana, where her mother married for the third time. A few years later, her second husband caught up with her again. When her new husband heard about it, he tracked down his new wife's stalker, found him sitting in the local bar, walked in, lifted him off the ground by his ear, and escorted him to his vehicle with some stern advice about never setting foot in Montana again.

Sue went to university in San Jose, California, and finished a Master's degree in speech pathology. After six years in the California public school system, she decided a new career was needed, and she was now in Japan studying a form of traditional Chinese medicine, moxibustion. For a few months she studied and learned the theory and practice of heating acupuncture points with a stainless steel tube into which a burning punk of dried mugwort was inserted. The hot tube is stroked gently along the meridians of *chi* on the back, arms, legs, and chest. When a blocked acupuncture point is encountered, the heat creates an excruciating microdot of pain seeming to come from an infinitely minute source. The skilled practitioner recognizes the patient's reaction at once, uncontrollable spasms, tears, and cries for mercy. A couple of more strokes over the same area results in a subsidence of the pain and a relief so profound the patient actually feels his or her health has improved. The blockage at the acupuncture point has been cleared, and the practitioner moves on to the next one. The American Cancer Society says "available scientific evidence does not support claims that moxibustion is effective in preventing or treating cancer or any other disease." But that doesn't mean it doesn't work. You know the saying, "absence of evidence is not evidence of absence." And besides, that sounds like something the pharmaceutical industry, the second most profitable business on the planet, would pay them to say, doesn't it? If you play ball in that lucrative game, everybody's your friend and everybody gets paid. When Sue finished her course, she received an enormous diploma covered in *kanji*. The smaller the country, the bigger the passport stamp. The shorter the course of study, the bigger the diploma.

Sue lived in Japan longer than I did, but she never accepted the realities of renting in Tokyo. She refused to pay exorbitant fees and gift-money to secure a long-term apartment, preferring instead to do house-sits, or rent single rooms in boarding houses, or find other short-term sharing arrangements, rare but possible. She moved so often she had a regular mover, a little old Japanese man with a tiny truck who charged reasonable fees, and she employed him every couple of months. I remember visiting her at six apartments and houses around town, another way of getting to know the city and its neighbourhoods, and she had two or three more apartments in the half-year she lived there after I left. I wonder if she was driven by childhood memories of midnight moves in and out of dusty motels in the American southwest.

Sue was much more dedicated to work than I was. In addition to convincing her to have sex with me, I needed to convince her to stop working so much for so little. Her devotion to work was making her unavailable to me. This was annoying and obviously wrong. She taught a labour-intensive correspondence course, the Writing Program, which she referred to as the "R. P." She read and marked many papers every week for not much money. English teachers new to Japan are occasionally roped into low-paying jobs until they realize they can make a lot more money if they are choosier about their employers. I wanted to spend more time with Sue enjoying what Tokyo had to offer, and no one really likes unremunerative labour. I helped her look for less intense, more lucrative jobs.

Spring came wafting up from the south followed by the rain and then by the heat. Sue introduced me to her friends and I introduced her to mine. We met between and after classes at cafes and restaurants all over Tokyo. A favourite was the large, elegant, European-styled cafe in the Isetan department store in Shinjuku, a location handy for both of us. You could relax in a comfortable, cosmopolitan atmosphere for the price of a cup of strong coffee or creamy tea. In the same store I saw a small show of half a dozen paintings by Diego Velázquez, the Baroque portrait artist of the Spanish Golden Age. These shows were common amongst the bigger department stores. They were always offering a variety of services and exhibits in fierce competition with each other. A friend of mine taught Jazzercise classes at Isetan.

There are always line-ups in large urban centres, but in Tokyo they are well managed and move quickly, not least owing to the practice, all over Japan, of bountiful staffing. Where there are five staff in a business in Canada, there are eight in Japan. The salaries of those five Canadians are split amongst the eight Japanese workers, but in Japan they judged the financial health of their society not by how much money was made by those who were working, ignoring the cost to society of those who weren't, but by how many people were working overall. Salaries were low but unemployment was lower. Finding a staff member in a store in Canada can be a maddening and fruitless task. In Japan you are left alone to browse but you have only to mutter *sumimasen*, "excuse me," and you are immediately assisted in a manner so polite it is breathtaking to westerners. I don't think Japanese customers realize how lucky they are in their home markets.

Shinjuku-san-chome was also home to a tiny basement noodle restaurant that David and Jude showed me, and I went there at least once a week for a year and a half. They served *kuro udon*, "black noodles," thick buckwheat noodles in rich, dark *miso* soup with meat, or for me, tofu. Cheap, healthy, and filling. The same two young women worked there the entire time I lived in Tokyo. They didn't speak a word of English, but they usually seemed happy to see me. I never had to wait for a seat, and I was always the only westerner there. There wasn't a fork in the place.

The Japanese will eat just about anything that comes out of the ocean, but I won't. I was ninety-five per cent vegetarian. In two years in Japan, I had sushi once, against my will. I decided to try fried squid once. I was not expecting the chef to pull a live squid out of a bucket and rip it apart in front of me, but that's what happened. The plate came with what I thought was cabbage, it was crunchy and fresh and tasty. Then I noticed that each thin shred had a pair of eyes. Tokyo has hundreds of fruit boutiques, small shops selling only fruit, each one encased in soft, webbed, foam packaging, each one perfect and expensive. Tofu was the only thing cheaper in Tokyo than in Canada, and you bought it at the side-street windows fronting the little shops where it was made early in the morning. The mom-and-pop proprietors spent half their day with their arms immersed in ice-cold water, chilled to the bone in winter. Tokyo has thousands of little coffee-shop restaurants that serve the vilest spaghetti, the foulest curries, the whitest, most insubstantial bread I have ever seen, all thoroughly inedible, worse than anything you ever ate out of a can or a freezer. A typical Japanese restaurant would serve you tasty, healthy food, but these western-inspired establishments served a wretched imitation of their original types.

Mochi is a thick, gooey, heavy cake of pounded glutinous rice. It is so thick I could only eat two of them at most. It is consumed year-round but traditionally eaten at New Year's. In the past it was prepared in advance of the holidays by Japanese housewives so that, with a supply of ready food on hand, they would be freed from the kitchen and have time to participate in the New Year's celebrations. One of my students was a divorced mother, the only one I was aware of, and one day after the holidays she told me her teenage son had gone skiing for three days with his high school class. For three days they skied all day and partied all night. When he returned on the bus at six o'clock in the morning, utterly exhausted, he went to bed, slept twelve hours, and woke up at supper time, ravenous. His mother told him to go back to bed or his days and nights would be upside-down. He slept another twelve hours through to the next morning, woke up ferociously hungry and ate twenty-four *mochi*. Teenagers.

Sue and I heard of, and went to, a new business in Roppongi where you could sit in comfortable chairs in a private booth and watch a VHS video, impressive new technology. You could pause the video at any time and buzz for the attendant to bring you tea. We went to a school bowling party in the biggest bowling alley I have ever seen, dozens of lanes, every one reserved and in use. Jude won the top prize, for Lowest Score. Sue refused to go to a swimming party with the same school staff because she said the owners just wanted to see the female *gaijin* teachers in bathing suits. We went three or four times, on Saturday nights, to the enormous lobby lounge in the New Otani Hotel where for a small cover charge you could hear three or four sets of live big band music in luxurious surroundings.

Sue knew of a *genmai* restaurant in Shibuya. *Genmai*, brown rice, was a staple for North American hippies, but in Japan it is peasant food, and it was not easy to find in restaurants in Tokyo. Over-processed foods were the norm. Even food in the ethnic restaurants of Tokyo tasted decidedly Japanese. They are usually owned and run by Japanese people, there are so few immigrants in Japan, and they cater to familiar tastes. When we found this small health food restaurant in Shibuya, we went weekly. One day when I was dining alone I saw a western man sitting at another table. We made slight eye contact, but we both decided we would rather eat in peace and made no further social effort, neither of us in the mood. He looked a little weird to me, anyway. A week or two later I saw him again, but this time he was with a stunningly beautiful woman. I began to feel much friendlier. They motioned me to join them and I happily complied.

Vicente was a broadcaster from Brazil just starting a contract at NHK, the Japan Broadcasting Corporation, beaming news from Yoyogi to South America in Portuguese. His beautiful wife, Edna, had been a model. Vicente, not a particularly attractive man himself, was polyglot, fluent in five languages, Portuguese, English, French, Italian, and Spanish, although I had no way of testing his claims. He was urbane, sophisticated, witty, well-read, a man of taste and talent. Edna had many of these same qualities, but I never quite got past the more obvious aspects of her body and soul. To me she was sweet-natured and eye-poppingly gorgeous. Was I supposed to dig deeper? I introduced them to Sue, and afterwards we got together on many occasions. They took to Sue with great affection especially after I left Japan, perhaps not a coincidence, and the three of them became inseparable. Sue visited them at least once in Brazil in later years. We usually went out to eat, but we spent one evening at their apartment having a gourmet dinner prepared by Edna. Vicente was also a talented photographer. He had made several nudes of his breathtaking wife, and they adorned the walls of their apartment. This was too much for me. I was not that mature.

One day, I saw Vicente carrying a book, in English, one I had heard of but was not familiar with. I enquired about it. He said, "You have not read Powell? You call yourself a teacher of English and you have not read Powell?" His charm always more than made up for any offence I might take at his displays of uber-urbanity. He had an honest claim to it. He read in five languages. I didn't get around to reading Anthony Powell for another seven years, but I eventually took four months off and read all twelve volumes of *A Dance to the Music of Time*. By then I had the advantage of Spurling's 300-page "Who's Who" at my side to explain the cultural landscape of Powell's England and his 50-year *roman-fleuve*, the plots, the paintings, the places, and the characters, all four hundred of them.

Sue had an audiotape of Jane Fonda's new and very popular workout routine, a copy of which I soon acquired. It was thirty, sixty, or ninety minutes long, and it was a vigorous set of exercises. Jane Fonda is credited with being a major, early influence in the baby-boom fitness craze. She released the videotape of her workout in 1982 expecting it to flop. VCR players were new and quite expensive, but people started to buy them, in part, so they could exercise at home to Jane Fonda's videos. She sold seventeen million copies over the years. I loved working out at home. In the humid summer afternoons in Tokyo, I would sweat rivers and then throw a bucket of water over myself outside, a summertime *samurai* thing. One morning, prancing blissfully in my tiny apartment to Jane's tape, I twisted my back so badly I had to crawl, in great pain, to the nearest restaurant to use the telephone and beg Sue to come over as soon as possible and give me an emergency moxibustion treatment. That was the end of my affair with Jane Fonda.

Sue knew an American woman whose husband was the manager of AFN, the American Forces Network, my favourite radio station, at the US Air Base in Yokota thirty miles west of Tokyo. We were invited to their home, in military housing, on July 4. At the base, 14,000-strong, we found the entire complement of off-duty personnel engaged in fire-cracking celebration of Independence Day. There were flaxen-haired children playing and arguing and shouting, "Uh-huh!" "Nuh-uh!" "Uh-huh!" "Nuh-uh!" running around letting off bottle rockets and roman candles. This was a change from the shouts of *"Gaijin! Gaijin!"* that you heard when encountering groups of Japanese children. In addition to the bangs and flashes of the firecrackers, you could see, and what was more vivid, hear, the massive and deadly planes of the United States Air Force taking off in the distance, ever vigilant. I had never been on an air base before. The sheer power of it was overwhelming. After an hour of boisterous celebration of independence and freedom, combined with the visible proofs of the death-dealing wizardry deemed necessary to defend and promote these high ideals, I was beginning to feel uncomfortable. I was glad to start for our friends' quarters for a break from the planes and the propaganda.

Military housing is a grim prospect in any country, and the uninviting rows of identical fronts we encountered were not promising. Inside, however, Sue's friends had tastefully decorated their quarters with fabrics, plants, candles, wood, leather, art, and crafts. We drank herb tea in a deeply relaxing atmosphere completely insulated from the jets and the jingo just outside the door. The radio station manager had a Master's degree in communications and was a captain, maybe a major. He ran the only English-language station in town, so he broadcast several genres of music to multiple target audiences, the reason I liked the station so much. You could listen to classical, jazz, pop, country and western, etc, every day for a couple of hours each. His job seemed like a very benign role to play in the armed forces although I imagine planning for the use of his broadcast facilities during emergencies was non-stop and gloomy.

I bought reserved tickets weeks in advance, which you could do in Japan, for the opening of the third *Star Wars* movie, *Return of the Jedi*. Sue and I waded through warm spring rains to see it, and for our troubles we were presented with Ewoks. We saw Ben Kingsley in *Gandhi*. Our arty and intellectual friends sniffed at it, but I liked it. Gandhi was another of my brown heroes. When he was asked what he thought of western civilization, he said he thought it would be a good idea, and I, race traitor, agreed with him. We went to see *Octopussy*, the James Bond movie, where, before it started, I made my friends promise to keep the groaning and the eye-rolling to a minimum. My students asked me what "Octopussy" meant. Here I was pressed. I told them that "octo" came from octopus and a "pussy" was a baby cat, a kitten. I left it at that. Sue and I saw *Flashdance* and afterwards danced together, hopping and skipping, down the hot and humid streets of Takadanobaba at midnight.

In Tokyo, I could have seen live performances by Joni Mitchell, David Bowie, Dire Straits, the Police, or Journey, but I've never been a rock-concert guy. I probably should have been. I grew up with the evolution of the mega rock concert. I wanted to see Elton John in Vancouver eight years earlier, in 1975, but he was one of the two or three hottest pop musicians of the day, and the ticket price had been raised to six dollars from the norm of five, a shocking amount, and I refused to go. I could buy one of his albums for four dollars and listen to it a hundred times. I couldn't justify the expense. Instead, I went to as many classical concerts in Tokyo as I could, in beautiful halls. I saw Beethoven's Ninth Symphony impressively performed by an orchestra and choir whose names I have forgotten. I saw a French piano soloist on a world tour whose name I have also forgotten, performing Haydn and Debussy. I saw the dazzling Berlin Philharmonic Octet, as well as an evening of opera standards and highlights, and an expensive, but unimpressive, performance of *Romeo and Juliet* by the Bolshoi Ballet.

The crowds at these kinds of events tend to be better behaved than at rock concerts although you won't find nearly as many people in Japan high on drugs at a stadium concert as you would anywhere else in the world. The Japanese have no sense of humour about even the softest of drugs. They put Paul McCartney in jail for ten days in 1980 for possession of a little pot, well, seven ounces. They cancelled his tour and banned his music from radio and television. Paul McCartney, MBE, Sir Paul, the sweetest guy in the world. This is blatant hypocrisy in a country with such a serious alcohol problem. Six nights a week the bars, the streets, and the subways are full of drunks, beer and whisky for the salarymen, beer and *shochu* for the working men. I know. On my first trip to Japan, I was one of them. Intoxicated men urinating and vomiting in the streets, falling asleep on the train home, are a common sight everywhere in Japan.

I did go with David and Jude and their friend Lindley to see Joe Jackson perform, in his Night and Day Tour, at Nakano Sun Plaza. The theatre had reserved seating, a must-have for my taste. Lindley was a friend of David and Jude's, but I don't know how they met. He wasn't an English teacher. He was a finance and planning manager at Exxon Corporation's Tokyo office, part of Japan's privileged corporate and embassy elite, one not much given to associating with English-teaching riff-raff. He was exactly my age but much over-qualified for my company. Before I met him, he had already earned a Bachelor's degree *magna cum laude*, as well as an MPA, both from Princeton University, and an Advanced Professional Certificate in Finance from NYU's Stern School of Business. I had a fake two-year diploma in chemistry handwritten by a secretary. Tall, dark, and a little stout, he looked older than his thirty years whereas I still looked younger than mine. That, at least, was as it should be. He was New-England, Ivy-League stock "on a blue-chip highway," as David said. He was also a friendly, peaceful, and generous man. We went a few times to his almost uncomfortably spacious apartment, expensive and beautifully furnished, in the pricey Aoyama neighbourhood for dinner or a party or to relax after an evening out. He had a big cathode-ray TV, probably twenty-six inches, and a VCR, possibly a Betamax, each, incredibly, with its own remote control. This was impressive *tech nouveau*.

We went to see *Missing*, a movie about the revolting and horrifying behaviour of that scowling eagle, the United States, especially Nixon and the CIA, in the 1973 Chilean coup d'état. It was one of the fifteen or more regime changes, one of the most blatant, in which the US took part in the twentieth century, usually in support of whatever military groups were willing to pose as anti-communist for pay. Hiding behind the cant and false piety of democracy, a political system, the United States has made it clear again and again that it will oppose, militarily if necessary, any obstacle to capitalism, an economic system, even if it means the unashamed support of dictatorship and monopoly. If the ruling capitalists of the west fear that a country is using democracy to achieve economic equality, that country's government is not long for this earth. Representative democracy as practised by the Americans does not include the right to undermine or change the economic system that benefits those who own and run both systems. The short definition for this kind of political behaviour is fascism, except that the primacy of the state is replaced by the primacy of the corporation and the cartel. In Chile, the socialist president, Salvador Allende, committed suicide in the presidential palace, and General Augusto Pinochet joined the long list of murderous dictators that have been put in place by the United States. Pinochet ruled Chile as president for seventeen years and as commander-in-chief of the army for twenty-five. By the end of his life, he was an international pariah facing hundreds of charges for human rights violations and the theft of millions of dollars of public money. When we wandered out of the theatre stunned and saddened by the story, Lindley said, "You must be very proud, or at least relieved, to be Canadian." He had interviewed for the CIA when he graduated from Princeton.

Lindley told me his goal was to work in New York in investment banking. I didn't know what that was, but it sounded bad to me. Only a month after I left Japan, Lindley left as well and spent a dozen years at Salomon Brothers in their Global Power Group, manipulating energy resources around the world. Global Power. It sounds absolutely frightening. I hardly heard a word about him for the next twenty-five years, but David and Jude kept in touch with him off and on. He was their friend. For me he was a brief acquaintance. In the mid-nineties he left Wall Street. In a move that must have been a surprise to some, he started working on a Master of Divinity degree at the Union Theological Seminary in New York, followed by a Doctor of Divinity, at Princeton, and he is now the Rev. Dr. Lindley DeGarmo, Pastor and Head of Staff at the Towson Presbyterian Church in Towson, Maryland, a comfortable, well-educated, white suburb of Baltimore. The most common surnames there among the deceased are Smith, Miller, Jones, Johnson, Williams, Brown, and White. The Presbyterian Church (USA) is part of the Reformed tradition, another word for Calvinist. It is ninety-three per cent white, fifty-eight per cent female, and has been losing members steadily for thirty years. It has not experienced an increase in its proportion of non-white members for the last fifteen.

On the church website Rev. DeGarmo lists hobbies such as golf and wine tasting. He also lists memberships in five private clubs, one or two of them five-diamond golf clubs. The others are arts and social clubs that are not embarrassed to state that "integrity, civic purpose and gracious company" are their objectives. Membership involves no mention of, or need for, a contrite or Christian heart. In general, the mainline Protestant churches support civil rights and equality for women. The Reverend's duties as a pastor, then, include a commitment to social justice, but I wonder how much social inequality you can see from the verandas of Lindley's exclusive clubs. This is a man I liked but could never understand. All that love and caring and giving, the commitment, the generosity and largeness of spirit, the hard work, combined with conspicuous worldly achievement and the unflappable acceptance of bountiful material reward. These were two groups of ideas that never came together for me.

In Lindley's world, the Protestant world, church is a part of society and a part of the state. Active membership in the right congregation makes you a better person in a better, more successful civilization. Religion and material success are both good and both may be pursued and enjoyed. Prosperity requires no apology. For me, neither church nor society are goods. They are both transitory, closer to necessary evils, and religious life is an inherently subversive practice of personal transformation, a reproach to both church and society. All prayer is dissent, not from reality, but from convention. All religion is revolt, not against reality, but against unnecessary suffering and can play no part in its worldly propagation.

The wealthy priest never comes off well in literature, the missionary only rarely. The bishop is always the bad guy. The princes of the church are often the purest evil. Torquemada, Borgia, Medici, Richelieu, Marcinkus. Granted, all Catholics. The good priest is always the poor one in the story, or the friar or the hermit. Lindley, practical-minded and experienced in corporate movements, probably finds many generous donors on the manicured fairways of the clubs he frequents, but my distrustful view of philanthropy is that it is a thin, chilly wrap of public relations thrown over the more traditional goals of the moneyed classes, keeping the pool of labour poor and conservative, skilled but uneducated, un-unionized, unhealthy, uninsured, distracted and angry about manufactured and overblown issues like gun rights, taxes, gay marriage, health care, illegal immigration, foreign crusades, the war on this, the war on that, so they have no choice but to show up for work every day for minimum wage or join the army. And when they get uppity, the factories are moved to Mexico and China.

I grew up in a society where to do was everything and to be was nothing. When everyone is unemployed and hungry, when economies are depressed, you have no choice. Unless you do something, you can't be anything at all. But seeing the emotional and cultural effects of this one-sided approach, I naturally evolved the opposite philosophy that to be was everything and to do was nothing, that there is no lower form of human activity than the pursuit of money at the unwarranted and unjustified expense of others. There is no such thing as enlightened self-interest. The trickle down effect only trickles up. Try as I might I cannot associate elite levels of white wealth and authority with social goodness. I don't suppose the rich are the sole possessors of every vice, and the poor of every virtue, but in my small experience of repugnant prosperity, rich men are not good men. Too often, those who do well do bad.

But maybe these grasping, hard-working white people have something. Life in a closed system is unsustainable, and in the end all systems are closed. Life consumes all the resources of the system in which it arises and then consumes itself and dies away, or it changes and rises again in another system. Every species is a process, and every stage a species reaches, every form it takes, is the echo of a previous extinction. When you see a recognizable form, you are looking at an illusion, something never born. You need not apologize, then, for the inevitable, but you may be held accountable one day for your participation in the means.

The Protestant Work Ethic, and that's the last time I will capitalize that, is the Great Mistake of the Protestants. It replaced the remote, magisterial, organizational fear, greed, dogma, authoritarianism, corruption, and abuse of the Catholic Church with local, self-directed, individual fear, greed, dogma, authoritarianism, corruption, and abuse. It was a step forward but only a step. It was the midwife of capitalism and bears that heavy responsibility. Its noble commitments and spectacular achievements are old and tarnished now, after four hundred years of preaching by the Anglo-Saxon Hordes of the New World, development and devastation in their wake. The endless, unfalsifiable tautology: "We are right because we are successful. We are successful because we are right." Judging by results rather than by principles. It is a philosophy of grasping born in a world where everything was free to the hand that could grasp it.

For me, an old hippie and wannabe mystic, there are no such things as conservative religion and established church. These phrases are reductionist oxymorons. The duty of every religionist is not to support the status quo but to put him or herself out of a job by creating a physical world so infused with spirit that churches and societies are irrelevant. For me, not born into a tradition of high education or social capital, and too stoned to found such a tradition in my family, the trademarks of Protestant wealth and society are oppression, personal, social, and political, and the conspicuous absence of not only holiness, but a framework for its arising. I associate WASP wealth and authority with their brutal acquisition and entrenchment, exclusion and privilege, the lies and hypocrisy fabricated to justify and preserve them in the hands of those bold enough to get hold of them. You can't invest in and support a system that ass-rapes the planet and its people Monday through Saturday, and then tell me you love God on Sunday. If the water is not clean enough to drink, it is not clean enough to baptize. As for the proprietary colonies of Chesapeake Bay, Maryland and its neighbour Virginia, they were the cradle of American slavery. They and the Presbyterians, tepid abolitionists at best, aren't finished paying for that yet.

But I am not a fanatic. Lindley and I were both hungry, and we fed ourselves with the food we found at hand. I've been known to backslide. I could probably be persuaded to change my views if I were invited to become a member of a comfortable, wealthy, philanthropic social class. "I will change my faith and my bedding, but thou must pay for it." If I think about it at all, I must cling to the idea for the sake of my sanity that my spirit runs deep, but I know it is not large. In another year or so, I would realize that the pathetic attempts I was making in my late twenties to simplify my life were only making it small.

Tokyo Disneyland opened that spring, but for some reason we were never tempted to go.

I also met Tatsuro at the *genmai* restaurant and his intense American wife, a friend of Sue's. Tatsuro was a professor of something at Keio University. His subject of research seemed to involve a lot of dance, music, sex, myth, and different cultures, and he was truly an outlier in Japanese society. He wrote books with names like *The Spirit Journey of the Body Expression*, *Sexuality of Transvestism*, *Polysexual Love*, and *The Climactic Point of Body*. I met him many times for coffee and brown rice. I don't think I realized the depths I was dealing with in Tatsuro.

In addition to going to the gym and my short affair with Jane Fonda's workout tapes, and doing yoga, and bicycling, David and Jude and I played racquetball as often as we could manage. It was popular in the eighties. There was a new club next to the New Otani Hotel, only one subway stop from my house and a brisk walk along the moat down the east side of Akasaka Palace. We took a couple of classes, and we were always the best players, easily trouncing the other beginners. But when we played the instructor, she would first let us get a few points off her, and then she would tighten down her game and wipe the floor with us to keep us humble. One day I noticed a very special membership card in a glass case in the reception area. It was the first one issued by the club, Member No. 1. It was made out to President Gerald Ford.

Next to the racquetball club was the new tower of the Akasaka Prince Hotel. It was brand new, only a few weeks old, thirty-five storeys high, clad in gleaming aluminum outside, and decorated in gleaming white inside. And it was practically empty. They had few customers for many weeks after opening until it became better known. I used to go to the empty lounge on the top floor, order a bottle of Perrier water, and alternately read my book and gaze out the window at the breathtaking view. When I was finished, I would take the empty elevator to the lobby in an uninterrupted free fall of thirty-five storeys. Sometimes twice, just for fun.

My shirt-tail cousin Dale was living in Manila, and his parents stopped in Tokyo for a couple of nights on their way to visit him and his new wife. I didn't have a telephone, but my mother had given Wayne and Edith my address. They asked the front desk clerk at the Akasaka Prince Hotel, where they were occupying a gleaming white room for the opening special price of about thirty dollars a night, to assist them. Using my address, the front desk clerk found a telephone number for my landlord, Mr. Nakai, the veterinarian, and Mr. Nakai knocked on my door one evening to tell me, to my great surprise, that there was a telephone call waiting for me at his house next door. I had no idea anyone from Canada was planning a visit. I took Wayne and Edith around Tokyo as best I could the next day telling them of my experiences in Japan, but not all of them, showing them my little haunts, including lunch at the black noodle joint, where Wayne, an Alberta farmer, was completely flummoxed by chopsticks. We asked for a fork, but they said they didn't have one. By the end of the meal, the entire front of his shirt was covered in *miso*, and everyone in the restaurant was highly entertained.

The real estate market in Tokyo is so wild that the new Akasaka Prince Hotel was closed after only thirty years of operation and was dismantled from the inside, from the top down. The top couple of floors were preserved intact as the floors directly beneath were dismantled and the top floors progressively lowered on jacks. The building thus preserved its overall form while appearing to shrink in height over a period of two years. The partial building was used to house refugees from the Fukushima nuclear disaster in 2011. All thirty-five storeys were gone by 2013. It will be replaced by an office building of about thirty-five storeys.

I read constantly and everywhere, on the subway, on buses, in cafes and restaurants, and at home. I had no telephone or TV. When I wasn't teaching a class or doing yoga or with friends, I was reading. There were only two good English bookstores in Tokyo and Kinokuniya was the best. It was only two stops away from my house and was as good as any good bookstore in North America. I read, as always, literature, history, and religion. Apart from studying at university, I read more in that year and a half in Tokyo than at any other time in my life. It was heaven.

I met Rupert soon after I arrived in Tokyo. He was a tall, slim, roguishly handsome, slightly dodgy Englishman of David and Jude's acquaintance. At our second meeting he asked me for a loan of 10,000 yen, about fifty dollars. I complied, hesitatingly, to try to be agreeable in my new social surroundings. When I told Jude about it, she laughed and said he owes every *gaijin* in Tokyo 10,000 yen. I liked Rupert, but I wasn't going to let him get away with it. After about a month I cornered him. I told him I would not be fleeced. He didn't have the authority to impose a tax on others simply for the privilege of meeting him. I told him I would harry him for the rest of my time in Tokyo until he paid up, and we were now part of the same social circle. I must have been convincingly stern because a few days later he produced the necessary and we got along well afterwards. He was a guy you could yell at for bad behaviour. He wouldn't take offence.

 Rupert was even lazier than I was. His apartment was near mine, and he knew I was always home at 10:00 a.m. It was amazing the number of times he just happened to drop by while I was making French toast. He had been a car salesman in England in the 1970s, not a lucrative time for the auto industry in the UK, and he discovered he could make more money teaching English in Japan. He also discovered that a small percentage of Japanese women like having sex with western men. It was a small percentage, but in a city the size of Tokyo that made for a very large number, and Rupert spent his time in Japan swimmin' in women, taking them back to his little apartment for the night. After classes and in night clubs, pretty girls with downcast eyes offered in simple English to sleep with him in the plainest terms. "Do you want me?" He scratched the number off the telephone in his apartment, so they couldn't make a note of it and call him later. One night he picked up a young beauty at a disco. He said she picked him up. They went back to his place and did the right thing. In the morning she opened her backpack and pulled out her high school uniform, the standard sailor suit, to get dressed and ready for school. This was not what she had been wearing the night before. This nearly gave the 30-year-old Rupert heart failure. There are certain ages when a man can have sex with a woman half his age and get away with it, but thirty is not one of them. He hustled her to the subway under a raincoat, praying the neighbours wouldn't see.

 Rupert also took advantage of Japan's easy access to other, even more sexually alluring, countries in South East Asia, Thailand and the Philippines. With little or no preparation or knowledge beforehand, he would simply land at the airport, ask for the location of the nearest backpacker beach and get on a bus. Once there he would find a hammock for rent, hire a steady hooker, and drink and do drugs and have sex for a week, invariably returning home with what he referred to as a drippy dick. He was kind of a hero of mine. I was only mildly envious of his sexual escapades, and next to him I felt quite upright and responsible. At first I couldn't figure out why cute and curious Japanese girls seemed so eager to leap into bed with Rupert. He was a bit of a wet blanket overall. We went to the same public bath, but we were on different schedules, and in a year and a half I only ever saw him there once. But when I did run into him one night at the *sento*, I figured out why the girls always wanted to see him again.

Sex is different in Japan. In 1983, dating and courting were still very old fashioned. If you agreed to go on a date with someone three times, you were effectively engaged. Most single people lived at home with their parents. Full-on sex before marriage was unlikely to happen except in a love hotel. The sex business, on the other hand, was and is huge. Prostitution was made illegal in 1958, but since then every possible loophole has been explored and exploited in the Japanese sex business. Turkish baths, *toruko-buro*, are a standard. You get soaped from head to toe by a young woman who then has sex with you. Very clean, very Japanese, positively hygienic. Another plus is that sex workers in Japan tend not to be involved with drugs. I never went to a Turkish bath, but I heard reports from a couple of westerners who did. You either had to be accompanied by a Japanese man or be fluent in Japanese. Otherwise, foreigners are not welcome. In the 1980s, the Turkish embassy in Tokyo launched a campaign to convince the Japanese to stop calling brothels Turkish baths. They were successful, and in a nationwide contest a new name was chosen, Soaplands. There are a couple of hundred of them in Tokyo. Japan's national pension cheques are issued on the fifteenth of the month, and on that day elderly Japanese men are seen in greater frequency on the streets of Yoshiwara, the Tokyo neighbourhood where the soaplands are most common.

Setting and costuming in the sex business play a big role in Japan. You can be entertained in bars by very expensive hostesses whose only job is to talk to you, pour your drinks, light your cigarettes, and laugh at your jokes. You can purchase all manner of fantasy and fetish in specialized brothels, some that don't even involve sex. You can simply have a nap with a pretty girl wearing a quirky costume, or buy a pair of her unwashed underwear.

One of my western friends told me his Japanese colleagues made plans one day to go to a live sex show over the lunch hour, so he went along too.

There were ten rows of ten chairs packed tightly into a room with a small stage. A woman came out, danced a little, and asked for a volunteer from the audience. An eager man leapt up and dropped his trousers. His naked buttocks pumped up and down vigorously in short, rapid strokes until he was exhausted, but he was too shy to finish the job. He was jeered off the stage, and another man was called upon to deliver the goods. "Damnedest thing I ever saw," said Bob. The show was in Kabuki-cho, the red-light district in Shinjuku, not far from my favourite bookstore. Of course the sex business can be much worse than that, involving things you don't want to think about. I wandered through Kabuki-cho a couple of times. It's tawdry at night and depressing during the day, tempting only in the last resort.

One other disturbing feature of the sex business in Japan was that you could buy rather upsetting bondage-sex magazines at kiddie-eye-level at the corner store. The photographs themselves were censored, everyone's genitals brushed out, but given the frequent display of sex dungeons, machines, weapons, and ropes, this was little consolation. Although the knot-making was fabulous. The Boy Scouts would be fascinated by that alone. In spite of all this worrying material openly displayed, every Playboy and Penthouse magazine that entered the country had the models' crotches mechanically scraped off, by, I imagined, a warehouse full of middle-aged Japanese women working at rows of desks in the customs houses, each armed with something resembling a modified, old-fashioned, desktop, wooden-handled, mechanical date stamp, scraping away pubic hair, which it was still possible to find in 1983.

Even Shizuka, my conservative Japanese girlfriend, had a couple of stories about strange sex in Japan. There was a new love hotel in Shibuya in the late seventies, instantly famous, built in the form of a castle, with fantasy rooms for hourly sexual encounters, usually between unmarried couples, boyfriends and girlfriends, businessmen and their mistresses. Shizuka knew a girl from college who worked there part time, and out of curiosity she spent a busy shift with her as a housekeeper, changing the sheets. She also accompanied her father on a corporate retreat where part of the entertainment for his employees was a sex show involving vaginas, cigarettes, and ping-pong balls. Shizuka was still in her early twenties. She wanted to talk to the principal performer. They chatted after the show, and the older woman told Shizuka that she couldn't have sex for twenty-four hours before a performance otherwise she didn't have the bounce necessary to execute her vaginal gymnastics.

Manga is huge in Japan. These are comics in multiple genres, fantasy, sci-fi, sports, comedy, etc, usually very thick volumes in black-and-white on very cheap paper. You could find yourself standing next to a young schoolgirl in the subway reading a cutesy romance story or the foulest imaginable sex and violence. In either case the girls and women in these comics were drawn with very large, round eyes, and very large breasts. What the young boys were reading was unspeakable.

There were movie posters in Shinjuku, near my house, that were sickening, advertising movies of horrific sex and violence, Japanese productions in association with European and Asian companies, movies that would never be allowed in Canada. The themes in Japan's pornography industry, which still showed their productions in movie houses and openly advertised them, were frequently of kidnapping, confinement, bondage, rape, torture, murder, and incest. This was new to me, and alarming. This incredibly conservative and polite society, refined in so many ways, where you couldn't legally look at a pin-up girl's crotch in a magazine, had a thriving industry and market for the lowest passions in the form of the most revolting depictions of film sex and violence, truly obscene and offensive, ever-so-slightly censored with blurry patches, illegal in most other countries of the world. What a society. What a dark shadow. Where young people are not permitted an open and healthy sexual outlet, there are very sad consequences.

Japan's population is aging fast. Their birth rate is the sixth lowest in the world, second only to Germany for larger countries. Monaco and Singapore don't really count. The current population of 126 million is falling and could fall by one-third over the next fifty years. Soon, one in three Japanese people will be over sixty-five. There have been cases of land and houses going unclaimed, their owners dying alone, their relatives unknown or non-existent. In 2012, adult diapers outsold baby diapers.

As far as real sex and relationships go, life in Japan is so conservative and expensive and so filled with lifelong grinding obligations that many young people have lost interest in sex, dating, marriage, and having children. Surveys in 2013 showed that forty-five per cent of women between the ages of sixteen and twenty-four, and twenty-five per cent of males, "were not interested in or *despised* sexual contact." One-half of unmarried people under thirty-four were not in any kind of romantic relationship. A third of people under thirty had never dated at all. The phrase most commonly heard among young people talking about sex and marriage is *men-*

dokusai, "I can't be bothered." Currently a young woman in Japan has a one in four chance of never marrying and a four in ten chance of never having children. A small percentage of men in Japan have stimulated a lot of discussion about "recluses," "geeks," and "parasite singles," 35-year-old men who still live at home and have never dated. Men and women in Japan are learning to live without sex, or at least without human contact.

Western scientists and engineers working in robotics have long snickered at their Japanese counterparts for their obsession with developing human-like robots designed for companionship. Japan is a country that needs them. Work and family life there have become so difficult and unattractive, downright miserable in many ways, that people would rather snuggle up to a robot or a pillow in the form of a person, play sexy video games, or watch what is now, hands down, the most innovative and wacky pornography in the world, much of it hilarious, much of it very disturbing.

Initially, it was thought that the repulsions of Japan's onerous, conservative, and complicated society had driven its young people away from the desire to participate in it, preserve it, or advance it along traditional lines. Now, it appears there is also an inherent attraction to the new lifestyles that are emerging. "Celibacy syndrome." People like being single. They like technology-based companionship and sex. They prefer it.

It is possible the Classic Maya Collapse of a thousand years ago in Central America was the result of a people who were experiencing a declining marginal return on participation in an intolerably demanding and ugly society forced upon them by previous generations. They simply lost interest. They downed their shit-shovels, packed up their gourds, left their cities of stone, and walked into the jungle. The Japanese may be the Mayans of the twenty-first century, walking away from their elders with their boyfriend pillows, their blow-up dolls, and their sex-bots under their arms. Some say that in this they are merely the bellwether for all developed nations, re-imagining the social-sexual life of the human species.

13 Tokyo Confidential, Two

In spite of the bondage magazines and the nauseating posters I had to walk by nearly every day, the seamier side of life in Japan and its difficult future didn't mean much to me. I had daydreams of taking short trips out of the country, perhaps not dissimilar to Rupert's, or perhaps of a more healthful nature. It seemed a shame not to explore more of Asia since I was already there.

I thought of visiting my cousin in the Philippines, but Benigno Aquino was assassinated at the Manila International Airport in August, and the People Power Revolution began with the aim of finally being rid of President Ferdinand Marcos. It turned into a three-year campaign of non-violent civil resistance. Marcos had ruled the Philippines for more than twenty years, authoritarian, corrupt, despotic, and repressive. He was accused of human rights violations and the theft of billions in public money. Marcos's ridiculous wife, Imelda, the Iron Butterfly, owned 3,000 pairs of shoes. In a snap election in 1986, Aquino's widow, Corazón, was elected president. After weeks of tension and uncertainty, while Corazón took meditative refuge in a Carmelite convent, and the army squabbled, Marcos, to everyone's surprise, stepped down and left the Philippines. The Marcoses were foul and murderous co-dictators, so they were of course supported by the United States and given asylum in Hawaii. They had billions of dollars in Swiss banks. A billion friends. Ferdinand died in 1989. Imelda was pardoned by Corazón Aquino. She returned to the Philippines and has spent the last thirty years fighting nearly a thousand civil lawsuits and criminal cases brought against her, as well as being elected twice to the Philippine House of Representatives, currently incumbent for Ilocos Norte. Her billions in Switzerland have never been recovered by the state. Imelda's shoes were stored, badly, at the presidential palace and the National Museum, and half of them have been destroyed by termites, flooding, and mould. My cousin Dale told me things weren't that bad in Manila and I should come for a visit anyway, but I never did.

I spent the first half of my second visit to Japan paying off bills and the second half saving money. Living and working in Tokyo, even for a pampered *gaijin* teacher, can be stressful. The city is enormous and polluted and crowded. The Japanese are notoriously xenophobic, "a handful," as

David remarked in his laconic way. If you get tired of Tokyo's pleasures, you will soon weary of its challenges. Jude grew tired of Japan long before David did. When I first arrived to sleep on their *tatami* floor, Jude was showing signs of stress, and they were both looking forward to their long, nine-week holiday in the warm embrace of David's comfortable family in Calgary, while I raced around Tokyo in the rain happily covering their many well-paid classes.

When David and Jude had flown off to Canada, I received a pleasant invitation from a few of their friends to join them for an evening out. I was happy to go, but I suspected, and was right, that it would turn into a three-hour *gaijin* bitch session about life in Japan. These were all agreeable, educated people who had been in Tokyo for a couple of years and were now sick of it. I had just arrived, and I knew I would likely be joining their ranks eventually, but I didn't want to start complaining after only a couple of weeks. As the evening wore on and my new friends got drunker and more voluble in their stories and complaints, I noticed several Japanese people in the bar looking askance at us. Surely some of them spoke a little English. That's why we were there.

I met many expatriates working in Japan who spent all the money they made hoping to relieve stress by enjoying their new wealth. Unfortunately, when you enjoy your wealth in this way, you also part with it. Having squandered much of their money on pleasures that paled quickly, whether travel or shopping, they now had to work longer to make up the deficit. There are some old Japan hands in the country, but most westerners stay no more than a year or two. Exercising some care, you can go home with impressive savings. Without care you go home with nothing or you have to stay and work twice as long, meeting those same old daily challenges. I met a few people who had worked in Japan for a year or two and then gone home, only to return within a year. They found there was nothing for them at home but lower pay, longer hours, and fewer pleasures. Hell, I was one of them, although I considered my second visit to Japan a continuation of my badly bungled first trip.

The easy living of the expatriate is not always a trap, but it always comes with conditions and restrictions. The longer you stay in a foreign place, the fewer contacts you have in your home country. Opportunities at home do not come up if you are not there to make them and take them. You drift away from your family and your friends. The longer you stay away, the harder it is to go home. At a certain point you have to decide if you are going to do what it takes to make your adopted country your home country. Some foreigners marry, usually men taking Japanese wives, rarely the other way around, creating a new family. Some start businesses, finding new friends and colleagues. Some, not many, are qualified to work in professions other than teaching. If you master the language, a four-year project for even the most diligent, your horizons will expand. Many simply renewed their teaching contracts, year after year, but there aren't many old teachers in Japan. Schools and students prefer their teachers young. You see a sad self-indulgence in the eyes of the older members of the low-level ex-pat community. These are people who know they will never belong in Japanese culture and who can't go home. Their life will never be as good anywhere else, and they know their current circumstances cannot last. You can spend two easy, lucrative years in Japan, but if you stay any longer you face the same life decisions you would at home, further education, career, marriage, family, none of which is easier in a foreign country. I came down firmly in the it's-better-not-to-stay-too-long camp.

With my eye always on my bank account, my budget allowed for nothing more than weekend trips. I would have to miss the Philippines and Thailand.

Bob was from Australia and had been in Japan for nearly ten years. His wife Miwako, "Miki," was Japanese, and they had a three-year-old boy. Bob was teaching English, but he was now fluent in Japanese and would eventually, over the next thirty years, work in Japan for the Australian Tourist Commission, the Australian Embassy in Tokyo, and as a representative for the state government of South Australia, as well as in high-quality translation services. He made Japan his new home by balancing his home culture with that of his adopted country.

Forty miles due south of my little house in Samon-cho, Miki's parents owned a tall, rambling, rickety wooden beach house in Nobi, on the east side of the Miura Peninsula. One summer weekend, with a typhoon spinning somewhere off the coast, eight or nine of us took the train down and lounged and sunbathed and barbequed and swam and walked and chatted. I did yoga on a sheltered balcony while everyone else drank, and we all enjoyed the summer cottage as much as anyone has ever enjoyed a weekend at the beach. At midnight it was still very warm, and Sue and I walked along the road next to the wide, south-facing bay. From there, southward, lay nothing but water, the Western Pacific Ocean. Journeying in that direction, skirting the Mariana Trench, you wouldn't hit landfall again for 2,600 miles, not until the island of New Guinea. From there it is another 11,000 uninterrupted, watery miles to South America, halfway around the world. It's a big ocean. The distant typhoon had whipped the water into a swelling and frightening mass level with the top of the seawall. The wall seemed a small thing to hold back the entire Pacific Ocean.

I went to Nikko National Park again, spectacular in the fall, and after a long hike, on the spur of the moment, I decided to stay overnight at an *onsen* inn, a hot springs hotel, in the little town of Yumoto, where hot, smelly water bubbles out of the ground everywhere you look. I soaked myself in the hot pools and slept on an uncomfortable cotton futon on *tatami* mats, with a rock-hard pillow. In the morning I dined on cold rice and weeds, with a raw egg on top, at a long table with thirty Japanese people, all of us dressed in identical, floor-length *yukata*, hotel housecoats. I took another long, beautiful hike that day, and decided to stay over again.

Mount Nantai, in Nikko National Park, "Manly Mountain," is one of Japan's "100 Famous Mountains." It's a volcano and may still be active. It's the fiftieth-or-so highest mountain in Japan. You can walk to the top. You can also walk to the top of Mt. Fuji, Japan's highest mountain, but that walk is much more painful. I was feeling so outdoorsy I thought I'd give Mt. Nantai a try the next day. It was late in the season and the elderly front desk clerk thought a walk to the top might not be a good idea. There was snow in the forecast. We communicated with hardly a shared comprehensible word between us, but he drew me a little map in case I was crazy enough to try the climb. He emphasized in particular a short patch of the trail, attempting to get me to understand the finesse and caution that would be required when I got to it. He looked grave and warned me about this brief section several times, jabbing at the map with his pencil. I smiled and nodded, but I had no idea what he was talking about.

The next morning it was snowing and grey in Yumoto, and I wandered around the little village, chilly, wondering if the skies would clear, which they did. I decided to go for the summit, and back in my room, in a flurry, I grabbed a snack and some water and bolted through the lobby for the bus. I saw the front desk clerk and indicated to him I was heading for Mt. Nantai. He gave me a look that says, in any language, "It's been nice knowing you."

I took the bus halfway back to Lake Chuzenji, to the trailhead, and started my walk in rising temperatures and clearing, sunny skies. I walked across open rice paddies and then plunged suddenly into dense forest and up a steep switchback trail. Typically, for me, I was going about it backwards, approaching from the west rather than taking the more common route from the south. Finally, after a couple of hours, the trail began to skirt a high, vertical rock wall to my right. I couldn't see the top. Then the trail simply stopped. I found myself at a dead end, the high rock wall to my immediate right, the trail behind me, and nowhere to go. In front of me was a sheer drop, nothing but fresh air and the tops of trees. Astutely, I remembered the front desk clerk's map, and I fished it out. This must be the place he was talking about.

Unfortunately, I could make absolutely nothing of his map. To my right there was a wall, behind me the trail, to my left a steep hill down, in front of me nothing but the tops and near-tops of coniferous trees, firs and cedars. The giant rock wall continued on, curving away in front of me, tickled by the tops of the conifers, and I was dying to know what lay in that direction. There was no way up the wall to my right and nothing behind me, so the only way up the mountain had to be ahead of me. It seemed improbable there was anything around the curved wall in front of me, but I couldn't resist. I set off awkwardly, stepping very carefully into the high branches of the nearest tree.

And from there to the next one and then to the next. I had my bulky shoulder bag with me, and it interfered constantly with my forward progress. I was also slapped and scratched frequently by the whipping rough branches of the trees, trees that had never experienced the touch of a human hand before. After about forty minutes of this, I had walked through the tops of eight or ten trees and was nearly exhausted. I finally realized the absurdity of waving around in the tops of trees, standing on thin branches fifty feet off the ground. This tree-top dance also exacted a considerable expenditure of energy to keep from falling out of them. I didn't have the strength to go forward much longer, and there was nothing promising in view in that direction. I knew it would take me half an hour to retrace my steps and I accepted, with resignation, that I might have to admit defeat and wander back down the trail to the rice paddies. And to the restaurant I had passed, which was starting to seem like a good idea. When I finally stepped out of the trees back onto the end of the trail, I was considerably worse for wear, scratched and sweating and winded. I had kissed the treetops of Asia, seventeen years before Ang Lee's ethereal *Crouching Tiger, Hidden Dragon*, but I had not flown amongst them. I was no Chow Yun-fat. I had been smacked for my impertinence.

I rested for a moment and then, frustrated, looking up at the wall again, I realized, slowly, that I was standing at the foot of a half-chimney. A natural curve, just bigger than an adult body, was set into the wall, rising straight up and out of view. Looking closely now, I started to see handholds, some natural, some perhaps scraped out of the rock by climbers. I got out my map again. My God, I thought, this is what the old guy was talking about. He was trying to point out this chimney. I rested a little more and then started up, alone and free climbing, with my shoulder bag banging into my legs the whole time, giving me the yips. I'm afraid of heights. I had no idea how far up it went, and once I was up a few feet, going back down again was not an attractive option. After twenty feet or so, where the view was incredible, and terrifying, to my absolute delight I met a dangling steel cable anchored from above. It was not visible from the trail below. I used it to walk myself up the rest of the chimney, finally spilling out and collapsing onto the low shoulder of a windy, rocky ridge. I didn't mind travelling alone back then, and now in my old age I prefer it, but I have made some tremendously stupid decisions for lack of a second set of eyes.

I was still a long way from the top, but it was now an easy ridge walk up and along a narrow spine of rock. It was cold and increasingly cloudy here unlike the sunny rice paddies, and even the forest, on the west side of the mountain. I walked another hour through icy wisps of cloud to the cold and windy shrine at the summit. After a short rest I followed the arrows painted on the rocks and made my way slowly down the long, steep rock fall on the south side. Very hard on the quadriceps. I crossed one or two gravel roads, the only ones I ever saw in Japan, and finally sat down on one of them to hitchhike. A friendly man gave me a ride. He said he was surprised I was hiking so late in the season. In the summer, the mountain is alive with hikers and pilgrims, but I had seen no more than two or three people all day. He gave me a ride to Chuzenji town, and I took the bus back to Yumoto. At the inn I saw the old front desk clerk. He seemed surprised to see me alive. I got out the map, pointed to his squiggles, and gave him an emphatic "A-ha!" I made hand-over-hand climbing motions. We laughed and nodded together, and he welcomed me back.

When I got back to Tokyo, I discovered I had left my bicycle unlocked in the middle of the sidewalk for three full days. My trip to Nikko had been a last-minute decision, and when I got there, wanting to stay longer, I telephoned a couple of my employers to say I would be missing a day of work. One day. I hadn't missed a scheduled day of work since I had arrived in

Tokyo, a year earlier. Reporting for class a day or two later, at Sony Language Lab, Mr. Namikawa intercepted me and gave me a stern lecture on the inappropriateness of my behaviour. It was the closest thing I ever got to a dressing down in two years of otherwise regal treatment from my many employers. Japanese employers generally suck up to their foreign teachers, so the seriousness of this matter was apparent. I was in a pampered profession, I was much in demand, and no one likes being reprimanded. My face flushed and I rebelled inwardly at my uncomfortable meeting with Mr. Namikawa, but I was making a lot of money at Sony, so this was dirt I had to eat. Taking a vacation is practically a sin in Japan. Missing work on short notice for such self-indulgence as a day in the country is truly disrespectful. I should have called in sick. That would have rendered the matter a non-issue. I realized then that the price of a well-paid sixteen-hour workweek is never having a day off. I never asked for another one.

Nikko is such a lovely place I went a third time, taking Sue just for the day, so she could see it. It was a long day, but we did two beautiful hikes along the boardwalks through marshes and ponds, and then through open, easy woods. I had to browbeat her into moving quickly along on the second hike. We were losing the light, and she didn't seem to understand that you really can't hike in the woods after dark. We had brought flashlights with us this time, but it was still inadvisable. She was cranky with me, but I was willing to be unpopular with her in this cause. She should have known better, and for good reason.

A few weeks earlier, Sue and I took a long day hike on the outskirts of Tokyo. It was raining a little in the morning, and we couldn't decide if we wanted to go. We dawdled along, finally making it to the trailhead around 1:00 p.m. We dawdled further at a quaint shop and tea house in the woods where the proprietor, a woman in her thirties, served us tea and wouldn't take a penny for it. She offered us umbrellas in spite of knowing we wouldn't be returning by the same route, but we declined. We finally started our lazy way up the long hill and through the beautiful open forest. When we got to a shrine in the middle of the forest, the trees much closer now, it was nearly dark and we weren't quite sure of the way down, other than to retrace our steps which we hadn't wanted to do. A passing hiker, a gruff, older woman, grunted and pointed vaguely but headed off in another direction. We walked through the twilight and were relieved to find another small shrine, this one on our map, and we were pretty sure now of the route back down. Unfortunately, not a shred of light was left in the sky, and we could hardly see our hands in front of our faces. At the top of the last leg down, there was a small sign which I was just able to make out.

The most common, as well as the most dangerous, species of snake in Japan is the venomous *mamushi*. It is a pit viper like the rattlesnake, the copperhead, and the cottonmouth. The venom is hemorrhagic, and the treatment, assuming you can get to it, is a week in the hospital, possibly in intensive care, a month of out-patient treatments, and several months to full recovery. Every year in Japan, 2,500 people are bitten and ten die. In British Columbia there haven't been more than two or three deaths due to rattlesnake bite in the last seventy-five years. The small sign I saw as the dark closed around us was without graphics and completely in Japanese. I had learned just enough of the language to read *Beware of the mamushi*. I then wished I hadn't seen it. It took us more than an hour in the pitch black, without flashlights, to work our way down the otherwise short trail to the road, taking baby steps, constantly frighted and jolted as the trail dropped out beneath our feet in unseen dips, crisscrossed by roots. We held hands the whole way but not like lovers. Like beginners on ice skates we clutched at each other, white-knuckled and chest-high, terrified of falling and breaking a leg in the dark, or stepping on a *mamushi*.

Sue went home for several weeks over Christmas in 1983. There were plenty of holidays for me as well, so I wasn't working much. I had been busy and then sick for my first Christmas, the previous year, but now, in good health and good spirits, I bounced around Tokyo to churches and masses and carol concerts and sing-alongs, belting out the songs in fine voice with only the occasional squeak and blat. After a while, though, for the first time in Tokyo, I grew bored and restless, and I was very happy to go out to the airport to meet Sue when she finally came back.

Just after Sue left for the US, when the weather was still good, Sue's friend Ricki and I took the "Romancecar" to Mt. Fuji to hike for the day. Romance Car isn't quite as exciting as it sounds. It's just the amusingly inappropriate name in English, a common occurrence in Japan, that someone at the Odakyu railroad company had chosen to call their express train from Shinjuku to Hakone, the main tourist town in the Mt. Fuji area.

Speeding south from Tokyo on the Romance Car, I gazed out the window at the astonishing energy, organization, and cooperation that is Japan. It was still very early in the morning, and I sighed with a small scrap of regret as the landscape swept past, musing aloud, "Everywhere I look about me I see activity and industry, and I feel so detached from it." This was a feeling I had had before. Ricki was a self-professed counsellor of some kind. Neuro-linguistic Programming. Eckankar. Who knows. She was looking for business and an opportunity to show her chops. She said, "I can help you with that." She held out the promise, after a course of counselling, of a more meaningful integration into my environment. She was older than I, and I suspected she was a woman of many resources, but I parried with, "You would presume to tamper with my highest ideals?"

I turned thirty in 1983, and I could not anticipate, design, or build a single thing I used in my daily life. I made little or no contribution to the endeavours of society other than as a gilded teacher of English in a non-English-speaking country. My skill was being able to speak the language of the land of my birth. No great achievement, that. For thirteen years, puffing and grimacing, I had been concerned, if not obsessed, with alternatives, and I was coming to the slippery conclusion that there were no such things as countercultures or subcultures. There is no mainstream and there is no alternative, because there is only one frail human family. There is one comity, one polity, and everyone feeds off it, the wise and the foolish, the poor and the rich, the bottom-feeders and the high-roosting gobblers. The poor steal from it as do the rich, but the rich have always stolen more. They're better at it.

I was coming to the realization, of questionable usefulness, without quite knowing it, that it was not necessary to create an alternate course once the mainstream was found wanting. I didn't grasp this realization deeply, but I felt it and I lived its effects. I had no home in either camp. As I met the coming years I wandered and I read, I practised yoga and I meditated, I drank and I leaned. I leaned on schools for an excuse not to have to work for a living, on couples for warmth and stability, on single women for love and sex and affection. I borrowed money from governments and family and paid it back. I always paid my bills but I never had a lick of ambition beyond that. My whole life passed without ever wanting a career, a house, a wife, children, or family. Never, not once in my life, did those desires arise. Many years later, I told my new friend Larry that I had moved eighty times. He said, "So you were never home-less. You were always home-full."

From the station at Odawara, only an hour south of Shinjuku, we transferred to the cute little cars of the Hakone Tozan Train, Japan's only mountain train. It travels fifteen kilometres west and half a kilometre up. The line rises so steeply there are three switchbacks along the way. I had found a map and a little trail to hike, and we got off at a tiny station before the switchbacks started. From there we walked up and into the woods, past shrines, through magnificent groves of tall, creaking bamboo in magical light, and then west in and out along the sides of the hills with Mt. Fuji peaking at us in the distance.

Fuji-Hakone-Izu National Park is huge, five hundred square miles, and it is a popular place for suicides, especially the dense, quiet forest northwest of Mt. Fuji. The annual frequency varies considerably, but in the twentieth century there were, on average, about a hundred suicides a year. Signs such as *Please reconsider!* and *Please consult the police before you decide to die!* are nailed to trees throughout the forest. I also heard of more emotional messaging. *Star-crossed lovers! Please do not commit suicide here. It is not romantic! In the spring your bodies can be smelled half a kilometre away!*

We walked for several sunny hours encountering no dead bodies and very few live ones, the valley far below us to the south. We finally descended to the edge of the Hayakawa River where we spent an hour or two, separately, at one of the many hot springs there. There is no mixed nude bathing anymore. By the time we got back to Shinjuku, I had such a headache. Leisure activities in Japan can be exhausting.

Every few weeks the earth shook letting off pressure. Office buildings and their contents rattled, filing cabinets walked across the floor, the supertall skyscrapers of Shinjuku swayed back and forth, and the wooden frame of my house, or Sue's, everyone's, clattered in the night. If there wasn't a small earthquake for six or seven weeks, the tension in Tokyo increased slowly, in the back of everyone's mind, knowing that the next one, when it came, would be bigger. Better to have small frequent temblors than large isolated ones.

Nineteen eighty-three was the sixtieth anniversary of the Great Kanto earthquake of 1923. It wasn't as strong as the 2011 Tohoku earthquake that destroyed the Fukushima Daiichi Nuclear Power Plant, but its epicentre was only seventy miles from downtown Tokyo. There was a small tsunami. A train with a hundred passengers and an entire train station were pushed into the sea, but the greatest damage was from fire. The earthquake happened at noon, and lunchtime cooking fires immediately started firestorms that swept across the city, fanned by the winds of a typhoon that was happening at the same time. Water mains were broken, and it took two days to put out the flames. All Yokohama was a plain of fire. Forty thousand people took refuge in an open area of downtown Tokyo which was then engulfed in a 300-foot-high fire *tornado*, incinerating them all. More than 100,000 people died overall, 600,000 houses and apartments were destroyed, and two million people were left homeless. The *Daibutsu* statue in Kamakura, the face of Japan, 185,000 pounds, and forty miles from the epicentre, shifted two feet forward. In contrast, and with better technology for measuring the effects, the Tohoku earthquake, which the Japanese call the Great East Japan earthquake, moved the entire island of Honshu, Japan's main island, eight feet to the east and shifted the earth's axis off-tilt by six inches.

After the 1923 earthquake, thousands of Koreans, Chinese, Okinawans, and Japanese people who spoke with regional dialects were mass murdered by mobs driven mad by the tragedy and by rumours that foreigners were starting fires and poisoning wells. The police and the army took advantage of the chaos to murder socialist and communist political leaders. Unsanitary conditions led to high rates of typhoid fever.

And strangely, my friend Mark's mother, Jessica, was two years old in 1923 and living in Yokohama. When the earthquake struck, she was handed out the window by her much older brother, to a nanny in the yard on the other side. The building collapsed and an uncle that Mark never met was killed. Jessica survived the Great Kanto earthquake by a matter of seconds thanks to the quick thinking of her brother and at the cost of his life. Thirty-five years later Mark was born in Canada. He is named for his uncle, and he is married to Yoriko, who was born in Yokohama.

In 1983, the Great Kanto earthquake was still the deadliest in Japanese history and the most powerful ever recorded in the region. The Japanese are a superstitious bunch. Sales of earthquake kits went through the roof. Everyone in Tokyo had their fingers crossed hoping to get through the sixtieth anniversary without a repeat of the disaster.

I spent New Year's Eve in a far western suburb of Tokyo with Japanese and western friends. We slept the night in a freezing cold house and rose in the pre-dawn dark to walk to a park at the edge of town and watch the sun rise on 1984 and the sky lighten on Mt. Fuji to the southwest. Midnight had passed, the sun rose, and it was official. Tokyo had escaped the unlucky sixtieth anniversary year. I was home by noon and exhausted from a poor sleep the night before and an early morning. I took to my bed for hours that afternoon, and when I awoke around 5:00 p.m. I realized I could just make the last New Year's mass of the day at the Franciscan Chapel Center in

Roppongi, so I scooted out the door for the bus. By 6:00 p.m. I was settling, still half asleep, into my first mass of 1984, Sunday, January the First. When I place the period at the end of this sentence, it will be thirty years ago today.

At 6:03 p.m. a 6.5 earthquake struck the southern coast of Honshu and rocked the pews of the Chapel Center back and forth and shook the walls. It was felt in Hokkaido, five hundred miles away. The priest stopped. After a moment, as the ceiling shook, he said, "I think we should all, uhm…stay inside for now?" It's hard to decide what to do in an earthquake and hard to stop the heart from pounding. When the ground stops shaking, the relief is immense. We were all reminded, powerfully, that earthquakes don't know what year it is.

I worked no more than four hours a day, often less, five days a week, any time between 7:50 a.m. and 9:00 p.m. I went frequently to the gym and met friends for lunch and coffee, often five times a week. There were errands to be done, groceries to be got in, the baskets on my mama-san bicycle laden front and back, and I spent as much time as I could with Sue. The weekends were relaxed with small entertainments, just walking and bicycling, exploring new parts of Tokyo, going to the cheap movie house in Shinjuku, The Royal. There were many dinners out, occasional concerts and short trips out of town, hiking, sightseeing, etc. When I wasn't actually using my hands or speaking to someone, I was holding a book and reading. And four hours a day I was practising yoga and meditating and saying prayers.

I wanted to keep the Liturgy of the Hours, the Catholic prayers said seven times a day, Matins, Lauds, Terce, Sext, None, Vespers, and Compline. For me they tended to bunch up in the morning since I would not be rising in the middle of the night for Matins, or even at dawn for Lauds, but the rest were easy enough to schedule.

In Victoria Fr. John asked me if I had thought about the priesthood, and oh, I had. I had thought about it non-stop since I was a teenager. Not the Catholic priesthood, obviously, and not priesthood so much as monkhood. In Grade 11 I told my English teacher, Mrs. Chevraux, that if I could sit under a tree and read a book for the rest of my life that's what I would do. My social studies teacher, Mr. Bates, told us Karl Marx was broke for much of his life and spent twenty years in the British Museum Reading Room. I envied Karl his poverty. Although he and Mrs. Marx, Jenny, lost four children to it. My fascination with the idea of a life of retreat and meditation, utter simplicity, and profound quiet, of isolation, was only increased by early reading, at seventeen, of *The Glass Bead Game* and *Siddhartha* and *Steppenwolf*. Soon after *The Outsider* and *Seven Pillars of Wisdom* reinforced the idea of the unavoidability, for some, of an existence apart, regardless of one's actual involvement in worldly activity, as well as the idea that transcendence and healing can arise from suffering and despair. Herman Hesse, Colin Wilson, and T. E. Lawrence, not an eastern author among them, were all writing in and of a state of spiritual despair brought on by twentieth-century wars. Add to that the inrush of eastern gurus in the 1960s and the quantum leaps of the psychotropic experiences of my teen years, and it was practically inevitable that I would wind up a confused, skinny, white kid sitting in Lotus posture. The blessings I have known.

I told Fr. John that the idea of studying for the priesthood was strange and appealing to me in an improbable way. I wanted to learn everything I could about my new avocation. Maybe it would also be my vocation. I wondered about the usefulness of studying philosophy and theology for nine years, if as a priest, all you then did was spend your time marrying and burying your flock, maybe doing the books at the parish office, going to meetings. Calling Bingo? The more priests I met, the more it seemed like a club rather than a profession, diverse daily occupations where the salary was low but the perks never ended.

I leaned more towards monkhood where it wasn't necessary to be a priest. You could be a brother in a religious order without ever going to university. I didn't feel I needed to over-credentialize my spiritual longings. One priest said to me, "No, no, you don't want to be a brother. In the past they were the uneducated members of the monasteries, the servants. Now some of them have PhDs in theology without ever becoming priests, but that's pointless. Why do all that study and not become a priest? That's like going to law school and not writing the bar exam. You want to study. It's getting better, but still, in general, if you don't do a couple of degrees you're just a bellhop in the monastery. You carry the priests' bags. The pecking order is slowly breaking down, but it's still very much alive." It had only been fifteen years since the reforms of Vatican II. The church wasn't modern yet.

I also mentioned to Fr. John that I had no family money, or money of my own, to pay for many years of study. And where would I go? They sent their candidates to schools in Ottawa, Edmonton, and occasionally Mission, BC. He told me not to worry too much about money. If I could convince the Bishop that I was sincere, and Fr. John would weigh heavily in my corner in that battle, money would not be a problem. He gave me a little sideways nod. "There's money around."

Brother Paul was, and is, a Franciscan friar in Victoria, not a priest, and he could be seen walking vigorously in his much-repaired brown robe and rope belt back and forth from the friary on Joan Crescent to the cathedral downtown. He was a familiar sight to downtown workers and the residents of Rockland. He walked by my house on Rockland Avenue nearly every day while I sat at my kitchen table studying chemistry. He was fifty-nine in 1982, and he is ninety-two now, in 2014, and uses a walker. I had been seeing him for years on the streets of Victoria and had always wanted to speak to him, but I never had the courage to approach him or the desire to be lectured, which is so often the result of conversation with religionists. In the summer of '82, when I was studying to become a Catholic, I felt safe in finally approaching him one day in front of the cathedral, where he was sweeping. He surprised me with a volley of energetic and small "c" catholic opinion. He told me the Catholic Church and its fulfilment would never be complete until the west was joined with the east, or rejoined, since Jesus was a man of the east. I was pleasantly gobsmacked to hear him say so. I asked him how he had become a friar. He told me he was diagnosed with multiple sclerosis in his early twenties when he came back from the war, World War II, and his doctor told him he must lead a quiet life. He took this advice seriously and joined the Franciscans. He has done physical exercise, calmly, every day of his life since. And now he is ninety-two. I wonder about that diagnosis.

So I wasn't really interested in becoming a priest, but it was an amusing notion. I indulged in harmless daydreams of becoming a parlour priest. I would have great sympathy with the poor during the week, and on the weekends I would dine in elegant comfort in the homes of rich and wrinkled Oak Bay Catholics. "Nothing makes people laugh like money, the rich get wrinkles from laughing." But I was more interested in the religious orders than in parish life.

There is an order of Benedictines in Mission, BC, forty-five miles east of Vancouver on two hundred spectacular acres in the Fraser Valley. Westminster Abbey was founded in 1939 by monks from Mount Angel Abbey in Oregon. Benedictine abbots are appointed for life, and in its first sixty-six years there were only two at Westminster. A seminary was added almost from the beginning. The college accepts only candidates for the priesthood, and there has been a Faculty of Theology since 1951. If I went to Christ the King Seminary at Westminster Abbey, I could do all the training I would need on the west coast and not have to freeze my ass off in Edmonton or Ottawa for six years. Or I could bypass the academic requirements altogether and simply enter the monastery directly, and provisionally, as a postulant and then as a novice. This staged process allows for two years of immersion in the community before anything resembling a solemn vow is required. I imagine nearly everyone I knew in Tokyo or at home quietly thought I was out of my mind. Although most people seemed willing to accept that there were different strokes for different folks. I wasn't the guy studying transvestism, or the guy who sold cars, or the guy going back to Canada to study linguistics, or the person studying moxibustion, or even the guy in love with Japanese pussy. I was the guy who did yoga and wanted to explore the possibility of deeper spiritual realization by becoming a monk. This isn't something you can buy. You can't just spend your money. You have to spend your life. Most people in my circle of acquaintance probably thought, "Well, who am I to judge?" What else could they say?

As for family, my grandmother asked me with obvious concern if my interest in monastic life would mean that I would be separated from my family. I was surprised. I wasn't concerned about leaving my family. I always assumed my mother had a warm general feeling towards me, but my father and I would gladly have pushed each other off a cliff if no one was looking. My sister was married and was a mother. She had her own problems.

My motives and the strength of my motivation were questionable, as they had been during my previous efforts at poking at community life at Ananda Cooperative Village and Self-Realization Fellowship. The thought of going back to Canada made me ill. Edmonton and Ottawa are deep freezes in the winter, and I really hated the snow and cold. When Yogi Bhajan came from India to the west, he settled in Canada. After the first winter, he left for the southern US. At the World Symposium on Humanity in 1976 he said, "You can't achieve enlightenment while shovelling snow." He was joking, of course. My friend Brian, the photographer, says, "If you live in Canada and you don't shovel snow, you're not a real Canadian."

I wrote to Fr. Wilfrid, the prior at Westminster Abbey. He was sixty-six years old, and he had already been prior of the abbey for thirty years, a tenure he extended to fifty-three years by the time he died. I asked him about acquiring books of prayer, and he mailed me a thick copy of *Morning and Evening Prayer*, a much shorter book than the full 8,000 pages of *The Liturgy of the Hours*, but it was still a few hundred pages long. There were at least four coloured ribbons to mark the passages, and six would have been better, to keep all the daily prayers and the Feast days and Saints' days sorted out. I bought both volumes of the *St. Joseph Weekday Missal* in order to be able to say the mass every day at home. I also bought the *Secular Franciscan Companion*, a pocket-sized book of prayers to carry with me during the day. One thing about the Catholics, they have a prayer for everything, and every day of the year is marked for the possibility of holiness. I still have the *Franciscan Companion*. It props up the back of my laptop to keep it from overheating. Between readings in these three books of prayers, saying the rosary, and the *mala*, the Hindu rosary, and meditation, I was spending every day in frequent, regular prayer. I didn't feel too bad about letting my mind wander off listening to *CBS Radio Mystery Theater* while I performed eighty or ninety minutes of physical yoga postures. This routine was a resurgence, with a few additions, of the regimen I had begun at Ananda Cooperative Village in 1977. There had been a bad break in my practice of spiritual exercises while studying at Camosun College, and smoking dope and drinking, and chasing women, doubtless the work of Satan, and it was deeply satisfying to return to its benefits, clear eyes, calm mind, and open heart. Devotion and realization are interdependent. If you can generate a little devotion, receptive and grateful, grounded, lucid, and intelligent, you will see a little of the true nature of mind, which will generate more devotion, which generates greater insight, and so on. It's a dynamo. Devotion comes from wisdom and wisdom comes from devotion. Get on and hang on, even though you know you will be thrown.

The intelligent reader will notice a muddle of activities, tendencies, and motivations in my lifestyle. I was lazy, disobedient, insubordinate, wayward, disgusted by authority and societal norms, and profoundly addicted to sex, intoxication, and general naughtiness. These were not qualities likely to place me in any great stead with a religious organization. Then why was I so attracted to them? For me disobedience, insubordination, and waywardness were the natural result of transcendent practice, of disgust with society and authority. The sex and naughtiness I was less sure about, but even the Devil knows that heaven is a better place than hell. At heart I knew I would fail with the Catholics as I had before with the yogis, but I also knew I had to try. I would hazard any road for a chance at a life less ordinary. The simple, tidy activity of religious practice has called to me my entire life, and I have responded to that call in my own way, the only way I could.

In Tokyo, at the Franciscan Chapel Centre, I told Fr. William, nervously, that I wanted to become a Franciscan friar. You can't start unless you say it out loud, and sometimes it surprises you. I couldn't join the Order of Friars Minor in Japan. I would have to go back to Canada to do that. Fr. William was a missionary from New York, a member of the Holy Name Province, the largest in the US. Over the eighteen months I was in Tokyo, I went to the Chapel Center as often as I could, but it wasn't always a comfortable experience. Many of the people I met there I found to be unsettling, bizarre personalities, from academics to military personnel, to the families of US Embassy staff. Their large housing complex was right next door.

I went to a short retreat one weekend at the Center led by an animated, big-hearted Irish woman named Sister Bridget. Try as I might I can find no record of her on the Internet, but what I remember is that she had had an epiphany as a young woman and hadn't stopped talking about it ever since. She travelled the world shaking hands and giving retreats, often to groups of priests, sharing the joy and the wisdom she had received from her visions. At the end of our time together, she stood in the centre of a circle formed by the retreatants and addressed each of us individually with clasped hands and a blessing. The notable feature of this greeting would be that somehow she would be able to impart to each person the particular blessing they needed without actually knowing anything about them. When she got to me, she took my hands in hers and after only a breath or two she shuddered and shrank back from me while continuing to hold on. She was speechless for a moment but was finally able to ask the Lord God, her voice breaking a little, to keep me in the faith, and I suspect, under her breath, out of jail. She had felt the crazy. It was a bit awkward.

One Sunday, I saw Fr. William in the hall at the Center. Mass was starting in a few minutes and he was busy. Without a word he took me by the arm and shoved me into a room saying, "Neil, Sean. Sean, Neil," and left. A man about my age was lying on a bed reading, and we laughed and introduced ourselves again. He was a monk from St. Benedict's Monastery at Snowmass, Colorado, near Aspen. He was a man on a serious journey. He had graduated from the Military Academy at West Point, in nuclear engineering. He was an officer familiar with missiles and silos and the battle plans of strategic and all-out nuclear war, Mutual Assured Destruction. Later in his twenties, he had a change of heart and left the army. He said the resistance to his resignation was intense and uncomfortable. He told me the ones who understood his feelings best were the older officers who had been on the battlefield. The harsher criticism came from younger officers who had never fought, and their wives. On leaving the army he became a monk. I said, "You have had a lot of experience with authority." Why was a Benedictine monk staying at a Franciscan chapel in Tokyo? Monks and nuns who follow the Rule of St. Benedict take a vow of stability, the promise never to leave the monastery they enter. He told me he had received permission to examine his heart and conscience away from the order, perhaps he was still only a novice, and he was now on his way to a Buddhist community in Kyoto. This was surprising from several points of view. I told him I was doing just the opposite. After years of practising yoga, I was going back to Canada, or to the US I hoped, to infiltrate the Catholics, the Franciscans preferably. I added, with my usual bit of sass, that I was hoping to get them straightened out on a few sticky points of doctrine. He said with a smile, "You might want to lie low at first."

Fr. William threw me into company on another occasion, this time with a beautiful young American student studying in Japan, a girl he was keeping an eye on for her parents back home. She was nineteen or twenty, modest, a vision of young Catholic sweetness. I don't think he was testing me, but it was a test nonetheless. He invited the two of us to join him for an evening at the New Otani Hotel. Fr. William knew the old, white, resident pastor and his wife. They led generically Christian Sunday services in the hotel's little chapel in the middle of ten acres of exquisite gardens. In return for these light duties, they received full-time housing at the very expensive hotel. The five of us watched and listened to the big band in the lounge and chatted as best we could, given the difference in our ages. At twenty-nine, I was about as handsome as I was ever going to be in a nice suit and a natty shirt and tie, and Michele was almost unbearably adorable. To the old, generic preacher and his wife Fr. William said, "Look at these two. Aren't they pretty people? Aren't they just the prettiest people?" Old people, like young people, don't care what they say. I had the decency to squirm a little. Over the years, Michele did multiple degrees in art history including a PhD at Columbia University. She has taught around the world. And I? Well, read on, if you like.

Sue never set foot in the Franciscan Chapel Center. She wanted nothing to do with a church whose leadership denied heaven to anyone born before Jesus or any non-Catholic born after. She understood that a majority of Catholics disagreed with Rome on many important issues, and like me, were merely waiting for the curia to come to their senses. She knew I was only really interested in the church's mystical and meditative traditions, but those generally well-hidden features weren't enough to draw her across the threshold. I had been disappointed, if not betrayed, by my New Age gurus and experiences, Hindu and Buddhist, and it had driven me into the arms of a more familiar, but just as strange, mother. Sue had had no such unhappy experiences in her New Agey life and thus had no similar motivations. I kept hoping I had finally found the home I was looking for, but events would prove, ultimately, that I had been a wanderer for too long to settle down now.

Sometime in 1983, I decided to start fasting one day a week. After many months of having nothing but juice on Fridays, I was emaciated, no bigger than a swizzle stick, quite saintly in appearance I thought. I showed up for morning mass at the Chapel Center one Saturday, and I was the only one there. I had eaten nothing since Thursday evening, not even water that morning, and I was a tad woozy. When Fr. William saw there would only be the two of us for mass, he hesitated. I think he wanted just for a second to cancel, but you know, "Where two or three are gathered together in my name...." I was a little nervous. There was no one else to cover for me if I lost my way in the order of the mass. A lot of people at any given service are just mumbling, and being new, I was occasionally one of them. I was very spaced out, and Fr. William had to prompt me a couple of times. I have never wanted to think of myself as an alcoholic, but I was definitely a big, stinking drunk, so I always walked by the cup of wine offered at mass without partaking. No one really believes it changes into the blood of Christ at consecration. It's wine. Not to mention the germs. But this morning I had no choice when Fr. William handed me the cup. I hadn't had a drink of alcohol in a year, or a bite of food in thirty-six hours. When the few drops of rich red wine, and the alcohol, hit my tongue, my mouth and brain exploded in a sensuous, and sensual, commotion of flavour and feeling. I was flushed. I tingled in waves from head to toe. And it wasn't the Holy Spirit. It was the wine, God's other gift. I knew the effect was enhanced by my fasting state, but I reeled at the impact. I faltered through to the end of the mass and then wobbled out of the Chapel Center in search of breakfast and coffee.

Not many people stay in Japan for life. In early 1984, David and Jude started packing. After four steady years in Tokyo, teaching English and saving money, they were moving to Calgary to start a new chapter in their life together. They were married in 1981 at the Shinjuku Ward Office. I had spent most of my time over the last year with Sue and some of her friends, but David and Jude and I, and Sue, were often together for movies and dinners and walking and exercise. David and Jude never went hiking with me, though. They weren't hikers. They lived only a few blocks away from me, and it comforted me to know they were always there. They had been a shoulder for me to cry on during my first visit to Japan, and they had got me sorted out for my second. Poor David and his unsuspecting "English girlfriend." When I wrote to him from Victoria in 1980 asking about life in Japan, he would have been wiser not to reply. He and Jude wound up first with a drunken, moaning mess on their floor and then, two years later, a religious nut doing yoga and clacking his rosary. I loved them like a puppy dog.

I, too, had thought about leaving Tokyo in 1984, but I wasn't sure just when that might happen. You always ask yourself how many more semesters of income you need to meet your financial goals, or how many more you can stand. I didn't think I could take another brutally hot and humid Tokyo summer. I was also becoming frustrated by the routine and the general pointlessness of my work, tired of having the same simple conversation over and over again with my students. I was getting sick of teaching, and of Tokyo, but less so of Tokyo than teaching. Not long after David and Jude made their decision, I made the difficult decision to leave Japan as well, and I began the three-month process of winding up my jobs and students and apartment, and making arrangements for what I would do on returning to Canada. The decision was difficult because I didn't want to go and I didn't want to stay. My last three months were a bit of a haze.

Over a period of eighteen months in Tokyo, I had a dozen employers to keep track of, a dozen classroom and office locations to find and go to, not to mention Sue's many apartments. I had a few hundred students and a couple of dozen friends and acquaintances, and throughout that time I never kept an appointment book, barely an address book. Once I knew where and when something was supposed to happen, there was no need to keep a written record of it. I kept it all in my head and generally had no problem. But as my interest waned near the end of my stay, I became sloppy and forgetful. I never missed a class, but I was late, nearly absent, for a couple of party dates with students. As the *sensei* I was always something of an honoured guest. To forget about these social events was very disrespectful to them, and embarrassing for me. I think I was coming to the conclusion that I really didn't like Japanese society very much, and I was getting tired of pretending to be interested. There had been a spring in my step for well over a year. Tokyo owed me a good time, and it had obliged. I had been happy here, on my second visit. But now I found I was, not depressed, but enervated. So I dragged myself with a half-hearted smile through the forms and commitments of my last days.

David and Jude didn't sit around hoping someone would throw them a going away party. To celebrate four amazing years in Japan, they rented a banquet room at Miki's parents' hotel in Ikebukuro, with a cash bar, and sent out a hundred invitations to four years' worth of friends and colleagues. Parties in Japan tend to be well organized, like everything else. They start and end on time, and everyone shows up at the requested hour. David shared a natural affinity for the Japanese approach to tidy organization. He decided on a Red and Yellow theme for the party and once the music started, which he had pre-recorded and timed to the minute, a hundred people in red and yellow clothing, Japanese and westerners, let their hair down, and danced and drank and hooted and hollered for exactly four hours, and then went home. It was fuckin' awesome. A couple of weeks later, I accompanied David and Jude part of the way to Narita Airport. They insisted I turn back when they transferred to the last train that would take them the rest of the way there. At Narita they boarded a plane for China. Some of the money they had saved in Tokyo would be spent in China, Greece, Egypt, and England before they arrived home in Calgary.

I gave long notice to all of my employers and students, and to Mr. Nakai, my landlord. At Yotsuya Gaigo Gakuin I presented Mr. Owada and the staff with a large gift basket of fruit and deli items, by way of thanks. I said, "Mariko won't marry me so there's no point in staying." She gave me a little pout and muttered, "You said last time." It had been more than three years since I teased her in that same way. I didn't throw myself a party, and neither did anyone else, but I had a dozen small dinners to say good-bye to friends and students. The last time I saw Lindley he told me he was also going home. He would succeed first in the field of investment banking and then become a Protestant minister. I would fail first at becoming a Catholic minister, or a Catholic anything, and then, after my vague fashion, continue to wander.

We were both leaving our girlfriends behind. Lindley went out with a beautiful woman named Reiko. Unlike most Japanese women, for whom simpering is a way of life, she seemed, in some ways, as hard as nails. She would have to be. She worked for the American Express Company in their Department of Serious Management, putting in a full twelve-hour executive day, on-call 24/7. If something was happening in Stockholm that was affecting business in Tokyo, she was in the office, never mind the eight-hour time difference.

And I was leaving Sue, very reluctantly. Not unlike how I had left Maura when I went to California in 1977 to become a yogi, except that Maura was glad to see me go. Sue and I still had nothing but warm feelings for each other unless there was something she wasn't telling me. We had no great complaints or grievances about our relationship, and I knew it was hard for her to see me go although I was pretty sure she knew she could live without me. We had had a lovely time together in many ways but she was three years older than I, which may as well have been ten. She knew I needed to go off and make several hundred more mistakes in life before I would be of any use to her or any other wise woman. She had her own goals, spiritual and otherwise, and they did not overlap with mine. Even if we had wanted to stay together, I couldn't move to the US to live with her, to make a life together, to work, and have a family. I had no skills, no college degrees. And I didn't want a family. Not many people from the US want to move to Canada anymore, not since the Vietnam war ended, and neither did Sue. She didn't want to have to re-credentialize her career, whatever form it might now take, and look for work in cold, unfamiliar climes and systems. What could she do in Canada? Canadians spoke French and lived in igloos. A love affair in Japan is often a time-limited tale, a shipboard romance on a very slow boat.

I sold my bicycle and stereo and household goods. The school semester ended at the end of March, and after I taught a little more early-morning English to Mr. Mukai, and we discussed hot liquid sodium for the last time, I took the subway back to my empty apartment. There, I and my backpack waited for Sue, who was going to come to the airport with me. Rupert stopped in as he frequently did around breakfast time, but this time to say good-bye. Mr. Nakai waited until the last moment and then showed up at my door with a final bill for gas and electricity, about a hundred and twenty dollars, and then went back to his house. I didn't have the right change to pay the bills. I didn't want to leave less than the total, and I was damned if I was going to leave more. Tokyo landlords were very obnoxious when it came to squeezing their tenants, and I had no love for them. I had nothing against Mr. Nakai, but in a fluster, in a rare moment of larceny, surprising even myself, I walked out the door with Sue to get a taxi and left the bills unpaid on the counter, something about which I was thoroughly ashamed afterwards. I have daydreamed a few times of travelling back to Tokyo and paying Mr. Nakai the money I owe him. The interest by now would be frightening. Conveniently, it never occurred to me to mail it to him.

We were going to take the Tokyo Monorail to Haneda Airport, but it was too late now. We had to take a cab. At the airport Sue walked me to the gate, and we parted there quickly and awkwardly. When she turned and walked away, I went through the gate and slumped immediately to the floor. I was so confused and upset I wanted to cry, but couldn't, and I realized at that moment that I was dead beat, spent, and coming down with the Mother of All Colds.

Tokyo is a noisy city. Every day you encountered vans and trucks with enormous speakers mounted on top of them carrying politicians and advertisers, blaring out their messages at deafening volumes. I hated this vulgar and unnecessary assault on my peace and quiet as a pedestrian. In private life there is no politer nation than Japan, but rudeness in public often prevails. In the extremes of urban transportation, there was no choice but to put up with trying circumstances, but the struggles and stresses of the subways and trains weren't nearly as annoying as the uncalled for and inexcusable noise pollution in the streets.

There were other sounds that were now as familiar to me as anything I had known at home. The clacking of subway and train wheels, the endless nervous clicking of the ticket-takers' punches at the turnstiles, the sound in the fall and winter of the *imo* man, the vendor of roasted sweet potatoes, his traditional chant blasting out, unfortunately, from a speaker on his wheeled cart, "Ee-mōōōō, ee-mōōō, ee-mō, ee-mō, ee-mō, ee-mōōōōōōō!"

Japanese men are ferocious smokers. Smoking was more common among Japanese men than among North American men by a factor of two, less common among Japanese woman. There was no such thing as a non-smoking section in a restaurant. Whenever Sue and I went to a restaurant, we always asked to sit in the non-smoking section, which sent the hostesses and waiters into a confusion. It was our clever and niggling way of contributing to the adult education of the population, raising awareness about healthy choices and fairness. Smoking wasn't permitted in the subway stations, but some Japanese men defied the rules and defiled the air. I had had cigarette smoke blown in my face for two years, even in the health food restaurant in Shibuya, and I was not going to miss that disgusting experience.

I bought my second and last 35-mm SLR camera in Tokyo. It was a used Minolta from a little shop in Ginza. I bought one very short and one very long lens to go with it, and I have hundreds of photographs of Tokyo from the early eighties. I had enough money to get dozens and dozens of rolls of film developed. I usually had contact sheets printed. From them I could then choose the better images for making larger prints. It was the first period of my life for which I had such a comprehensive visual record.

When I made my way home through the streets of Tokyo, in the dark at the end of the day, I felt safe and at home. Because I bicycled so frequently, I knew my neighbourhood very well. With the barest of information, I would venture to any part of Tokyo and beyond, without a care. Japanese language and culture can send your head spinning, but once you come to terms with them, Japan is an easy place to live, especially the big cities. "Tokyo is very convenient," as my students never tired of saying.

In early April, especially in Ueno and Shinjuku Parks, the cherry blossoms formed pink and white clouds in the trees, and drifts of petals on the ground. In May, Sue and I spent an entire day surrounded by purple irises at the ponds in the enormous park at *Meiji-jingu*, the shrine dedicated to the Meiji emperor of the nineteenth century. In June, I bicycled many times by pastel hydrangeas the size of volleyballs in the park surrounding the National Stadium. The autumn leaves viewed from the "highway of forty-eight hairpin turns" at Nikko National Park were so breathtaking I went three times to see them. The memory of walking through two feet of fallen leaves in Shinjuku Park with David and Jude will be with me as long as my memory functions.

I spent one and a half summers, three autumns, three Christmases, and one and a half springs in Tokyo. My Samon-cho barber, after going to him for a year, was disgusted at the low level of my Japanese. I was no better at language acquisition than the rich, mahjong-playing Japanese wives of Tamagawa and Manhattan.

By the time I left Japan for the last time, in early April 1984, it had been four and a half years since I met Shizuka at the kitchen table at the Victoria Buddhist Dharma Society Centre on Leonard Street. The brief harmony of my relationship with her was short and intense, but she introduced me to an extended melody, one that has lingered on and accompanied me for the rest of my life. It took me six months to write 80,000 words, seven chapters, and a hundred and fifty pages about Shizuka and Japan. Together the stories form a full forty per cent of this volume. The memories rise slowly and submerge again in my mind, and in my life, like the tip of an iceberg, the little part you see and the big part you don't.

In spite of my tic-tac-toe work schedule and having to bob and weave around an enormous city in a foreign country, from early morning to late at night, maybe because of it, my time in Tokyo was vivid and carefree. I had been an ESL prima donna on light duty, and I had been well paid for it. Some aspects of life and work in Tokyo were difficult, some disturbing, but on deeper acquaintance it was, on my second visit, a far friendlier and kinder experience than I might have imagined.

I was hurt and sad and muddled about leaving Sue, but I had what I wanted, didn't I? I was debt-free and I had a pocketful of money. I had a plane ticket out of town.

But I didn't feel good about it, and I didn't know where I was going. I had uneasy suspicions about the immediate future that I was happy to ignore for now, but the unrest and distortions that were to come over the next sixteen months were beyond my ability to imagine.

14 Briefly by the Bay

There was just enough room behind the last row of seats on the 747 to do yoga, so that's what I did for an hour starting not long after the plane took off and headed northeast into the oncoming night. The flight attendants politely asked me what I was doing and then left me alone. By the time I was at Michael and Mia's door in San Francisco, twelve hours later, I was exhausted and full-on sick and stayed that way for the next ten block-headed days.

Larry and Cathy had gone to the Caribbean to work as skipper and crew for a charter yacht company, and Michael and Mia were feeding their fish while they were gone. This was opportune and convenient. I took over fish-feeding duties and lived in Larry and Cathy's third-floor apartment for the month of April. Michael said he was sure they wouldn't mind.

April is practically summer in San Francisco. July and August aren't. When my head finally cleared, I had day after day to explore the city in depth, in gorgeous weather. I let out a great sigh knowing I had left Japan and its volcanoes and the constant threat of apocalyptic earthquakes. But I had merely gone from the west side of the Pacific Rim to the east.

Standing with Mike and Mia in their kitchen on April 24, just after lunch, a 5.7 earthquake struck that was felt from Bakersfield to Sacramento, from San Francisco to Reno. The tall old house was heavy and solid, but it shook violently. The kitchen door let onto the exterior stairs at the back of the house, but they did not tempt us to use them to run outside. They were very tall and wooden and rickety. Even on the second floor, we were so high up, so far from the tiny sunken yard below, we risked staying inside rather than attempt an escape by that means. The stairs might have been the first thing to separate from the building, and no one wanted to be on them if that happened. We stood wide-eyed, hearts pounding, either in the door frames to the hall and the bedroom, or reeling like drunkards in the kitchen until the shaking stopped. It was a big one. Out of the frying pan, into the fire.

While in Tokyo, in addition to the Benedictines, I had been writing to the Franciscans in both the US and Canada. The Franciscan Province of St. Barbara is headquartered in Oakland. They pursue their charism and their program of aiding the poor in Washington, Oregon, California, Arizona, and New Mexico. The friars first came to the America Southwest in 1539 to convert the heathens and put them to work in their fields and workshops. They built twenty-one missions along the old El Camino Real from San Diego to Sonoma, now the Historic Missions Trail, Highway 101. These church-community-farms were built in beautiful locations along with, later, retreat centres, social service centres, and parishes, many of them with very attractive buildings and grounds. I still had a deep appreciation for California and its fine weather, and once again I wanted to talk to someone in sunny climes about my New Age and medieval love of meditation.

There was a Franciscan volunteer program run out of the San Damiano Retreat in Danville, a town in the hot San Ramon Valley just over the hills east of Oakland. My contact there, Mr. Ambrose, was trying to find me a place to wash dishes for a few months. He suggested going to the Province's Native missions in Arizona and New Mexico, but his description of them was grim. Desert isolation, lack of education, few jobs, unemployment rates up to eighty-five per cent, illness, violence, substance abuse, suicide, and widespread poverty. And unbearable heat in the coming summer. Mr. Ambrose made no judgment of my reluctance to go to these places. I wasn't a friar. Or a missionary. I wasn't finished converting myself yet. I was looking for a retreat, not an outpost.

Also, I knew nothing about Native Americans except what I had seen driving through the bleak reservations of southern and central Alberta. In Calgary, a few years earlier, I had seen a disturbing television news report about the abuse of Lysol Disinfectant Spray at the Siksika Nation Reserve near Gleichen and Cluny, the second largest reserve in Canada. My family drove by these towns, and this reserve, every time we visited my grandfather's farm near Brooks. In the late seventies, the stores on the reserve were no longer allowed to stock and sell Lysol. People were discharging the aerosol contents into water and drinking it. This is a vicious way to get wasted. There is nothing high about it. The video coverage showed the ditch behind the reserve's main store, littered with empty Lysol cans. The locals called this depression Happy Valley. I was not up to immersion in the cultures of the Apache, the Yaqui, the Mescalero, and the Tohono O'odham of the American Southwest. This culture, one type of which I had grown up next door to, and was completely isolated from, was more foreign to me than those of India or Japan. The friars of St. Barbara would have to make their amends to the Natives of Arizona and New Mexico without my assistance.

I preferred the look and sound of Santa Barbara, the Queen of the Missions, or perhaps I could mow lawns in Monterey, Malibu, Huntington Beach, or Oceanside, or even Los Angeles, for six months or a year. I would not be averse to a waterfront stay.

I also wanted to talk to Fr. Michael about joining the Franciscans of California. He was the vocations director, based out of St. Elizabeth's Parish in Oakland, and I took the BART train to Fruitvale one day to meet him. I was still very sick. It was a beautiful day in the Bay Area, and Fr. Michael wanted to sit outside in the walled garden. The sunny, dry garden was exploding with new spring life, and my nose ran like a faucet for an hour and a half while we talked, and roasted, in unshaded chairs. I had not brought a hat with me, and I thought my hair would start on fire. I was overheated and gasping for the cool, dark quiet and comfort of those little rooms that I knew were in the church's rectory just a few feet away, or even in the crypt, if there was one. Sick or healthy, without three months of carefully increased incremental exposure, a sudden thirty minutes in the sun renders me practically unconscious. I wouldn't survive a week in Arizona. I'm too Nordic and pale for that.

And again, Fr. Michael told me there was nothing to be done. Unless I could find a way to transform my otherwise very desirable Canadian citizenship into that of another country, I couldn't join a religious order anywhere but in Canada. This was bitterly disappointing to me. And unfair, dammit! This was the only thing I wanted to do, and I was prevented by nothing more than a geographical accident of birth.

There was one way to get around these policies of national exclusion, but it wasn't easy. I could go to university in the US, something Fr. Michael thought was a very good idea. He was an academic, and he couldn't hide his disappointment at my lack of education. He said spending a year at a retreat was "a year out." He believed that action would be better for me than contemplation. I disagreed with him in general, but on a purely practical level, if I were armed with a couple of degrees I could then make application to immigrate to the US as an HQW, a Highly Qualified Worker. This was not an attractive option to me. Years of hard work in school under the constant threat of uncertain funding. How does a friar, after taking a vow of poverty, pay off student loans? I was confusing a vow of poverty with a vow of unemployment. As Fr. Michael was filling out a form with my tombstone data, we discovered we were exactly the same age, born on the same Sunday in 1953. He seemed quite taken by this coincidence. I was less impressed, but I was hot and sick. And cranky. No one was telling me what I wanted to hear. He invited me to a dinner and talk at the Franciscan School of Theology in Berkeley.

I had had a very satisfying Christmas in Tokyo. Sue was away and I was a little restless, but I went to all the Christmas celebrations and events at the Franciscan Chapel Center and at other locations around town. I found the services and carolling more enjoyable and gratifying than I had ever known. After a fulfilling Christmas Day mass, only slightly distracted by young Michele crowded close next to me, I bought a large gift basket at a store in Roppongi and made my way to the house of friends of friends. I spent the rest of the day there in the glow of mixed Japanese and American family warmth.

Now, in April, I was having an equally good Easter. I went to mass every day in San Francisco, here and there, my wicked cold permitting. Over Holy Week and Easter Week, I went every day to Mission San Francisco de Asis, not far from Michael and Mia's. The founding of the church, also known as Mission Dolores, predates the US Declaration of Independence by five days. It is the oldest intact building in San Francisco. Its thick adobe walls kept it upright during the 1906 San Francisco Earthquake even though the epicentre was only eleven miles away. The quake destroyed eighty per cent of the city all around it. In the basilica next door, on Good Friday, I watched women weeping and touching the life-sized cross and corpus as it was carried down the centre aisle. I was not so emotional as that, I am Norwegian-Scottish after all, but it was interesting to participate in several services with a heavy Hispanic presence.

In Tokyo, Sue had given me a navy blue, crewneck, pullover sweater once owned by her brother. I think it was military issue of some kind. He was in the National Guard. It was not thick, but it was strong and tightly woven of high-quality wool. It fit me like a glove. When I wore a shirt underneath, the shirt collar stuck up half an inch above the sweater in an even circle around the neck. For reasons that I consider to be coincidental, I had taken to wearing white shirts and trousers while I was living in Tokyo. When I wore a white shirt under this sweater, the combined effect of navy blue and a sliver of white collar had a distinctly clerical look, especially with my emaciated frame and the suit jacket I routinely wore. A couple of times people greeted me on the street with, "Good day, Father." As I said, coincidental.

My former girlfriend Shea was in San Francisco on a little holiday with her parents, who lived in Saskatchewan, and I met the three of them and showed them around town. I had taken Shea and her father and her brother sailing three summers before, and now I took them all to Fisherman's Wharf, and Tommy's Joynt, and to the top of the Fairmont Hotel to enjoy the view for the price of a drink. Shea told me later that her mother, a no-nonsense prairie Protestant, had whispered to her, "What's with the collar?"

What Shea wanted to say was, "He thinks that shit that goes through his head is God talking to him," but she was too kind for that. Instead she said, "Oh, he thinks he wants to be a priest."

Her mother said, "Ha! He may as well be. He looks like one."

When they all left San Francisco, Shea invited me to stay with her in Vancouver, where she was now living, should I find myself passing that way.

The Franciscan School of Theology is the only freestanding Franciscan graduate theological school in North America. It is a member of the Graduate Theological Union, an affiliate of the University of California, Berkeley. It's on Euclid Avenue just north of the main campus on what is called Holy Hill, a quiet, tree-lined neighbourhood so named for the number of seminaries in the area. I had no trouble finding the school, a good-sized stucco building painted brick red, and I spent an evening in close company with thirty or so friars and young men interested in the Franciscan religious life. By the time the dinner and talks were over, I was very uncomfortable, sweltering and suffocating, and I begged leave to get some air outside. Fr. Michael was at the dinner, and I met several other local and visiting friars. These were all pleasant men, quite academic, and people I knew I had almost nothing in common with. I rode the BART train home with fewer illusions and with a fellow aspirant who also lived in the Castro district. He was so insipidly gay it was difficult to talk with him. And I am gay positive. He asked me out on a date. I declined. I was sure he thought of the Franciscan community, without much error, as a place to meet men.

I have always enjoyed the company of intelligent gay men. They tend to be gentle and open-minded, usually with a good sense of humour, and they don't talk so much about sports. I don't, however, like precious, excessively effeminate gay men even though they make funny characters in television sitcoms, any more than I like excessively macho straight men. In both cases it seems like an insecure overemphasis of sexuality. And unless

I'm actually having sex with you, or you're on TV, I don't care about your sexuality. Keep it to yourself.

By the end of the month, Mr. Ambrose, the volunteer coordinator, had only one option for me. The retreats and missions of Southern California were staffed up with volunteers, but there was a place for me at St. Mary's Retreat in Toledo, Washington, if I cared to go north. This was far too close to the forty-ninth parallel for me, but I had spent a month in San Francisco and nothing else had materialized. I accepted his offer.

I had spent the sunny month of April at leisure in the great city of San Francisco, free to explore, walking for miles, and taking the bus and the streetcar everywhere, my camera in hand, money in my pocket. I had an apartment to myself and good friends, Michael and Mia, close by. In the evenings we often lay together on their bed and watched blurry episodes of *Barney Miller* on their tiny television. I telephoned and wrote frequently to Sue and sent her presents in the mail. I had meditated in peace and participated in numerous satisfying church services. I was disappointed at not being able to find a volunteer position in California, and I had made no headway with the Franciscans of the Province of St. Barbara. I was feeling very calm and very peaceful, but also a trifle leaden in the gut, no closer at all to a resolution. My shaky plans were falling apart one after another. And now I was heading in the wrong direction. North.

The Franciscans I had written to in Western Canada belonged to the Province of Christ the King. They are a small group with retreat centres near Calgary and Regina, active also in Edmonton and Vancouver. Their retirement friary is in Victoria, the one I had been to many times. I spoke with a friar there before going to Japan, asking about a Franciscan vocation. He gave me a civil welcome and provided me with some information and advice. He also told me that only about one in four postulants actually succeeded in becoming a friar. I told him as nicely as I could that when there is a seventy-five per cent failure rate, it is usually the fault of the system, not the participating aspirant. I asked him if there was one particular stumbling block that accounted for this dismal success rate. His answer was one word. "Sex." When I passed through Victoria again a couple of years later, I was informed that the priest I had talked to before was now living and working in Florida, the Sunshine State. "How on earth did he manage that?" I asked, surprised.

"He talks a good story," was the reply.

While I was in San Francisco I telephoned the vocations director for the Franciscans of Western Canada, Fr. Martin, a man I had written from Tokyo. I wanted to give him an idea of my plans for the next few months and ask him about the advisability of showing up on their doorstep sometime soon, at St. Michael's Retreat in Lumsden, Saskatchewan, just east of Regina. He seemed unconcerned about my plans. He said, "I ran into your primary reference recently, Fr. John, your good friend in Victoria, and when I mentioned you, he couldn't say enough to your credit." Pause. And then, "You must be quite an actor." This was a cool slice of cucumber on his part, but it was also amusing in a backhanded and close-bitten way. Just my style.

I wrote to Karen, my old high school girlfriend, the auburn-haired artist. She was living in Regina and was the director of an art gallery, a job she had had for six years and would keep for another thirty. She had been married, but she ditched her no-good husband. She had a three-year-old boy. I asked her if I could stay at her place for a time while I negotiated with the Franciscans of Lumsden. Her response was, more or less, "What?"

When the utility bills showed up in Larry and Cathy's mailbox, I opened them and paid them and left the receipts on their dresser along with a few balloons and little presents by way of thanks.

The train for the north left near midnight, and I took a taxi to a huge station in San Francisco's Mission Bay industrial district. I had seen this area at night from a great vantage in Bernal Heights just to the west, after smoking pot for hours while watching *Das Boot* at friends of Michael's. The freeways and the port facilities, the maritime piers, many of them covered and jutting out into the water, the giant cranes, industrial sites, warehouses, and commercial real estate, ran north and south on the west side of San Francisco Bay, eight miles of lit-up waterfront lands, with the port of Oakland and its nineteen miles of waterfront only another mile to the east. It was an astonishing sight, remarkable day or night, straight or stoned. If you thought only of San Francisco's tourist attractions, the hills, the trolley cars, Chinatown, Haight-Ashbury, you might forget, or never know, that in its early days the bay was said to be a port in which all the fleets of the world could find anchorage.

I had never seen this train station before, and I have the barest memory of it from a single glimpse at night. It must have been the Caltrain Station at Fourth and King, the new station that had replaced the crumbling, 60-year-old Southern Pacific Depot only eight years earlier. From here I took a coach bus to Oakland where I boarded the Amtrak *Coast Starlight* one more time and rode it north to Centralia, Washington, a journey of twenty slow, bumpy, uncomfortable hours without a bed.

15   Holy Toledo

Vince, the director of the retreat, picked me up at the Amtrak station in Centralia for the twenty-mile ride south to St. Mary's Retreat on Spencer Road, just northwest of the little town of Toledo on the Cowlitz River. The Cowlitz drains the slopes of Mt. Rainier, Mount St. Helens, and Mt. Adams into the Columbia. These mountains are all enormous stratovolcanoes in the Cascade Volcanic Arc. Exactly four years earlier Mount St. Helens had blown its top.

Mount Rainier is the tallest of the three at over 14,000 feet, taller than Mt. Fuji. It, too, had erupted only ninety years earlier, in 1894, and it is considered to be one of the most dangerous volcanoes in the world because of the proximity of large population centres and the amount of glacial ice on its peak. When ice and lava meet, the result is the explosive production of toxic and suffocating ash, more widespread in its effects and therefore more deadly than molten rock. Mount Rainier is the most topographically prominent mountain in the lower forty-eight states. It sticks up more from its surroundings than K2 in the Himalayas, the world's second-highest mountain. From the retreat Mt. Rainier was about forty miles northeast as the crow flies, and Mount St. Helens was thirty miles southeast, with Mt. Adams just out of sight beyond it.

That night Vince showed me to a little house on the property which I was to have to myself, for now. The next morning I entered the main retreat building and made my way to the staff dining and lounge area on the east side, and there on the horizon, very close, and stunningly beautiful, were Mt. Rainier and Mount St. Helens. From the large bank of windows, obviously designed and built to let in as much light as possible in this grey climate, these magnificent peaks dominated the eastern horizon along sightlines angled slightly to the north and to the south. Seeing them every day, I could understand why people bowed before mountains and imagined them to be the natural home of the gods.

The Mission of St. Francis Xavier, named for the sixteenth-century Jesuit missionary, was the first in Washington State, founded on the Cowlitz prairie in 1838, five years before Fort Victoria in British Columbia. Fr. Modeste Demers, later Bishop of Victoria, was one of the two founding priests, and he designed and directed the construction of the church and the cemetery. The Franciscans took over the mission in 1908, and the Franciscan Sisters oversaw the school, first started in 1864, until it closed in 1973. The school was converted into St. Mary's Retreat, and it was still under the authority of the Sisters of St. Francis, headquartered in Redwood City south of San Francisco.

On my first morning at the retreat, I met the old nuns, Sisters Grace, Miriam, and Teresina. There was little contact, none really, with the two old priests at the church next door, and I never met them, not once. I could have introduced myself to them, but I was warned off by Vince. He described them as old, conservative, and espousing the Church's more dismal doctrines. There were two maintenance men and a young housekeeper, as well as a contract cook who worked only when meals were needed for retreatants. Business was not brisk.

Most of my time over the next two and a half months was spent very casually helping the maintenance men with outdoor tasks such as mowing the lawn, shingling a roof, putting in a fence post, digging a hole, or filling one in. When there was a retreat group in residence, I helped in the kitchen and dining room.

A few large additions to the small campus had been built not long before the school closed, and they were only fifteen years old, still fairly new. There was a modern kitchen, a new gymnasium, library, and staff quarters, along with new heating and air conditioning. The staff quarters, for nuns and single teachers, had been made into pleasant individual rooms for retreatants, and there were, as well, dozens of single beds separated only by privacy curtains in a huge open area designed to accommodate large groups.

There was an adjoining classroom building of three concrete storeys that had been built in the 1930s. It was still in excellent shape fifty years later. It was so solidly constructed it looked like it might last until the End of Days. But it was now empty.

It seemed pretty obvious that a lot of economical effort had been made to transform the school into a functioning retreat centre, but it was unlikely it would succeed financially. Apart from a small amount of retreat activity, it was exactly what it appeared to be, an empty, unused school. No one was looking forward to the day the accountants were scheduled to show up to discuss the books.

I started with some hope, at least, of living in devout unity, but it wasn't long before I realized that St. Mary's was not a spiritual community. It was half a dozen unhappy people who didn't like each other, living and working together. It never occurred to me that that might be the definition of a spiritual community. I thought I could find a situation like that just about anywhere.

Sister Grace felt that she was the boss. She was the oldest nun, and she had been an old-school sergeant-major-teacher-principal-nun for a long time. She was used to being obeyed. At St. Mary's no one was officially in charge. They were all now part of something new called a management team, and the lack of clear lines of authority caused a great deal of tension. Sister Grace was also an elderly, emaciated, insulin-dependent diabetic. Nonetheless, she rose early and worked hard all day. When the others wanted to take a break, and did, or do something else, and wandered off, she became very angry. She complained that no one was helping her, which was true some of the time, but her real complaint was that she wasn't in charge. There had been some unfriendly exchanges amongst the inmates.

I also found out fairly quickly that the pretty housekeeper was having sex with one of the maintenance men. He was ruggedly handsome and twice her age. She spent most nights in his quarters above the garage instead of in her own above the laundry. This was unacceptable to the nuns, and they were very annoyed, but this was 1984, not 1964, and there was nothing they could do about it. They couldn't legally fire them, and they couldn't forbid them. Moreover, the maintenance man was an experienced machinist who had worked in the aeronautics industry, and his skills were essential to the mechanics of the operation. They couldn't afford to lose him even if they could easily find another housekeeper.

In short order I realized I had nothing in common with any of these people, and they had no particular reason to like me. I should have been more concerned when Vince, the director, said, on the drive home from the train station, "Don't feel you have to stay if you decide you don't like the place. There's no obligation at all. No, really." What he meant was, "Run. Go. Go now. Run for your life. These people are crazy." He left before I did. He was actively looking for other employment. The nuns and the general unhappiness of the place drove him away. Vince might have been a sympathetic ear for me, but he kept his distance knowing he was leaving soon. He was unhappy and anxious to go. One of the few things he told me about himself was that he had landed at Normandy on D+2, June 8, 1944, eighteen years old and scared shitless. He was five years older than my father.

It rained five days out of six the entire time I was at St. Mary's. I had heard that pioneer women arriving at last in the Seattle area, threw themselves to the ground in tears, not out of joy or relief after their long and arduous journey, but on realizing that their new home was in a part of the world where the rain falls two hundred days of the year. Of the dozen places in the contiguous USA with the highest total yearly precipitation averages, nine of them are in the state of Washington. The other three are in Oregon, its border only twenty-five miles from the retreat. There was a reason I wanted to stay in California.

I liked my little moss-covered house under the big conifers, away from the main building, but one day I was told they wanted to rent the house to retreatants. I moved into the fairly spacious studio suite above the gymnasium. It had obviously been the coach's quarters. After a drab day at the retreat, I would myself retreat to the empty gym, grab a basketball and shoot hoops by myself for half an hour, then read for a couple of hours in the library, always history, before retiring to my little coach's corner to do yoga.

I was bored out of my skull in no time. And lonely. God, I hadn't been that lonely since my long, last, dismal winter at Camosun College. I wrote constantly to Sue and telephoned her frequently in spite of the expense. At the end of May and again at the end of June, Sister Miriam presented me with a telephone bill for a hundred and ten dollars, a fortune, which I paid without blinking. Sister Miriam knew I was miserable.

Things picked up a little in the summer. More groups began to arrive, and we catered for crowds of fifteen to fifty. The cook was my height and weighed three hundred pounds and never stopped talking. Her husband was over four hundred pounds and was subject to fits of narcolepsy. The cook brought her own staff, one or two, when she had a big group to cook for, but I and the other retreat staff did dishes and kept the self-serve stations stocked and set up, and we cleaned the dining room. The cook's little redheaded ten-year-old daughter was often present, and she openly pestered me in the kitchen with saucy sexual innuendo, uncorrected by her mother. It was very uncomfortable.

We had a small group of mid-week retreatants in residence once, just for the day, all Washington State employees. After lunch I passed the two group leaders in the hallway while they discussed the upcoming after-

Ch. 15 — Holy Toledo — 315

noon's events. They were two tall, paunchy men in their thirties dressed in casual clothing, khaki pants and Hush Puppies, pale blue or pale yellow shirts, both holding clipboards and pens in their hands. They spoke in soft, self-satisfied tones, praising trifles in the sick-making jargon of bureaucrats the world over. I knew nothing of government, less than nothing, but I knew enough to mutter then and there a small prayer. "Please, God. Whatever happens, don't let me become a bureaucrat. Don't let it come to that." Five years later, I was starting the Master of Public Administration program at the University of Victoria to learn a new language, bureaucratese.

We had a special concert in the gym one day given by a visiting Catholic celebrity, John Michael Talbot. He was a hip, young, former rocker now in Franciscan robes, and he was very popular on the Christian Gospel circuit. I had never heard of him, but I had heard of his earlier folk rock band, Mason Proffit. They were big enough in the late sixties and early seventies to open for the Doobie Brothers, Steely Dan, John Denver, and the Eagles. John Michael was a year younger than I. He dropped out of school at fifteen and toured the country playing three hundred gigs a year, surrounded by groupies and drugs. He made five studio albums with his band. Then he saw the light and became a Catholic. Now he was writing and playing syrupy Christian folk music. But he was very talented. And tireless. He used some of his rock 'n' roll money to found a Christian community, the Brothers and Sisters of Charity, and he has, to date, recorded over fifty albums of Gospel music and written two dozen books. In 2008, much of his community in Arkansas was destroyed by fire, and he started again, travelling nine months of the year performing and raising money to rebuild. He married in 1989 with permission from the Church.

When the concert was over, I was charged with getting John Michael safely to an address somewhere near Bothell, Washington, a bedroom suburb of Seattle a hundred and twenty miles north of Toledo. We began the journey at eight o'clock at night. Two hours later I dropped him at Pat Boone's daughter's house. It must have been Cheryl Lynn's place. I was invited in to rest a little before starting back and was introduced to Cherry's husband, Dan O'Neill, the founder of Mercy Corps, the humanitarian aid agency, then only five years old. Cherry and the kids were away, and after a few minutes I headed back to St. Mary's leaving Dan and John Michael giggling and bouncing up and down on a mini-trampoline in the living room of the spacious and expensive house. There was a photograph on the mantle of Pat Boone with Pope John Paul II.

I became a frequent driver and runner of errands at the retreat. The nuns had a couple of Chrysler K cars, and I was often sent into town for this and that, sometimes to pick up retreatants. I was also encouraged to take a car on my day off and explore the local countryside, as long as I didn't leave the gas tank empty. The nuns didn't want me getting morose. This was a perk I wasn't expecting, and I took advantage of it.

Mount St. Helens was the biggest and closest natural disaster I had any experience of, and I wanted to see as much of it as I could. I went to both of the new visitor centres devoted to describing and explaining the 1980 eruption, one built near the retreat and one near the summit of what was left of the mountain. The eruption blew thirteen hundred feet of elevation off the top of the peak and left behind a mile-wide crater. I drove around the entire mountain on rough roads, not always sure where I was. The eruption is the deadliest on record in North America, and it was an astonishing event to contemplate, as well as the new landscape it left behind.

On another day I went to the Ape Cave. It's on the south side of Mount St. Helens, and it is the longest continuous lava tube in the continental United States. It's an unusual formation for the area since stratovolcanoes don't typically produce them. I admit I was a little nervous at first going down into the dark alone. I had never been in a cave before. But it is no more than a walk in the park at night. The floor is flat, sandy, and gently sloping which makes for an easy stroll. As long as your flashlight holds out, you're fine. I only saw one other person down there, a cute young girl, a summer student park ranger. One of her duties was to walk to the bottom of the cave every day to make sure nothing was amiss. I thought she would be a little nervous herself about being down there alone. I wouldn't be surprised if cave inspection procedures have changed since then.

The nuns rarely used their own cars, so I made free with them. I drove often into Chehalis and Centralia to go to the movies by myself. I went into Portland for the Rose Festival. Portland is seventy miles from the ocean but thanks to dredging in the Columbia River, ocean freighters and navy ships can dock in downtown Portland on the Willamette River, a tributary of the Columbia, and thanks to locks and canals, barges can reach four hundred miles inland to Lewiston, Idaho, most of this traffic for the export of prairie wheat. Almost all of North America's inland waterways are on the east coast and around the Mississippi River. On the west coast the only navigable rivers of any length are the Columbia, the Sacramento, and the San Joaquin.

Portland's climate is ideal for growing roses. Rose City is its nickname. The US Navy usually lends a hand at the annual Rose Festival, and a few spare ships steam up the river to light up the wharves along NW Front Avenue next to the midway. In 1984, there was also a visiting Canadian ship at the back of the line. I wouldn't have known it then, but it was almost certainly an *Iroquois*-class destroyer. At 5,600 tons it was tiny compared with the US Navy behemoths in front of it, but I was pleased to see that there was a line-up of three dozen well-dressed young American women waiting their turn for a tour of the ship, each one to be accompanied in person by an eager Canadian sailor.

I drove the two miles from the retreat to Toledo to rent VHS tapes and a video player, since they didn't have one at the retreat, for the occasional staff movie night. I accompanied Sister Teresina into Seattle a couple of times. One night, we stayed over at a parish somewhere. I was asked to fetch something from one of the priest's studies and saw there, to my pleasant surprise, a copy of *Autobiography of a Yogi*. Sister Teresina, although over sixty, was the youngest of the nuns, the fun nun, and she obviously didn't care much for older company. She had her own car, and she was always gone, gadding about here and there. Sister Miriam was about the same age but more level-headed. She was a science teacher, now retired. She told me she had a Master's degree in biology, something that surprised me since I never, in three months, heard her utter anything but the most mundane remarks. And Sister Grace was the Holy Terror.

There was a celebration in the summer, an anniversary, in honour of what I don't recall, and a few very elderly nuns and priests came up from the Bay Area. One of them was Fr. Alfred Boeddeker. He had founded the St. Anthony Dining Room in 1950 to feed the poor of San Francisco's Tenderloin. One friar, one loaf of bread. That's how it started. When he wasn't running the program, he was mopping the floors. His foundation grew to include emergency housing, drug and alcohol rehabilitation, a medical clinic, and a farm. They have since served 40 million meals. In 1984, he was eighty-one years old and famous in the Bay Area. He was doted on at St. Mary's. One evening, Fr. Alfred was milling awkwardly about the crowded staff lounge in his brown robe. I heard someone ask him if there was something he wanted. He said, "I want to go home." He lived in the Tenderloin, the poorest part of San Francisco, for forty-four years. These were the Catholics I liked.

The next day, a very old nun, close to ninety, was sitting in the dining room, looking out at the magnificent view of the volcanoes. She said to me in her old, thin voice, "I remember when we planted those trees, back in the thirties." There was a substantial row of them between the main building and the laundry. I said, "You planned with a long eye back then, Sister. It must be very satisfying to see them so tall now." She said, "Well, we just planted them there so we wouldn't have to look at the boys' underwear drying on the clothesline." St. Mary's was a residential school.

I had started 1984 in a state of guarded pessimism, wondering how the year would unfold, what with my new, radically unconventional goals. I, a dyed-in-the-wool bohemian, an aging and experienced hippie, and you know what I mean, was angling to enter the ranks of the ultraconservative, the straight and the narrow-minded. I couldn't infiltrate Self-Realization Fellowship, but surely I could find a place in an inclusive church of my own culture.

And now, only six months later, I was miserable, lonely, dispirited, disillusioned, and depressed. I began to think there might be a flaw in my plan. How on earth could I possibly survive in such dismal and petty company? How could I have gone looking for a spiritual community and found *this*? Grudging, dysfunctional, uncooperative, childish, passive-aggressive, and small-minded. Not only was there nothing spiritual about life at St. Mary's, there wasn't even anything vaguely religious about it. It was less than ordinary people leading immature lives. And I was one of them. And now I remembered Vince's advice on the day he picked me up at the train station. "Don't feel you have to stay if you decide you don't like the place. There's no obligation at all. No, really."

I hadn't wanted to run away at the first sign of stupidity. I had lived long enough to know that when stupidity happens around me, it is often enough my own fault. But there was nothing here for me. And worse, I was starting to think there might not be anything good about the Catholics at all. My church sponsor in Victoria, Kay, told me that when she converted in the 1930s, she went, soon after, to a conference of skilful and enlightened Catholic practitioners. There she was told by a knowing friend, "Enjoy this now, Kay. This is the cream of Catholic spirituality. You won't see this again, not in everyday parish life."

I continued to read. *Revelations of Divine Love* by Julian of Norwich, *Dark Night of the Soul* by St. John of the Cross, the anonymous *Cloud of Unknowing*, *The Book of Margery Kempe*, snippets of St. Hildegard of

Bingen and St. Teresa of Ávila, *The Story of a Soul* by St. Thérèse of Lisieux, history and commentary by Thomas Merton, *The Great Code* by Northrop Frye, and the lives of the saints. One young priest I talked to said, "That's what I should be reading! I always seem to wind up reading things like *When Good Things Happen to Bad People*, or is it the other way around?"

I began to mope, never an attractive quality in a 30-year-old. I could hardly drag myself out of bed. Work was pointless. Conversation with my fellows was utterly lifeless. I felt no more connection with the people around me than I did with the furniture in the hallways. The skies were grey. The rain never stopped. As my spirit flagged my cover story got flimsier by the week. It seemed obvious to me that it was obvious to everyone that I was marvellously self-deluded and laughably unsuited to my cautiously stated goals, now expressed with ever more hesitation. Looking back I am sure now that no one gave me or my problems a second thought, which is what they deserved.

I had skimmed through California with little to offer and little to show for my time and trouble. I had found the retreat I was looking for, and now I was retreating. I had begun an honourable, but unrealistic, course of action that would, over the coming months, result in nothing but defeats. I was selfish and vague and I wandered. *Soy vago y vago*. I led with my jaw, and I was knocked hard and thrown back upon myself. And now I was dismayed to discover that there was no self there. Only feet of clay and a naive individuality that crumbled to the touch. I didn't see how I could get much more miserable than I was, but it was just the beginning. This would change of course. It would get better, but I didn't know that then. If I had known that I was going to be seriously depressed for another year, would I have stopped? Did I have the power to change that?

I stayed almost as long as I had intended at St. Mary's, three months, but I cut out a couple of weeks early. Vince had left, and I couldn't bear another day. I didn't go down on my knees before the altar and ask God for help or guidance. That wasn't the way I prayed. I bought a bus ticket.

The next stop on this fading, pathetic journey, one I nevertheless felt obliged to play out to its bitter end, was Westminster Abbey in Mission, BC.

16 Summer, Sudden and Short

Shea was a forgiving soul. She had taken in stride the drearier aspects of my personality during the winter of our unfortunate relationship in Victoria more than two years earlier. We were better friends than lovers. Shea had grown up in Estevan, in southern Saskatchewan, and she had got a job as a Border Services Officer right out of high school. A couple of years of that was enough, and she was now going to Simon Fraser University to finish a degree in criminology. She was living in an old, brick apartment building, vaguely Edwardian, on Salsbury Avenue in Vancouver. And she was happy. She shared the apartment with a physicist named Tom, and they were more or less in love. She was attracted to scientists. They had another roommate who was out of town, there was plenty of room in their sweltering apartment, and no one cared if I slept on their couch for a couple of weeks during the heat wave.

Summer had come to the Pacific Northwest in a blaze. For the next six weeks it was eighty degrees Fahrenheit, and much more, every day. The winter had been very long and the spring practically absent, but after three days of warm weather, the mossy rainfolk of the west coast began to complain that it was too hot.

There was also a bus strike. I found myself in Vancouver, a big city, without transportation. I rented a bicycle for a week, and within the first few blocks of riding it, I caught the front wheel on a rough edge of roadway on a residential street and fell over sideways, hard. I wasn't wearing a helmet. A man was working in his front yard only a few feet away from my crash, and he picked me up and helped me into his house. I was bleeding, scratched and bruised, dazed by the fall. He immediately turned his attention to a skilful assessment and repair of the damage to my newly rented bicycle while his wife cleaned me up in the kitchen and gave me two large glasses of orange juice to drink. After a rest of twenty-five minutes, I was able to continue my journey, both my bicycle and my abrasions buffed out by the Samaritans of West Point Grey. Before crashing I had been heading for a New Age health clinic on trendy West Fourth Avenue for no particular reason other than to examine their programs and bulletin boards, and I decided I was well enough to carry on. By the time I arrived at the clinic, the exertion of cycling had reopened my cuts and scratches, and I presented myself at the reception counter bleeding freely from multiple superficial wounds to the head.

Salsbury is a quiet street one block off Commercial Drive, the main road through Vancouver's Little Italy, an area now also populated by East Asians, South Asians, Latinos, and African Americans. English is a minority language in the area. There are European-styled cafes, and very few restaurant chains, as well as bars and boutiques, alternative shops, and entertainment venues. As time went by, there was to appear a large counterculture demographic including political activists, lesbians, hippies, punks, and artists, leaning towards a car-free, street-market lifestyle. The battle between the encroaching squalor of the Downtown Eastside and upward gentrification continues. But in 1984 it was still mostly espresso bars filled with old Italian men making sucking noises at passing girls, a generation of Mediterranean ass-pinchers.

Shea was happy and I was too, or I had been. Since I had last seen Shea, I had spent a successful and cheerful eighteen months in Japan and had turned myself inside out only a couple of times over my fretful spiritual imaginings. I was especially happy to put St. Mary's Retreat behind me. The obvious question, now and always, was, "Why don't you just shut up and do what you want to do regarding your so-called practice? Why be so critical of yourself and the world around you? Why don't you just stay at home and sweep your own door? Be still, live simply, pay your bills, mind your own business, and be at peace?" It would take many more years before I found the inner resources necessary to live in a manner so clear and simple. Thirty years ago I still needed outside reassurance. Rarely does anyone go it alone. I wanted to belong. I wasn't looking for certainty. I didn't need that. I just wanted a home, a conducive environment, and an effective system. I could turn the mangle, but I wanted someone else to balance the cheque book. In the end, my 45-year, ongoing practice of yoga and meditation was, and still is, a solitary undertaking, and I do not now regret a moment of that solitude, not even the years I spent doing yoga with a beer in my hand, watching *Murphy Brown* on TV, a contemplative animal. "I love Jesus but I drink a little." Regardless of the distractions, wherever the road took me, I always did my practice, with occasional modifications. Like the medieval Catholic Hunting Mass, a four-minute service for the convenience of those engaged in hunting, my practice was at times abbreviated, and nearly always imperfect, but it was always there, always part of my life, the biggest part. With every step of the way a part of your true self is revealed and fulfilled.

My Tokyo girlfriend, Sue, was a fixer. She was always trying to fix herself, and me, and her opinion was that I needed a lot of fixing. She seemed concerned that I was twenty-eight years old before I ever used the word "emotion" in a conversation. She sympathized deeply with my fancy for meditative resourcing, and my reliance upon it, but she also thought I had a lot of rough edges that could be ground down using other New Age modalities. At her suggestion I had gone for several acupuncture treatments with her favourite practitioner in San Francisco, Dr. Pang, and I boiled up horrifying concoctions of his herbal recipes on Michael and Mia's stove. I took no over-the-counter drugstore preparations to try to get over my wretched cold in April, and given how bad my illness was and how long it lasted, I doubt that gagging down Dr. Pang's foul brown potions of herbs and snake skins was of any help.

Talking with Sue on the telephone over the last couple of months, while she continued to live in little rooms in Tokyo, telling her about my profoundly disappointing experiences of late, she opined repeatedly and emphatically that I would without doubt benefit immensely from therapy. I thought meditation *was* therapy. She said I should go to workshops, do the sorts of things that progressive people do. In other words, I should do the things that she liked to do.

One of the most maddening and unappealing aspects of daily living and social intercourse, as I have experienced them, is the deadening and sickening amount of time one is required to listen to other people tell you why what they are doing is wise and right and why what you are doing is ludicrous, pointless, foolish, and wrong, and that what you should be doing is what they are doing instead of what it is you are doing. All advertising falls into this category which, with rigorous training and experience, can be put out of your mind, but where can you run when this ego-disease strikes every member of your family and community? My life is three-quarters over now, or more, and I have heard enough talk like this to last me to the end. God grant me quiet.

I was very reluctant to become a seeker by workshop, a style of self-exploration that I found to be far too subject to cliché, thinly rewarding, often risible. Plus I simply couldn't afford it. But everything seemed to be slipping through my hands, and I was getting to the point where spending all my income, or savings, to try once again to save my sanity, might be the only thing left for me to do. If you have a bad headache you might spend your last three dollars on Aspirin. Vancouver is a rich oasis of New Age nuttiness, and I had no trouble finding progressive and alternative activities to choose from. I signed up for a writing workshop at UBC, not creative writing, but journaling, something called the Progoff Intensive Journal Program for Self-Development.

But there was something else I had to do first, and it was time to get it over with.

I had written a few times to Fr. Wilfrid, the prior at Westminster Abbey, enquiring about the religious life. He had sent me prayer books in Japan. I had sent him money to pay for them. I had told him a little of my history and of my hopes. I was heading his way, and he knew I was coming.

I took the bus the slow forty miles from Vancouver to Mission and then, from the street-stop there, a taxi a couple of more miles to the Abbey. It was set in two hundred acres of beautiful farm and woodlands on a bench above the Fraser River. The new abbey church, in tall, narrow, vertical skirts of concrete and stained glass, was not to everyone's taste, but it was impressive nonetheless and had been dedicated only two years earlier. It cost four million dollars to build in the early eighties. One of the priests at the abbey told me he was amazed how easy it was to raise the money to pay for it. All the buildings of the monastery, most of them adjoining one another, were concrete, built to last, with red tiled roofs. It was July and the entire site couldn't have shown in better light.

I was told the story of the abbey's impressive 100-foot bell tower. Kenyon Reynolds was a millionaire at thirty-four thanks to early and spectacular successes in gas exploration and engineering in Texas. He sold out to Standard Oil and spent the next twenty years in easy living. When his wife, "a Catholic saint," died suddenly in 1945, he helped build the new abbey in Mission by paying for one-third of it. He then gave away his fortune of seventeen million (2014) dollars and entered the abbey. He became a monk and priest at age fifty-nine, well past the usual cut-off age for acceptance. His wife's family paid for the bell tower, and it is named for her. He was now ninety-two years old and had been a Benedictine monk for thirty years. I saw him in the choir, small, bent over, and deaf. He sang the prayers of the liturgy wearing a big set of headphones.

I thought of the monastic life or life in a religious order as a perfectly justifiable and dignified alternative for failing in the material world. To fail at them both was a bit embarrassing. At Ananda Cooperative Village one of the inversion platitudes was that people thought they came to the yoga community to renounce money when in reality they came because money had renounced them. I found this a bit harsh. If you genuinely have no interest in money, you are unlikely to acquire any because of your reasonable and understandable inattention to it. Even those who want nothing but money often find it hard to come by. I encountered this mean inconsistency more than a few times. The religious orders didn't want material losers. They wanted people who had either succeeded in life or those who had the mindset to do so. They didn't want incompetents. This is understandable. Even a religious order lives in a material world. But it is wrong. It denies entry to those who have perfectly legitimate spiritual reasons for rejecting the world, people who rarely find themselves in a higher tax bracket as a result of worldly disengagement.

I didn't have seventeen million dollars to donate, to smooth my acceptance with the Benedictines, and I probably wouldn't have given it away if I had.

I arrived in time for lunch and ate in silence with the monks at long tables while one of their number on a raised platform read briefly from the Rule of St. Benedict and then finished the last few pages of what I recognized as Tim Severin's *The Brendan Voyage*, the account of his 4,500-mile journey sailing an ox-hide dinghy from Ireland to Newfoundland, retracing the steps of the Irish sailor-saint.

After lunch I helped with the dishes in the big kitchen in the basement, and then Fr. Wilfrid introduced me to Fr. Placidus who was tasked with giving me a tour of the monastery. And a very thorough tour it was. Fr. Placidus had been the rector of the minor seminary, the high school, and he still taught there. He was also the monastery's choir director. He was disappointed to learn that my musical education had been neglected, and if admitted to their ranks, I would make no substantial addition to the recitative air of the liturgy. He was gentle and soft-spoken, aptly named, and he took me over every inch of the monastery, talking about its history and introducing me to everyone we saw. He obviously loved his home and the way it had grown over the thirty years he had been there.

He pointed out the monastery's many works of art with especial pride. Fr. Dunstan was the abbey's resident artist. He painted colourful and moving frescoes around the abbey as well as sculpting a series of striking concrete bas-reliefs affixed to walls and pillars. His sculptures started out as fairly flat profiles, quite Egyptian, but his recent work was much more muscular and three-dimensional.

Fr. Placidus and I stopped in a corridor to look at an open guesthouse room. We chatted briefly with the cleaners and then turned to continue down the hallway. There was a door in the hall, a fire door, and it was propped open. Next to it was a side panel of floor-to-ceiling glass. I was so focussed on a close examination of everything that was presented to me, so keen not to miss anything, that I was utterly unaware of the glass just to my right. It was also very clean, to all intents invisible. I turned and took a full-energy stride face first straight into it. I reeled at the impact and was nearly knocked off my feet. In ten minutes, I had a headache that I thought would be the end of me.

I would have been happier with a much more abbreviated tour of the monastery, but Fr. Placidus was determined I should see every inch of it. It was his turn to work in the fields that afternoon, and it's possible he preferred to chat with someone new to the monastery than to bale hay for four or five hours in the hot sun. It was nearly supper by the time we were done.

There was more pre-supper liturgy in the church followed by more pork chops and Jell-O and reading of the Rule in the refectory. I did more dishes. This was followed by the hour that all the monks are required to spend together in the evening in communal recreation. Some chatted, some read the paper. I retired at last to the room I had been assigned. I was spent and my head was killing me, but it was still too early to go to bed. I wasn't expecting him, but there was a knock at the door and Fr. Wilfrid came in. We talked for at least an hour. I asked him if there was an Aspirin, or a fistful of them, somewhere in the monastery. He said he couldn't think of where he might find one. This was surely cruelty. There was obviously an infirmary in a monastery that ran a school for boys.

Fr. Wilfrid was sixty-seven years old, and he was as bright and lively as I was at thirty-one, maybe more, suffering as I was from a pounding headache. To his experienced eye, to anyone really, I was obviously labouring under a pile of second thoughts, backtracking like a character racing out of the frame of an old-fashioned animated cartoon, accompanied by the rattle of a wooden cowbell and the sound of a bullet. He ended our conversation by saying he felt it would be better if I entered the community as a student in the college, the major seminary. I was clearly too intelligent to remain uneducated and clearly unsuited to enter directly as a postulant brother. I told him I had no money for school and no desire to borrow any. This was an impasse that was as good as a verdict.

I spent the entire night with an agonizing headache and rose in the morning from no more than a few minutes of sleep. I attended the liturgy at five or six o'clock, then the mass, then had breakfast with the monks, washed some more dishes, and caught a ride back to Vancouver with the organist.

Here is a passage from the Rule of St. Benedict that I probably should have read before I went to the monastery: "Let easy admission not be given to one who newly cometh to change his life; but, as the Apostle saith, 'Try the spirits, whether they be of God' (1 *Jn* 4:1). If, therefore, the newcomer keepeth on knocking, and after four or five days it is seen that he patiently beareth the harsh treatment offered him and the difficulty of admission, and that he persevereth in his request, let admission be granted him."

I had been torturing myself and others off and on for the last six years with my noble daydreams of monastic life. I felt like I had been knocking on the door for a long time. I didn't think it was necessary to thump any longer.

Twelve years later, in 1996, Fr. Placidus was charged with six counts of indecent assault, gross indecency, and buggery involving seminary boys aged twelve to fourteen years. He denied the charges but admitted to having consensual sex with an eighteen-year-old high school student. It took a few years, but he was finally acquitted by a judge, not by a jury, because of "inconsistencies and contradictions" in the evidence, and he continued his life at the monastery cleared of the charges.

Fr. Placidus, a priest and a teacher, although acquitted, did admit to having "consensual" sex with a high school boy under his charge. In Canada you must be eighteen to be able to consent to sex in an "exploitative" relationship, sex with someone in a position of authority, trust, or dependency, a teacher, a coach, a babysitter, counsellor, or minister. In this the law is blind to all but the age of the participant. By the numbers alone, Fr. Placidus's high school romance was not illegal, but he had taken a vow of chastity, and he was in a strict and secretive position of influence and authority over a teenaged lover less than half his age. Who, other than the law, where common sense is foolishness, can consider this kind of relationship consensual? Even if not criminal, it was still predatory, professionally inappropriate, and profoundly disturbing, disgusting in any light. It seemed that in nearly every school I attended, or saw, there were teachers, usually men, having sex with their students, girls and boys. How much more widespread must this have been before there were avenues of complaint and redress? It is horrifying to contemplate the routine, silent, and unspoken, but not unknown, abuse and rape of millions of nameless children over the centuries. What did these children grow up to be? How did they contribute as adults?

My God, who were these men who couldn't keep their hands off the little boys? In 2013, Pope Francis called them "monsters" and blamed clericalism, cronyism, careerism, and corruption among these men of the cloth. The formation of priests in seminaries is seen by many, if not all involved, as an empty joke. You smile and nod, you keep your head down, and when you are formed, at last, you are in an entrenched position of authority over young people for the rest of your life. One of Fr. Placidus's former students remarked, "Monastic life is like prison in that you remain forever the same age you were when you entered. My memories of the monks, with very few exceptions, are of petty, immature men, with little insight, almost all still stuck in adolescence, many, if not most, homosexual." By the 1970s, in North America, you were more likely to be expelled from a seminary for complaining about homosexuality than for practising it. Not only did the bishops not prosecute the offenders, they actively aided and abetted them, protected and hid them. How much the bishops thought of their colleagues, how little of their victims. How did a place of worship and meditation, of scholarship, philosophy, and ethics, of charity, become a club, and then a haven, for brutes and rapists? What parent now would leave their child alone with a celibate of any religion? I knew there was a dark side to the Catholic Church. I wanted to belong to the light side.

I took refuge on Shea and Tom's couch and collapsed in a mixture of disappointment and relief. All my life I have been aware of, and believed in, the wellspring of inner aliveness, call it God if you want. That awareness arose when I was eight years old. I found, though, that it was much harder to believe in churches. They were blueprints for beautiful divisions, exquisite and horrible maps I could not read. I was naive, selfish, unrealistic, and confused.

The sun shone day after day. I rode my rented bicycle as far as I could, but it was too damn hot. I preferred hanging out at the Italian espresso bars on Commercial Drive. While watching the Los Angeles Olympics on television at eleven o'clock at night, Tom and I smoked dope and listened to Huey Lewis and the News sing "I Want a New Drug." All the windows of the apartment were open. The air was hot and still. Athletes from nine countries tested positive for banned substances that year, and one-third of the US cycling team received blood doping transfusions before the games. The amped-up cyclists won nine medals, their first since 1912. Sixteen countries boycotted the games for political reasons.

I went to UBC for three or four days to participate in the Progoff Writing Workshop. It was helpful, but afterwards it was unlikely I would continue the practice of journaling at home. It wasn't that helpful. Until now.

I hadn't seen my old friend and drama teacher, Ink, since the summer of 1980 when Shizuka and I went to Vancouver for a visit. He was still working in theatre, often for the well-known BC impresario Fran Dowie, a man who had appeared in vaudeville acts at the age of twelve on stage at the Orpheum Theatre on Granville Street.

Ink and I had visited each other when we could and corresponded regularly with pen and paper for fourteen years. I knew he had been ill recently. He was living in the Okanagan, and I wrote to him from Japan and St. Mary's with a cheerful, "Hang on, Ink. I'll be in BC in the summer and I'll stop in Kelowna for a visit." I didn't know how sick he was.

I called our mutual friend Willie, Enid's old boyfriend, the farrier, and Willie's new partner told me on the telephone, rather abruptly, that Ink had died in the spring. He was forty-seven. I was stunned by the news. Ink was one of the most alive people I had ever met. I asked Willie if I could meet him for a few hours and catch up with him on Ink's last days. Willie was always a busy man, and he now had many new expensive responsibilities in the form of a new spouse and her children, but he told me I could accompany him on his rounds of the Fraser Valley the next day. He would be driving from farm to farm shoeing horses. We would have plenty of time to talk between appointments.

I met Willie very early in the morning at the Hastings Racecourse only a mile-and-a-half walk from Shea's apartment. He had duties there every day at six in the morning. We then spent eleven hours driving around the Lower Mainland talking and smoking dope in his giant old Detroit sedan filled with the tools of his trade. Willie was a smoker of tobacco, and he routinely added a few sprinkles of pot to his roll-your-owns. I couldn't take inhaling tobacco smoke, so with his permission I rolled a single joint for myself. It had been some time since I had much experience with pot. I rolled a big joint that would have been an appropriate size for the low-quality skunk pot of the 1970s. But it was 1984, and marijuana had come a long way. Willie looked at the joint I was rolling. "That's pretty strong pot, you know." By the time I had smoked half the joint I was, what's the word? blasted? for the rest of the day. Conversation dwindled after that.

As for Ink, Willie told me he was having dinner with him one day when he, Ink, threw down his fork and said, "Man, my guts haven't been right for a year." He was diagnosed with oesophageal cancer and died about a year later. Willie said Ink was cracking jokes in his hospital bed, entertaining everyone in the room, two days before he died.

I watched Willie shoe a few horses, which was interesting at first, but it soon became routine. The farm dogs often ate the clippings. Willie's spouse and one of the kids were away for a few days, so there was a bed I could use for the night. Early the next morning Willie dropped me at the racetrack in East Vancouver. I haven't seen him since that day. He was older than I. He would be an old man now.

After a couple of weeks in Vancouver, I took the Pacific Coach Lines bus to Victoria. There was still no local transportation available, the city buses were on strike there as well. I stayed at Ron's.

Ron lived down the hill from me when we were children in Calgary. Michael, now living in San Francisco, my perpetual provider of couch accommodation there, lived two doors up from Ron, on the corner. Michael and his brother, Dennis, played guitars, as did I, after a fashion. Ron had a drum kit. We made ourselves into a basement band called The Conquerors. I was the first owner of an electric guitar and amplifier in our little group, so I was indispensible to the band although it was obvious I had no musical talent.

I took a dislike to Ron as a child. He was a year younger, and I had skipped a grade in school so I was two grades ahead of him, an enormous gulf at that age. I thought he was very spoiled although his parents seemed to be no more well off than mine. Drawing on approximately equal resources, his share of his family's fortune seemed excessive to me. This alone would be sufficient cause for irritation. I recall uttering childish threats in his direction on a couple of occasions, things I would never have carried out. It was just eleven-year-old bluster. And it's just as well. By the time he stopped growing he was six foot four, and I gave out long before that.

Ron has always told the story of his monkey, but I'm sure I never saw the creature. His father or older brother acquired a small monkey somewhere, and for the time it lived with them, it was a mischievous, sex-crazed fiend. If the little primate succeeded in making his way to your shoulder, he would immediately begin humping your ear. This provided untold raptures to twelve-year-old boys when Ron invited girls to his basement to see his monkey and the beast invariably performed according to expectation. The shrieking of girls at the touch of monkey penis to the ear must have been monumental.

Ron never went to university and consequently did quite well in life, in his way. He studied graphic design in Grade 12 and worked in that area off and on until he found another way to make money in his thirties. For a while after high school, Ron and Michael worked at the CPR Ogden Shops, the railway's largest locomotive maintenance and overhaul facility. It was on a quarter section of land, a hundred and sixty acres, just a few hundred yards east of Ron and Michael's neighbouring houses on Crestwood Road. The shops were often referred to as Ogden University, a derisory reference to the likely academic and employment future of the children in our working class neighbourhood.

The shops employed hundreds of men. As a child I used to see these aromatic men in dark and dirty clothing, heads down, smoking and walking slowly home with their lunch buckets under their arms when the whistle blew at 4:00 p.m. It was a depressing sight. Many of them were European men, displaced persons who had come to Canada after World War II. My parents called them DPs, and not kindly. They brought their families, learned to speak a kind of English, bought cheap houses as soon as they could, and as my father said, "slept on the floor and ate macaroni," until years of peace, employment, and steady income helped to right the wrongs of the past. Many of these older men were skilled in the art of the snot rocket.

But the money was good at the shops, and the duties were not always onerous. They were often oddly specific. I never knew what Ron and Michael did there, but I imagine it was just as eccentric, in a unionized way, as what Michael and I did a few years later at the Alyth Yards just up the road. While I was banished to Sedgewick for a couple of years, Michael and Dennis and Ron pulled together a bar band, and they played nights and weekends wherever they could. They kept their day jobs but lived on the money they made playing music. To annoy their mortgage-paying, family-man coworkers, they walked around at work with fat, uncashed CPR paycheques in their shirt pockets.

Ron's parents moved to a farm south of Calgary, and the house in Ogden was let to Ron. He was nineteen years old with a good income and little or no rent and a whole house to himself and his friends. Times were good.

Ron was a gentle soul, open to new ideas and the warmth of true companions. He was interested in the usual attractions of the day that were likely to appeal to a young musician, drugs, rock concerts, women, bits of New Age spirituality, vegetarianism. Alberta wasn't quite geared up for vegetarians yet. Ron told me that once, while on tour with his bar band, he ordered a fruit salad at a hotel restaurant in Medicine Hat. When it arrived, it consisted of a single leaf of lettuce onto which a small can of Dole Fruit Cocktail had been upended.

Ron was smart. He looked about him and saw a generation of young folkies and hippies rebelling against the ways of their parents. It was all long hair, sandals, drugs, protest, tune in, turn on, drop out, make love not war, peace and love, man. In a couple of logical and therefore brilliant and unexpected steps, he concluded that the next generation would, inexplicably but inevitably, shave their heads, wear big boots, and be intolerant, racist, and violent. In 1972, he predicted with ease the flourishing of the small subculture of punks and skinheads into a worldwide phenomenon by the late seventies and early eighties. The punks still had sex, drugs, and rock 'n' roll, but the sex became dangerous, the drugs hard, and the music stark and mean.

When I started studying science at Camosun College in Victoria in the fall of 1979, I was sitting in a health food restaurant in Fernwood called the Prancing Pony. These seventy-seven years there has been no getting away from that damn book, *The Lord of the Rings*. I was reading my biology textbook before heading to a night class. An enormously tall man entered the restaurant with a few friends and immediately started walking slowly towards me, never taking his eyes from my face. I wondered what this giant man wanted and then realized it was Ron. I had seen him, briefly, just a couple of years earlier in Calgary, but I didn't know he had moved to Victoria, and I had no expectation of ever seeing him again. After that night, whenever I was living in Victoria, we had lunch every couple of weeks. For thirty years.

Ron had decided, like so many Albertans, that he would move to the gentler climate of the west coast. In 1984, he had been in Victoria for five years. He was one of that peculiar class of people for whom there is nothing more important in life than simply living in Victoria. It's an understandable feeling. The horrific weather of the Canadian prairies can drive you mad, and for some people just living in Victoria can be the defining goal and the central experience of their life, like being a mother or gay or a surfer. For some mothers, for some gay people, or surfers, being a mother, or being gay, or a surfer, is their avocation, their vocation, and their destiny, all in one. For others, living in Victoria and being part of the west coast lifestyle is similar. It is all you know about them and all you need to know. For them it is an experience profound enough to take them through life without any further demand for self-definition. It is who they are. "What do you do?" "I'm a mother," or "I'm gay," or "I'm a surfer," or "I live in Victoria." Everything else is beside the point. If you happened to be all four, a gay woman surfer with children living in Victoria, that might constitute a sufficiency too grand to bear.

In August 1984, I showed up at Ron's small, one-bedroom apartment near Dallas Road, across from Ross Bay Cemetery, and slept on his couch for a couple of weeks. He loaned me his bicycle, but it was so big it was impossible for me to ride. Ron went to Alberta for a visit and left me in charge of his apartment and his car, which was a lifesaver, given the buses were on strike. I visited Kay, my Catholic sponsor of exactly two years earlier, and we drank gallons of tea together, with cat hair.

The sunny weather continued, and I had lunch with five or six sets of old friends of former days, including Professor Howard and Fr. John, of course. I went to the university and wandered the halls in late August wondering if I should enrol in something. I wasn't going to join the Franciscans or the Benedictines. What was I going to do now? I wouldn't borrow money to study theology, but I might have to resort once more to student loans if I were to try to finish a degree in science. God knows, I didn't want to go back to studying. I had come to the conclusion that while hard work can be amusing and rewarding for short periods of time, it was no way to spend your life. The conservation of energy was my guiding principle.

Somehow, I had wound up with several chemistry courses under my belt, a subject I had hated in high school but one that turned out to be more interesting than I thought when I went to Camosun College. But chemistry was too much. The working materials were toxic and dangerous, and I was only just competent in the lab, hardly adept. You could also be the victim of accidents that were not your fault. Once in chemistry lab, I stepped away from my station for a second, heard an enormous bang, and turned back around to find my neighbour's apparatus had blown up and there was concentrated nitric acid all over my bench, equipment, and books. I had a suspicion, true or not, that wet chemistry was very hard on the health overall. The jobs were unappealing.

I thought about biology. Lots of girls in that department. I loitered around the empty halls of the biology building looking at brochures and calendars and bulletin boards. I found a professor in his office and stuck my head in to ask a few questions about the department. He was a Glaswegian man, and he was in a very bad mood. After only a few words, I fled the building.

I hadn't worked for pay in five months, not since March, and I was starting to run out of money. I didn't want to go to university, but it was hard to imagine working in Victoria. Jobs were scarce, I had few skills, and it was expensive to live there. Winter was coming. How could I make money? I had only one idea left.

Roland and his wife, Brenda, were vacationing in Victoria. Roland was the younger brother of my good friend, Bernd, from school days of long ago. They were a family of post-war German immigrants living in the Calgary suburb of Ogden. Bernd's mother was in her thirties. She was dark and slim and attractive, very direct in her speech. She used to wear fantastically short shorts, bare legs and bare feet, and button-front shirts only casually closed at the top. She tied the tails in a knot well above her belly button revealing a flat, strong midriff. No one else's mom dressed like this. She spoke English with an enticing accent. When she called Bernd's name, it sounded like "Bairnt." We pronounced Bernd just the way it looked, "Burned." She would stand in the kitchen talking, smoking a cigarette, with her arms crossed beneath her breasts. We were thirteen years old and had a little homework group that met, happily, at Bernd's house after school. We always looked forward to seeing what Bernd and Roland's mom was wearing. Roland and Ron had been very good friends, and Roland played bass guitar in the garage bands and bar bands of high school and afterwards. In Victoria, Ron and I had a great time visiting with Roland and Brenda and their two young boys. We spent one sunny, sandy day at the beach, at Witty's Lagoon, one of the few times I ever saw Ron take one drink too many.

I had left a few boxes of books and household items in Kay's empty basement while I was in Japan, and now I threw them into the back of Roland's enormous truck. The family of four and my boxes went east from Victoria across the Strait of Georgia, through the valleys, and over the mountain passes to Calgary.

I stopped in Vancouver again for a day or two, and then followed them by train all the way to the prairies.

17 The Last Time I Saw Calgary

I treated myself to a Cabin for One. This was a bit of luxury in which I wanted to indulge. I suspected it would be a very long time before I travelled anywhere by train again. Passenger rail in Canada was a dying industry, and it wasn't long before there was no regular train service at all between Vancouver and Calgary. It was another fifteen years before I was on a train again, one from Victoria Falls to Bulawayo. The trains in both Canada and East Africa speed along at an average of about thirty miles an hour. My tiny Via Rail sleeper room smelled slightly of urine, like Mr. Bloom's breakfast kidneys, but it was coming from the toilet under the seat. I had a much better time on the National Railways of Zimbabwe, and I'll tell you all about it, by and by.

I found I couldn't sleep during the night because of the rocking motion of the cars and then, exhausted, I slept all the next day and missed much of the spectacular scenery of the Rocky Mountains. When we arrived at the CPR station in Calgary in the late afternoon, on a beautiful day in early September, I was thoroughly rested, and at the same time stunned with fatigue by my inverted night and day. In typical Canadian fashion, in the time-honoured tradition of Canadian businesses showing no respect whatsoever for their paying customers, before we were allowed to disembark, we had to wait another hour on the train while it was run, very slowly, through an enormous washing contraption only a few maddening yards from our final destination at the passenger station.

I made my way to my sister and brother-in-law's, another new house for them, this one on Sixtieth Street in the Temple district of northeast Calgary. They had a dinner date with friends from out of town and were not at home, but they told me where to find the key hidden in the yard, and I let myself in. In no time I was ill at ease on that bright sunny evening, uncomfortable in their comfortable home, bored and lonely with their two cats, and restless. My sister's refrigerator has never been empty, but I wasn't hungry. For the first time in two and a half years, I reached for the beer I saw there in long rows of brown, stubby bottles. I downed four of them on an empty stomach and went to bed spectacularly drunk and miserable, before Linda and Eric arrived home. I had the worst goddamn hangover the next day. I realized that this had been a mistake, pretended it never happened, and managed, somehow, to stay on the wagon through a very bad winter until the next summer.

Linda and Eric's English friends, Geoff and Clare, stayed overnight as well, rather than drive, tipsy, the fifty miles north to their small farm at Didsbury. Geoff was a talented mechanic and woodworker. He restored cars and furniture at his shop on the farm. Clare looked after the animals and was in ecstasy as long as what she was doing involved a goat. I had met them before. They were very eccentric. Ten years after seeing them again at my sister's in Calgary, they packed up and left the frozen foothills of Alberta and moved to Mazatlan, Mexico, the Pearl of the Pacific. As I type these words I am seated, coincidentally, in a rented apartment in downtown Mazatlan surrounded by the warm, colourful, neo-tropical streets of El Centro. Geoff and Clare and their kids and grandkids live nearby, a few miles up the beach. Geoff builds and installs fabulous woodwork in the many new condos always under construction in Mazatlan, and Clare rescues animals. The last time I saw her, she had two hundred and fifty baby parrots in her garage, confiscated by the authorities from bird smugglers and left in her care for rehabilitation. She was feeding them with an eyedropper. By the time she finished one round of two hundred and fifty, it was time to start another.

I was in Calgary with the nervous intention of living there for the first time in six and a half years. I wasn't sure what to expect. I hadn't been keeping up on current affairs. The only job I could get was driving a taxi, and I went immediately for the medical exam and the driving test, borrowing my easygoing brother-in-law's van for the purpose. This was good of him. A workingman's wife's brother is not always a welcome sight. Eric was a carpenter for the Calgary School Board. He rose early and commuted every working day for nearly forty years to carry out his duties. He wasn't halfway through his career yet. He got me hooked on watching *Doctor Who* on television every day after work.

They had a spare bedroom, and I paid rent for a few weeks. I found an apartment and moved out in a cold snap at the end of October. It was minus twenty-five degrees Fahrenheit.

My experience at the Progoff Writing Seminar in Vancouver had been positive enough that I signed up for a couple of more workshops, different ones, at the University of Calgary. I picked the longest and most expensive one and stopped going after two sessions. It, if not I, was pathetic. The other one was only a day long. Its subject was how to reduce stress. I wasn't stressed. I was trying to think of a reason to get out of bed in the morning or a reason to get into it at night. I was looking for the source of the obligation to draw breath. Enlightenment by workshop was not going to work for me.

I had been fascinated by my experience at the Ape Cave in Washington State, and I signed up for a short caving course at Mount Royal College. It involved one evening's lecture and one evening practising rappelling on the climbing wall at the gym. I was very nervous about rappelling, afraid of heights, but when I had done it once, I wanted to do it again and again. The next Saturday eight or nine of us drove in a college van to Rat's Nest Cave in Grotto Mountain, near Canmore, Alberta, just two peaks over from Squaw's Tit, an unfortunate name, unofficial, but in common use and still marked as such on many maps.

We hiked to the cave and suited up. Rat's Nest has a 75-foot vertical drop just inside the entrance, and this is why everyone needs to be trained to rappel. I had never thought of rappelling anywhere, ever, in my life. The steeper sides of mountains do not call to me. And now I was rappelling *inside* a mountain by the dim light of a helmet lamp. Rat's Nest is an undeveloped cave, no handrails, walkways, or interior lighting, with many twisting, narrow passages, so narrow there are some you have to struggle hard to get through. Some are negotiated standing, others head first or feet first, others lying on your back. It is an interesting moment when you realize you are lying on your back under a million tons of rock in the middle of a mountain, sandwiched between the floor and the ceiling with only an inch between your nose and the geology above you. It is not for the claustrophobic. We spent four hours underground and then drove to a pub in Canmore for a drink, tea for me. It was exhilarating. I felt like I could do anything after that experience. One day of caving was worth a dozen workshops.

That same weekend I saw my good friend, Jim, for the last time. I had met him in the fall of 1968 not long after moving to Sedgewick from Calgary. I was fifteen. He was a youthful thirty-four, two years younger than my mother, but I didn't know that. He never told me his age although I asked him repeatedly. He grew up on a farm north of Sedgewick and made money, with his two brothers, by setting a trap line on the way from home to school, a journey they often made on skies, catching weasels and other fur-bearing creatures in the winter, and gophers, crows, magpies, and grouse in the summer. During one of those winters the family was snow-bound on the farm for a month. It was a time of little money, kerosene lamps, box socials, whist drives, horse-drawn sleighs, and country concerts and dances. His grandparents had lived for a time in a sod house.

Jim went to university in the early 1950s, a rare occurrence for people in the Sedgewick area, did a degree in education, and left his homespun background behind him. By the time I met him he had been teaching for a dozen years. He lived in Yellowknife in the Northwest Territories which seemed unnecessarily remote for a man of his obvious talents, but he told me the money up north was good when he was looking for work. He was clearly a man of the world. He taught mostly woodworking, art, and photography, and academic courses when required. He was single, handsome, educated, well-read, and he had lived for two years in Europe teaching at the Canadian Armed Forces base in Marville, France. From there he routinely vacationed around Europe in a sports car with the top down. He had a narrow little moustache that lined the immediate top of his upper lip. It would be considered kind of douchey now, but it was pretty cool in 1968. He kept some kind of moustache all his life to hide a scar he got as a child in a run-in with a barbed wire fence.

Jim was sophisticated material compared with most of the people I met in my first couple of seasons in Sedgewick, and I was thrilled to find such a sophisticated friend. I noticed right away that one of his most important freedoms, and the source of his ongoing ability to learn and grow and travel was that, unlike so many men, especially rural men, he had avoided a young marriage. In those days if you found a woman willing to have sex with you, you got married, and that was the end of everything except work and family. One good year of marriage and forty-nine more of running out the clock. Twenty-two-year-old men with two children are not driving around Europe in a sports car.

Jim was hanging around the pool hall in Sedgewick in the fall of 1968, and we spotted each other right away. We were friends in an instant. He actually had a kind of sports car now, a red Corvair, with a rear-mounted, air-cooled engine. We drove around endlessly on country roads talking. He used to let me drive once we were out of town. I was a non-stop, if not scintillating conversationalist, and Jim was a breath of fresh air, a positive gale of it, in Sedgewick, Alberta.

He was on a paid sabbatical from his job in Yellowknife, one of the perks of teaching up north. He had arranged to go to UNAM, the National Autonomous University of Mexico, to study art for two semesters starting in September. He would then also be able to go to the 1968 Summer Olympics there, in October. This was an excellent plan. UNAM's spectacular main campus in Mexico City is a World Heritage site of richly detailed art and architecture with murals by Rivera and Siqueiros. But it all went bad.

Starting in July, there had been government raids on opposition groups, followed in August by enormous labour and student protests against the repressive Díaz Ordaz administration, with more in September and October, culminating in the Tlatelolco Massacre only a week before the Olympics started. The military fired into the crowds killing hundreds of students and civilian protestors, as well as bystanders. UNAM was shut down, and Jim's sabbatical was cancelled. He spent the fall in Sedgewick searching for somewhere else to go to salvage his study-vacation, his time away from the Northwest Territories. He eventually arranged to spend a semester at the University of Hawaii.

We spent most of that fall together, and we wrote frequently after he left for Hawaii in January. He came back to Sedgewick the next May with nothing to do before returning to Yellowknife in September, and we spent more time together. I believe my parents were concerned about this relationship between their fifteen-year-old son and a grown man, but Jim was a member of a family long established in the community. His elderly parents lived across the street. He was trusted and respected. He was a teacher.

We drove four or five times, or more, to Calgary and Edmonton just to see movies. We would stay in a hotel and eat pizza and drink beer. And talk. I can't remember a time in my young life when I was ever out of conversation. I thought of Jim as a great friend. I revelled in his sophisticated company. He was older, which was appealing in itself, and it also had other advantages. He had enough money to own a car, and he could buy beer. I suspected early on that he might be gay, and I imagine many other people did as well. I knew nothing about homosexuality, but I knew that in a small town in the sixties if you were thirty-five and single, you were gay. And looking back, I suppose he was. But it was never an issue between us. Never. Not once. Not even a hint. There was nothing effeminate about him. He was an avid sports fan and an accomplished curler, golfer, and baseball player. He had the respect of his redneck neighbours for those preferences and achievements. I think Jim was very tightly closeted and completely resigned to the fact. He was keenly aware that if he were outed it would destroy his career, his family, and his life. There was nothing noble about being loud and proud in the 1950s and '60s in Alberta.

It was a strange friendship. I saw Jim a lot for a couple of years when I was a teenager, and off and on as a young adult. We always drank together. I think Jim drank a lot but in a controlled fashion, moderate to heavy, but steadily. I drank excessively and orgiastically. Drinking is the standard approach for encouraging frisky behaviour, but even when I was over twenty-one Jim never changed his mood or his tone in his dealings with me. Nothing untoward ever arose. And we spent a lot of time alone. We had no mutual friends. Is it a testament to my winning personality that a man twice my age wanted to spend time in my company? Some would be reluctant to accept such an explanation. Why else would a single, 34-year-old man want to spend hours of unstructured time with a fifteen-year-old? What else would he want besides sex? Conversation? From a fifteen-year-old? Some things are destined to remain a mystery, and my relationship with Jim is one of them.

It wasn't my first intense relationship with an older man. When I was fourteen, living in Calgary, I absolutely adored my drama teacher, Louis. He was about twenty-five, and he was definitely gay, but I wasn't sure then. It rarely crossed mind. It wasn't something you thought much about in Grade 10, at least not in 1967. I didn't spend much time alone with him, but I did sleep on his couch a couple of times when I was visiting Calgary from Sedgewick in Grades 11 and 12. I had a couple of girlfriends in Calgary that I couldn't shut up about, so it was obvious I was straight. He never showed any sign of sexual interest in me. What I liked about him, again, was that he was single, unburdened by family, free to come and go as he pleased. His income was all his own. He wore a Nehru jacket and drove a brand new Pontiac Firebird. The only other adult men I knew were stolid and conservative, weighed down for life by wives and children, as were eight of my nine uncles, and obviously, the fathers of all my friends. My one unmarried uncle was not suited to the marriage market, otherwise he probably would have been married, too. Louis and Jim were the first single men I met who had free and happy lives of their own outside marriage. They introduced me to the idea, by example, that marriage was not inevitable and that being a bachelor was a lot of fun. That they were both gay was irrelevant to the argument.

In Calgary, in 1984, Jim and I went for lunch and to the movies and talked about books and travels, things we always did and talked about. He mentioned that he was having trouble with his liver, something I thought must have stemmed from long winters of drinking in Yellowknife. They played a drinking game while curling, two highballs downed for every end played. He didn't know what his ailment was and neither did his doctors. I encouraged him to look for solutions outside mainstream medicine. This seemed like a reasonable suggestion to me if his doctors didn't know what it was, but Jim was of a generation that took little responsibility for, and paid little attention to, its health. He said that fixing his liver was his doctors' job, not his.

Exactly five years later, Jim became the first recipient in Alberta of a liver transplant, at the University of Alberta Hospital. To the press he commented that he had complete confidence in the expertise of his medical team, a statement I'm not sure I could ever make. We wrote short letters and sent cards to each other for years, but I never saw him again after our brief visit in Calgary in 1984. Without the transplant he would have died in short order. With it he lived another fifteen years and died in 2004 at the age of sixty-nine.

And what had happened to Calgary, the money-mad, booming oil town of the 1970s? In that decade, over a period of only seven years, the price of oil had gone up 1,300 per cent. The result was hundreds of oil companies all rapidly expanding, an influx of workers from all over the country, a billion dollars of construction permits issued in one year in Calgary alone, more than in New York City, the creation of more multimillionaires than the province had ever seen, zero vacancy rates for apartments, a spike in crime, widespread speculation in real estate and oil ventures, giant office towers, and private jets. It was a party that would never end.

But end it did. In the early eighties, Alberta's economy, along with that of the US and much of the rest of the world, crashed hard into recession. The price of oil was still very high due to the disruptions and chaos of the Iranian Revolution and the Iran-Iraq War, but the industry was also overexpanded. Oil exploration activity, Alberta's bread and butter, and caviar, ground to a fraction of its previous highs. On top of the recession, Pierre Trudeau's National Energy Policy of double taxation on oil, implemented in 1981, siphoned billions of dollars out of the Alberta economy and guaranteed the absence of a live, breathing, elected federal liberal politician in the Canadian west for years to come. Bumper stickers appeared that read *Let the Eastern bastards freeze in the dark*. Interest rates were ratcheted vigorously upwards to combat years of double-digit inflation. The prime rate was over ten per cent. My grandmother told me she bought a guaranteed investment certificate from a credit union that paid twenty-two per cent per annum. For the first time in ten years, more people were leaving the province than were coming into it. Unemployment rose to ten per cent and stayed there. Bankruptcies went up fifty per cent. Thousands of houses were foreclosed by the banks or were sold for a dollar. The owners simply walked away from their mortgages, sometimes leaving the furniture inside the house and the new Corvette in the garage. In 1982, Canada's largest oil company, Dome Petroleum, was saved from collapse at the last second by taxpayers and banks. There were millions of square feet of empty office space in Edmonton and Calgary. Work on an office building under construction on the west side of downtown Calgary ground to a halt. It remained half-finished for years, something I had never seen before. In the US it was the worst recession since the Great Depression. I saw other bumper stickers that read *Please God, bring back the Boom Times. I promise I won't piss it all away this time.* At the University of Calgary, there was a sticker on every paper towel dispenser on campus. They read *Please use only one.* Apart from *Arbeit Macht Frei*, this was the most depressing sign I had ever seen. Coming down from the frenzy of the seventies, Alberta now led the nation in suicides.

Needless to say, the taxi business was slow. The best I could hope for was one or two days a week where I made the same amount of money as my worst day of the week in the winter of 1977–78. The other days were hardly worth showing up for. I was able to earn enough to cover rent and food but very little else. Plus, and worse, it was depressing. Making money hand over fist makes driving a taxi fast and engaging and satisfying. Sitting for hours every day without a paying customer is not the same experience. I found a taxi owner to work for without any difficulty, about the best that could be said for the job, and went to work right away. I tried to keep my upper lip stiff, paid my sister some rent, and moved down to Fourteenth Avenue and Seventh Street in the Beltline, the familiar neighbourhood of my years as a misbehaving young adult. It was a small, characterless, one-bedroom, walk-up apartment with a few pieces of cheap furniture. It might have been made pleasant to occupy but for nearly everything else that was happening in my life.

My first driving partner was a one-legged biker covered in tattoos, and the second was very obviously mentally ill and potentially violent. These were not the happy, easygoing people I had known and worked with in the seventies. My brief encounters at the beginning and end of each shift, with either of my disturbing new partners, were always nerve-racking. Fortunately, the owner of the taxi was not hard to get along with, merely taciturn, a breath of still air compared with his employees.

When I was twenty-three and making a fortune, driving a taxi had been a bit of a lark, irrelevant to my dignity. Now, at thirty-one, making nothing, it was very low-rent. A year earlier I wore a suit and tie and made as much money as I cared to work for. I ate lunch in the finest hotel in Tokyo with the CEO of a major corporation. Something had gone badly wrong in the meantime. I had worked my way to the bottom.

When you are young, your own stateliness is rarely at the forefront of your mind. You lay your dignity down lightly knowing there will be plenty of time and leisure to pick it up again. I was starting to see now that if you lay your dignity down too often, it may be that one day claiming it again is more than you can manage.

I took to leaving work early, as soon as I had enough money in my pocket to make my weekly budget. I went home to relax and do yoga and watch TV in the afternoons. I enjoyed these free hours but not as much as I wanted to.

There was one bright light in this otherwise dismal fall. David and Jude were in Calgary after their long holiday travelling through China and Egypt and Greece and England, and it was wonderful to see them again. They had rented a house which now, a few months later, they were about to purchase from the landlord. Jude was still looking for a job, but David had found a few hours a week teaching English at Mount Royal College, in their ESL program, and he had enrolled in linguistics at the University of Calgary to start in September. He was a year older than I and had never been to university, but he now started in earnest, the only way he ever did anything, and he tore through a BA and an MA and became the manager of MRC's ESL program, and later the registrar of the college, which is now a university. Jude found a job in her field, social work and counselling, finished a Master's degree, and became an honoured employee at the Southern Alberta Institute of Technology, a school I once went to. Later, she became a very successful private consultant, a provider of soft-skills organizational workshops. And they still live in the same house.

They offered to rent me a bedroom in their basement, but I was hesitant. I could feel the darkness of depression settling over me, and I did not wish to subject them to that. I skirted the issue of my declining mood by saying,

"I think we'll be friends a lot longer if I don't live in your basement." We played racquetball at a local club and at the university, we went for meals in Chinatown, we spent time at their parents' cabin at Sylvan Lake while the leaves changed colour and fell and the weather grew first chilly and then cold and snowy.

By the fall Sue had left Tokyo and moved to Helena, Montana, to start a moxibustion business. She lived at home with her mother and her second step-father, the one who picked her wicked first step-father up by the ear and threw him bodily out of the state. It is four hundred miles from Helena to Calgary and a long day on the bus, but Sue made the journey. I was delighted to see her. We spent a week together, and I used my taxi as personal transportation to show her the city. We had supper at David and Jude's and talked of the glory days of Tokyo and of the future.

The future was a problem. There didn't seem to be one. Before Sue had even left for the long trip back to Helena, I was again immobile on the couch of my little apartment, depressed beyond anything I had known. I took her to the bus station, and she left me to work out my own salvation.

I received a telephone call from Fr. Martin, a surprise, asking me if I was still coming to Lumsden to court the Franciscans. I said no.

It turned out that the corner of Fourteenth Avenue and Seventh Street was the gay hustler stroll. The Beltline neighbourhood is an innocuous rectangular grid of one hundred blocks of low apartment buildings in southwest Calgary, from Centre Street to Fourteenth Street and Tenth Avenue to Seventeenth Avenue, a flat expanse between the hills of Mount Royal to the south and the railroad tracks, downtown, and the Bow River to the north. For reasons known only to gay hustlers, I now shared my little corner of the neighbourhood with the Wesley United Church and the young men who stood shivering in the cold. They dressed in tight jeans and light vinyl jackets to attract their customers. Occasionally, they shivered in fear as cars of homophobic rednecks circled the block threatening and jeering.

My favourite health food restaurant was only a couple of blocks away, but it had gone downhill over the years, and I didn't have the money to eat there anyway. One day while waiting in a service station for a tire to get fixed, I bought a paperback copy of *The Name of the Rose*, an unexpected find on a spinning wire bookrack in a small garage in Inglewood. It had been published in English only the year before. I spent the next couple of weeks immersed in Umberto Eco's semiotic evocation of weird and frightening medieval religious life, the rich and complicated imagery of the cultural and historical setting for his plot centred around the multiple murders of monks in a Benedictine monastery. It was a doubly uncomfortable read for me given my recent experiences. Walking to the health food restaurant one dark, snowy evening, my mind was many thousands of miles and many centuries away, in northern Italy in AD 1327, musing over the gruesome murders of Eco's novel, the grotesque characters, coarse and deformed and diseased, the prosecutors of the Inquisition, the burnings at the stake, the ignorance and fear, and the dangerous labyrinth of rooms and passages in the monastery's massive library tower, the only place where the mystery of the murders could be solved. There was a huge, aggressive dog always on a leash in the small front yard of one of the remaining houses near my apartment, and on this night, distracted by my fantastic thoughts, I forgot about his presence. I wandered too close to the low fence as I passed the house, and he rushed at me from out of the dark. My head snapped to the right just as he leapt at me, and his wild eyes and bared teeth and snarling bark peaked no more than a foot from my face. My field of vision was filled with all the demons of medieval Europe. I expected in that second to be dragged to hell by this black monster. His head jerked violently back as he reached the end of his leash just inches from my face, and I screamed out loud. That damn book together with that damn dog frightened a year off my life.

By New Year's Eve, I was as low as I had ever been. I'm surprised I made it through the night.

I was never much interested in the University of Calgary, but I had been playing racquetball there with David and some of his friends through the fall. The campus was much improved by the wealth of Alberta's boom years, in spite of the current lack of paper towels. I came to the very reluctant conclusion that I had no choice but to go back to university and finish some kind of degree in science. I realized that if I didn't, I was going to be a parking lot attendant by the time I was forty.

In the first few days of January, I managed to find two courses, and two only, that would suit my needs. I registered as an undeclared student belonging to no faculty, with no major. I resigned for the last time from the taxi business. I could have kept driving a shift or two each week to make a little money, but I wanted a complete separation from that now much-degraded commerce. I would rather starve. Or borrow money.

I took introductory courses in zoology and microbiology, studies of life from its biggest to its smallest forms, courses I could easily use as options in just about any degree in science. These were big classes in a big university. This was new to me. The professors gave their lectures in large amphitheatres speaking into microphones, something that hadn't been necessary at Camosun College with its classes of ten or twelve students in small rooms. The professor of zoology was calm, well-dressed, reserved, well-prepared, and professional. The professor of microbiology was disorganized and haphazard in his lectures, not very helpful, and he leered in the most obvious and disgusting way at the young women in the class. The labs were well run by efficient teaching assistants with PhDs.

After more than two years of being very thin, I quickly began to gain weight until none of my clothes fit, and I was reduced to wearing my only pair of cheap sweat pants every day. I had no more than a dollar in my pocket at any time, and I never went out, not if it cost money, except to buy basic groceries. I managed to make friends with a couple of pretty girls in my classes, and three or four times a week I sat with them after lectures and labs for an hour or two in a coffee shop on campus. They both had boyfriends, but a little friendly flirting was not out of the question. Being able to chat with them for a few hours was the brightest part of my week. Our little coffee klatch meant a lot to me. Later in the day, I would meet David to play no-mercy racquetball and lift weights until all my joints ached, although it had no effect on my weight gain. In the afternoon I came home to do yoga and watch *Late Night with David Letterman* on my new VCR. The talk show had debuted two years earlier and was considered edgy and unpredictable and had become a cult hit with college students. I found it laboured and tedious. I watched a dozen episodes and never laughed once. I stopped taping it. Letterman has made fifteen million dollars a year, or more, for the last thirty years, making very weak jokes.

Taking classes was the only sensible thing I could do, but I was still in a very dark mood. I studied at home and stuffed myself with enormous bowls of salty and buttery popcorn while watching my rented TV. I hid in my apartment and watched the rent-boys from my window shivering on the winter nights. The temperatures ranged from very cold to bitterly cold, and I no longer had the use of a car, my taxi, to do personal errands. It was physical torture to drag heavy bags of groceries home from the Safeway store in sub-zero temperatures. I had to take two buses to get to the university, and the waiting and the transfers were miserably cold. I had been willing to take a vow of poverty in a religious order, although admittedly they now possessed every amenity of modern life, and preferably one in California, but a life of actual poverty in Canada was turning into a very grim existence.

One Saturday, my wallet was stolen from a locker at the gym at the university. It contained exactly one paper dollar and a brand new bus pass. I could live without the dollar, but reacquiring all of the identification was time-consuming and cost me money I didn't have. The loss of the bus pass was tragic.

I made an effort to be unconcerned in company. It was bad enough being depressed. There was no point in being depressing as well. Why give others opportunities to pity me? And who would notice? Well, Jude would. She was a gifted counsellor, and she read me easily. She became concerned at my indecision and disappointment, my lack of spirit. She knew a suicide when she saw one. She came to my apartment building and banged on my door while I concealed myself inside and pretended to be out, hiding, afraid to answer, embarrassed and depressed at the state of my body, mind, and soul. From a depth of daily anguish lived out alone in my apartment, I emerged a few times a week with a cautious smile on my face to go to classes and meet friends. When I got home again, it was the same blank nothing, no strength within, no opportunity without.

The semester came to an end, and I wrote my two exams and got my two A's, easy enough with such a light workload. I had no summer job lined up. I had no money or resources even to look for one, not even clothes to wear. I was thirty-one years old and had barely a penny in my pocket. I lacked nothing less than everything. With my last few dollars, I treated myself to a movie at the old Plaza Theatre on Kensington Road. But nothing I could do would improve my mood. Things that at any other time in my life would have held a simple, satisfying joy were now ash in the mouth. I walked home from the theatre across the Tenth Street bridge and looked down at the ice still packed thick and broken on the Bow River in April. I thought, "I can't even jump off this bridge. I would bounce off the ice." It was a cold humour. I began to imagine the terrors of the water beneath and hurried home. When eternity is impressed upon the mind in vivid terms, it is a fearful prospect. It was probably wrong of me, but I didn't want to die. I wasn't fit to die. There would be time left yet to repent.

I had finished school. I had no more than a few dollars in my pocket, and for a day or two I continued in my apartment without a clue about the immediate future, enjoying nothing more than the warming air of springtime. That magic feeling, nowhere to go. When the telephone rang I would not have guessed, not until I had made a few false stabs, that it was my mother calling. I had not an inkling of what she was about to say. She offered me a job.

It never occurred to me that my parents were sensitive to, or even cognizant of, my situation. I assumed they were blissfully unaware of my life, my feelings, my illusions. It seemed to me they always had been. I didn't give them enough credit, I guess. They were aware, perhaps not keenly, but aware, that their son was falling apart at the seams. My parents' current business, still fairly new, was busy to the point of a frantic rush, and if I wanted to come home for the summer, there would be plenty for me to do. And there would be a salary of some kind. I was astonished. I shouldn't have been, maybe, but I was. I said to my mother, "Does Dad know about this?" They would be driving to Lethbridge in a few days on business and could stop in Calgary on their way back and pick me and my things up, the inevitable twenty boxes of books and junk that I hauled around with me for most of my life.

An appeal to my parents had not occurred to me as a solution to the dire fiscal and employment problems I was facing, but now that the option was offered, out of the blue, I accepted without hesitation. In another couple of days, I was riding in the cab of my father's heavy-duty diesel pickup truck heading for Sedgewick, Alberta. It was the same trip I had made half a lifetime ago.

In 2013, I read Moss Hart's autobiography. He wrote: "I had lived for so long as a stranger [to] my family that it had never occurred to me to seek counsel or comfort among them.... I am by no means certain that blood is thicker than water, but [poverty and unemployment] can thicken it as nothing else can. I warmed my hands and my heart in their affection and wondered why I had never found solace with them before. There is nothing like tasting the grit of fear for rediscovering that the umbilical cord is made of piano wire."

It had been a long, unhappy winter.

18   Another Hangover

My first hangover in Sedgewick had been in the fall of 1978 when I was passing through town, unemployed, and took a job at the Co-op as a manager trainee, or in reality, a stock clerk. Now I was going to Sedgewick as a full-blown charity case, not a penny in my pocket, saved from destitution by my energetic parents, a situation so embarrassing to both of us it was never discussed, never even mentioned. And what's more natural than a son working in the family business?

Sedgewick has been good to my father. And he is grateful. His small business as an agent for Imperial Oil, a Canadian company founded in 1880 and quickly bought out by Standard Oil, was the most lucrative of the four he had over the years. But it was a tough business. In the spring he worked twenty hours a day. I don't know how he did it. Out of his tiny office and warehouse, and the huge tanks and sheds in the yard, he and my mother, and no more than four or five employees, sold bulk fuels and fertilizers, as well as small amounts of pesticides and herbicides. They probably only made a profit of a penny a litre selling gas and diesel, but the other products were much more lucrative, particularly anhydrous ammonia.

Anhydrous ammonia is household ammonia, window cleaner, but tremendously concentrated, without the water. In the early twentieth century Fritz Haber and later Carl Bosch, the nephew of the inventor of the spark plug, both German Nobel prize winners, figured out how to capture atmospheric nitrogen on an industrial scale using high pressure chemistry. Natural sources of organic nitrogen, typically Chilean guano, were no longer required, and the Haber-Bosch process has been used ever since to produce, in this day, almost 200 million tons of ammonia a year, half of it in the form of synthetic fertilizers that are applied to the food base of nearly four billion people around the world. The production of ammonia also consumes more than one per cent of all man-made power, a significant part of the world's energy budget. Ammonia is very big business.

It is also caustic and dangerous. Anhydrous ammonia boils at minus twenty-eight degrees Fahrenheit, so it is transported and stored under high pressure as a liquid. Body moisture will absorb ammonia as liquid or gas on contact, turning the skin, flesh, and organs to goo until the ammonia is diluted or all the human tissue is consumed. Ammonia freeze-dries everything. The eyes and lungs are particularly vulnerable in a spill. For the next several weeks, I frequently caught whiffs of the strong, pungent odor of a few parts per million of ammonia in the air around the equipment parked at my father's bulk plant.

The ammonia was delivered from the manufacturing plant in Fort Saskatchewan, just northeast of Edmonton, in pressurized railcars and transferred to storage tanks and smaller tanks on rubber wheels at a railway siding two miles east of Sedgewick, day or night. The rolling tanks are then pulled behind tractors in the farmers' fields. The liquid, which turns to gas upon release, is transferred by plastic tubing to an array of knives pulled behind the tank. The knives cut into the subsoil, and when the gas hits the moisture in the soil, it is converted again to liquid. The nitrogen is deposited and available to plants when the ground is later seeded, usually with wheat. I had little to do with the handling and transfer of ammonia and was just as glad. Even a minor accident, a small misstep, could result in horrific injuries. I wondered how attentive my father and his employees could be at two o'clock in the morning after working all day, handling a dangerous chemical at an unmanned railway siding in the dark.

Local demand was high on a daily basis and supply was adequate but delivery was fitful. My father pleaded with railway officials on the telephone to release his cars of ammonia that were stuck on a siding only thirty maddening miles away. His customers clamoured for product, and he led slow, overnight convoys of ungainly farm tanks over a hundred miles up the highway in the dark to fill them directly at the plant in Fort Saskatchewan, coming home even more slowly, full and heavy, at dawn. Occasionally, I would enter the office from the yard on the hot, sunny days, taking off my gloves, the screen door slamming, and find my father with his head back, fast asleep in his chair for two or three minutes until the telephone rang again or the radio squawked, "Hello, Bob!" and one of his drivers had good news or bad, often enough bad. When one of his feeder-tank trucks blew an engine, he had it towed to Camrose within the hour, fifty miles away, and paid a team of heavy-duty mechanics overtime rates to work all night and have the entire engine rebuilt by morning. The truck was back in service by the time his employees were out of bed the next day and finished their breakfast, not a minute of delivery time lost. One word from a man, or a woman, who can pay the price of capital and labour will set dozens of others in motion, or thousands.

He dealt with lawyers and bankers and government inspectors. He barked at his lawyer on the telephone for her outrageous bills, thousands of dollars to manage his contracts, but he liked her name, Shafter. On his way to Edmonton for this or that he would stop in Camrose and parley with his bankers. He had a million-dollar rolling line of credit to buffer his outrageous outlays for product and to provide temporary financial protection until the damn farmers paid their bills. He was a good customer and the bankers liked him. The interest rate on money was nearly twenty per cent. They always bought him lunch when he dropped in, and I know he took a cranky pride in sitting down in his working clothes with these suit-and-tie men to lecture them on their dishonest occupation. They would console him and then laugh all the way back to the bank.

When the government inspectors came by in their fleets of cheap Chevrolets to test the accuracy of his pumps or the safety standards of his pesticide storage, it was all my father could do to keep his conservative, entrepreneurial thoughts to himself. He was pleased though when the pump inspector informed him that his meters were cheating his customers slightly but not enough to require an adjustment by law.

He was castigated, politely and timidly, by an environmental inspector for having met exactly none of the requirements for safe storage of the small amount of herbicides and pesticides he sold. This was a side business for my father, and to him the amounts and the regulations were irrelevant. He told the inspector, politely and seething, to go back to his office and write his report and see where that got him. There were no spill events in my father's pesticide storage. In general, an Edmonton bureaucrat in Sedgewick was what the locals referred to as target practice, especially if he was East Indian. My father and nearly everyone else in the area called East Indian people "Pakis," and were prejudiced against them, unreasoning and disgraceful. Sedgewick's town doctor was of South Asian descent, and my parents travelled with him and his wife on several occasions, skiing at Taos and partying in Las Vegas. Dr. Meer was a privileged and fun-loving South African. He had no accent and was a graduate of Trinity College Dublin, one of the seven ancient universities of Britain and Ireland. His wife was tall, attractive, and Irish. Exceptions in racial prejudice can be made in certain cases.

My mother worked at the bulk plant in an office even smaller than my father's. She sat at a dumb-tube computer which spent its nights under a plastic cozy to keep out the dust. It was tied into Imperial Oil's headquarters in Toronto, which are now in Calgary, feeding them data on daily sales. My mother was an early adopter of computer technology. I was astonished to see her sitting and working at a computer. I had never laid hands on one. Units of sale were an issue. Litres, gallons, pounds, kilograms, and temperature were all factors in the calculations. One of my jobs was to climb to the top of the fuel tanks and lower a 30-foot measuring stick into them to determine the height, and thus the volume, of the contents, not forgetting to note the air temperature.

It is almost impossible to conceive of the importance and the value of oil to the world, and to Canada and Alberta. Crude oil and natural gas are the first and third most traded commodities in the world. Coffee is second. Canada has thirteen per cent of the world's oil reserves, almost all of them in Alberta, behind only Venezuela and Saudi Arabia. Market capitalization and revenues in the oil industry are in the trillions of dollars. My father had tried once before to buy Imperial Oil's bulk plant in Sedgewick but had been unsuccessful. He made another attempt a couple of years later and succeeded. He knew he could only work this hard for five years, and he was determined to make it pay.

Imperial Oil was and is Canada's second largest oil company. It sponsored *Hockey Night in Canada* for forty-one years, and the advertising campaign to sell Esso gas, "Put a Tiger in Your Tank," would be known by any Canadian alive in the 1960s. The company is a monster. If you could get on and hang on, if you could stand it, it was a fast-rolling gravy train. A good portion of my parents' net worth and retirement income originated with the amassing of assets in the early 1980s with the money they made in just a few years of association with Imperial Oil, more especially as dealers of chemical agricultural fertilizers.

I could not help but be impressed by, and proud of, my parents' energy and hard work and sagacity in snagging this smelly and dusty business jewel in such a place as Sedgewick, Alberta. The oil patch was in crisis, the industry was floundering, the world was in recession, but they had found a small niche where prosperity was still possible. The high cost of money, though, was a wrench in the works. My parents paid thousands of dollars in inflated interest rates for business operating loans that would otherwise have gone into their pockets. This was unfortunate but unavoidable.

It wasn't necessary to train me to handle anhydrous ammonia or drive the trucks and haul the tanks necessary for delivering it to the farms. There were experienced and handy men in my father's employ for those jobs. It probably wasn't even possible to train me. I had a knack for the practical misapplication of any process requiring more than one or two steps, and I was prone to breakage and accidents. I was largely untrainable, and it was safer just to have me schlepping bags of dry fertilizer around, and cases of oil, or barrels of it, which I could barely manage, or filling up the gas trucks, or accompanying the drivers as a swamper, a helper. I was good for simple tasks under close supervision. In spite of the number of my father's cars I had damaged as a teenager, I had figured out how to drive a pickup truck, and I had been a successful cab driver. So I drove frequently into Edmonton and Camrose to pick up barrels of chemicals and replacement parts, glad to get out on the road, away from the office and the yard and the warehouse for a while.

I wasn't completely useless. With my cousin Jim, who had come to Sedgewick to take a job with his Uncle Bob, I helped rotate the axles on several of the rolling tanks when they became deformed from constant heavy use. I cleaned things. I detailed the ammonia trucks when the spring rush was over.

My father's few employees worked as many hours of the day as were necessary to get the job done, many days of double shifts, expecting nothing different. Everyone was tired and tempers were strained, but I never heard a word of complaint about the hours or compensation. Weeks later, when the rush was over, my mother cut the ammonia drivers bonus cheques for thousands of dollars. When my father presented the cheques to them, without a hint of ceremony, all he said was, "Good enough?" Obviously pleased, they each muttered, "Thanks, Bob," and that was that. No need for further negotiation.

Activity in the summer would slow down, a few holidays would be taken, a family reunion, camping by the lake, a golf tournament maybe, and in the fall a smaller rush would begin again.

I couldn't hope to match my father's enthusiasm and commitment to his business. I knew what it was to make money self-employed. I had been a cab driver in Calgary in the seventies in the oil boom and an ESL teacher in the eighties in Tokyo when Japan was "Number One!" Well paid piecework makes you long for work. You can't wait to get back to it. When you own your own business and times are good, when it is successful, you can see the money rolling in, and every hour you are awake and busy is gold in your pocket. It is a sweet thing to be useful to your own profit. Many other men wouldn't have made as much money as my father did in this business, but he knew how to maximize his limited time and resources. He knew that close attention and non-stop process improvement were the keys to efficiency and revenue. He had an innate feel for Total Quality Control although I doubt he had ever heard of Juran or Deming. I hadn't, not yet. Moreover, he was able to convince his customers, quietly and reasonably, to pay their bills, a rare gift. If his life had started differently or taken a different course, he might have ascended to positions of responsibility in greater combinations of skill and capital than small businesses in Sedgewick, possibly in a political setting. He belonged to the Kinsmen, the Masons, and the Legion, and was on the town council. He became mayor the next year. He moved from Calgary to Sedgewick so he could be, in his words, a bigger fish in a smaller pond. When he was young, he didn't have the background, the education, no more than eight years of public school, or the connections, to move easily in established or venture circles, but he valued work and community, and his eye for detail and his commitment to improvement were bound to lead him to greater comforts than he had known growing up in a small farmhouse in Southern Alberta with nine brothers and sisters. And besides, when he was young, he had brats to feed.

If a man writes a book about his life and doesn't call his father a son of a bitch at least once, he's just not being honest. My father may have been Good Ol' Bob to his customers and friends, his community and electors, but he was kind of a prick at home, a street angel and a house devil. We fought for years, almost without reserve, until I left home at sixteen. We would have fought physically but that he was twice my size and there would be no point. Spanking was considered normal in those days, as was hitting women, although I would bet my liver my father never hit my mother. And he stopped spanking me when I became a young teenager. You can't spank a teenager. There's nothing educational or corrective about that. That's just violence. At least one of my teenaged cousins got into a knock-down fist fight with his father, tired of listening to his constant, irrelevant criticisms. If my father had continued to hit me as a teenager, I might have killed him in his sleep with a baseball bat. Fortunately for both of us, it never came to that. But the threats of violence never stopped, and that was enough to piss me off. He was a young parent with no interest in children, and when confronted with a difficult child his only talents were to ignore and bully. I think he realized that if he could just hang on a little longer I would be gone, and he was right. When I was sixteen he was happy to finance me, and my sister, out of the house. He was thirty-nine. My mother was thirty-seven. In a couple of more years Alberta's economy soared, and his business, then a clothing store, picked up, and he and my mother lived the rest of their lives without children, free to make money and have fun in whatever way they could.

Until now. Here I was. Back again. I had left home when I was still in high school. I guess I could come home for a couple of months on a bum. The first employer in the history of the world was a father, the first employee his son. My father asked me more than once to join him in his next business. I know why. It was so he could pass the business on to me without the trouble of having to sell it, also so he could be the boss until the day he died.

My father and mother were working hard and socking money away, but you can't work double shifts every day of the week and not be a little cranky. In some ways I liked my dad. There were parts of his sense of humour that resonated with me culturally and genetically. Even though we had been strangers for much of my childhood, there was a strong, shared experience and understanding between us, seen from radically different points of view. We were both twentieth-century, prairie men, Alberta-born. We had grown up under the same sky, in the same landscape, and had watched the towns and cities around us grow and change, although a generation apart. We breathed the same dry air, and if push came to shove we would salute the same flag. On nearly every other matter we disagreed entirely. Name a subject. We disagreed.

We made some effort not to quarrel that spring. I spent about ten weeks in Sedgewick, and we only snapped at each other a couple of times. He was stressed and would drink a little. There's always a bottle of rye in a small-business office in rural Alberta. When office hours are over, the front door is closed, but not locked, and half a dozen men will stop in for a game of cards, or several, and a drink, or several, on their way home. My father was always happy to oblige. He enjoyed it immensely, I would say. He loved small town life. When the usual suspects showed up and the cards and the whisky came out, I headed for home. Rednecks are bad enough to deal with during business hours. I was damned if I was going to listen to those fat, sweaty bastards in endless repetition of unlettered grievance on my own time. I would head home to do yoga, chat with my mother, help her make supper, and watch classic movies on their new satellite receiver. The dish was in the back yard, as big as anything built by NASA.

My father often came home for supper a couple of hours later, a little worse for wear. I never held it against him. I had never seen anyone work so hard and deal with so much shit. One evening after a hot, sweaty day at work, home for an early supper, he grabbed a beer from the refrigerator and downed it in one thirsty gulp then grabbed another and did the same. With his head tipped back he viewed the ceiling above him for a moment and couldn't help but see the light fixture there. When he was finished his beer he said, "Has that always been there?" He then walked to his La-Z-Boy recliner and fell fast asleep for ten minutes while steam came out of my mother's ears. After supper he went back to work.

My grandmother and her new husband, Jack, both retired and happily opening envelopes at the end of every month, envelopes containing pension cheques and investment dividends, were living in Edmonton. They used to come to Sedgewick and stay for weekends and short visits in a little travel trailer in my mother and father's back yard. Helen could visit her daughters, and Jack could play golf for much lower green fees than in Edmonton. This pissed my father off, and he didn't need any more stress. My mother's sister, Barb, and her husband, Ray, lived up the road. I had some sympathetic company amongst these easygoing folk, and I could wander over and vent with them when living and working with my very intense father got to be too much.

Another example of domestic manners during the summer of 1985.

I was tired and sore one night and wanted nothing more than to do yoga and go to bed early. My mother was out somewhere, which was unusual, and my father was still across the road at the office talking, and no doubt drinking, with the Imperial Oil rep from Edmonton. I was in bed by nine o'clock and in a deep sleep by 9:30 when the telephone rang. It rang twenty times before I was able to achieve any kind of waking consciousness, accept that it was not going stop, and drag myself up from my happy bed to answer it. It was my father, about one-third drunk, calling from the office. The following ridiculous conversation, irritated and aggressive on both sides, took place.

I, the ferret: "Hello?"

Bob, the mastiff: "Uhhhhhhhhhhhhhhhhhhhhhhhh, is your mother back yet?"

"No."

"Shit." He wasn't expecting this.

"What? What is it? What do you need? What's going on?"

"Well, we're still over here, and uh…we haven't had anything to eat. We're hungry, dammit."

"Go to the highway." There was a restaurant at the service station on the highway. My father had eaten there five hundred times.

"Highway's closed."

"What time is it?"

"Nine thirty. What the hell are you doing?"

"I was in bed."

"What the hell are you doing in bed at 9:30?"

"I was tired."

"Well…can you make us something to eat?"

I wanted to say, "Are you fucking crazy?" but I settled for, "Are you kidding me?"

"C'mon!"

"Make it yourself!"

"Oh, hell, you're better at that stuff than I am."

"No way!"

"C'mon! For Christ's sake make us something to eat."

"Why didn't you go to the highway earlier? What have you been doing all night?"

"Well, you know. Talking business and having a drink."

"Goddamn it. What do you want?"

"Oh, I don't know."

"There's nothing to eat. We have to go shopping."

"C'mon. Just some soup and sandwiches…and crackers…and put some coffee on."

"Jesus Christ. Alright. Give me twenty minutes."

"Okay. We'll have another drink and be over in a bit. He's a nice guy. You'll like him."

I hung up. "Fuckin' jerk."

He was a Clydesdale, and I was a rabbit pilfering hay in the corner of his stall.

Well, my parents had saved my life. There was no denying that. One of my old high school acquaintances, an obnoxious redneck, needless to say, saw me in the office one day. "What are *you* doin' back in town? Broke?"

"Yeah."

I saw Danny, the driller from my very short career on the oil rigs. He was bouncing his child on his huge knee in my father's office. He told me he had seen guys work all their lives and never get rich.

I wasn't happy in Sedgewick, that would have been unrealistic, but I was grateful. The summers there are usually hot, the days long and clear and dry. I saw a small twister one very hot day, a hundred feet high. At five in the afternoon, like clockwork, enormous brilliant white and then black thunderclouds formed bringing with them a skyful of lightning and thunder, sometimes with rain, sometimes without. One night the northern lights played faintly across the sky in a 1,000-mile dance. I was grateful, but I wasn't going to thank my parents too profusely. That would be embarrassing for both of us. I endured and enjoyed my time in Sedgewick as best I could. I tried to be cooperative if not helpful, and when I couldn't do either, I tried to stay out of the way. At the end of June, my father gave me a decent paycheque for a couple of months' work, as well as free room and board, and I made plans to bolt.

In the spring, at U of C, I had pondered the future and come to the conclusion that I had to find another area of study. I couldn't bear the thought of continuing in chemistry, but a new subject would have to be something in which my first two years of chemistry would count. I couldn't start again. I couldn't face that. It would also help if it were a program with a professional leaning, meaning a bit more industry-specific than academic chemistry or biochemistry or physics, holding out the promise of some kind of dedicated employment at the end, something vocational.

I was still faintly interested in health, nutrition, vegetarianism, herbs, and natural healing, and now I thought I might have to reassert and operationalize these vague interests. The University of Alberta in Edmonton had a program in food science. So did the University of British Columbia in Vancouver, a much nicer city, but I was starting to see the benefits of being close to home when teetering so often on the edge of financial collapse. The U of A Interdisciplinary Food Science program was administered by the Faculty of Agriculture and offered jointly by the Faculties of Agriculture, Science, and Home Economics. I was more academically interested in nutrition than food technology, but I was squeamish about being a male student in the Faculty of Home Economics. That just didn't seem right. And I didn't want to be a dietitian. I applied to U of A and because I was such a good student, if nothing else, I was accepted immediately. It came to pass in the summer of 1985, fourteen years after leaving high school, that I was to enter the U of A Faculty of Agriculture. This is not something that anyone familiar with my history, at any point in my life, was likely to have predicted. I, least of all. Not many in the general public know what food science is, and I have relatives who still think I am a cook.

I would be required to take an introductory course in food science, Food Science 200. Fortunately, it was offered in a three-week period in the summer for people in exactly my situation, transferring to the program in September. Here was my out. My grandmother and Jack were going to Eastern Canada for a month and I could stay, free of course, in their very comfortable high-rise apartment across the river from the campus while they were away. I took my parents' money and moved to my grandmother's in early July. I sat in a very elementary three-hour class five days a week, for three weeks, and passed Food Science 200. I applied, without much hope, to live in the mature students' housing at U of A, otherwise I would soon be looking for some kind of miserable shared student accommodation. I had only lived in a student residence once before, during my brief semester as a sixteen-year-old at Camrose Lutheran College in 1970, and it wasn't that appealing, but the promise of a room to myself and mature neighbours, not to mention the convenience of being on campus during Edmonton's harsh winters, was worth investigating.

Anne was in Edmonton. This was Gordon's former girlfriend from long-ago days at the XN Ranch. She had left the mountain hippies behind and gone back to school where she mowed down a BSc in zoology, and she was now crushing a Master's degree in the same subject. She already had a job lined up for September lecturing at the University of Lethbridge and would soon go off to medical school. We connected by mail, then over drinks, and then in the shower. She was in the mood for casual sex, and so was I.

Klondike Days, Edmonton's summer festival, was upon us. Anne said, "Have you ever seen kd lang perform?" I said, "No, I've never heard of her." She said, "Then we're going." Anne and I saw kd lang at a big, expensive hotel in downtown Edmonton, possibly the Four Seasons, when kd was twenty-four years old and used to wear two different cowgirl boots. She thought she was the reincarnation of Patsy Cline. We danced the whole night in a packed ballroom. I hadn't had that much fun in a very long time.

I showed up at the exhibition site a couple of days before Klondike Days started and got a job slinging beer for ten days at the beer gardens in the 17,000-seat Northlands Coliseum. There was a beer strike that summer, and the festival organizers scrambled to truck in American beer in time for opening day. By then, the strike in Alberta was over and Canadian beer was once more available, but all we had was truckloads of that watery piss Americans call beer, and no self-respecting Canadian would drink it. It was an embarrassing state of affairs, and the beer gardens were a bust that year.

While I was slinging beer, I got to see the music acts that were booked in the afternoons and evenings. I think the Saturday night headliner was Tammy Wynette. There was another band from Hawaii called The Krush and they played two shows a day. After seeing them do exactly the same show twenty times in ten days, I hated them. They did a parody, in drag, of Madonna's "Like a Virgin," and I kept thinking, "Who is Madonna?"

One slow afternoon at work, I was leaning on a low divider wearing my K-Days bow tie and straw boater hat. As I twirled my empty tray, I saw Wayne Gretzky and a couple of his pals, other cement-head hockey players, stroll across the polished concrete at centre ice. Gretzky was twenty-four years old, and six weeks earlier he had captained the Edmonton Oilers to their second straight National Hockey League Stanley Cup Championship with three more to come over the next five seasons. At a hundred and sixty-five pounds, he was twenty-four pounds lighter than the NHL average, but he passed the puck better than anyone. He was always two steps ahead of his opponent. He never skated after the puck. He skated to where it was going to be. Gretzky walked by within a few feet of me throwing a set of keys up and down in the air. I was so out of touch with Canadian sport I didn't recognize him, but I thought he looked familiar. After they had passed, a cute young girl, another waiter, ran over to me shouting breathlessly, "I just saw Wayne Gretzky! He was here! He was here! I think he was booking a VIP table for tonight!"

I said, "Yeah, I think I just saw him."

When he and his friends walked across the floor of the Coliseum, they looked like they owned every inch of it. And they did. Gretzky, Messier, Anderson, Coffey, Smith, McSorley, Kurri, Fuhr, and Sather. I didn't give two shits about professional hockey, and even I knew these names. In the 1980s in Edmonton, the Oilers were royalty. They ruled the city. Gretzky's wedding to Janet Jones in 1988 was called The Royal Wedding. Later that same year, when Peter Pocklington, the owner of the Oilers, needed money to shore up his other failing business interests, he traded Gretzky to the Los Angeles Kings for fifteen million dollars. Pocklington became the most hated man in Canada, and he was burned in effigy in front of the Coliseum.

The city went into mourning. In Gretzky's first appearance in Edmonton after his trade to LA, he received a four-minute standing ovation from a sold-out audience at the Coliseum, even after it was learned that Gretzky was himself in favour of the trade and had participated in the negotiations. In spite of it all, Edmonton loved Wayne Gretzky. They called him the Great One, or even, sometimes, with affection, Plain Wayne. He was no looker. When he left the ice in 1999, his jersey number, 99, was retired league-wide, the only player ever to be so honoured. In his twenty-year career in the NHL, ten of them with the Oilers, Gretzky set sixty-one new records and was awarded at least thirty-one trophies, prizes, and honours, including the Companion of the Order of Canada, the country's second highest national order for merit.

My depression had lightened a little in Sedgewick, but it was still there, overlaid and intermixed with anger and disappointment. My appetite was voracious. I had no money to speak of, no lover, no future. For months I had been fat, broke, lonely, and useless. Now, staying by myself at my grandmother's deluxe air-conditioned apartment, swimming in the big, fancy pool, baking in the sauna, seeing and making love with Anne, working at Klondike Days, away from Sedgewick, I strolled the warm summer streets of Edmonton with a little money in my pocket, unobserved and unjudged, unknown and unblamed. I started to take an interest outside myself, in people and places. I curbed my appetite and lost weight. I began to see that I must make a motion of the mind, an exertion of the spirit, and I thought, "Fuck this, fuck it, fuck it to hell and back! I am sick of this. I am sick of being depressed. Enough!" It can take a lot of despair before courage is found. In a moment that I remember clearly on a summer night in Edmonton, I made a decision to turn my thoughts in a positive and energetic direction, to submit to what is unavoidable and to banish the impossible from my thoughts, to reengage in some kind of active life, to look for new objects of interest. Fr. Michael in Oakland had been right. I could not spend my life in retreat. Not yet.

Anne and I took our casual relationship to Calgary on the bus. We were in fine fettle, light of heart. We laughed and partied. We made plans to do one thing and then did another. What did it matter? It was summer and summer in Alberta is a beautiful thing. We had no immediate obligations, and no reason whatever not to be happy. We then split up and went our separate ways to visit a dozen other friends and family. I heard Shelagh was in town dancing in a reunion with the Young Canadians at the Stampede. She was my old drinking buddy and one-off lover from my days in the Television, Stage and Radio Arts program at SAIT, a woman I was deeply attracted to. I called her, and we connected for a few hours, delicious hours for me. I had always loved that skinny, happy redhead.

From Calgary I took the bus to Helena, Montana, and visited Sue for a week. Her moxibustion business was slow, but she usually had one or two appointments a day to keep her busy. When she was working, I toured on my own around Helena, the capital of Montana, a small, pretty, old Gold Rush town. Sue's office was just off Last Chance Gulch, the city's main street. In 1888, there were more millionaires in Helena per capita than any other city in the world, and there remain to this day beautiful buildings and neighbourhoods of Victorian houses, the Painted Ladies, as pretty as San Francisco. Sue had bought an old International Harvester Scout, an early version of the American gas-guzzling SUV, and I used it to drive around the neighbouring countryside. I hiked up Mt. Ascension and took a boat ride on the Missouri River.

It was a warm and friendly week with Sue. I went to a pet shop and bought soft, but strong, cat collars to use as effective and economical handcuffs. When her mother went out, we chased each other around the house. We tied each other up and giggled and fucked the daylights out of each other. By the time I left, we both knew we would probably never see each other again. And we never did.

I took the bus back to Calgary and then to Regina, Saskatchewan. My old high school girlfriend, Karen, lived there, and she had invited me for a visit, or I invited myself, I don't remember which. We had written back and forth a few times while I was in Tokyo, and she wondered why I was so interested in the Franciscans of Lumsden, just thirty miles to the east of Regina. When I got there, we renewed our relationship with the aid of a beanbag chair in a way that made me realize for the rest of my life that I preferred redheads to friars.

It had taken a long time, but not much of substance, to turn me around, to rehydrate my inelastic spirit. A little easy living, some warm summer weather, some sex, and some re-established goals. It seemed unfair that my life should be saved by fifteen hundred dollars, a plan, and some pussy, or ruined by the lack of them, although I suspected my problems ran deeper than that, but there it was. Back in Edmonton on the eve of classes, I was delighted to learn that my student loan had come through, course scheduling appeared to be satisfactory with no bloody night classes, and more importantly I had been assigned a room in the mature student housing at Pembina Hall. No roommate. Thank God.

This was the same 1914 building where my grandmother had lived as a 50-year-old co-ed in the early sixties. It had been a place of offices, classrooms, accommodation for both professors and students, and for a while in 1918, a makeshift hospital where seventy-two people died during the Spanish flu pandemic. It was one of only three lovely old pre-World War I buildings remaining on campus, built of red brick with rows of windows framed with wide sandstone. The three buildings had been renovated recently and were now in good shape, handsome and stately behind trees and ivy, the most collegiate looking buildings I ever occupied, beautiful in the changing fall colours. I would have a room to myself and mature company just outside my door when desired or needed.

The Agriculture Building was only fifty yards from Pembina Hall. I could run to most of my classes wearing just a light coat, even in the dead of winter, or to the cafeteria or the bookstore. Physics, statistics, and the library were a little farther afield across the Quad. Nutrition classes and Sunday cafeteria, however, were a serious march of four or five bone-chilling blocks, almost unendurable in winter.

In mid-July I had been deeply concerned about transfer credit. Universities have a tendency to discount the work and standards of their fellow institutions, sometimes justifiably, sometimes haughtily, especially across provinces. International transfers are worse. Assigning equivalents is a translation nightmare, and the forgery of documents is not uncommon. Wherever you are transferring from, course equivalents are always a hot topic, closely watched, and they change frequently. They are the bane of those who, like me, like to switch back and forth and go to multiple schools.

I submitted my transcripts from SAIT, UVic, U of C, and most importantly, Camosun College. I telephoned Professor Howard in Victoria and told him of my plans to continue studying science, and that I was trying to mount a convincing offensive in support of maximum transfer credit. Would he mind sending a letter of recommendation directly to the dean's office? I asked Graham and Rintje as well. Howard, in his usual carefree and blissful way, told me I should just take introductory biochemistry again. I would learn much from a second survey and cement my early foundations. My response to him was, more or less, "Jesus, Howard, I'm going to be thirty-two years old next month. I need a degree, and I need it as fast as I can get it."

I telephoned the dean's office at the U of A Faculty of Agriculture every couple of days to enquire about the status of my assessment. It occurred to me that if it went badly there was a possibility I would not continue with my application to U of A. School had its charms, it was a poor man's country club, but it wasn't that much fun. I couldn't bear the thought of having to repeat any of my earlier courses in science just because U of A was too snooty to recognize my previous work at a junior college. Classes were starting in a few weeks. Once the decision on transfer credit was handed down, there would be no time for an appeal.

In only a few days, one of my calls yielded results. The sniffy secretary on the other end of the line read off the names of the courses for which I had been granted credit. When I heard the long list of courses I would not have to take, I stuffed my fist into my mouth to suppress my glee, to keep from laughing out loud. I rolled onto my back like a child, kicking my feet into the air in my grandmother's posh apartment overlooking the leafy campus just across the beautiful valley of the North Saskatchewan River. To my indescribable delight they had erred in my favour and given me one or two more courses than I could have expected under the most favourable circumstances. The secretary then told me, in a state of grave dudgeon, that my numerous telephone calls and unsolicited letters of recommendation had made me no friends in the dean's office. They did not like being pushed.

The normal procedure was for an applicant to stand with his hat in his hand and wait quietly for judgment. For this custom of academe I cared not one small, dry fart. I still had a fresh face, but I wasn't a fresh-faced nineteen-year-old. I was damned if I was going to allow my five semesters of work at Camosun College, two and a half years, be they ever so humble, to be judged without significant personal input. I was convinced to a certainty, and was probably wrong, that the secretaries and administrators in the dean's office were no more than high school graduates, as was I, not counting the handmade diploma given to me by (Mrs.) Kay Kelly. I imagined these uneducated gatekeepers, arbitrary and obstructive, sitting on their twats in their cubicles all day knowing no more of my special genius than could be gleaned from a handful of abbreviations on a couple of sheets of embossed paper. As far as I was concerned, they could, in the words of old Götz Iron Hand, "lick my arse."

I was then told that the dean wanted to see me. Uh oh. I hadn't even started, and I was already being called into the principal's office. I presented myself a couple of days later and gave him a humble, verbal précis of my concerns, my reasoning and motivation, for besieging and upsetting his office staff. He seemed undisturbed. Frankly, I think he just wanted to meet this brassy new transfer student with the perfect GPA. Over the next two years, I walked by the dean's office a thousand times, but it was recessed from the main thoroughfare, and I never looked in. They had served their purpose. There is no lower form of life than a bureaucrat, except, possibly, a university bureaucrat. Or as I was soon to learn, a teaching assistant.

September broke and thousands of young people converged on the University of Alberta campus. I wasn't young anymore, but I had a youthful look and thirty-two didn't seem to be too old to be finishing a degree. There was always a certain justifiable nobility in going back to school. There was even a fine old dormitory specially reserved for mature students. We commanded, as a type, some small recognition and respect for our humility, our dedication to life-long learning, our desire to improve ourselves, etc, etc, etc.

School was something I knew well, something I knew I could do, something I knew I would be successful at, and I was badly in need of some kind of success. I also knew that in a large faculty, in a difficult subject, in honours physics or mathematics, in astronomy or engineering, or theology, the preferred study of the needy, I would have to work very hard to be in the top ten of my class. But I had, for various reasons, sheer laziness mostly, perhaps also taking a page from my father's book, chosen to be a big fish in a small pond, and I was about to become, for the next two years, the Wayne Gretzky of the University of Alberta Food Science Department.

19   The First Year

I exaggerate, of course. But it was a very good year. I was taking a full load, and I went to work right away. I studied genetics, industrial food processing, food microbiology, food chemistry, statistics, food engineering, quality control, brewing and enology, more food microbiology, and physics. I remained steady in my scholarly habits throughout. The result was predictable and satisfying. With a stable and unbroken approach to preparation, attendance, and review, time-consuming but tolerable, my work was always done, I was always on top of proceedings, and there was little need to mope or fret. The system is designed to grant success to those who show up and do the work. I was free at all other times to probe the depths of my attraction to misbehaviour.

At the beginning of any school year, especially in a dormitory, there is always an atmosphere of probing and jockeying, of tender negotiation, as singles seek out partners for the coming year. The mingling of two whims, the contact of two skins. A long, cold winter of long hours of study, with very little pocket money, is made a different world when you have someone close at hand to rub feet with at night.

I started my new life quickly and uncharacteristically. I volunteered to help at a fundraising dance given by the Pembina Hall social club. It turned out to be a rollicking success, sold out, and I met a lot of my fellow dorm residents in a responsible and cheerful setting. The group that was booked to play was a Beatles tribute band called "1964." This seemed an odd and risky choice to me. I thought a New Wave or Punk band would have a better chance of competing for frosh-week dollars than a costume band covering the silly love songs of the mop tops of a previous generation, a band I had grown up with. How wrong I was. "1964: The Tribute" had been founded the year before and they were an immediate success. *Rolling Stone* magazine called them the "best Beatles tribute on Earth." Thirty years later they're still selling out seven shows a month. That's thirty years of Beatles haircuts for them. The performances were authentic and endearing. The vocals and mannerisms, even the likenesses, were uncanny. Fifteen hundred people who weren't born until 1964 screamed and danced and sang along with "I Love You, Yeah, Yeah, Yeah!" It was a tremendous success. Early Beatles music fit perfectly with the resurgence of catchy, unchallenging, sugary pop music in the mid-1980s, Prince, Michael Jackson, Cyndi Lauper, Phil Collins, Whitney Houston, Lionel Ritchie, Madonna, a-ha, and Wham! No one misses the mid-80s musically.

I made a deliberate decision to make every effort to find a girlfriend, and soon. For many months, until recently, I had been nervous and timid around women, naturally unwilling to share my inexplicable ambitions, bizarre and shifting, my atavistic fascination with "impulses long suppressed by society's current rules," not to mention the long period of penury and depression. But now, at U of A, I was on a level playing field again, and no one here knew about my previous questionable appetites. I could start over with a group of intelligent, mature people without mention of the failures and embarrassments of earlier days. There was no need to identify with, or advertise, anything from my past other than that which would advance my interests, professionally and socially. And there was no reason my native charms should not net me intimate company for the coming months. Any woman in the building could easily get to know me better.

Ferda, "Fair-uh-da," was a cute young woman, petite and fit, living in the dorm, of Turkish background but thoroughly Canadian. She was an aerobics instructor, and we caught each other's eye. We found ourselves in close company a couple of times in a matter of a few days, and just when I thought we were about to come to an arrangement, she veered sharply away from me in favour of a well-heeled medical student from Vancouver. She knew her assets could attract better spoils than I offered. I was still wearing sweat pants.

Next on my list of possibles was Sharon. She was older, quite a bit older. I was thirty-two. She was in her mid-forties. She was from Victoria, BC, and had a job, a house, and grown children. She was doing graduate work in clothing and textiles to further her knowledge of art conservation, mostly working with museum collections. A relationship with her, an older woman, would not be notorious, but it would be noticeable. And not something I had experienced before. She was slim, petite, and quiet with bountiful hair and deep, magnetic eyes. A woman in her forties knows her own mind, sometimes, and if her mind is made up, a lot of wooing is not necessary. On our first date we went to the movies and then went back to her room, down the hall from mine, and had sex, a pleasant surprise. There was no need for reticence. She had made up her mind. We kept at it for the rest of the semester. Sharon decided she liked the look of me, and I have found that a woman never looks quite so attractive as when she is admiring me. No more than three or four women in my life have told me that I was all their dreams come true, but Sharon was one of them. She insisted on taking me to West Edmonton Mall to shop for new clothes. She couldn't have me walking around in sweat pants. I was desperate enough to accept a new pair of trousers, and I tried on expensive and trendy Doc Martens shoes, which Sharon was willing to buy for me, but I was not that much of a gold-digger. I felt like quite the kept man as it was.

I knew I would want and need to be entertained over the winter beyond the joys of Arnold Schwarzenegger movies showing at the Student Union Building, and I bought two sets of season tickets at two theatres, the Citadel downtown and the U of A Department of Drama closer to home. At the Citadel Theatre Sharon and I saw the best production of *The Tempest* ever mounted, done in a Japanese *kabuki* style, as well as an entertaining musical based on *Treasure Island*, called *Pieces of Eight*. The Citadel was hosting this latter's world premiere after which it promptly died. We saw *Top Girls*, an evening of sexual politics in a disturbing setting of fantasy and reality, including dinner with Pope Joan. We saw *Private Lives*. At U of A we saw productions featuring young actors with more presence and talent than I had ever possessed in my eleven years of performing on stage.

I had come to a pretty pass, a fork in the road, and I was forced down the one more travelled. I was working once again in a system where, for someone of my academic abilities, some kind of success was practically guaranteed. I would finish this degree at the top of my class and be offered a job, even with the resume of a demented hobo, because that's the way the world works. It was a world I wanted nothing to do with, but I had no choice. The universe had proved singularly unwilling to reward my noble, otherworldly leanings, and I was miffed at having to crawl back to a system I disdained, at being reduced to having to wrench my living from it like any other plebeian. If I couldn't have the former, if I was forced to settle for the latter, I would have it spades. I always knew I was a great deal more devilish in practice than I was in theory, but now I truly went overboard. Virtue had gone out of me.

I liked Sharon. She was smart and experienced and comfortable in her own skin, gentle and feminine. She was a grown-up. Her personality was fully formed and needed none of the experimental extremes of youth, although she was sexually agreeable in every way. She was fond of risky public sex. We made love one night amongst the dripping plants under the glass in the hot and humid conservatory of the Agriculture Building, and one afternoon in the open lounge on the third floor of our residence, discoverable at any moment. I was stunned by her adventurousness, and I couldn't have been more pleased, but I came to the realization, in early days, that our relationship was unsustainable for reasons it would be ungentlemanly of me to reveal. Yes, I hear the irony in my use of that word.

I had been dazzled by my visit to Karen in the summer in Regina. She had grown into a talented, competent woman, over-competent, in charge of her life, and unfortunately, everyone else's. At thirty-three she was already being honoured for her vigorous contributions to the art community.

She had graduated from university in painting and ceramics. She worked for a couple of years in and out of community art studios, at this and that, and then at twenty-six, she landed a job as the director and curator of a public art gallery in Regina. She has been the boss there ever since, thirty-six whirlwind years of kicking ass on the cultural landscape in the public sector. In that generally underfunded, polite, and timid world of unproductive meetings and tepid compromises, she, as a fresh young art administrator, was on the short list for every committee appointment in town and was frequently consulted by a variety of organizations, in spite of, or perhaps because of, her unhesitating tendency to encourage and guide her colleagues in matters of professional deportment in very direct terms, for example, "Try finding a job you can handle!" Karen felt as strongly about art as Beryl had about TESL.

When asked by her remote and uninvolved overseers if she had a strategic plan for the gallery, the management flavour of the moment, she responded, "Yes!" and hung up. Due to a chronic lack of money resources, no such document existed or was ever likely to. At a presentation by a visiting artist from Ontario, after enduring the praise of an endless list of male artists, she barked at him from the audience, "Are there no *women* artists in Toronto?!" She could be loud and vehement when moved. When courted to jury a corporate art competition, she resigned at the first meeting and walked out, disgusted by the ignorance and conservatism of the organizers. Needless to say she educated them a little before she left.

At a banquet, fed up with an intoxicated, leering fellow attendee, she flashed her breasts at him and told him to take a picture. She marched on the courthouse and the Legislature in angry support of women's rights. In 1967, when Karen was fifteen, Pierre Trudeau had said, "There's no place for the state in the bedrooms of the nation." It was no great stretch to extend this proscription to the uteri of the nation. She supported an underground railroad to procure abortions for pregnant teens. Henry Morgentaler was a particular hero.

She was five feet tall and one hundred pounds of red-headed razor wire, in shoulder pads during the day and a cocktail dress at night. She grew up in rural Saskatchewan watching Doris Day movies. By the age of fourteen, in Calgary, she was the president of the local Rolling Stones fan club, and by twenty-five you would be well advised to guard your jewels and your jugular if you found yourself in public or private debate with her on issues of art, politics, or feminism. She was a force of art and nature.

She was also an excellent cook and kept a small but beautiful house. She knew the value of domestic skills and the satisfaction of esthetic surroundings. On a small salary and exposed to virtually the totality of the distinctive, and decidedly non-commercial, world of contemporary Saskatchewan art, and frequently in contact with visiting artists, she was able to spy out opportunities for the astute purchase of desirable, sometimes notable, works for her personal collection. She continued to produce paintings of her own over the years, hundreds eventually, selling some, at an unhurried rate. They adorned the walls of her house exhibiting a progression of artistic exploration. They were usually figurative, some abstract in later years, always absorbing.

In addition to her quick, analytical mind and bright conversation, her unerring eye for form and colour, and her striking personal style, these latter things mysterious to me, what was most appealing, in the strongest possible way, was her obvious attraction and devotion to me, also a mystery, not to mention her spectacular collection of costume lingerie. On nearly every evening of our visit in the summer, and for years to come, one or both of us was dressed in full fantasy kit, upended on the furniture.

Karen and I had held hands behind the lab bench in chemistry class when we were fourteen years old, lived together briefly and impossibly at seventeen, and had connected off and on a couple of times after that. Our youthful lovemaking had been inept and unsatisfying. Now, in her early thirties, she was the complete package. She was a mother, an artist, a community leader, a feminist and philosopher, an activist, a woman who had taken and discarded an unacceptable husband, living on her own and paying a mortgage, a woman who knew her mind, a woman who took no shit from anyone. A woman skilled in the boudoir. Jude called her the

Widow Spanky. This relationship dominated my life for the next eight years.

The first of my many sins in my new life of renewed self-indulgence was a tendency to lie to women and the trip to Saskatoon at Thanksgiving.

A joke about Saskatoon that bears repeating here, and I will be the judge of that, goes like this.

In the early twentieth century, two women, mature, of a certain age, were travelling together by train. They had been dozing when they came to a stop at a substantial station on the wide prairies. They had missed seeing the station sign, and upon waking they didn't know where they were. Margaret said, "Betty, I'm just going to go down to the platform and ask someone where we are."

Betty said, "Alright, dear."

On the platform Margaret approached a man and asked him the name of the town.

He said, "Saskatoon, Saskatchewan."

She nodded, smiled, and thanked him.

When she got back on the train, she seated herself beside her friend but remained silent until Betty said, "Well, what did he say, Margaret?"

She replied, "I don't know, dear. He didn't speak English."

Karen and I arranged to meet at the Bessborough Hotel, the Bez, in downtown Saskatoon, overlooking the South Saskatchewan River. It was fifty years old, built in the grand chateau style of Canadian railway hotels, this one a Bavarian castle with towers and turrets. It had two hundred rooms, and at ten storeys it was the tallest building in Saskatoon until 1979. Karen knew how to hunt for a deal and which room to book, a corner room with a good view, turreted and atmospheric.

I studied genetics on the seven-hour bus ride from Edmonton to Saskatoon, and Karen drove up from Regina with a picnic basket full of snacks and strawberries and champagne. I had never been in the company of a woman who made such a positive effort to be romantic. At the same time she was a ferocious feminist and community activist. I loved being with her. She worked in all the established systems, and she broke all the rules. For her, art and life, and the art of living, were about the conscientious and unrelenting establishment of a fair and equal community through uncompromising justice, unfettered exploration, and the assiduous application of intelligence and skill in vocation and avocation. What on earth did she see in me? I know all of her friends asked themselves the same question.

For the next holiday, Remembrance Day, I flew to Regina. The memorable phrase of the weekend was, "Well, I've never done *that* before."

I booked a flight first to Phoenix for part of the long winter break and then another one from there to Regina. I had been looking forward to long, slow Sunday dinners over the fall in my grandmother's warm company, in her comfortable apartment, seated handy to Jack's open bar. Jack had gained a lot of weight when he married my grandmother a couple of years earlier, and he gave me a dozen good shirts he could no longer get into. This completed my new gigolo wardrobe. When Jack and Helen came back from their holiday in Eastern Canada in the summer, they set out again to visit friends in Arizona for ten days. When they returned in September, I said, "How did you like Phoenix?"

They replied, "We loved it!"

"You should move there," I said, not seriously.

They responded in unison with wide smiles, "We are!"

They had bought a mobile home in a clean, well-run park in Mesa, a park owned by, and full of, Canadians. The park's number one rule was *No Canadian Flags*. They had searched for apartments, mobiles homes, and condominiums in their ten days in Phoenix but had found nothing affordable or acceptable. On their last morning in town, they heard of another place for sale and were convinced by their friends to stop and see it on their way to the airport. They liked the look of the park. The very old man who owned the mobile, his wife now gone, was moving back to Nebraska to be, and die, near his family. He was asking $10,000. He said, "Give me eight thousand. You can have the whole damn place and everything in it except my clothes." My grandmother wrote him a cheque. In Edmonton they gave up their apartment, stored everything for the winter, and drove back to Phoenix.

So much for warm family Sunday dinners at my grandmother's. I told her I had no idea they were looking for a place down south. She said, "It's what we've wanted all our lives. It's our dream come true." I don't recall her ever speaking of such dreams within my hearing, not in thirty years.

I was glad to go south for a week at Christmas, but it wasn't easy to get to Phoenix. The Western Airlines plane stopped first in Calgary and then circled Salt Lake City for an hour in a blinding snow storm. We tried to land in Ogden, Utah, but failed and went back to Salt Lake City where we finally succeeded in touching down between blasts of Arctic air. We were delayed for hours waiting for our final connection to Phoenix.

I was reading Boswell's *Life of Samuel Johnson*. A young woman sitting next to me in the airport asked me about it. She was a third or fourth-year university student majoring in English. Dr. Johnson was, among many other things, the sole author, in 1755, of *A Dictionary of the English Language*, the most important dictionary of English for the next one hundred and seventy-five years. Boswell's biography of him has been called the greatest ever written in English. Johnson wrote of Boswell, "One would think the man had been hired to spy upon me." My airport seatmate, studying English at university for three or four years now, had never heard of Samuel Johnson or James Boswell. In America, English literature begins with James Fenimore Cooper and *The Leatherstocking Tales*.

Only five hundred miles farther south, in Phoenix at last, I stepped off the plane into summer and was met by Helen and Jack. They were miffed at having to wait so long for my delayed arrival and were keen to get home for cocktails. Their mobile home was clean and set in a large, tidy mobile home park, but the square footage of the one-bedroom manufactured home was small. I slept behind the couch, not on it, for the next eight nights. We all realized right away that it was going to be a long visit. Three nights would have been enough, but I have never liked short trips. I have always felt that if you are going to go somewhere you should stay long enough to get a feel for the place.

My grandmother was married to Hector Alexander for forty-six years until he died in 1979. A few years later I asked her if she would consider marrying again. She said, "I don't think so! I'm think I'm done with all that." Then she met Jack Turpin, a widower, through friends in Edmonton. He took her dancing and to Hawaii, and he told her he loved her every day. I was living in Tokyo when they married in 1983. Jack had a few more years left, and they spent them together in Arizona in the winter and in Sedgewick in the summer where they bought a little house.

We went golfing in Mesa, where I won the daily prize for the longest, and luckiest, putt. We went shopping, we cooked meals, or my grandmother did, we watched *Wheel of Fortune* on TV. We drove by the spectacular display of Christmas lights at the impressive Church of Jesus Christ of Latter-day Saints, the Mormons, just a mile or two away. And every day at precisely 5:00 p.m., it was Happy Hour. We pulled oranges from the tree at the front door, and you could buy vodka by the gallon for a couple of dollars at the supermarket. The screwdrivers disappeared pretty fast around the Deserama Mobile Ranch. My grandparents were never drunk in the evening, but they were never sober, two drinks for my grandmother, four for Jack.

I swore drunkenly at the television during Ronald Reagan's Christmas address, "Liar! Thief! Murderer!" until my grandmother tut-tutted me. Reagan and his creepy insect wife and his cowboy economics.

Yentl was playing on TV. I was not a fan of Barbara Streisand, but I wanted to watch it. I hadn't seen it. I was more interested in the young and pretty Amy Irving. We watched fifteen minutes or so, and Jack grumbled and swore and finally barked, "Why the hell am I watching this goddamn thing?!" We had to change the channel. I was surprised by his angry outburst. He was normally an easygoing man. My grandmother whispered in my ear, "Jack really hates Jews."

In July, I had attended my cousin Jackie's wedding in Edmonton. It was a beautiful summer day at the Old Timers' Cabin on the hill on the south side of the river. There were colourful hot air balloons floating in the bright blue sky. Jackie's sister Sheryl made me do the Chicken Dance, something for which I have never forgiven her. I decided that night that I was now rehabilitated from my excesses. I was mature, I was going to live again in a manner more familiar to the other members of my family and society, I was going to survive by blending in. That meant I could drink again. Over the summer, I occasionally had a beer and a sandwich on a hot day. There's nothing better. I drank sparingly with Anne and Shelagh and Sue and other friends and then with greater gusto with Karen in Regina. That fall I used to take the new Edmonton Light Rail Transit in a quick and easy route to a liquor store downtown, stock up on cheap wine, and have a glass a day as a reward for my diligent study habits. Only rarely did I have more than two. Until I got to Phoenix. I was now up to a couple of vodkas and four or five beers a night.

I convinced Helen and Jack to drive a hundred miles south to the bisected Saguaro National Park, the section on the west side of Tucson, to visit the Arizona-Sonora Desert Museum. It's a hundred acres of zoo, aquarium, botanical garden, and natural history museum. There are a couple of miles of easy walking trails through twenty acres of desert landscape, with two hundred animal species in residence and a thousand varieties of plants. I was fascinated by the desert. I had to see it. The entry fee was six dollars, and Helen and Jack, frugal seniors, were outraged by the cost. They refused to pay, so I, a starving student, bought all the tickets, reluctantly. I was glad I did. It is a fabulous site, and fifteen years later I went again. I couldn't convince them to go to Old Tucson Studios, the small theme park and western movie studio just down the road, but that was fine with me, it was too expensive. They enjoyed their irregular day out, walking a couple of miles along the paths, through the artificial cave and the hummingbird conservatory, the long drive. My grandmother was pleased with herself, but it was a bit hard on them. On the highway back to Mesa, she said, "I think I can say with certainty that we'll all be ready for a drink when we get home." She was seventy-two that year.

I realized I needed to get out of the house on my own. I found a place that would rent me a cheap, beaten down old car, and Jack fearlessly ponied up a credit card for the deposit. For a few days I drove around the Valley of the Sun in a decrepit, ten-year-old AMC Gremlin. When I first picked it up, the gas tank was empty, and it rode so low and rough it was like a buckboard, a real backbreaker. I thought the suspension must have been removed. I was about to turn around and take it back to the dodgy little business where I had acquired it, Mitch's Auto Sales, "All Kinds of Financing Available," when I drove over some railway tracks. There was an enormous bang from beneath the car, an explosion, frightening. I was certain it would result in the disablement, if not the destruction, of the vehicle, but to my great surprise, as I continued along for another fearful hundred yards, the suspension came to life and the car, and I, floated upwards and stayed there. I don't know what happened when I hit the tracks, but it resuscitated the shock absorbers, and I was able to keep going.

I went to the Heard Museum. It was at least seventy-five degrees Fahrenheit that day, and I was perspiring in my shirtsleeves. The elderly volunteer at the front entry of the museum had an electric heater going under her desk. She was chilly. People who are regularly exposed to temperatures of a hundred and twenty degrees have the most foolish notions about the weather. At the Heard I learned that the first snowbirds to come to Arizona were the Athabascan peoples who migrated from the Canadian sub-arctic to the American Southwest starting in the 1300s, when Benedictine monasteries dotted the landscape of Europe. They might have been more or less welcome than the current flock of seasonal visitors. The bumper stickers I saw, *Welcome to Arizona. Now go home!* seemed a little ungrateful. Every winter 300,000 northerners come to Arizona and bring a billion dollars with them to dump into the local economy of racists, xenophobes, and homophobes. Arizona opposed Martin Luther King Day for nearly ten years, by a large majority. It was the second last state to approve the holiday.

Their intransigence sparked a patchy boycott of the state which Arizonans were able to ignore until the National Football League pulled the Super Bowl from Phoenix in 1993, costing the tourist industry $500 million. The people of Arizona, a solid three-quarters of them white, continue to struggle with illegal immigration across their border with Mexico, as well as with gay rights and same-sex marriage, passing repressive and heavily criticized laws out of touch with much of the rest of the country.

Phoenix is the sixth most populous city in the US, soon to be the fourth, growing at a steady rate of four per cent a year. It is also one of the biggest in terms of area. The Valley of the Sun is five hundred square miles of flat, hot concrete. Looking at my map, I wanted to drive here or there only to discover that it was miles and miles of straight roads and occasional freeways to get anywhere, exhausting and unrewarding. It was no wonder my grandparents ventured no farther from their mobile home park than the supermarket and the local golf course.

I drove eighty miles north one day to Arcosanti, the experimental town founded by Paolo Soleri in 1970. He wanted to demonstrate how urban conditions could be improved while minimizing the destructive impact on the earth using a concept he called "arcology," architecture and ecology combined. The skyline of the earth-formed, concrete, compact, 25-acre community, on its rocky hill, is mostly curves and non-right angles in an organic layout, no grid at all. There are thirteen major structures and a population of around a hundred, mostly students and volunteers, which fluctuates depending on the scheduling of workshops and events. There are some resident workers making metal and ceramic bells for sale. There are greenhouses, gardens, and fields where the average salary is minimum wage. South-facing half domes, apses, and barrel vaults work well in this climate. They let in more light and heat in winter and less in summer. I took a guided tour and had lunch in the cafeteria where I ordered a quesadilla, pronouncing the l's hard, like gorilla or flotilla. I wandered around on my own and struck off over the desert until I saw signs warning of rattlesnakes.

The community has been puttering along for over forty years. A fire in the parking lot on a busy day in 1978 burned up two hundred cars. The last major structure was built in 1989. If they had an urgent need of survival such as that found at an Israeli kibbutz, food in peace and security in war, or the intense, inward, protective religious focus of an ashram, the community would develop much more quickly. As it is, it seems to be no more than a long-running demonstration project of conceptual architecture, an interesting jumble of ideas and prototype buildings in the desert unlikely to turn into a large, established community anytime soon. Soleri's followers might disagree. He died in 2013 at the age of ninety-three.

At Arcosanti I was amazed to see a model of a low, light, sprawling, organic-looking structure that Soleri had designed to cover and house the large space occupied by the railway tracks in downtown Regina, Saskatchewan. More than a dozen tracks, side-by-side, half a mile long, congeal in a thready bicep in the centre of the city. The goal was to remove and relocate the tracks, something that had been on Regina's civic mind for a long time, and create a large, protected, even warm, living space beneath an architectural carapace, something to keep the winter out and the townsfolk from freezing. Keeping the winter out is always on the agenda in a place where the temperatures drop to minus fifty degrees.

My next stop was this same frigid city on the prairies where Karen and I ate and drank and went to parties and accomplished our erotic contortions in front of the cats in front of the fire. The landscape of my indulgence had never been so esthetic and satisfying. I gained fifteen pounds in three weeks and returned to Edmonton sated and exhausted.

I was busted, of course. Sharon was fooled once or twice over the fall, shame on me, but not a third time, the more shame to my account. She expressed no outrage, only disappointment, and remained friendly, as did I. She had a more deserving suitor waiting in the wings and when my lying, orgiastic, bohemian sins were revealed, I was replaced within a week by an actual Bohemian, a man from Czechoslovakia. Frank was working at the university and finishing a PhD in electrical engineering. He was a better man than I in about a hundred different ways, but I asked Sharon how she could go out with a man who called her Sha-rone'. They married a couple of years later. I believe Frank was grateful for my revolting behaviour.

It was January in Edmonton. The days were short, black, and very cold. And now I had no one to snuggle with at night. I kept working, kept drinking, and the spring came on, but very slowly. My courses were all of a piece, notably successful.

There are advantages to being a quick learner. In early days, when it became obvious to my classmates that I was acing the quizzes and labs and tests, I was approached by young and pretty girls to help them, and we formed a study group that met every day. I didn't need a study group, but I did like pretty girls, and I found that if I could explain the course material to someone else it meant I understood it myself. I almost always had every aspect of our subjects worked out in advance, and I would cement the details in my mind by devising clear and simple ways to explain them to others.

From the beginning of the school year, I was very much in love with Connie, a woman in food science I met on the first day of statistics class. She was older than the other kids, almost my age. She had very long brown hair often in a single thick braid, a tall, athletic body, and a ruggedly pretty face with a small but ready smile. She was a pretty cowgirl, an equestrienne. She trained in show jumping and, possibly, dressage. She was a horse ballerina. It only happened on one occasion that she came straight to class from riding lessons and didn't have time to change out of her skin-tight breeches and tall dress boots, but I have to admit I was deeply moved. I liked costumes.

Connie was married to an older man, a professor at the university, and they had a little boy. She lived out of town in a real house with a man who had a real job and a good income. She dropped her child at daycare every day and drove a new Toyota into the city. She was thus not a typically impoverished student. She was also American. She was either from or had lived in Tucson, Arizona, where she went for a while to the other U of A.

I couldn't say why she was attracted to me, but to my great delight she was. She was circumspect in her conversation about her home life, she didn't complain, but I learned in snippets that things were difficult. She and her husband divorced just a few years later. We began to flirt immediately, and in a very short time we developed a floppy relationship. We held hands across the table in the cafeteria gazing endlessly into each other's eyes. We always sat together, wherever we found ourselves, practically in each other's laps. In the lab, both of us facing the teaching assistant at the front, I sat on a lab stool with my legs apart, and she stood leaning against me, her bottom in my crotch. I rested my hands deep in the front pockets of her jeans and my chin on her shoulder. We couldn't keep our hands off each other. This public sexual tension was exciting for both of us. We were a lot like teenagers and just as sickening.

I flat-out adored Connie, and for her it was perhaps just nice to know there was someone who did. We were handsy and touchy, but kissing was not on the menu. I managed to steal a kiss only two or three times in two years. I saw her off-campus only once, at a student party when I graduated. We sat cheek to cheek and held hands for three hours and never left each other's side. She finished the program the next year. We never made love although I thought that would be the right thing to do. Her husband worked on campus, but she never seemed to worry about running into him. He never came to the Agriculture Building or the cafeteria, the scenes of our drooling romance. Although one day, as we walked along together, she jumped a clear five feet away from me as she stopped to chat briefly with someone she knew, a friend of her husband's.

This long, steady, funny relationship, an emotional affair, an affair of the heart, was an interesting and diverting way to pass the long hours of classes and studying. My heart leapt every time she came into view. Every time. It was unconsummated without much expectation of ever being so. For Connie, in a tepid marriage, it was a relational disorder of some kind. For her I was safe, risk-free, sugar-free candy. For me, someone whose normal progress through life was one disorder after another, it was mead, sweet and golden.

Classes droned on. The teaching assistants were an interesting, and annoying, bunch. Some were PhD graduates who weren't quite employable as lecturers but who were capable of running large laboratory departments in the mainstream sciences, such as chemistry and biology. In the smaller departments, like food science, the TAs were newly minted graduate students who only a year earlier had still been short of a BSc, and with no more experience or talent for teaching in a laboratory than the glassware you would find in one. I had TAs whose first language was French, Thai, and Czech. Some of them barely spoke English.

As the academic year wound down, I looked vigorously and earnestly for career-related summer employment. What I did in the summer between my third and fourth years was crucial. This would be my last chance before graduation to establish contact with, and gain experience in, some part of the food industry. It was possible, even likely, that wherever I worked this summer would be where I worked when I finished my degree the next spring. Now was the time to meet industry people and impress them.

I wanted to work in brewing or winemaking. This was a dangerous field for me, but it paid well, better than many other areas of food science. Specifically, I wanted to work at Molson's Brewery in Regina, so I could learn how to make beer and live with Karen for the summer, but they couldn't be convinced to hire someone from out of the province.

I tried the Calgary Brewery with no luck.

I called Molson's Brewery in Edmonton but the man on the phone, the one in charge of handing out summer jobs, was gruff and ignorant. He responded only in grunts and monosyllables. I nearly hung up on him. How could I work for that kind of primitive?

I got an interview at Labatt's Brewery in Edmonton. A day or two before it was scheduled to take place, I called to confirm the appointment. The man I eventually talked to, Michael, said, "Oh, don't bother coming in, we hired someone last week." It was someone I knew, a woman in my classes. He hadn't thought it necessary to interview me, or inform me, or the others who had been scheduled, that they were cancelling the rest of the interviews. If I hadn't called to confirm, I would have gone to the brewery in the far south of the city on the day of my appointment and been told this news in person. This was unbelievably inappropriate and unprofessional. Even I knew that. And stupid. How would they know they hadn't missed a much better candidate if they didn't interview everyone? Hiring a summer student was obviously not important enough to them to maintain good business practice, or even good manners. When I asked Michael if he thought this was fair or wise, he basically said, "Tough." I was livid. I wrote on a small piece of paper, "Fuck your dead asshole, Mikey," and pinned it to my bulletin board. I was pleased to read it several times a day for the next few weeks. I imagined meeting this arrogant jackass one night at a food science event and planting a lead pipe, several times, into his obligingly soft skull. I found this helpful.

I interviewed, on campus, for a large dairy in Calgary, Palm Dairies. I was offered a job, not a great one, just a production-line monkey. The pay was not spectacular, but it was acceptable. I didn't want the job, but I decided I had better take it. Not much else was on the horizon. I telephoned the office in Calgary and asked for the applicable manager. He had not been at the interviews. When I got through to him, I thanked him politely and told him I was happy to accept the job. He barked at me over the telephone, "Yeah, you can have the job but I'll tell you, I won't hesitate a minute to fire you if I don't see you toeing the line!"

My response was, "Uhm, uh, uh…pardon?"

He said, "I've seen your resume. My guys offered you the job, and I'll go along with that for now, but that can change! Get that through your head!" There was nothing wrong with my resume.

"Okay, uh, well, uh…thank you."

My God, who were these corporate creeps?

I went to the departmental administrative officer. He was an accessible and knowledgeable man. I told him about my experiences so far with prospective employers, the Neanderthal, the liar, and the psychopath. I asked him if this kind of behaviour was common in the food industry. He shook his head and commiserated with me. He said that much of the food industry in Alberta, the secondary processing, was founded by farmers, primary producers. Many of them were hard, conservative men, and a rough, anti-education attitude often still prevailed. He told me to hang in there.

Jesus.

I interviewed with a bottling company that had a small plant in Edmonton, HPI Beverages. They were a private-label supplier to, among others, Loblaw's, Canada's largest food retailer, but all I saw was a small, unimpressive facility. They offered me a position working both in quality control and on the floor. It wasn't well paid, but at least it wasn't a full-time production job wearing a hairnet. With resignation I accepted their offer and wrote a letter to Palm Dairies politely declining their uncivil terms.

Then, at nearly the last moment, I received an offer to work at the Alpha Milk Company's new cheese manufacturing plant in Medicine Hat, a full-time position in the quality control lab. This was the one I was looking for. If I couldn't work in brewing, the dairies were the next best thing, and starting in the lab was much better than starting on the production floor. The man at the bottling company was very pleasant, and I was sorry to have to tell him that I wouldn't be able to work for him. He was surprised and disappointed and then a little miffed, but the job hadn't started yet, and I told him as sincerely as I could that I really had no choice. A lab job in a dairy? Excellent. I had to get dairy experience this summer since that was an industry I could likely break into upon graduation. I didn't want to make soda pop. It's not really food.

My father had a second car he wasn't using, and I asked him if I could borrow it for the summer. He loved that car. And so did I. It was a 1977, light green Chrysler New Yorker Brougham with a matching light green fabric interior and an 8-track tape player, four doors and air-conditioned, a 440 cubic-inch, eight-cylinder hardtop. It got eleven miles to the gallon in the city. It had power everything. It was a land yacht. You weren't behind the wheel, you were at the helm. It was a big, pretty, 4,000-pound, slab-sided behemoth with fender skirts and cruise control. It was a thing of planet-eating beauty. When my parents bought it they flew to Toronto, took delivery of it at Chrysler's Windsor Assembly Plant, a little south of

Detroit, and drove it 2,000 miles back to Alberta. Canadian-built cars were of higher quality than those built in American plants. Most of them were exported to the US. It was no secret that Chrysler executives working in the US routinely ordered their personal vehicles from the Windsor plant.

Before the school year ended, I took up with Pam.

I am almost finished listing the names and talking about the qualities of the women I attempted to seduce, and lied to, during this period of time. I'm not sure why I felt it was necessary to have sex with as many women as possible while I was going to school, but I did feel it was necessary.

I really did.

20   Say Cheese

Pam was studying nutrition in the Faculty of Home Economics, and she took a couple of courses in the Food Science Department in the Faculty of Agriculture. We were in a brewing and winemaking class together. We had noticed each other, and I liked the look of her. She was my height and slim. She had delicate hands, long fingers, lean legs, slim feet, small bottom, small top. She had short hair and a playful face, an easy smile. And eyes? Again, no idea. We both sat in the corner of the small classroom, in close proximity amongst the crowded jumble of desks, close enough to whisper, but I was busy when it came to women, and although I could think of many things to whisper in her ear, I was usually tired. Near the end of the semester, we started to talk.

I don't remember the pretext for our first date, but I know it went until six o'clock in the morning and ended with kisses. We spent most of the next seventeen months together.

Pam had a little boy six years old. This was unfortunate, but it was becoming increasingly difficult to find women my age who didn't have children. I had no experience of children, no feeling or affinity for them, no desire to have any. I had never owned a pet. In the fifteen years that I had been an adult, I had never once thought about having children. I was certain that progeny was something I could live happily without all my days. If I wanted heirs, I'd put them on. But I was a 32-year old student with no money, and I was short. I had enough going against me. If I ruled out single women with children as potential sweethearts the game would become even more difficult. Besides, I liked Pam. Holding her family status against her wasn't going to get me anywhere, and it would be rather wicked of me besides.

By now I was beginning to suspect that I was destined to break up with every woman I fell in love with. I loved falling in love, but in every case it was just a matter of time. I had seen no great models of relationships in my life. I hadn't met a couple who didn't hate each other after five or ten years, or sooner. The divorce rate was approaching fifty per cent. Those who stayed together had horrible relationships, utterly sickening. It seemed to me that people only stayed together for children, or for business interests, and for no other good reason. Commitment in a relationship seemed to me to be nothing more than dishonesty and laziness. In my own experience it was only a matter of a few months, or even a few weeks, before a woman exhibited the craziness that would eventually drive me away. The romantic notion that there was someone special for everyone, the right man or Ms. Right, was clearly absurd. I knew I would never be able to live my entire life with one woman. In my early thirties I was averaging about a year and a half per relationship. I felt that my having just one at a time might be the best anyone could hope for.

As long as I was able to have good sex with a woman, and lots of it, I would be able to put up with the nesting, the useless home improvement projects, the jam-making, the garden parties, the endless shopping, the accessorizing, the empty vanities and patent absurdities of material living, the vicious and unnerving mood swings, the cauldron of natural cruelty specifically formulated to extinguish my peace of mind, the waste and depletion of energy in constant checking-in and wallowing in emotional silliness, the perpetual revisiting of old gaffes, boxed in by judgment and criticism, having to treat every trifle seriously in order not to appear insensitive, the contradictory and quarrelsome opinions fogging the quiet calm of reasonable, everyday expectation with the poison of mindless irrationality, often before breakfast. In all my life I never found a woman who wanted to meditate, rarely met one who could stand to see a man happy. Mind you, I wasn't looking very hard. I was hungry, and I fed myself with the food I found at hand. When the talk turned to marriage or the flow of sex was reduced, I became a lot less interested in monogamous female company. A woman who won't have sex with you is an investment yielding little interest. Every relationship I had was a relationship with my own clinging desires.

My sins against womankind are the result of the tension between my unwillingness to ally myself with it and my inability to stay away. I won't speculate on the direction those sins might have taken had I been more willing to throw in with their lot. How had I lived alongside women for so long and knew so little about them? My education in these matters has been long and painful and continues to this day. The faults and failings in this crucial area of my life, so important, have been a scandal, and it is embarrassing to me, as it should be, to state them here so plainly. But why else have I come this far?

When I hesitated to exert any effort to have a relationship with the adorable Laverne in the fall of 1978, I was thinking there was no point in wooing her because I would have to leave her anyway. I was applying to SRF in California to become a yogi-monk. All those old daydreams of easy religious living had now been put painfully to rest. I loved women and physical intimacy, as well as emotional intimacy, as long as it was emotion of the comfortable kind, not the disturbing kind. So I stopped thinking and worrying about failure with women, which I now viewed as inevitable, and focussed instead on the joyful aspects of new relationships. I knew now that I would part with every woman I met, if only because I never wanted to have children, and there was nothing to be done about it. If I wanted to have relationships, I would have to meet new women, since new relationships were the only kind I could tolerate. I would have to woo. And besides, what better time or place is there to have lots of sex than when you're in college? I mean, c'mon.

Pam rented a small, old house not far from the U of A campus, and she had a business that ran itself. She owned a daycare centre in a space she leased at a public school in a low-income area of Edmonton. After she started this enterprise, she decided to go back to school, and she hired someone to run the daycare for her. Her personal income from the business was therefore minimal, but the daycare was there for her to take up again if she felt like it, or if it became necessary. We had a couple of delicious weeks together before I moved to Medicine Hat, and we made plans to visit over the summer.

I had cousins in Medicine Hat, and I was able to connect with two of them. When I first arrived, I slept on Arnold's floor for a few nights, until I found an apartment. Arnold was a year older than I, and we had spent a lot of time together when we were young. As a child, I had twenty-five cousins on my father's side, the Hansens, twenty-seven including my sister and me.

My father's father's parents were born in Norway before Canada became a country, and they died there in 1943 and 1950, both just over eighty years old. My grandfather John and four of his brothers, George, Hans, Helmer, and Norvald, left their home in Fluberg, eighty miles north of Oslo, not far from Lillehammer, to settle in Canada. Hans changed his mind about life on the Canadian prairies and went back to Norway.

Of my great-grandparents' eight living children, then, four of the brothers spent their lives in Canada, and two brothers and two sisters in Norway. John's youngest sister was three years old when he left home at twenty-one. One day, not long ago, I was talking to my father about those early days. He said, more or less, "Can you imagine that little girl, my dad's sister, my aunt Mina? She was three years old when he left home in 1914. She stood on the platform in that little village in Norway, two or three times over her childhood years, and watched five of her brothers get on the train and leave home. When she was three, three of her brothers were still young, seven and nine and eleven years old, but the other three were old enough to be her father. These were the boys and men she had known all her young life. They were her *brothers*, the boys who provoked her and the men who protected her. They were more than half of her family. My God, it must have broken her heart to see them go." In 1975, in Norway, my father finally met his Uncle Hans, the one who went back, and his Aunts Anna and Mina, and his Uncle Oskar, and all of his other cousins and their children.

Before coming to Canada, John went first to the United States. For him it was a once in a lifetime journey. He never set foot in Europe again, not once. When he talked about Norway, he always called it the Old Country.

John married Sophia Abrahamson in 1916, in Kansas, the day before his twenty-third birthday, and within the week they moved to southern Alberta to homestead. John's brother Helmer married Sophia's sister Emma, and they joined John and Sophie near Brooks, Alberta, in the County of Newell. Other members of Sophia's family settled in the area, her brother and parents. It was a place where only a few years earlier the Blackfoot and the Crow had hunted bison. Brooks is in an area of thousands of square miles of semi-arid, treeless steppe called Palliser's Triangle, the driest part of the Canadian prairies, surveyed by John Palliser in the 1850s. His opinion was that it was too dry to be farmed, and it remained sparsely populated for the next fifty years. The mixed and shortgrass prairie supported cattle for a time, but it was soon overgrazed.

It was later determined that the soil of Palliser's Triangle was indeed rich and would likely support the growing of wheat if it could be treed and irrigated. Enter, just before World War I, the Fourth Duke of Sutherland, Cromartie Sutherland-Leveson-Gower. In addition to being a duke, he was somehow also a marquess, twice an earl, a viscount, a lord, and a baron. He was a man of enormous wealth, the second-largest private landowner in Europe. Only the Czar of Russia owned more land. Late in his life, he lost confidence in the viability of his vast family estates in Britain and Europe, 1.5 million acres, and he began disposing of his properties in Britain, transferring his wealth to Canada.

Cromartie, His Grace, was a major shareholder in the CPR, and he became the leading investor in irrigation agriculture in southern Alberta. He bought ten square miles of land for himself, 7,000 acres, just east of Brooks, along with buildings, equipment, and cattle in the thousands. The CPR had received 25 million acres from the crown in land grants in partial payment for building the railway, and without settlers it was useless to them. They had hoped that the West would be populated immediately upon the opening of the railway, but much of this land had lain idle for a generation.

Starting in 1904, the CPR began creating irrigation systems along the Bow River. Downstream from the Bassano Dam, the Eastern Irrigation District was established to water the farms of southeastern Alberta. The Duke brought thirty families from England and Scotland to colonize his land, and the CPR built ready-made farms. In a few years most of the land was under crops. The CPR was now advertising in Great Britain not just for farmers, but for labourers and tradesmen, offering free passage to Brooks, Alberta.

The Duke visited his holdings in Canada only once, and he died young, in 1913. The spacious craftsmen-style bungalow that was built for him three miles east of Brooks, a comfortable home with a far more imposing interior than exterior, was then occupied by a series of managers who ran the colony profitably for another thirty years. The Fifth Duke of Sutherland, however, lost interest in his Canadian holdings. Doubly pressured by the Dust Bowl and the Great Depression, he sold the land in 1935. What remains is an Alberta Provincial Historic Resource in the form of the bungalow, and the unincorporated community of Millicent, named for the Duke's wife, and the village of Rosemary, named for their daughter. There is also the village of Duchess, the nearest settlement to my grandfather's farm, named for a daughter-in-law of Queen Victoria, and the hamlet of Patricia, named for the Duchess's daughter. All of these names are remembrances of British government in Canada and British investment in southeastern Alberta.

There also remain 285,000 acres of irrigated cropland fed by the Bow River through 2,500 miles of canals, pipes, and drains. There are also 35,000 acres of wetlands and 400,000 planted trees. In the early days crops were irrigated by flooding them, a tremendously labour-intensive practice. Now they are sprinkled, a system that requires only a third of the water for the same return in crops. Only four per cent of Alberta's farm lands are irrigated, and that four per cent produce twenty per cent of the agricultural product of the province. The CPR, the Duke, and the homesteaders, including my grandparents and great-aunts and uncles, built a garden in John Palliser's barren triangle, a thousand farms growing wheat for the last one hundred years.

My great-grandfather's name was Hans Hagen, but only one of his sons was named Hagen, and not the oldest one. All the others were Hansens, "sons of Hans." The girls, all four of them, were named Hagen. More research will be required before I understand why the names were divided up in that way. Last names in Scandinavia seem to be quite mutable.

So my great-grandfather had eight children, and my grandfather had ten, and my father's three Canadian uncles had another twenty-one between them. They were determined to be fruitful. Of my father's twenty-one cousins nearly all of them married and had families ranging in size from one to six kids.

My father's mother, Sophia Abrahamson, was born in Kansas in 1892. In 1942, her ancestry on both sides was traced by Dr. Theo Jorgenson, a professor of history at St. Olaf's College in Northfield, Minnesota, to an area of southern Norway called Kvinesdal, more specifically, West Narvestad, a wide spot on the Kvina River, at the foot of lumpy mountains. It is an area from which many people emigrated to the US in the mid-1800s. My great-great-great-great-great-grandparents, Soren and Anna, were farmers in Narvestad in 1700. Later, some of them became whalers. The handful of small mountain homesteads in that area date back to the period AD 700–1000, the pre-Christian Viking Age, thirteen hundred years ago, the last years of the Iron Age in Northern Europe. It is not unreasonable to imagine my amphibious Norse ancestors manning the oars of the shallow-draft boats that traded and raided, and sometimes settled, from the Baltic to the Black and Caspian Seas, from the North Sea to the Mediterranean, up the rivers of France and Germany and Russia, to Britain and Ireland, and across the North Atlantic Ocean to Iceland and Greenland and Canada. I can also imagine the short, difficult lives they must have led in the narrow, isolated valleys of the mountains of Norway, short and painful lives circumscribed by acute injury and illness and sudden death, a gut-wrenching diet and generations of steady poverty made occasionally worse by the capriciousness of events beyond their control or understanding. They would have lived in close relation with the land, the sea, the stars, the weather, and the seasons, skilled in a handful of arts and engineering without an inkling of the natural science that lay beneath them, the mathematics, physics, and biology that are now taught to children who couldn't survive for a week under the conditions their forebears endured for centuries. They lived not only before electricity, anesthetics, and antibiotics, but before aspirin, antihistamines, and antipsychotics. I wonder what they would have thought had they been able to see their pampered descendants living in the noisy and polluted twenty-first century, a thousand years in the future.

The family farm in the New World, the home quarter, was ten miles north of Brooks, Alberta, close to the village of Duchess. My grandmother's first eight children were born on the farm. My father was the last one. His younger brother and sister were born in the hospitals of Bassano and Brooks.

The farm was right next to an irrigation canal that we always just called "the ditch" and was referred to locally as the Hansen Ditch. No more than a hundred yards away from the back door of the farmhouse, through an open stand of tall trees, the muddy water ran through a culvert under a gravel road and then over a small concrete spillway. The tiny waterfall created a wide spot in the canal, a swimming hole, which could be entered by slipping down the bank or you could dive in from the spillway. The water was so brown you couldn't see more than a foot beneath the surface. The slow-moving canal water was never cold in summer, and when the air temperature reached eighty degrees Fahrenheit, or ninety, there was always a handful of bright-white kids in the dark brown water, like small dumplings in gravy. It wasn't quite a Huck Finn childhood, but thinking about it now I believe I did go shirtless and barefoot in sleeveless coveralls and a straw hat. My nose in summer was always burnt bright red and scabbed over. And like Tom Sawyer, I hated work more than I hated anything else.

In the winter we skated on the stock pond, and it was tolerable to minus twenty degrees Fahrenheit as long as the wind wasn't blowing. There were no hills for tobogganing.

It was a hundred and twenty miles from our house in Calgary to the farm, and we visited three or four times a year, often enough that the feeling of driving up the long, straight lane to the farmhouse, lined with light-green deciduous trees, with or without snow, and pulling the car to a stop behind the house, is as memorable to me as anything from my childhood.

The farmhouse had two bedrooms on the main floor and two on the upper, to be shared by two adults, six boys, and four girls. By the time I came along, none of my aunts and uncles was still living on the farm, and one of the bedrooms on the main floor was used as a dining room. The upstairs bedrooms were still used for kids though, the constantly visiting cousins, one for the girls and one for the boys.

The house was heated with coal until the mid-1960s when the coal stove in the living room was replaced by a television. The only heat on the upper floor came through a round, wrought iron grill in the ceiling of the living room that allowed the warm air to communicate with the little bodies that had been sent to their beds in the rooms above. It was also a perfect spy hole for another kind of communication, eavesdropping on the grown-ups.

My grandmother baked twenty loaves of white bread a week in a coal-fired oven when her kids were at home. There were up to a dozen people at her table, infants to adults, three times a day for twenty years, and she was either pregnant or nursing for two decades. In the 1960s, on a holiday evening, at Christmas or Easter, or in the summer, there might be twenty people in the house, kids and grandkids. I rarely saw my grandmother sitting down and if I did, she was knitting mitts and scarves.

There was no indoor plumbing, which meant a long trip to the outhouse, daunting in winter. Who can go when it's twenty below? Water was drawn in a bucket from a cistern covered with a square plywood lid, just outside the back door. When I visited as a child, I was drafted to bring buckets of coal up the short, steep stairs from the small basement, in addition to water from the well, but not until I was older. No one wanted a city kid down the well.

When we visited the farm, there were often other aunts and uncles and cousins converged on the homestead, sometimes by design, sometimes by accident, and I knew my twenty-five cousins well. At the age of ten, I was exactly the average age and also the median. Thirteen of the cousins, starting with my sister, were older, and thirteen were younger. In 1963, we ranged in age from one to twenty-two with only one more cousin to come. Some of them were already teenagers and grown-ups, and I went to ten weddings as a child. The youngest ones were babies. Many were around my own age, eighteen of us from five to fifteen. Gail, Darlene, Jeannie, Bob, Dianne, Dale, Linda, Arnold, me, Sheryl, Brian, Jim, Jack, Carl, Eric, Connie, Joan, and Brad. We had everything in common, except that some of us were country cousins and some of us were city cousins, a source of mild rivalry and amusement.

There were Hansen family reunions every summer, outdoor potluck picnics, alternating one year in Brooks and the next year in Calgary. It was always a hot day, and we visited and ate and played baseball. The kids wandered off in groups to explore the surrounding area. The men sat together and talked about work and money and politics, and the women gathered separately and talked about people, especially their children. I wandered back and forth between them and tired quickly and equally of their conversation. Then the men drank beer, chewed snus, and played stook while the women cleaned up and waited for the men to finish so they could go home. The Hansen men were ever gamblers, a gene I didn't inherit. I went to every family reunion until 1974 when I moved to British Columbia. It's a long way from Victoria to Brooks, and it takes time and money to make the journey, two things I rarely had together. In my long years of vague wandering I often had time, but no money, and when I had money, rarely, there was no time. For a few years in the nineties I had both commodities, but by then it had been so long since I had seen anyone on that side of my family I had lost touch with nearly everyone, and I had a refractory wife who refused to go. She wanted nothing to do with my family, especially a family of unreconstructed chain-smokers living in the dirty little hamlets, however rich, of the fly-over province of Alberta. She was from Ontario.

My grandparents sold the farm in 1969. Four years later, at the age of eighty, my grandfather slipped on ice and died of complications from the fall. My grandmother outlived him by seventeen years. By the summer of 1986, when I moved to Medicine Hat to work at the cheese plant, I hadn't set foot in Brooks in a dozen years. I probably hadn't seen my cousin Arnold in all that time.

Arnold worked hard in the oil industry where he had become fat and successful and divorced. He had a new house in a new suburb, and he had plenty of room to let me stay while I looked for an apartment for the summer. I had another cousin in the city as well. Sheryl had lived most of her young life in Red Deer but was now teaching in Medicine Hat. She was out of town when I arrived. I found a basement suite in a house, but the young renters upstairs were so noisy when they came home from their jobs at one o'clock in the morning, I was forced to move out in only three weeks. I was exhausted at work, and I couldn't afford to be. My employer had problems that he expected me to investigate and solve with energy and diligence, every day.

When Sheryl was back in town, she told me she was leaving again for the rest of the summer and she wanted to sublet her place to me, only two blocks from my noisy apartment. She also had a basement suite, but it was fully furnished, and her upstairs neighbour, also a teacher, would be gone for most of the summer as well. I was thus well accommodated until the end of August.

My grandmother was living in Brooks in a home for seniors. I had last seen her four years earlier at her ninetieth birthday party just before leaving for Japan. In Medicine Hat, sixty-seven miles from Brooks, I was as close to the place of my birth as I had been for many years, and as close as I was ever going to get again. I told my parents I would go see her. My mother said, "Take her out for a drive. She loves to get out of the home."

On a hot summer Sunday after a weekend debauch, driving home from Calgary or Edmonton, I stopped in Brooks and found my grandmother's lodge. When I went to her room, she wasn't there, but I turned and saw her walking slowly towards me down the hallway, holding on to the rail, coming back from lunch. She was ninety-three and very frail. We chatted awhile in her room. I had to tell her a couple of times that I was "Bobby's boy." Her short-term memory was impaired, and she would repeat herself after only a few minutes. I think she thought I was getting ready to leave, but I said, "Grandma, do you want to go out for a drive?" She practically sparkled. "Oh, yes."

I told her I wanted to drive by the farm, and she agreed to that. I hadn't seen the farm in more than fifteen years, but I knew where it was. It was a simple route from Brooks. North, a little west, and north again, a drive of ten miles that I had made a hundred times as a child. When we reached the farm, I stopped on the gravel road just before the ditch and gazed at the long entry lane lined with trees, and at the stand of tall trees next to the irrigation canal. The old house was still there. My grandmother looked at the house and the farm. She said, "That's not it."

I said gently, "Oh, I think it is, Grandma."

She said, "No. No, that's not it." But I knew it was.

I asked her how they managed to survive when they first arrived in the area during the First World War, and she told me they worked for farmers who were already established as well as planting the home quarter. I asked her about the Dirty Thirties, so many years of so little income, and so many kids. She said they always had the garden, and chickens and eggs, and they slaughtered a steer in the fall. Her memory of those days, fifty and sixty years earlier, was keen and detailed, but she couldn't remember what anyone had said just a few minutes ago. And I think her eyesight was also very poor by now.

We drove into Duchess to see if my aunt Shirley, my dad's youngest sibling, and her husband, my uncle Fred, were home, but no one answered the door. I had never been to their house in Duchess, but between my grandmother and me, we thought we had the right place. Back in Brooks I called another aunt and uncle, Gordon and Ethel. They were home, and they invited us over for dinner. In front of their house, I opened the passenger door of my giant New Yorker to help my grandmother out. I turned away from her for a second to lock the door, and when I turned back around I found she was falling over straight backwards, stiff from the heels. She was already at an angle of forty degrees acute to the vertical, but I stuck out an arm, arrested her fall, and gently put her upright again. She was as light as a feather. She had on a flowered dress, and when it was mentioned at dinner I asked her when she had bought it. She said, "This? I bought this twenty years ago." I said, "So you bought it when you were seventy-three." It seemed an unimaginable age. She was sixty-one years old when I was born, and she died twenty-four years ago, in 1990, four years after I saw her at her seniors' residence in Brooks, which was the last time. And now I am sixty-one years old.

We had spent the afternoon and early evening together, and when I took her home to her little room at the lodge, just before I left she said, "And you're Bobby's boy?" I never saw her again. I was living in Victoria when she died, going to school, as always in those days, and I had no time or money to go to the funeral. I have no quarrel with death, but I'm not big on funerals.

While I was staying at Arnold's place, we talked a lot and drank beer and vodka in the evenings, catching up on the intervening years. He had turned into a cranky old redneck, but we had enough good memories to carry us through. His father, my dad's older brother Billy, farmed south of Medicine Hat in the 1960s near a little place, a hamlet, called Seven Persons. My Uncle Billy and Aunt Ruth and their five kids themselves constituted seven persons but not the titular seven. My sister and I were great friends with the two older cousins, Dianne and Arnold, and we spent time on their hot, dry farm in the summers, sleeping on the unbearably hot second floor of the small farmhouse, seven kids in two bedrooms. Dianne was the only girl, and she was delighted when my sister, Linda, would come to stay. Her four younger brothers were a handful. And Linda loved to visit. Dianne had a horse.

My Uncle Billy, he was always Billy, eventually became a successful farmer, but money was tight in the '60s. Kids' birthdays were modest events.

There was only one bedroom on the main floor, for the grown-ups. One day I and a couple of the little cousins were in the bedroom. It had two doors, one onto the kitchen and one onto the small front hallway, so it was used as a shortcut and throughway. My aunt came in from the kitchen and said, "Alright, you boys, get out of here. I've got to change my blouse." Carl, the second youngest, about ten years old, replied, "It's okay, Mom, we won't laugh." Then we all ducked and ran.

There was no running water. Baths were taken in a portable tub in the kitchen with water heated on the stove. My country cousins were a deal stronger than I was from fetching buckets of water from the hand pump fifty yards from the house. The kids fed the animals and milked the cows early in the morning and cranked the separator by hand. Arnold was barely thirteen, but he helped his father tune the combine, and he drove the grain truck, slowly, next to the combine as it swathed the grain in the fields. At the age of twelve and thirteen, the kids were driving tractors and the family car. The boys stacked bales of hay all day. These farm kids had a much more immediate understanding of the importance of their contribution to the family. They were an essential part of it. In Calgary I complained about my birthday and Christmas presents. Why didn't we have more money? My father criticized me endlessly about the way I polished his shoes. And I really tried! Who cared about shoe polish, anyway? Polish you own damn shoes if you don't like it. My inept way of mowing the lawn and shovelling snow were constant sources of aggravation to his persnickety standards. I was ten years old. How good at it could I be? His favourite topic of conversation, when he spoke to me at all, was a long list of my shortcomings. Who cared about cutting grass you couldn't eat? Compared with farm life how irrelevant was a fucking lawn? To this day I despise yard work.

One day, the cousins walked us a mile or two across the prairie to a small railway trestle, and we climbed up the giant, dark-brown wooden beams, perched ourselves under the tracks, and waited for the train. When it roared overhead the dusty trestle, its beams reeking of coal tar creosote heated by the sun, shook and rattled, and we hung on for dear life and laughed and screamed our lungs out. On Saturday night, we went with Dianne and her older boyfriend to the drive-in movies in Medicine Hat and afterwards parked the car in the country under the black velvet night and the myriad stars listening to *Brown Eyed Girl* on the radio. It was the summer of 1967.

Arnold and I had decided, at the age of twelve, that we would be scientists when we grew up. Now I was doing a degree in science, but Arnold wasn't impressed. He worked in the oil patch, and he was smart and self-educated. He had no respect for the newly minted engineers the company sent out to him to be taught things in the field he had figured out for himself and had known for a decade. He was one of those guys we all meet in the workplace, an angry man who thinks he is the only person left on the face of the earth putting in an honest day's work. Everyone else is a slacker, a lazy, useless, thieving bureaucrat, an artist, or a fag. He might have just been in a bad mood, but I was starting to sense a pattern. He told me a couple of great stories, though, both to do with our shared family name.

Arnold was divorced, and he had a new girlfriend who lived in Lethbridge, a Canadian woman of Japanese ancestry. I never met her. She may have been a descendant of Japanese Canadians interned during World War II, some of whom were sent to southern Alberta to work in the sugar beet fields. She was a teacher, and Arnold warned me strongly about getting involved with a teacher. He said he had never seen a whinier bunch of complainers in all his life. He couldn't stand to be around them. I should have paid more heed. He and his girlfriend were vacationing in Europe. In Copenhagen, they neglected to book a hotel in advance, and after a long day they found themselves in the unfortunate position of looking for a room without reservations. Standing exhausted at the front desk of the first hotel they entered, the clerk informed them that without reservations there was no room at the inn, nor was there likely to be any nearby. He did, however, offer to phone around to other hotels on their behalf. He asked my cousin for his name. On hearing the words "Arnie Hansen," he put the phone down. He said, "You know, Mr. Hansen, I just remembered our manager is out of town for a couple of days. You can have his suite, no extra charge. Welcome to Copenhagen." They speak very good English in Denmark.

The fine old Hansen name didn't always work in Arnold's favour in Scandinavia. They boarded a small cruise ship somewhere in Norway for a short journey around the fjords. He told me he was pretty disappointed with their cabin when they finally found it. It was small and hot and noisy, buried in the bowels of the ship. His opinion was that he had paid a lot of money and received very little in return. This couldn't be right. They fled the cabin for the fresh air of the decks and found themselves having a cocktail in conversation with an English-speaking Norwegian woman who was in charge of a very old man. She explained that he was her grandfather and she was accompanying him on the first trip he had ever taken in his life, the first time he had ever been away from home. The old fellow spoke to his granddaughter in Norwegian and she translated. "Oh, he is going on about his cabin. He is very impressed about it. He says it is much nicer than he expected. He is so proud. Am I using this word, 'proud'? *Ja, ja, Bestepappa*! *Ja, ja*! And now he says he thinks, too, it is very cheap." Arnold said, "What's your grandfather's name, by the way?" The woman replied, "Arnie Hansen." My cousin Arnold muttered an involuntary "Son of a bitch," but to his everlasting credit he said no more about it.

I was now the Quality Control Supervisor at the Alpha Milk Company cheese manufacturing plant on Industrial Avenue in Medicine Hat. Until recently, it had been a meat packing plant and was now just converted. Production had begun, but there was, as yet, no full-time technician in the lab. The lab supervisor from the Lethbridge plant, a smart and friendly young Asian woman, came to Medicine Hat, stayed for a week, and got me sorted out on the routine. There were two dozen tests I had to perform regularly at various stages of the production process, and it kept me running all day, taking samples at specific times in different places, juggling supplies and procedures and timing. When things didn't go right on the floor, other investigations and tests were required.

Many of the employees at the new plant were old Alpha Company hands who had agreed to move to Medicine Hat from vanishing jobs in Red Deer, so although the plant was new a lot of the staff already knew each other. As a new person, a university summer student, therefore already suspect, I had to insert myself carefully into the organization, as well as assert myself when it came to educating my fellow workers about quality control techniques and protocols, for example, not using the lab as a smoking room.

There were two 7,000-litre vats on the tiled manufacturing floor, enormous storage tanks, a pasteurizer and separator, presses and cutters, and a kilometre or two of pipes, all stainless steel, all thoroughly washed every night. The control panel for much of the engineering equipment had a plastic plaque on it that read *Computor*. The packaging department was in the basement.

There was to be a Saturday Open House in celebration of the opening of the new plant, and we scrubbed the place top to bottom and manned our stations to give talks and demonstrations to the public. I set up a couple of small tests to show groups of touring children what it was I did in the laboratory. "Does anyone know what bacteria are? Well, almost all of them are harmless, but some are quite good. Some of them make cheese for us. But a few are quite bad. My job is to make sure we keep the good ones working for us and the bad ones out!" Then they all got an ice cream treat, and the next batch trooped in.

The staff party afterwards was where we all really got to know each other. A girl from the packaging department jumped off my lap when she saw her husband coming into the bar looking for her at one o'clock in the morning. Fortunately, he was madder at her than he was at me. It took an hour to find my car the next morning. And the rest of the summer went on swimmingly.

I was always tired at work. I slept for forty minutes every day at noon in the back of my car in the parking lot until it got too hot. I stopped at the Silver Buckle strip bar almost daily after work. It was on the way home. Then I exercised on a mini-trampoline and watched rented videos. I mowed Arnold's lawn when he was away on holidays. I ate rather poorly, drank rather excessively, gained fifteen pounds, again, and was on the road every weekend to Regina or Edmonton or Calgary to get laid. Pam was disappointed when she discovered she was sharing me with Karen, and she became scarce later in the summer.

Driving home from Edmonton one weekend, I found myself in Sedgewick for a little visit one Sunday, and the day wore away. I was exhausted from this and that, and I lingered too long, reluctant to be on the road again even in my huge, comfortable car. I still had two hundred and fifty miles to drive to get home to Medicine Hat, and work to face in the morning. I took Highway 41 for the first time, the Buffalo Trail. It runs four hundred and twenty-five miles south just inside the Alberta border with Saskatchewan, from the little town of La Corey, near Cold Lake, all the way to the US border, passing close by Medicine Hat. It was only twenty miles longer than the shortest route home, and who can resist a new road?

Unfortunately, the northern half was in poor shape, and it was slow and rough going. Farther south was easier driving, and close to the Red Deer and South Saskatchewan River crossings the evening sky was transformed into a vision, Blake to the west, El Greco to the east. I fancied I could see a faint image of the sawtooth horizon of the Rocky Mountains in the west, two hundred miles away. The setting sun was nowhere to be seen, but the entire western horizon, north and south for hundreds of miles, was bathed in a preternatural effulgence, a brilliant and radiant splendour, a light so heaven-filled it would rouse the soul of a dead man. To my left, in the east, very close, uncomfortably close, was a wall of black cloud from the ground to the sky, running north and south, again, for hundreds of miles, constantly streaked with lightning strikes. I watched it closely and uneasily trying to determine its direction of travel. I still had some distance to go, and I couldn't imagine driving through any part of that dense and pitch-black electric storm. My head swivelled to the right and left for many miles, from the bright light of the western horizon to the coal-black wall of cloud to the east. It was a shining moment, as close to a meteorological religious experience as you ever need to get. I knew I was blessed to have seen such a thing. I hardly saw another car all day. If I had been a Native American of the past, or even a prairie pioneer living in a sod hut, standing two-footed on the earth, instead of driving a Chrysler New Yorker at sixty miles an hour on cruise control, I might have fallen to my knees and wept at the terrible beauty of the world all around me.

I loved cruise control. I had never had it before in any of my old cars. The roads in Alberta and Saskatchewan can be very straight, and for very long distances. There are only a couple of bends in the road from Medicine Hat to Regina, a road I drove many times over the summer. I often left on a Friday afternoon right after work. Once outside the city and travelling at speed, I would set the cruise control for about seventy-five miles an hour, turn sideways and put my feet up on the long bench seat and command the power steering with minute movements of one finger. After about a hundred and twenty miles of straight road, there was a curve just before entering Swift Current, affectionately known as Rapid Raisin, and I would lower my legs once more into the foot well, for safety's sake. I stopped at McDonald's in Swift Current for take-out supper and dined on the four basic food groups, fish burger, French fries, milkshake, and coffee. The coffee would see me through to the next curve, another hundred miles down the highway at Moose Jaw. It was the only time I ever ate at McDonald's. They were giving away little toys that summer, and I gave them to Devon when I got to Regina. Devon, Karen's son, was five years old. I was thirty-two. We had some things in common.

I enjoyed that summer, but I had a full-time job seeking pleasure, so it was doubly hard work having a full-time job in a lab, too, where what I learned, mostly, was how to pour really strong acid out of really big bottles, *really* carefully. I learned other things as well. One day, by making a bad decision, and causing a potentially expensive problem, I discovered there were discrepancies in the sensitivities of various common methods of testing for antibiotics in milk. I panicked a bit at first, but through a neat trick I managed to dodge the bullet of my own mistake and avoid giving the company any cause for financial concern. Alpha's director of lab operations instructed me to investigate the matter further. I set up a blind testing scheme and sent samples off to different labs. The results of the various tests demonstrated a need for further investigations into testing standards, etc, etc, and everybody thought I was pretty smart. I got calls from a couple of lab directors around the province, thanking me for spotting the problem. It was a little victory snatched from the jaws of my own stupidity. For a couple of days, I was a boy genius. Lucky is what I was.

The Alberta Department of Agriculture offered a five-hundred dollar competitive bursary to Food Science students who submitted an acceptable written report describing and analyzing issues encountered in summer employment in the food industry. Five hundred dollars was just enough to motivate me, and for purely mercenary reasons I decided to submit a report. I laboured away at it for a week, and typed it all out one Saturday on a rented electric typewriter. It was a good educational experience. I dug into the workings of the business and the history of the industry and deepened my understanding of them both. I knew it was a good report. After a very long day of typing, utterly satisfied with myself, I walked joyfully downtown to see a new movie. It was *Top Gun*. I ate popcorn in the balcony and sang "Danger Zone" along with Kenny Loggins.

At the end of August, the boys on the production floor gave me a plaque with all of our names engraved on it. They said at first they were going to get me a bottle of booze, but they changed their minds. They knew I would just drink it and forget who they all were. I was sent off from my summer job at the Alpha Milk Company generally considered by all to be a fine fellow with a bright future ahead of me.

21 The Pursued, the Pursuing, the Busy, and the Tired

I stopped in Sedgewick on my way back to Edmonton to surrender the New Yorker to my father, with great sadness and gratitude, and found a letter waiting for me. It was from the University of Alberta, and it was very cryptic, nothing but a single small sheet of paper, too small for the envelope, a sort of laundry ticket with "$2,000.00" typed onto it and then "Stetson Scholarship in Agriculture," and not another word. I howled with delight when I finally concluded it had to be an award notice for a scholarship, one I hadn't even applied for, the sweetest kind.

I submitted my Bursary Report to the Food Science Department, and a week later both the administrative officer and the head of the department told me it was the best report they had read in the eight years the program had been running.

It had never occurred to me that getting A's in school was worth money. Now, starting my fourth year, I realized I must never let scholarship money go unpursued. I had straight A's, a dial tone straight to the ears and hearts of university bureaucrats working in awards offices. In the last year of my first university degree, I received four scholarships totalling $4,500, a magnificent sum in 1986, as much as a student loan and one I didn't have to pay back. I earnestly believed I deserved one other scholarship as well, but it went to the woman who got the summer job with the execrable Mikey at Labatt's Brewery. Her summer salary was considerably higher than mine, and it had afforded her much greater savings than I had managed to sock away, although some of that failure may have been my own fault. She didn't need the scholarship money as much as I did. The departmental administrative officer tried to console me. He said, "We couldn't give *all* of them to you."

I even received a warm letter of congratulations on my many awards from my local MP, thanks I'm sure to his alert staff. Arnold Malone was a Professional Agrologist, an agricultural educator, and a twenty-year Progressive Conservative parliamentarian. Unfortunately, for him, he laboured in a political era dominated by the Liberals, and he was never a cabinet minister. In those days no one could outshine the folksy and flamboyant

Ontario farmer Eugene Whelan as Minister of Agriculture. He was no relation to Ed Whalen, the folksy and flamboyant Calgary sportscaster mentioned briefly, but conspicuously, in Volume 1 of these many memoirs.

I received a rare scholarship from the Institute of Food Technologists in the United States. I was the only Canadian so honoured in 1986, and the first ever at U of A. My food chemistry professor had surprised me and submitted the application on my behalf. My picture, cheek by jowl with those of many other students, was printed in IFT's monthly journal. As a result of this exposure, I received at least a couple of calls from universities in the US recruiting me for postgraduate work, at Duke and Michigan.

I applied for and was awarded a Postgraduate Scholarship from the Natural Sciences and Engineering Research Council of Canada, an NSERC Scholarship, very fancy indeed. NSERCs are highly prized. The awards are made to individuals, and they can be used at any university. You show up at the door, wherever you want to go, with money in your hand.

I was now the Golden Boy of the department. Focussed activity finds its footing everywhere, and the result is confidence. Or over-confidence.

I was asked to join, or at least try out for, the Dairy Judging Team, a small group of senior students that travels annually to dairy judging competitions held in different cities, usually in the US. I didn't have time to do the training, and it was a lot of unpaid work other than the trip itself, so I declined. When our team came back from the final competition in Washington, DC, one of them, a little redneck girl, said, "I have never seen so many Negroes in my life!"

To my professor of food engineering, when he congratulated me on my many recent successes, I laughed and quoted Merrick, or Vidal, or Rochefoucauld. "It is not enough that I succeed. Others must fail."

I was as surprised as anyone by the events of the last year or so. One day at my parents' house, I said, "I seem to be a success story waiting to happen." I was reluctantly, but not cautiously, optimistic. The spirit was upon me. I began to envision highly coloured fruit within my grasp. My father's pithy observation was, "You don't have to make it big. You just have to make it." No need to charge through life. Walking will get you to the end. He had seen it all before, and for both our sakes he didn't want me showing up at his door again, broke.

A year earlier, entering U of A, I had had to take yet another English qualifying exam. I walked across the quad to the exam room pumping myself up with incantations of, "You're bright! You're clever! You have something to say about everything!" Repeat. Happily, one of the subjects was something dear to my heart. "Should beauty pageants be abolished? Discuss." Ah, the treatment of women as objects in society. Dear reader, given certain events bared, certain patterns revealed, in the last eight hundred and fifty pages, you might wonder at my attraction to, or interest in, this subject, my motivation or sincerity or competence to comment. I was fascinated by women as objects, of course. They formed fifty per cent of my external environment and ninety per cent of my internal landscape. I couldn't get them out of my head. I couldn't help but be fascinated by women as objects, and as people, and as persons, and as a social group, and as an idea, and as spiritual beings. I was leery of imagining or discussing, never mind pronouncing on, women's role in life and society, but no more than I was about the role of men in life and society. I had no idea how to present myself usefully, or respectfully, or appealingly overall, to women as individuals, or as a category of human beings, or what the struggle for power between men and women meant historically or politically or academically, but I had read a little.

When I was driving a taxi in Calgary, broke and depressed in the fall two years earlier, I had special-ordered *The Woman's Encyclopedia of Myths and Secrets* by Barbara G. Walker. It is an astonishing work, not without its critics, of eleven hundred pages, twenty-five years in preparation, containing over thirteen hundred entries, a unique and comprehensive sourcebook focussing on women in mythology, anthropology, religion, and sexuality. I read it constantly sitting in my underused taxi.

God knows I loved beautiful women. I was a slave to physical lust my whole life long, tortured and self-tortured, but I knew which parts of my obsessions were wrong and which were not. This knowledge didn't always lead me into paths of righteous, or even polite, behaviour, but I did know the difference. In a glib, mildly provocative style, a style you might recognize today, I filled the pages of the English qualifying exam booklet with a knowledgeable, sincere, indignant, and skillful condemnation of beauty pageants. When I was finished, I handed it to the invigilator and smiled. I said, "F for Flawless," and flounced out the door. I checked the Pass/Fail grades posted a few days later, and found I had passed the test.

It was possible to have your paper reviewed in person by one of the many graduate students of English who were employed to mark them. I went to the trouble of booking an appointment. The people who utilized this service were usually those who had failed to pass the exam and were in need of corrective coaching. I was simply curious. The articulate, slightly pudgy English major with glasses and a beard sitting across from me leafed through my paper and pointed out a couple of things that had been circled by the person who graded it. He said they were transition passages that would normally require a more formal approach in academic writing, but they were hardly serious matters. He then began reading quietly from the beginning. As he progressed he muttered, "Oh, yes. This is good. Oh, yeah, this is quite good. Oh, very good." I noticed there was an "S" at the top of the front page, handwritten and circled in red ink. I asked him about it. He said, "Oh, right, that's not an official mark or anything. It's just something some of us scribble when we come across a good paper. 'S' stands for, quite informally, mind you, 'Superior.'"

Here was the air that sang my praise, but on the summit of fortune one abides not long.

I was still no fan of writing papers. I found writing lab reports to be quite enough. But I was the obvious candidate to compete in a nationwide food science essay contest, an event scheduled to be held at exactly the same time, adjusted for Canada's six time zones, at universities across the country. I knew the woman who had won the competition the year before. She was my lab partner in genetics, a U of A student who had done the Food Science Department proud and brought the prize home. She told me the only reason she won was because she had, in an amazing coincidence, written a paper on that year's assigned topic just a few weeks before the competition. At the appointed time she showed up, sat down, was amazed to see that the subject was one fresh in her mind, decided it wasn't necessary to recuse herself on those grounds, and simply rewrote her previous paper from memory. I, however, showed up at the department on a deserted Saturday and sat for three hours writing wildly about a topic I knew nothing about, food irradiation. It was a hot topic then, but I knew more about beauty pageants than food irradiation. When I was done it was a spill event as bad as Chernobyl. Not "F for Flawless," but "FA for Fucking Awful." I apologized to the administrative officer for letting the department down. He told me to think nothing of it. I ate my humble pie, humbly, and went back to my daily duties.

On cold winter nights, I spent hours in the library poring over university catalogues from around the world and filling out applications with pen and ink. I was going to graduate, something that had never happened before in all my years of study. What on earth would I do after that? I was genuinely interested in the sexy science of fermentation as a possible area of further study. Fermentation was an old friend to the human race, 7,000 years old in food production, and was making new friends in the twentieth century in pharmaceuticals and biotechnology. It seemed a respectable alternative to chemistry. It was real science with a glass of wine or a vaccine or a vitamin to your credit at the end of the day. Most of the entry-level employment opportunities, scant as they were, especially in Canada, were in brewing and winemaking, quality control jobs babysitting engineering processes already well established. If, however, you could put in a mildly impressive couple of years in Master's level research, there was always the chance that an American brewery, or even a Canadian one, would recruit you right off campus at $80,000 a year, very good money in those days. This seemed like something I should investigate.

The University of British Columbia had a food science department with links to the fruit and winemaking industries in the Okanagan Valley. They had a research centre in Summerland, a great name for a town and a nice place to live. There were universities in the UK notable for their work in fermentation and brewing, the University of Birmingham, and Heriot-Watt University in Edinburgh. I applied for a Commonwealth Scholarship that would facilitate my going to universities just about anywhere in the fifty-three countries of the Commonwealth. Living in frozen Edmonton, I naturally began to fantasize about the University of the West Indies, formerly a college of the University of London, and their programs in sugar research. They were scattered around the Caribbean on little English-speaking "British" campuses. Once again I was daydreaming about island hopping in a tropical paradise, about sailboats and warm blue seas. I could take up cricket. Closer to home, but still international, there was viticulture and enology at the University of California Davis, an essential research partner in the California winemaking industry.

My application for a Commonwealth Scholarship was turned down. Brewing? Maybe not the noblest of research topics. I wasn't too surprised but just a little. I was on a roll after all. But I was still hopeful. The NSERC Scholarship appeared at first to be portable. I could use it in the US. UC Davis was happy to hear it. A Canadian who showed up with money in his pocket was a rare bird in those parts. But later, I received a letter from NSERC telling me in apologetic, but firm, tones that there had been an error. My scholarship was not internationally portable and could only be used at a university in Canada. Upon receiving this news, I went immediately to the Power Plant Pub, only a short walk from my dormitory residence, to have several drinks.

There was one other possibility that I felt I should investigate, very cautiously, the always tempting chimera of the MD degree, that implausible, fire-breathing monster. If you could get through one, the money to be made was spectacular, but the cost and the workload were outrageous. People who get straight A's can count on getting interviews at medical schools, if not admission, and I made my applications. As a U of A graduand, I got an immediate interview at U of A's Faculty of Medicine, before even writing the MCAT, the Medical College Admission Test, but the test would have to be taken eventually. In the summer, to prepare, I bought one of those thick, expensive, MCAT practice books on cheap newsprint, but when I finally removed its cellophane wrapping, reluctantly, and began examining the contents, I found I couldn't remember the first thing about the most basic topics in physics or biology, never mind math. I decided to ask myself four questions. Do I like to work hard? Do I like to get woken up in the middle of the night? Would I want to do a spinal tap right after breakfast? Do I really give a shit about other people's health? The answer to all of these questions was, "No, thank you!" The pre-med and medical students I had met were ambitious, aggressive, and often obnoxious. If you had an assignment that depended on your reading a particular article in the library and you found the journal was missing or the article torn from its pages, it was generally suspected, right or wrong, that a medical student was the miscreant responsible. I saw them dog-tired and asleep on their books in the library. I heard some of them slept overnight on cots in their labs. After four years of medical training, a group photo of a graduating class of doctors, still mostly male, looked like a test-tube rack of clones, arrogant, defensive, exhausted, and entitled. Not to mention their snippy starter wives. The phrase "medical men" had not long been out of use. This hardly seemed like a lifestyle I would be attracted to. I threw the MCAT practice book in the garbage and declined my interview at the U of A Faculty of Medicine. All of my other applications became null and void when the various schools I had applied to didn't receive my MCAT results. Seven years later I started working at the BC Ministry of Health and spent most of the next twelve years working with physicians. Some of them were as sweet as pie, but not all of them.

I had elected to live in Pembina Hall again because it was easy, a common motivation for me, but it lacked the novelty and warmth of the first year. I found far fewer simpatico souls there in the second year. The notion that it was a residence for *mature* students had been put quickly to rest from the beginning. The minimum age was twenty-one. Most of the residents were in their twenties, their young twenties. In my opinion the minimum age should have been thirty-one. Still, I had enjoyed easy and entertaining, only occasionally annoying, company for the eight months I was there in the winter of 1985–86. It was a daunting prospect now, however, to face another winter in Edmonton, in spite of the beautiful autumn colours and the ivy and the brick. In September 1986 I sat in my room looking out the window onto the quad and shook my head, wondering how I was going to get through another eight months of miserable deep-freeze temperatures.

If it's true that the best universities have real winters, then U of A was the best in North America. It was three hundred and fifty miles north of the US border, the most northerly campus in Canada, except for Athabasca University, but AU was brand new, tiny, and focussed on distance education. They had two graduates at their first convocation. Student enrollment at U of A was over 25,000.

It was a long walk of four or five blocks to our nutrition class at 7:45 in the morning, and for three long months, December, January, and February, we walked through snow and wind, or ice fog, under pitch black skies in minus 40-degree temperatures. At those icy depths the cold seeks by every opening to penetrate to the core of the body, the mind ceases to function at the higher levels, and you become nothing more than meat and chemicals and behaviours bent on survival. Limbs and extremities are expendable. They wrap tightly around the vital inner organs to protect them. The body hunches. Humidity control in the overheated buildings was poor or nonexistent and hovered around ten per cent for many months. Your skin, nails, eyes, nose, throat, and lungs were parched and desiccated, flaking, cracked, and bleeding. We were the freeze-dried mummies of Northern Alberta.

I had only a medium load left to finish my degree. I was taking three courses that fall with another four scheduled for January, computing, nutrition, more engineering, and a research project. I decided I had better try to keep busy or I might take up residence in the Power Plant Pub and hibernate there for the entire winter.

In early September I stumbled upon an opportunity to make some easy money, an offer to act as the designated driver for a stag party of Edmonton police officers. I found the job through a young man in the dormitory who had a brother or two on the force. My task was to drive people home from a party at a local country and western bar, in a passenger van, making as many trips as necessary to get everyone safely home. This sounded like a responsible, upstanding plan and job.

I showed up at the bar around 11:00 p.m. I hadn't been in a place like this since the night Woody and I drunkenly stormed the back door of the Ranchmen's Steakhouse in Calgary in 1974. There was line dancing, there was sawdust, there was horrible music. There were smiling, pretty girls in fetching country outfits and men smoking and swearing and spitting on the floor. Cowboy boots as far as the eye could see. I started driving small groups of people to different parts of town. I had only completed three or four trips when it appeared that everyone had been accounted for. All that remained was the core group of organizers, all police officers. The bar was closing and the lights were on full now, never a pretty sight at 2:00 a.m. I was thinking I would only need to make one more trip. I would be home no later than three in the morning. It had been a pretty painless night, except for the country and western music, and for my four hours of work I was to receive a flat ninety dollars, a very good return. I was looking forward to getting this last group of people out the door, into the van, and down the road. I was to be profoundly disappointed.

Four or five men no older than I, my employers for the night, all cops, lingered and dawdled about the club for another hour, and smoked and spat on the floor, drunk and posturing, making aggressive sexual comments to women as the bar was closing. It was not for me, or the bar owners, to hurry them along. Sometimes I waited off to the side. Sometimes I stood with them, chatting a bit when possible, hovering, disgusted by their disgusting behaviour. One of them was very sour, the small one, belligerent and threatening. Short man syndrome, I suppose. One of them was tall and strong and seemed to be the one in charge. He acted as spokesman for the group, proposing and managing events, and giving me driving directions in the van.

When we were all finally in the van, I breathed a sigh of relief hoping to get these meatheads home and out of my hair, but it just got worse. No one had any intention of going home. The party had simply become mobile. What was to follow was another four hours of driving around Edmonton in the middle of the night looking for trouble. And I was the wheelman.

Our first stop was the Fruit Loop, a big alley on the west side of downtown where the gay hustlers worked. This van full of drunk, off-duty, out-of-uniform police officers instructed me to drive quietly, without lights, down various streets and alleys until we came upon a lone male hooker. These bullies, these wretches, these fucking assholes then piled out of the van and verbally abused and harassed the man in makeup until they were satisfied with their performance. They didn't hit him or even push him, as far as I could tell, but they leaned into him as a group and made aggressive motions and swore loudly at him and insulted him. I sat at the wheel and couldn't believe what I was seeing and hearing. It was sickening. They pulled out their badges. They demanded ID. I imagined this wasn't the first time they had engaged in this kind of fun.

On the road again, with no particular destination in mind yet, I was told to drive up and down various streets on the bad side of town. They were surveilling hotspots, places where they might find trouble or stir it up. We drove quietly, again without lights, along dark, empty residential streets in the poor area north of downtown, not far from Pam's daycare. We pulled up a little distance from a small, nasty, old house with several large motorcycles parked in front. It was a biker-gang house. The van door slid open and the cops slipped out. I was told to wait and be ready to go when they got back. I heard and then saw them pushing over all the motorcycles in the yard. They ran back to the van and piled in laughing and excited, whispering loudly "Go, go, go!" and we made our getaway.

These two little adventures took at least an hour each. It involved a lot of driving around, and swearing and blustering and bragging. The leader sat in the front with me and seemed less drunk than the rest of his comrades. I asked him why we were doing all of this ridiculous stuff. He said something about blowing off steam. Stress was a serious issue in police work. They had all talked at one time or another about eating their guns, suicide.

They decided it would be hilarious to go to the police station, so I drove downtown to 9620 - 103A Avenue where they, drunk, and I, not, spent an hour strutting around Edmonton's new police headquarters, only three years old then. Passing the chaplain's office, I saw the door was open, and I ducked in to grab his business card. I am looking at it now, as I write this, twenty-eight years later. "Rev. Bruce Cowley, Police Chaplain." My drunken, aggressive, law-breaking, partying cops were badly in need of his services. The reverend eventually retired to Victoria.

I made small suggestions, which began to border on small complaints, about getting home, but the sun was coming up before I drove the last of these foul bastards home for the night. These men weren't just drunk and negative. They were angry, hate-filled human beings. They were also police officers armed with authority and weapons. What was I going to say to them? It was a very disturbing night.

As I was dropping off the last of them, the leader, I asked for my pay. He said, "Oh, I don't have it on me. Don't worry about it. We'll get it to you. It won't be long." The only thing worse than spending eight hours in the company of these blackguards was not getting paid for it. It was nine in the morning before I was in bed. My four-hour job had turned into ten.

I wondered if I would ever see the money, but a week later one of them showed up at the dormitory, off-duty, visited a bit with his brother, and then gave me a hundred and fifteen dollars cash, a quarter more than what had been agreed upon. He seemed very sheepish now. Seeing and participating, most unwillingly, in this sickening abuse of power, in this brute company, constituted one of the most disgusting nights I have ever spent in my life, and it made me awfully wary of the Edmonton Police Department.

I had a few savings, some scholarship money, and a student loan, but I had a lifestyle that would eat up as much money as I could find. Plus, I had time on my hands. I thought I might try to get a part-time job. In the first week of September, I walked across the quad to the large cafeteria in the Central Academic Building. Being older, I presented a more responsible front compared with the nineteen-year-olds who were applying, and I was hired immediately. For a couple of weeks, I did kitchen clean-up in the late afternoons and evenings. This was a shitty job, and it did put some stress on my academic day, so I decided to quit. I told the boss I had misjudged my school workload and I really didn't have time during the week to work in the cafeteria. He countered my resignation with an offer to make me the weekend supervisor. This meant that I, and one other person, set up a limited service on Saturdays and Sundays selling soggy sandwiches, and coffee and sugary drinks. We also fired up the ovens and cooked pizzas. I was nearly always drunk on Friday nights which made Saturday mornings torture, getting up early to open the cafeteria which was then not busy at all for most of the weekend. Typically, I was also out late on Saturday nights, so Sundays were even worse. Occasionally business was so slow, and I was so bored on the job, I actually looked for something useful to do. I was not infrequently asleep at the cash register. I was not a model employee.

I hadn't seen Pam since July, but we wound up in the same computing science class in September. This was something of a coincidence. U of A is a big school. It was a little awkward at first. For a while, she would scurry away right after class and wouldn't talk to me, but eventually she warmed to me again and we found ourselves making love in my room after computing and before lunch. I was pleased, and surprised, that she forgave me my sins. I must have been good company.

I was tired of school and tired of living at Pembina Hall. I spent the next eight months staying three or four nights a week with Pam at her house, with her and her six-year-old son. I kept my room at the university for study and retreat. We played a little house. Pam had thrown away all the ratty, old cupboard handles and drawer handles in her kitchen when she painted it, but when she bought new ones, twenty-two of them, she found installing them was too much for her. There wasn't a handle on anything in the kitchen. It was constantly annoying and hard on the fingertips. I spent half a day manually drilling holes and screwing in the handles that had lain untouched at the back of a drawer for a year. We cooked, we cleaned, we went to classes, we went out for meals and movies, and we drank.

Every Saturday and Sunday morning, horribly hung-over, I walked the two miles to the campus, through snow and wind and ice when winter came, and worked at the cafeteria for the day. With the money I made in the summer and at the cafeteria, from loans and scholarships, I now always had a couple of hundred dollars in my pocket, unusual for most students, and very unusual for me. We ate out frequently, often at two popular restaurants on Whyte Avenue, Greek and Chinese, ones frequented by members of the Edmonton Oilers. I was delighted to have spending money. One of the things I hated most about going to school was the poverty. Sometimes Pam's little boy was with us. Sometimes he was with his father. We were as happy as you could be for two people in our situation. We visited friends. We had lots of sex. We had enough money to party non-stop but not enough to take a vacation. Our daily obligations were only mildly onerous and would have been even easier without the hangovers.

Pam was smart, but I always did a little better in school than she did. I worked harder and she was no slave to grades. She wasn't applying for scholarships or grad school, and she had a child to look after. But she surprised me in computing class when she showed a knack for programming that I clearly lacked. She could spit out lines of BASIC and COBOL that left me blank. I couldn't figure out how I could get straight A's in every area of science and be completely in the dark when it came to computer coding. This was something that would bite me hard in the ass in later years.

Pam fit me like a glove. Her pleasant company and good humour, her lightness of being and considerable physical appeal, should have been enough to tear me away from Karen. But it wasn't. Pam had a six-year-old boy, and I could not imagine another ten or fifteen years of dealing with that. I could not allow myself to fall into that trap. I visited Karen in Regina in the fall and on holidays, but less so after Christmas. I continued to lie to Pam about my activities and whereabouts, but not without regret. I wasn't finished being a total shit just yet, but it was starting to wear on me. To my amazement Pam never found me out.

Karen also had a child about the same age as Pam's. My involvement with Karen was not an inconsistency on my part. I had no intention of ever settling down with her, either. I just liked her.

I hadn't seen Connie all summer, of course, and when I started school again in September I wondered whether she would want to continue playing emotional footsie. It was going to be another long winter, after all. On the first day of classes I saw her on the second-floor walkway between the Student Union Building and the Agriculture Building. I was thrilled to see her and a little nervous. She gave me a few minutes of guarded conversation, forcing herself to appear unconcerned, and then, when she saw that I was willing, she indicated to me by a small combination of signs, from eyes and lips and hands, that she too wanted to be able to look forward to another year of sighs and whispers and warm touches. What possible reason could there be to deny ourselves these silly pleasures? Marriage is a contract based on law, not love, and adultery is not a crime of the heart. It is a property crime, an artefact of backward and ailing societies, instituted by ignorant men, men who owned their women like they owned their kine.

I was sick of my cafeteria job long before the New Year, and I quit in January. My excuse was that I had a major project to undertake, worth half a dozen course credits, a final series of experiments to conduct and write up. It was a bugbear for all fourth-year students. I cast around the department looking for a supervisor and was taken on by Dr. Lech Ozimek, a dairy scientist from Poland. He had a suggestion for a project, and he went to some trouble to get me going on it. I had pretty much lost the will to finish the damn degree at all, and I was now on cranky autopilot. I couldn't concentrate, I didn't care about anything, I was always mildly angry, and I was always hung-over. Professor O. had to guide me through the project like an infant. I had no idea how to design it or what the results meant when I was finally looking at them, but of course I wrote it all up very nicely and got my A. I calculated to the hour and to the percentage point how long and how hard I would have to work in each of my courses to get through the program with an acceptable grade point average. If I didn't have to do an assignment, I didn't do it. I dragged myself through the last year, especially the last term, and finished with a four-year GPA of 8.6, out of 9.0. I got my first A-, an Asian C, in the last semester of my fourth year of university.

I was mad for a girl named Kathy, a beautiful 21-year-old I had known in the program for two years. I would have walked fifty miles over bad ground just to look at her. She was svelte with fabulous breasts, hips, and legs, a model's body, but not tall. "Slim with a nice rack" is, I believe, the expression. At twenty-one she had been in possession of this magnificent form for no more than five or six years. When granted to a fifteen-year-old girl, it is not one likely to remain long inexperienced. She had short, dark hair, a dark humour, a lesbian vibe, and an alabaster face of otherworldly symmetry. When I commented, in as casual a voice as I could manage, on the remarkable regularity of her features, she replied only, with her signature scowl, "Superstore face." Kathy came with a friend, a tall, strong, athletic woman, a swimmer. This made my tail wag. Coming home from a food and wine-tasting event one night, we three found ourselves in my dorm room, where we read erotic poetry to each other and massaged each other's feet. The next thing I knew tops and bras and bottoms were flying in every direction, and I was able to indulge in every high school boy's fantasy. They were both twelve years younger than I, and you will know by now that I was not made of stone. It was natural that I should appreciate every year of the difference in our ages, but at thirty-three, I was not the seducer. I wasn't that aggressive. This was mutual monkey business, and we were all amateurs. I chased Kathy, Kathy chased Deonna, and Deonna chased me at close carnal quarters in a slippery circle without beginning or end, circumscribed only by the bounds of imagination and anatomy. The last month or two of my fourth year of university was a flavourful, sybaritic splendor, a heavenly delight.

But even the gods belong to the world of suffering.

Spring's restive blessings were in the air, and Nature was as pregnant as she could be. It is an expectant, irritable time on the prairies as you wait in an agony of frustration, with many false starts, for the slow delivery from winter, for break-up, for the snow and ice to go once more. Go! Just go! Cabin fever. The city is unbelievably filthy from the thousands of cubic yards of sand and dirt and gravel that are strewn upon the snow as it falls over the winter and refuses to melt, not for seven long months. When the snow finally recedes, the city's treasures beneath are revealed, dead grass and 20,000 fresh-frozen dog turds. The sun now shone pretentiously bright in the thin prairie air, and reflected painfully into the eyes from the two inches of melted snow and mud that covered every square inch of the roads. Every road and every vehicle was wet and brown. When the water dried after a few more days, the streets billowed with dust.

The year-end decadence of student life, not just mine, combined with the stress of final exams, makes for an edgy time at any university. I walked the hallways of the school hung-over, sated, and muttering to myself, "I could have been in medicine, or law, or accounting, something that would make some money. What the hell am I doing in food science?" It was embarrassing. It needn't have been, but it was.

I had money left on my cafeteria card which would expire into nothingness at the end of the semester if I didn't use it, so I went to the residence commissary and swiped the last of it on an enormous box of chocolates, pounds of them. I opened the box, took one or two, and left it in the empty third-floor residence lounge. When I passed through the lounge again thirty minutes later, the table was littered with dozens of tiny, brown, pleated paper cups, all empty. Every one of the chocolates was gone, consumed by passing mature students studying for final exams, stress-eating. A sensible, older female resident in her last year of law school dropped into the lounge to check her lottery numbers in the newspaper. She said, "If I've won the lottery I'm not going to class this afternoon." She was glum. Any normal human being would rather have been T-boned at an intersection than go to another class.

I had a job lined up, for the summer at least. The Alpha Milk Company was willing to take me on again, this time at their main lab in Red Deer. They thought I might turn out to be a good long-term bet, or not. The summer could turn into something more permanent. I borrowed my father's New Yorker again. He always kept it registered and insured even though he never drove it. I moved to Red Deer. After only three weeks, I saw a man I didn't know sitting in the boss's office. He was the manager of a flavour manufacturing facility in Vancouver, and he was in need of a lab supervisor. He looked like the kind of guy who would piss me off eventually, but when he offered me the job, a permanent position, I took it.

But not before attending the graduating students' dinner. I was tapped to give the toast to the professors. I was no great public speaker, not without a script, or even with one, so I went to the library and looked up a few jokes. On the evening of the dinner, Kathy and Deonna wore little black dresses, stockings, and lipstick. Deonna was taller than I and now, in heels, so was Kathy. The three of us arrived together. When the hour came, I went to the podium with a few drinks in me. I chewed the professors out, then I patted them on the head, and then I threw us both a bone, professors and students alike. I said it was damned difficult to be a student sometimes, and the professors seemed to think it was their job to make it more difficult than it needed to be. But you know the saying, "If you make your students think they're thinking, they'll love you. If you actually make them think, they'll hate you." I allowed that we couldn't do it without them, and they always gave us enough to get us through, but no sooner than we needed it. When I was done, after eight or nine minutes of raillery, I ended my toast to the professors with an actual toast, a limerick, and I raised my glass to drink their health expecting all present to join in, but of the fifteen or so graduating students seven of them were Asians from Asia. They sat motionless in their seats, staring blankly, not seeming to know what was expected of them. The very serious and sober Professor Marc Laguerre was tasked with responding to my Lucky Jim toast. He said he detected a note of burnout in my address. Yeah, he did.

I was in British Columbia by the time my graduation ceremony rolled around in June, and I didn't attend. It's possible I might not have attended no matter where I was. For me university was a necessary evil, nothing more. The place is full of schoolmasters. As is hell.

There are a dozen other situations, events, moments, and people from that last year at U of A that I would like to describe, mostly people, people far more interesting than I am, quirkier, braver, more dedicated, with higher ideals, fewer weaknesses and appetites, fewer illusions, less self-absorbed. People with more interesting backgrounds, speaking more than one language, from rich cultures. People from Syria, Malta, Jamaica, New Zealand, Iceland, Thailand, Czechoslovakia, and Quebec. One day sitting in the lounge, several of us were talking about our ancestors insofar as we knew them. One said, "My grandfather was a senator." Another said,

"Mine were born in Russia." And then one young Chinese man surprised us all when he said, "My grandparents don't know how to multiply."

There were a few rapscallions and scallywags, like the fourth-year student in the Food Science Department who photocopied someone else's work for every assignment he was required to submit. And who can forget the well-heeled jackass living in the basement at Pembina Hall who ran a cable up the outside of the building, at considerable personal risk, it was winter, and piped porn videos into all the TV lounges one night?

There were religious nuts and evangelizers. There were calm and wise grown-ups. There were recluses and oddballs and innocents.

Couples came together in romance and split up and reformed into new combinations. There was at least one threesome everyone was intrigued by, two handsome young men and an attractive redhead. This woman was in one of my classes. The professor marked quizzes and labs and assignments and left them in a cardboard box outside the door of the classroom. People always gathered there to pick them up as soon as they were marked, anxious to see how they had done. When you have no money, grades are your riches. The redhead never bothered to pick any of hers up. At the end of the semester, there were still sixteen papers in the box, all hers. She had done most of the assignments, she came to most of the classes, she wrote the finals. Beyond that, she simply did not care. I admired her greatly. And not just because she was comfortable with two lovers.

There was at least one genius in Pembina Hall, a good-looking young man who sat in the bathtub reading Proust in the evenings. He finished a Master's thesis in mathematics in a single semester.

I was no genius. No new Laws of Nature would flow from me. I was only good at imagining myself outside existing bounds, breaking rules, declaring myself above restraint, judging and reviling the dogs that guarded the flock in which I was so safe and so uncomfortable. "You can't do anything with someone who goes where he pleases and doesn't want anything on God's earth except his own way."

I wasn't much good at unravelling truth, but I recognized it when it was presented plainly to me, and thus I was not a completely unappreciated blessing to mankind. My fellow students asked me, once again, how I could be so damn brilliant, acing every test. I wanted to tell them they were grasping at the ungraspable. The solution to success in study, or any human endeavour, is a supra-real process, stepwise thought combined with thought-free awareness. It is like the quantum change of position of an electron. First you do and then you be. Then you do again, then you be again. When all the possibilities of the universe collapse into actualities, you do. Then you be, meaning you reflect and meditate. The number of possibilities in the next set of possibilities then increases, so you have a greater likelihood of finding the next thing to do that is in harmony with the unconditioned reality you have allowed to flow into a state of potentiality. The explanation is sequential, but the events, like quantum transitions, are not. This is how Kekulé divined the flexiform structure of the benzene ring, a pivotal event in nineteenth-century chemistry.

Because the body is morphogenetic, you can build better connections in the brain that allow you to approach conditioned reality using the resources of higher consciousness. The source and the result together form a state of dynamic acceptance. This all seemed pretty obvious to me, and it was the same thing I had told my fellow students at Camosun College seven years earlier. "Don't fight the material. You don't always have to understand it. Don't expect to. Just *be* with it."

I might have gone on to say that the Christian idea of individuals going to heaven makes no sense to a Buddhist, a Vedantist, or the quantum consciousness of a scientist. Everybody goes or nobody goes. There's no picking and choosing based on membership, or even on merit. Life is one hundred per cent inclusive. This truth is the source of universal compassion, the infinite love of the guru, and straight-up evolution. Consciousness chooses out of possibilities and then makes actual events. It is a natural conclusion that we choose our own reality. But it is not the choice of individual egos. Free will is not an ego-based concept. It is part of a mystic consciousness that is identical with God's will.

How many times did I have to explain this? I was no genius, but I was not deficient of penetration. I had been giving this lecture for years. I had written it on the tail of my lab coat with a ballpoint pen, for all to see. I was, however, tired and hung-over, and I wasn't feeling philosophically expansive, so I just told my fellow students the secret to writing good exams was to get plenty of oral sex.

You're welcome.

I couldn't keep an educated distance from my worst self, and I was indifferent to the effects I might have on those around me. Making someone else feel better emotionally was not on my daily to-do list. I wouldn't think less of myself for being bad, but I knew my inclinations fatally undermined my better intentions. This is the tosser's lament.

I didn't come here to be perfect, and I know you know that, but I wonder if you are not tired of hearing me crow and seeing me misbehave?

I am.

Going to school had not been a straightforward task for me. I first enrolled in post-secondary education at the Southern Alberta Institute of Technology in September of 1973 at the age of twenty. It was now June 1987. Over the last fourteen years, I had spent sixty-four months, that's sixteen semesters and eight academic years, in five colleges and universities, in Television, Stage and Radio Arts, in theatre, in carpentry, and in general science, and I finally had a degree which might now prove to be of some practical value.

I lived in a time when weakness did not necessarily lead to ruin. In a few more months I would be thirty-four years old, and it had been evident for many years, to many an observer, that I was mentally and emotionally incapable of pursuing a career, or even holding down a job. What were the odds of that changing now?

There wasn't a chance in hell I would ever become a food scientist.

22   The Bribery of Paris

After the graduating students' dinner, I stood in the lobby of the Agriculture Building chatting briefly with Professor Pavel "Paul" Jelen, a Czech academic who knew how to work a room. He had had a couple of drinks himself, and he pumped my hand, shouting congratulations into my face ("Professor Yellin'"), laughing and pumping and spitting on me. I told him I was glad the damn thing, the degree, was over. He yelled, "Oh, the work is just starting for you, my boy! Just starting! The degree is nothing! Now you really get down to it!" I sensed a dip in the road.

"I still feel like I don't really know anything."

"Oh, you probably don't! You can't learn much in four years! You need to do graduate work to get a handle on anything specific!"

I told him about my new job in Vancouver at Universal Flavours Canada. He was thrilled to hear it.

"Excellent!" he shouted and spat. "The flavour houses! Interesting work! Good pay! Good for you! Work your way up in the flavour houses, my boy! That's the place to be! Best of luck to you!"

I went in search of paper towel.

I informed my father that I and the New Yorker were moving to the west coast. He quivered at the thought of his beautiful car so far away from home, nine hundred miles, and he encouraged me to "keep it between the green," but he said nothing more. He wanted me working and the loss, probably temporary, of his Brougham was worth the sacrifice if it would keep me on the straight and narrow.

I wanted to move to the coast, badly. I wanted nothing more to do with the prairies. I had spent an aberrant and unwanted three years there finishing school. If I had had a plan, moving to the Lower Mainland of BC would have been the perfection of it. People all over Canada would kill their mothers for a job on the west coast, and I was offered one, out of the blue, immediately upon graduation, even with my shabby work history. In a ten-minute interview at the Alpha lab in Red Deer, with my lab boss's blessing, Denis, pronounced "Dennis," the manager at Universal Flavors, offered me a good starting salary as lab supervisor in their flavour manufacturing facility in Abbotsford, forty miles east of Vancouver. Their head office was in Toronto. The parent company was Universal Foods, a 100-year-old, billion-dollar flavour house based in Milwaukee. I think I clinched the interview when I said, "My goal is to see a significant improvement in my lifestyle over the next five years." I may have been convincing, but I was kidding myself as well as Denis. The real truth was that I could never take the pursuit of money, or a job, seriously.

The Abbotsford plant was a modest few thousand square feet of office space, lab, warehouse, production room, frozen storage, and dispensary. Production consisted mostly of mixing and cooking ingredients in a large kettle to make ice cream and soda pop flavourings, as well as chocolate coatings in a giant grinding machine. There was a lab supervisor currently on staff, but she had only agreed to work for a limited period of time while the manager looked for someone else. She was quitting for good. She had other plans. The job was mine to lose. The supervisor stayed on for a week or two and got me sorted out on the routine.

I liked her. She was smart and experienced, a UBC graduate in food science. She also worked in some volunteer capacity with the Canadian Institute of Food Science and Technology. In an amusing twist, my reputation in Abbotsford and Vancouver had preceded me. When I was awarded the US Institute of Food Technologists Junior/Senior scholarship the previous year, the IFT office staff in Chicago had no idea where to send the plaque that commemorated the event. They assumed the CIFST office in Vancouver would be close enough since it, and U of A, were both somewhere in the wilds of Western Canada, although nine hundred miles apart. My plaque had wound up in the custody of my new friend, the lab supervisor, as part of her administrative role at CIFST. It had been sitting on a desk in her basement for many months. She had made no great effort to track me down at U of A, and now I had come to her. She presented me with my tablet in the lab at Universal Flavors. I had known nothing of this lettered slab, but I and my plaque were destined to be together.

When the lab supervisor left, I scrubbed and detailed the lab top to bottom. I was surprised how dirty a lab could get, and how trained food scientists could let them continue in that state where contamination in testing is an issue. A spotless lab in a food manufacturing facility seemed like a baseline obligation to me. I also insisted that filing equipment be purchased, and I organized and filed the reams of production papers that had accumulated in haphazard layers in a cardboard box over the previous several months. A food manufacturing facility without a documented production history is unacceptable. Surely there were government inspections? The departing supervisor was a more creative thinker than I was, but no one could fault me for a lack of detailed organization.

Much of my job involved taste-testing, and everything we produced was made with sugar. I kept a toothbrush in the lab and was brushing three or four times a day. I feared for my teeth. I was in the sugar business now. It was an odd turn of events. This was a business and an industry against which I had inveighed for years, calling our century the Age of the White Death, declaring that sugar makes you stupid. My vague interest in health, nutrition, vegetarianism, herbs, and natural healing had somehow ended in my employment in a sugar factory. I was not expecting that.

During four years of studying chemistry and food science, especially in the last two years, I had come to the lazy conclusion that the world and its food supply was hopelessly and irreversibly poisoned by the chemical and manufacturing industries. The numbers were overwhelming. The ammonia alone. Only a year before I graduated, the Chernobyl nuclear disaster contaminated thousands of farms, farm animals, crops, wild game, and vegetation in thirty countries across Europe. In 2011, twenty-five years later, restrictions on foodstuffs were still in place in the UK, Sweden, Finland, and Germany, and of course, Russia and Ukraine. Why bother trying to eat healthily when every consumable is modified, adulterated, poisoned, and irradiated, accidentally or on purpose, on a worldwide scale by the time it reaches your plate and palate? My professors at U of A spent their lives leaving no natural piece of food undisturbed. Their profession revolved around canning, drying, freezing, processing, genetically modifying, and irradiating every piece of food they could lay their hands on. "Let no food remain unaltered" was their creed. Food in its natural state was of no interest to them. This was laudable activity in some cases. Food has to be preserved.

I was just as mystified, however, by some of the illogical aspects of the study of nutrition. In 1897, Eijkman found that chickens fed a diet of polished rice developed an illness akin to beriberi, a serious nerve disease in humans, not uncommon in the nineteenth century. When the birds were fed unpolished rice, brown rice, they got better. It took another thirty years of research before Vitamin B_1, the preventative agent, was synthesized in the lab. Now we can enjoy eating white rice, as long as we take Vitamin B_1 pills, instead of having to eat brown rice. I would never quibble with the ongoing need for basic research in nutritional science, but it seems a shame that public education and common sense have to suffer at the same time.

The untangling of secrets by means of natural science is motivated by a burden of suffering, by pain and fear, and the result has been an unnaturally grotesque and bewildering assault on nature. My days in the classrooms and labs of Camosun College and U of A had jaded me. I was now myself a purveyor of white death. I had dropped any pretense to vegetarianism and was chowing down on steak sandwiches every week. What did it matter?

I found an unfurnished one-bedroom apartment near my new flavour house. The building was a little older, but the suite had hardwood floors in good condition and new paint. I went to Wal-Mart and IKEA and bought minimal, but new, furniture. I bought posters of prints by A. Y. Jackson, Picasso, Van Gogh, Gauguin, Giotto, and others, and had them mounted on foamcore so they hung nicely on my fresh white walls. With nothing in the living room but a large, thin rug in a light and swirling charcoal design, and a contemporary IKEA table in the dining room, my apartment looked like an art gallery, bright with clean lines.

I joined a racquetball club and smashed the ball around by myself. I went to aerobics classes. I thought about joining an amateur theatre. I thought about going to the local junior college to take business courses or accounting or art history. I wasn't quite sure how to spend my spare time. I went to restaurants constantly. The summer of 1987 was unusually hot on the coast, and I drove all over the Lower Mainland exploring, hiking, and swimming. The valley was lush, the lakes warm, and the trails dry. The distances rapidly ate up the gas in my enormous land yacht. I discovered that what I had thought was a good salary didn't go far after the bills were paid. I drove into Vancouver frequently and ate and drank freely in pricey bars and restaurants, often picking up the tab myself, surprising old friends who had thought I might never get a real job. We lounged about for hours in the harmless summer fantasy of Vancouver's brummagem café society. I went to the theatre. I had credit cards now, for the very first time, and I plunged in.

I was enjoying the art and politics, the diversity and ethnicity of East Vancouver. I reconnected with four or five sets of old friends in the big city, people I had known in Calgary and Victoria who had wound up in Vancouver. One of these sets of friends, Shea and Tom, who had put me up when I was passing through in 1984, moved to Mount Vernon in Washington State that summer, sixty miles south of Abbotsford, and I helped them move and visited them there. I was frequently crossing the Canada-US border, only three miles from Abbotsford, to buy cheap gas and dairy products. Canadians, as well as Green Bay Packers football fans and the citizens of the state of Wisconsin, have been called cheeseheads for a long time.

By an astonishing coincidence, I was now living only eleven miles from Westminster Abbey near Mission, the scene of so much drama and anguish three summers ago. I drove by the monastery once and looked in to the church, but I didn't stay long. It was as close as I would ever get.

Mostly, I was drinking. Between the hangovers and the sugar, there were days when I could not brush my teeth often enough.

I shopped around for a more economical car knowing that the day would eventually come when I would have to return the Chrysler to my father. I didn't want to buy it from him. Its luxury was a tasty indulgence for me but not a good match. It was an old man's car and too expensive to run. People stared at me at intersections when they saw me at the wheel. I now had a good job, and a young Asian salesman at the Toyota dealership in Abbotsford was keen to finance me into a brand new subcompact, a Tercel. Nineteen eighty-seven was a good year for the Tercel, and if I had bought it I would have spent five difficult years paying for it, knowing my work history, but it would likely have provided reliable transportation for twenty. I came perilously close to signing the papers, but I hesitated at the last moment. I have never bought a new car in my life. I knew my ability to commit to a job was shaky, to say the least, and what's more, I was beginning to sense that something was rotten in the city of Abbotsford.

I hated my boss almost from the start. He was upbeat and energetic and that gave him an air of competence and likeability, but it couldn't mask a massive underlying accrual of self-satisfaction and arrogance. What he lacked in self-awareness, he made up for in self-esteem. He was the kind of man who walked into a room, took off his coat, and without looking, held it out behind him in one hand without a hint of doubt that someone would take it for him. His presence deprived the room and its occupants of air. He was ten pounds of shit in a five-pound bag, a day-long plague. He was the star of the Jesus Denis Christ Show, and it never stopped. There aren't horns, claws, hooves, and mucous enough to describe him.

He was from Glasgow and had been a policeman for a while. He was ultraconservative, noisily opinionated, a thinker in blocks of pronouncements, and I wasn't. We were oil and water. I got along with him about as well as I got along with my ultraconservative father. He was an unwelcome villain in my already overcrowded dramas. Every day I sincerely wished he would go home, draw a hot bath, and open a vein. I was projecting onto him the very things I saw in myself, and hated, but I would never concede superiority to this ass as long as I could think of a reason to deny it.

I had a problem with authority figures in general and that summer with Social Credit conservatives in particular. Denis was a big fan of Bill Vander Zalm, the rabidly anti-socialist, soon-to-be-scandalized-and-disgraced premier of British Columbia. After years of political supremacy, Vander Zalm singlehandedly destroyed the Social Credit party in BC by a "foolish, ill-advised…apparent or real conflict of interest or breach of ethics." But for now, for Bill and Denis, everything was "faaaantastic" as long as they and their ilk held the purse strings. By the end of the summer, I was ready to wring Denis's neck with my bare hands. It would have been a short fight. He was an ex-cop. He was tough, and I wasn't. I was just angry.

I was miserable in Abbotsford. My job was not unbearable, but I had a beef with the nine to five routine, and I hated my boss's guts. He grew more offensive and repulsive every day. He was a man as false as hell who expected his every word to be taken as gospel. I couldn't stand to be around him. My salary evaporated with my lifestyle. I was losing focus, and I had little enough to begin with. I was restless, uncomfortable, and lonely at home. The drinking started to get out of hand.

And what was I going to do about the girls? About all my beautiful women?

Pam came out for a visit and so did Kathy and Karen. Not all at the same time.

Still, it wasn't enough, and how could I choose between them?

I agonized all summer about work and women. What could I do with Pam? She had way too much family in and around Edmonton, many of them forty miles down the road towards Sedgewick, parents, grandparents, brothers, aunts and uncles, and cousins. She had a son. And I was not a family guy. One day in the spring, she had pressed me about marriage and it scared the daylights out of me. I was sincerely troubled by my feelings for her. I liked her, and I loved her. We had been tangled together for a year and a half, long enough to be genuinely intertwined. I just didn't want to have children. Every month, I was sick at the thought that Pam might be pregnant. At the age of thirty-three, I went to the doctor to enquire for the first time about getting a vasectomy, but he told me to come back in five years. I was still too young. Neither did I want to get married. I would rather be dragged to hell than dragged to the altar. Marriage in the morning, last rites in the afternoon. The days of trading marriage for sex were long past. The yodel was over, but that one-note ululation continued to echo down the canyons of love. The idea that what was forbidden the day before marriage was a duty the day after was ancient and absurd. It remains strangely commonplace, and shouldn't, to say that most women still want to be married and some men still don't. I didn't. Why was it worse of me to say "give me sex" than it was of Pam to say "give me a ring?" Having to explain and justify my feelings about marriage and family was a constant anguish. Why were they inexplicable and unjustifiable? It was a dreary dance. I was ahead of my time.

Also, Pam's university degree had been an interesting project for her, a laugh, a possibility, but she showed no sign of using it to improve her lifestyle. She seemed willing to throw four years of study away. She graduated in nutrition that spring but had no desire to be a dietitian, the usual application of that particular parchment. If she didn't go down that road, a degree in nutrition was of no more use than a degree in English, or less. It was too specific. I was so appalled by the agony of going to school that I was determined, however imperfectly, however unlikely, to use the results of it as a springboard to a better job, a career of some kind. After all my name in Japanese was "board spring," wasn't it? Pam wasn't showing much ambition. She liked partying and loafing as much as I did, and I needed a partner who would help me get out of bed in the morning if I was going to survive the grind of the working world.

With Kathy? She was a broke student, at odds with a difficult father and family, and still had a year of university left. She was paranormally gorgeous, and I was drawn magnetically and disturbingly to her, but she was young, and apparently gay/bisexual. Although she made herself available to me, she didn't seem that interested. She was sick of men drooling over her, and I was too old for her. For my part, being with her was an unsettling perfection. As attracted to her as I was, I saw nothing but complications in that direction. She had a dark interior view, she rarely smiled, and she had a sexual nature that would require more time for her to survey and map, to navigate and accept. Our brief relationship had been intensely delicious, wonderfully naughty and exploratory, but she was an unknown quantity. I knew our paths could not run together for long. Deonna was in Europe most of that summer, and I lost touch with her altogether. A dozen years later, under serendipitous circumstances, I had an opportunity to speak to Kathy on the telephone. She was living only a few miles away from me. Connie, my classroom emotional lover from U of A, with her new husband, was visiting me, and my new wife, in Victoria. She was sitting in my living room, talking to Kathy on the phone, but Kathy would not permit her to hand the receiver to me. She refused to speak to me. I shouted across the room, teasing, hoping Kathy would hear me on the other end of the line, "Is it because we went to college together?"

Karen had invited me to move to Regina when I finished school, and she ardently encouraged the plan in a pleasant and flatteringly persistent way. I despised the prairies and their dark-side-of-the-moon winters, but I loved Karen, and I had known the considerable warmth and welcome of her accomplished and intense personality, her colourful, art-filled little house, the glow of her fireplace, her tasty cooking, the drinking and the parties and the champagne, and the hours of endlessly creative sex on her beanbag chair.

I knew Karen was devoted to me and would be as fine a partner as I was likely to get. She would never cheat on me, she was too busy. She was well-established in her career and her community and always would be. She had a wide, ready-made circle of friends, acquaintances, and neighbours I could slip into socially. I knew many of these people already, and Karen was convinced that what I needed was community.

She would always work, and she owned her own house. The cost of living in Regina was a fraction of that on the coast. If we both had good jobs, we would have more income than we could spend. Her mortgage payment was four hundred dollars a month. If there was a new Lexus in the garage at home and I had underground parking at work maybe I could stand the winters.

She had a son, though, and that was unnerving, but I had got to know Devon over the last two years. I was used to him, if nothing else. I had spent six hours with him one Christmas Day sipping beer and assembling the Robin Hood castle he got from Santa Claus.

Karen said, "Move to Regina, honey. You'll get a job right away. There are so few qualified people in the province you will be in immediate demand." In two years I had been to Regina at least a dozen times. I was at home there, be it ever so ghastly. There were many reasons to go in that direction and no ultimately imperative reasons not to.

I had had seven lovers over the last two years, none of them a one-night stand. And I loved them all. Hand to God. Selfish people are capable of great love. It's what they want. It's all they want. Love isn't the measles. You are not immune after a single fever. Every one of these lovers was a soul mate. They had no choice. They all had souls, however much trodden upon by my small sneakers. In every case I surrendered my heart forever, and then left. I could have been happy with any one of them if I had known how to be happy, but I didn't.

Before me was the Judgment of Paris, and I was in a state of paresis. It was a judgment of Cupid which I could not make without a blush of cupidity, a concupiscent pragmatism, not my most attractive feature, in a crowd of unattractive features. Marriage, or its simulacrum, was indeed a contract in law.

I talked to Pam. I wrote to Kathy. I called Karen.

By the beginning of September, I was already packed. I knew my time and my future at Universal Flavors was over. I had to fire my boss. I told Denis to his face that I had met guys like him before, but I had never worked for one, and I never would. It was an acrimonious parting, the worst quit I ever experienced in a lifetime of quits. Later someone remarked, "That's okay. If you find yourself in a job that isn't right for you, don't walk away from it, run!" Upon hearing this I was satisfied, once again, that I had exercised the right option, transcendentally so.

I gave notice on my apartment, shipped a few boxes of things on the bus, packed up the New Yorker, got into it and drove away from Abbotsford, heading east. But not before I had torn cartilage in my knee again, this time in an aerobics class, and I limped painfully for several weeks. Every few years I was losing weeks of mobility to my cranky knee. It had started eleven years earlier slipping and falling on the golf course in Dawson Creek. Later, in Brisco, I had fallen through a hole in the floor at the sawmill and landed straight and hard on the same knee. Only a few weeks later, I was helping John jack up a car at the auto wreckers. We ill-judged the balance of the car, it fell over, and the jack flew out and hit me on the very same joint. Three years later, there was the motorcycle accident, and now I was down and limping again, the result of vigorous rhythmic tiptoeing in an aerobics class with twenty women in Spandex.

I stopped in Calgary to visit here and there. It was September and I was moving to Saskatchewan. I had failed miserably to escape the prairies, failed miserably at my first career job in the food industry. But I knew there were treats waiting for me in Regina and I wasn't going to give up on my career just yet.

As I drove east that fall, across the beautiful mountains and valleys of British Columbia, and the foothills and prairies of Alberta and Saskatchewan, there was also a change in the moral landscape. My endless days and nights of chasing skirts were over forever.

I was just as glad.

I was tired.

23 Meretricious

There was a big paper banner across the back of the house on Elphinstone Street in Regina when I pulled into the alley to park my giant car next to Karen's small garage, which she had renovated into a studio. It said *Welcome Home, Honey.* Moving to Regina was an imperfect solution, but it felt like a decision I could live with, and one that had been made just in time. I had no desire now, or plan, to stir from this safe haven. Home, I was.

I had finished my bloody degree, and I would now use it to find a better job and work at that job for the rest of my life, enjoying a family and the good things that money can buy in our society. Also, Karen had told me that I was the only man she ever knew who opened a woman's shirt like it was a picnic basket, and now every day would be a picnic.

The fall was lazy. I raked leaves and grass. I negotiated my housekeeping duties and rent with Karen. My contribution, however small, was important and provided welcome financial relief to her precise budget. One day I came into the house to find Karen in close consultation at the kitchen table with her financial advisor. He was explaining to her what Black Monday was and why her portfolio had lost twenty-three per cent of its value in a single day, October 19, 1987. Being sans portfolio myself, I had no similar concerns.

I needed a job. I applied here and there. The big dairy in town, Dairy Producers Co-op, in their shiny new plant, needed someone to cover one of their lab tech's vacation leave, and I managed to get two weeks of well paid employment there. I had hoped something more might come of it, but no.

I was still limping on my painful knee, and eight hours a day on my feet was torture. On the first day, early in the day, I was being shown how to calibrate the computerized, direct, in-line milk fat standardization system, somewhat overwhelmed by control valves, and flow and density meters. I began to flag, and I thought it must surely be time for coffee. I really needed to sit down. When I looked at my watch, it was nowhere near ten o'clock. It was twenty to nine. I had been on the job for forty minutes, and I was exhausted.

The woman training me was as unhappy as it is possible to be. She had a university degree in something, and she was stuck in a shitty lab job in a dairy with no likelihood of every breaking out of it. There was no room in food industry management for women. In addition there was so little communication and respect between union and management that she didn't know, and was barely thankful when she found out, that her bosses had bothered to hire extra help. They had not told her I was coming in. She thought she was going to have to cover all the functions of the lab by herself while her partner was away on vacation, and she was dreading the frantic pace that would involve. The managers took some interest in me because I was a man and therefore eligible to join management ranks. I also had a pretty dazzling academic record which I took no pains to cover up, so there was also the possibility that I might not only join them one day, but surpass them. They eye-balled me suspiciously.

But there were simply no positions at the dairy. This was unfortunate. There wasn't much else going on in Regina in the food industry. Karen's notion that "there are so few qualified people in the province you will be in immediate demand" was overly optimistic, if not unrealistic. People who already have jobs are often very out of touch with the realities of the employment scene.

I found another odd job that fall working at the Canadian Western Agribition, Regina's fall agricultural fair. The Department of the Secretary of State of Canada, State Ceremonial, National Exhibitions and Regional Fairs, schlepped around an exhibit called "Spirit of Enterprise," from one town fair to another, and hired local people to act as hosts. For ten days we stood in front of a variety of interesting products made somewhere in Canada and talked them up to passersby. The federal project officer in charge, Jeannine, gave me flirty smiles in the interview and made me the unofficial team leader, sort of the Head Vanna White. At the fair we greeted the public, schmoozing and answering questions. I may have missed my calling. Still, and again, it was hard standing on my biting knee for hours at a time.

One of my ten-day colleagues was an older man who had worked for years for the government of Saskatchewan and was now unemployed. He and hundreds of others had been fired recently in the privatization and downsizing programs of the conservative eighties. He was "given the opportunity to work in the private sector."

Grant Devine was the eleventh premier of the province and the first Conservative premier since 1934. After fifty years of socialist and centrist government, the people of Saskatchewan, the land of the co-operative, the home of Canadian Medicare, the home of Tommy Douglas, decided to get into bed with the virulently anti-socialist Ronald Reagan and Brian Mulroney. Why fight it? Devine won back-to-back terms of office, in 1982 and 1986. His ten years in power were marked by mass sell-offs of government assets and enterprises, sometimes at ridiculous losses, mass firings of public servants, white-elephant and snake-oil economic development projects, fiscal mismanagement, stalled growth, outrageous debt, and criminal scandal.

In the 1991 election, the unofficial anti-Conservative campaign slogan was "Open the books and punish the crooks." The Conservatives won only ten seats in 1991 and lost the popular vote by a margin of two to one, a drop of seventy-five per cent from 1986. They won only five seats in 1996, and after that the party disappeared altogether from the political landscape. Grant Devine was the Bill Vander Zalm of Saskatchewan. He oversaw, and was the major cause of, the implosion of an entire political party at the height of its power, a rare gift. Most Conservatives flocked to the new Saskatchewan Party in the late nineties, and they finally won the government back in 2007, sixteen years after the Devine disgrace.

When Grant Devine announced his intention, in 2004, of re-entering politics and running for federal office for the Conservative Party of Canada, his political legacy was still so toxic he was expelled from the party by the executive council rather than be allowed to represent them.

In 1987, with hundreds of Saskatchewan public servants newly unemployed, it was unlikely there would be any job openings in the provincial government. But one day there was an ad for a temporary food science job in the local office of the Federal Department of Agriculture. I applied, got an interview, and started on Monday, January 4, 1988.

Only four years earlier I had muttered a heartfelt prayer in the hallway at St. Mary's retreat in Toledo, Washington. "Please, God. Whatever happens, don't let me become a bureaucrat. Don't let it come to that." And what I had been trying to avoid was precisely what happened.

In spite of my general misgivings, I had to look on this job as good news. The Federal Government. The Iron Rice Bowl. Like it or not, want it or not, this was a bit of luck. It was amazing to have landed the job, under the circumstances, and it was an opportunity to succeed or even excel. Upon graduating I had been offered a good job in a flavour house, and blown it. Now, right off the street, with no professional connections in Regina at all, I was offered an even better job, in some ways, the Mother of All Sinecures, a professional position in a small niche of the lumbering Juggernaut of Important Mediocrity. In this case, protecting the public through inspection of the food supply. I told myself I would be more of a science officer than a bureaucrat. The Federal Government! Given Regina's low cost of living, they were an employer of good pay, good benefits, and many perks, a place where no one really worked, and no one was ever fired. Fate wanted me to succeed, or at least survive in comfort. But there was no job I could not sabotage.

It was close to fifty degrees below zero the morning I started, pitch black outside at 8:00 a.m., and hot and dry on the fourth floor of the Agriculture Canada offices on Broad Street. I started my first day in the federal government with a meeting with my new boss, Don. I was seated across the desk from him in his corner office. Don had a wide outlook on life and an appreciation of life's many absurdities. He was given to chortling, and he chortled now. "There's a question I would like to ask you that I wasn't allowed to ask in the interview, and it's this. Are you the kind of guy who can go home at five o'clock, look back on the day, and realize you haven't done a damn thing?" In other words, did I have unrealistic expectations about the effectiveness or immediacy of my daily work? Was I suited to the long view of government?

I was fairly certain I could do nothing all day for good pay, and if pressed, not care very much about it, so long as no one else did. I was pretty sure that's what everyone in government did, anyway. But I didn't say that. I wasn't sure what to say.

I had a question for Don. Had he telephoned my previous employer, Denis, in Abbotsford? Yes, he had. He said it was an interesting conversation. He had had to close the door of his office. I told him that I had fired Denis by quitting, and that it was his performance that was inadequate, not mine. Knowing Denis would not give me a reference, quite the reverse, there was no other way to frame the circumstances, and no point in trying. I told Don I was surprised I had still been hired at Agriculture Canada. He said he had decided not to worry about Denis's strong opinion of me.

Don was an interesting guy. He was too straightforward and honest to be a manager in government, but he told me he was forced by circumstances to apply for the job he now had. He and his colleagues realized that if one of them didn't apply for, and win, the manager's job, it was going to go to a prick that no one wanted to work for. Don drew the short straw, won the job, and he was now the federal Program Manager of Food Inspection in Saskatchewan. I was the newly minted Program Officer in Dairy, Fruit and Vegetable.

Don was, and had been, a meat guy, and he would happily have spent many more years kicking around the province's ranches, feed lots, stockyards, auction houses, slaughterhouses, and packing plants, in his cowboy boots, watching cows, pigs, and chickens get killed and cut up, but he had had to leave all that delicious freedom behind and take a desk job. He was a couple of years older than I, and he had gone straight through university after high school, in spite of attempting to drink every beer made in the province of Saskatchewan during that time. He and dozens of other new graduates were snapped up in one of the last waves of mass federal government recruitment. He had fifteen years of pensionable service under his belt. I had none.

Don was short and quite round in the belly. I know you're not supposed to describe people by simply likening them to famous faces, actors of stage and screen, magazine icons, etc. It's considered lazy and unworkmanlike in a writer. But, truth be told, Don was a dead ringer for a young Wilfrid Brimley, well known by the 1980s for his big moustache and his many "Grandpa" roles in film and television. If that helps. He did butter sculptures and played the mandolin. Don, not Wilfrid. He laughed a lot. I liked him. One day he put a mirror on the wall in the office and a sign under it that read *Employee of the Month*. His unimaginative boss, a young rule-bound hayseed, made him take it down.

Don also talked a lot. Some bureaucrats figure out that if you're always talking, you never have to do anything. If you're always planning for tomorrow, you never have to do anything today. In my first few weeks, I was frequently on edge. There was always a meeting coming up, and I was new. I wanted to be prepared. I knew nothing about public administration, the mechanics of government, and nothing much about the Saskatchewan food industry, although there was no one in the office who knew more about general food science than I did. I was the only graduate in that discipline. Most of the office staff were soil and crop guys. And I mean guys. There wasn't a single woman in the managerial or professional levels, the privileged boys' club, and there wasn't a single man in the secretarial or clerical ranks, the pink and angry ghetto. And bitchy.

"Raylene, are you coming to the bar after work?"

"I don't know. Is *she* coming? Because if *she's* coming then *I'm* not going."

"Alright. Maybe next time."

To prepare for these many meetings, I read and researched and consulted my colleagues with persistence and diligence. And invariably, when the meeting convened, Don started talking and didn't shut up until it was over. He liked to make his points in order, in point form, starting usually with "a," but there was never a "b." He liked to have his ducks in a row but there was only ever one duck. He was unconcerned. He had no gift for self-doubt. I soon realized that preparing for meetings was no more than an abstract good, something you could do to improve yourself, but it was hardly a practical necessity. No one ever asked me a question, and Don never stopped talking. Decisions were rare. The first principle of bureaucracy is that bullshit, if left alone, will go on forever by itself.

I had never had an office job before, a desk job. It was my very first one. I had worked for government as a summer labourer of one sort or another, building sidewalks for the town of Sedgewick, and as gay eye candy at the BC Provincial Museum. Being an ESL teacher was the only pen-and-paper job I had ever had, and that was more of a performance position. I had never worked in a cubicle with thirty or forty other people on the same floor, also in cubicles. I went to the store and bought a couple of new suits and an overcoat and new shoes. I looked pretty sharp. Too sharp, actually, for an agriculture office.

There was no computer in my cubicle, or anyone's. The desktop computer had only just been invented. I had taken a couple of university courses in computing, one of them using dumb tubes and one using the brand new Apple Macintosh Plus. The three shiny, new computing labs at U of A were full of brand new Macs, none of them with hard drives. All you could hear in the crowded labs was the boop-boop-boop of 3.5" ROM disks being flipped endlessly in and out of the floppy drives. In 1986, a Mac Plus cost $2,600, about $5,000 in 2014 money. No one at Agriculture Canada knew how to use a computer of any kind except a couple of nerds on the second floor who babysat the mini-computer down there. In 1988, a mini-computer was the size of a Toyota Corolla. It sat with its lights blinking in its own air-conditioned room and had less computing power than a preschooler's Fisher-Price learning tablet does today.

Needless to say, the federal government was a nightmare of unending bureaucratic bullshit. The personnel manual, laid on its back, was nearly four feet high. You couldn't do anything without first crawling up your supervisor's ass to look for permission. We had to have a meeting before we could make a phone call. We needed a legal opinion before we could write a letter. We had no idea what our powers really were, or if it would be a good idea to exercise them. Mostly, we just had meetings and talked about things that would never happen. We had little to do and little to lose, so there was always a lot to say.

And we got to travel around quite a bit. I saw a lot of Saskatchewan in 1988. When we weren't bored out of our skulls in the over-heated office, we were out on inspections, or going to conferences, or to other government offices to visit, to chat, and to, uhm, liaise, or exchange information or expertise. Or something. I'm not sure. I was mostly at sea.

I went frequently with Henry, the skinny, skittish fruit and vegetable inspector, to pore over and grade random samples at the local warehouses. Saskatchewan's fruit and vegetable industry in the 1980s was worth about $200 million a year, half of it imported. Inspection was used for both food safety and business arbitration purposes. If the local importers had a complaint about quality, Agriculture Canada inspectors provided a timely quality assessment service which the sellers and the buyers agreed to abide by. Food-borne illness in fruit and vegetables is rare compared with dairy sources and very rare compared with meat, so health inspections for food safety purposes, although routine, were actually less pressing than those for commercial arbitration.

I went on several inspection tours with Keith, the easygoing dairy inspector. I enjoyed these. Most of them were out of town. I was especially glad to go to the big dairy plant in Regina where I could quietly show my former, temporary bosses that I was now their boss, sort of. They teased us mercilessly, making fun of bureaucrats. We visited just about every dairy in the province. We took samples of bird shit and tasted butter. There were, and are, thousands of pounds of butter in frozen storage across the country.

Keith was a joker. He had a situational joke that I heard him use two or three times in the office. It never failed. He would encounter a woman in the elevator or in the hallway and say, "Hi, Jane. Hey, I had a dream about you last night." She would inevitably say, "Did you?" And Keith would say, "No, you wouldn't let me." It worked every time, a modern classic.

Honey is fairly big business in Saskatchewan, or was, and we went to the honey producers' convention in Saskatoon where the topic of bee mites and their devastating effects on bee colonies was at the forefront of everyone's mind. We went to honey farms to take samples and do testing. At one farm, in January, it was fifty below with a strong wind blowing as we made our way from the car to the barn. At first Henry and I were in the lee of the barn, protected from the wind, but when we turned the corner and were hit with a 30-mile-an-hour wind at fifty below zero, I thought I would die. You wouldn't last twenty minutes without shelter in that weather. We took our frozen samples and ate our bag lunches with the young farmer and his wife and their small children in the kitchen of their new mobile home. It was flat prairie for hundreds of miles in every direction.

Don and I took a car one day to Swift Current and looked over the cattle yards there, a nostalgia tour for Don. We chatted with the head of the operation, an old friend of his. While we sat across from him, his desk phone rang, and he picked it up and told the person on the other end of the line that he couldn't talk now, he had guys in his office wearing *ties*. We stayed overnight. kd lang was performing in Rapid Raisin, but I didn't have the energy to go see her. The next day, we visited the cheddar cheese plant, but it wasn't an official inspection. On the way back to Regina, we stopped at the big slaughterhouse outside Moose Jaw. Don knew I was not a meat-eater, a vegetarian of sorts, quite content working in dairy, fruit and vegetable, but he felt I needed to be more well-rounded and get to know every aspect of the food industry in Saskatchewan. In short, the bastard made me take a tour of the slaughterhouse without warning me in advance. We drove up to the plant, and the next thing I knew I was on the killing floor watching the legs kicking and the blood draining, three dead cows every minute. I have never forgotten those images. I remember the man who walked us through the plant. He was wearing a belt buckle the size of an automobile licence plate. Don said it was a rodeo prize.

I went to Ontario for a week. Don sent me to a HAACP course at the Transport Canada Training Institute, now called NavCentre, in Cornwall, a small city on the St. Lawrence River near Montreal, a city so bilingual they speak bad English as well as they speak bad French. That's HAACP, Hazard Analysis Critical Control Point. It's a logic-tool, preventive system for minimizing hazards in food production. It was cooked up by NASA and the Pillsbury Company in the 1960s to make sure astronauts didn't get food poisoning in space. After the course I spent a night in Ottawa, seventy miles away, and the next day introduced myself, nervously, to any bigwig I could find at Agriculture Canada headquarters. Nothing had been arranged in advance. Don told me simply to go to headquarters and make myself known. Don was better at self-promotion than I was, by a damn sight. One high-ranking bureaucrat whose office I bumbled through said, "On a course at Cornwall? Good. Get whatever training you can get your hands on. The days of easy money for that sort of thing are over."

What I remember fondly about Ottawa was the dinner I had at the taxpayers' expense at a very nice Afghan restaurant near the Parliament Buildings. I went to a play at the National Arts Centre, but I don't remember what it was. I wandered the sumptuous public areas of the Chateau Laurier Hotel and heard snippets of relentlessly political discussion emanating from every table and corner, every plush chair and bench. In my mind I compared these rich and highly charged surroundings with the tiny, bare cubicle in Regina that I shared with the increasingly grumpy Henry.

Agriculture Canada was no better than Dairy Producers Co-operative when it came to labour relations and organizational behaviour. When I started on January 4, the two inspectors who were under me on the organization chart, Henry and Keith, had no idea I had been hired. My position was a temporary assignment, so there wasn't much need for them to worry yet, but the plan was obviously to make the position permanent. To them this only meant another layer of management and another boss. There was definitely a divide. They were in the union. I was in a professional association. My job required a university degree, their jobs didn't. On my first day, I went out vegetable-inspecting with Henry and he told me, testily, that he had not been consulted or informed about my appointment. "Great," thought I. He was bitter because, for lack of a degree, he would never rise above a union position. Don's response, not unfriendly but clear, was that Henry was free to go back to university any time he wanted.

Henry was civil for a while, but he was as dull as a dial tone and grew less friendly and cooperative over time. After a few months, he stopped speaking to me altogether. After I had been out on several dozen inspections, and to all the winter conferences in the province, I found myself with nothing left to do but read endlessly in my cubicle. Technical reports, journals, trade magazines, scientific papers, history, policy, conference proceedings, anything I could find, and there were hundreds of things to read in the office. The ongoing inspection programs ran themselves and required no input or refinement from me. There were no projects to do, and none were proposed by my boss. I discovered later, to my naive surprise, that he expected me to propose them. I was new. He might have mentioned that.

When I got back from Ottawa and the HAACP course, I presented a shortened, two-day version of it to all the inspectors in the province. I did a marvelous job of the written materials. I made up large, clear handbooks for each of the inspectors, quite professional-looking, with no help from the typing pool. They did no work for temporary employees. I was deeply engaged in designing the teaching modules, and I even enjoyed presenting them. This was something I could do and had done before. It didn't much matter. Most of the inspectors still thought I was a dick. I was too high-tone for them. They wanted to keep the working atmosphere working class. They were proud of their blue-collar background, and their hard-earned skills and experience. They wanted no fancy college talk from me.

Don liked me, though, and I think the reason he did is because I had a more polished and up-to-date education, and look, than the rednecks of a previous generation who were still running the companies in secondary food processing in Saskatchewan, and the uneducated, button-pushing high school dropouts who worked for them in their new plants. Swedish Tetra Pak technology had finally come to Canada, and the brand new machines caused much scratching of heads on the production floor in Regina, among the staff and the inspectors. The food industry was modernizing, and Don wanted someone shinier and more professional on his organization chart.

Don was a short, pudgy cowboy, but he was also an artist and a musician. He had a good sense of humour, he was smart, and he longed, discreetly, for a higher level of culture. I heard him mention a desire for adventure travel. He was a Renaissance meat inspector. I didn't attempt to make hay out of my previous life experience. I wasn't the world's most interesting man, and I was too polite to let him know or feel that I was his superior in every way. But on a personal level, I think Don liked the idea that I had lived and worked in Israel and Japan and California, that I had travelled, that I had an eclectic background, and that my spouse was an artist and the director of an art gallery. Maybe not. I was turning out to be useless on the job. He began to reconsider the need for having a Dairy, Fruit and Vegetable Program Officer in Regina. Maybe they didn't need one after all.

I didn't know how to push in government, how to promote myself, how to propose, plan, and execute projects that would be considered valuable in an enormous, and to me, incomprehensible organization. I was hoping Don would teach me those things. It's not like he didn't have time. For his part, he wanted me to bring those abilities with me to the job. Other than a mutual affability, we shared no middle ground.

My mood deteriorated as I became more disillusioned and disgusted by government work. I know it is easier to abuse your fellows than to praise them. Praise, it is said, takes more intelligence and requires a finer analysis. Also, often enough, we find unpleasant truths in ourselves that we cannot accept, and we project them onto those around us. We don't see the world as it is, we create it based on desire and aversion, an endless cycle of pleasure and pain, and then populate it with ideas and judgments. Our relationship is not with what is in front of us, but with the thoughts and stories we have created in our minds about what we see. Sometimes, though, you just have to accept that other people can be dicks, too. Unfortunately, sometimes, people are exactly what you read into them.

My coworkers were a distasteful bunch. In 1988, the Regina office of Agriculture Canada was not an enlightened workplace. The pervading atmosphere of racism and sexism among the all-white staff was discouraging and occasionally sickening. Offensively inappropriate language, behaviour, and jokes were the norm. The men constantly put the women down and so did the women, an office of Anita Bryants and Phyllis Schlaflys. "Indians" and minorities of every kind were routinely disparaged in the self-satisfied terms of grubby prejudice. Other topics of conversation seldom varied from the fascinating themes of mortgages, pensions, and lawn care. Some of my colleagues had never had a bite of ethnic food and had no more personality than the letters in their names. The list on the sign-out board was *Al, Barry, Bill, Bob, Chuck, Don, Ernie, Frank, George, Harry, Henry, John, Keith, Ken, Les, Neil, Peter, Richard, Stan, Vic, Walt.* It was a pasty, paunchy, all-white, all-male circle jerk. The most frequent entry next to these names was "SBB," meaning "Should Be Back." By the end of the day, I couldn't wait to get away from most of these narrow-minded, hidebound bigots. I mention this unpleasant aspect of working at Agriculture Canada only because it is true, the weeping wound of a sad culture. I cannot blame my coworkers for my own failings, but I was in no mood to blame myself. Again, what the hell was I doing in food science? Fuckin' rednecks. I didn't have to worry. I wouldn't be in it long.

At the largest financial and real estate company in Regina, the office culture was no better. The private sector has rarely led the way in workplace reform. I was told that there, as usual, all the professional and managerial positions were occupied by men. Women made up the typing pool.

When young, male university graduates were hired, they received much of their training from women in senior clerical positions who had been with the company for years, women who made nowhere near the salary of the pups they were training. The new hires received memberships to golf and fitness clubs. The women did not. When the women in the company complained of this to the management, in the late eighties, they were given, as a group, a fifty-dollar gift certificate to a bowling alley.

Things were looking up in one regard. On January 1, 1988, smoking was banned in Canadian federal government offices. I started my bureaucratic career only three days later. Hallelujah! I couldn't imagine what it must have been like to work in an office of forty people with half of them smoking at their desks all day long. I got a taste of it at the enormous MacDonald's Consolidated grocery warehouse, a place I visited several times with Henry, where the office staff worked in a single large room, dozens of desks flush with one another and an overflowing ashtray on every desk. Federal rules did not yet extend to the private sector. The air was thick with smoke all day long, worse than a honky-tonk saloon. The place was filthy. I couldn't have worked there for a minute. The small waiting area was packed with nervous salesmen itching and squirming to make a sale to Safeway, whacked out on caffeine, yapping like little dogs. A single sale would make their week. Unfortunately, at Agriculture Canada, the new rules still allowed for the designation of a smoking room somewhere in the office. In an act of counterproductive, but inevitable stupidity, the lunchroom was designated the smoking room. Every employee who smoked now converged on the break room to light up. This made the lunchroom unbearable, and toxic, for the intelligent half of the staff, the non-smokers. On my worst days, I feel that if every smoker on the planet were to put a bullet in their head tomorrow, after we got all of the bastards buried, the world would be a finer place. But that's only on my worst days.

I got to the point where I could hardly stand going into the office. "SBB" was frequently scrawled next to my name on the sign-out board while I sat in a coffee shop somewhere nearby. There was nothing to do in the office but read, and there weren't many friendly faces. Don went to some effort to give me the advantage. Arguing down opposition from his fellow managers and his boss, he extended my position by a month, but when I finally interviewed for the permanent version of my own job, I failed to make the minimum number of points. I came in second to a young man working in the Saskatoon office in a position similar to mine. But he also failed the interview. Everyone did. How could I have possibly failed? I had been on the job for seven months. I had the edge. It wasn't that complicated. I had a fatal aptitude for being bad at interviews. God knows the jobs I might have got, and the trouble I'd have known, if I had been good at them.

I could make nothing of Agriculture Canada. I over-thought it, and I missed the point. As far as I could tell, there was no job there at all. It was as phoney as a three-dollar bill. I guess I did have an over-attachment to the immediacy of my daily activities. The long view of government was too long for me. And worse, I despised the organizational culture. I was working in an office of backward, narrow-minded people whose only job was to *keep* their jobs, living lives of fretful self-preservation. I didn't fit in. Apart from the right to suck air, I had nothing in common with these people. I didn't know who they were, what they wanted, how they thought, or what the fuck they were doing.

Government payroll had ballooned to spectacular levels over the last twenty years. In the 1960s, Canada began producing university graduates at unprecedented levels, far higher than could be absorbed by Canadian business and industry. The various levels of expanding government had stepped in to hire these graduates in an elaborate form of welfare for the over-educated. And now the party was coming to an end. The great swathing of new graduates in annual federal recruiting was over, limitless national travel was sharply curtailed, programs that hadn't been evaluated in years, if ever, were under the microscope, and new management information systems were discovering alarming gaps and variations in productivity. Downsizing was in the wind. The biggest question on the managers' minds was, "Is *anyone* in this office doing enough work to justify their job classification?" It was government. It was waste and lies and shit, as dishonest as a marriage.

When I failed the final interview, and my temporary position was up at the end of July, I packed up the few things in my desk and walked out of the over-air-conditioned office hardly saying good-bye to anyone other than Don, and the good-natured Keith, and Ben the egg man, and Ken the very eccentric livestock auction man.

This is your reward for playing the game. That was the introduction to a half-page ad I saw in the newspaper one day in Calgary when I was nineteen years old. There was a picture of a new car under the words. I was happily unemployed, and I shook my head and thought, "Gee, I guess I'll have to get a job, so I can finance the car I need to drive to my job, the one I have to get in order to pay for my new car." To my friends I said, "Does anyone see the circular logic in this 'game'?" At nineteen, in 1972, I could see only the weaknesses in this kind of reasoning and how it played to our basest desires. A sordid game it was. I had been raised on materialism, and I saw that the structure of materialism was as fragile and ephemeral as the seed ball of a dandelion. If that was the game, then it was not a game for me. Even at nineteen, I knew I was a drunk and a fool, but I wasn't *that* kind of fool, enslaved by possessive instinct. How soft does your toilet paper need to be?

I never pursued a career, never wanted one, because I could never suspend my disbelief in the underlying political and social myths, the community, the structure, or the process, and I had no hankering for the rewards. A worker, a taxpayer, a consumer. I couldn't wear those masks. Surely it would be wrong of me to dissimulate. I was intolerant of such pursuits, and I was what I was because I would not engage in them. I could not make that bitterness sweet, and it made my virtues look like shortcomings.

Sixteen years later, I found that I had asked for very little from life, and I had received very little from it. I had also forgotten, or never learned, how to give. It had only occasionally occurred to me to do good for its own sake, and it had been discouraging to discover that even those who want to do good are required to make a career, a game, of it.

There was nothing unsound about the philosophies I loved. It was my lazy personality combined with an incomplete understanding and an unproductive misinterpretation of them that formed the problem. I was as incapable of pursuing the paths I loved as I was of pursuing the ones I despised. I wanted to do something out of the ordinary, and I wound up doing nothing. *Soy vago y vago.*

I was to discover, over time, that I can work alone with numbers and words quite contentedly, twelve hours a day for weeks at a time before I finally collapse, but when I'm tired I can't work with, or even be around other people for ten minutes, especially in the afternoon. I don't like people in groups very much, a state that I suspect has arisen in me because they so rarely agree with me, and I never figured out how to hide those feelings. As Don said, "Sincerity is everything. Once you can fake that, you've got it made." I have never accepted the notion that working with other people was obligatory or inevitable. I disagreed with Karen. Community was not what I needed.

My last two jobs had been complete disasters. I couldn't work in production of any kind, or in a trade, or an art, not in a lab, or in an office. Six years earlier, at Camosun College, Professor Howard had asked, "So, Neil, even if you do graduate, what do you think you will do? How long will you last in a lab?" "Good question, Howard," said I. Agriculture Canada was my thirtieth job in eighteen years. The options were thinning out. All I had ever been successful at was going to school and teaching, and I didn't care much for either of those. And I wasn't qualified to teach. In 1988, I still believed, I had no choice, that I could fit in to some kind of employment situation. I just had to find the right one. In spite of the evidence, I had to believe that not being able to stand any of my previous thirty jobs was a matter of a series of specific flaws, not a general malaise. My strategy seemed to be to lose every battle, and somehow still win the war. But my essential nature was planless. I could not follow a plan of my own. It was unlikely I would follow the plans of others.

Things seemed a little desperate, but I still had the degree, and I wasn't going to write it off just yet. For me, it was Cinderella's glass slipper. It was in my hand. It would be a long time, though, before I found her pretty foot, that pale, underfed, shoeless char.

I was as particular as a prince, but not as charming.

24   Trophy Husband

Karen and I went out every week. We went to the movies, to art openings, to galleries, art events, and the theatre, to friends' places and parties, to restaurants and bars. Every Thursday we met the same small group of educated, interesting, unworldly women for turkey dinner at the Eaton's cafeteria in the mall downtown, followed by shopping and then a trip to a grungy but convenient bar. Beer was two dollars and fifty cents, and I always had four.

Karen shopped every week. She came home frequently carrying three or four shiny bags, like a woman in a magazine cartoon. I saw her buy dresses that she wore once and never wore again. She shopped manically at the edge of her budget. Still does.

Most of Karen's friends worked in art, social work, community development, healthcare, teaching, every manner of tax-funded employment. She knew no one in industry and very few people in business except the wealthy lawyers, doctors, and accountants who bought art. An art opening is a social chiaroscuro of wealth and creativity. The artists are creative enough not to be intimidated by wealth, and the people with enough money to buy art are not intimidated by creativity. You wind up with a roomful of confident, self-possessed people, some perfectly lovely, some creeps, some both, feeding off each other, no one quite sure at any given moment who is black and who is white. It's a yeasty, sexy mix of art and property. Add wine and stir.

Every month Karen put on a cocktail dress, and I put on a shiny suit and a skinny tie, and we drank at art galleries, ballrooms, and people's homes. Then I drove us home drunk in the New Yorker. We either had brief, outrageous sex, or argued and fought, or both.

Generally, we had a good first fall and winter. At my new job, though, I was away from home at least once a week, sometimes twice, inspecting dairies, going to meetings and conferences, and attending to made-up, out-of-town, bureaucratic busywork. Karen travelled once in a while as well, judging art shows, going to meetings, meeting artists, visiting studios, looking at art, talking about art. She was often out on weeknights. Having a spouse who is away can be a nice break, but it's also stressful. Routines get disturbed. Partners are simply less available.

It also became clear very soon after I arrived that Karen was not going to let me have my own relationship with her son, Devon. She felt, not incorrectly, that I was too inexperienced and generally uninterested in children to be able to foster the kinds of values she wanted to instill in the home. In this, however, she was only partly right. When Devon and I were alone, we got along fine. When the three of us were together, he skilfully played Karen and I against each other in order to get what he wanted or just for the childish but understandable thrill of being able to create discord. Like many young children of divorce, he thought his mom and dad were going to get back together. While he was waiting, he would make good use of his time. He never lost an opportunity to manipulate Karen into being pissed off at me for whatever reason he could think up. In this, Karen was as blind as only a mother can be. She felt she needed to position herself between Devon and me rather than let us work out our own relationship. There would be no loss of control in this important area. Parenting was not a household chore for which my services were required. Living with a seven-year-old who had his mother wrapped around his finger got old very quickly. "When it comes to influencing a child, a woman who is happy with her husband is worth a dozen women who worship their children."

For all of Karen's high ideals about art and politics and community, when it came to childrearing, she was a lazy parent. Devon's behaviour would decline without check for many weeks until she snapped and yelled at him in the most frightening way. Devon would then make an effort to take his shoes off at the door and do his homework, but over time, without a structured routine of disciplined or even logical activity, he would inevitably resort to the easy indulgence he saw in the adults around him. Artists and bohemians and anarchists often have high ideals, and are fun to drink with, but how many second-generation artists and bohemians and anarchists are there? Devon knew I had a degree in science, and whenever he had a question, he would first pose it to his mother, disbelieve her responce, and then, to her frustration, ask me the same question. Often enough, I gave him the same answer, but his mother was an artist, and he distrusted her grasp of technical realities. It didn't matter that she was the one who worked and ran an art gallery while I stayed home and vacuumed. I was a man, and I was a scientist.

In addition to the parties, we lived a domestic life, too. The sparse work schedule of my first autumn in Regina was padded out by household projects, fixing the fence, putting a roof on Devon's playhouse, mounting whirligigs on the roof of the garage. Karen had taken to making wooden folk-art, whirligigs, key-hook holders, bookends, wall plaques, varieties of yard art, often in the shape of, and brightly painted with, plump women wearing nothing but red lipstick and flirty smiles. She was co-opting the familiar peasant medium in the service of women's culture, something she believed in, and something in which she was an obvious creative force. She contrasted the naive style of the folk art form with her own provocative strain of feminism.

Karen was largely unconcerned about my career. She told me I could work at the 7-Eleven convenience store at the end of the block, for all she cared, as long as I brought in enough money to help pay the bills. What she wanted from me was a steady date on Saturday nights, a pretty face across the room she could go home with. It was her career that was important, not mine. There was some logic in this attitude. When two people harness themselves to professional challenges, they progress at different rates. Tensions will arise. If two people simply agree that one of them is in charge, there will be fewer stresses. Are you the diamond or are you the setting? When I got the job at Agriculture Canada, she was pleased for me, but only because it was something I wanted. If I made a good income as a boring bureaucrat, that was fine, but it didn't really matter to her.

Karen's mother was a teacher of six-year-olds, a job she executed daily for forty years. Her father was, among other things, in the end, a downtown, back-alley alcoholic, a drinker of after shave. In Karen's life, women worked and men were a gamble. She was the "adult child of an alcoholic," a phrase much in use in the eighties. According to Janet Woititz's 1983 book, these adult children fear losing control and try to control the behaviour and feelings of others, and thus can misinterpret assertiveness in their friends and family. They can become addicted to chaos and drama, which gives them their adrenaline fix and feelings of power and control. They are often in relationships with people they feel they can rescue, confusing love with pity, and will do anything to save a relationship rather than face the pain of abandonment even if the relationship is unhealthy. And they can often become abusers of alcohol themselves.

In 2014, twenty-two years after Karen and I split up, I was talking with her one day about the eighties. I said, "I was a leaner and you were an enabler." She paused a moment to think about that, then sighed and said, "All my useless men."

Karen was in charge of the universe, and of me. I felt like an employee in The Karen Group of Worldwide Companies. I told her I couldn't live being so constantly controlled and managed, so constantly under her thumb. She was surprised. Did I think she would give up control of her life to me? To anyone? To any *man*? I told her I didn't want control of her life. I wanted control of mine. She did not understand assertiveness. Later, I asked her if counselling might not be a good idea. She said, "That's a wonderful idea, honey. You would definitely benefit from counselling." And she wasn't making a joke. I had meant counselling for *us*, not me. The pronoun was unstated, but obvious, and it had not occurred to her. She hadn't even heard it.

I wasn't much of a trophy husband, but even if I were, my mangy head wouldn't be on the wall for long.

By the spring, many cracks had begun to show. I was aghast at how snippy and demanding and controlling Karen was. Over the years, we went to a hundred movies, and she never let me pick one. It doesn't sound like much, but it's part of a pattern, and it's wearing. Aghast also at how difficult it was to live with a child committed to sabotage and destruction. I also knew, very soon, that my job at Agriculture Canada was doomed to fail. The daily weight was too much for my narrow shoulders.

June of 1988 was a record hot month in Regina. On June 5, it was a hundred and six degrees Fahrenheit, thirty-eight degrees higher than average. I was mowing the lawn and started to feel woozy before it occurred to me to check the thermometer. Starting in the middle of May, there were twenty-nine sweltering days in a row of higher than average temperatures. In the month of June, four days out of five were above average, meaning scorching hot. Our tiny house turned into an oven. We all slept on the concrete floor in the basement, but not well. We went to the movies and to malls because they were air-conditioned. We looked forward to going to work to get some sleep at our desks in our chilly over-air-conditioned offices. There wasn't an air conditioner in Regina left for sale. I knew my parents had an extra one in their basement, a heavy, old, but refurbished, 10,000 BTU window shaker, and I telephoned them and begged them to sell it to us and send it on the bus as soon as possible. When it arrived a few days later, I was so desperate to get it going I picked it up off the floor by myself and placed it in the kitchen window. The packing slip said "104 pounds." That's a lot for me.

The heat and the arguing became intolerable, and for a week or two in the spring I bolted for refuge to the spare basement bedroom of a friend who lived nearby. I actually moved out, I and my thirty boxes of personal goods. I was working. I needed my clothes. When Karen and I talked again, it was not easy to reconcile, but neither of us wanted to give up on each other yet. We were both glad to put our fighting behind us, and I moved back after just a few days.

If you know yourself, you need not always be advancing, particularly if you are of a shirking temperament. You can retreat with equal confidence. I am not the kind of person who shatters for lack of the fiction of an occupation, but when I lost my job at the end of July, I was more affected than at many times in the past. I left the house that same night, after Karen was in bed, about ten o'clock, and went to the second-worst bar in town, a truly awful place. I drank there by myself until it closed.

The next day Karen said, "Are you all right, hon?"

I was free during the day now, so I did the weekly shopping and built a big closet in the basement, as well as a shoe rack, and shelving. There was always painting and drilling and planing to be done, something peeling or stuck, some electrical inconvenience to be overcome. There was one electrical outlet in each room of the house. When it was built in 1927, all anyone owned with a cord and a plug was a lamp and a radio. I dealt with plumbing, badly, and with the sump pump when it seized up. I cleaned the rain gutters. In a land so dry, it seemed unfair that we often had a flooded basement, but in a land so flat, there was nowhere for the water to go when it rained. I cooked and vacuumed and raked leaves and shovelled snow.

And I read. I discovered I needed glasses for the first time in my life. The optometrist said I had probably been reading with one eye for fifteen years. At the end of the day, Karen and I would climb into bed and read to each other. We read biographies, philosophy, and religion. She was the most interesting conversationalist I ever had sex with.

And we stayed home and watched TV and VHS movies rented from the video store.

Karen's friends were artists, social workers, socialists, communists, lesbians, homosexuals, designers, teachers, academics, counsellors, musicians, public servants, and workers in non-governmental organizations. In the 1960s, Canada bemoaned the brain drain, the exodus of our best and brightest to the United States. The US got our scientists and engineers, and we got their draft dodgers, poets, and sociologists. That was the joke. Saskatchewan was the home of Canadian socialism, and many left-leaning US citizens of the reverse brain drain wound up here, attracted to the birthplace of the cooperative movement and universal healthcare, to feminism, unionism, to reform of any kind. They were heady days. Now, at the end of the eighties, the people of Saskatchewan had turned back into slaves voting for their masters. They seemed ready to throw it all away, a hundred years of cooperative development on the Canadian prairies, in exchange for the trade beads of right wing economic policy. Many people in the lefty community were now disappointed, disillusioned, and angry. Wouldn't we all like to throw a Molotov cocktail, just once? Many of them were humourless. I had always believed that the moment you are unable to laugh at yourself you are on shaky ontological ground. I was lectured and disapproved of by many of Karen's friends because I was not sufficiently respectful of their emblems of belief. I was a true anarchist, an iconoclast. I didn't care about anyone's emblems of belief. I liked many of these people, but they could be a touchy bunch.

I wasn't ready to work at 7-Eleven or be a parking lot attendant just yet. There seemed to be three long-term options. The one I wanted most dearly was to find another job, one I could live with, but I feared that would now be impossible in Regina.

Far down the short list of options was going to grad school in food science. I still had the NSERC scholarship. When I finished the BSc, I couldn't face the idea of going to grad school. I needed money. I had to get a job. But that wasn't working out. I was allowed to defer the NSERC for up to two years, and that's what I did. I could take it up again anytime until September 1989.

Or I could go to grad school in a different discipline. I could do a professional graduate degree, perhaps in administration. At Agriculture Canada I had been stunned by how little I knew about organizations and administration. I enrolled in a night class in accounting at the University of Regina, something I thought might be useful no matter which direction I wound up going.

I began a long fall and winter of researching different schools and programs, and the ridiculous charade of looking for jobs so I could justify receiving unemployment insurance cheques every two weeks for the next many months.

One job that seemed to come up in the newspapers quite regularly was that of pharmaceutical sales representative. The big drug companies always needed someone to drive around the province selling drugs out of the trunk of their car. This seemed like something I would be suited to. The pay wasn't bad, and the duties were only mildly onerous. I liked driving from town to town. It's gets you out of the house. Plenty of time to be alone and listen to CBC Radio. There were always sales territories available in Saskatchewan because no one wanted to work there. Saskatchewan was the entry-level province for sales employment in Big Pharma. Once you had a year or two under your belt, you transferred to a more desirable climate and province, and another job opened up in Saskatchewan.

I had a recent degree in science, and there was lab and government work on my resume, so I got a few interviews. Once or twice I even got a second one. But even in my nice suit, in spite of my earnest protestations, it was not hard for interviewers to tell that I was not a serious candidate. Desperate, yes, but not earnest. The private sector was unimpressed by me. This was a sphere of human activity in which my skill set was irrelevant. In the world of professional sales, amongst my peers, it was unlikely I would "astonish the weak minds of those about me." These were not weak-minded men. They were in a morally weak business, but they had an undeviating devotion to their profession and commercial goals. They and I both knew my strengths would not play to the rites and rituals, the religion, of sales. I had had thirty jobs. This was difficult to hide. The interviewers wanted to know why, at thirty-five, I was looking for an entry-level position. My answer, not spoken aloud, was, "I'm not." I would have taken a job with a drug company if they had offered me one, although it's unlikely I would have kept it long.

I did not want to go back to school. I only had one degree, but it had taken me eight years to get it. I had had enough of that.

I spent an hour every day going through the Regina *Leader-Post* and the *Globe and Mail*, then sitting at my by-now electronic, not electric, typewriter in the basement. It was chilly downstairs in the winter, tapping out brief letters to prospective employers, ones I knew I would never hear back from. There were very few jobs available locally. Sometimes, it was difficult to find enough of them to apply for to meet the minimum weekly number of applications required by the Unemployment Insurance office. The notion of employment became such a hopeless and ridiculous fantasy I started writing funny letters to companies in the US, Europe, South America, and the Caribbean, to multinational corporations, hospitals, universities, offshore banks, the United Nations, responding to the pompous, overblown ads you see for upper-level positions in large concerns, especially in the *Globe and Mail*, especially on Saturdays. I applied to be a Chief Executive Officer, or a Vice-President of Business Banking, or a Chief Financial Officer, or a Dean of Admissions. What did it matter? I just needed to be able to add the name of a company to my application log, something I could present to a federal bureaucrat should I be called into the UI office. I received one reply from a vice-president of something in the Caribbean. He said he liked my letter and wished me good luck.

I had quit and failed my first two jobs out of university, and as far as employment in the private sector was concerned, that was the death knell. No private company would touch me. I had demonstrated clearly, by my mid-thirties, that I had no mainstream goals, that I didn't get along well with people in groups, and I couldn't get out of bed in the morning. There was only one employer left, one whose eyes were already so woolly I might succeed in throwing another fleece over them.

The government.

I noticed there was one question that I was never asked in a government interview, one they weren't allowed to ask, one they weren't shy about asking in the private sector. "How old are you?" I could pass for a younger man, I could doctor my resume, I could spin my experience as long as I wasn't compelled to confess to twenty years of vague, non-productive wandering. There was no choice but to target the public sector for future income.

Every university I applied to for a graduate position in food science was delighted to have me and my NSERC, but I ended negotiations with all of them. I couldn't bear the thought of a lifetime of academic work, or any, and I was now too old to find work in the private sector even if I did manage to get through a Master's degree in science.

I abandoned the notion of employment in both Regina and food science. I made plans for an alternative fall and winter.

I started applying to schools of public administration.

There was no school of public administration in Regina. I applied to universities in Halifax, Fredericton, Ottawa, Kingston, and Victoria. They all accepted me, and they all offered money in one form or another. I wanted to try living in a different part of Canada. I like to wander. I like new places. Eastern Canada is much older than western Canada. There would be history to be discovered there. It was tempting to go east.

But in the end, I couldn't get away from Victoria. I knew the city and the west coast, and I loved the area. It is the warmest part of Canada, a huge concern for a climatic coward. It is on the ocean, and I missed the water so much. We had two small humidifiers going constantly in the house in Regina. Otherwise, the air was so dry your eyeballs would shrivel into wrinkled orbs the size of dried peas and fall out of their sockets. The University of Victoria also offered a full, no-strings-attached, graduate fellowship. It was $25,000 free and clear, no teaching assistant duties required. I couldn't say no.

I finished the accounting course at the top of a class of three hundred and five. It wasn't too hard. I was only taking one course. In January, I enrolled in another night class, microeconomics, and drove to the campus in fifty-below weather on square, frozen tires. I got public administration textbooks out of the library and read them cover to cover, more than 2,000 pages. At Agriculture Canada I had failed miserably at understanding the mechanics of government and organizational behaviour, and now I would master them, if only academically.

One course in accounting wasn't enough to keep me busy, and I took the opportunity of weeks and weeks of free time to enroll in another course, darkroom photography. I had two dozen rolls of film still undeveloped from my last days in Japan, and California and Washington. After four years of sitting in a cardboard box, hundreds of pictures from halfway around the world came slowly to light.

I decided I would find an organization to volunteer with for the winter. I looked around, here and there, asking various groups what it was they did and what they needed, and if there was anything I could do to help. I was fascinated by international development. I loved every culture but my own, and I love to wander, in daydreams if not in reality, to lands far away. These were trips I might have been able to take if I hadn't spent half my time daydreaming about them. One day, not far from my house, I walked into the office of Save the Children Canada and met Philip and Edith. Philip was the regional director, and Edith was the clerical support, an office of two. They were lovely people, a breath of fresh air compared with some of the spiky and humourless ideologues I had been talking to lately, progressives indeed. And their office was the closest one to my home, just across from the Safeway store and Mullen's Hardware.

I spent the next twelve months volunteering in a variety of capacities with Save the Children Canada. I went to weekly volunteer meetings. I took pictures, went to conferences, and wrote short articles for the newsletter. I chauffeured visiting speakers around Regina, promoting international development. One of them was a man named Andrew Ignatieff. He worked for Save the Children Canada in South America. I recognized the last name from George Ignatieff, the well-known Canadian diplomat, an Ambassador to the United Nations, among many other things. He, I learned, was Andrew's father. I drove Andrew around Regina, not in my embarrassing New Yorker, I had finally returned it to my father, with thanks and 15,000 miles on it, but in my embarrassing lemon-yellow Renault Le Car which I had bought for five hundred dollars from Karen's gynecologist. Andrew and I talked about work and success, or in my case the lack of them. Traction had been an issue for me. He told me he had experienced his own challenges working in the long, successful, high-toned shadow of his famous father and that of an over-achieving brother named Michael, who lived in the UK.

I acted as secretary at inter-agency meetings, I helped organize fund-raising events, I appeared on TV and radio, although I never became the media darling I hoped I would, and I sold layettes from a table in the mall. I didn't know what a layette was at first. In the end, volunteerism comes down to a willingness to sell knitted goods in the mall with old ladies to raise money for starving children.

Overall, it was a wonderful experience. I read a lot, I met a lot of people, I did a lot of different things, and I learned a lot about international development. Philip, the Regional Director for Western Canada, was still in his twenties, and international development was his chosen career. It was a career in which, for a short time, he had a delightful leg up. He had just won a year-long free pass on Canadian Airlines International. Before it was bought by Air Canada in 2000, it was Canada's second-largest airline, and they flew to a hundred and five cities in Canada and seventeen countries. His wife, Gillian, had entered the contest, and in a moment of madness she wrote Philip's name on the entry form instead of her own. The prize was for a single pass only, and the rules of the contest dictated that it be made out to the name on the entry form, to Philip. He was able to travel for a year, at no expense to himself or his employer, anywhere Canadian Airlines flew. He could have flown to Asia, Europe, or South America on any weekend, but wisely, out of deference to his wife, he never did. He used his pass soberly, going to NGO meetings all over Canada, and for project site visits. He went to Peru to visit Save the Children development projects there. I helped him process and print pictures he had taken while in Peru, and one of them won an award in a local photography contest. We split the prize, but somehow I felt guilty taking the money. Philip was known to telephone the airport an hour before an intended flight, enquire about seating availability, and show up five minutes before they retracted the Jetway. The Canadian Airlines staff at the Regina airport knew him well, and they would simply wave to him as he ran through the terminal and boarded the jet, unticketed.

By the end of 1988, I had come to the conclusion that the drinking was becoming unmanageable again. I found myself doing yoga every night with a beer in my hand, watching TV. So I crawled back up on the wagon. It was so much easier to quit drinking than to drink moderately. I was still angry, occasionally, about money and my lack of employment, but in general, I spent 1989 with a clearer head, and in a much less argumentative, and more hopeful, character.

I finished microeconomics and enrolled in systems analysis in May, but the instructor was intolerable, and I dropped the course after a couple of weeks, something I had never done before, not in eight years of going to post-secondary schools. There was a photograph in the front of the systems analysis textbook showing row upon row of low-walled cubicles in an enormous room, each one occupied by a single person sitting at a computer terminal. The caption read: "These people are knowledge workers in the information society. You, too, can be a knowledge worker in the information society by studying systems analysis." I looked at the hundreds of cubicles in the football-field-sized room in the photograph and thought to myself, "I'd rather be shot." On the Drop Form, under "Why are you dropping the course?" I wrote, "Fed up." I also wrote to the Dean of Something outlining the instructor's haphazard and unprofessional approach to teaching systems analysis.

The University of Regina gave me a Certificate in Administration anyway. You only needed four courses to qualify for one, and you could earn two courses by applying for transfer credit for academic work done elsewhere, which I did. People were always giving me paper, but none of it was money.

The days and the weeks and the months rolled by in a largely unvaried succession of love and bickering, contentment and frustration, easy work, lunches, coffee dates, parties, and pleasure outings. One night in the nearly empty bar of the Hotel Saskatchewan, Regina's grand railway hotel, this one not quite as grand as many of them, I saw Eric Malling sitting at a table with a couple of other people. I admired his work tremendously, and I thought about saying a few words to him, but I was sick with a cold, I should have been in bed really, and I just didn't have the energy. He was a major force in Canadian journalism, and he received many broadcasting awards while he was host of the television newsmagazine shows *the fifth estate* and *W5*. His interviewing style was aggressive, contrarian, and conclusive. He uncovered illegality and corruption. His investigations sent criminals to jail and forced government ministers to resign. I saw him interview the murderous dictator of Nicaragua, Anastasio Somoza. He made him look like a fool, and he made it look easy. He was forty-two when I saw him in Regina. Ten years later, he fell down his basement stairs and died. They say he drank.

I still watched television news in 1989, but that was soon to come to an end forever. In 1992, I turned off my TV and never turned it back on again, not to watch news.

In 1985, the Internet Domain Name System was created, but I knew nothing about that. Nelson Mandela rejected an offer from South African President P. W. Botha to be released from prison, preferring to remain in jail rather than submit to the conditions attached. He wasn't freed until 1990, twenty years after I wrote my high school essay on apartheid. Gorbachev became leader of the Soviet Union. Rick Hansen set out on his two-year, 25,000-mile wheelchair trip around the world. He raised $26 million for spinal cord research and leveraged it into $300 million. I was asked a dozen times if I was related to him. The Greenpeace vessel *Rainbow Warrior* was bombed and sunk in Auckland Harbour by French DGSE agents, the French CIA. Robert Ballard found the wreck of the *Titanic*.

In 1986, I was walking through the cafeteria at U of A and on the big projection screen was live coverage of the crash of the Space Shuttle *Challenger*. I hardly knew it existed. Baby Doc Duvalier fled Haiti ending thirty years of father-son dictatorship. Microsoft went public. The Chernobyl disaster killed at least 4,000 people and resulted in $7 billion in damages. Traces of radioactive deposits were found in nearly every country in the northern hemisphere. Prince Andrew married Fergie. A cargo ship called *Khian Sea* departed from the US carrying 14,000 tons of toxic waste and wandered the oceans for sixteen months trying to find a place to dump its cargo. It wound up in Haiti. Desmond Tutu became the first black Anglican Church bishop in South Africa, and *The Oprah Winfrey Show* premiered in Chicago. The Iran-Contra affair came to light. The US was secretly selling arms to Iran in exchange for the release of hostages and also to fund the Nicaraguan Contras, something that had been prohibited by Congress. For this, Ronald Reagan was rebuked the next year by his own special commission, and the US was found in contravention of international law by the International Court of Justice.

In 1987, the Dow Jones Industrial Average broke 2000 points for the first time. Terry Waite, the special envoy of the Archbishop of Canterbury in Lebanon, was kidnapped and not released for four years. AZT was approved by the FDA for treatment of HIV. *The Simpsons* cartoon first appeared as short clips in the middle of *The Tracey Ullman Show*. Mathias Rust, eighteen years old, created an "imaginary bridge" to the east by landing a private plane in Red Square in Moscow. He was tried and detained for a year. New Zealand created the world's first Nuclear Free Zone. Canada introduced a one-dollar coin stamped with the image of the common loon, and it was immediately dubbed the "loonie." Only weeks after I moved to the west coast from Edmonton, an F4 tornado hit the city and destroyed a trailer park. Twenty-seven people were killed and hundreds were injured. Hundreds more were left homeless and jobless. I telephoned Pam from Abbotsford to make sure she was okay. Rudolf Hess committed suicide at the age of ninety-three in his cell at Spandau Prison which was then torn down. After six hundred and forty years, the UK's highest Order of Chivalry, the Order of the Garter, was opened to women. Reagan and Gorbachev signed a treaty that banned intermediate-range cruise missiles. The First Intifada began.

In 1988, the Soviet Union began major economic restructuring, *perestroika*. In four more years, the country would cease to exist. After more than eight years of fighting, the Soviet Army began to withdraw from Afghanistan, and the eight-year Iran-Iraq war ended in military stalemate. Osama bin Laden founded Al-Qaeda. George Bush Sr. became President of the United States. Benazir Bhutto became the first female Prime Minister of Pakistan.

Nineteen seventy-nine was a hell of a year and so was 1989. By the end of the eighties, the Cold War was coming to an end. In the USSR, decades of bankrupting military spending, and now economic recession, resulted in the advent of reformist policies. Decades of authoritarian rule and a resurgence of nationalism resulted in the overthrow of communism in most of the Eastern Bloc. Over the next two years, fifteen countries declared their independence from the Soviet Union, and communism was abandoned in half a dozen other countries. China had been opening up and reforming its economic policies for a decade, but political protest and reform died, along with 3,000 protesters, at Tiananmen Square. In China, order is more important than freedom. The Berlin Wall came down. After two generations, Germany was reunified. By the early 1990s, electoral democracy was the official political system in half the countries of the world.

Developing countries faced multiple debt crises in the 1980s. Multinational manufacturing corporations moved their plants from the developed world to Thailand, Mexico, South Korea, Taiwan, and China.

There were riots, rebellions, and revolutions, international wars, civil wars, guerilla wars, coups, and nuclear threats. There were national emergencies, assassinations, and hijackings. There was independence for some nations. There were volcanoes, earthquakes, droughts, hurricanes, tsunamis, tornadoes, fires, floods, famines, and epidemics. There were plane crashes and a shuttle crash. There was Bhopal, Chernobyl, and the *Exxon Valdez*. In the eighties, if you weren't depressed, you weren't paying attention.

I remember little enough from the summer of 1989. Tiananmen Square, *Seinfeld*, sunny days, picnics, and potlucks. The days were routine until it was time to go. By the middle of July, I was excited about moving back to the coast. I feared, as always, the miserable process of finding accommodation in Victoria at the end of August, just before the start of a new school year. I needed to give myself extra time, and I rolled out of Regina ten days before the end of the month with a full load of household items packed into Lucky Le Car.

Lucky earned his nickname. I wasn't sure he would make it to Moose Jaw, but he toddled along, across the prairies and over the mountains, at fifty miles an hour, making fifty miles to the gallon. I bought him in 1988 for five hundred dollars. In 1998, I sold him to the auto wreckers for scrap and drove him to their yard. They gave me twenty-five dollars. Only once in ten years did he let me down.

Exactly two years earlier, I had moved from the coast to the prairies, from Abbotsford to Regina, running away from jobs and relationships I didn't want. Now I was making the same trip in the opposite direction, from Regina to Victoria, for the same reason. I was a Western Canadian pinball.

I had had some hope that life with Karen would be satisfying, a form worth preserving. I still thought so. I had every intention of returning. I still lived in Regina. I was still with Karen, we were still a couple. But distance makes the heart grow blander, and the joy I felt driving west was awkwardly disproportionate to a man supposedly committed to his spouse and his spouse's house.

Distance can sharpen the appetite, too. We weren't very happy together, but we couldn't stand to be apart for more than a few weeks. Karen flew out for Thanksgiving, and I flew back for Remembrance Day.

I was home for Christmas.

Afterword

In 2003, I found myself in the company of a social worker, a counsellor, for many hours of interviews. This was not my idea. In her semi-skilled hands, I could not help but reveal a life of some confusion. She told me she could recommend a number of self-help books that she thought would be of value to me. I said, "That's not necessary. I read literature."

She said, "Well, it's not really the same."

I said, "English literature *is* self-help literature. That's what literature *is*."

In the first five pages of *Adam Bede*, George Eliot says more about religion and work, two of the devils that tortured me, and says it better, than I have in the last nine hundred. The book was assigned reading in my Grade 11 literature class at Sedgewick Central High School. I read a few pages of it, at fifteen, and put it down, unable to start, never mind finish. I doubted Mrs. Chevraux's sanity in assigning such a work. I know it wasn't her goal to make literature distasteful to young people, but the selection seemed likely to have that effect. The choice probably wasn't hers. J. D. Salinger, Saul Bellow, or Joseph Heller would have played better to sixteen-year-olds in 1968. Softly, softly catchy monkey. I got ten per cent on my report card that semester, a D-!

It was another forty-five years before I got around to reading *Adam Bede*, and I read *Romola*, *The Mill on the Floss*, and *Silas Marner* first. It took over twenty hours to get through *Adam Bede*, and I had to stop many times to wonder, at the age of sixty, at Eliot's breadth of understanding and beauty of expression. She writes of the pulse and the inevitable pluralism of intense emotion, of love and family, of generations, of conscious effort and unconscious strain, of knowledge, need, and industry, of invisible right, hidden dread, and tragedy, matters of concern to everyone with breath in their lungs and blood in their veins. She writes of female beauty, as I frequently have in this second volume.

Hetty Sorrel was "of the order of beauty which seems made to turn the heads not only of men, but of all intelligent mammals.... It is...a beauty with which you can never be angry, but that you feel ready to crush for inability to comprehend the state of mind into which it throws you.... [The] wondrous harmonies [of her beauty] searched the subtlest windings of your soul, the delicate fibres of life where no memory can penetrate...binding together your whole being past and present in one unspeakable vibration, melting you in one moment with all the tenderness, all the love that has been scattered through the toilsome years...blending your present joy with past sorrow and your present sorrow with all your past joy.... Beauty has an impersonal expression beyond and far above the one woman's soul that it clothes.... It seems to be a far-off mighty love that has come near to us, and made speech for itself...."

That's what I wanted to say, but I can't write like that.

There are a hundred points of departure in *Adam Bede* for a genuinely improving self-help sermon, one recognizable not only to a nineteenth-century Methodist, but to a twenty-first century yogi and hedonist.

If you're feeling the need for inspiration and peace, and you think you might find it in a book, I recommend you walk past the bleating self-help section in the bookstore and continue on until you come upon the older ink.

In Chapters 3 and 4 I may have seemed hard on Geshe-la, the Tibetan lama, and his major-domo, Sister Margaret. My defence is that I wrote about my experiences with these two strange people in the only way I could: as they happened, as honestly as I could, as I saw them and understood them, and from my point of view. When Geshe-la died in 2008 at the age of eighty-five, he left behind two Dharma centres, hundreds of students, sixty years of teaching, thirty-four of them in the west, and two hundred fifty-six cassette tapes of lectures. Sister Margaret worked for many years as a Buddhist Chaplain at the University of Victoria, the Vancouver Island Regional Correctional Centre, and the William Head Institution. In 1998, she became Lama Margaret. Others had a different experience of these remarkable people. If I have made them out to be bad or mad, it is a passing reference only, nine months out of long lives. If I have been wrong in matters of fact, I apologize.

In the newsy sections of this volume, the parts where I offer a whirl of headlines, like a Shrine Temple parade of miniature cars, some of which I was aware, many of which I was not, I have most often put forward the tragic. Why not the noble and uplifting, the helpful and hopeful? Because, partially, kindness and virtue are what I expect from life. To me they are the norm. They are what is innate in us. All else is anomaly. We love kindness and virtue, but we learn little from them. It is the hard lessons that jar us and wake us and give us knowledge, direction, and opportunity to exercise the muscles of the heart. "Memory is a thermometer that records only fevers." It is mishaps that mark the path to enlightenment.

I still have no band of researchers, proofreaders, editors, or designers, except the clever builders of computer templates for text and graphics at CreateSpace.com. Thank you to those unknown workers in art and science.

Believe me, I wish I had an editor. Oscar Wilde wrote, "I have spent most of the day putting in a comma and the rest of the day taking it out." There are 15,699 commas in this volume, and they have, individually and collectively, nearly driven me mad. I prefer the Oxford comma, and yes, the double possessive.

And where would any of us be without Wikipedia?

When it comes to a real person, a person I know, I offer thanks, again, to Larry Chalmers, whose early advice I continue to take to heart when my brain will let me.

Even More About the Author

Neil Hansen still lives in Victoria, BC, in the same bachelor suite, in the same non-profit, 55+, low-income housing project started by the Anglican Church Women in the late 1960s. He is still grateful to them.

He has lived there now for four years.

It is an above-average length of stay for him.

To Say Nothing
A Diary of Memory
Vol. 3
by Neil Hansen

Coming to an outhouse near you soon

The third volume of To Say Nothing will be available in 2017.

Another ten years. But not so many schools, so many places to live, not so many jobs, so many apartments, so many roommates, and girlfriends.

Once again, from the prairies to the ocean, this time to stay. The difficulties of unintended self-knowledge and the struggles of a small man dealing with bigger, longer-term problems, including a small woman, and then, much later, small children.

The variety of daily experience contracts somewhat as three more years of academic work command the attention of the wanderer, followed by eleven years of steady employment, the first and last time that will ever happen, as well as by a marriage, and ditto that.

The 1990s see an increase in routine, but much will change in spite of it.

The travels continue. Months of camping and adventures in Africa and Mexico. The US and Hawaii. No all-inclusive resorts for Neil. He is a tepidly intrepid voyager. The flea-ridden hostels of Zanzibar and Harare, Key West and New Orleans, the trails of British Columbia, and the swells of the Pacific Ocean, are more to his taste.

On and off the wagon.

In any life sometimes funny things just happen.

The very odd things you can count on.

Made in the USA
Lexington, KY
16 August 2014